THE CHRISTIAN LIFE HYMNAL

HENDRICKSON
Worship

HENDRICKSON PUBLISHERS, INC.
PEABODY, MASSACHUSETTS

ISBN 978-1-56563-952-2 — Burgundy
ISBN 978-1-56563-955-3 — Royal Blue

Copyright © 2006 Martingale Music, LLC
Under Exclusive License to Hendrickson Publishers Marketing, LLC, Peabody, Massachusetts
All Rights Reserved. Printed in China. International Copyright Secured.
Eighth Printing — August 2023

Acknowledgements

Editor — Eric Wyse

Associate Editors — Brenda Boswell, Tom Calvani

Senior Managing Editor — Danny R. Jones

Managing Editor — Paul Nelson

Consulting Editor — James C. Gibson

Design Editor — Carl Seal

Typesetters — Rick Domenico, Andrew High, Paul Nelson, Brent Roberts, Carl Seal

Proofreaders — Bonnie Moore, Jere Adams, Ben Ryan, Natasha Smith

Art Direction and Design — Dawn Rodgers

Copyright Administration — Jill Johnson, Music Services, Inc.

For Hendrickson Publishers Marketing, LLC — Ray Hendrickson, President

Production — Ann Droppers, Dave Pietrantonio

TABLE OF CONTENTS — THE CHRISTIAN LIFE HYMNAL

GOD
Trinity ..... 1 – 9
Father ..... 10 – 36
Jesus Christ
    Praise and Adoration ..... 37 – 71
    Advent ..... 72 – 82
    Birth ..... 83 – 139
    Epiphany ..... 140 – 144
    Life and Ministry ..... 145 – 152
    Passion and Death ..... 153 – 180
    Resurrection ..... 181 – 192
    Ascension and Reign ..... 193 – 209
    Return ..... 210 – 215
Holy Spirit ..... 216 – 229

WORD OF GOD ..... 230 – 234

WORK OF GOD
Creation ..... 235 – 245
Redemption
    Salvation ..... 246 – 271
    Love, Grace and Mercy ..... 272 – 290
    Repentance and Commitment ..... 291 – 315

GOD'S PEOPLE
Church
    Foundation and Nature ..... 316 – 322
    Baptism ..... 323 – 325
    Lord's Supper ..... 326 – 333
    Fellowship of Believers ..... 334 – 336
    Renewal ..... 337 – 342
    Evangelism and Missions ..... 343 – 361
Christian Life
    Hope and Assurance ..... 362 – 409
    Faith and Trust ..... 410 – 435
    Loyalty and Courage ..... 436 – 454
    Prayer and Guidance ..... 455 – 472
    Service and Stewardship ..... 473 – 506
    Testimony ..... 507 – 543
    Marriage and Family ..... 544 – 546
    Heaven and Eternity ..... 547 – 572
Special Times and Seasons
    Morning ..... 573 – 574
    Evening ..... 575 – 580
    Opening ..... 581 – 584
    Closing ..... 585 – 588
    Harvest and Thanksgiving ..... 589 – 595
    New Year 596
    National ..... 597 – 607

SERVICE MUSIC ..... 608 – 641

INDEXES FOR THE HYMNS
Scriptural Allusion Index ..... 644 – 648
Tune Name Index ..... 648 – 651
Metrical Tune Index ..... 651 – 654
Authors, Composers, Arrangers and Sources Index ..... 654 – 659
Church Year Index ..... 659 – 661
Topical Index ..... 662 – 677
Hymn Title and First Line Index (with Key) ..... 678 – 684

FOREWORD

*G*OD'S PEOPLE have always had a song. The first strains of their melody are a response, springing from the deepest emotions, amazed that the Creator of the universe would take delight in lavishing grace on poor, fallen people and even rejoice over them with singing. From that moment on, the redeemed of the Lord struggle to find adequate words to express what their hearts can barely contain. At last, their voices rise in a joyful refrain uniting body, soul and spirit in worship of the Living God.

There is no more wonderful sound than that of believers in glorious adoration and worship. Music gives our praises wings and frees the heart to say what must be said. Yet, the songs of the church have other important functions as well. The Song of Moses recorded in Deuteronomy 32 is a history lesson and a warning to the people of Israel. Our memories are fallen, so we need songs of testimony that rehearse God's faithfulness and trace His gracious working throughout history. Many of the Psalms are such detailed reminders.

For centuries, the church has relied on hymns as a source of doctrinal instruction. Since theology results in doxology, a right understanding of the orthodox elements of faith are essential for true worship. Many times my own heart has been inflamed with renewed passion while singing hymns such as, "And Can It Be," "The Church's One Foundation," and "Rock of Ages." The truth of God's Word set to music can, by the Spirit, penetrate the heart and engage the mind, resulting in a thoughtful and worshipful response.

In recent years, new songs of praise have filled our churches, giving voice to hearts yearning to express worship. These songs are a refreshing gift. At the same time, we have a wealth of hymns and a powerful history of spiritual songs that must not be forgotten. *The Christian Life Hymnal* gathers all of these musical expressions of redemption and faith together in a new volume for today's church. There is a new generation that would be blessed to discover our rich heritage of hymnody and learn texts that have helped shape the spiritual underpinnings of those who have gone before us.

So sing on! Sing to remember God's faithfulness. Sing to rehearse God's truth. Sing to worship our Savior. Sing with hope in the darkest of nights. Sing with joy at the break of dawn. Sing on to the glory of God!

Steve Green

— Steve Green, Recording Artist and Author

*L*et the word of Christ dwell in you richly as you teach and admonish one another with all wisdom,

and as you sing psalms, hymns and spiritual songs with gratitude in your hearts to God.

— *Colossians 3:16 NIV*

iv

Holy, Holy, Holy!

Holy, holy, holy is the Lord, the all-powerful God, who was and is and is coming! – Revelation 4:8 CEV

1. Ho - ly, ho - ly, ho - ly! Lord, God Al - might - y!
2. Ho - ly, ho - ly, ho - ly! All the saints a - dore Thee,
3. Ho - ly, ho - ly, ho - ly! Though the dark - ness hide Thee,
4. Ho - ly, ho - ly, ho - ly! Lord, God Al - might - y!

Ear - ly in the morn - ing our song shall rise to Thee.
cast - ing down their gold - en crowns a - round the glass - y sea;
though the eye of sin - ful - ness Thy glo - ry may not see,
All Thy works shall praise Thy name in earth and sky and sea.

Ho - ly, ho - ly, ho - ly! Mer - ci - ful and might - y!
cher - u - bim and ser - a - phim fall - ing down be - fore Thee,
on - ly Thou art ho - ly; there is none be - side Thee,
Ho - ly, ho - ly, ho - ly! Mer - ci - ful and might - y,

God in three Per - sons, bless - ed Trin - i - ty!
which wert, and art, and ev - er - more shalt be.
per - fect in pow'r, in love and pur - i - ty.
God in three Per - sons, bless - ed Trin - i - ty!

WORDS: Reginald Heber, 1826
MUSIC: *Nicaea*, John Bacchus Dykes, 1861

11.12.12.10

2 God, Our Father, We Adore Thee!

True worshippers shall worship the Father in spirit and in truth. – John 4:23 KJV

1. God, our Fa-ther, we a-dore Thee! We, Thy chil-dren, bless Thy name!
2. Son E-ter-nal, we a-dore Thee! Lamb up-on the throne on high!
3. Ho-ly Spir-it, we a-dore Thee! Par-a-clete and heav'n-ly guest!
4. Fa-ther, Son, and Ho-ly Spir-it– Three in One! We give Thee praise!

Cho-sen in the Christ be-fore Thee, we are "ho-ly, with-out blame."
Lamb of God, we bow be-fore Thee, Thou hast brought Thy peo-ple nigh!
Sent from God and from the Sav-ior, Thou hast led us in-to rest.
For the rich-es we in-her-it, heart and voice to Thee we raise!

We a-dore Thee! We a-dore Thee! Ab-ba's prais-es we pro-claim!
We a-dore Thee! We a-dore Thee! Son of God, who came to die!
We a-dore Thee! We a-dore Thee! By Thy grace for-ev-er blest;
We a-dore Thee! We a-dore Thee! Thee we bless through end-less days!

We a-dore Thee! We a-dore Thee! Ab-ba's prais-es we pro-claim!
We a-dore Thee! We a-dore Thee! Son of God, who came to die!
we a-dore Thee! We a-dore Thee! By Thy grace for-ev-er blest!
We a-dore Thee! We a-dore Thee! Thee we bless through end-less days!

WORDS: Sts. 1, 2, 4 George West Frazer, 1904; St. 3 Alfred Samuel Loizeaux, 1952
MUSIC: *Beecher,* John Zundel, 1870

8.7.8.7 D

Holy God, We Praise Thy Name

In the midst of the assembly I will sing praise to You. – Hebrews 2:12 NJKV

1. Ho - ly God, we praise Thy name; Lord of all, we
2. Hark! The loud ce - les - tial hymn an - gel choirs a -
3. Lo! The ap - os - tol - ic train join the sa - cred
4. Ho - ly Fa - ther, Ho - ly Son, Ho - ly Spir - it,

bow be - fore Thee; all on earth Thy scep - ter claim,
bove are rais - ing, cher - u - bim and ser - a - phim,
name to hal - low; proph - ets swell the loud re - frain,
Three we name Thee; while in es - sence on - ly One,

all in heav'n a - bove a - dore Thee; in - fi - nite Thy
in un - ceas - ing cho - rus prais - ing; fill the heav'ns with
and the white - robed mar - tyrs fol - low; and from morn to
un - di - vid - ed God we claim Thee; and a - dor - ing

vast do - main, ev - er - last - ing is Thy reign.
sweet ac - cord: Ho - ly, ho - ly, ho - ly, Lord.
set of sun, through the Church the song goes on.
bend the knee, while we own the mys - ter - y.

WORDS: Para. of *Te Deum*, attr. Ignaz Franz, ca. 1774; tr. Clarence Alphonsus Walworth, 1853
MUSIC: *Grosser Gott, Wir Loben Dich*, from *Katholisches Gesangbuch*, Vienna, 1686, anon.

7.8.7.8.7.7

Come, Thou Almighty King

I am the Alpha and the Omega...Who is, and Who was, and Who is to come, the Almighty. – Revelation 1:8 NIV

1. Come, Thou Al - might - y King, help us Thy
2. Come, Thou In - car - nate Word, gird on Thy
3. Come, Ho - ly Com - fort - er, Thy sa - cred
4. To Thee, great One in Three, e - ter - nal

name to sing, help us to praise:
might - y sword, our prayer at - tend;
wit - ness bear in this glad hour:
prais - es be, hence, ev - er - more.

Fa - ther all glo - ri - ous, o'er all vic - to - ri - ous,
come, and Thy peo - ple bless, and give Thy Word suc - cess,
Thou who al - might - y art, now rule in ev - 'ry heart,
Thy sov - 'reign maj - es - ty may we in glo - ry see,

come and reign o - ver us, An - cient of Days!
Spir - it of ho - li - ness, on us de - scend!
and ne'er from us de - part, Spir - it of pow'r!
and to e - ter - ni - ty love and a - dore!

WORDS: English tr., anon., ca. 1757
MUSIC: *Italian Hymn*, from *The Collection of Psalms and Hymn Tunes*
Sung at the Chapel of the Lock Hospital, Felice de Giardini, 1769
Another harmonization of this tune, No. 344.

6.6.4.6.6.6.4

Thou, Whose Almighty Word

Deal bountifully with Thy servant, that I might live and keep Thy word. – Psalm 119:17 KJV

1. Thou, whose al - might - y Word cha - os and dark - ness heard, and took their flight; hear us, we hum - bly pray, and, where the gos - pel day sheds not its glo - rious ray, let there be light!

2. Thou who didst come to bring on Thy re - deem - ing wing heal - ing and sight, health to the sick in mind, sight to the in - ly blind, O now to all man - kind, let there be light!

3. Spir - it of truth and love, life - giv - ing, ho - ly Dove, speed forth Thy flight! Move on the wa - ters' face bear - ing the lamp of grace, and in earth's dark - est place, let there be light!

4. Ho - ly and bless - ed Three, glo - ri - ous Trin - i - ty, Wis - dom, Love, Might; bound - less as o - cean's tide, roll - ing in full - est pride through the world far and wide, let there be light!

WORDS: John Marriott, 1813, alt.
MUSIC: *Moscow*, Felice de Giardini, 1769; harm. *The New Hymnal*, 1916,
from *Hymns Ancient and Modern*, 1875, and Lowell Mason, 1833

6.6.4.6.6.6.4

I Bind Unto Myself Today

His truth shall be thy shield and buckler. – Psalm 91:4 KJV

Unison

1. I bind un-to my-self to-day the strong name
2. I bind this day to me for-ev-er, by pow'r of
3. I bind un-to my-self to-day the pow'r of
5. I bind un-to my-self the name, the strong name

of the Trin-i-ty, by in-vo-ca-tion
faith, Christ's In-car-na-tion; His bap-tism in the
God to hold and lead, His eye to watch, His
of the Trin-i-ty, by in-vo-ca-tion

Stanza 1 ends here.

of the same, the Three in One, and One in Three.
Jor-dan Riv-er; His death on cross for my sal-va-tion;
might to stay, His ear to heark-en, to my need;
of the same, the Three in One, and One in Three.

2. His burst-ing from the spic-ed tomb; His rid-ing
3. the wis-dom of my God to teach, His hand to
5. Of whom all na-ture hath cre-a-ted e-ter-nal

WORDS: Attr. St. Patrick; adapt. Cecil Frances Humphreys Alexander, 1889
MUSIC: *St. Patrick's Breastplate*, traditional Irish melody; arr. Charles Villiers Stanford, 1902, 1906

L.M.D.

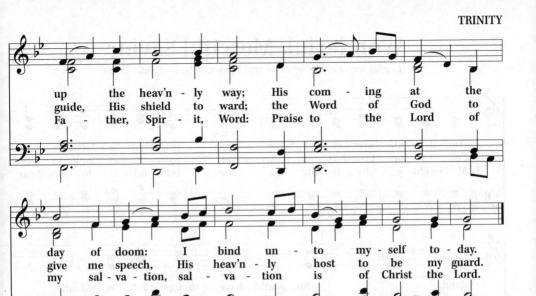

up the heav'n - ly way; His com - ing at the
guide, His shield to - ward; the Word of God to
Fa - ther, Spir - it, Word: Praise to the Lord of

day of doom: I bind un - to my - self to - day.
give me speech, His heav'n - ly host to be my guard.
my sal - va - tion, sal - va - tion is of Christ the Lord.

For stanza 4, continue with "Christ Be with Me"; then return for stanza 5.

Christ Be with Me

Harmony

4. Christ be with me, Christ with - in me, Christ be -
   Christ be - neath me, Christ a - bove me, Christ in

hind me, Christ be - fore me, Christ be - side me, Christ to
qui - et, Christ in dan - ger, Christ in hearts of all that

win me, Christ to com - fort and re - store me.
love me, Christ in mouth of friend and strang - er.

For stanza 5, return to "I Bind Unto Myself Today."

WORDS: Attr. St. Patrick c. 386 - 460; adapt. Cecil Frances Humphreys Alexander, 1889
MUSIC: *Deirdre*, traditional Irish melody; adapt. Charles Villiers Stanford, 1904

L.M.D.

7 Wonderful, Merciful Savior

In His great mercy He has given us new birth into a living hope. – 1 Peter 1:3 NIV

1. Won-der-ful, mer-ci-ful Sav-ior, pre-cious Re-deem-er and Friend; who would have thought that a Lamb could res-cue the souls of men? Oh, You res-cue the souls of men.

2. Coun-se-lor, Com-fort-er, Keep-er, Spir-it we long to em-brace; You of-fer hope when our hearts have hope-less-ly lost the way, oh, we hope-less-ly lost the way. *(to Refrain)*

3. Al-might-y, In-fi-nite Fa-ther, faith-ful-ly lov-ing Your own; here in our weak-ness You find us fall-ing be-fore Your throne, oh, we're fall-ing be-fore Your throne. *(to Refrain)*

(to verse 2)

Refrain

You are the One that we praise, You are the One we a-dore;

WORDS: Dawn Rodgers and Eric Wyse, 1989
MUSIC: *Vine Ridge,* Dawn Rodgers, 1989; arr. Eric Wyse, 2000

Irregular with Refrain

You give the heal-ing and grace our hearts al-ways hun-ger for, oh, our hearts al-ways hun-ger for.

Praise Ye the Triune God! 8

I will...praise Thy name for Thy lovingkindness and for Thy truth. – Psalm 138:2 KJV

1. Praise ye the Fa-ther! For His lov-ing kind-ness, ten-der-ly
2. Praise ye the Sav-ior! Great is His com-pas-sion, gra-cious-ly
3. Praise ye the Spir-it! Com-fort-er of Is-rael, sent of the

cares He for His err-ing chil-dren; praise Him, ye an-gels,
cares He for His cho-sen peo-ple; young men and maid-ens,
Fa-ther and the Son to bless us; praise ye the Fa-ther,

praise Him in the heav-ens, praise ye Je-ho-vah!
old-er ones and chil-dren, praise ye the Sav-ior!
Son and Ho-ly Spir-it, praise ye the Tri-une God!

WORDS: Elizabeth Rundle Charles, ca. 1858
MUSIC: *Flemming*, Friedrich Ferdinand Flemming, 1811

11.11.11.6

Worthy of Worship

For great is the Lord and most worthy of praise. – 1 Chronicles 16:25 NIV

1. Wor-thy of wor-ship, wor-thy of praise, wor-thy of hon-or and glo-ry; wor-thy of all the glad songs we can sing, wor-thy of all of the off-'rings we bring.
2. Wor-thy of rev-'rence, wor-thy of fear, wor-thy of love and de-vo-tion; wor-thy of bow-ing and bend-ing of knees, wor-thy of all this and add-ed to these:
3. Al-might-y Fa-ther, Mas-ter and Lord, King of all kings and Re-deem-er, won-der-ful Coun-se-lor, Com-fort-er, Friend, Sav-ior and Source of our life with-out end.

Refrain

You are wor-thy, Fa-ther, Cre-a-tor. You are wor-thy, Sav-ior, Sus-tain-er. You are wor-thy, wor-thy and won-der-ful; wor-thy of wor-ship and praise.

WORDS: Terry W. York, 1988
MUSIC: *Judson,* Mark Blankenship, 1988

Irregular with Refrain

O Worship the King

Yours is the kingdom O Lord, and You are exalted as head above all. – 1 Chronicles 29:11 ESV

1. O wor - ship the King, all glo - rious a - bove,
2. O tell of His might, O sing of His grace,
3. Thy boun - ti - ful care what tongue can re - cite?
4. Frail chil - dren of dust, and fee - ble as frail,

and grate - ful - ly sing His won - der - ful love;
whose robe is the light, whose can - o - py space!
It breathes in the air, it shines in the light,
in Thee do we trust, nor find Thee to fail:

our Shield and De - fend - er, the An - cient of Days,
His char - iots of wrath the deep thun - der - clouds form,
it streams from the hills, it de - scends to the plain,
Thy mer - cies how ten - der, how firm to the end,

pa - vil - ioned in splen - dor, and gird - ed with praise.
and dark is His path on the wings of the storm.
and sweet - ly dis - tills in the dew and the rain.
our Mak - er, De - fend - er, Re - deem - er and Friend.

WORDS: Robert Grant, 1833, alt.; based on Psalm 104:1-6
MUSIC: *Lyons,* attr. Johann Michael Haydn, 1770; arr. William Gardiner, 1815

10.10.11.11

11 Praise to the Lord, the Almighty

Then you will delight yourself in the Almighty and lift up your face to God. – Job 22:26 ESV

1. Praise to the Lord, the Al-might-y, the King of cre-a-tion!
2. Praise to the Lord, who o'er all things so won-drous-ly reign-eth,
3. Praise to the Lord, who doth pros-per thy work and de-fend thee;
4. Praise to the Lord, O let all that is in me a-dore Him!

O my soul, praise Him, for He is thy health and sal-va-tion!
shel-ters thee un-der His wings, yea, so gent-ly sus-tain-eth!
sure-ly His good-ness and mer-cy here dai-ly at-tend thee.
All that hath life and breath, come now with prais-es be-fore Him.

All ye who hear, now to His tem-ple draw near;
Hast thou not seen, how thy de-sires e'er have been
Pon-der a-new what the Al-might-y can do,
Let the "A-men" sound from His peo-ple a-gain,

join me in glad ad-o-ra-tion.
grant-ed in what He or-dain-eth?
if with His love He be-friend thee.
glad-ly for-ev-er a-dore Him.

WORDS: Joachim Neander, 1680, alt.; based on Psalms 150 & 103:1-6; tr. Catherine Winkworth, 1863, alt.
MUSIC: *Lobe Den Herren*, anon. in *Straslund Gesangbuch*, 1665; harm. W. Sterndale Bennett, 1863

Irregular

Praise, My Soul, the King of Heaven 12

I will sing praise to Thy name, O Thou most High. – Psalm 9:2 KJV

1. Praise, my soul, the King of heav - en; to His
2. Praise Him for His grace and fa - vor to our
3. Fa - ther - like He tends and spares us; well our
4. Frail as sum - mer's flow'r we flour - ish, blows the
5. An - gels, help us to a - dore Him; ye be -

feet thy trib - ute bring. Ran - somed, healed, re - stored, for - giv - en,
fore - bears¹ in dis - tress; praise Him still the same as ev - er,
fee - ble frame He knows; in His hand He gent - ly bears us,
wind and it is gone; but while mor - tals rise and per - ish
hold Him face to face; sun and moon bow down be - fore Him,

ev - er - more His prais - es sing: Al - le - lu - ia,
slow to chide, and swift to bless: Al - le - lu - ia,
res - cues us from all our foes. Al - le - lu - ia,
God en - dures un - chang - ing on; Al - le - lu - ia,
dwell - ers all in time and space. Al - le - lu - ia,

Al - le - lu - ia! Praise the ev - er - last - ing King.
Al - le - lu - ia! Glo - rious in His faith - ful - ness.
Al - le - lu - ia! Wide - ly yet His mer - cy flows.
Al - le - lu - ia! Praise the high E - ter - nal One!
Al - le - lu - ia! Praise with us the God of grace.

1. forebears: ancestors

WORDS: Henry Francis Lyte, 1834, alt.; based on Psalm 103
MUSIC: *Lauda Anima*, John Goss, 1869

8.7.8.7.8.7

13 Come, Thou Fount of Every Blessing

Every good and perfect gift comes down from the Father. – James 1:17 CEV

1. Come, Thou fount of ev-ery bless-ing, tune my heart to sing Thy grace;
2. Here I raise mine Eb-e-ne-zer[1] hith-er by Thy help I'm come;
3. O to grace how great a debt-or dai-ly I'm con-strained[3] to be!

streams of mer-cy, nev-er ceas-ing, call for songs of loud-est praise.
and I hope, by Thy good plea-sure, safe-ly to ar-rive at home.
Let Thy good-ness, like a fet-ter,[4] bind my wan-dering heart to Thee.

Teach me some me-lo-dious son-net, sung by flam-ing tongues a-bove.
Je-sus sought me when a strang-er, wan-dering from the fold of God;
Prone to wan-der, Lord, I feel it, prone to leave the God I love;

Praise the mount! I'm fixed up-on it, mount of Thy re-deem-ing love.
He, to res-cue me from dan-ger, in-ter-posed[2] His pre-cious blood.
here's my heart, O take and seal it, seal it for Thy courts a-bove.

1. Ebenezer: According to 1 Samuel 7:12, a stone commemorating God's deliverance of His people, literally, "stone of help."
2. interposed: placed between   3. constrained: obligated   4. fetter: shackle, chain

WORDS: Robert Robinson, 1758
MUSIC: *Nettleton*, from Wyeth's *Repository of Sacred Music, Part Second,* 1813

8.7.8.7 D

Come, Thou Fount of Every Blessing 14

Every good and perfect gift comes down from the Father. — James 1:17 CEV

1. Come, Thou fount of ev - 'ry bless - ing, tune my heart to
2. Here I raise mine Eb - e - ne - zer[1] hith - er by Thy
3. O to grace how great a debt - or dai - ly I'm con -

sing Thy grace; streams of mer - cy, nev - er ceas - ing,
help I'm come; and I hope, by Thy good plea - sure,
strained[2] to be! Let Thy good - ness, like a fet - ter,[3]

Refrain

call for songs of loud - est praise.
safe - ly to ar - rive at home. I am bound for the king-dom, won't you
bind my wan - d'ring heart to Thee.

go to glo - ry with me? Hal - le - lu - jah! Praise the Lord.

1. Ebenezer: *According to 1 Samuel 7:12, a stone commemorating God's deliverance of His people, literally, "stone of help."*
2. constrained: *obligated*
3. fetter: *shackle, chain*

WORDS: Robert Robinson, 1758
MUSIC: *Warrenton*, from *The Sacred Harp*, 1844; arr. Eric Wyse, 2005
8.7.8.7 with Refrain

15 Unto the Hills

I will lift up mine eyes unto the hills, from whence cometh my help. – Psalm 121:1 KJV

1. Un - to the hills a - round do I lift up my long - ing eyes:
2. He will not suf - fer that thy foot be moved: Safe shalt thou be.
3. Je - ho - vah is Him - self thy Keep - er true, Thy change - less shade;
4. From ev - 'ry e - vil shall He keep thy soul, from ev - 'ry sin:

O whence for me shall my sal - va - tion come, from whence a - rise?
No care - less slum - ber shall His eye - lids close, who keep - eth thee.
Je - ho - vah thy de - fense on thy right hand Him - self hath made.
Je - ho - vah shall pre - serve thy go - ing out, thy com - ing in.

From God the Lord doth come my cer - tain aid,
Be - hold, He sleep - eth not, He slum - b'reth ne'er,
And thee no sun by day shall ev - er smite,
A - bove thee watch - ing, He whom we a - dore

from God the Lord who heav'n and earth hath made.
who keep - eth Is - rael in His ho - ly care.
no moon shall harm thee in the si - lent night.
shall keep thee hence - forth, yea, for - ev - er - more.

WORDS: John Douglas Southerland Campbell, 1866; based on Psalm 121
MUSIC: *Sandon*, Charles Henry Purday, 1860

10.4.10.4.10.10

The God of Abraham Praise

16

I am the God of Abraham. – Exodus 3:6 ESV

1. The God of A-br'ham praise, who reigns en-throned a-bove;
2. He by Him-self hath sworn: We on His oath de-pend;
3. There dwells the Lord, our King, the Lord, our righ-teous-ness,
4. The God who reigns on high the great arch-an-gels sing,
5. The whole tri-um-phant host give thanks to God on high;

An-cient of Ev-er-last-ing Days, and God of love;
we shall, on ea-gle-wings up-borne, to heav'n a-scend:
tri-um-phant o'er the world and sin, the Prince of Peace;
and "Ho-ly, ho-ly, ho-ly," cry, "Al-might-y King!
"Hail, Fa-ther, Son, and Ho-ly Ghost" they ev-er cry;

the Lord, the great I Am, by earth and heav'n con-fessed:
We shall be-hold His face, we shall His pow'r a-dore,
on Zi-on's sa-cred height His king-dom He main-tains,
Who was, and is, the same, and ev-er-more shall be:
hail, A-br'ham's God and mine! I join the heav'n-ly lays;

We bow and bless the sa-cred name for-ev-er blest.
and sing the won-ders of His grace for-ev-er-more.
and, glo-r'ous with His saints in light, for-ev-er reigns.
E-ter-nal Fa-ther, great I Am, we wor-ship Thee."
all might and maj-es-ty are Thine, and end-less praise.

WORDS: Daniel ben Judah, 1404; tr. Thomas Olivers, 1770, alt.
MUSIC: *Leoni*, Hebrew melody; adapt. Thomas Olivers and Meyer Lyon, 1770

6.6.8.4 D

17 God the Omnipotent!

Alleluia! For the Lord God Omnipotent reigneth. – Revelation 19:6 KJV

1. God the Om-nip-o-tent! King, who or-dain-est
2. God the All-mer-ci-ful! Earth hath for-sak-en
3. God the All-righ-teous One! We have de-fied Thee;
4. God the All-prov-i-dent! Earth by Thy chas-tening,
5. So shall Thy chil-dren, with thank-ful de-vo-tion,

thun-der Thy clar-ion, the light-ning Thy sword;
Thy ways All-ho-ly and slight-ed Thy Word;
yet to e-ter-ni-ty stand-eth Thy Word;
yet shall to free-dom and truth be re-stored;
praise Him who saved them from per-il and sword;

show forth Thy pit-y on high where Thou reign-est:
bid not Thy wrath in its ter-rors a-wak-en:
false-hood and wrong shall not tar-ry be-side Thee:
through the thick dark-ness Thy king-dom is hast-ening:
sing-ing in cho-rus from o-cean to o-cean,

Give to us peace in our time, O Lord.
Give to us peace in our time, O Lord.
Give to us peace in our time, O Lord.
Thou wilt give peace in Thy time, O Lord.
peace to the na-tions, and praise to the Lord.

WORDS: Sts. 1, 2 Henry Fothergill Chorley, 1842, alt.; and Sts. 3 - 5 John Ellerton, 1870
MUSIC: *Russian Hymn*, Alexis Fyodorovich Lvov, 1833

11.10.11.9

Immortal, Invisible, God Only Wise   18

Now to the King eternal, immortal, invisible, to God who alone is wise. – 1 Timothy 1:17 NKJV

1. Im - mor - tal, in - vis - i - ble, God on - ly wise,
2. Un - rest - ing, un - hast - ing, and si - lent as light,
3. To all, life Thou giv - est, to both great and small;
4. Great Fa - ther of glo - ry, pure Fa - ther of light,

in light in - ac - ces - si - ble hid from our eyes,
nor want - ing, nor wast - ing, Thou rul - est in might;
in all life Thou liv - est, the true life of all;
Thine an - gels a - dore Thee, all veil - ing their sight;

most bless - ed, most glo - rious, the An - cient of Days,
Thy jus - tice like moun - tains high soar - ing a - bove
we blos - som and flour - ish as leaves on the tree,
all laud we would ren - der, O help us to see

Al - might - y, vic - to - rious, Thy great name we praise.
Thy clouds which are foun - tains of good - ness and love.
and with - er and per - ish, but naught chang - eth Thee.
'tis on - ly the splen - dor of light hid - eth Thee.

WORDS: Walter Chalmers Smith, 1876, alt.
MUSIC: *St. Denio*, Welsh melody from *Canaidau y Cyssegr*, 1839; adapt. and harm. John Roberts, 1839   11.11.11.11

19 From All That Dwell Below the Skies

O give thanks unto the Lord, call upon His name, make known His deeds among the peoples. – 1 Chronicles 16:8 ESV

1. From all that dwell be-low the skies let the Cre-a-tor's praise a-rise; Al-le-lu-ia! Al-le-lu-ia! Let the Re-deem-er's name be sung through ev-'ry land by ev-'ry tongue.

2. In ev-'ry land be-gin the song; to ev-'ry land the strains be-long. Al-le-lu-ia! Al-le-lu-ia! In cheer-ful sound all voic-es raise and fill the world with joy-ful praise.

3. E-ter-nal are Thy mer-cies, Lord; e-ter-nal truth at-tends Thy Word. Al-le-lu-ia! Al-le-lu-ia! Thy praise shall sound from shore to shore till suns shall rise and set no more.

Refrain

Al-le-lu - ia! Al-le-lu - ia! Al-le-

WORDS: Sts. 1, 3 Isaac Watts, 1719, alt.; based on Psalm 117; St. 2 anon.
MUSIC: *Lasst Uns Erfreuen*, from *Geistliche Kirchengesäng*, 1623; harm. Ralph Vaughan Williams, 1906   L.M. with Alleluias
This tune in a lower key, No. 236.

lu - ia!   Al - le - lu - ia!   Al - le - lu - ia!

From All That Dwell Below the Skies   20

O give thanks unto the Lord, call upon His name, make known His deeds among the peoples. – 1 Chronicles 16:8 ESV

1. From all that dwell be - low the skies
2. In ev - 'ry land be - gin the song;
3. E - ter - nal are Thy mer - cies, Lord;

let the Cre - a - tor's praise a - rise;
to ev - 'ry land the strains be - long.
e - ter - nal truth at - tends Thy Word.

let the Re - deem - er's name be sung
In cheer - ful sound all voic - es raise
Thy praise shall sound from shore to shore

through ev - 'ry land by ev - 'ry tongue.
and fill the world with joy - ful praise.
till suns shall rise and set no more.

WORDS: Sts. 1, 3 Isaac Watts, 1719, alt.; based on Psalm 117; St. 2 anon.
MUSIC: *Duke Street*, attr. John Hatton, 1793   L.M.

21 All People That on Earth Do Dwell

Make a joyful noise to the Lord, all ye lands! – Psalm 100:1 KJV

1. All people that on earth do dwell,
2. The Lord, ye know is God indeed;
3. O enter then His gates with praise,
4. For why? The Lord our God is good,
5. To Father, Son, and Holy Ghost,

sing to the Lord with cheerful voice:
without our aid He did us make:
approach with joy His courts unto;
His mercy is for ever sure;
the God whom heav'n and earth adore,

Him serve with fear, His praise forth tell,
We are His flock, He doth us feed,
praise, laud, and bless His name always,
His truth at all times firmly stood,
from earth and from the angel host

come ye before Him and rejoice.
and for His sheep He doth us take.
for it is seemly so to do.
and shall from age to age endure.
be praise and glory evermore.

WORDS: Attr. William Kethe, 1561; based on Psalm 100
MUSIC: *Old 100th (original)*, melody from *Pseaumes Octante Trois de David*, 1551, alt.; harm. Louis Bourgeois, 1551   L.M.
This tune in a higher key, No. 622; another harmonization of this tune, No. 544.

A Mighty Fortress Is Our God

22

The Lord of hosts is with us; the God of Jacob is our fortress. – Psalm 46:7 ESV

1. A might-y for-tress is our God, a bul-wark nev-er fail - ing;
2. Did we in our own strength con-fide, our striv-ing would be los - ing;
3. And though this world, with dev - ils filled, should threat-en to un-do us,
4. That Word a-bove all earth - ly pow'rs, no thanks to them, a-bid - eth;

our help - er He a - mid the flood of mor - tal ills pre - vail - ing.
were not the right Man on our side, the Man of God's own choos - ing.
we will not fear, for God hath willed His truth to tri - umph through us.
the Spir - it and the gifts are ours through Him who with us sid - eth;

For still our an-cient foe doth seek to work us woe; his craft and pow'r are
Dost ask who that may be? Christ Je - sus, it is He; Lord Sab - a - oth His
The prince of dark-ness grim, we trem-ble not for him; his rage we can en -
let goods and kin-dred go, this mor-tal life al - so; the bod - y they may

great; and armed with cru - el hate, on earth is not his e - qual.
name, from age to age the same, and He must win the bat - tle.
dure, for lo! his doom is sure; one lit - tle word shall fell him.
kill, God's truth a - bid - eth still, His king-dom is for - ev - er!

WORDS: Martin Luther, 1529, based on Psalm 46; tr. Frederic Henry Hedge, 1853
MUSIC: *Ein Feste Burg* (Isometric), Martin Luther, 1529

Irregular

23 A Mighty Fortress Is Our God

The Lord of hosts is with us; the God of Jacob is our fortress. – Psalm 46:7 ESV

1. A might-y for-tress is our God, a bul-wark
2. Did we in our own strength con-fide, our striv-ing
3. And though this world with dev-ils filled, should threat-en
4. That Word a-bove all earth-ly pow'rs, no thanks to

nev-er fail - ing; our help-er He a-mid the flood
would be los - ing; were not the right Man on our side,
to un-do us, we will not fear, for God hath willed
them, a-bid - eth; the Spir-it and the gifts are ours

of mor-tal ills pre-vail - ing. For still our an-cient foe
the Man of God's own choos - ing. Dost ask who that may be?
His truth to tri-umph through us. The prince of dark-ness grim,
through Him who with us sid - eth; let goods and kin-dred go,

doth seek to work us woe; his craft and pow'r are great;
Christ Je-sus, it is He; Lord Sab-a-oth His name,
we trem-ble not for him; his rage we can en-dure,
this mor-tal life al-so; the bod-y they may kill,

WORDS: Martin Luther, 1529, based on Psalm 46; tr. Frederic Henry Hedge, 1853
MUSIC: *Ein Feste Burg* (Rhythmic), Martin Luther, 1529

Irregular

and armed with cru - el hate, on earth is not his e - qual.
from age to age the same, and He must win the bat - tle.
for lo! his doom is sure; one lit - tle word shall fell him.
God's truth a - bid - eth still, His king - dom is for - ev - er!

Rejoice, Ye Pure in Heart 24

Be glad in the Lord and rejoice, ye righteous. – Psalm 32:11 KJV

1. Re - joice, ye pure in heart, re - joice, give thanks, and sing;
2. With all the an - gel choirs, with all the saints on earth,
3. Yes, on through life's long path, still sing - ing as ye go;
4. Still lift your stan - dard high, still march in firm ar - ray;
5. Then on, ye pure in heart! Re - joice, give thanks, and sing!

your glo - rious ban - ner wave on high, the cross of Christ your King.
pour out the strains of joy and bliss, true rap - ture, no - blest mirth!
from youth to age, by night and day, in glad - ness and in woe.
as war - riors through the dark - ness toil till dawns the gold - en day.
Your glo - r'ous ban - ner wave on high, the cross of Christ your King.

Refrain

Re - joice, re - joice, re - joice, give thanks, and sing!
Re - joice, re - joice,

WORDS: Edward Hayes Plumptre, 1865, alt.
MUSIC: *Marion*, Arthur Henry Messiter, 1883

S.M. with Refrain

25 Praise the Lord! His Glories Show

Praise the name of the Lord...His glory is above the earth and heaven. – Psalm 148:13 KJV

1. Praise the Lord! His glo-ries show: Al - le - lu - ia!
2. Earth to heav'n and heav'n to earth: Al - le - lu - ia!
3. Praise the Lord, His mer-cies trace: Al - le - lu - ia!
4. Strings and voic-es, hands and hearts: Al - le - lu - ia!

Saints with-in His courts be - low: Al - le - lu - ia!
Tell His won-ders, sing His worth: Al - le - lu - ia!
Praise His prov-i-dence and grace: Al - le - lu - ia!
In the con-cert, bear your parts: Al - le - lu - ia!

An - gels round His throne a - bove: Al - le - lu - ia!
Age to age and shore to shore: Al - le - lu - ia!
All that He for us hath done: Al - le - lu - ia!
All that breathe, your Lord a - dore; Al - le - lu - ia!

All that see and share His love: Al - le - lu - ia!
Praise Him, praise Him ev - er - more: Al - le - lu - ia!
All He sends us through His Son; Al - le - lu - ia!
Praise Him, praise Him ev - er - more: Al - le - lu - ia!

WORDS: Henry Frances Lyte, 1834, alt.; based on Psalm 150.
MUSIC: *Llanfair*, Robert Williams, 1817; harm. John Roberts, 1837
Another harmonization of this tune, No. 245; this tune in a higher key, No. 193.

7.7.7.7 with Alleluias

O Praise Ye the Lord!

All the ends of the earth have seen the salvation of our God. – Psalm 98:3 KJV

1. O praise ye the Lord! Praise Him in the height;
2. O praise ye the Lord! Praise Him up-on earth,
3. O praise ye the Lord All things that give sound;
4. O praise ye the Lord! Thanks-giv-ing and song

re - joice in His Word, ye an-gels of light;
in tune - ful ac - cord, ye heirs of new birth;
each ju - bi - lant chord re - ech - o a - round;
to Him be out - poured all a - ges a - long;

ye heav - ens a - dore Him, by Whom ye were made,
praise Him who hath brought you His grace from a - bove,
loud or - gans His glo - ry forth - tell in deep tone,
for love in cre - a - tion, for heav - en re - stored,

and wor - ship be - fore Him in bright-ness ar - rayed.
praise Him who hath taught you to sing of His love.
and sweet harp the sto - ry of what He hath done.
for grace of sal - va - tion, O praise ye the Lord!

WORDS: Henry Williams Baker, 1875, alt.; based on Psalms 148, 150
MUSIC: *Laudate Dominum (Parry)*, Charles Hubert Hastings Parry, 1897

10.10.11.11

27 How Great Thou Art!

O great and mighty God...great in counsel and mighty in deed. – Jeremiah 32:18-19 ESV

1. O Lord, my God, when I in awe-some won-der con-sid-er
2. When through the woods and for-est glades I wan-der and hear the
3. And when I think that God, His Son not spar-ing, sent Him to
4. When Christ shall come with shout of ac-cla-ma-tion and take me

all the worlds Thy hands have made; I see the stars, I hear the
birds sing sweet-ly in the trees; when I look down from loft-y
die, I scarce can take it in, that on the cross, my bur-den
home, what joy shall fill my heart! Then I shall bow in hum-ble

roll-ing thun-der, Thy pow'r through-out the u-ni-verse dis-played.
moun-tain gran-deur, and hear the brook and feel the gen-tle breeze.
glad-ly bear-ing, He bled and died to take a-way my sin.
ad-o-ra-tion, and there pro-claim, "My God, how great Thou art!"

Refrain

Then sings my soul, my Sav-ior God, to Thee, "How great Thou

WORDS: Carl Boberg, 1886; tr. and adapt. Stuart K. Hine, 1953
MUSIC: *O Store Gud*, adapt. Stuart K. Hine, 1953

11.10.11.10 with Refrain

art, how great Thou art!" Then sings my soul, my Sav-ior God, to

Thee, "How great Thou art, how great Thou art!"

O God, Our Help in Ages Past 28

Lord, Thou hast been our dwelling place in all generations. – Psalm 90:1 KJV

1. O God, our help in a-ges past, our hope for years to come,
2. Un-der the shad-ow of Thy throne, Thy saints have dwelt se-cure;
3. Be-fore the hills in or-der stood, or earth re-ceived her frame,
4. A thou-sand a-ges in Thy sight are like an eve-ning gone;
5. Time, like an ev-er-roll-ing stream, bears all its sons a-way;
6. O God, our help in a-ges past, our hope for years to come,

our shel-ter from the storm-y blast, and our e-ter-nal home!
suf-fi-cient is Thine arm a-lone, and our de-fense is sure.
from ev-er-last-ing Thou art God, to end-less years the same.
short as the watch that ends the night be-fore the ris-ing sun.
they fly, for-got-ten, as a dream dies at the o-p'ning day.
be Thou our guide while life shall last, and our e-ter-nal home.

WORDS: Isaac Watts, 1719; based on Psalm 90:1-5
MUSIC: *St. Anne*, from *A Supplement to the New Version*, attr. William Croft, 1708; harm. William Henry Monk, 1861   C.M.
This tune in a higher key, No. 198.

29 Sing Praise to God Who Reigns Above

Proclaim the name of the Lord; ascribe greatness to our God. – Deuteronomy 32:3 ESV

1. Sing praise to God who reigns above, the God of all cre-a-tion, the God of pow'r, the God of love, the God of our sal-va-tion; with healing balm my soul He fills and ev-'ry faith-less

2. What God's al-might-y pow'r hath made, His gra-cious mer-cy keep-eth; by morn-ing glow or eve-ning shade His watch-ful eye ne'er sleep-eth. With-in the king-dom of His might, lo! All is just and

3. The Lord is nev-er far a-way, but through all grief dis-tress-ing, an ev-er pres-ent help and stay, our peace and joy and bless-ing; as with a moth-er's ten-der hand He leads His own, His

4. Thus all my toil-some way a-long I sing a-loud Thy prais-es that all may hear the grate-ful song my voice un-wea-ried rais-es. Be joy-ful in the Lord, my heart, both soul and bod-y

5. O ye who name Christ's ho-ly name, give God all praise and glo-ry; let all who own His pow'r pro-claim a-round the won-drous sto-ry! Cast each false i-dol from its throne, the Lord is God, and

WORDS: Johann Jacob Schütz, 1675; tr. Frances Elizabeth Cox, 1858, alt.
MUSIC: *Mit Freuden Zart*, Bohemian Brethren's *Kirchengasänge*, Berlin, 1566; harm. Henrich Reimann, 1895   8.7.8.7.8.8.7

mur - mur stills; to God all praise and glo - ry!
all is right; to God all praise and glo - ry!
cho - sen band; to God all praise and glo - ry!
take your part; to God all praise and glo - ry!
He a - lone; to God all praise and glo - ry!

Begin, My Tongue, Some Heavenly Theme 30

My tongue will sing of Your Word. – Psalm 119:172 ESV

1. Be - gin, my tongue, some heav'n - ly theme and
2. Tell of His won - drous faith - ful - ness and
3. His ve - ry Word of grace is strong as
4. O might I hear Thy heav'n - ly tongue but

speak some bound - less thing: The might - y works or
sound His pow'r a - broad; sing the sweet prom - ise
that which built the skies; the voice that rolls the
whis - per, "Thou art mine!" Those gen - tle words shall

might - ier Name of our e - ter - nal King.
of His grace, the love and truth of God.
stars a - long speaks all the prom - is - es.
raise my song to notes al - most di - vine.

WORDS: Isaac Watts, 1707
MUSIC: *Manoah*, Henry Wellington Greatorex, 1851
This tune in a lower key, No. 332

C.M.

31 To God Be the Glory

To our God and Father...be the glory forever and ever. – Galatians 1:3 - 5 ESV

1. To God be the glo - ry, great things He hath done; so loved He the
2. O per - fect re - demp - tion, the pur - chase of blood, to ev - 'ry be -
3. Great things He hath taught us, great things He hath done, and great our re -

world that He gave us His Son, who yield - ed His life an a -
liev - er the prom - ise of God; the vil - est of - fend - er who
joic - ing through Je - sus the Son; but pur - er, and high - er, and

tone - ment for sin, and o - pened the life-gate that all may go in.
tru - ly be - lieves, that mo - ment from Je - sus a par - don re - ceives.
great - er will be our won - der, our vic - t'ry, when Je - sus we see.

Refrain

Praise the Lord, praise the Lord, let the earth hear His voice! Praise the Lord,

praise the Lord, let the peo - ple re - joice! O come to the Fa - ther, through

WORDS: Fanny Jane Crosby, 1875
MUSIC: *To God Be the Glory*, William Howard Doane, 1875

11.11.11.11 with Refrain

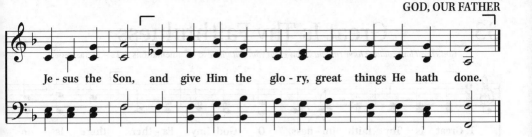

Je - sus the Son, and give Him the glo - ry, great things He hath done.

We Praise Thee, O God 32

Sing unto the Lord, and give thanks at the remembrance of His holiness. – Psalm 30:4 KJV

1. We praise Thee, O God, our Re - deem - er, Cre - a - tor;
2. We wor - ship Thee, God of our fa - thers; we bless Thee.
3. With voic - es u - nit - ed our prais - es we of - fer,

in grate - ful de - vo - tion our trib - ute we bring.
Through life's storm and tem - pest our guide Thou hast been.
to Thee great Je - ho - vah glad an - thems we raise.

We lay it be - fore Thee; we kneel and a - dore Thee.
When per - ils o'er - take us, es - cape Thou wilt make us
Thy strong arm will guide us; our God is be - side us.

We bless Thy ho - ly name; glad prais - es we sing.
and with Thy help, O Lord, our bat - tles we win.
To Thee, our great Re - deem - er, for - ev - er be praise.

WORDS: Anon. 1626; tr. Julia Bulkley Cady Cory, 1882
MUSIC: *Kremser,* attr. Adrianus Valerius, 1625; arr. Edward Kremser, 1877

12.11.12.11

33 Great Is Thy Faithfulness

God's loyal love couldn't have run out...How great your faithfulness! – Lamentations 3:22 - 23 The Message

1. Great is Thy faith - ful - ness, O God my Fa - ther, there is no
2. Sum - mer and win - ter, and spring - time and har - vest, sun, moon and
3. Par - don for sin and a peace that en - dur - eth, Thy own dear

shad - ow of turn - ing with Thee; Thou chang - est not, Thy com -
stars in their cours - es a - bove join with all na - ture in
pres - ence to cheer and to guide; strength for to - day and bright

pas - sions they fail not; as Thou hast been Thou for - ev - er wilt be.
man - i - fold wit - ness to Thy great faith - ful - ness, mer - cy and love.
hope for to - mor - row, bless - ings all mine, with ten thou-sand be - side!

Refrain

Great is Thy faith - ful - ness! Great is Thy faith - ful - ness! Morn - ing by

morn - ing new mer - cies I see; all I have need - ed Thy

WORDS: Thomas Obediah Chisholm, 1923
MUSIC: *Faithfulness*, William Marion Runyan, 1923

11.10.11.10 with Refrain

hand hath pro - vid - ed; great is Thy faith - ful - ness, Lord un - to me!

Stand Up and Bless the Lord 34

Stand up and bless the Lord your God from everlasting to everlasting. – Nehemiah 9:5 ESV

1. Stand up and bless the Lord, ye peo - ple
2. Though high a - bove all praise, a - bove all
3. O for the liv - ing flame from His own
4. God is our strength and song, and His sal -
5. Stand up and bless the Lord; the Lord your

of His choice; stand up and bless the
bless - ing high, who would not fear His
al - tar brought, to touch our lips, our
va - tion ours; then be His love in
God a - dore; stand up and bless His

Lord your God with heart and soul and voice.
ho - ly name, and laud and mag - ni - fy?
minds in - spire, and wing to heav'n our thought!
Christ pro - claimed with all our ran - somed pow'rs.
glo - rious name, hence - forth for - ev - er - more.

WORDS: James Montgomery, 1824
MUSIC: *St. Michael (Old 134th)*, melody Louis Bourgeois from *Genevan Psalter,* 1551; adapt. William Crotch, 1836   S.M.

35 O Bless the Lord, My Soul!

Bless the Lord, O my soul! O Lord, my God, Thou are very great. – Psalm 104:1 KJV

1. O bless the Lord, my soul! His grace to thee pro - claim!
2. O bless the Lord, my soul! His mer - cies bear in mind!
3. He will not al - ways chide; He will with pa - tience wait;
4. He par - dons all thy sins, pro - longs thy fee - ble breath;
5. He clothes thee with His love, up - holds thee with His truth;
6. Then bless His ho - ly name, whose grace hath made thee whole,

And all that is with - in me join to bless His ho - ly name!
For - get not all His ben - e - fits! The Lord to thee is kind.
His wrath is ev - er slow to rise and read - y to a - bate.
He heal - eth thine in - fir - mi - ties and ran - soms thee from death.
and like the ea - gle He re - news the vig - or of thy youth.
whose lov - ing - kind - ness crowns thy days: O bless the Lord, my soul!

WORDS: James Montgomery, 1819
MUSIC: *St. Thomas*, Aaron Williams, 1770; harm. Lowell Mason, n.d.
This tune in a lower key, No. 320.

S.M.

36 Bless the Lord, O My Soul

Bless the Lord, O my soul: And all that is within me, bless His holy name! – Psalm 103:1 KJV

Bless the Lord, O my soul; bless the Lord, O my soul;

and all that is with - in me bless His ho - ly name.

WORDS: Psalm 103:1
MUSIC: *Bless the Lord*, anon., n.d.

Irregular

Blessed Be the Name

Blessed be His glorious name forever! – Psalm 72:19 KJV

37

1. O for a thou-sand tongues to sing, bless-ed be the name of the Lord!
2. Je - sus, the name that calms my fears, bless-ed be the name of the Lord!
3. He breaks the pow'r of can - celed sin, bless-ed be the name of the Lord!
4. I nev - er shall for - get that day, bless-ed be the name of the Lord!

The glo - ries of my God and King, bless-ed be the name of the Lord!
'Tis mu - sic in the sin - ner's ears, bless-ed be the name of the Lord!
His blood can make the foul - est clean, bless-ed be the name of the Lord!
When Je - sus washed my sins a - way, bless-ed be the name of the Lord!

Refrain

Bless-ed be the name, bless-ed be the name, bless-ed be the name of the Lord!

Bless-ed be the name, bless-ed be the name, bless-ed be the name of the Lord!

WORDS: Charles Wesley, 1739, alt.; Ref. Ralph Erskine Hudson, 1887
MUSIC: *Blessed Name,* American camp meeting melody, Anon., 19th c.; arr. Ralph Erskine Hudson, 1887   L.M. with Refrain

38 Glorious Is Thy Name

Now therefore, our God, we give You thanks and praise Your glorious name. – 1 Chronicles 29:13 HCSB

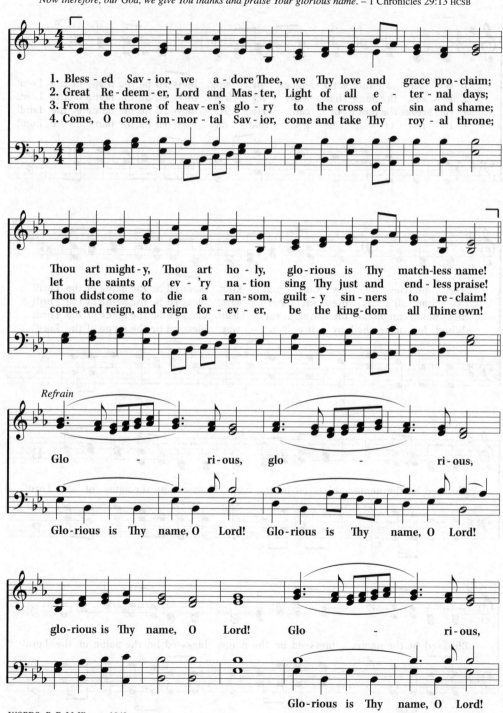

1. Bless-ed Sav-ior, we a-dore Thee, we Thy love and grace pro-claim;
2. Great Re-deem-er, Lord and Mas-ter, Light of all e-ter-nal days;
3. From the throne of heav-en's glo-ry to the cross of sin and shame;
4. Come, O come, im-mor-tal Sav-ior, come and take Thy roy-al throne;

Thou art might-y, Thou art ho-ly, glo-rious is Thy match-less name!
let the saints of ev-'ry na-tion sing Thy just and end-less praise!
Thou didst come to die a ran-som, guilt-y sin-ners to re-claim!
come, and reign, and reign for-ev-er, be the king-dom all Thine own!

Refrain

Glo - ri-ous, glo - ri-ous,
Glo-rious is Thy name, O Lord! Glo-rious is Thy name, O Lord!

glo-rious is Thy name, O Lord! Glo - ri-ous,

Glo-rious is Thy name, O Lord!

WORDS: B. B. McKinney, 1942
MUSIC: *Glorious Name*, B. B. McKinney, 1942

8.7.8.7 with Refrain

glo - ri-ous, glo-rious is Thy name, O Lord!

Glo-rious is Thy name, O Lord!

Jesus Shall Reign

39

We have a building from God, a house…eternal in the heavens. – 2 Corinthians 5:1 HCSB

1. Je - sus shall reign wher - e'er the sun does its suc -
2. To Him shall end - less prayer be made, and end - less
3. Peo - ple and realms of ev - 'ry tongue dwell on His
4. Bless - ings a - bound wher - e'er He reigns; the pris - 'ners
5. Let ev - 'ry crea - ture rise and bring hon - or and

ces - sive jour - neys run; His king - dom spread from
prais - es crown His head; His name like sweet per -
love with sweet - est song; and in - fant voic - es
leap to lose their chains, the wea - ry find e -
glo - ry to our King; an - gels de - scend with

shore to shore, till moons shall wax and wane no more.
fume shall rise with ev - 'ry morn - ing sac - ri - fice.
shall pro - claim their ear - ly bless - ings on His name.
ter - nal rest, and all who suf - fer want are blest.
songs a - gain, and earth re - peat the loud "A - men."

WORDS: Isaac Watts, 1719, alt.; based on Psalm 72
MUSIC: *Duke Street*, John Hatton, 1793

L.M.

40 Love Divine, All Loves Excelling

God is love. Whoever lives in love lives in God, and God in him. – 1 John 4:16 NIV

1. Love di-vine, all loves ex-cel-ling, joy of heav'n, to earth come down;
2. Breathe, O breathe Thy lov-ing Spir-it in-to ev-'ry trou-bled breast!
3. Come, Al-might-y to de-liv-er, let us all Thy life re-ceive;
4. Fin-ish, then, Thy new cre-a-tion; pure and spot-less let us be.

fix in us Thy hum-ble dwell-ing; all Thy faith-ful mer-cies crown!
Let us all in Thee in-her-it; let us find that sec-ond rest.
sud-den-ly re-turn and nev-er, nev-er-more Thy tem-ples leave.
Let us see Thy great sal-va-tion per-fect-ly re-stored in Thee;

Je-sus, Thou art all com-pas-sion, pure, un-bound-ed love Thou art;
Take a-way our bent to sin-ning; Al-pha and O-me-ga be;
Thee we would be al-ways bless-ing, serve Thee as Thy hosts a-bove,
changed from glo-ry in-to glo-ry, till in heav'n we take our place,

vis-it us with Thy sal-va-tion; en-ter ev-'ry trem-bling heart.
end of faith, as its be-gin-ning, set our hearts at lib-er-ty.
pray and praise Thee with-out ceas-ing, glo-ry in Thy per-fect love.
till we cast our crowns be-fore Thee, lost in won-der, love, and praise.

WORDS: Charles Wesley, 1747
MUSIC: *Beecher*, John Zundel, 1870

8.7.8.7 D

Love Divine, All Loves Excelling

41

God is love. Whoever lives in love lives in God, and God in him. – 1 John 4:16 NIV

1. Love di - vine, all loves ex - cel-ling, joy of heav'n, to earth come down;
2. Breathe, O breathe Thy lov - ing Spir - it in - to ev - 'ry trou - bled breast!
3. Come, Al - might - y to de - liv - er, let us all Thy life re - ceive;
4. Fin - ish, then, Thy new cre - a - tion; pure and spot - less let us be.

fix in us Thy hum - ble dwell - ing; all Thy faith - ful mer - cies crown!
Let us all in Thee in - her - it; let us find that sec - ond rest.
sud - den - ly re - turn and nev - er, nev - er - more Thy tem - ples leave.
Let us see Thy great sal - va - tion per - fect - ly re - stored in Thee;

Je - sus, Thou art all com - pas-sion, pure, un-bound - ed love Thou art;
Take a - way our bent to sin - ning; Al - pha and O - me - ga be;
Thee we would be al - ways bless-ing, serve Thee as Thy hosts a - bove,
changed from glo - ry in - to glo - ry, till in heav'n we take our place,

vis - it us with Thy sal - va - tion; en - ter ev - 'ry trem - bling heart.
end of faith, as its be - gin - ning, set our hearts at lib - er - ty.
pray and praise Thee with - out ceas - ing, glo - ry in Thy per - fect love.
till we cast our crowns be - fore Thee, lost in won - der, love, and praise.

WORDS: Charles Wesley, 1747
MUSIC: *Blaenwern*, William Penfro Rowlands, 1905

8.7.8.7 D

42 Love Divine, All Loves Excelling

God is love. Whoever lives in love lives in God, and God in him. – 1 John 4:16 NIV

1. Love di- vine, all loves ex- cel- ling, joy of heav'n, to earth come down; fix in us Thy hum- ble dwell- ing; all Thy faith- ful mer- cies crown! Je- sus, Thou art all com- pas- sion, pure, un- bound- ed love Thou art; vis- it us with

2. Breathe, O breathe Thy lov- ing Spir- it in- to ev- 'ry trou- bled breast! Let us all in Thee in- her- it; let us find that sec- ond rest. Take a- way our bent to sin- ning; Al- pha and O- me- ga be; end of faith, as

3. Come, Al- might- y to de- liv- er, let us all Thy life re- ceive; sud- den- ly re- turn and nev- er, nev- er- more Thy tem- ples leave. Thee we would be al- ways bless- ing, serve Thee as Thy hosts a- bove, pray and praise Thee

4. Fin- ish, then, Thy new cre- a- tion; pure and spot- less let us be. Let us see Thy great sal- va- tion per- fect- ly re- stored in Thee; changed from glo- ry in- to glo- ry, till in heav'n we take our place, till we cast our

WORDS: Charles Wesley, 1747
MUSIC: *Hyfrydol,* Rowland Hugh Prichard, ca. 1830; harm. *The English Hymnal,* 1906

8.7.8.7 D

This tune in a lower key (E♭), No. 74 ; with another harmonization (D), No. 248.

Thy sal - va - tion; en - ter ev - 'ry trem - bling heart.
its be - gin - ning, set our hearts at lib - er - ty.
with - out ceas - ing, glo - ry in Thy per - fect love.
crowns be - fore Thee, lost in won - der, love, and praise.

Join All the Glorious Names 43

God…is far above every ruler, authority, and above every name that is named. – Ephesians 1:21 ESV

1. Join all the glo - rious names of wis - dom, love, and pow'r,
2. Great Proph - et of my God, my tongue would bless Thy name:
3. Je - sus, my great High Priest, of - fered His blood and died;
4. Be Thou my Coun - sel - or, my Pat - tern, and my Guide,
5. My dear Al - might - y Lord, my Con - qu'ror and my King,

that ev - er mor - tals knew, that an - gels ev - er bore: All are too
By Thee the joy - ful news of our sal - va - tion came: The joy - ful
my guilt - y con-science seeks no sac - ri - fice be - side: His pow'r - ful
and through this des - ert land still keep me near Thy side; O let my
Thy scep - ter and Thy sword, Thy reign-ing grace, I sing; Thine is the

poor to speak His worth, too poor to set my Sav - ior forth.
news of sins for - giv'n, of hell sub - dued, and peace with heav'n.
blood did once a - tone, and now it pleads be - fore the throne.
feet ne'er run a - stray nor rove nor seek the crook - ed way.
pow'r; be - hold I sit in will - ing bonds be - neath Thy feet.

WORDS: Isaac Watts, 1707
MUSIC: *Darwall's 148th*, John Darwall, 1770
Another harmonization of this tune, No. 206.

6.6.6.6.8.8

44 O Could I Speak the Matchless Worth

We have seen His glory...who came from the Father, full of grace and truth. – John 1:14 NIV

1. O could I speak the match-less worth, O could I sound the glo-ries forth which in my Sav-ior shine! I'd sing His glo-rious righ-teous-ness, and mag-ni-fy the won-drous grace which made sal-va-tion mine, which made sal-va-tion mine.

2. I'd sing the pre-cious blood He spilt, my ran-som from the dread-ful guilt of sin, and wrath di-vine; I'd sing His glo-rious ho-li-ness, in which all-per-fect, heav'n-ly dress my soul shall ev-er shine, my soul shall ev-er shine.

3. I'd sing the char-ac-ter He bears and all the forms of love He wears, ex-alt-ed on His throne; in loft-iest songs of sweet-est praise, I would to ev-er-last-ing days make all His glo-ries known, make all His glo-ries known.

4. Soon the de-light-ful day will come when my dear Lord will bring me home, and I shall see His face; then with my Sav-ior, Broth-er, Friend, a blest e-ter-ni-ty I'll spend, tri-um-phant in His grace, tri-um-phant in His grace.

WORDS: Samuel Medley, 1789
MUSIC: *Ariel*, Wolfgang Amadeus Mozart, 1791; adapt. Lowell Mason, 1836

8.8.6.8.8.6 with Repeat

Come, Christians, Join to Sing

Sing psalms, hymns, and spiritual songs, as you praise the Lord with all your heart. – Ephesians 5:19 CEV

1. Come, Chris-tians, join to sing Al - le - lu - ia, A - men!
2. Come, lift your hearts on high; Al - le - lu - ia, A - men!
3. Praise yet our Christ a - gain; Al - le - lu - ia, A - men!

Loud praise to Christ our King; Al - le - lu - ia, A - men!
Let prais - es fill the sky; Al - le - lu - ia, A - men!
Life shall not end the strain; Al - le - lu - ia, A - men!

Let all with heart and voice be - fore His throne re - joice;
He is our Guide and Friend; to us He'll con - de - scend;
On heav - en's bliss - ful shore His good - ness we'll a - dore,

praise is His gra - cious choice; Al - le - lu - ia, A - men!
His love shall nev - er end, Al - le - lu - ia, A - men!
sing - ing for - ev - er - more, Al - le - lu - ia, A - men!

WORDS: Christian Henry Bateman, 1843
MUSIC: *Madrid*, Spanish melody, ca. 1824

6.6.6.6 D

46 Crown Him with Many Crowns

His eyes were like flames of fire, and on His head were many crowns. – Revelation 19:12 NIV

1. Crown Him with man - y crowns, the Lamb up - on His throne.
2. Crown Him the Son of God, be - fore the worlds be - gan,
3. Crown Him the Lord of love, be - hold His hands and side,
4. Crown Him the Lord of life, who tri - umphed o'er the grave,
5. Crown Him the Lord of peace, whose pow'r a scep - ter sways
6. Crown Him the Lord of heav'n, One with the Fa - ther known,
7. Crown Him the Lord of years, the Po - ten - tate of time,

Hark! How the heav'n - ly an - them drowns all mu - sic but its own.
and ye who tread where He hath trod, crown Him the Son of Man;
those wounds, yet vis - i - ble a - bove, in beau - ty glo - ri - fied.
and rose vic - to - rious in the strife for those He came to save.
from pole to pole, that wars may cease, and all be prayer and praise.
One with the Spir - it through Him giv'n from yon - der glo - rious throne.
Cre - a - tor of the roll - ing spheres, in - ef - fa - bly[1] sub - lime.[2]

A - wake, my soul, and sing of Him who died for thee,
who ev - 'ry grief hath known that wrings the hu - man breast,
No an - gel in the sky can ful - ly bear that sight,
His glo - ries now we sing, who died and rose on high,
His reign shall know no end, and 'round His pierc - ed feet
To Thee be end - less praise for Thou for us hast died.
All hail, Re - deem - er, hail! For Thou hast died for me;

1. *ineffably: not able to put into words*
2. *sublime: grandeur, excellence and beauty that results in honor, admiration and awe*

WORDS: Sts. 1, 4-7 Matthew Bridges, 1852; Sts. 2, 3 Godfrey Thring, 1874
MUSIC: *Diademata*, George Job Elvey, 1868
S.M.D.
This tune in a lower key, No. 449; another harmonization of this tune, in a lower key, No. 488.

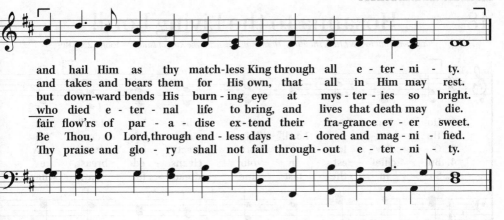

and hail Him as thy match-less King through all e-ter-ni-ty.
and takes and bears them for His own, that all in Him may rest.
but down-ward bends His burn-ing eye at mys-ter-ies so bright.
who died e-ter-nal life to bring, and lives that death may die.
fair flow'rs of par-a-dise ex-tend their fra-grance ev-er sweet.
Be Thou, O Lord, through end-less days a-dored and mag-ni-fied.
Thy praise and glo-ry shall not fail through-out e-ter-ni-ty.

O Come, Let Us Adore Him   47

We have come to worship Him. – Matthew 2:2 NIV

1. O come, let us a-dore Him, O come, let us a-dore Him,
2. We'll praise His name for-ev-er, we'll praise His name for-ev-er,
3. We'll give Him all the glo-ry, we'll give Him all the glo-ry,
4. For He a-lone is wor-thy, for He a-lone is wor-thy,

O come, let us a-dore Him, Christ the Lord.
we'll praise His name for-ev-er, Christ the Lord.
we'll give Him all the glo-ry, Christ the Lord.
for He a-lone is wor-thy, Christ the Lord.

WORDS: Traditional
MUSIC: *Adeste Fideles* (Ref. only), from Wade's *Cantus Diversi*, 1751

7.7.10

48 Hosanna to the Living Lord!

They...went out to meet Him, shouting, "Hosanna!...Blessed is the King of Israel!" – John 12:13 NIV

1. Ho - san - na to the liv - ing Lord! Ho -
2. "Ho - san - na, Lord!" Thine an - gels cry; "Ho -
3. O Sav - ior, with pro - tect - ing care now
4. But chief - est, in our cleans - ed breast, e -
5. So in the last and dread - ful day, when

san - na to the In - car - nate Word! To Christ, Cre - a - tor,
san - na, Lord!" Thy saints re - ply; a - bove, be - neath us,
bide in this Thy house of prayer, as - sem - bled in Thy
ter - nal, bid Thy Spir - it rest; and make our se - cret
earth and heav'n shall melt a - way, Thy flock, re - deemed from

Sav - ior, King, let earth, let heav'n ho - san - na sing!
and a - round, both dead and liv - ing swell the sound;
sa - cred name, where we Thy part - ing prom - ise claim,
soul to be a tem - ple pure and wor - thy Thee!
sin - ful stain, shall swell the sound of praise a - gain.

Refrain

Ho - san - na, Lord! Ho - san - na in the high - est!

WORDS: Reginald Heber, 1811
MUSIC: *Hosanna*, John Bacchus Dykes, 1865

L.M. with Refrain

O for a Thousand Tongues to Sing 49

Every tongue confess that Jesus Christ is Lord, to the glory of God the Father. – Philippians 2:11 NIV

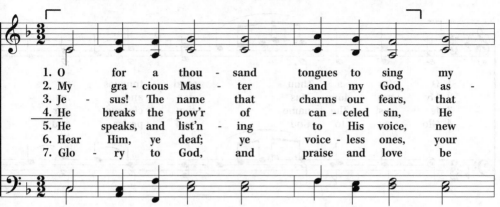

1. O for a thou - sand tongues to sing my
2. My gra - cious Mas - ter and my God, as -
3. Je - sus! The name that charms our fears, that
4. He breaks the pow'r of can - celed sin, He
5. He speaks, and list'n - ing to His voice, new
6. Hear Him, ye deaf; ye voice - less ones, your
7. Glo - ry to God, and praise and love be

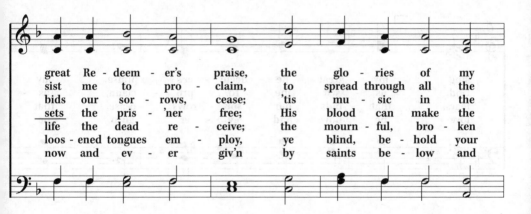

great Re - deem - er's praise, the glo - ries of my
sist me to pro - claim, to spread through all the
bids our sor - rows, cease; 'tis mu - sic in the
sets the pris - 'ner free; His blood can make the
life the dead re - ceive; the mourn - ful, bro - ken
loos - ened tongues em - ploy, ye blind, be - hold your
now and ev - er giv'n by saints be - low and

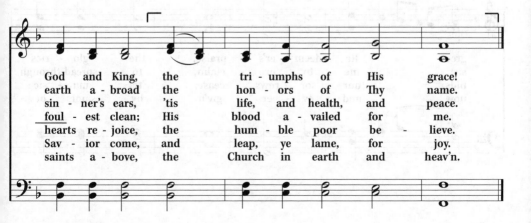

God and King, the tri - umphs of His grace!
earth a - broad the hon - ors of Thy name.
sin - ner's ears, 'tis life, and health, and peace.
foul - est clean; His blood a - vailed for me.
hearts re - joice, the hum - ble poor be - lieve.
Sav - ior come, and leap, ye lame, for joy.
saints a - bove, the Church in earth and heav'n.

WORDS: Charles Wesley, 1739
MUSIC: *Azmon*, Carl Gotthelf Gläser, 1828; arr. Lowell Mason, 1839

C.M.

50 O for a Thousand Tongues to Sing

Every tongue confess that Jesus Christ is Lord, to the glory of God the Father. – Philippians 2:11 NIV

1. O for a thou - sand tongues to
2. My gra - cious Mas - ter and my
3. Je - sus! The name that charms our
4. Glo - ry to God and praise and

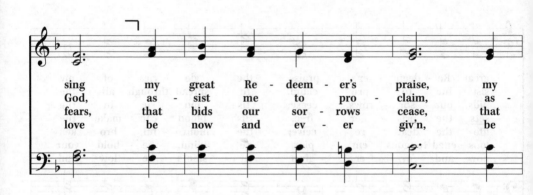

sing my great Re - deem - er's praise, my
God, as - sist me to pro - claim, as -
fears, that bids our sor - rows cease, that
love be now and ev - er giv'n, be

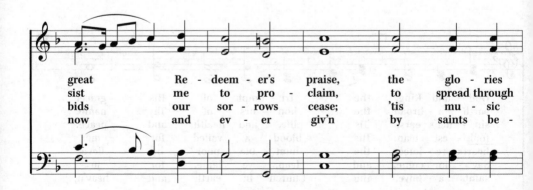

great Re - deem - er's praise, the glo - ries
sist me to pro - claim, to spread through
bids our sor - rows cease; 'tis mu - sic
now and ev - er giv'n by saints be -

WORDS: Charles Wesley, 1739
MUSIC: *Lyngham*, Thomas Jarman, ca. 1803

C.M. with Repeat

51 May Jesus Christ Be Praised!

Praise the God and Father of our Lord Jesus Christ. – Ephesians 1:3 CEV

1. When morn - ing gilds the skies, my heart, a - wak - ing, cries,
2. When mirth for mu - sic longs, this is my song of songs;
3. No love - lier an - ti - phon in all high heav'n is known
4. Ye na - tions of man - kind, in this your con - cord find:
5. Sing, suns and stars of space, sing, ye that see His face,

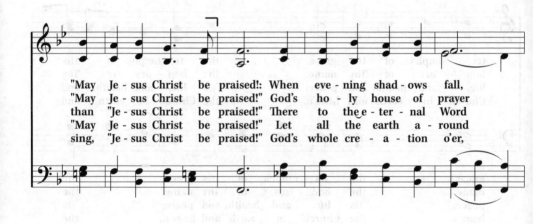

"May Je - sus Christ be praised!: When eve - ning shad - ows fall,
"May Je - sus Christ be praised!" God's ho - ly house of prayer
than "Je - sus Christ be praised!" There to the e - ter - nal Word
"May Je - sus Christ be praised!" Let all the earth a - round
sing, "Je - sus Christ be praised!" God's whole cre - a - tion o'er,

this rings my cur - few call, "May Je - sus Christ be praised!"
hath none that can com - pare with, "Je - sus Christ be praised!"
the e - ter - nal psalm is heard: "May Je - sus Christ be praised!"
ring joy - ous with the sound: "May Je - sus Christ be praised!"
both now and ev - er - more shall Je - sus Christ be praised!

WORDS: German, ca. 18th c.; tr. Robert Seymour Bridges, 1899, alt.
MUSIC: *Laudes Domini*, Joseph Barnby, 1868

6.6.6.6.6.6

As the Deer

The Lord is my strength and my shield; my heart trusted...and I am helped – Psalm 28:7 KJV

1. As the deer pants for the wa-ter, so my soul longs af-ter
2. You're my Friend and You are my Broth-er, e-ven though You are a
3. I want You more than gold or sil-ver, on-ly You can sat-is-

You. You a-lone are my heart's de-sire, and I
King. I love You more than an-y oth-er, so much
fy. You a-lone are the real joy giv-er, and the

Refrain

long to wor-ship You.
more than an-y-thing. You a-lone are my Strength, my Shield; to
ap-ple of my eye.

You a-lone may my spir-it yield. You a-lone are my

heart's de-sire, and I long to wor-ship You.

WORDS: Martin Nystrom, 1984
MUSIC: *As the Deer*, Martin Nystrom, 1984

Irregular with Refrain

53 Fairest Lord Jesus

His face was shining as bright as the sun. – Revelation 1:16 CEV

1. Fair - est Lord Je - sus, rul - er of all na - ture, O Thou of
2. Fair are the mead - ows, fair - er still the wood - lands, robed in the
3. Fair is the sun - shine, fair - er still the moon - light, and all the
4. Beau - ti - ful Sav - ior! Lord of the na - tions! Son of

God and man the Son, Thee will I cher - ish,
bloom - ing garb of spring; Je - sus is fair - er,
twin - kling, star - ry host; Je - sus shines bright - er,
God and Son of Man! Glo - ry and hon - or,

Thee will I hon - or, Thou my soul's glo - ry, joy, and crown!
Je - sus is pur - er, who makes the woe - ful heart to sing.
Je - sus shines pur - er, than all the an - gels heav'n can boast.
praise, ad - o - ra - tion, now and for - ev - er - more be Thine!

WORDS: *Münster Gesangbuch*, 1677; tr. Joseph August Seiss, 1873
MUSIC: *Crusader's Hymn* (*St. Elizabeth*); melody from *Schlesische Volkslieder*, 1842; harm. Thomas Tertius Noble, 1918 Irregular

54 Beautiful Savior

Who is this who looks down like the dawn, beautiful as the moon, bright as the sun. – Song of Solomon 6:10 ESV

1. Beau - ti - ful Sav - ior, King of Cre - a - tion,
2. Fair are the mead - ows, fair are the wood - lands,
3. Fair is the sun - shine, fair is the moon - light,
4. Beau - ti - ful Sav - ior, Lord of the na - tions,

WORDS: German Jesuits, 17th c.; Jospeh August Seiss, 1873
MUSIC: *Schönster Herr Jesu*, melody from *Munster Gesangbuch*, 1677; harm. *The English Hymnal*, 1906 Irregular
*This original translation of the German text, and the altered translation "Fairest Lord Jesus" are both
interchangeable with the tunes CRUSADER'S HYMN (St. Elizabeth) and SCHONSTER HERR JESU.

Son of God and Son of Man! Tru-ly I'd love Thee,
robed in the flow-ers of bloom-ing spring; Je-sus is fair-er,
bright the spar-kling stars on high; Je-sus shines bright-er,
Son of God and Son of Man! Glo-ry and hon-or,

tru-ly I'd serve Thee, light of my soul my joy, my crown.
Je-sus is pur-er, He makes our sor-row-ing spir-it sing.
Je-sus shines pur-er than all the an-gels in the sky.
praise, ad-o-ra-tion, now and for-ev-er-more be Thine!

Jesus, the Very Thought of Thee   55

Consider Him who endured such opposition from sinful men. – Hebrews 12:3 NIV

1. Je-sus, the ver-y thought of Thee with sweet-ness fills my breast;
2. No voice can sing, no heart can frame, nor can the mem-'ry find
3. O hope of ev-'ry con-trite heart, O joy of all the meek,
4. But what to those who find? Ah, this no tongue or pen can show;
5. Je-sus, our on-ly joy be Thou, as Thou our prize wilt be;

but sweet-er far Thy face to see and in Thy pres-ence rest.
a sweet-er sound than Thy blest name, O Sav-ior of man-kind.
to those who fall, how kind Thou art! How good to those who seek!
the love of Je-sus, what it is none but His loved ones know.
Je-sus, be Thou our glo-ry now and through e-ter-ni-ty.

WORDS: Attr. Bernard of Clairvaux, ca. 12th c.; tr. Edward Caswell, 1849
MUSIC: *St. Agnes*, John Bacchus Dykes, 1866
This tune in a lower key, No. 331   C.M.

56 When in Our Music God Is Glorified

It is for God's glory so that God's Son may be glorified through it. – John 11:4 NIV

Unison

1. When in our mu-sic God is glo-ri-fied,
2. How of-ten, mak-ing mu-sic, we have found
3. So has the Church in spo-ken word and song
4. And did not Je-sus sing a psalm that night
5. Let ev-'ry in-stru-ment be tuned for praise!

and ad-o-ra-tion leaves no room for pride,
a new di-men-sion in the world of sound,
in faith and love, through cen-tu-ries of wrong,
when ut-most e-vil strove a-gainst the Light?
Let all re-joice who have a voice to raise!

it is as though the whole cre-a-tion cried
as wor-ship moved us to a more pro-found
borne wit-ness to the truth in ev-'ry tongue,
Then let us sing, for whom He won the fight:
And may God give us faith to sing al-ways

Refrain

Al - le - lu - ia! lu - ia!

WORDS: Fred Pratt Green, 1971
MUSIC: *Engelberg*, Charles Villiers Stanford, 1904, alt.

10.10.10 with Alleluias

All Hail the Power of Jesus' Name! 57

You are worthy, our Lord and God, to receive glory and honor and power. – Revelation 4:11 NIV

1. All hail the pow'r of Je - sus' name! Let an - gels pros-trate[1] fall;
2. Crown Him, ye mar - tyrs of your God, who from His al - tar call;
3. Ye cho - sen seed of Is - rael's race, ye ran - somed from the fall,
4. Sin - ners, whose love can not for - get the worm-wood and the gall,
5. Let ev - 'ry kin - dred, ev - 'ry tribe, on this ter - res - tr'al ball,[3]
6. O that with yon - der[4] sa - cred throng we at His feet may fall;

bring forth the roy - al di - a - dem,[2] and crown Him Lord of all;
ex - tol the Stem of Jes - se's rod, and crown Him Lord of all;
hail Him who saves you by His grace, and crown Him Lord of all;
go, spread your tro - phies at His feet, and crown Him Lord of all;
to Him all maj - es - ty as - cribe, and crown Him Lord of all;
we'll join the ev - er - last - ing song,[5] and crown Him Lord of all;

bring forth the roy - al di - a - dem, and crown Him Lord of all.
ex - tol the Stem of Jes - se's rod, and crown Him Lord of all.
hail Him who saves you by His grace, and crown Him Lord of all.
go, spread your tro - phies at His feet, and crown Him Lord of all.
to Him all maj - es - ty as - cribe, and crown Him Lord of all.
we'll join the ev - er - last - ing song, and crown Him Lord of all.

1. prostrate: *lying face down*
2. diadem: *crown*
3. terrestrial ball: *the planet earth*
4. yonder: *heavenly afterlife*
5. everlasting song: *"Holy, holy, holy..." of Revelation 4:8*

WORDS: Sts. 1 - 5 Edward Perronet, 1779, alt.; St. 6 John Rippon, 1787
MUSIC: *Coronation*, Oliver Holden, 1793
C.M with Repeat

58 All Hail the Power of Jesus' Name!

You are worthy, our Lord and God, to receive glory and honor and power. – Revelation 4:11 NIV

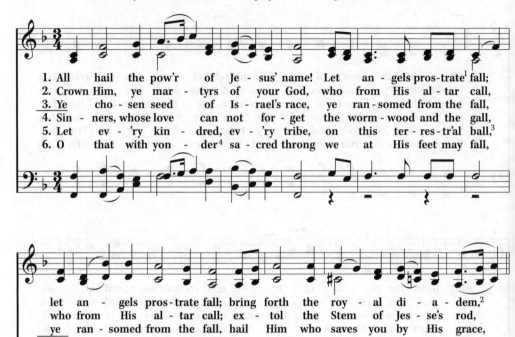

1. All hail the pow'r of Je - sus' name! Let an - gels pros-trate[1] fall;
2. Crown Him, ye mar - tyrs of your God, who from His al - tar call,
3. Ye cho - sen seed of Is - rael's race, ye ran - somed from the fall,
4. Sin - ners, whose love can not for - get the worm - wood and the gall,
5. Let ev - 'ry kin - dred, ev - 'ry tribe, on this ter - res - tr'al ball,[3]
6. O that with yon - der[4] sa - cred throng we at His feet may fall,

let an - gels pros-trate fall; bring forth the roy - al di - a - dem,[2]
who from His al - tar call; ex - tol the Stem of Jes - se's rod,
ye ran - somed from the fall, hail Him who saves you by His grace,
the worm - wood and the gall, go, spread your tro - phies at His feet,
on this ter - res - tr'al ball, to Him all maj - es - ty as - cribe,
we at His feet may fall; we'll join the ev - er - last - ing song,[5]

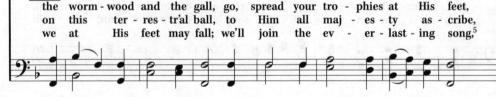

Refrain

And crown Him, crown Him,
And crown Him, crown Him, crown Him, crown Him, crown Him,

crown

1. *prostrate: lying face down*
2. *diadem: crown*
3. *terrestrial ball: the planet earth*
4. *yonder: heavenly afterlife*
5. *everlasting song: "Holy, holy, holy..." of Revelation 4:8*

WORDS: Sts. 1-5 Edward Perronet, 1779, alt.; St. 6 John Rippon, 1787
MUSIC: *Diadem*, James Ellor, 1838

8.6.8 with Repeat and Refrain

All Hail the Power of Jesus' Name!   59

You are worthy, our Lord and God, to receive glory and honor and power. – Revelation 4:11 NIV

1. All hail the pow'r of Jesus' name! Let angels
2. Crown Him, ye martyrs of your God, who from His
3. Ye chosen seed of Israel's race, ye ransomed
4. Sinners, whose love can not forget the wormwood
5. Let ev'ry kindred, ev'ry tribe, on this ter-
6. O that with yonder[4] sacred throng we at His

prostrate[1] fall; bring forth the royal diadem,[2]
altar call; extol the Stem of Jesse's rod,
from the fall, hail Him who saves you by His grace,
and the gall, go, spread your trophies at His feet,
res-tr'al ball,[3] to Him all majesty ascribe,
feet may fall; we'll join the everlasting song,[5]

Refrain

And crown Him, crown Him, crown Him, crown Him, Lord of all!

1. prostrate: lying face down
2. diadem: crown
3. terrestrial ball: the planet earth
4. yonder: heavenly afterlife
5. everlasting song: "Holy, holy, holy..." of Revelation 4:8

WORDS: Sts. 1-5 Edward Perronet, 1779, alt.; St. 6 John Rippon, 1787
MUSIC: *Miles Lane*, William Shrubsole, 1779

8.6.8 with Refrain

60 I Love Thee

I will love Thee, O Lord, my strength. – Psalm 18:1 KJV

1. I love Thee, I love Thee, I love Thee, my Lord;
2. I'm hap-py, I'm hap-py, oh, won-drous ac-count!
3. O Je-sus, my Sav-ior, with Thee I am blest,
4. Oh, who's like my Sav-ior? He's Sa-lem's bright King;

I love Thee, my Sav-ior, I love Thee, my God;
My joys are im-mor-tal, I stand on the mount:
my life and sal-va-tion, my joy and my rest:
He smiles and He loves me and helps me to sing:

I love Thee, I love Thee, and that Thou dost know;
I gaze on my trea-sure and long to be there,
Thy name be my theme, and Thy love be my song;
I'll praise Him, I'll praise Him with notes loud and clear,

but how much I love Thee my ac-tions will show.
with Je-sus and an-gels and kin-dred so dear.
Thy grace shall in-spire both my heart and my tongue.
while riv-ers of plea-sure my spir-it shall cheer.

WORDS: Anon., Jeremiah Ingalls' *Christian Harmony*, 1805
MUSIC: *I Love Thee*, anon., Jeremiah Ingalls' *Christian Harmony*, 1805

11.11.11.11

My Jesus, I Love Thee

61

Yea, Lord; Thou knowest that I love Thee. – John 21:15 KJV

1. My Jesus, I love Thee, I know Thou art mine;
   for Thee, all the follies of sin I resign;
   my gracious Redeemer, my Savior art Thou;
   if ever I loved Thee, my Jesus, 'tis now.

2. I love Thee because Thou hast first loved me,
   and purchased my pardon on Calvary's tree;
   I love Thee for wearing the thorns on Thy brow;
   if ever I loved Thee, my Jesus, 'tis now.

3. I'll love Thee in life, I will love Thee in death,
   and praise Thee as long as Thou lendest me breath;
   and say, when the death-dew lies cold on my brow;
   if ever I loved Thee, my Jesus, 'tis now.

4. In mansions of glory and endless delight,
   I'll ever adore Thee in heaven so bright;
   and singing Thy praises, before Thee I'll bow;
   if ever I loved Thee, my Jesus, 'tis now.

WORDS: William Ralph Featherstone, 1864
MUSIC: *Gordon,* Adoniram Judson Gordon, 1876

11.11.11.11

62 Oh, How I Love Jesus

Though you have not seen Him, you love Him. – 1 Peter 1:8 KJV

1. There is a name I love to hear, I
2. It tells me of a Sav - ior's love, Who
3. It tells me what my Fa - ther has in
4. It tells of One whose lov - ing heart can

love to sing its worth; it sounds as mu - sic
died to set me free; it tells me of His
store for ev - 'ry day; and though I tread a
feel my deep - est woe; Who in each sor - row

in my ear, the sweet - est name on earth.
pre - cious blood, the sin - ner's per - fect plea.
dark - some path, yields sun - shine all the way.
bears a part, that none can bear be - low.

Refrain

Oh, how I love Je - sus, oh, how I love Je - sus,

oh, how I love Je - sus, be - cause He first loved me.

WORDS: Frederick Whitfield, 1855
MUSIC: *Oh, How I Love Jesus*, American melody, 19th c.

C.M. with Refrain

He Is Exalted

For Thou, Lord, art high above all the earth: Thou art exalted far above all gods. – Psalm 97:9 KJV

He is ex-alt-ed, the King is ex-alt-ed on high; I will praise Him.

He is ex-alt-ed, for-ev-er ex-alt-ed and I will praise His name!

1. He is the Lord, for-ev-er His truth shall reign;
2. You are the Lord, for-ev-er Your truth shall reign;

heav-en and earth re-joice in His ho-ly name.
heav-en and earth re-joice in Your ho-ly name.

He is ex-alt-ed, the King is ex-alt-ed on high.
You are ex-alt-ed, for-ev-er ex-alt-ed on high.

WORDS: Twila Paris, 1985
MUSIC: *He Is Exalted*, Twila Paris, 1985

Irregular

64 Praise Him! Praise Him!

Great is the Lord, and most worthy of praise. – Psalm 48:1 NIV

1. Praise Him! Praise Him! Je - sus, our bless - ed Re - deem - er!
2. Praise Him! Praise Him! Je - sus our bless - ed Re - deem - er!
3. Praise Him! Praise Him! Je - sus our bless - ed Re - deem - er!

Sing, O earth, His won - der - ful love pro - claim!
For our sins, He suf - fered and bled and died;
Heav'n - ly por - tals loud with ho - san - nas ring!

Hail Him! Hail Him! High - est arch - an - gels in glo - ry,
He our Rock, our hope of e - ter - nal sal - va - tion,
Je - sus, Sav - ior, reign - eth for - ev - er and ev - er;

strength and hon - or give to His ho - ly name!
hail Him! Hail Him! Je - sus the cru - ci - fied;
crown Him! Crown Him! Proph - et and Priest and King!

Like a shep - herd, Je - sus will guard His chil - dren,
sound His prais - es! Je - sus who bore our sor - rows,
Christ is com - ing, o - ver the world vic - to - rious,

WORDS: Fanny Jane Crosby, 1869
MUSIC: *Joyful Song,* Chester G. Allen, 1869

Irregular with Refrain

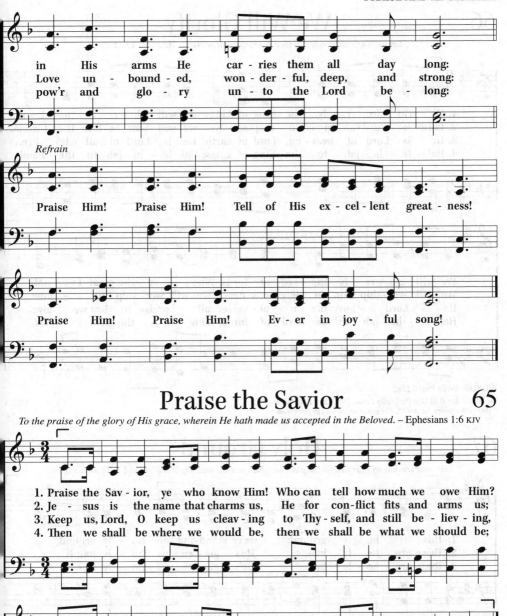

in His arms He car - ries them all day long:
Love un - bound - ed, won - der - ful, deep, and strong:
pow'r and glo - ry un - to the Lord be - long:

Refrain

Praise Him! Praise Him! Tell of His ex - cel - lent great - ness!

Praise Him! Praise Him! Ev - er in joy - ful song!

Praise the Savior 65

To the praise of the glory of His grace, wherein He hath made us accepted in the Beloved. – Ephesians 1:6 KJV

1. Praise the Sav - ior, ye who know Him! Who can tell how much we owe Him?
2. Je - sus is the name that charms us, He for con - flict fits and arms us;
3. Keep us, Lord, O keep us cleav - ing to Thy - self, and still be - liev - ing,
4. Then we shall be where we would be, then we shall be what we should be;

Glad - ly let us ren - der to Him all we are and have.
noth - ing moves and noth - ing harms us while we trust in Him.
till the hour of our re - ceiv - ing prom - ised joys with Thee.
things that are not now, nor could be, soon shall be our own.

WORDS: Thomas Kelly, 1806
MUSIC: *Acclaim*, traditional German melody, n.d.

8.8.8.5

66

We Will Glorify

Let us continually offer to God a sacrifice of praise. – Hebrews 13:15 NIV

1. We will glo-ri-fy the King of kings; we will glo-ri-fy the Lamb.
2. Lord Je-ho-vah reigns in maj-es-ty; we will bow be-fore His throne.
3. He is Lord of heav-en, Lord of earth; He is Lord of all who live.
4. Hal-le-lu-jah to the King of kings; Hal-le-lu-jah to the Lamb.

We will glo-ri-fy the Lord of lords, Who is the great I AM.
We will wor-ship Him in right-teous-ness, we will wor-ship Him a-lone.
He is Lord a-bove the u-ni-verse; all praise to Him we give.
Hal-le-lu-jah to the Lord of lords, Who is the great I AM.

WORDS: Twila Paris, 1982
MUSIC: *We Will Glorify*, Twila Paris, 1982; arr. Eric Wyse, 2005

9.7.9.6

67

Holy Ground

Take your sandals off your feet, for the place on which you are standing is holy ground. – Exodus 3:5 ESV

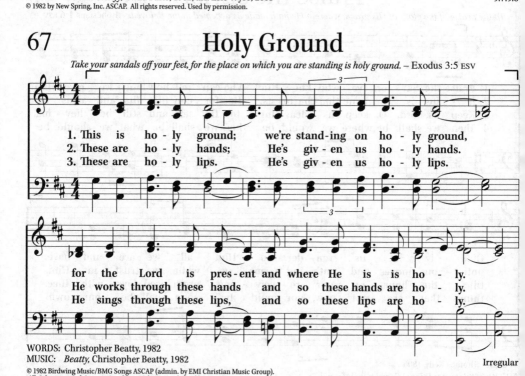

1. This is ho-ly ground; we're stand-ing on ho-ly ground,
2. These are ho-ly hands; He's giv-en us ho-ly hands.
3. These are ho-ly lips. He's giv-en us ho-ly lips.

for the Lord is pres-ent and where He is is ho-ly.
He works through these hands and so these hands are ho-ly.
He sings through these lips, and so these lips are ho-ly.

WORDS: Christopher Beatty, 1982
MUSIC: *Beatty*, Christopher Beatty, 1982

Irregular

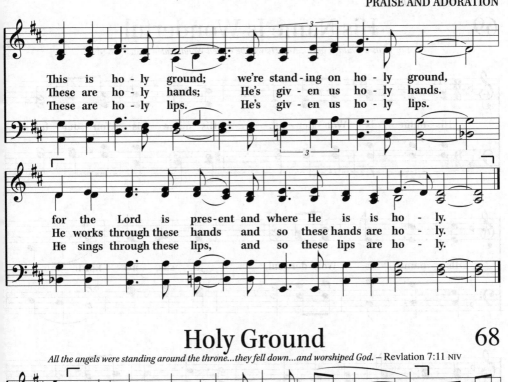

This is ho-ly ground; we're stand-ing on ho-ly ground,
These are ho-ly hands; He's giv-en us ho-ly hands.
These are ho-ly lips. He's giv-en us ho-ly lips.

for the Lord is pres-ent and where He is is ho-ly.
He works through these hands and so these hands are ho-ly.
He sings through these lips, and so these lips are ho-ly.

Holy Ground

68

All the angels were standing around the throne...they fell down...and worshiped God. – Revlation 7:11 NIV

We are stand-ing on ho-ly ground, and I

know that there are an-gels all a-round. Let us praise Je-sus

now. We are stand-ing in His pres-ence on ho-ly ground.

WORDS: Geron Davis, 1979
MUSIC: *Holy Ground,* Geron Davis, 1979

Irregular

69 His Name Is Wonderful

For to us a Child is born...And He will be called Wonderful. – Isaiah 9:6 NIV

His name is Won-der-ful, His name is Won-der-ful,

His name is Won-der-ful, Je-sus, my Lord.

He is the Might-y King, Mas-ter of ev-'ry-thing,

His name is Won-der-ful, Je-sus, my Lord.

He's the Great Shep-herd, the Rock of all a-ges, Al-might-y

WORDS: Audrey Mieir, 1959
MUSIC: *Mieir*, Audrey Mieir, 1959

Irregular

God is He. Bow down be-fore Him, love and a-

dore Him, His name is Won-der-ful, Je-sus, my Lord.

We Worship and Adore You 70

They sang praises with gladness and they bowed down and worshipped. – 2 Chronicles 29:30 ESV

1. We wor-ship and a-dore You, bow-ing down be-fore You,
2. Lord Je-sus, we a-dore You, bow-ing down be-fore You;

songs of prais-es sing-ing, Hal-le-lu-jahs ring-ing. Hal - le-
gifts and prais-es bring-ing, Hal-le-lu-jahs sing-ing.

Refrain

lu-jah, Hal - le-lu-jah, Hal - le-lu-jah. A - men.

WORDS: St. 1 traditional, n.d.; St. 2 Danny R. Jones, 2005
MUSIC: *Worship and Adore,* traditional, n.d.

Irregular with Refrain

71 Shout to the Lord

Shout your praises to God, everybody! Let loose and sing. – Psalm 98:4 The Message

My Je-sus, my Sav-ior, Lord, there is none like You.

All of my days I want to praise the won-ders of Your

might-y love. My com-fort, my shel-ter,

tow-er of ref - uge and strength. Let ev-'ry breath,

all that I am, nev-er cease to wor-ship You.

WORDS: Darlene Zschech, 1993
MUSIC: *Shout to the Lord*, Darlene Zschech, 1993; arr. Eric Wyse, 2005

Irregular with Refrain

72 O Come, O Come, Emmanuel

The Virgin will give birth to a Son, and will call Him Emmanuel. – Isaiah 7:14 NIV

1. O come, O come, Emmanuel, and ransom captive Israel that mourns in lonely exile here, until the Son of God appear.

2. O come, Thou Wisdom from on high, Who ord'rest all things mightily; to us the path of knowledge show, and teach us in her ways to go.

3. O come, Thou Rod of Jesse, free Thine own from Satan's tyranny; from depths of hell Thy people save and give them vic'try o'er the grave.

4. O come, Thou Day-spring, come and cheer our spirits by Thine advent here; and drive away the shades of night, and pierce the clouds and bring us light!

5. O come, Thou Key of David, come, and open wide our heav'nly home; make safe the way that leads on high, and close the path to misery.

6. O come, O come, great Lord of might, Who to Thy tribes on Sinai's height in ancient times once gave the law in cloud and majesty and awe.

7. O come, Desire of nations, bind all peoples in one heart and mind; bid envy, strife and quarrels cease; fill all the world with heaven's peace.

WORDS: Latin, 12th c.; Sts. 1, 3 - 5 tr. John Mason Neale, 1851; Sts. 2, 7 tr. Henry Sloan Coffin, 1916
MUSIC: *Veni Emmanuel,* 15th c. plainsong, adapt. Thomas Helmore, 1854

L.M. with Refrain

While We Are Waiting, Come   73

Come, Lord Jesus. – Revelation 22:20 NIV

1. While we are wait - ing, come; while we are
2. With pow'r and glo - ry, come, with pow'r and
3. Come, Sav - ior, quick - ly come; come, Sav - ior,

wait - ing, come. Je - sus, our Lord, Em -
glo - ry, come. Je - sus, our Lord, Em -
quick - ly come. Je - sus, our Lord, Em -

man - u - el, while we are wait - ing, come.
man - u - el, while we are wait - ing, come.
man - u - el, while we are wait - ing, come.

WORDS: Claire Cloninger, 1986
MUSIC: *Waiting,* Don Cason, 1986
S.M.

74 Come, Thou Long-Expected Jesus

What God promised our fathers He has fulfilled for us, their children, by raising up Jesus. – Acts 13:32-33 NIV

1. Come, Thou long-ex-pect-ed Je-sus, born to set Thy peo-ple free; from our fears and sins re-lease us; let us find our rest in Thee. Is-rael's strength and con-so-la-tion, hope of all the

2. Born Thy peo-ple to de-liv-er, born a Child and yet a King, born to reign in us for-ev-er, now Thy gra-cious king-dom bring. By Thine own e-ter-nal Spir-it, rule in all our

WORDS: Charles Wesley, 1744
MUSIC: *Hyfrydol*, Rowland Hugh Prichard, ca. 1830; harm. *The English Hymnal*, 1906
Another harmonization of this tune in a lower key, No. 248; in a higher key, No. 42

8.7.8.7 D

earth Thou art; dear de - sire of ev - 'ry
hearts a - lone; by Thine all - suf - fi - cient

na - tion, joy of ev - 'ry long - ing heart.
mer - it, raise us to Thy glo - rious throne.

Come, Thou Long-Expected Jesus   75

What God promised our fathers He has fulfilled for us, their children, by raising up Jesus. – Acts 13:32-33 NIV

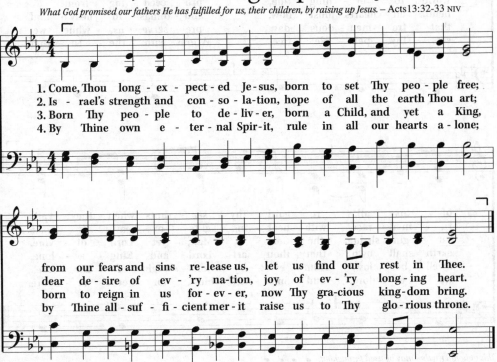

1. Come, Thou long - ex - pect - ed Je - sus, born to set Thy peo - ple free;
2. Is - rael's strength and con - so - la - tion, hope of all the earth Thou art;
3. Born Thy peo - ple to de - liv - er, born a Child, and yet a King,
4. By Thine own e - ter - nal Spir - it, rule in all our hearts a - lone;

from our fears and sins re - lease us, let us find our rest in Thee.
dear de - sire of ev - 'ry na - tion, joy of ev - 'ry long - ing heart.
born to reign in us for - ev - er, now Thy gra - cious king - dom bring.
by Thine all - suf - fi - cient mer - it raise us to Thy glo - rious throne.

WORDS: Charles Wesley, 1744
MUSIC: *Stuttgart*, Christian Friedrich Witt, 1715; adapt. Henry John Gauntlett, 1861   8.7.8.7

76 Creator of the Stars of Night

And God created the two great lights...and the stars. – Genesis 1:16 ESV

Unison

1. Cre - a - tor of the stars of night, Thy peo - ple's
2. Thou, griev - ing at the bit - ter cry of all cre -
3. Thou cam - est, Bride-groom of the bride, as drew the
4. At Thy great name, ex - alt - ed now, all knees must
5. To Thee, O Ho - ly One, we pray, our judge in
6. All praise, e - ter - nal Son, to Thee, whose ad - vent

ev - er - last - ing light, O Je - sus, Sav - ior
a - tion doomed to die, didst come to save a
world to ev - 'ning - tide, pro - ceed - ing from a
bend, all hearts must bow, and things in heav'n and
that tre - men - dous day, pre - serve us, while we
sets Thy peo - ple free, Whom with the Fa - ther

of us all, re - gard Thy ser - vants when they call.
ru - ined race with heal - ing gifts of heav'n - ly grace.
Vir - gin shrine, the Son of Man, yet Lord di - vine.
earth shall own that Thou art Lord and King a - lone.
dwell be - low, from ev - 'ry on - slaught of the foe.
we a - dore, and Spir - it blest, for ev - er - more.

This optional rhythm may be used throughout:

WORDS: Latin, 7th c.; John Mason Neale, 1852
MUSIC: *Conditor Alme Siderum*, Sarum plainsong, Mode IV

L.M.

Lift Up Your Heads, Ye Mighty Gates! 77

Lift up your heads, O ye gates; and be ye lifted up, ye everlasting doors. – Psalm 24:7 KJV

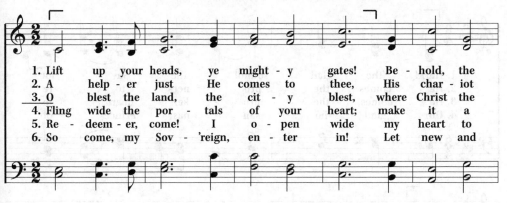

1. Lift up your heads, ye might - y gates! Be - hold, the
2. A help - er just He comes to thee, His char - iot
3. O blest the land, the cit - y blest, where Christ the
4. Fling wide the por - tals of your heart; make it a
5. Re - deem - er, come! I o - pen wide my heart to
6. So come, my Sov - 'reign, en - ter in! Let new and

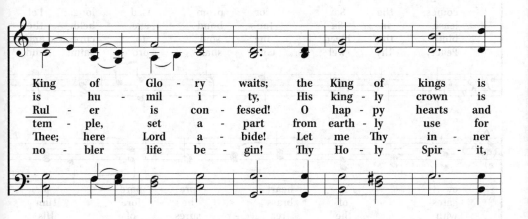

King of Glo - ry waits; the King of kings is
is hu - mil - i - ty, His king - ly crown is
Rul - er is con - fessed! O hap - py hearts and
tem - ple, set a - part from earth - ly use for
Thee; here Lord a - bide! Let me Thy in - ner
no - bler life be - gin! Thy Ho - ly Spir - it,

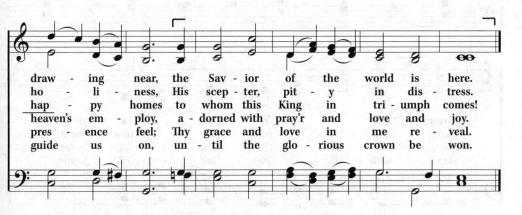

draw - ing near, the Sav - ior of the world is here.
ho - li - ness, His scep - ter, pit - y in dis - tress.
hap - py homes to whom this King in tri - umph comes!
heaven's em - ploy, a - dorned with pray'r and love and joy.
pres - ence feel; Thy grace and love in me re - veal.
guide us on, un - til the glo - rious crown be won.

WORDS: Based on Psalm 24, Georg Weissel, 1642; tr. Catherine Winkworth, 1855, alt.
MUSIC: *Truro,* from *Psalmodia Evangelica,* 1789   L.M.

78 Hark the Glad Sound! The Savior Comes

Our God has given us a mighty Savior from the family of David His servant. – Luke 1:69 CEV

1. Hark! The glad sound! The Savior comes, the Savior promised long: Let ev-'ry heart prepare a throne and ev-'ry voice a song.

2. He comes the pris-'ners to release in Satan's bond-age held; the gates of brass be-fore Him burst, the i-ron fet-ters yield.

3. He comes, the bro-ken heart to bind, the bleed-ing soul to cure; and with the trea-sures of His grace to bless the hum-ble poor.

4. Our glad ho-san-nas, Prince of Peace, Thy wel-come shall pro-claim; and heav-en's e-ter-nal arch-es ring with Thy be-lov-ed name.

WORDS: Philip Doddridge, 1735
MUSIC: *Richmond*, Thomas Haweis, 1792

C.M.

Hail to the Lord's Anointed

Yes, all kings shall fall down before Him; all nations shall serve Him. – Psalm 72:11 NKJV

1. Hail to the Lord's A - noint - ed, great Da - vid's great - er Son!
2. He comes with suc - cor[1] speed - y to those who suf - fer wrong,
3. He shall come down like show - ers up - on the fruit - ful earth,
4. Kings shall bow down be - fore Him, and gold and in - cense bring;
5. O'er ev - 'ry foe vic - to - rious, He on His throne shall rest;

Hail, in the time ap - point - ed, His reign on earth be - gun!
to help the poor and need - y, and bid the weak be strong;
and love, joy, hope, like flow - ers, spring in His path to birth:
all na - tions shall a - dore Him, His praise all peo - ple sing;
from age to age more glo - rious, all - bless - ing and all - blest:

He comes to break op - pres - sion, to set the cap - tive free;
to give them songs for sigh - ing, their dark - ness turn to light,
Be - fore Him on the moun - tains shall peace, the her - ald, go;
to Him shall prayer un - ceas - ing and dai - ly vows as - cend;
The tide of time shall nev - er His cov - e - nant re - move;

to take a - way trans - gres - sion, and rule in eq - ui - ty.
whose souls, con - demned and dy - ing, were pre - cious in His sight.
and righ - teous - ness in foun - tains from hill to val - ley flow.
His king - dom still in - creas - ing, a king - dom with - out end.
His name shall stand for - ev - er, His change - less name of Love.

1. succor: help, relief or aid

WORDS: Based on Psalm 72, James Montgomery, 1821
MUSIC: *Es Flog Ein Kleins Waldvögelein*, 19th c. German folk song; adapt. and harm. Henry Walford Davies, 1923   7.6.7.6 D

80 Of the Father's Heart Begotten

"I am the Alpha and Omega," says the Lord God. – Revelation 1:8 NIV

1. Of the Fa-ther's heart be-got - ten, e're the world from cha - os rose, He is Al - pha: from that foun - tain, all that is and hath been flows. He is O - me - ga: of all things yet to come the mys - tic Close;

2. By His Word was all cre - a - ted; He com-mands and lo! 'tis done; earth and sky and bound-less o - cean, u - ni-verse of Three in One, all that sees the moon's soft ra - diance, all that breathes be - neath the sun.

3. He as-sumed this mor-tal bod - y, frail and fee - ble, doomed to die, that the race from dust cre - a - ted, might not per - ish ut - ter - ly, which the dread-ful Law has sen - tenced in the depths of hell to lie.

4. This is He whom seers and sag - es sang in a - ges long gone by; this is He of old re-veal - ed in the page of proph - e - cy; lo! He comes, the prom - ised Sav - ior; let the world His prais - es cry;

This optional rhythm may be used throughout: ♩ ♩ ♩♩♩ ♩ |

WORDS: Marcus Aurelius Clemens Prudentius, 4th c.; tr. Martin Pope and Roby Furley Davis, 1905, alt.
MUSIC: *Divinum Mysterium* (triple meter), plainsong, 13th c.; adapt. *Piae Cantiones*, 1582; harm. Eric Wyse, 2005   8.7.8.7.8.7.7
This tune in duple meter, a lower key and another harmonization, No. 86.

ev - er - more and ev - er - more.
Ev - er - more and ev - er - more.
Ev - er - more and ev - er - more.
ev - er - more and ev - er - more.

"Comfort, Comfort Ye My People" 81

"Comfort ye, comfort ye My people," saith your God. – Isaiah 40:1 KJV

1. "Com-fort, com - fort ye My peo - ple, speak ye peace," thus saith our God;
2. Hark, the voice of one that cri - eth in the des - ert far and near,
3. Make ye straight what long was crook - ed, make the rough - er plac - es plain;

"com-fort those who sit in dark - ness, mourn - ing 'neath their sor - rows' load.
bid - ding all to true re - pent - ance since the king - dom now is here.
let your hearts be true and hum - ble, as be - fits His ho - ly reign.

Speak ye to Je - su - sa - lem of the peace that waits for them;
O that warn - ing cry o - bey! Now pre - pare for God a - way;
For the glo - ry of the Lord now o'er earth is shed a - broad,

tell her that her sins I cov - er, and her war - fare now is o - ver."
let the val - leys rise to meet Him and the hills bow down to greet Him.
and all flesh shall see the to - ken that His Word is nev - er bro - ken.

WORDS: Johannes G. Olearius, 1671; based on Isaiah 40:1-8; tr. Catherine Winkworth, 1863, alt.
MUSIC: *Psalm 42,* Louis Bourgeois, 1551; harm. Claude Goudimel, 1564

8.7.8.7.7.7.8.8

82 Let All Mortal Flesh Keep Silence

Be silent, O all flesh, before the Lord. – Zechariah 2:13 KJV

1. Let all mor-tal flesh keep si-lence, and with fear and trem-bling stand; pon-der noth-ing earth-ly mind-ed, for with bless-ing in His hand, Christ, our God, to earth de-scend - eth, our full hom-age to de - mand.

2. King of kings, yet born of Ma-ry, as of old on earth He stood, Lord of lords, in hu-man ves-ture, in the Bod-y and the Blood, He will give to all the faith - ful His own Self for heav'n-ly food.

3. Rank on rank the host of heav-en spreads its van-guard on the way, as the Light of light de - scend-eth from the realms of end-less day, that the pow'rs of hell may van - ish as the dark-ness clears a - way.

4. At His feet the six-wing-ed ser-aph; cher-u-bim, with sleep-less eye, veil their fac-es to the Pres-ence, as with cease-less voice they cry, "Al-le-lu-ia, Al - le-lu - ia! Al-le-lu - ia, Lord Most High!"

WORDS: *Liturgy of St. James*, 4th c.; adapt. Gerard Moultrie, 1864
MUSIC: *Picardy*, 17th c.; harm. Ralph Vaughan Williams, 1906

8.7.8.7.8.7

Once in Royal David's City

Joseph [and Mary] also went up from Galilee, from the town of Nazareth, to Judea, to the city of David. – Luke 2:4 ESV

1. Once in roy - al Da - vid's cit - y stood a low - ly cat - tle
2. He came down to earth from heav - en, Who is God and Lord of
3. And, through all His won - drous child-hood, He would hon - or and o -
4. For He is our child - hood's pat - tern, day by day like us He
5. And our eyes at last shall see Him, through His own re - deem - ing
6. Not in that poor low - ly sta - ble, with the ox - en stand - ing

shed, where a Moth - er laid her Ba - by in a man - ger for His bed;
all, and His shel - ter was a sta - ble, and His cra - dle was a stall;
bey, love and watch the low - ly Maid - en in whose gen - tle arms He lay;
grew; He was lit - tle, weak and help - less, tears and smiles like us He knew;
love; for that Child so dear and gen - tle, is our Lord in heav'n a - bove,
by, we shall see Him; but in heav - en, set at God's right hand on high;

Ma - ry was that Moth - er mild, Je - sus Christ her lit - tle Child.
with the poor, and mean, and low - ly lived on earth our Sav - ior ho - ly.
Chris-tian chil - dren all should be kind, o - be - dient, good as He.
and He feel - eth for our sad-ness, and He shar - eth in our glad-ness.
and He leads His chil-dren on to the place where He is gone.
when like stars His chil-dren crowned, all in white shall wait a - round.

WORDS: Cecil Frances Humphreys Alexander, 1848
MUSIC: *Irby,* Henry John Gauntlett, 1849; harm. Arthur Henry Mann, 1919

8.7.8.7.7.7

84 Lo, How a Rose E'er Blooming

The root of Jesse, who shall stand as a signal...His resting place shall be glorious. – Isaiah 11:10 ESV

1. Lo, how a Rose e'er bloom-ing from ten-der stem hath sprung, of Jes-se's lin-'age com-ing, as those of old have sung. It came, a blos-som bright, a-mid the cold of win-ter, when half-spent was the night.

2. I - sa - iah 'twas fore-told it, the Rose I have in mind; with Ma-ry we be-hold it, the Vir-gin Moth-er kind. To show God's love a-right, she bore to us a Sav-ior, when half-spent was the night.

3. The shep-herds heard the sto-ry pro-claimed by an - gels bright. how Christ, the Lord of Glo-ry was born on earth this night. To Beth-le-hem they sped and in the man-ger found Him, as an-gel hear-alds said.

4. This flow'r whose fra-grance ten-der with sweet-ness fills the air, dis-pel in glo-rious splen-dor the dark-ness ev - 'ry-where. True man, yet ver-y God, from sin and death He saves us and light-ens ev-'ry load.

WORDS: German carol, 16th c.; tr. Theodore Baker, 1897, Harriet Reynolds Krauth Spaeth, 1875
MUSIC: *Es Ist Ein Ros*, from *Alte Catholische Geistliche Kirchengesäng*, 1599; harm. Michael Praetorius, 1609   7.6.7.6.6.7.6
This tune in a lower key, No. 85.

A Great and Mighty Wonder

She was found to be with child through the Holy Spirit. – Matthew 1:18 NIV

1. A great and might-y won-der, a full and ho-ly cure!
2. The Word be-comes in-car-nate and yet re-mains on high!
3. While thus they sing Your Mon-arch, those bright an-gel-ic bands;
4. Since all He comes to ran-som, by all be He a-dored,

The Vir-gin bears the In-fant, with vir-gin-hon-or pure.
And cher-u-bim sing an-thems to shepherds from the sky.
re-joice, ye vales and moun-tains, ye o-ceans, clap your hands.
the In-fant born in Beth-l'em, the Sav-ior and the Lord.

Refrain

Re-peat the hymn a-gain! "To God on high be

glo-ry, and peace on earth to men."

WORDS: St. Germanus, c. 734; tr. John Mason Neale, 1862
MUSIC: *Es Ist Ein Ros*, from *Alte Catholische Geistliche Kirchengesäng*, 1599;
      harm. Michael Praetorius, 1609   7.6.7.6. with Refrain
This tune in a higher key, No. 84

86 Of the Father's Love Begotten

In the beginning was the Word, and the Word was with God, and the Word was God. – John 1:1 NIV

Unison

1. Of the Fa - ther's love be - got - ten, ere the worlds be - gan to be,
2. O that birth for - ev - er bless - ed! When the Vir - gin, full of grace,
3. O ye heights of heav'n a - dore Him; an - gel hosts His prais - es sing;
4. Christ, to Thee, with God the Fa - ther, and, O Ho - ly Ghost, to Thee,

He is Al - pha and O - me - ga, He the source, the end - ing He,
by the Ho - ly Ghost con - ceiv - ing, bore the Sav - ior of our race;
pow'rs, do - min - ions, bow be - fore Him, and ex - tol our God and King;
hymn and chant and high thanks-giv - ing and un - wea - ried prais - es be;

of the things that are, that have been, and that fu - ture
and the Babe, the world's Re - deem - er, first re - vealed His
let no tongue on earth be si - lent, ev - 'ry voice in
hon - or, glo - ry, and do - min - ion, and e - ter - nal

years shall see, ev - er - more and ev - er - more!
sa - cred face, ev - er - more and ev - er - more!
con - cert ring, ev - er - more and ev - er - more!
vic - to - ry, ev - er - more and ev - er - more!

This optional rhythm may be used throughout: ♩ ♪ ♩ ♪

WORDS: Marcus Aurelius Clemens Prudentius, 4th c.; Sts. 1-3 tr. John Mason Neale, 1854; St. 4, Henry Williams Baker, 1859, alt.
MUSIC: *Divinum Mysterium,* (duple meter), plainsong, 13th c.; adapt. *Piae Cantiones,* 1582;   8.7.8.7.8.7.7
This tune in triple meter, a higher key and another harmonization, No. 80.

Unto Us Is Born a Son

For to us a child is born, to us a son is given. – Isaiah 9:6a ESV

1. Un - to us is born a Son, King of choirs su -
per - nal: [1] see on earth His life be - gun, of lords the Lord e -
ter - nal, of lords the Lord e - ter - nal.

2. Christ, from heav'n de - scend - ing low, comes on earth a
strang - er; ox and ass their own - er know, be - cra - dled in the
man - ger, be - cra - dled in the man - ger.

3. This did He - rod sore af - fray, and griev - ous - ly be -
wild - er, so he gave the word to slay, and slew the lit - tle
chil - der, and slew the lit - tle chil - der.

4. Of His love and mer - cy mild this the Christ - mas
sto - ry; O that Ma - ry's gen - tle Child might lead us up to
glo - ry, might lead us up to glo - ry.

5. A and O and O and A, cum cant - i - bus in
chor - o, let our mer - ry or - gan go. Ben - e - dic - a - mus
Dom - i - nus, ben - e - dic - a - mus Dom - i - no.

Al - pha and O - me - ga He, sing we now to -
geth - er, let our mer - ry or - gan go. O bless the Lord for -
ev - er, O bless the Lord for - ev - er.

1. supernal: heavenly

WORDS: Latin, from *The Moosburg Gradual,* c. 1360; Sts. 1-4 tr. George Ratcliffe Woodward, 1910; St. 5 tr. Eric Wyse, 2005
MUSIC: *Puer Nobis Nascitur,* melody from *Piae Cantiones*; 1582; harm. Eric Wyse, 2005
7.6.7.7 with Repeat

88 Break Forth, O Beauteous Heavenly Light

Nations shall come to Your light, and kings to the brightness of Your rising. – Isaiah 60:3 ESV

1. Break forth, O beau-teous heav'n-ly light, and ush-er in the morn-ing; O shep-herds, shrink not with af-fright, but hear the an-gel's warn-ing. This Child, now weak in in-fan-cy, our con-fi-dence and joy shall be, the pow'r of Sa-tan break-ing,

2. Break forth, O beau-teous heav'n-ly light, to her-ald our sal-va-tion; He stoops to earth: The God of might, our hope and ex-pec-ta-tion. He comes in hu-man flesh to dwell, our God with us, Em-man-u-el, the night of dark-ness end-ing,

WORDS: St. 1 Johann Rist, 1641; St. 2 A. T. Russell, 1851; tr. John Troutbeck, ca. 1885
MUSIC: *Ermuntre Dich Mein Schwacher*, Johann Schop, 1641; harm. Johann Sebastian Bach, 1734

8.7.8.7.8.8.7.7

our   peace   e - ter - nal   mak   -   ing.
our   fall - en   race   be - friend   -   ing.

Silent Night! 89

Ye shall have a song, as in the night when a holy solemnity is kept. — Isaiah 30:29 KJV

1. Si - lent night! Ho - ly night! All is calm, all is bright,
2. Si - lent night! Ho - ly night! Shep - herds quake at the sight,
3. Si - lent night! Ho - ly night! Son of God, love's pure light
4. Si - lent night! Ho - ly night! Won - drous star, lend thy light;

round yon vir - gin moth - er and child! Ho - ly In - fant, so ten - der and mild,
glo - ries stream from heav - en a - far, heav'n - ly hosts sing: "Al - le - lu - ia;
ra - d'ant beams from Thy ho - ly face, with the dawn of re - deem - ing grace.
with the an - gels let us sing, "Al - le - lu - ia to our King;

sleep in heav - en - ly peace, sleep in heav - en - ly peace.
Christ the Sav - ior is born, Christ the Sav - ior is born."
Je - sus, Lord, at Thy birth, Je - sus, Lord, at Thy birth.
Christ the Sav - ior is born, Christ the Sav - ior is born."

WORDS: Joseph Mohr, 1816; trans. John Freeman Young, 1863; and others.
MUSIC: *Stille Nacht*, Franz Xaver Gruber, 1818   Irregular

O Come, All Ye Faithful

"Let's go to Bethlehem and see this thing that has happened, which the Lord has told us about." – Luke 2:15 NIV

1. O come, all ye faith-ful, joy-ful and tri-um-phant,
2. — God of God, Light from Light e-ter-nal.
3. — Lo! Star-led chief-tains, ma-gi, Christ a-dor-ing,
4. — Child, for us sin-ners, poor and in the man-ger,
5. — Sing, choirs of an-gels, sing in ex-ul-ta-tion,
6. — Yea, Lord, we greet Thee, born this hap-py morn-ing,

O come, ye, O come ye to Beth-le-hem!
— Lo, He ab-hors not the Vir-gin's womb;
— of-fer Him frank-in-cense and gold and myrrh.
— we would em-brace Thee with love and awe;
— Sing, all ye cit-i-zens of heav'n a-bove!
— Je-sus to Thee be all glo-ry giv'n;

Come and be-hold Him, born the King of an-gels!
ver-y God, be-got-ten, not cre-a-ted.
We to the Christ-child bring our hearts' ob-la-tions:
who would not love Thee, lov-ing us so dear-ly?
Glo-ry to God, all glo-ry in the high-est!
Word of the Fa-ther, now in flesh ap-pear-ing!

Refrain

O Come, let us a-dore Him. O Come, let us a-dore Him.

WORDS: John Francis Wade, ca. 1743; tr. Frederick Oakley, 1841, and others

Irregular with Refrain

MUSIC: *Adeste Fideles,* John Francis Wade, ca. 1743; harm. from *Collections of Motetts or Antiphons,* 1792

O come, let us a - dore Him, Christ the Lord!

Love Came Down at Christmas 91

We are happy because God sent our Lord Jesus Christ to make peace with us. – Romans 5:11 CEV

Love came down at Christ - mas, love all
Wor - ship we the God - head, love in -
Love shall be our to - ken; love be

love - ly, love di - vine; love was born at
car - nate, love di - vine; wor - ship we our
yours and love be mine, love to God and

Christ - mas, star and an - gels gave the sign.
Je - sus: But where-with for sa - cred sign?
neigh - bor, love for plea and gift and sign.

WORDS: Christina Georgina Rossetti, 1885, alt.
MUSIC: *Gartan,* traditional Irish melody

6.7.6.7

92 Joy to the World! The Lord Is Come

The Lord has made known His salvation. – Psalm 98:2 KJV

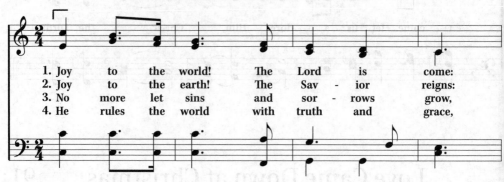

1. Joy to the world! The Lord is come:
2. Joy to the earth! The Sav - ior reigns:
3. No more let sins and sor - rows grow,
4. He rules the world with truth and grace,

Let earth re - ceive her King;
Let all their songs em - ploy;
nor thorns in - fest the ground;
and makes the na - tions prove

let ev - 'ry heart pre - pare Him room,
while fields and floods, rocks, hills, and plains
He comes to make His bless - ings flow
the glo - ries of His righ - teous - ness

WORDS: Isaac Watts, 1719, alt.; based on Psalm 98
MUSIC: *Antioch,* attr. Charles Rider, n.d., William Holford, 1834; adapt. Lowell Mason, 1836

C.M. with Repeat

93 Hark! The Herald Angels Sing

Suddenly many other angels came down from heaven and joined in praising God. – Luke 2:13 CEV

1. Hark! The her-ald an-gels sing, "Glo-ry to the new-born King;
2. Christ, by high-est heav'n a-dored; Christ, the ev-er-last-ing Lord!
3. Hail the heav'n-born Prince of Peace! Hail the Sun of Righ-teous-ness!

peace on earth, and mer-cy mild, God and sin-ners rec-on-ciled!"
Late in time be-hold Him come, off-spring of the Vir-gin's womb.
Light and life to all He brings, ris'n with heal-ing in His wings.

Joy-ful, all ye na-tions, rise, join the tri-umph of the skies;
Veiled in flesh the God-head see; hail th'in-car-nate De-i-ty,
Mild He lays His glo-ry by, born that we no more may die,

with th'an-gel-ic host pro-claim, "Christ is born in Beth-le-hem!"
pleased as man with us to dwell, Je-sus, our Em-man-u-el.
born to raise us from the earth, born to give us sec-ond birth.

Refrain

Hark! The her-ald an-gels sing, "Glo-ry to the new-born King."

WORDS: Charles Wesley, 1739; George Whitefield, 1753, and others, alt.
MUSIC: *Mendelssohn*, Felix Mendelssohn, 1840; arr. William Hayman Cummings, 1856

7.7.7.7 D with Refrain

Good Christian Friends, Rejoice

Rejoice in the Lord always. I will say it again: Rejoice! – Philippians 4:4 NIV

1. Good Chris-tian friends, re - joice with heart and soul and voice;
2. Good Chris-tian friends, re - joice with heart and soul and voice;
3. Good Chris-tian friends, re - joice with heart and soul and voice;

give ye heed to what we say: Je - sus Christ is born to - day;
now ye hear of end - less bliss; Je - sus Christ was born for this!
now ye need not fear the grave: Je - sus Christ was born to save!

ox and ass be - fore Him bow, and He is in the man - ger now.
He hath o - pened heav - en's door, and we are blest for - ev - er - more.
Calls you one and calls you all to gain His ev - er - last - ing hall.

Christ is born to - day! Christ is born to - day!
Christ was born for this! Christ was born for this!
Christ was born to save! Christ was born to save!

WORDS: Latin carol, 14th c.; tr. John Mason Neale, 1853, alt.
MUSIC: *In Dulci Jubilo*, German melody, 14th c.

Irregular

95 O Little Town of Bethlehem

Bethlehem...from you shall come...one...whose origin is from of old, from ancient days. – Micah 5:2 ESV

1. O lit-tle town of Beth-le-hem, how still we see thee lie!
2. For Christ is born of Ma - ry; and gath-ered all a-bove,
3. How si-lent-ly, how si-lent-ly the won-drous gift is giv'n!
4. Where chil-dren pure and hap - py pray to the Bless-ed Child,
5. O ho-ly Child of Beth-le-hem, de-scend to us, we pray;

A - bove thy deep and dream-less sleep the si - lent stars go by;
while mor-tals sleep, the an-gels keep their watch of won - d'ring love.
So God im-parts to hu-man hearts the bless-ings of His heav'n.
where mis-er - y cries out to Thee, Son of the Moth-er mild;
cast out our sin, and en - ter in, be born in us to - day.

yet in thy dark streets shin - eth the ev - er - last-ing Light;
O morn-ing stars to - geth - er, pro-claim the ho - ly birth!
No ear may hear His com - ing, but in this world of sin,
where char - i - ty stands watch - ing and faith holds wide the door,
We hear the Christ-mas an - gels, the great glad ti - dings tell;

the hopes and fears of all the years are met in thee to - night.
And prais - es sing to God the King, and peace to all on earth.
where meek souls will re - ceive Him still the dear Christ en - ters in.
the dark night wakes, the glo - ry breaks, and Christ-mas comes once more.
O come to us, a - bide with us, our Lord, Em - man - u - el.

WORDS: Phillips Brooks, 1868, alt.
MUSIC: *St. Louis*, Lewis Henry Redner, 1868

C.M.D

O Little Town of Bethlehem

Bethlehem...from you shall come...one...whose origin is from old, from ancient days. – Micah 5:2 ESV

1. O lit - tle town of Beth - le - hem, how still we see thee lie!
2. For Christ is born of Ma - ry; and gath - ered all a - bove,
3. How si - lent - ly, how si - lent - ly the won - drous gift is giv'n!
4. Where chil - dren pure and hap - py pray to the bless - ed Child,
5. O ho - ly Child of Beth - le - hem, de - scend to us, we pray;

A - bove thy deep and dream - less sleep the si - lent stars go by;
while mor - tals sleep, the an - gels keep their watch of won - d'ring love.
So God im - parts to hu - man hearts the bless - ings of His heav'n.
where mis - er - y cries out to Thee, Son of the Moth - er mild;
cast out our sin, and en - ter in, be born in us to - day.

yet in thy dark streets shin - eth the ev - er - last - ing Light;
O morn - ing stars to - geth - er, pro - claim the ho - ly Birth!
No ear may hear His com - ing, but in this world of sin,
where char - i - ty stands watch - ing and faith holds wide the door,
We hear the Christ - mas an - gels, the great glad ti - dings tell;

the hopes and fears of all the years are met in thee to - night.
And prais - es sing to God the King, and peace to all on earth.
where meek souls will re - ceive Him still the dear Christ en - ters in.
the dark night wakes, the glo - ry breaks, and Christ - mas comes once more.
O come to us, a - bide with us, our Lord, Em - man - u - el!

WORDS: Phillips Brooks, 1868
MUSIC: *Forest Green*, English melody, n.d.; arr. Ralph Vaughn Williams, 1906
This tune in a lower key, No. 242.

C.M.D.

97

The First Noel

The shepherds returned, glorifying and praising God for all the things they had heard and seen. – Luke 2:20 NIV

1. The first No - el the an - gel did say was to cer - tain poor
2. They look - ed up and saw a star shin - ing in the
3. And by the light of that same star three wise men
4. Then let us all with one ac - cord sing prais - es

shep - herds in fields as they lay; in fields where they lay
east, be - yond them far, and to the earth it
came from coun - try far; to seek for a king was
to our heav'n - ly Lord; that hath made heav'n and

keep - ing their sheep, on a cold win - ter's night that was so deep.
gave great light, and so it con - tin - ued both day and night.
their in - tent, and to fol - low the star wher - ev - er it went.
earth of naught, and with His blood man - kind hath bought.

Refrain

No - well, No - well, No - well, No - well,

*In this carol, Noel (Latin natalis) means birthday and Nowell (Latin novellae) means news.

WORDS: English carol, 19th c.
MUSIC: *The First Noel,* 19th c. English carol; arr. John Stainer, 1871

Irregular with Refrain

born is the King of Is - ra - el.

Angels, from the Realms of Glory 98

Bethlehem...out of you will come a ruler who will be the shepherd of my people. – Matthew 2:6 NIV

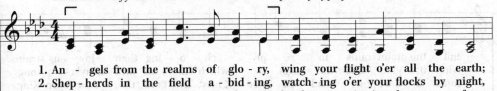

1. An - gels from the realms of glo - ry, wing your flight o'er all the earth;
2. Shep - herds in the field a - bid - ing, watch - ing o'er your flocks by night,
3. Sag - es, leave your con - tem - pla - tions, bright - er vi - sions beam a - far;
4. Saints, be - fore the al - tar bend - ing, watch - ing long in hope and fear;
5. Though an in - fant now we view Him, He shall fill His Fa - ther's throne,

ye who sang cre - a - tion's sto - ry, now pro - claim Mes - si - ah's birth:
God with us is now re - sid - ing; yon - der shines the in - fant Light:
seek the great De - sire of Na - tions; ye have seen His na - tal star:
sud - den - ly the Lord, de - scend - ing, in His tem - ple shall ap - pear.
gath - er all the na - tions to Him; ev - 'ry knee shall then bow down.

Refrain

Come and wor - ship, come and wor - ship, wor - ship Christ, the new - born King.

WORDS: Sts. 1-4 James Montgomery, 1816; St. 5 *The Christmas Box*, 1825
MUSIC: *Regent Square*, Henry Thomas Smart, 1867
This tune in a lower key, No. 317.

8.7.8.7 with Refrain

99 Angels We Have Heard on High

A great company...appeared with the angel...saying, "Glory to God." – Luke 2:13-14 NIV

1. An - gels we have heard on high sweet - ly sing - ing o'er the plains,
2. Shep - herds, why this ju - bi - lee? Why your joy - ous strains pro - long?
3. Come to Beth - le - hem and see Him whose birth the an - gels sing;
4. See Him in a man - ger laid, whom the choirs of an - gels praise;

and the moun - tains in re - ply ech - o - ing their joy - ous strains.
What the glad - some tid - ings be which in - spire your heav'n - ly song?
come, a - dore on bend - ed knee Christ the Lord, the new - born King.
Ma - ry, Jo - seph, lend your aid, while our hearts in love we raise.

Refrain

Glo - - - - - - - - - - - ri - a,

in ex - cel - sis De - o! Glo - - - - - - - ri - a,

in ex - cel - sis De - o!

WORDS: French carol; tr. James Chadwick, 1862
MUSIC: *Gloria*, French carol, 18th c.

7.7.7.7 with Refrain

It Came upon the Midnight Clear

The angel said to them, "Do not be afraid. I bring you good news of great joy." – Luke 2:10 CEV

1. It came up-on the mid-night clear, that glo-r'ous song of old,
2. Still through the clo-ven skies they come with peace-ful wings un-furled,
3. Yet with the woes of sin and strife the world has suf-fered long;
4. And ye, be-neath life's crush-ing load whose forms are bend-ing low,
5. For lo! The days are hast'n-ing on, by proph-ets seen of old,

from an-gels bend-ing near the earth to touch their harps of gold:
and still their heav'n-ly mu-sic floats o'er all the wea-ry world;
be-neath the heav'n-ly hymn have rolled two thou-sand years of wrong;
who toil a-long the climb-ing way with pain-ful steps and slow;
when with the ev-er-cir-cling years shall come the time fore-told,

"Peace on the earth, good-will to men, from heaven's all gra-cious King."
a-bove its sad and low-ly plains they bend on hov'r-ing wing,
and war-ring hu-man-kind bears not the ti-dings which they bring;
look now, for glad and gold-en hours come swift-ly on the wing:
when the new heav'n and earth shall own the Prince of Peace their King,

The world in sol-emn still-ness lay to hear the an-gels sing.
and ev-er o'er its Ba-bel-sounds the bless-ed an-gels sing.
O hush the noise and cease your strife and hear the an-gels sing!
O rest be-side the wea-ry road, and hear the an-gels sing.
and all the world send back the song which now the an-gels sing.

WORDS: Edmund Hamilton Sears, 1849
MUSIC: *Carol,* Richard Storrs Willis, 1850

C.M.D.

Joy Has Dawned

A light to bring revelation to the Gentiles, and the glory of Your people Israel. – Luke 2:32 NKJV

1. Joy has dawned upon the world, promised from creation;
2. Sounds of wonder fill the sky, with the songs of angels;
3. Shepherds bow before the Lamb, gazing at the glory;
4. Son of Adam, Son of Man, given as a ransom;

God's salvation now unfurled, hope for ev'ry nation.
as the mighty Prince of Life shelters in a stable.
gifts of men from distant lands prophesy the story.
reconciling God and Man, Christ our mighty Champion!

Not with fanfares from above, not with scenes of glory,
Hands that set each star in place, shaped the earth in darkness
Gold, a King is born today; incense, God is with us;
What a Savior, what a Friend, what a glorious mys-t'ry!

but a humble gift of love; Jesus, born of Mary.
cling now to a mother's breast, vul-n'ra-ble and help-less.
myrrh, His death will make a way and by His blood He'll win us.
Once a Babe in Bethlehem now the Lord of his-t'ry.

WORDS: Keith Getty and Stuart Townend, 2004
MUSIC: *Joy Has Dawned*, Keith Getty and Stuart Townend, 2004; arr. Eric Wyse, 2005

7.6.7.6 D

He Is Born

You will be with child and give birth to a son, and you are to give Him the name Jesus. – Luke 1:31 NIV

Refrain

He is born, the di - vine Christ child, play on the o - boe and bag - pipes mer - ri - ly! He is born, the Ho - ly Child, sing we all of the Sav - ior mild.

Fine

1. Through long a - ges of the past proph - ets have fore - told His com - ing;
2. Oh, how love - ly, oh, how pure is this per - fect Child of heav - en;
3. Je - sus, Lord of all the world, com - ing as a child a - mong us;

D.C. al Fine

through long a - ges of the past, now the time has come at last!
oh, how love - ly, oh, how pure, gra - cious gift of God sent down.
Je - sus, Lord of all the world, grant to us your heav'n - ly peace.

WORDS: Traditional French carol, 19th c.
MUSIC: *Il Est Né*, traditional French carol, 19th c.; arr. Eric Wyse, 2005

7.8.7.7 with Refrain

O Come, Little Children

Let the little children come to Me, and do not hinder them. – Luke 18:16 NIV

1. O come, lit-tle chil-dren, O come, one and all,
2. He's born in a sta-ble for you and for me,
3. See Ma-ry and Jo-seph, with love-beam-ing eyes,
4. Kneel down and a-dore Him with shep-herds to-day,
5. Dear Christ Child, what gifts can we chil-dren be-stow

to Beth-le-hem haste, to the man-ger so small;
draw near by the bright gleam-ing star-light to see,
are gaz-ing up-on the rude bed where He lies;
lift up lit-tle hands now and praise Him as they;
by which our af-fec-tion and glad-ness to show?

God's Son for a gift has been sent you this night
in swad-dling clothes ly-ing so meek and so mild,
the shep-herds are kneel-ing, with hearts full of love,
re-joice that a Sav-ior from sin you can boast,
No rich-es and trea-sures of val-ue can be,

to be your Re-deem-er, your joy, and de-light.
and pur-er than an-gels, the heav-en-ly Child.
while an-gels sing loud "Hal-le-lu-jahs" a-bove.
and join in the song of the heav-en-ly host.
but hearts that be-lieve are ac-cept-ed with Thee.

WORDS: Christian von Schraid, ca. 1840
MUSIC: *O Come, Little Children*, Johann Abraham Peter Schultz, 18th c.

11.11.11.11

Away in a Manger

You will find a baby wrapped in cloths and lying in a manger. – Luke 2:12 NIV

1. A - way in a man - ger, no crib for a bed,
2. The cat - tle are low - ing, the poor Ba - by wakes,
3. Be near me, Lord Je - sus, I ask Thee to stay

the lit - tle Lord Je - sus laid down His sweet head;
but lit - tle Lord Je - sus, no cry - ing He makes;
close by me for - ev - er, and love me, I pray;

the stars in the bright sky looked down where He lay,
I love Thee, Lord Je - sus! Look down from the sky,
bless all the dear chil - dren in Thy ten - der care,

the lit - tle Lord Je - sus, a - sleep on the hay.
and stay by my cra - dle till morn - ing is nigh.
and fit us for heav - en, to live with Thee there.

WORDS: Sts. 1-2, traditional carol; St. 3 attr. John Thomas McFarland, ca. 1906
MUSIC: *Cradle Song*, William James Kirkpatrick, 1895

11.11.11.11

Away in a Manger

You will find a baby wrapped in cloths and lying in a manger. – Luke 2:12 NIV

1. A - way in a man - ger, no crib for a bed, the lit - tle Lord
2. The cat - tle are low - ing, the poor Ba - by wakes, but lit - tle Lord
3. Be near me, Lord Je - sus, I ask Thee to stay close by me for -

Je - sus laid down His sweet head; the stars in the sky looked
Je - sus, no cry - ing He makes; I love Thee, Lord Je - sus! Look
ev - er, and love me, I pray; bless all the dear chil - dren in

down where He lay, the lit - tle Lord Je - sus, a - sleep on the hay.
down from the sky, and stay by my cra - dle till morn - ing is nigh.
Thy ten - der care, and fit us for heav - en, to live with Thee there.

WORDS: Sts. 1-2, traditional carol; St. 3 attr. John Thomas McFarland, ca. 1906
MUSIC: *Away in a Manger, (Mueller)* James Ramsey Murray, 1887

11.11.11.11

106   Come As a Child

The shepherds said...Let's go to Bethlehem and see this thing that has happened. – Luke 2:15 NIV

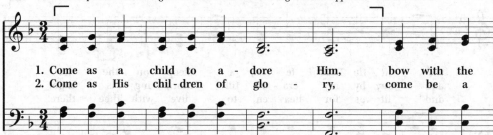

1. Come as a child to a - dore Him, bow with the
2. Come as His chil - dren of glo - ry, come be a

NOTE: This can be sung simultaneously with Away in a Manger (Mueller)

WORDS: Claire Cloninger, 1991
MUSIC: *Cloninger,* Dawn Rodgers, Eric Wyse, 1991; arr. Eric Wyse, 2006

8.8.10.8

shep - herds be - fore Him. Wel - come the Babe in the
part of His sto - ry, lift ev - 'ry hope in your

man - ger a - gain, come as a child to Beth - le - hem.
heart to Him, come as a child to Beth - le - hem.

Still, Still, Still 107

While they were there, the time came for the Baby to be born. – Luke 2:6 NIV

1, 4. Still, still, still, the Babe from heav - en sleeps; His
2. Dream, dream, dream, while shep - herds watch the sky, and
3. Deep, deep, deep, the love of God is deep; Who

moth - er Ma - ry soft - ly sing - ing, through the night her com - fort
choirs of an - gels with - out num - ber praise You as You sweet - ly
glad - ly sent the Son, His trea - sure that our hearts would live for -

bring - ing; still, still, still, the Babe from heav - en sleeps.
slum - ber; dream, dream, dream, while shep - herds watch the sky.
ev - er; deep, deep, deep, the love of God is deep.

WORDS: Traditional Austrian carol; tr. Dawn Rodgers, Eric Wyse, 2005
MUSIC: *Still, Still, Still,* traditional Austrian melody; arr. Eric Wyse, 2005
9.9.8.9

Savior's Lullaby

The virgin will be with child and will give birth to a son, and...will call Him Immanuel. – Matthew 1:23 NIV

Unison

1. Un - der a vel - vet blan-ket of star-light, cho - rus of an - gels in the air;
2. There is a shep-herd kneel-ing be-side You, bring-ing his wool to warm Your bed;

kissed by Your fa - ther, held by Your mam - ma, an - i - mals sleep-ing un - a - ware;
there is a king, the heav-ens to guide him, giv-ing his gold to crown Your head;

close Your eyes, sleep to - night while the world longs for Your Light.
close Your eyes, sleep to - night, how our hearts long for Your Light.

Refrain Harmony

Al - le - lu - ia, al - le - lu - ia, here is the gift our hearts can bring;

al - le - lu - ia, al - le - lu - ia, lul - la - by, Re-

WORDS: Dawn Rodgers, 2002
MUSIC: *Martingale*, Dawn Rodgers, 2002

Irregular with Refrain

deem - er King. Al - le - lu, Al - le - lu - lu - lu.

Gentle Mary Laid Her Child 109

She gave birth to her firstborn, a son. She wrapped Him in cloths and placed Him in a manger. – Luke 2:7 NIV

1. Gen - tle Ma - ry laid her Child low - ly in a man - ger;
2. An - gels sang a - bout His birth; wise men sought and found Him;
3. Gen - tle Ma - ry laid her Child low - ly in a man - ger;

there He lay, the Un - de - filed, to the world a strang - er:
heav - en's star shone bright - ly forth, glo - ry all a - round Him:
He is still the Un - de - filed, but no more a strang - er:

Such a Babe in such a place, can He be the Sav - ior?
Shep - herds saw the won - drous sight, heard the an - gels sing - ing;
Son of God, of hum - ble birth, beau - ti - ful the sto - ry;

Ask the saved of all the race who have found His fa - vor.
all the plains were lit that night, all the hills were ring - ing.
praise His name in all the earth, hail the King of Glo - ry!

WORDS: Joseph Simpson Cook, 1919
MUSIC: *Tempest Adest Floridum*, from *Piae Cantiones*, 1582; arr. John Stainer, 1871

7.6.7.6 D

What Child Is This?

And His name shall be called Wonderful Counselor, Mighty God, Everlasting Father, Prince of Peace. – Isaiah 9:6b ESV

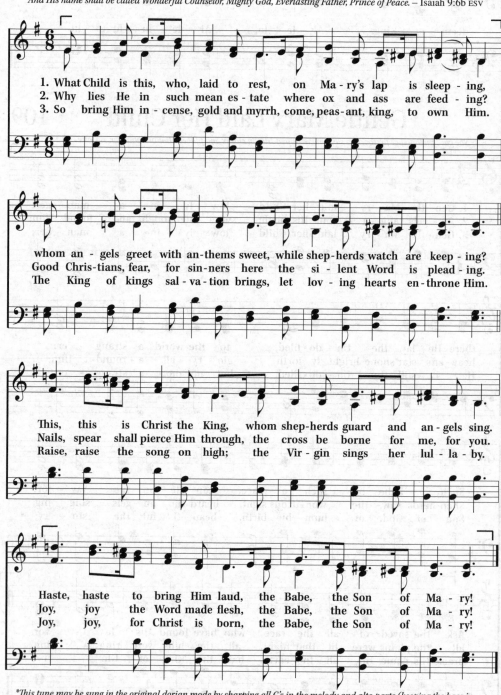

1. What Child is this, who, laid to rest, on Ma-ry's lap is sleep-ing,
2. Why lies He in such mean es-tate where ox and ass are feed-ing?
3. So bring Him in-cense, gold and myrrh, come, peas-ant, king, to own Him.

whom an-gels greet with an-thems sweet, while shep-herds watch are keep-ing?
Good Chris-tians, fear, for sin-ners here the si-lent Word is plead-ing.
The King of kings sal-va-tion brings, let lov-ing hearts en-throne Him.

This, this is Christ the King, whom shep-herds guard and an-gels sing.
Nails, spear shall pierce Him through, the cross be borne for me, for you.
Raise, raise the song on high; the Vir-gin sings her lul-la-by.

Haste, haste to bring Him laud, the Babe, the Son of Ma-ry!
Joy, joy the Word made flesh, the Babe, the Son of Ma-ry!
Joy, joy, for Christ is born, the Babe, the Son of Ma-ry!

This tune may be sung in the original dorian mode by sharping all C's in the melody and alto parts (keeping the bass in measures 3 and 11 unaltered).

WORDS: William Chatterton Dix, ca. 1865
MUSIC: *Greensleeves*, traditional English melody, 16th c.; harm. John Stainer, 1871, alt.

8.7.8.7.6.8.6.7

All My Heart This Night Rejoices

I will praise Thee, O Lord my God, with all my heart: and I will glorify Thy name for evermore. – Psalm 86:12 KJV

1. All my heart this night re-joic-es as I
2. Hark! A voice from yon-der man-ger, soft and
3. Come, then, let us hast-en yon-der! Here let
4. Bless-ed Sav-ior, let me find Thee! Keep Thou
5. Thee, O Lord, with care I'll cher-ish; live to

hear, far and near, sweet-est an-gel voic-es:
sweet, doth en-treat, "Flee from woe and dan-ger!
all, great and small, kneel in awe and won-der!
me, close to Thee; cast me not be-hind Thee!
Thee, and with Thee dy-ing, shall not per-ish;

"Christ is born!" their choirs are sing-ing, till the
Peo-ple come! From all doth grieve you, you are
Love Him who with love is yearn-ing, hail the
Life of Life, my heart Thou still-est; calm I
but shall dwell with Thee for-ev-er, far on

air ev-'ry-where now with joy is ring-ing."
freed; all you need I will sure-ly give you."
star that from far bright with hope is burn-ing!
rest on Thy breast: All this void Thou fill-est.
high in the joy that can al-ter nev-er.

WORDS: *Fröhlich Soll Mein Herze Springen*, Paulus Gerhardt, 1653; tr. Catherine Winkworth, 1858, alt.
MUSIC: *Warum Sollt' Ich Mich Denn Grämen*, Johann Georg Ebeling, 1666

8.3.3.6 D

Christians, Awake!

All who heard it were amazed at what the shepherds said to them. – Luke 2:18 NIV

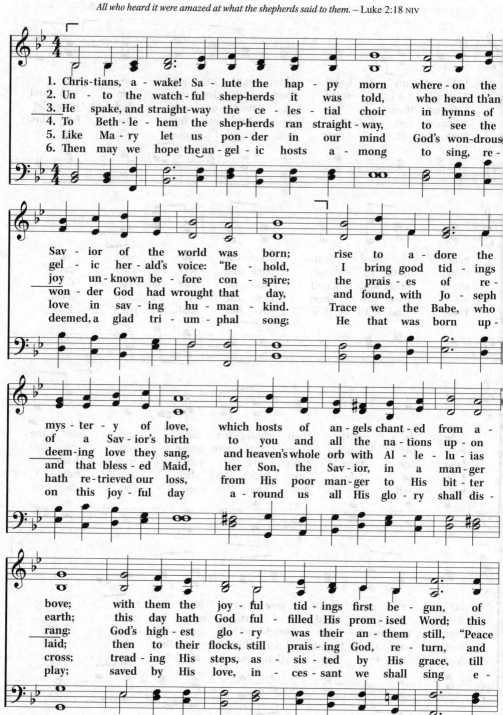

1. Chris-tians, a-wake! Sa-lute the hap-py morn where-on the Sav-ior of the world was born; rise to a-dore the mys-ter-y of love, which hosts of an-gels chant-ed from a-bove; with them the joy-ful tid-ings first be-gun, of

2. Un-to the watch-ful shep-herds it was told, who heard th'an-gel-ic her-ald's voice: "Be-hold, I bring good tid-ings of a Sav-ior's birth to you and all the na-tions up-on earth; this day hath God ful-filled His prom-ised Word; this

3. He spake, and straight-way the ce-les-tial choir in hymns of joy un-known be-fore con-spire; the prais-es of re-deem-ing love they sang, and heaven's whole orb with Al-le-lu-ias rang: God's high-est glo-ry was their an-them still, "Peace

4. To Beth-le-hem the shep-herds ran straight-way, to see the won-der God had wrought that day, and found, with Jo-seph and that bless-ed Maid, her Son, the Sav-ior, in a man-ger laid; then to their flocks, still prais-ing God, re-turn, and

5. Like Ma-ry let us pon-der in our mind God's won-drous love in sav-ing hu-man-kind. Trace we the Babe, who hath re-trieved our loss, from His poor man-ger to His bit-ter cross; tread-ing His steps, as-sis-ted by His grace, till

6. Then may we hope the an-gel-ic hosts a-mong to sing, re-deem, a glad tri-um-phal song; He that was born up-on this joy-ful day a-round us all His glo-ry shall dis-play; saved by His love, in-ces-sant we shall sing e-

WORDS: John Byrom, 1749, alt.
MUSIC: *Stockport (Yorkshire),* John Wainwright, 1750

10.10.10.10.10.10

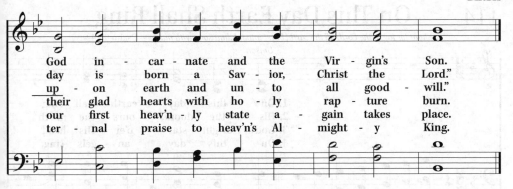

God in - car - nate and the Vir - gin's Son.
day is born a Sav - ior, Christ the Lord."
up - on earth and un - to all good - will."
their glad hearts with ho - ly rap - ture burn.
our first heav'n - ly state a - gain takes place.
ter - nal praise to heav'n's Al - might - y King.

O Thou Joyful, O Thou Wonderful 113

O give thanks to the Lord; call upon His name: make known His deeds among the peoples. – Psalm 105:1 NKJV

1. O thou joy - ful, O thou won - der - ful grace re - veal - ing
2. O thou joy - ful, O thou won - der - ful love re - veal - ing
3. O thou joy - ful, O thou won - der - ful peace re - veal - ing

Christ - mas - tide! Je - sus came to win us from all sin with -
Christ - mas - tide! Loud ho - san - nas sing - ing, and all prais - es
Christ - mas - tide! Dark - ness dis - ap - pear - eth, God's own Light now

in us; glo - ri - fy the Ho - ly Child!
bring - ing, may Thy love with us a - bide!
near - eth, peace and joy to all be - tide!

WORDS: Sts 1, Johannes Daniel Falk, 1816; Sts. 2, 3 anon.; tr. Henry Katterjohn, 1919
MUSIC: *O Sanctissima*, from Tattersall's *Psalmody*, 1792   Irregular

On This Day Earth Shall Ring

Shout for joy to the Lord, all the earth, burst into jubilant song with music. – Psalm 98:4 NIV

Unison

1. On this day earth shall ring
2. His the doom, ours the mirth[2]
3. God's bright star o'er His head,
4. On this day an-gels sing,

with the song chil-dren sing to the Lord, Christ our King,
when He came down to earth, Beth-le-hem saw His birth;
wise men three to Him led, kneel-ing low by His bed,
with their song earth shall ring, prais-ing Christ, Heav-en's King,

born on earth to save us, Him the Fa-ther gave us:
ox and ass be-side Him from the cold would hide Him:
lay their gifts be-fore Him, praise Him and a-dore Him:
born on earth to save us, peace and love He gave us:

Refrain

I-de-o - o - o,[1] i-de-o - o - o,

1. The word ideo *(pronounced ee-day-oh) is Latin for* therefore.
2. Mirth: joyfulness, gaiety, laughter

WORDS: *Piae Cantiones,* 1582; tr. Jane M. Joseph, 1924
MUSIC: *Personent Hodie,* from *Piae Cantiones,* 1582; arr. Gustav Theodore Holst, 1925   6.6.6.6.6 with Refrain

i - de - o glo - ri - a in ex - cel - sis De - o!

Child in the Manger 115

They hurried off and found Mary and Joseph, and the baby, who was lying in the manger. – Luke 2:16 NIV

1. Child in the man - ger, In - fant of Ma - ry,
2. Mon - archs have ten - der, del - i - cate chil - dren
3. But the most ho - ly Child of sal - va - tion
4. Proph - ets fore - told Him, In - fant of won - der;

out - cast and strang - er, Lord of all! Child who in - her - its
nour - ished in splen - dor, day by day; death soon shall ban - ish
gent - ly and low - ly lived be - low; now as our glo - rious
an - gels be - held Him on His throne; wor - thy our Sav - ior

all our trans - gres - sions, all our de - mer - its on Him fall.
hon - or and beau - ty; plea - sure shall van - ish, forms de - cay.
might - y Re - deem - er, see Him vic - to - rious o'er each foe.
of all their prais - es; hap - py for - ev - er are His own.

WORDS: Mary MacDougal MacDonald of Mull, 19th c.; tr. Lachlan McBean, 1888
MUSIC: *Bunesson,* Hebridean melody from the Isle of Mull, n.d.

5.5.5.3 D

116 God Rest Ye Merry, Gentlemen

Joseph, the husband of Mary, of whom was born Jesus, who is called Christ. – Matthew 1:16 NIV

1. God rest ye mer - ry, gen - tle - men, let noth - ing you dis - may,
2. From God our heav'n - ly Fa - ther, a bless - ed an - gel came,
3. "Fear not," then said the an - gel, "let noth - ing you af - fright;
4. The shep - herds at those ti - dings re - joic - ed much in mind,
5. But when to Beth - le - hem they came, where this dear in - fant lay,
6. Now to the Lord sing prais - es all you with - in this place,

re - mem - ber Christ, our Sav - ior was born on Christ-mas day,
and un - to cer - tain shep - herds brought tid - ings of the same;
this day is born a Sav - ior of a pure Vir - gin bright,
and left their flocks a - feed - ing in temp - est, storm and wind,
they found Him in a man - ger where ox - en feed on hay;
and with true love and char - i - ty each oth - er now em - brace.

to save us all from Sa - tan's pow'r when we were gone a - stray:
how that in Beth - le - hem was born the Son of God by name.
to free all those who trust in Him from Sa - tan's pow'r and might."
and went to Beth - l'em straight - way this bless - ed Babe to find.
His Moth - er Ma - ry, kneel - ing un - to the Lord did pray.
This ho - ly tide of Christ - mas doth bring re - deem - ing grace.

Refrain

O tid - ings of com - fort and joy, com-fort and joy,

WORDS: English carol, 18th c.
MUSIC: *God Rest Ye Merry*, English carol, 18th c.; arr. John Stainer, 1871

Irregular with Refrain

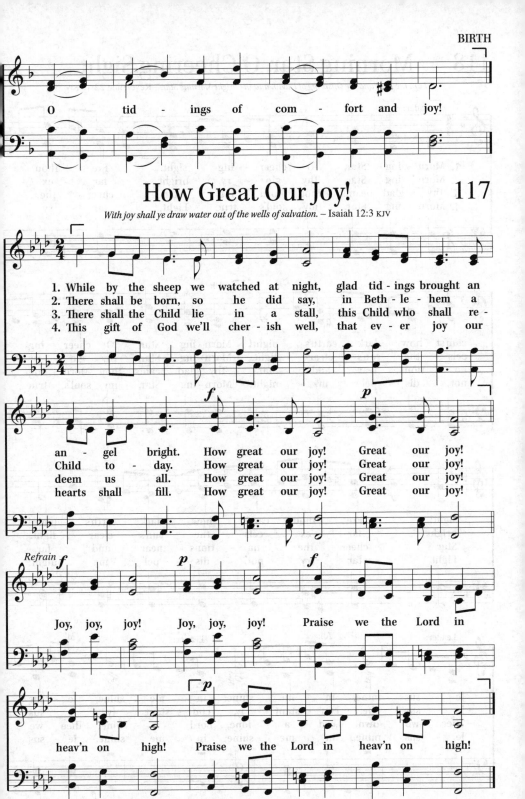

O tidings of comfort and joy!

How Great Our Joy! 117

With joy shall ye draw water out of the wells of salvation. – Isaiah 12:3 KJV

1. While by the sheep we watched at night, glad tidings brought an
2. There shall be born, so he did say, in Bethlehem a
3. There shall the Child lie in a stall, this Child who shall re-
4. This gift of God we'll cherish well, that ever joy our

f   *p*

angel bright. How great our joy! Great our joy!
Child today. How great our joy! Great our joy!
deem us all. How great our joy! Great our joy!
hearts shall fill. How great our joy! Great our joy!

Refrain *f*   *p*   *f*

Joy, joy, joy! Joy, joy, joy! Praise we the Lord in

p

heav'n on high! Praise we the Lord in heav'n on high!

WORDS: Traditional German carol; tr. Theodore Baker, 19th c.
MUSIC: *Jüngst*, traditional German carol; arr. Hugo Jüngst, 1890

Irregular with Refrain

118 Morning Star, O Cheering Sight

I am the Root and the Offspring of David, and the bright Morning Star. – Revelation 22:16 NIV

Leader:

1. Morn - ing Star, O cheer - ing sight! Ere Thou
2. Morn - ing Star, Thy glo - ry bright far ex -
3. Thy glad beams, Thou Morn - ing Star cheer the
4. Morn - ing Star, my soul's true Light, tar - ry

All:

cam'st how dark earth's night! Morn - ing Star, O cheer - ing
cels the sun's clear light. Morn - ing Star, Thy glo - ry
na - tions near and far. Thy glad beams, Thou Morn - ing
not, dis - pel my night; Morn - ing Star, my soul's true

sight! Ere Thou cam'st how dark earth's night!
bright far ex - cels the sun's clear light.
Star cheer the na - tions near and far.
Light, tar - ry not, dis - pel my night;

Leader: All: Leader: All:

Je - sus mine, in me shine; in me shine, Je - sus
Je - sus be, con - stant - ly, con - stant - ly, Je - sus
Thee we own, Lord a - lone, Lord a - lone, Thee we
Je - sus mine, in me shine; in me shine, Je - sus

WORDS: Johann Scheffler, 1657; tr. Bennet Harvey, Jr. 1885
MUSIC: *Hagan*, F. F. Hagen, 1836

7.7.7.7. with Repeat

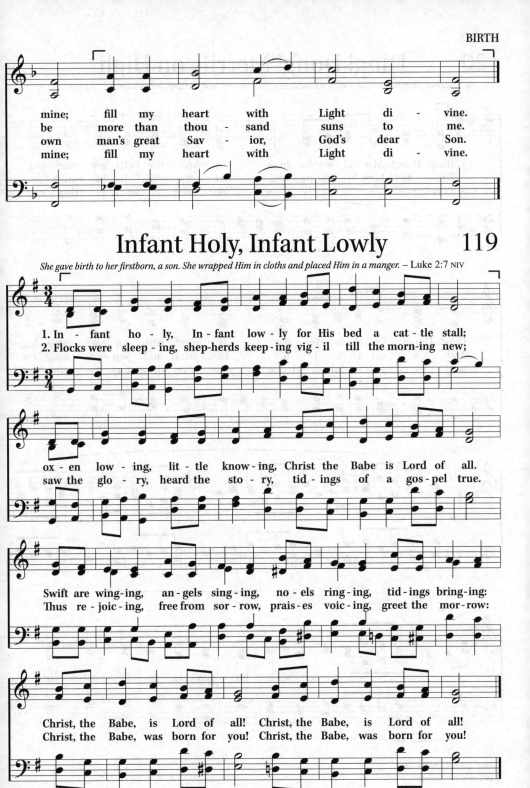

mine;   fill   my   heart   with   Light   di - vine.
be   more than thou - sand   suns   to   me.
own man's great Sav - ior,   God's dear Son.
mine;   fill   my   heart   with   Light   di - vine.

Infant Holy, Infant Lowly   119

She gave birth to her firstborn, a son. She wrapped Him in cloths and placed Him in a manger. – Luke 2:7 NIV

1. In - fant ho - ly, In - fant low - ly for His bed a cat - tle stall;
2. Flocks were sleep - ing, shep-herds keep - ing vig - il till the morn-ing new;

ox - en low - ing, lit - tle know - ing, Christ the Babe is Lord of all.
saw the glo - ry, heard the sto - ry, tid - ings of a gos - pel true.

Swift are wing - ing, an - gels sing - ing, no - els ring - ing, tid - ings bring-ing:
Thus re - joic - ing, free from sor - row, prais - es voic - ing, greet the mor - row:

Christ, the Babe, is Lord of all! Christ, the Babe, is Lord of all!
Christ, the Babe, was born for you! Christ, the Babe, was born for you!

WORDS: Traditional Polish carol; tr. Edith Margaret Gellibrand Reed, 1921
MUSIC: *W Zlobie Lezy*, Traditional Polish carol

8.7.8.7.8.8.7 with Repeat

120 Ding! Dong! Merrily on High

And suddenly there was with the angel a multitude of the heavenly host praising God and saying... – Luke 2:13 KJV

1. Ding! Dong! Mer - ri - ly on high   in heav'n the bells are ring - ing.
2. E'en so here be - low be - low   let stee - ple bells be swung - en,
3. Pray you, du - ti - ful - ly prime   Your mat - in chime, ye ring - ers;

Ding! Dong! Ve - ri - ly the sky   is rent[1] with an - gel sing - ing.
And "i - o,[2] i - o, i - o,"   by priest and peo - ple sung - en.
may ye beau - ti - ful - ly rhyme   your eve - time song, ye sing - ers.

Refrain

Glo - - - - - - - ri - a, ho - san - na in ex - cel - sis!

1. *rent: opened, split or torn*
2. *io: Latin for "hurrah!"*

WORDS: G.R. Woodward, early 20th c.
MUSIC: *Branle de l'officiel,* Thoinot Arbeau in *Orchesographie,* 1588; harm. Eric Wyse, 2005
7.7.7.7 with Refrain

See, Amid the Winter's Snow

"I bring you good news of great joy...a Savior has been born." – Luke 2:10-11 NIV

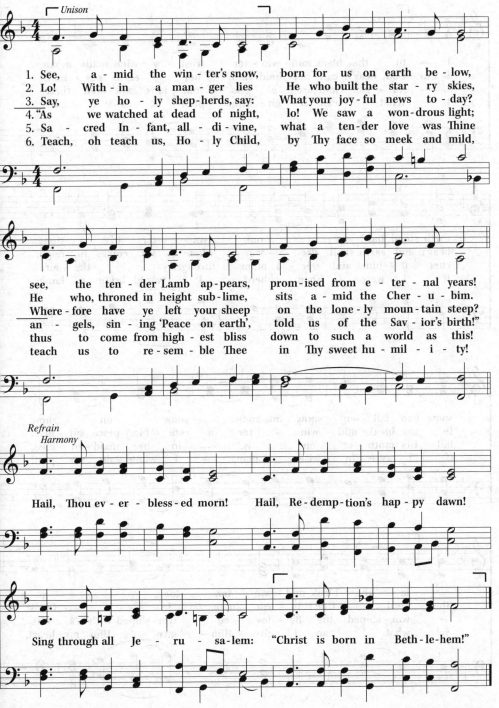

Unison

1. See, a - mid the win - ter's snow, born for us on earth be - low,
2. Lo! With - in a man - ger lies He who built the star - ry skies,
3. Say, ye ho - ly shep - herds, say: What your joy - ful news to - day?
4. "As we watched at dead of night, lo! We saw a won - drous light;
5. Sa - cred In - fant, all - di - vine, what a ten - der love was Thine
6. Teach, oh teach us, Ho - ly Child, by Thy face so meek and mild,

see, the ten - der Lamb ap - pears, prom - ised from e - ter - nal years!
He who, throned in height sub - lime, sits a - mid the Cher - u - bim.
Where - fore have ye left your sheep on the lone - ly moun - tain steep?
an - gels, sing - ing 'Peace on earth', told us of the Sav - ior's birth!"
thus to come from high - est bliss down to such a world as this!
teach us to re - sem - ble Thee in Thy sweet hu - mil - i - ty!

Refrain
Harmony

Hail, Thou ev - er - bless - ed morn! Hail, Re - demp - tion's hap - py dawn!

Sing through all Je - ru - sa - lem: "Christ is born in Beth - le - hem!"

WORDS: Edward Caswall, 1851
MUSIC: *Humility (Oxford)*, John Goss, 1871

7.7.7.7 with Refrain

In the Bleak Midwinter

Mary treasured up all these things, and pondered them in her heart. – Luke 2:19 NIV

1. — In the bleak mid-win-ter frost-y wind made moan,
2. Our God, heav'n can-not hold Him, nor earth sus-tain;
3. — An-gels and arch-an-gels may have gath-ered there,
4. — What can I give Him, poor as I am?

earth stood hard as i-ron, wa-ter like a stone;
heav'n and earth shall flee a-way when He comes to reign;
cher-u-bim and ser-a-phim thronged the air;
If I were a shep-herd, I would bring a lamb;

snow had fall-en, snow on snow, — snow on snow,
In the bleak mid-win-ter a sta-ble place suf-ficed
but His moth-er on-ly, — in her maid-en bliss,
if I were a wise man, — I would do my part;

— in the bleak mid-win-ter, long, a-go.
the Lord God in-car-nate, Je-sus Christ.
— wor-shiped the Be-lov-ed wor-shiped with a kiss.
yet what I can I give Him— give Him my heart.

WORDS: Christina Georgina Rossetti, 1872
MUSIC: *Cranham*, Gustav Theodore Holst, 1906

Irregular

What Can I Give Him?

And she brought forth her firstborn son...and laid Him in a manger. – Luke 2:7 KJV

1. — In the bleak mid-win-ter frost-y wind made moan,
2. Our God, heav'n can-not hold Him, nor earth sus-tain;
3. — An-gels and arch-an-gels may have gath-ered there,
4. — What can I give Him, poor as I am?

— earth stood hard as i-ron, wa-ter like a stone;
— heav'n and earth shall flee a-way when He comes to reign;
— cher-u-bim and ser-a-phim thronged the air;
If I were a shep-herd, I would bring a lamb;

— snow had fall-en, snow on snow, snow on snow,
— in the bleak mid-win-ter a sta-ble place suf-ficed,
— but His moth-er on-ly in her maid-en bliss
if I were a wise-man, I would do my part;

— in the bleak mid-win-ter, long a-go.
the Lord God Al-might-y, Je-sus Christ.
wor-shiped the Be-lov-ed with a kiss.
yet what can I give Him? Give Him my heart.

WORDS: Christina Georgina Rossetti, 1872, alt.
MUSIC: *Castle*, Don Cason, 1986; new harm. 2005

Irregular

124 While Shepherds Watched Their Flocks

There were shepherds living out in the fields nearby, keeping watch over their flocks at night. – Luke 2:8 NIV

1. While shep-herds watched their flocks by night, all seat-ed on the ground
2. "Fear not," said he (for might-y dread had seized their trou-bled mind)
3. "To you, in Da-vid's town this day is born of Da-vid's line,
4. "The heav'n-ly Babe you there shall find to hu-man view dis-played
5. Thus spake the ser-aph, and forth-with ap-peared a shin-ing throng
6. "All glo-ry be to God on high, and to the earth be peace;

the an-gel of the Lord came down and glo-ry shone a-round.
"glad tid-ings of great joy I bring to you and all man-kind."
the Sav-ior, who is Christ the Lord, and this shall be the sign:"
all mean-ly wrapped in swath-ing bands,[1] and in a man-ger laid."
of an-gels prais-ing God, who thus ad-dressed their joy-ful song:
Good will to all from high-est heav'n be-gin and nev-er cease."

1. *swathing bands: layers of fabric*
WORDS: Nahum Tate, 1700
MUSIC: *Winchester Old,* melody from Este's Psalter, 1592

C.M.

125 While Shepherds Watched Their Flocks

There were shepherds living out in the fields nearby, keeping watch over their flocks at night. – Luke 2:8 NIV

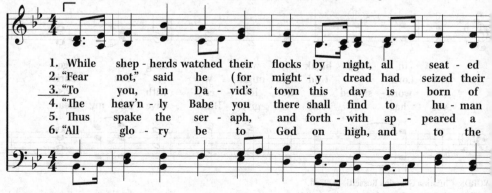

1. While shep-herds watched their flocks by night, all seat-ed
2. "Fear not," said he (for might-y dread had seized their
3. "To you, in Da-vid's town this day is born of
4. "The heav'n-ly Babe you there shall find to hu-man
5. Thus spake the ser-aph, and forth-with ap-peared a
6. "All glo-ry be to God on high, and to the

WORDS: Nahum Tate, 1700
MUSIC: *Christmas,* George Frederic Handel, from an air in *Siroe,* 1728; arr. Lowell Mason, 1821

C.M. with Repeat

on the ground,   the   an - gel   of   the   Lord came   down
trou - bled mind);   "glad   tid - ings   of   great   joy   I   bring
Da - vid's line,   the   Sav - ior, who   is   Christ   the   Lord,
view dis - played   all   mean - ly wrapped in   swath - ing[1]   bands,
shin - ing throng   of   an - gels prais - ing   God, who   thus
earth be peace: Good   will to   all   from high - est   heav'n

and glo - ry shone a - round,   and   glo - ry shone a - round.
to you and all man - kind,   to   you and all man - kind."
and this shall be the sign: And   this shall be the sign:"
and in a man - ger laid,   and   in a man - ger laid."
ad - dressed their joy - ful song,   ad - dressed their joy - ful song.
be - gin and nev - er cease,   be - gin and nev - er cease!"

1. swathing bands: layers of fabric

I Heard the Bells on Christmas Day   126

Glory to God in the highest, and on earth peace to men on whom His favor rests. – Luke 2:14 NIV

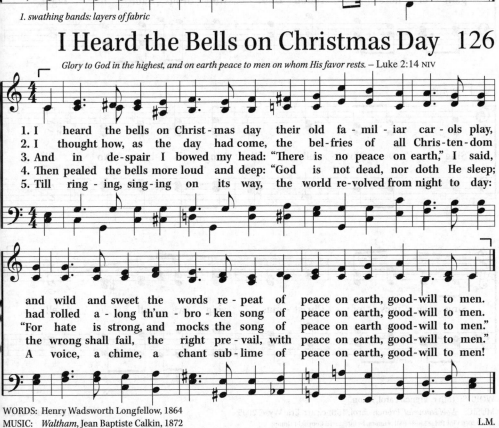

1. I   heard   the bells on Christ - mas day   their old fa - mil - iar car - ols play,
2. I   thought how, as   the   day had come, the   bel - fries of   all Chris - ten - dom
3. And   in   de - spair I bowed my head: "There   is   no peace on earth," I   said,
4. Then pealed the bells more loud   and deep: "God   is   not dead, nor doth He sleep;
5. Till   ring - ing, sing - ing on   its way,   the world re - volved from night to   day:

and wild and sweet   the words re - peat   of   peace on earth, good - will to men.
had rolled a - long th'un - bro - ken song   of   peace on earth, good - will to men.
"For hate   is strong, and mocks the song   of   peace on earth good - will to men."
the wrong shall fail,   the   right pre - vail, with   peace on earth, good - will to men."
A   voice, a chime, a   chant sub - lime   of   peace on earth, good - will to men!

WORDS: Henry Wadsworth Longfellow, 1864
MUSIC: *Waltham*, Jean Baptiste Calkin, 1872

L.M.

127 Sing We Now of Christmas

Then they opened their treasures and presented Him with gifts of gold and of incense and of myrrh. – Matthew 2:11b NIV

1. Sing we now of Christ-mas, No-el, sing we here!
2. From the East-ern king-doms come the wise men far,
3. From the dis-tant moun-tains, hear the trum-pet sound,
4. Come, let us sur-round Him on this ho-ly night,

Sing our grate-ful prais-es to the Babe so dear.
bear-ing an-cient trea-sure, fol-low-ing yon-der star.
with an-gel-ic bless-ings on the si-lent town.
gath-er here a-round Him, won-drous Babe of Light.

Refrain

Sing we No-el! The King is born, No-el!

Sing we now of Christ-mas, sing we all, No-el!

WORDS: 15th c. French carol, Anon.
MUSIC: *Noel Nouvelet*. French carol, 15th c.; arr. Eric Wyse, 2005
Arr. © 2006 Vine Ridge Music BMI. (admin. by Integrated Copyright Group)

6.5.6.5 with Refrain

On Christmas Night All Christians Sing 128

You shall know that I, the LORD, am your Savior and your Redeemer. – Isaiah 60:16 KJV

Unison

1. On Christ-mas night all Chris-tians sing, to hear the news the
2. Then why should we on earth be sad, since our Re-deem - er
3. When sin de-parts be-fore His grace, then life and health come
4. All out of dark-ness we have light which made the an - gels

Harmony

an - gels bring; on Christ-mas night all Chris - tians sing, to
made us glad; then why should we on earth be sad, since
in its place; when sin de - parts be - fore His grace, then
sing this night; all out of dark - ness we have light, which

Unison

hear the news the an - gels bring: news of great joy, news
our Re-deem - er made us glad, when from our sin He
life and health come in its place; heav - en and earth with
made the an - gels sing this night: "Glo - ry to God and

Harmony

of great mirth, news of our mer - ci - ful King's birth.
set us free, all for to gain our lib - er - ty?
joy may sing, all for to see the new - born King.
peace to all, for - ev - er - more, Al - le - lu - ia!"

WORDS: Traditional English carol; attr. Luke Wadding, 17th c., alt.
MUSIC: *Sussex Carol*; arr. Ralph Vaughan Williams, 1919

8.8.8.8 with Repeat

129 O Holy Night!

The Holy One to be born will be called the Son of God. – Luke 1:35 NIV

1. O ho - ly night! The stars are bright - ly shin -
2. Led by the light of faith se - rene - ly beam -
3. Tru - ly He taught us to love one an - oth -

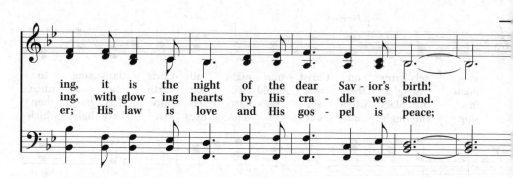

ing, it is the night of the dear Sav - ior's birth!
ing, with glow - ing hearts by His cra - dle we stand.
er; His law is love and His gos - pel is peace;

Long lay the world in sin and er - ror pin - ing, till He ap -
So led by light of a star sweet - ly gleam - ing, here came the
chains shall He break, for the slave is our broth - er, and in His

peared and the soul felt its worth. A thrill of hope, the
wise men from O - ri - ent land. The King of kings lay
name all op - pres - sion shall cease. Sweet hymns of joy in

WORDS: Placide Cappeau, 1847; tr. John Sullivan Dwight, 1855
MUSIC: *Cantique De Noel*, Adolphe-Charles Adam, 1847

Irregular

weary world re-joic-es, for yon-der breaks a new and glo-rious
thus in low-ly man-ger, in all our tri-als born to be our
grate-ful cho-rus raise we; let all with-in us praise His ho-ly

morn! Fall on your knees, O hear the an-gel
Friend; He knows our need, to our weak - ness is no
name. Christ is the Lord! O, praise His name for-

voic - es! O night di - vine, O
strang - er. Be - hold your King, be -
ev - er! His pow'r and glo - ry

night when Christ was born! O night di y -
fore Him low - ly bend! Be - hold your
ev - er - more pro - claim! His pow'r and

vine, O night, O night di - vine!
King, be - fore Him low - ly bend!
glo - ry ev - er - more pro - claim!

130 That Beautiful Name

She will give birth to a son, and you are to give Him the name Jesus. – Matthew 1:21 NIV

1. I know of a name, a beau-ti-ful name, that an-gels brought down to earth; they whis-pered it low, one night long a-go, to a maid-en of low-ly birth.
2. I know of a name, a beau-ti-ful name, that un-to a Babe was giv-en; the stars glit-tered bright through-out that glad night, and an-gels praised God in heav'n.
3. The One of that name my Sav-ior be-came, my Sav-ior of Cal-va-ry; my sins nailed Him there, my bur-dens to bear, He suf-fered all this for me.
4. I love that blest name, that won-der-ful name, made high-er than all in heav-en; 'twas whis-pered, I know, in my heart long a-go, to Je-sus my life I've giv'n.

Refrain

That beau-ti-ful name, that beau-ti-ful name from sin has pow'r to free us! That beau-ti-ful name, that

WORDS: Jean Perry, 1916
MUSIC: *Beautiful Name*, Mabel Johnston Camp, 1916

Irregular with Refrain

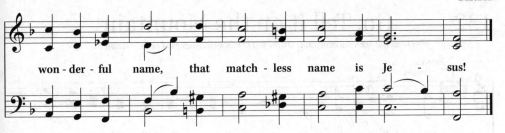

won - der - ful name, that match - less name is Je - sus!

Worship the Newborn King 131

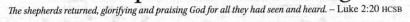

The shepherds returned, glorifying and praising God for all they had seen and heard. – Luke 2:20 HCSB

1. Wor - ship the new - born King, wor - ship the
2. Come hear the an - gels sing, come, hear the
3. Go, tell to all the news, go, tell to

new - born King; Je - sus is our Em -
an - gels sing; Je - sus is our Em -
all the news; Je - sus is our Em -

man - u - el, wor-ship the new - born King.
man - u - el, wor-ship the new - born King.
man - u - el, wor-ship the new - born King.

WORDS: Claire Cloninger, 2005
MUSIC: *Waiting,* Don Cason, 1986
S.M.

132 Go, Tell It on the Mountain

How beautiful upon the mountains are the feet of him who brings good news. – Isaiah 52:7 ESV

Refrain
Unison

Go, tell it on the moun - tain, o - ver the hills and ev - 'ry-where;

Fine

go, tell it on the moun - tain that Je - sus Christ is born!

Harmony

1. While shep - herds kept their watch - ing o'er si - lent flocks by night,
2. The shep - herds feared and trem - bled when, lo! a - bove the earth
3. Down in a low - ly man - ger the hum - ble Christ was born,
4. — When I was a seek - er, I sought both night and day;

D.C. al Fine

be - hold, through - out the heav - ens there shone a ho - ly light.
rang out the an - gel cho - rus that hailed our Sav - ior's birth.
and God sent us sal - va - tion that bless - ed Christ-mas morn.
I asked the Lord to help me, and He showed me the way.

WORDS: Negro spiritual, 19th c.; adapt. John Work, Jr. 1907
MUSIC: *Go Tell It*, Negro spiritual, 19th c.

7.6.7.6 with Refrain

Rise Up, Shepherd, and Follow

An angel of the Lord appeared to them, and the glory of the Lord shone around them. – Luke 2:9 NIV

1. There's a star in the East on Christ-mas morn,
2. If you take good heed to the an-gel's words,

rise up, shep-herd, and fol-low, it will lead to the place where the
rise up, shep-herd, and fol-low, you'll for-get your flock, you'll for-

Christ was born, rise up, shep-herd, and fol-low.
get your herd, rise up, shep-herd, and fol-low.

Refrain

Fol-low, fol-low, rise up, shep-herd, and fol-low,

fol-low the Star of Beth-le-hem, rise up, shep-herd, and fol-low.

WORDS: Negro spiritual, n.d.
MUSIC: *Follow,* Negro spiritual, n.d.

10.7.10.7 with Refrain

134 Bring a Torch, Jeannette, Isabella!

They saw the child with His mother Mary, and they bowed down and worshipped Him. – Matthew 2:11a NIV

1. Bring a torch, Jeannette, Isabella! Bring a torch, to the cradle run! It is Jesus, good folk of the village; Christ is born and Mary's calling. Ah! Ah! Beautiful is the mother! Ah! Ah! Beautiful is her Son!

2. It is wrong when the child is sleeping, it is wrong to talk so loud; silence, all, as you gather around, lest your noise should waken Jesus. Hush! Hush! See how fast He slumbers; hush! Hush! See how fast He sleeps!

3. Hasten now, good folk of the village; hasten now the Christ Child to see. You will find Him asleep in the manger; quietly come and whisper softly. Hush! Hush! Peacefully now He slumbers; hush! Hush! Peacefully now He sleeps.

4. Softly to the little stable, softly for a moment come; look and see how charming is Jesus, how He is pure, so fair and lovely. Hush! Hush! See how the Child is sleeping; hush! Hush! See how He smiles in dreams.

WORDS: Traditional French Provençal carol, 1836; adapt. Émile Blémont, 1901; tr. Edward Cuthbert Nunn, 1901 alt.
MUSIC: *Bring a Torch*, traditional French Provençal carol, 14th c.; adapt. Edward Cuthbert Nunn, 1901
Irregular

There's a Song in the Air!

Blessed are you among women, and blessed is the child you will bear. – Luke 1:42 NIV

1. There's a song in the air! There's a star in the sky!
2. There's a tu - mult of joy o'er the won - der - ful birth,
3. In the light of that star lie the a - ges im - pearled;
4. We re - joice in the light, and we ech - o the song

There's a Moth - er's deep prayer and a Ba - by's low cry!
for the Vir - gin's sweet boy is the Lord of the earth.
and that song from a - far has swept o - ver the world.
that comes down through the night from the heav - en - ly throng.

And the star rains its fire while the beau - ti - ful sing,
Oh! The star rains its fire while the beau - ti - ful sing,
Ev - 'ry hearth is a - flame, and the beau - ti - ful sing
Oh! We shout to the love - ly e - van - gel they bring,

for the man - ger of Beth - le - hem cra - dles a King!
for the man - ger of Beth - le - hem cra - dles a King!
in the homes of the na - tions that Je - sus is King!
and we greet in His cra - dle our Sav - ior and King!

WORDS: Josiah Gilbert Holland, 1872
MUSIC: *Christmas Song*, Karl Pomeroy Harrington, 1904

6.6.6.6.12.12

136 The Birthday of a King

After Jesus was born...the Magi asked, "Where is the one who has been born king of the Jews?" – Matthew 2:1-2a NIV

1. In the lit-tle vil-lage of Beth-le-hem, there lay a Child one day; and the sky was bright with a ho-ly light o'er the place where Je-sus lay.

2. 'Twas a hum-ble birth-place, but O how much God gave to us that day, from the man-ger bed what a path has led, what a per-fect, ho-ly way.

Refrain

Al-le-lu-ia! O how the an-gels sang. Al-le-lu-ia! How it rang! And the sky was bright with a ho-ly light, 'twas the birth-day of a King.

WORDS: William Harold Neidlinger, 1890
MUSIC: *Neidlinger*, William Harold Neidlinger, 1890

10.6.10.7 with Refrain

Thou Didst Leave Thy Throne

Being found in appearance as a man, He humbled Himself and became obedient to death. – Philippians 2:8 NIV

1. Thou didst leave Thy throne and Thy king - ly crown, when Thou
2. Heav - en's arch - es rang when the an - gels sang, pro -
3. The fox - es found rest, and the birds their nest in the
4. Thou cam - est, O Lord, with the liv - ing Word that should
5. When the heav - ens shall ring, and the an - gels sing, at Thy

cam - est to earth for me; but in Beth - le - hem's home was there
claim - ing Thy roy - al de - gree;[1] but of low - ly birth didst Thou
shade of the for - est tree; but Thy couch was the sod, O Thou
set Thy peo - ple free; but with mock - ing scorn, and with
com - ing to vic - to - ry, let Thy voice call me home, say - ing

found no room for Thy ho - ly na - tiv - i - ty.
come to earth, and in great hu - mil - i - ty.
Son of God, in the des - erts of Gal - i - lee.
crown of thorn, they bore Thee to Cal - va - ry.
"Yet there is room, there is room at My side for thee."

Refrain

1.–4. O, come to my heart, Lord Je - sus, there is room in my heart for Thee.
5. My heart shall re - joice, Lord Je - sus, when Thou com - est and call - est for me.

1. degree: descent, lineage

WORDS: Emily Elizabeth Steele Elliot, 1864
MUSIC: *Margaret*, Timothy Richard Matthews, 1876

Irregular with Refrain

138 We Wish You a Merry Christmas

And we declare unto you glad tidings. – Acts 13:32 KJV

1. We wish you a mer-ry Christ-mas, we wish you a mer-ry
2. We sing you this Christ-mas bless-ing, great joy now we are con-
3. May God's grace and peace be with you, may God's grace and peace be

Christ-mas, we wish you a mer-ry Christ-mas, and a
fess-ing; best wish-es to you ad-dress-ing for a
with you, may God's grace and peace be with you through-

Refrain

hap-py New Year!
hap-py New Year! Glad tid-ings we bring to you, and your
out the New Year!

kin, glad tid-ings for Christ-mas and a hap-py New Year!

WORDS: Traditional English carol; Sts. 2-3, Danny R. Jones and Eric Wyse, 2005
MUSIC: *We Wish You a Merry Christmas,* traditional English carol

Irregular with Refrain

Good King Wenceslas

When you give a banquet, invite the poor, the crippled...the blind, and you will be blessed. – Luke 14:13-14 NIV

1. Good King Wen - ces - las looked out on the feast of Ste - phen,
2. "Hith - er, page, and stand by me, if you know it, tell - ing,
3. "Bring me drink and bring me meat, bring me pine logs hith - er,
4. "Sire, the night is dark - er now, and the wind blows strong - er,
5. In his ma - ster's steps he trod, where the snow lay dent - ed;

when the snow lay round a - bout, deep and crisp and e - ven;
yon - der pea - sant, who is he? Where and what his dwell - ing?"
you and I will see him eat, when we bear them thigh - er."
fails my heart, I know not how; I can go no long - er."
heat was in the ve - ry sod which the saint had print - ed.

bright - ly shone the moon that night, though the frost was cru - el,
"Sire, he lives a good league hence, un - der - neath the moun - tain,
Page and mon - arch, forth they went, forth they went to - geth - er,
"Mark my foot - steps, my good page, tread now in them bold - ly,
There - fore, Chris - tians all be sure, wealth or rank pos - sess - ing,

when a poor man came in sight, gath - 'ring win - ter fu - el.
right a - gainst the for - est fence, by Saint Ag - nes' foun - tain."
through the cold wind's wild la - ment and the bit - ter weath - er.
you shal find the win - ter's rage freeze thy - self less cold - ly."
you who now will bless the poor shall your - selves find bless - ing.

WORDS: John Mason Neale, 1853, alt.
MUSIC: *Tempus Adest Floridum*, from *Piae Cantiones*, 1582; arr. John Stainer, 1871

7.6.7.6 D

140 We Three Kings of Orient Are

We saw His star in the east and have come to worship Him. – Matthew 2:2b NIV

1. We three kings of O-ri-ent are, bear-ing gifts we
2. Born a King on Beth-le-hem's plain, gold I bring to
3. Frank-in-cense to of-fer have I, in-cense owns a
4. Myrrh is mine, its bit-ter per-fume breathes a life of
5. Glo-r'ous now be-hold Him a-rise, King and God and

tra-verse a-far, field and foun-tain, moor and moun-tain,
crown Him a-gain, King for-ev-er, ceas-ing nev-er
De-i-ty nigh; prayer and prais-ing, glad-ly rais-ing,
gath-er-ing gloom; sor-rowing, sigh-ing, bleed-ing, dy-ing,
Sac-ri-fice; "Al-le-lu-ia! Al-le-lu-ia!"

Refrain

fol-low-ing yon-der star.
o-ver us all to reign. O
wor-ship Him, God on high. star of won-der,
sealed in the stone-cold tomb.
Sounds through the earth and skies.

star of night, star with roy-al beau-ty bright, west-ward

WORDS: John Henry Hopkins, Jr., 1857
MUSIC: *Kings of Orient*, John Henry Hopkins, Jr., 1857

8.8.8.6 with Refrain

lead - ing, still pro - ceed - ing, guide us to thy per - fect light.

As With Gladness Men of Old 141

He will be great and will be called the Son of the Most High. – Luke 1:32 NIV

1. As with glad - ness men of old did the guid - ing star be - hold;
2. As with joy - ful steps they sped to that low - ly man - ger - bed;
3. As they of - fered gifts most rare at that man - ger rude and bare;
4. Ho - ly Je - sus, ev - 'ry day keep us in the nar - row way;
5. In the heav'n - ly coun - try bright, need they no cre - a - ted light;

as with joy they hailed its light, lead - ing on - ward, beam-ing bright;
there to bend the knee be - fore Him whom heav'n and earth a - dore;
so may we with ho - ly joy, pure and free from sin's al - loy,
and, when earth - ly things are past, bring our ran-somed souls at last
Thou its light, its joy, its crown, Thou its sun which goes not down:

so, most gra - cious Lord, may we ev - er - more be led to Thee.
so may we with will - ing feet ev - er seek the mer - cy - seat.
all our cost - l'est trea - sures bring, Christ, to Thee, our heav'n-ly King.
where they need no star to guide, where no clouds Thy glo - ry hide.
There for - ev - er may we sing al - le - lu - ias to our King.

WORDS: William Chatterton Dix, 1860
MUSIC: *Dix*, Conrad Kocher, 1838; arr. William Henry Monk, 1865
This tune in a higher key, No. 595.

7.7.7.7.7.7

142 Brightest and Best of the Stars

The morning stars sang together and all the sons of God shouted for joy. – Job 38:7 ESV

1. Bright - est and best of the stars of the morn - ing,
2. Cold on His cra - dle the dew - drops are shin - ing,
3. Shall we then yield Him, in cost - ly de - vo - tion,
4. Vain - ly we of - fer each am - ple o - bla - tion,
5. Bright - est and best of the stars of the morn - ing,

dawn on our dark - ness, and lend us Thine aid;
low lies His head with the beasts of the stall;
o - dors of E - dom, and of - f'rings di - vine,
vain - ly with gifts would His fa - vor se - cure;
dawn on our dark - ness, and lend us Thine aid;

star of the east, the hor - i - zon a - dorn - ing
an - gels a - dore Him in slum - ber re - clin - ing,
gems of the moun - tain, and pearls of the o - cean,
rich - er by far is the heart's ad - o - ra - tion,
star of the east, the hor - i - zon a - dorn - ing,

guide where our in - fant Re - deem - er is laid.
Mak - er and Mon - arch and Sav - ior of all.
myrrh from the for - est, and gold from the mine?
dear - er to God are the prayers of the poor.
guide where our in - fant Re - deem - er is laid.

WORDS: Reginald Heber, 1811, alt.
MUSIC: *Morning Star*, James Proctor Harding, 1892

11.10.11.10

Worship the Lord in the Beauty of Holiness 143

Worship the Lord in the beauty of holiness. – Psalm 29:2 KJV

1. Wor - ship the Lord in the beau - ty of ho - li - ness,
2. Low at His feet lay Thy bur - den of care - ful - ness,
3. Fear not to en - ter His courts in the slen - der - ness
4. These though we bring them in trem - bling and fear - ful - ness,
5. Wor - ship the Lord in the beau - ty of ho - li - ness,

bow down be - fore Him, His glo - ry pro - claim;
high on His heart He will bear it for thee;
of the poor wealth thou woulds reck - on as thine;
He will ac - cept for the name that is dear,
bow down be - fore Him, His glo - ry pro - claim;

gold of o - be - dience and in - cense of low - li - ness,
com - fort thy sor - rows and an - swer thy prayer - ful - ness,
truth in its beau - ty, and love in its ten - der - ness,
morn - ings of joy give for ev - 'nings of tear - ful - ness,
gold of o - be - dience and in - cense of low - li - ness,

bring and a - dore Him the Lord is His name.
guid - ing thy steps as may best for thee be.
these are the of - f'rings to lay on His shrine.
trust for our trem - bling, and hope for our fear.
bring and a - dore Him the Lord is His name.

WORDS: John Samuel Bewley Monsell, 1863
MUSIC: *Was Lebet, Was Schewbet,* from *Reinhardt Manuscript,* 1754

12.10.12.10

144 Songs of Thankfulness and Praise

For in the days of David...there were...songs of praise and thanksgiving unto God. – Nehemiah 12:46 JKV

1. Songs of thank-ful-ness and praise, Je-sus, Lord, to Thee we raise,
2. Man-i-fest at Jor-dan's stream, Proph-et, Priest, and King su-preme,
3. Man-i-fest in mak-ing whole pal-sied limbs and faint-ing soul,
4. Sun and moon shall dark-ened be, stars shall fall, the heav'ns shall flee;
5. Grant us grace to see Thee, Lord, mir-rored in Thy ho-ly Word;

man-i-fest-ed by the star to the sag-es from a-far;
and at Ca-na, wed-ding guest in Thy God-head man-i-fest,
man-i-fest in val-iant fight, quell-ing all the dev-il's might,
Christ will then like light-'ning shine, all will see His glo-r'ous sign;
may we im-i-tate Thee now, and be pure, as pure art Thou,

branch of roy-al Da-vid's stem in Thy birth at Beth-le-hem,
man-i-fest in pow'r di-vine, chang-ing wa-ter in-to wine,
man-i-fest in gra-cious will, ev-er bring-ing good from ill,
all will then the trum-pet hear, all will see the Judge ap-pear;
that we like to Thee may be at Thy great e-piph-a-ny,

an-thems be to Thee ad-dressed, God in man made man-i-fest.
an-thems be to Thee ad-dressed, God in man made man-i-fest.
an-thems be to Thee ad-dressed, God in man made man-i-fest.
Thou by all wilt be con-fessed, God in man made man-i-fest.
and may praise Thee, ev-er blest, God in man made man-i-fest.

WORDS: Christopher Wordsworth, 1862
MUSIC: *Salzburg*, Jacob Hintze, 1678; harm. Johann Sebastian Bach, 18th c.

7.7.7.7 D

Who Is He in Yonder Stall?

He is Lord over all lords and King over all kings. – Revelation 17:14 CEV

1. Who is He   in yon - der stall,   at whose feet   the shep-herds fall?
2. Who is He   the peo - ple bless   for His words   of gen - tle - ness?
3. Who is He   who stands and weeps   at the   grave where Laz - 'rus sleeps?
4. Lo! At mid - night, who   is   He   prays in   dark Geth - sem - a - ne?
5. Who is He   who, from the grave,   comes to   heal   and help and save?

Who is He   in deep dis - tress,   fast - ing   in   the wil - der - ness?
Who is He   to whom they bring   all   the   sick   and sor - row - ing?
Who is He   the gath - 'ring throng   greet with loud,   tri - um-phant song?
Who is He   on yon - der tree   dies   in   grief   and ag - o - ny?
Who is He   that, from His throne,   rules through all   the world a - lone?

Refrain

'Tis the Lord!   O won-drous sto - ry!   'Tis the   Lord!   The King of glo - ry!

At His   feet   we hum-bly fall,   crown Him,   crown   Him Lord of   all!

WORDS: Benjamin Russell Hanby, 1866
MUSIC: *Lowliness,* Benjamin Russell Hanby, 1866

7.7.7.7 with Refrain

146 O Sing a Song of Bethlehem

He appeared in a body...was believed on in the world, was taken up in glory. – 1 Timothy 3:16 NIV

1. O sing a song of Beth-le-hem, of shep-herds watch-ing there,
2. O sing a song of Naz-a-reth, of sun-ny days of joy,
3. O sing a song of Gal-i-lee, of lake and woods and hill,
4. O sing a song of Cal-va-ry, its glo-ry and dis-may;

and of the news that came to them from an-gels in the air;
O sing of fra-grant flow-ers' breath, and of the sin-less Boy;
of Him who walked up-on the sea and bade its waves be still;
of Him who hung up-on the tree, and took our sins a-way;

the light that shone on Beth-le-hem fills all the world to-day;
for now the flow'rs of Naz-a-reth in ev-'ry heart may grow;
for though, like waves on Gal-i-lee, dark seas of trou-ble roll,
for He who died on Cal-va-ry is ris-en from the grave,

of Je-sus' birth and peace on earth the an-gels sing al-way.
now spreads the fame of His dear name on all the winds that blow.
when faith has heard the Mas-ter's Word, falls peace up-on the soul.
and Christ, our Lord, by heav'n a-dored, is might-y now to save.

WORDS: Louis Fitzgerald Benson, 1899
MUSIC: *Kingsfold;* from *English Country Songs*, 1893; traditional English melody collected by Lucy Broadwood;
    arr. and harm. Ralph Vaughan Williams, 1906

C.M.D.

This tune in a lower key, No. 147.

When Jesus Left His Father's Throne 147

Instead He gave up everything and became a slave, when He became like one of us. – Philippians 2:7 CEV

1. When Je-sus left His Fa-ther's throne, He chose a hum-ble birth;
2. Sweet were His words and kind His look, when moth-ers 'round Him pressed;
3. When Je-sus in-to Zi-on rode, the chil-dren sang a-round;

like us, un-hon-ored and un-known, He came to dwell on earth.
their in-fants in His arms He took, and on His bos-om blessed.
for joy they plucked the palms and strewed their gar-ments on the ground.

Like Him may we be found be-low, in wis-dom's path of peace;
Safe from the world's al-lur-ing harms, be-neath His watch-ful eye,
Ho-san-na our glad voic-es raise, ho-san-na to our King!

like Him in grace and knowl-edge grow, as years and strength in-crease.
thus in the cir-cle of His arms may we for-ev-er lie.
Should we for-get our Sav-ior's praise, the stones them-selves would sing.

WORDS: James Montgomery, 1816, alt.
MUSIC: *Kingsfold;* from *English Country Songs*, 1893; traditional English melody collected by Lucy Broadwood; arr. and harm. Ralph Vaughan Williams, 1906

C.M.D.

This tune in a higher key, No. 146.

148 Jesus, Thou Divine Companion

Whatever you did for one of the least of these brothers of mine, you did for Me. – Matthew 25:40 NIV

1. Je - sus, Thou di - vine Com-pan-ion, by Thy low - ly hu - man birth
2. They who tread the path of la - bor fol-low where Thy feet hath trod;
3. Ev - 'ry task, how - ev - er sim-ple, sets the soul that does it free;

Thou hast come to join the work-ers, bur-den - bear-ers of the earth.
they who work with - out com-plain-ing do the ho - ly work of God.
ev - 'ry deed of love and kind-ness done to the least is done to Thee.

Thou, the Car - pen - ter of Naz - 'reth, toil - ing for Thy dai - ly food,
Thou, the peace that pass - eth knowl-edge, dwell-est in the dai - ly strife;
Je - sus, Thou di - vine Com - pan - ion, help us all to work our best;

by Thy pa - tience and Thy cour-age, Thou hast taught us toil is good.
Thou, the Bread of heav'n, art bro-ken in the sac - ra - ment of life.
bless us in our dai - ly la - bor, lead us to our Sab-bath rest.

WORDS: Henry Jackson Van Dyke, 1909, alt.
MUSIC: *Pleading Savior*, melody from *The Christian Lyre*, 1831

8.7.8.7 D

Where Cross the Crowded Ways of Life 149

Go to the street corners and invite to the banquet anyone you find. – Matthew 22:9 NIV

1. Where cross the crowd-ed ways of life,
   where sound the cries of race and clan,
   a-bove the noise of self-ish strife
   we hear Thy voice, O Son of Man.

2. In haunts of wretch-ed-ness and need,
   on shad-owed thresh-olds dark with fears,
   from paths where hide the lures of greed,
   we catch the vi-sion of Thy tears.

3. The cup of wa-ter giv'n for Thee
   still holds the fresh-ness of Thy grace;
   yet long these mul-ti-tudes to see
   the sweet com-pas-sion of Thy face.

4. O Mas-ter, from the moun-tain side,
   make haste to heal these hearts of pain;
   a-mong these rest-less throngs a-bide,
   O tread the cit-y's streets a-gain;

5. Till all the world shall learn Thy love
   and fol-low where Thy feet have trod:
   Till glo-r'ous from Thy heav'n a-bove
   shall come the cit-y of our God.

WORDS: Frank Mason North, 1903
MUSIC: *Germany (Gardiner)*, from William Gardiner's *Sacred Melodies*, 1815

L.M.

150 One Day

When we were yet without strength, in due time Christ died for the ungodly. – Romans 5:6 NKJV

1. One day when heav - en was filled with His prais - es, one day when sin was as black as could be, Je - sus came forth to be born of a Vir - gin, dwelt a - mong men my ex - am - ple is He!

2. One day they led Him up Cal - va - ry's moun - tain, one day they nailed Him to die on the tree; suf - fer - ing an - guish, de - spised and re - ject - ed, bear - ing our sins, my Re - deem - er is He!

3. One day they left Him a - lone in the gar - den, one day He rest - ed, from suf - fer - ing free; an - gels came down o'er His tomb to keep vig - il hope of the hope - less, my Sav - ior is He!

4. One day the grave could con - ceal Him no long - er, one day the stone rolled a - way from the door; then He a - rose, o - ver death He had con - quered, now is as - cend - ed, my Lord ev - er - more!

5. One day the trum - pet will sound for His com - ing, one day the skies with His glo - ry will shine; won - der - ful day, my be - lov - ed ones bring - ing! Glo - ri - ous Sav - ior, this Je - sus is mine!

Refrain

Liv - ing He loved me, dy - ing He saved me, bur - ied He

WORDS: John Wilbur Chapman, 1910
MUSIC: *One Day,* Charles Howard Marsh, 1910

11.10.11.10 with Refrain

car - ried my sins far a - way; ris - ing He jus - ti - fied

free - ly, for - ev - er: One day He's com - ing, O glo - ri - ous day!

Lord, Who Throughout These Forty Days 151

After fasting forty days and forty nights, He was hungry. – Matthew 4:2 NIV

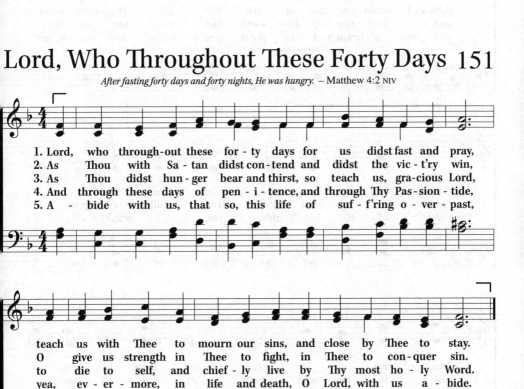

1. Lord, who through-out these for - ty days for us didst fast and pray,
2. As Thou with Sa - tan didst con-tend and didst the vic - t'ry win,
3. As Thou didst hun - ger bear and thirst, so teach us, gra-cious Lord,
4. And through these days of pen - i - tence, and through Thy Pas - sion - tide,
5. A - bide with us, that so, this life of suf - f'ring o - ver - past,

teach us with Thee to mourn our sins, and close by Thee to stay.
O give us strength in Thee to fight, in Thee to con - quer sin.
to die to self, and chief - ly live by Thy most ho - ly Word.
yea, ev - er - more, in life and death, O Lord, with us a - bide.
an Eas - ter of un - end - ing joy we may at - tain at last!

WORDS: Claudia Frances Ibotson Hernaman, 1873, alt.
MUSIC: *St. Flavian*, from Day's *Psalter*, 1562

C.M.

152 Tell Me the Stories of Jesus

This is the message God sent…telling the good news of peace through Jesus Christ. – Acts 10:36 NIV

1. Tell me the sto-ries of Je-sus I love to hear;
2. First let me hear how the chil-dren stood 'round His knee,
3. In-to the cit-y I'd fol-low, there take my stand,

things I would ask Him to tell me if He were here:
and I shall fan-cy His bless-ing rest-ing on me;
wav-ing a branch of the palm tree high in my hand;

Scenes by the way-side, tales of the sea,
words full of kind-ness, deeds full of grace,
one of His her-alds, yes, I would sing

sto-ries of Je-sus, tell them to me.
all in the love-light of Je-sus' face.
loud-est ho-san-nas, "Je-sus is King!"

WORDS: William Henry Parker, 1885
MUSIC: *Stories of Jesus,* Frederic Arthur Challinor, 1903

12.12.9.9

Hosanna, Loud Hosanna 153

Hosanna to the Son of David! – Matthew 21:15 NIV

1. Ho - san - na, loud ho - san - na, the lit - tle chil-dren sang;
2. From Ol - i - vet they fol - lowed 'mid an ex - ul - tant crowd,
3. "Ho - san - na in the high - est!" That an - cient song we sing,

through pil - lared court and tem - ple the love - ly an - them rang.
the vic - tor palm branch wav - ing, and chant - ing clear and loud.
for Christ is our Re - deem - er, the Lord of heav'n our King.

To Je - sus, who had blessed them, close fold - ed to His breast,
The Lord of earth and heav - en rode on in low - ly state,
O may we ev - er praise Him with heart and life and voice,

the chil - dren sang their prais - es, the sim - plest and the best.
nor scorned that lit - tle chil - dren should on His bid - ding wait.
and in His bliss - ful pres - ence e - ter - nal - ly re - joice!

WORDS: Jeanette Threlfall, 1873
MUSIC: *Ellacombe,* from *Gesangbuch der H.W.K. Hofkapelle,* 1784; harm. William Henry Monk, 1868
This tune in a higher key, No. 186.

7.6.7.6 D

154 All Glory, Laud, and Honor

Blessed is He who comes in the name of the Lord! Hosanna in the highest! – Matthew 21:9 NIV

1. All glo - ry, laud, and hon - or, to Thee, Re - deem - er, King,
2. The com - pa - ny of an - gels are prais - ing Thee on high,
3. To Thee, be - fore Thy pas - sion they sang their hymns of praise;

to whom the lips of chil - dren made sweet ho - san - nas ring:
and we with all cre - a - tion in cho - rus make re - ply:
to Thee, now high ex - alt - ed, our mel - o - dy we raise:

Thou art the King of Is - ra - el, Thou Da - vid's roy - al Son,
The peo - ple of the He - brews with palms be - fore Thee went;
Thou didst ac - cept their prais - es; ac - cept the prayers we bring,

Who in the Lord's name com - est, the King and bless - ed One.
our praise and pray'r and an - thems be - fore Thee we pre - sent.
Who in all good de - light - est, Thou good and gra - cious King.

WORDS: Theodulph of Orleans, ca. 820; tr. John Mason Neale, 1851
MUSIC: *St. Theodulph*, Melchior Teschner, 1615; arr. William Henry Monk, 1861, alt.
Another harmonization of this tune, No. 155.

7.6.7.6.D

All Glory, Laud, and Honor   155

Blessed is He who comes in the name of the Lord! Hosanna in the highest! – Matthew 21:9 NIV

Refrain

All glo-ry, laud, and hon-or, to Thee, Re-deem-er, King,

Fine

to whom the lips of chil-dren made sweet ho-san-nas ring:

1. Thou art the King of Is-ra-el, Thou Da-vid's roy-al Son,
2. The com-pa-ny of an-gels are prais-ing Thee on high,
3. The peo-ple of the He-brews with palms be-fore Thee went;
4. To Thee, be-fore Thy pas-sion, they sang their hymns of praise;
5. Thou didst ac-cept their prais-es; ac-cept the prayers we bring,

D.C.

Who in the Lord's name com-est, the King and bless-ed One.
and we, with all cre-a-tion, in cho-rus make re-ply.
our praise and prayer and an-thems be-fore Thee we pre-sent.
to Thee, now high ex-alt-ed, our mel-o-dy we raise.
Who in all good de-light-est, Thou good and gra-cious King.

WORDS: Theodulph of Orleans, ca. 820; tr. John Mason Neale, 1851
MUSIC: *St. Theodulph*, Melchior Teschner, 1615; arr. William Henry Monk, 1861, alt.   7.6.7.6 with Refrain
Another harmonization of this tune, No. 154.

156 Ride On! Ride On in Majesty!

Behold, your King is coming; righteous and having salvation, humble and mounted on a donkey. – Zechariah 9:9 ESV

1. Ride on! Ride on in maj-es-ty! Hark! All the tribes "ho-san-na" cry; O Sav-ior meek, pur-sue Thy road with palms and scat-tered gar-ments strowed.
2. Ride on! Ride on in maj-es-ty! In low-ly pomp ride on to die; O Christ, Thy tri-umphs now be-gin o'er cap-tive death and con-quered sin.
3. Ride on! Ride on in maj-es-ty! The an-gel ar-mies of the sky look down with sad and won-d'ring eyes to see th'ap-proach-ing sac-ri-fice.
4. Ride on! Ride on in maj-es-ty! Thy last and fierc-est strife is nigh; the Fa-ther on His sap-phire throne ex-pects His own a-noint-ed Son.
5. Ride on! Ride on in maj-es-ty! In low-ly pomp ride on to die; bow Thy meek head to mor-tal pain, then take, O God, Thy pow'r, and reign.

WORDS: Henry Hart Milman, 1827
MUSIC: *Winchester New*, adapt. *Musikalisches Handbuch*, Hamburg, 1690; harm. William Henry Monk, 1847, alt.   L.M.

157 How Deep the Father's Love for Us

This is how we've come to understand and experience love: Christ sacrificed His life for us. – I John 3:16 The Message

1. How deep the Fa-ther's love for us, how
2. Be-hold the Man up-on a cross, my
3. I will not boast in an-y-thing, no

WORDS: Stuart Townend, 1995
MUSIC: *Father's Love*, Stuart Townend, 1995; arr. Eric Wyse, 2005   Irregular

vast be-yond all mea - sure, that He should give His on - ly
sin up - on His shoul - ders; a - shamed, I hear my mock-ing
gifts, no pow'r, no wis - dom; but I will boast in Je - sus

Son to make a wretch His trea - sure. How
voice call out a - mong the scoff - ers. It
Christ, His death and res - ur - rec - tion. Why

great the pain of sear - ing loss; the Fa - ther turns
was my sin that held Him there un - til it was
should I gain from His re - ward? I can - not give

His face a - way, as wounds which mar the Cho - sen
ac - com - plished; His dy - ing breath has brought me
an an - swer, but this I know with all my

One bring man - y sons to glo - ry.
life: I know that it is fin - ished.
heart: His wounds have paid my ran - som.

158 Go to Dark Gethsemane

My soul is overwhelmed with sorrow to the point of death. Stay here and keep watch with me. – Matthew 26:38 NIV

1. Go to dark Gethsemane, ye that feel the tempter's pow'r;
2. Follow to the judgment hall, view the Lord of life arraigned;
3. Cal-v'ry's mournful mountain climb; there, adoring at His feet,
4. Early hasten to the tomb where they laid His breathless clay;

your Redeemer's conflict see, watch with Him one bitter hour,
O the wormwood and the gall! O the pangs His soul sustained!
mark that miracle of time, God's own sacrifice complete.
all is solitude and gloom. Who has taken Him away?

turn not from His griefs away; learn of Jesus Christ to pray.
Shun not suf-f'ring, shame, or loss; learn of Christ to bear the cross.
"It is fin-ished!" hear Him cry; learn of Jesus Christ to die.
Christ is ris'n! He meets our eyes; Sav-ior, teach us so to rise.

Note: Verse 4 should be omitted during Holy Week

WORDS: James Montgomery, 1820
MUSIC: *Redhead 76 (Gethsemane)*, from *Church Hymn Tunes, Ancient and Modern*, Richard Redhead, 1853   7.7.7.7.7.7
This tune in a higher key (E♭,) No. 227; (D) No. 290.

159 'Tis Midnight, and on Olive's Brow

And He said to them, "Sit here while I go over there and pray". – Matthew 26:36 NIV

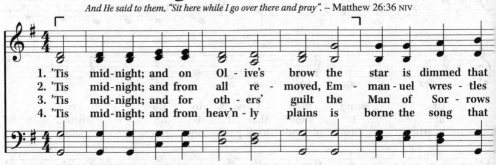

1. 'Tis mid-night; and on Ol-ive's brow the star is dimmed that
2. 'Tis mid-night; and from all re-moved, Em-man-uel wres-tles
3. 'Tis mid-night; and for oth-ers' guilt the Man of Sor-rows
4. 'Tis mid-night; and from heav'n-ly plains is borne the song that

WORDS: William Bingham Tappan, 1822
MUSIC: *Olive's Brow*, William Batchelder Bradbury, 1853   L.M

late-ly	shone,	'tis	mid-night;	in	the	gar-den
lone	with	fears;	e'en	that	dis-ci-ple	whom	He
weeps	in	blood;	yet	He	that	hath	in	an-guish
an-gels	know;	un-heard	by	mor-tals	are	the

now	the	suf-f'ring	Sav-ior	prays	a-lone.
loved	heeds	not	His	Mas-ter's	grief	and	tears.
knelt	is	not	for-sak-en	by	His	God.
strains	that	sweet-ly	soothe	the	Sav-ior's	woe.

There Is a Green Hill Far Away 160

Here they crucified Him, and with Him two others—one on each side. – John 19:18 NIV

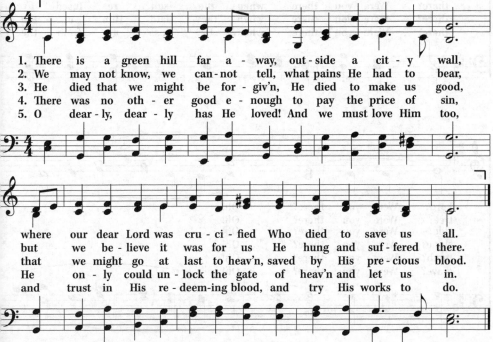

1. There	is	a	green hill	far a-way,	out-side	a	cit-y	wall,
2. We	may	not know,	we	can-not	tell,	what pains	He had	to	bear,
3. He	died that	we might	be for-giv'n,	He died	to make	us	good,
4. There	was	no oth-er	good e-nough	to pay	the price	of	sin,
5. O	dear-ly,	dear-ly	has He	loved! And	we must	love Him	too,

where	our	dear Lord was	cru-ci-fied	Who	died	to	save	us	all.
but	we	be-lieve it	was for us	He	hung and	suf-fered	there.
that	we might	go	at last	to heav'n, saved	by	His	pre-cious	blood.
He	on-ly	could un-lock	the gate	of	heav'n and	let	us	in.
and	trust in	His re-deem-ing blood,	and	try	His works	to	do.

WORDS: Cecil Frances Humphreys Alexander, 1847
MUSIC: *Horsley,* William Horsley, 1844
This tune in a higher key, No. 200.

C.M.

161 Were You There?

You...put Him to death by nailing Him to the cross. – Acts 2:23 NIV

1. Were you there when they cru - ci - fied my Lord? Were you
2. Were you there when they nailed Him to the tree? Were you
3. Were you there when they pierced Him in the side? Were you
4. Were you there when the sun re - fused to shine? Were you
5. Were you there when they laid Him in the tomb? Were you
6. Were you there when He rose up from the grave? Were you

there? Were you there when they cru - ci - fied my
there? Were you there when they nailed Him to the
there? Were you there when they pierced Him in the
there? Were you there when the sun re - fused to
there? Were you there when they laid Him in the
there? Were you there when He rose up from the

Lord? Were you there? Oh!
tree? Were you there? Oh!
side? Were you there? Oh!
shine? Were you there? Oh!
tomb? Were you there? Oh!
grave? Were you there? Oh!

WORDS: Negro spiritual, n.d.
MUSIC: *Were You There*, Negro spiritual, n.d.

Irregular

Some - times it caus - es me to trem - ble, trem - ble, trem - ble.
Some - times it caus - es me to trem - ble, trem - ble, trem - ble.
Some - times it caus - es me to trem - ble, trem - ble, trem - ble.
Some - times it caus - es me to trem - ble, trem - ble, trem - ble.
Some - times it caus - es me to trem - ble, trem - ble, trem - ble.
Some - times I feel like shout - ing glo - ry, glo - ry, glo - ry!

Were you there when they cru - ci - fied my Lord? Were you there?
Were you there when they nailed Him to the tree? Were you there?
Were you there when they pierced Him in the side? Were you there?
Were you there when the sun re - fused to shine? Were you there?
Were you there when they laid Him in the tomb? Were you there?
Were you there when He rose up from the grave? Were you there?

In the Cross of Christ I Glory   162

I will never brag about anything except the cross of our Lord Jesus Christ. – Galatians 6:14 CEV

1. In the cross of Christ I glo - ry, tow'r - ing o'er the wrecks of time;
2. When the woes of life o'er - take me, hopes de - ceive, and fears an - noy,
3. When the sun of bliss is beam - ing light and love up - on my way,
4. Bane and bless - ing, pain and plea - sure, by the cross are sanc - ti - fied;

all the light of sa - cred sto - ry gath - ers round its head sub - lime.
nev - er shall the cross for - sake me; lo! It glows with peace and joy.
from the cross the ra - diance stream - ing adds more lus - ter to the day.
peace is there that knows no mea - sure, joys that through all time a - bide.

WORDS: John Bowring, 1825
MUSIC: *Crucifixion*, John Stainer, 1887   8.7.8.7

163 In the Cross of Christ I Glory

I will never brag about anything except the cross of our Lord Jesus Christ. – Galatians 6:14 CEV

1. In the cross of Christ I glory, tow'r-ing o'er the
2. When the woes of life o'er-take me, hopes de-ceive, and
3. When the sun of bliss is beam-ing light and love up-
4. Bane and bless-ing, pain and plea-sure, by the cross are

wrecks of time; all the light of sa - cred
fears an - noy, nev - er shall the cross for -
on my way, from the cross the ra - diance
sanc - ti - fied; peace is there that knows no

sto - ry gath - ers round its head sub - lime.
sake me; lo! It glows with peace and joy.
stream-ing adds more lus - ter to the day.
mea - sure, joys that through all time a - bide.

WORDS: John Bowring, 1825
MUSIC: *Rathbun*, Ithamar D. Conkey, 1849

8.7.8.*

164 My Song Is Love Unknown

I want you to know all about Christ's love, although it is too wonderful to be measured. – Ephesians 3:19 CEV

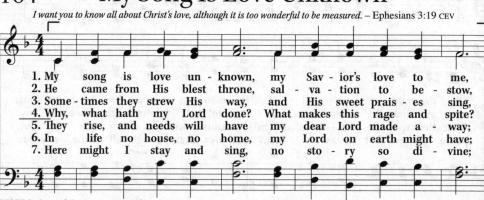

1. My song is love un - known, my Sav - ior's love to me,
2. He came from His blest throne, sal - va - tion to be - stow,
3. Some - times they strew His way, and His sweet prais - es sing,
4. Why, what hath my Lord done? What makes this rage and spite?
5. They rise, and needs will have my dear Lord made a - way;
6. In life no house, no home, my Lord on earth might have;
7. Here might I stay and sing, no sto - ry so di - vine;

WORDS: Samuel Crossman, 1664, alt.
MUSIC: *Rhosymedre*, John Edwards, 1840

6.6.6.6.8.8 with Repea

love to the love-less shown that they might love-ly be.
but men made strange, and none the longed-for Christ would know.
re-sound-ing all the day ho-san-nas to their King.
He made the lame to run, He gave the blind their sight.
a mur-der-er they save, the Prince of Life they slay.
in death no friend-ly tomb but what a strang-er gave.
nev-er was love, dear King, nev-er was grief like Thine.

Oh, who am I that for my sake my Lord should take frail
But oh, my Friend, my Friend in-deed, Who at my need His
Then "Cru-ci-fy!" is all their breath, and for His death they
Sweet in-ju-ries! Yet they at these them-selves dis-please, and
Yet stead-fast He to suf-f'ring goes, that He His foes from
What may I say? Heav'n was His home; but mine the tomb where-
This is my Friend, in Whose sweet praise I all my days could

flesh, and die? My Lord should take frail flesh, and die?
life did spend, Who at my need His life did spend.
thirst and cry, and for His death they thirst and cry.
'gainst Him rise, them-selves dis-please, and 'gainst Him rise.
thence might free, that He His foes from thence might free.
in He lay, but mine the tomb where-in He lay.
glad-ly spend, I all my days could glad-ly spend.

165 Lead Me to Calvary

I have died, but Christ lives in me. And I now live by faith in the Son of God. – Galatians 2:20 CEV

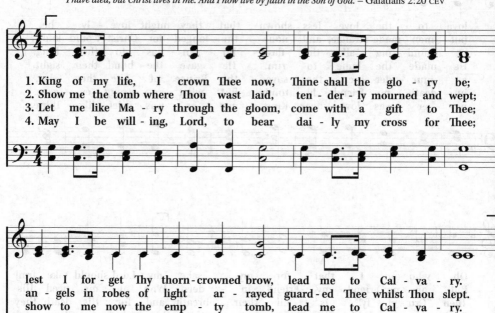

1. King of my life, I crown Thee now, Thine shall the glo-ry be;
2. Show me the tomb where Thou wast laid, ten-der-ly mourned and wept;
3. Let me like Ma-ry through the gloom, come with a gift to Thee;
4. May I be will-ing, Lord, to bear dai-ly my cross for Thee;

lest I for-get Thy thorn-crowned brow, lead me to Cal-va-ry.
an-gels in robes of light ar-rayed guard-ed Thee whilst Thou slept.
show to me now the emp-ty tomb, lead me to Cal-va-ry.
e-ven Thy cup of grief to share, Thou hast borne all for me.

Refrain

Lest I for-get Geth-sem-a-ne; lest I for-get Thine ag-o-ny;

lest I for-get Thy love for me, lead me to Cal-va-ry.

WORDS: Jennie Evelyn Hussey, 1921
MUSIC: *Duncannon*, William James Kirkpatrick, 1921

C.M. with Refrain

The Power of the Cross

166

For Christ did not send me to baptize, but to preach...lest the cross be emptied of its power. – 1 Corinthians 1:17 NIV

1. Oh, to see the dawn of the dark-est day; Christ on the road to
2. Oh, to see the pain writ-ten on Your face, bear-ing the awe-some
3. Now the day-light flees, now the ground be-neath quakes as its Mak-er
4. Oh, to see my name writ-ten in the wounds, for through Your suf-f'ring

Cal - va - ry; tried by sin-ful men, torn and beat-en then,
weight of sin; ev - 'ry bit - ter thought, ev - 'ry e - vil deed,
bows His head, cur-tain torn in two, dead are raised to life;
I am free; death is crushed to death, life is mine to live;

Refrain

nailed to a cross of wood.
crown-ing Your blood-stained brow. 1.–3. This the pow'r of the
"Fin - ished!" the vic - t'ry cry. 4. This the pow'r of the
won through Your self - less love.

cross; Christ be - came sin for us; took the
cross; Son of God, slain for us; what a

blame, bore the wrath. We stand for-giv-en at the cross.
love! What a cost! We stand for-giv-en at the cross.

WORDS: Keith Getty and Stuart Townend, 2004
MUSIC: *Power of the Cross*, Keith Getty and Stuart Townend, 2004; arr. Eric Wyse, 2005
© 2005 ThankYou Music (admin. worshiptogether.com songs).

5.5.8.5.5.6 with Refrain

167 The Old Rugged Cross

When they came to the place called The Skull, there they crucified Him. – Luke 23:33 NIV

1. On a hill far a-way stood an old rug-ged cross, the em-blem of suf-f'ring and shame; and I love that old cross where the dear-est and best for a world of lost sin-ners was slain.

2. Oh, that old rug-ged cross, so de-spised by the world, has a won-drous at-trac-tion for me; for the dear Lamb of God left His glo-ry a-bove, to bear it to dark Cal-va-ry.

3. In that old rug-ged cross, stained with blood so di-vine, such a won-der-ful beau-ty I see; for 'twas on that old cross Je-sus suf-fered and died, to par-don and sanc-ti-fy me.

4. To the old rug-ged cross I will ev-er be true, its shame and re-proach glad-ly bear; then He'll call me some day to my home far a-way, where His glo-ry for-ev-er I'll share.

Refrain

So I'll cher-ish the old rug-ged cross, the old rug-ged cross, till my tro-phies at last I lay down; I will cling to the old rug-ged cross, and ex-change it some day for a crown.

WORDS: George Bennard, 1913
MUSIC: *Old Rugged Cross,* George Bennard, 1913

Irregular with Refrain

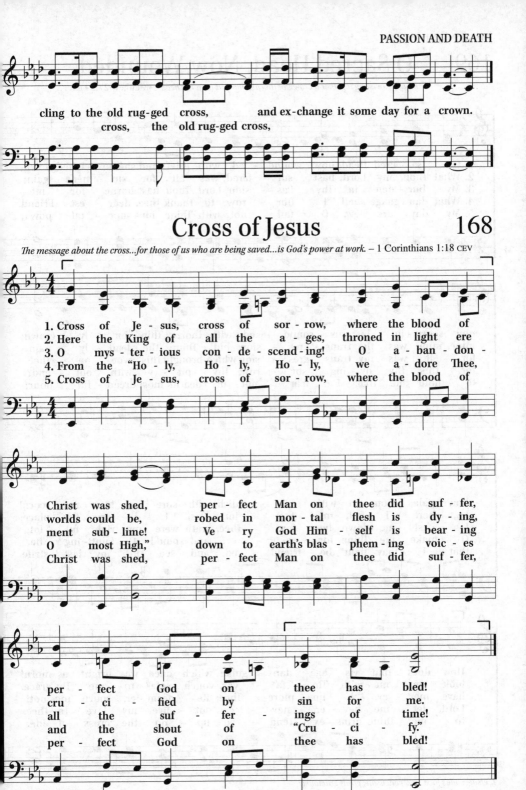

Cross of Jesus 168

The message about the cross...for those of us who are being saved...is God's power at work. – 1 Corinthians 1:18 CEV

cling to the old rug-ged cross, and ex-change it some day for a crown.
cross, the old rug-ged cross,

1. Cross of Je - sus, cross of sor - row, where the blood of
2. Here the King of all the a - ges, throned in light ere
3. O mys - ter - ious con - de - scend - ing! O a - ban - don -
4. From the "Ho - ly, Ho - ly, Ho - ly, we a - dore Thee,
5. Cross of Je - sus, cross of sor - row, where the blood of

Christ was shed, per - fect Man on thee did suf - fer,
worlds could be, robed in mor - tal flesh is dy - ing,
ment sub - lime! Ve - ry God Him - self is bear - ing
O most High," down to earth's blas - phem - ing voic - es
Christ was shed, per - fect Man on thee did suf - fer,

per - fect God on thee has bled!
cru - ci - fied by sin for me.
all the suf - fer - ings of time!
and the shout of "Cru - ci - fy."
per - fect God on thee has bled!

WORDS: William John Sparrow-Simpson, 1887
MUSIC: *Cross of Jesus,* John Stainer, 1887

8.7.8.7

169 O Sacred Head, Now Wounded

And after twisting together a crown of thorns, they put it on His head. – Matthew 27:29 ESV

1. O sa - cred Head, now wound - ed, with grief and shame weighed down,
2. What Thou, my Lord, hast suf - fered, was all for sin - ner's gain;
3. My bur - den in Thy Pas - sion, Lord, Thou hast borne for me,
4. What lan - guage shall I bor - row to thank Thee, dear - est Friend,
5. My days are few, O fail not, with Thine im - mor - tal pow'r,

now scorn - ful - ly sur - round - ed with thorns, Thine on - ly crown;
mine, mine was the trans - gres - sion, but Thine the dead - ly pain.
for it was my trans - gres - sion which brought this woe on Thee.
for this Thy dy - ing sor - row, Thy pit - y with - out end?
to hold me that I fear not in death's most dread - ful hour;

how pale Thou art with an - guish, with sore a - buse and scorn!
Lo, here I fall, my Sav - ior! 'Tis I de - serve Thy place;
I cast me down be - fore Thee, wrath were my right - ful lot;
O make me Thine for - ev - er; and should I faint - ing be,
that I may fight be - friend - ed, and see in my last strife

How does that vis - age¹ lan - guish, which once was bright as morn!
look on me with Thy fa - vor, vouch - safe² to me Thy grace.
have mer - cy, I im - plore Thee; Re - deem - er, spurn me not!
Lord, let me nev - er, nev - er out - live my love to Thee.
to me Thine arms ex - tend - ed up - on the cross of life.

1. visage: one's face   2. vouchsafe: grant graciously

WORDS: Sts. 1-4 attr. Bernard of Clairvaux, 1153,; German tr. Paul Gerhardt, 1656;
   English tr. James Waddel Alexander, 1830; St. 5 tr. Robert Seymour Bridges, 1899
MUSIC: *Passion Chorale*, Hans Leo Hassler, 1601; harm. Johann Sebastian Bach, 1729

7.6.7.6.D

Beneath the Cross of Jesus 170

Near the cross of Jesus stood His mother, His mother's sister...and Mary Magdalene. – John 19:25 NIV

1. Be - neath the cross of Je - sus I fain¹ would take my stand,
2. There lies be - neath its shad - ow, but on the far - ther side,
3. Up - on that cross of Je - sus mine eyes at times can see
4. I take, O cross, thy shad - ow for my a - bid - ing place;

the shad - ow of a might - y rock with - in a wea - ry land,
the dark - ness of an aw - ful grave that gapes both deep and wide;
the ve - ry dy - ing form of One who suf - fered there for me;
I ask no oth - er sun - shine than the sun - shine of His face;

a home with - in the wil - der - ness, a rest up - on the way
and there be - tween us stands the cross, two arms out-stretched to save,
and from my strick - en heart, with tears, two won - ders I con - fess:
con - tent to let the world go by, to know no gain nor loss,

from the burn - ing of the noon - time heat and the bur - den of the day.
like a watch - man set to guard the way from that e - ter - nal grave.
The won - ders of re - deem - ing love, and my un - wor - thi - ness.
my sin - ful self my on - ly shame, my glo - ry all the cross.

1. *fain: willingly*

WORDS: Elizabeth Cecelia Clephane, 1868, alt.
MUSIC: *St. Christopher*, Frederick Charles Maker, 1881   Irregular

171 When I Survey the Wondrous Cross

Christ has shown me that what I once thought was valuable is worthless. – Philippians 3:7 CEV

1. When I sur - vey the won - drous cross on which the
2. For - bid it, Lord, that I should boast, save in the
3. See, from His head, His hands, His feet, sor - row and
4. Were the whole realm of na - ture mine, that were a

Prince of Glo - ry died, my rich - est gain I
death of Christ, my God; all the vain things that
love flow min - gled down. Did e'er such love and
pres - ent far too small; love so a - maz - ing,

count but loss, and pour con - tempt on all my pride.
charm me most, I sac - ri - fice them to His blood.
sor - row meet, or thorns com - pose so rich a crown?
so di - vine, de - mands my soul, my life, my all.

WORDS: Isaac Watts, 1707
MUSIC: *Hamburg*, Gregorian chant, arr. Lowell Mason, 1824

L.M.

172 When I Survey the Wondrous Cross

Christ has shown me that what I once thought was valuable is worthless. – Philippians 3:7 CEV

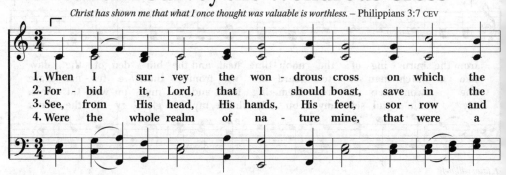

1. When I sur - vey the won - drous cross on which the
2. For - bid it, Lord, that I should boast, save in the
3. See, from His head, His hands, His feet, sor - row and
4. Were the whole realm of na - ture mine, that were a

WORDS: Isaac Watts, 1707
MUSIC: *Rockingham*, Anon.; arr. Edward Miller, 1790

L.M.

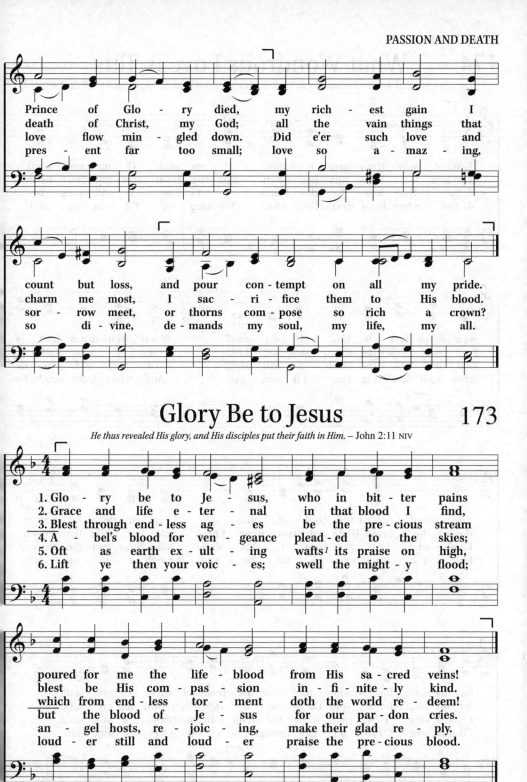

Prince of Glo - ry died, my rich - est gain I
death of Christ, my God; all the vain things that
love flow min - gled down. Did e'er such love and
pres - ent far too small; love so a - maz - ing,

count but loss, and pour con - tempt on all my pride.
charm me most, I sac - ri - fice them to His blood.
sor - row meet, or thorns com - pose so rich a crown?
so di - vine, de - mands my soul, my life, my all.

Glory Be to Jesus

173

He thus revealed His glory, and His disciples put their faith in Him. – John 2:11 NIV

1. Glo - ry be to Je - sus, who in bit - ter pains
2. Grace and life e - ter - nal in that blood I find,
3. Blest through end - less ag - es be the pre - cious stream
4. A - bel's blood for ven - geance plead - ed to the skies;
5. Oft as earth ex - ult - ing wafts[1] its praise on high,
6. Lift ye then your voic - es; swell the might - y flood;

poured for me the life - blood from His sa - cred veins!
blest be His com - pas - sion in - fi - nite - ly kind.
which from end - less tor - ment doth the world re - deem!
but the blood of Je - sus for our par - don cries.
an - gel hosts, re - joic - ing, make their glad re - ply.
loud - er still and loud - er praise the pre - cious blood.

1. wafts: gently moved by wind

WORDS: Attr. S. Alfonso, 18th c.; tr. Edward Caswall, 1857
MUSIC: *Wem in Leidenstagen*, Friedrich Filitz, 1847

6.5.6.5

174 What Wondrous Love Is This

This is love: not that we loved God, but that He loved us and sent His Son as an atoning sacrifice. – 1 John 4:10 NIV

1. What won-drous love is this, O my soul, O my soul, what
2. When I was sink-ing down, sink-ing down, sink-ing down, when
3. To God and to the Lamb I will sing, I will sing, to
4. And when from death I'm free, I'll sing on, I'll sing on, and

won-drous love is this, O my soul! What won-drous love is
I was sink-ing down, sink-ing down; when I was sink-ing
God and to the Lamb I will sing! To God and to the
when from death I'm free, I'll sing on! And when from death I'm

this that caused the Lord of bliss to bear the dread-ful curse
down be - neath God's righ-teous frown, Christ laid a - side His crown
Lamb, who is the great I AM, while mil-lions join the theme,
free, I'll sing and joy - ful be, and through e - ter - ni - ty

for my soul, for my soul, to bear the dread-ful curse for my soul!
for my soul, for my soul, Christ laid a - side His crown for my soul!
I will sing, I will sing, while mil-lions join the theme, I will sing!
I'll sing on, I'll sing on, and through e - ter - ni - ty I'll sing on!

WORDS: Appalachian folk hymn, 19th c.
MUSIC: *Wondrous Love*, from *Southern Harmony*, 1835   Irregular

Lamb of God

Look, the Lamb of God! – John 1:36 NIV

1. Your on-ly Son no sin to hide, but You have sent Him from Your
2. Your gift of Love they cru - ci - fied, they laughed and scorned Him as He
3. I was so lost, I should have died, but You have brought me to Your

side to walk up - on this guilt - y sod and to be -
died. The hum - ble King they named a fraud and sac - ri -
side to be led by Your staff and rod and to be

Refrain

come the Lamb of God. O Lamb of God, sweet Lamb of
ficed the Lamb of God.
called a lamb of God.

God. I love the Ho - ly Lamb of God. O wash me

in His pre - cious blood, 1.-2. my Je - sus Christ, the Lamb of God.
3. 'til I am just a lamb of God.

WORDS: Twila Paris, 1985
MUSIC: *Lamb of God*, Twila Paris, 1985

L.M. with Refrain

176 Ah, Holy Jesus

The Son of Man must suffer many things and be rejected. – Luke 9:22 ESV

1. Ah, ho-ly Je-sus, how hast Thou of-fend-ed,
   that man to judge Thee hath in hate pre-tend-ed? By foes de-
   rid-ed, by Thine own re-ject-ed, O most af-flict-ed.

2. Who was the guilt-y? Who brought this up-on Thee?
   A-las, my trea-son, Je-sus, hath un-done thee. 'Twas I, Lord
   Je-sus, I it was de-nied Thee: I cru-ci-fied Thee.

3. Lo, the Good Shep-herd for the sheep is of-fered;
   the slave hath sinned and the Son hath suf-fered; for our a-
   tone-ment, while we noth-ing heed-ed, God in-ter-ced-ed.

4. For me, kind Je-sus, was Thy in-car-na-tion,
   Thy mor-tal sor-row, and Thy life's ob-la-tion;[1] Thy death of
   an-guish and Thy bit-ter pas-sion, for my sal-va-tion.

5. There-fore, kind Je-sus, since I can-not pay Thee,
   I do a-dore Thee, and will ev-er pray Thee, think on Thy
   pit-y and Thy love un-swerv-ing, not my de-serv-ing.

*If desired, the G♯ in the tenor part may be lowered to G♮.   1. oblation: offering

WORDS: Johann Heermann, 1630; tr. Robert Seymour Bridges, 1899
MUSIC: *Herzliebster Jesu*, Johann Crüger, 1640, alt.

11.11.11.5

177 Alas! And Did My Savior Bleed?

Jesus was truly human, and He gave Himself to rescue all of us. – 1 Timothy 2:5 CEV

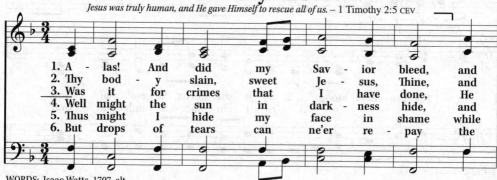

1. A-las! And did my Sav-ior bleed, and
2. Thy bod-y slain, sweet Je-sus, Thine, and
3. Was it for crimes that I have done, He
4. Well might the sun in dark-ness hide, and
5. Thus might I hide my face in shame, while
6. But drops of tears can ne'er re-pay the

WORDS: Isaac Watts, 1707, alt.
MUSIC: *Martyrdom*, attr. Hugh Wilson, 1827
Another harmonization of this tune, No. 368.

C.M.

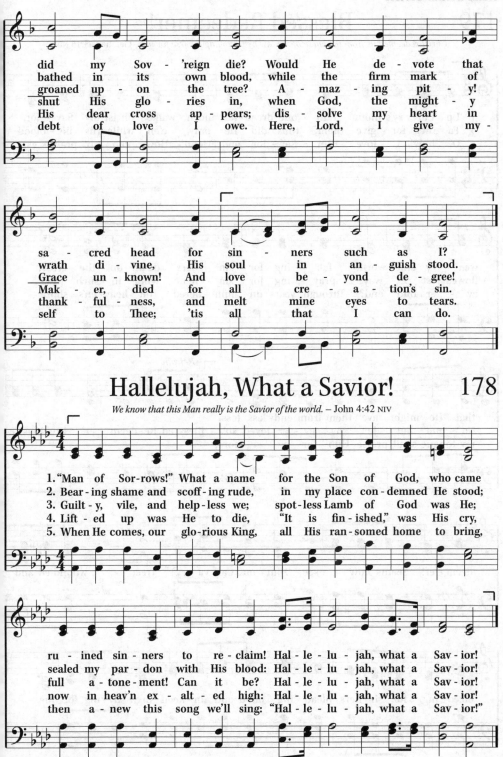

did my Sov - 'reign die? Would He de - vote that
bathed in its own blood, while the firm mark of
groaned up - on the tree? A - maz - ing pit - y!
shut His glo - ries in, when God, the might - y
His dear cross ap - pears; dis - solve my heart in
debt of love I owe. Here, Lord, I give my -

sa - cred head for sin - ners such as I?
wrath di - vine, His soul in an - guish stood.
Grace un - known! And love be - yond de - gree!
Mak - er, died for all cre - a - tion's sin.
thank - ful - ness, and melt mine eyes to tears.
self to Thee; 'tis all that I can do.

Hallelujah, What a Savior!   178

We know that this Man really is the Savior of the world. — John 4:42 NIV

1. "Man of Sor - rows!" What a name   for the Son of God, who came
2. Bear - ing shame and scoff - ing rude,   in my place con - demned He stood;
3. Guilt - y, vile, and help - less we;   spot - less Lamb of God was He;
4. Lift - ed up was He to die,   "It is fin - ished," was His cry,
5. When He comes, our glo - rious King,   all His ran - somed home to bring,

ru - ined sin - ners to re - claim! Hal - le - lu - jah, what a Sav - ior!
sealed my par - don with His blood: Hal - le - lu - jah, what a Sav - ior!
full a - tone - ment! Can it be? Hal - le - lu - jah, what a Sav - ior!
now in heav'n ex - alt - ed high: Hal - le - lu - jah, what a Sav - ior!
then a - new this song we'll sing: "Hal - le - lu - jah, what a Sav - ior!"

WORDS: Philip Paul Bliss, 1875
MUSIC: *Man of Sorrows,* Philip Paul Bliss, 1875

7.7.7.8

179 Blessed Redeemer!

Christ redeemed us from the curse of the law by becoming a curse for us. – Galatians 3:13 NIV

1. Up Cal-v'ry's moun-tain one dread-ful morn, walked Christ my Sav-ior,
2. "Fa-ther, for-give them," thus did He pray, e'en while His life-blood
3. O how I love Him, Sav-ior and Friend! How can my prais-es

wea-ry and worn; fac-ing for sin-ners death on the cross,
flowed fast a-way; pray-ing for sin-ners while in such woe:
ev-er find end? Through years un-num-bered on heav-en's shore,

Refrain

that He might save them from end-less loss.
No one but Je-sus ev-er loved so! Bless-ed Re-deem-er! Pre-cious Re-
my tongue shall praise Him for-ev-er-more.

deem-er! Seems now I see Him on Cal-va-ry's tree; wound-ed and

bleed-ing, for sin-ners plead-ing, blind and un-heed-ing, dy-ing for me.

WORDS: Avis Marguerite Burgeson Christiansen, 1920
MUSIC: *Redeemer*, Harry Dixon Loes, 1920

9.9.9.9 with Refrain

Christ, We Do All Adore Thee
180

The Lamb...is worthy to receive power, riches, wisdom, strength, honor, glory, and praise. – Revelation 5:12 CEV

Christ, we do all a - dore Thee, and we do praise Thee for - ev - er.

Christ, we do all a - dore Thee, and we do praise Thee for - ev - er,

for on the ho - ly cross hast Thou the world from sin re - deemed.

Christ, we do all a - dore Thee, and we do praise Thee for - ev - er.

*Instruments

Christ, we do all a - dore Thee!

These two measures may be omitted.

WORDS: *Adoramus Te*, English tr. Theodore Baker, 1899
MUSIC: *Adore Thee*, from *The Seven Last Words of Christ*, Theodore Dubois, 1867

Irregular

181 Come, Ye Faithful, Raise the Strain

I will sing to the Lord, for He is highly exalted. – Exodus 15:1 NIV

1. Come, ye faith - ful, raise the strain of tri - um - phant glad - ness!
2. 'Tis the spring of souls to - day: Christ hath burst His pris - on,
3. Now the queen of sea - sons, bright with the day of splen - dor,
4. Nei - ther might the gates of death, nor the tomb's dark por - tal,
5. "Al - le - lu - ia," now we cry to our King Im - mor - tal,

God hath brought His Is - ra - el in - to joy from sad - ness:
and from three days' sleep in death as a sun hath ris - en;
with the roy - al feast of feasts, comes its joy to ren - der;
nor the watch - ers, nor the seal hold Thee as a mor - tal:
who tri - um - phant burst the bars of the tomb's dark por - tal;

Loosed from Pha - raoh's bit - ter yoke Ja - cob's sons and daugh - ters,
all the win - ter of our sins, long and dark, is fly - ing.
comes to glad Je - ru - sa - lem, who with true af - fec - tion
But to - day a - midst Thine own. Thou didst stand, be - stow - ing
"Al - le - lu - ia," with the Son, God the Fa - ther prais - ing;

led them with un - moist - ened foot through the Red Sea wa - ters.
from His light, to whom we give laud and praise un - dy - ing.
wel - comes in un - wea - ried strains Je - sus' res - ur - rec - tion.
that Thy peace which ev - er - more pass - eth hu - man know - ing.
"Al - le - lu - ia," yet a - gain to the Spir - it rais - ing.

WORDS: John of Damascus, ca. 8th c., tr. John Mason Neale, 1859
MUSIC: *St. Kevin*, Arthur Seymour Sullivan, 1872

7.6.7.6 D

Christ Arose!

God raised Him from the dead...it was impossible for death to keep its hold on Him. – Acts 2:24 NIV

1. Low in the grave He lay, Je-sus my Sav-ior! Wait-ing the com-ing day,
2. Vain-ly they watch His bed, Je-sus my Sav-ior! Vain-ly they seal the dead,
3. Death can-not keep his prey, Je-sus my Sav-ior; He tore the bars a-way,

Je-sus my Lord!
Je-sus my Lord!
Je-sus my Lord!

Refrain

Up from the grave He a-rose, with a mighty tri-umph o'er His foes, He a-rose a vic-tor from the dark do-main, And He lives for-ev-er, with His saints to reign. He a-rose! He a-rose! Hal-le-lu-jah! Christ a-rose!

He a-rose, He a-rose!
He a-rose! He a-rose! He a-rose!

WORDS: Robert Lowry, 1874
MUSIC: *Christ Arose*, Robert Lowry, 1874

6.5.6.4 with Refrain

183 Jesus Christ Is Risen Today

You are looking for Jesus the Nazarene, who was crucified. He has risen! – Mark 16:6 NIV

1. Je - sus Christ is ris'n to - day, Al - le - lu - ia!
2. Hymns of praise then let us sing, Al - le - lu - ia!
3. But the pains which He en - dured, Al - le - lu - ia!
4. Sing we to our God a - bove, Al - le - lu - ia!

Our tri - um - phant ho - ly day, Al - le - lu - ia!
Un - to Christ, our heav'n - ly King, Al - le - lu - ia!
Our sal - va - tion hath pro - cured, Al - le - lu - ia!
Praise e - ter - nal as His love, Al - le - lu - ia!

Who did once, up - on the cross, Al - le - lu - ia!
Who en - dured the cross and grave, Al - le - lu - ia!
Now a - bove the sky He's King, Al - le - lu - ia!
Praise Him, all ye heav'n - ly host, Al - le - lu - ia!

Suf - fer to re - deem our loss, Al - le - lu - ia!
Sin - ners to re - deem and save, Al - le - lu - ia!
Where the an - gels ev - er sing, Al - le - lu - ia!
Fa - ther, Son, and Ho - ly Ghost, Al - le - lu - ia!

WORDS: Latin, 14th c; tr. *Lyra Davidica*, 1708; St. 4, Charles Wesley, 1739, alt.
MUSIC: *Easter Hymn*, from *Lyra Davidica*, 1708; adapt. from *The Compleat Psalmodist*, 1719, alt.   7.7.7.7 with Alleluias
This tune in a lower key, No. 184.

"Christ the Lord Is Risen Today"   184

He is not here; He has risen! – Luke 24:6 NIV

1. "Christ the Lord is ris'n to-day," Al - le - lu - ia!
2. Love's re-deem-ing work is done, Al - le - lu - ia!
3. Lives a-gain our glo-rious King, Al - le - lu - ia!
4. Soar we now where Christ was led, Al - le - lu - ia!

Sons of men and an-gels say, Al - le - lu - ia!
Fought the fight, the bat-tle won, Al - le - lu - ia!
Where, O death, is now thy sting? Al - le - lu - ia!
Fol-lowing our ex-alt-ed Head, Al - le - lu - ia!

Raise your joys and tri-umphs high, Al - le - lu - ia!
Death in vain for-bids Him rise, Al - le - lu - ia!
Once He died our souls to save, Al - le - lu - ia!
Made like Him, like Him we rise, Al - le - lu - ia!

Sing, ye heav'ns, and earth re-ply, Al - le - lu - ia!
Christ has o-pened par-a-dise, Al - le - lu - ia!
Where thy vic-to-ry, O grave? Al - le - lu - ia!
Ours the cross, the grave, the skies, Al - le - lu - ia!

WORDS: Charles Wesley, 1739
MUSIC: *Easter Hymn*, from *Lyra Davidica*, 1708; adapt. from *The Compleat Psalmodist*,1719, alt.   7.7.7.7. with Alleluias
This tune in a higher key, No. 183.

185 The Day of Resurrection!

At dawn on the first day of the week, Mary Magdalene and the other Mary went to look at the tomb. – Matthew 28:1 NIV

1. The day of res - ur - rec - tion! Earth, tell it out a - broad;
2. Our hearts be pure from e - vil, that we may see a - right
3. Now let the heav'ns be joy - ful! Let earth her song be - gin!

the Pass - o - ver of glad - ness, the Pass - o - ver of God.
the Lord in rays e - ter - nal of res - ur - rec - tion light;
The world re - sound in tri - umph, and all that is there - in;

From death to life e - ter - nal, from sin's do - min - ion free,
and, lis - t'ning to His ac - cents, may hear, so calm and plain,
let all things seen and un - seen their notes in glad - ness blend;

our Christ hath brought us o - ver, with hymns of vic - to - ry.
His own "all hail" and, hear - ing, may raise the vic - tor strain.
for Christ the Lord hath ris - en, our joy that hath no end.

WORDS: Greek hymn, John of Damascus, 8th c.; tr. John Mason Neale, 1862
MUSIC: *Lancashire*, Henry Thomas Smart, 1835
This tune in a higher key, No. 437.

7.6.7.6 D

The Day of Resurrection!

At dawn on the first day of the week, Mary Magdalene and the other Mary went to look at the tomb. – Matthew 28:1 NIV

1. The day of res - ur - rec - tion! Earth, tell it out a - broad;
2. Our hearts be pure from e - vil, that we may see a - right
3. Now let the heav'ns be joy - ful! Let earth her song be - gin!

the Pass - o - ver of glad - ness, the Pass - o - ver of God.
the Lord in rays e - ter - nal of res - ur - rec - tion light;
The world re - sound in tri - umph, and all that is there - in;

From death to life e - ter - nal, from sin's do - min - ion free,
and, lis - t'ning to His ac - cents, may hear, so calm and plain,
let all things seen and un - seen their notes in glad - ness blend;

our Christ hath brought us o - ver, with hymns of vic - to - ry.
His own "all hail" and, hear - ing, may raise the vic - tor strain.
for Christ the Lord hath ris - en, our joy that hath no end.

WORDS: Greek hymn, John of Damascus, 8th c.; tr. John Mason Neale, 1862
MUSIC: *Ellacombe*, from *Gesangbuch der H.W.K. Hofkapelle*, 1784; harm. William Henry Monk, 1868   7.6.7.6.D
This tune in a lower key, No. 153.

187 Hail Thee, Festival Day!

Blessed be the Lord this day. – 1 Kings 5:7 KJV

1. *(Easter)* Hail thee, Fes - ti-val day! Blest day that art hal-lowed for - ev - er;
1. *(Ascension)* Hail thee, Fes - ti-val day! Blest day that art hal-lowed for - ev - er;
1. *(Pentecost)* Hail thee, Fes - ti-val day! Blest day that art hal-lowed for - ev - er;

day where-on Christ a - rose, break-ing the king - dom of death.
day when our ris - en Lord rose in the heav - ens to reign.
day when the Ho - ly Ghost shone in the world with God's grace.

1. *(Easter)* Lo, the fair beau - ty of earth, from the
1. *(Ascension)* He who was nailed to the cross is
1. *(Pentecost)* Lo, in the like - ness of fire, on
3. *(All seasons)* God, the Al - might - y, the Lord, who
5. *(All seasons)* Spir - it of life and of pow'r, now

death of the win - ter a - ris - ing! Ev - 'ry good
Rul - er and Lord of all na - ture. All things cre -
those who a - wait His ap - pear - ing, He whom the
rul - est the earth and the heav - ens, guard us from
flow in us, fount of our be - ing, Light that dost

WORDS: Venantius Honorius Clementianus Fortunatus, ca. 6th c.; tr. Maurice Frederick Bell, 1906
MUSIC: *Salve Festa Dies*, Ralph Vaughan Williams, 1906

Irregular with Refrain

Repeat Refrain

gift	of the year	now with its Mas - ter re - turns:
at - ed on earth	sing to the glo - ry of God:
Lord fore - told	sud - den - ly, swift - ly de - scends:
harm with - out;	cleanse us from e - vil with - in:
light - en all,	life that in all dost a - bide:

2. *(Easter)* Rise from the grave now, O Lord, the Au - thor of
2. *(Ascension)* Dai - ly the lov - li - ness grows, a - dorned with the
2. *(Pentecost)* Hark! for in myr - i - ad tongues Christ's own, His
4. *(All seasons)* Je - sus, the health of the world, en - light - en our
6. *(All seasons)* Praise to the Giv - er of good! Thou love who art

life and cre - a - tion. Tread - ing the path - way of
glo - ry of blos - som; heav - en her gates un -
cho - sen a - pos - tles, preach to the ends of the
minds, Thou, Re - deem - er, Son of the Fa - ther su -
Au - thor of con - cord, [1] pour out Your balm on our

Repeat Refrain

death, new life You give to us all:
bars, fling - ing her in - cense of light:
earth Christ and His won - der - ful works:
preme, On - ly Be - got - ten of God:
souls, or - der our ways in Thy peace:

1. concord: harmony

Thine Be the Glory

"The Lord has risen indeed, and has appeared to Simon!" – Luke 24:34 ESV

1. Thine be the glo - ry, ris - en, con - qu'ring Son;
2. Lo! Je - sus meets us, ris - en from the tomb;
3. No more we doubt Thee, glo - rious Prince of life!

end - less is the vic - t'ry Thou o'er death hast won.
lov - ing - ly He greets us, scat - ters fear and gloom.
Life is nought with - out Thee; aid us in our strife;

An - gels in bright rai - ment[1] rolled the stone a - way,
Let His Church with glad - ness, hymns of tri - umph sing;
make us more than con - qu'rors, through Thy death - less love:

kept the fold - ed grave clothes where Thy bod - y lay.
for her Lord now liv - eth, death hath lost its sting.
Bring us safe through Jor - dan to Thy home a - bove.

Refrain

Thine is the glo - ry, ris - en con - qu'ring Son:

1. raiment: dress, clothing

WORDS: *A toi la gloire*, Edmund Louis Budry, 1884; tr. Richard Birch Hoyle, 1923
MUSIC: *Maccabaeus*, Air from *Judas Maccabaeus*, George Frederick Handel, 1747

10.11.11.11 with Refrain

Endless is the vic-t'ry, Thou o'er death hast won.

The Risen Christ

189

It is true! The Lord has risen. – Luke 24:34 NIV

1. O, Breath of God, come fill this place, re-vive our
2. O, Word of God, so clear and true, re-new our
3. O, love of God, so un-re-strained, re-fresh our
4. May God the Fa-ther, God the Son, and God the

hearts to know Your grace; and from our slum-ber make us
minds to trust in You; and give to us the Bread of
souls in Je-sus' name; let us re-flect Your sac-ri-
Spir-it make us one; in ho-li-ness let us u-

rise; that we may know the Ris-en Christ.
Life; that we may know the Ris-en Christ.
fice; that we may know the Ris-en Christ.
nite; that we may know the Ris-en Christ.

WORDS: Phil Madeira, 2003
MUSIC: *Risen Christ*, Keith Getty, 2003; arr. Eric Wyse, 2005

L.M.

190 Alleluia, Alleluia! Hearts to Heaven

Alleluia; salvation, and glory, and honour, and power, unto the Lord our God. – Revelation 19:1 KJV

1. Al - le - lu - ia, Al - le - lu - ia! Hearts to heav'n and voic - es raise:
2. Now the i - ron bars are bro - ken, Christ from death to life is born,
3. Christ is ris - en, Christ, the first fruits of the ho - ly har - vest field,
4. Christ is ris - en, we are ris - en! Shed up - on us heav'n - ly grace,
5. Al - le - lu - ia, Al - le - lu - ia! Glo - ry be to God on high;

Sing to God a hymn of glad - ness, sing to God a hymn of praise.
glo - rious life, and life im - mor - tal, on this ho - ly Eas - ter morn.
which will all its full a - bun - dance at His sec - ond com - ing yield:
rain and dew and gleams of glo - ry from the bright - ness of Thy face;
Al - le - lu - ia! To the Sav - ior who has won the vic - to - ry;

He, who on the cross a vic - tim, for the world's sal - va - tion bled,
Christ has tri - umphed, and we con - quer by His might - y en - ter - prise:
Then the gold - en ears of har - vest will their heads be - fore Him wave,
that with hearts in heav - en dwell - ing, here on earth may fruit - ful be,
Al - le - lu - ia! To the Spir - it, fount of love and sanc - ti - ty:

Je - sus Christ, the King of glo - ry, now is ris - en from the dead.
We with Him to life e - ter - nal by His res - ur - rec - tion rise.
ri - pened by His glo - rious sun - shine from the fur - rows of the grave.
and by an - gel hands be gath - ered, and be ev - er, Lord, with Thee.
Al - le - lu - ia, Al - le - lu - ia! To the Tri - une Maj - es - ty.

WORDS: Christopher Wordsworth, 1862
MUSIC: *Hymn to Joy,* Ludwig van Beethoven, 1824; adapt. Edward Hodges, 1864
This tune in a higher key, No. 235.

8.7.8.7 D

The Strife Is O'er

The bodies we now have...can die. But they will be changed into bodies that are eternal. – 1 Corinthians 15:54 CEV

Refrain (before stanza 1 and after stanza 5)

Al - le - lu - ia, Al - le - lu - ia, Al - le - lu - ia!

1. The strife is o'er, the bat - tle done, the vic - to -
2. The pow'rs of death have done their worst, but Christ their
3. The three sad days are quick - ly sped, He ris - es
4. He closed the yawn - ing gates of hell; the bars from
5. Lord, by the stripes which wound - ed Thee, from death's dread

ry of life is won; the song of tri - umph
le - gions hath dis - persed: Let shouts of ho - ly
glo - rious from the dead: All glo - ry to our
heav'n's high por - tals fell; let hymns of praise His
sting Thy ser - vants free, that we may live, and

has be - gun. "Al - le - lu - ia!"
joy out - burst. "Al - le - lu - ia!"
ris - en Head! "Al - le - lu - ia!"
tri - umphs tell! "Al - le - lu - ia!"
sing to Thee. "Al - le - lu - ia!"

WORDS: Latin hymn, ca. 1695; tr. Francis Pott, 1861
MUSIC: *Victory,* Giovanni Pierluigi da Palestrina, n.d., adapt. and arr. William Henry Monk, 1861

8.8.8 with Alleluias

Because He Lives

Because I live, you also will live. – John 14:19 NIV

1. God sent His Son, they called Him Je - sus,
2. How sweet to hold a new - born ba - by,
3. And then one day I'll cross the riv - er,

He came to love, heal, and for - give;
and feel the pride, and joy he gives;
I'll fight life's fi - nal war with pain;

He lived and died to buy my par - don,
but great - er still the calm as - sur - ance,
and then as death gives way to vic - tory,

an emp - ty grave is there to prove my Sav - ior lives.
this child can face un - cer - tain days be - cause He lives.
I'll see the lights of glo - ry and I'll know He lives.

WORDS: Gloria Gaither and William J. Gaither, 1970
MUSIC: *Resurrection*, William J. Gaither, 1970

Irregular with Refrain

Be - cause He lives I can face to - mor - row,

be - cause He lives, all fear is gone;

be - cause I know He holds the fu - ture.

And life is worth the liv - ing just be - cause He lives.

193 Hail the Day That Sees Him Rise

"When He ascended on high, He led captives in His train." – Ephesians 4:8 NIV

1. Hail the day that sees Him rise, Alleluia!
To His throne above the skies, Alleluia!
Christ, awhile to mortals giv'n, Alleluia!
Enters now His native heav'n, Alleluia!

2. See! He lifts His hands above, Alleluia!
See! He shows the prints of love, Alleluia!
Hark! His gracious lips bestow, Alleluia!
Blessings on His Church below, Alleluia!

3. Still for us He intercedes, Alleluia!
His prevailing death He pleads; Alleluia!
Near Himself prepares our place, Alleluia!
He the first fruits of our race, Alleluia!

4. Grant, though parted from our sight, Alleluia!
High above yon azure height, Alleluia!
Grant our hearts may there arise, Alleluia!
Fol-l'wing Thee beyond the skies, Alleluia!

5. There we shall with Thee remain, Alleluia!
Partners of Thy endless reign, Alleluia!
There Thy face unclouded see, Alleluia!
Find our heav'n of heav'ns in Thee, Alleluia!

WORDS: Charles Wesley, 1742, alt.
MUSIC: *Llanfair*, Robert Williams, 1817; harm. John Roberts, 1837
This tune in a lower key, No. 25; another harmonization in a lower key, No. 245.

7.7.7.7 with Alleluias

Blessing and Honor and Glory and Power 194

To Him be glory for ever and ever. Amen. – 2 Timothy 4:18 NIV

1. Bless - ing and hon - or and glo - ry and pow'r,
2. In - to the heav'n of the heav'ns hath He gone,
3. Sound - eth the heav'n of the heav'ns with His name;
4. Ev - er as - cen - deth the song and the joy;
5. Give we the glo - ry and praise to the Lamb;

wis - dom and rich - es and strength ev - er - more
sit - teth He now in the joy of the throne,
ring - eth the earth with His glo - ry and fame;
ev - er de - scen - deth the love from on high;
take we the robe and the harp and the palm;

give ye to Him who our bat - tle hath won
wear - eth He now of the king - dom the crown,
o - cean and moun - tain, stream, for - est, and flow'r
bless - ing and hon - or and glo - ry and praise,
sing we the song of the Lamb that was slain,

Whose are the king - dom, the crown, and the throne.
sing - eth He now the new song with His own.
ech - o His prais - es and tell of His pow'r.
this is the theme of the hymns that we raise.
dy - ing in weak - ness, but ris - ing to reign.

WORDS: Horatius Bonar, 1866
MUSIC: *O Quanta Qualia,* from *Antiphoner;* anon. 1681
Another harmonization of this tune in a lower key, No. 548.

10.10.10.10

195 Alleluia! Sing to Jesus

They were from every race, tribe, nation...and they stood before the...Lamb. – Revelation 7:9 CEV

1, 5. Al - le - lu - ia! Sing to Je - sus! His the
2. Al - le - lu - ia! Not as or - phans are we
3. Al - le - lu - ia! Bread of heav - en, Thou on
4. Al - le - lu - ia! King e - ter - nal, Thee the

scep - ter, His the throne. Al - le - lu - ia! His the
left in sor - row now; Al - le - lu - ia! He is
earth our food, our stay! Al - le - lu - ia! Here the
Lord of lords we own; Al - le - lu - ia! Born of

tri - umph, His the vic - to - ry a - lone.
near us, faith be - lieves, nor ques - tions how:
sin - ful flee to Thee from day to day:
Ma - ry, earth Thy foot - stool, heav'n Thy throne:

Hark! The songs of peace - ful Zi - on thun - der
Though the cloud from sight re - ceived Him when the
In - ter - ces - sor, Friend of sin - ners, earth's Re -
Thou with - in the veil hast en - tered, robed in

WORDS: William Chatterton Dix, 1867
MUSIC: *Hyfrydol*, Rowland H. Prichard, ca. 1830; harm. *The English Hymnal*, 1906
This tune in a higher key, No. 238; another harmonization, in a lower key, No. 248.

8.7.8.7 D

like   a   might - y   flood.   Je -   sus   out   of
for - ty   days   were   o'er,   shall   our   hearts   for -
deem - er,   plead   for   me,   where   the   songs   of
flesh   our   great   High   Priest;   Thou   on   earth   both

ev - 'ry   na - tion   hath   re - deemed   us   by   His   blood.
get   His   prom - ise,   "I   am   with   you   ev - er - more."
all   the   sin - less   sweep   a - cross   the   crys - tal   sea.
priest   and   vic - tim   in   the   eu - cha - ris - tic   feast.

He Is Lord

196

Jesus Christ is Lord. – Philippians 2:11 NIV

1. He is Lord,   He is Lord!   He is   ris - en from the dead and He   is Lord!
2. He is Lord,   He is Lord!   He is   high and lift - ed   up, for He   is Lord!
3. He is Lord,   He is Lord!   He will come a - gain in   glo - ry, He   is Lord!

Ev - 'ry   knee shall bow,   ev - 'ry   tongue con - fess   that   Je - sus Christ is   Lord!
Ev - 'ry   knee shall bow,   ev - 'ry   tongue con - fess   that   Je - sus Christ is   Lord!
Ev - 'ry   knee shall bow,   ev - 'ry   tongue con - fess   that   Je - sus Christ is   Lord!

WORDS: Based on Philippians 2:9-11; St. 1 traditional; Sts. 2-3 Danny R. Jones and Eric Wyse, 2005
MUSIC: *He Is Lord*, traditional
Words © 2006 Vine Ridge Music BMI . (admin. by Integrated Copyright Group)

Irregular

197

Majesty

For He received honor and glory from God...when the voice came to Him from the Majestic Glory. – 2 Peter 1:17 NIV

Maj-es-ty, wor-ship His maj-es-ty. Un-to Je-sus be all glo-ry, hon-or and praise. Maj-es-ty, king-dom au-thor-i-ty flow from His throne un-to His own, His an-them raise. So ex-alt, lift up on high the name of Je-sus. Mag-ni-fy, come glo-ri-fy Christ Je-sus, the King.

WORDS: Jack Hayford, 1980
MUSIC: *Majesty*, Jack Hayford, 1980
© 1981 New Spring Music, Inc. ASCAP

Irregular

Maj - es - ty, wor-ship His maj - es - ty. Je - sus, who

died, now glo - ri - fied, King of all kings.

O Christ, Our Hope

198

While we wait for the blessed hope-the glorious appearing of our great God and Savior, Jesus Christ. – Titus 2:12-14 NIV

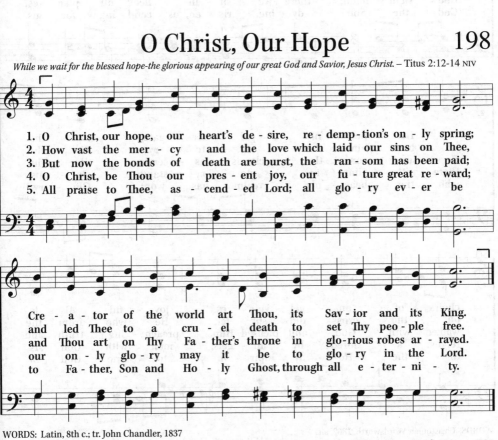

1. O Christ, our hope, our heart's de - sire, re - demp-tion's on - ly spring;
2. How vast the mer - cy and the love which laid our sins on Thee,
3. But now the bonds of death are burst, the ran - som has been paid;
4. O Christ, be Thou our pres - ent joy, our fu - ture great re - ward;
5. All praise to Thee, as - cend - ed Lord; all glo - ry ev - er be

Cre - a - tor of the world art Thou, its Sav - ior and its King.
and led Thee to a cru - el death to set Thy peo - ple free.
and Thou art on Thy Fa - ther's throne in glo - rious robes ar - rayed.
our on - ly glo - ry may it be to glo - ry in the Lord.
to Fa - ther, Son and Ho - ly Ghost, through all e - ter - ni - ty.

WORDS: Latin, 8th c.; tr. John Chandler, 1837
MUSIC: *St. Anne,* from *A Supplement to the New Version,* attr. William Croft, 1708; harm. William Henry Monk, 1861   C.M.
This tune in a lower key, No. 28.

199 See the Conqueror Mounts in Triumph

I saw heaven open, and behold, a white horse! The one sitting on it is called Faithful and True. – Revelation 19:11 ESV

1. See the Con-qu'ror mounts in tri-umph; see the King in
2. Who is this that comes in glo-ry, with the trump of
3. While He lifts His hands in bless-ing, He is part-ed
4. He has raised our hu-man na-ture on the clouds to
5. Glo-ry be to God the Fa-ther, glo-ry be to

roy-al state, rid-ing on the clouds, His char-iot,
ju-bi-lee? Lord of bat-tles, God of ar-mies,
from His friends, while their ea-ger eyes be-hold Him,
God's right hand; there we sit in heav-'nly plac-es,
God the Son, dy-ing, ris-en, as-cend-ing for us,

to His heav-'nly pal-ace gate. Hark! The
He has gained the vic-to-ry. He who
He up-on the clouds as-cends; He who
there with Him in glo-ry stand: Je-sus
who the heav-'nly realm has won; Glo-ry

choirs of an-gel voic-es joy-ful Al-le-
on the cross did suf-fer, He who from the
walked with God and pleased Him, preach-ing truth and
reigns, a-dored by an-gels; man with God is
to the Ho-ly Spir-it, to one God in

WORDS: Christopher Wordsworth, 1862, alt.
MUSIC: *In Babilone,* traditional Netherlands melody, ca. 1710; arr. Charles Winfield Douglas, 1918
Another harmonization of this tune, No. 201.

8.7.8.7 D

lu - ias sing, and the por - tals high are
grave a - rose, He has van - quished sin and
doom to come, He, our E - noch, is trans -
on the throne; might - y Lord, in Thine as -
per - sons Three; glo - ry both in earth and

lift - ed to re - ceive their heav - 'nly King.
Sa - tan, He by death has spoiled His foes.
lat - ed to His ev - er - last - ing home.
cen - sion we by faith be - hold our own.
heav - en, glo - ry, end - less glo - ry, be.

Majestic Sweetness Sits Enthroned   200

All...were amazed at the gracious words that came from His lips. – Luke 4:22 NIV

1. Ma - jes - tic sweet-ness sits en - throned up - on the Sav-ior's brow;
2. No mor - tal can with Him com - pare, who on the earth does reign;
3. To Him I owe my life and breath, and all the joys I have;
4. Since from His boun - ty I re - ceive such proofs of love di - vine;

His head with ra - diant glo - ries crowned, His lips with grace o'er - flow.
fair - er is He than all the fair that fill the heav'n - ly train.
He makes me tri - umph o - ver death, and saves me from the grave.
had I a thou-sand hearts to give, Lord, they should all be Thine.

WORDS: Samuel Stennett, 1787, alt.
MUSIC: *Horsley,* William Horsley, 1830
This tune in a lower key, No.160.

C.M.

201 Hail, Thou Once Despised Jesus!

He was despised and rejected by men; a man of sorrows, and acquainted with grief. – Isaiah 53:3 ESV

1. Hail, Thou once de - spis - ed Je - sus! Hail, Thou Gal - i -
2. Pas - chal Lamb, by God ap - point - ed, all our sins on
3. Je - sus, hail! En - throned in glo - ry, there for - ev - er
4. Wor - ship, hon - or, pow'r and bless - ing Thou art wor - thy

le - an King! Thou didst suf - fer to re - lease us;
Thee were laid; by al - might - y love a - noint - ed,
to a - bide; all the heav'n - ly hosts a - dore Thee,
to re - ceive; high - est prais - es, with - out ceas - ing,

Thou didst free sal - va - tion bring. Hail, Thou ag - o -
Thou hast full a - tone - ment made. All Thy peo - ple
seat - ed at Thy Fa - ther's side. There for sin - ners
right it is for us to give. Help, ye bright an -

niz - ing Sav - ior, bear - er of our sin and shame!
are for - giv - en through the vir - tue of Thy blood;
Thou art plead - ing; there Thou dost our place pre - pare;
gel - ic spir - its, bring your sweet - est, no - blest lays; [1]

1. lays: songs, melodies

WORDS: John Bakewell, 1757
MUSIC: *In Babilone,* traditional Netherlands melody, ca. 1710; arr. Julius Röntgen, ca. 1906
Another harmonization of this tune, No. 199.

8.7.8.7 D

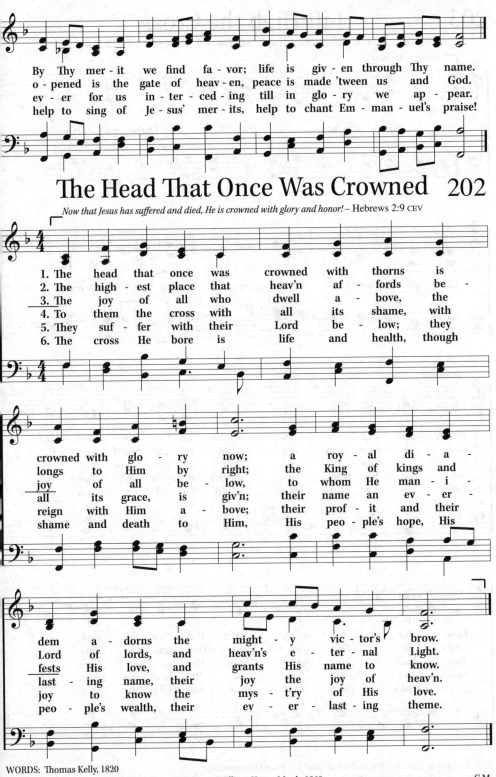

By Thy mer-it we find fa-vor; life is giv-en through Thy name.
o-pened is the gate of heav-en, peace is made 'tween us and God.
ev-er for us in-ter-ced-ing till in glo-ry we ap-pear.
help to sing of Je-sus' mer-its, help to chant Em-man-uel's praise!

The Head That Once Was Crowned 202

Now that Jesus has suffered and died, He is crowned with glory and honor! – Hebrews 2:9 CEV

1. The head that once was crowned with thorns is
2. The high-est place that heav'n af-fords be-
3. The joy of all who dwell a-bove, the
4. To them the cross with all its shame, with
5. They suf-fer with their Lord be-low; they
6. The cross He bore is life and health, though

crowned with glo-ry now; a roy-al di-a-
longs to Him by right; the King of kings and
joy of all be-low, to whom He man-i-
all its grace, is giv'n; their name an ev-er-
reign with Him a-bove; their prof-it and their
shame and death to Him, His peo-ple's hope, His

dem a-dorns the might-y vic-tor's brow.
Lord of lords, and heav'n's e-ter-nal Light.
fests His love, and grants His name to know.
last-ing name, their joy the joy of heav'n.
joy to know the mys-t'ry of His love.
peo-ple's wealth, their ev-er-last-ing theme.

WORDS: Thomas Kelly, 1820
MUSIC: *St. Magnus,* attr. Jeremiah Clark, 1707; harm. William Henry Monk, 1868

C.M.

203 Lift High the Cross

But I, when I am lifted up from the earth, will draw all men to Myself. – John 12:32 NIV

Refrain Unison

Lift high the cross, the love of Christ pro-claim

till all the world a-dore His sa-cred name.

Fine

Harmony

1. Come, now and fol-low where our Sav-ior trod, our
2. Led on their way by this tri-um-phant sign, the
3. O Lord, once lift-ed on the glo-rious tree, as
4. Set up Thy throne, that earth's de-spair may cease be-
5. For Thy blest cross which doth for all a-tone cre-

King vic-to-rious, Christ the Son of God.
hosts of God in con-qu'ring ranks com-bine.
Thou hast prom-ised, draw the world to Thee.
neath the shad-ow of its heal-ing peace.
a-tion's prais-es rise be-fore Thy throne.

D.C.

WORDS: George William Kitchin, 1887; alt. Michael Robert Newbolt, 1916
MUSIC: *Crucifer*, Sydney Hugo Nicholson, 1916

10.10 with Refrain

Look, Ye Saints! The Sight Is Glorious 204

The kingdom of this world belongs to our Lord and to His Chosen One! – Revelation 11:15 CEV

1. Look, ye saints! The sight is glo - rious: See the Man of Sor - rows now; from the fight re - turned vic - to - rious, ev - 'ry knee to Him shall bow. Crown Him, crown Him, crown Him, crown Him, crowns be - come the Vic - tor's brow.
2. Crown the Sav - ior! An - gels, crown Him; rich the tro - phies Je - sus brings; in the seat of pow'r en - throne Him, while the vault of heav - en rings. Crown Him, crown Him, crown Him, crown Him, crown the Sav - ior King of kings.
3. Sin - ners in de - ri - sion scorned Him, mock - ing thus the Sav - ior's claim; saints and an - gels crowd a - round Him, own His ti - tle, praise His name. Crown Him, crown Him, crown Him, crown Him, spread a - broad the Vic - tor's fame.
4. Hark, those bursts of ac - cla - ma - tion! Hark, those loud tri - um - phant chords! Je - sus takes the high - est sta - tion; O what joy the sight af - fords! Crown Him, crown Him, crown Him, crown Him, King of kings and Lord of lords!

WORDS: Thomas Kelly, 1809
MUSIC: *Regent Square*, Henry Thomas Smart, 1867
This tune in a higher key, No. 317

8.7.8.7.4.7 with Repeat

205 Look, Ye Saints! The Sight Is Glorious

The kingdom of this world belongs to our Lord and to His Chosen One! – Revelation 11:15 CEV

1. Look, ye saints! The sight is glorious: See the Man of Sorrows now; from the fight returned victorious, ev'ry knee to Him shall bow; Crown Him, crown Him, crown Him, crown Him, crown Him, crown Him. Crowns become

2. Crown the Savior! Angels, crown Him; rich the trophies Jesus brings; in the seat of pow'r enthrone Him, while the vault of heaven rings: Crown Him, crown Him, crown Him, crown Him, crown Him, crown Him. Crown the Sav-

3. Sinners in derision crowned Him, mocking thus the Savior's claim; saints and angels crowd around Him, own His title, praise His name: Crown Him, crown Him, crown Him, crown Him, crown Him, crown Him. Spread abroad

4. Hark, those bursts of acclamation! Hark, those loud triumphant chords! Jesus takes the highest station; O what joy the sight affords! Crown Him, crown Him, crown Him, crown Him, crown Him, crown Him. King of kings

WORDS: Thomas Kelly, 1809
MUSIC: *Bryn Calfaria*, William Owen, 1852

8.7.8.7.4.7 with Repeat

the Vic - tor's brow, crowns be - come the Vic - tor's brow.
ior King of kings, crown the Sav - ior King of kings.
the Vic - tor's fame, spread a - broad the Vic - tor's fame.
and Lord of lords! King of kings and Lord of lords!

Rejoice, the Lord Is King! 206

On the part of the robe that covered His thigh was written, "KING OF KINGS AND LORD OF LORDS." – Revelation 19:16 CEV

1. Re - joice, the Lord is King! Your Lord and King a - dore;
2. Je - sus, the Sav - ior, reigns, the God of truth and love;
3. His king - dom can - not fail, He rules o'er earth and heav'n,
4. He sits at God's right hand till all His foes sub - mit,
5. Re - joice in glo - rious hope! Je - sus the Judge shall come,

mor - tals give thanks and sing, and tri - umph ev - er - more; lift
when He had purged our stains He took His seat a - bove; lift
the keys of death and hell are to our Je - sus giv'n; lift
and bow to His com - mand, and fall be - neath His feet: lift
and take His ser - vants up to their e - ter - nal home. We

up your heart, lift up your voice; re - joice, a - gain I say, re - joice!
up your heart, lift up your voice; re - joice, a - gain I say, re - joice!
up your heart, lift up your voice; re - joice, a - gain I say, re - joice!
up your heart, lift up your voice; re - joice, a - gain I say, re - joice!
soon shall hear th'arch - an - gel's voice; the trump of God shall sound, re - joice!

WORDS: Charles Wesley, 1744
MUSIC: *Darwall's 148th*, John Darwall, 1770
Another harmonization of this tune, No. 43.

6.6.6.6.8.8

207   At the Name of Jesus

At the name of Jesus everyone will bow down, those in heaven, on earth, and under the earth. – Philippians 2:10 CEV

1. At the name of Je - sus, ev - 'ry knee shall bow,
2. Hum - bled for a sea - son, to re - ceive a name
3. Bore it up tri - um - phant with its hu - man light,
4. Name Him, Chris - tians, name Him, with love strong as death,
5. In your hearts en - throne Him; there let Him sub - due
6. Chris - tians, this Lord Je - sus shall re - turn a - gain,

ev - 'ry tongue con - fess Him King of glo - ry now;
from the lips of sin - ners un - to whom He came,
through all ranks of crea - tures, to the cen - tral height,
but with awe and won - der, and with bat - ed[1] breath;
all that is not ho - ly, all that is not true;
with His Fa - ther's glo - ry, with His an - gel train;

'tis the Fa - ther's plea - sure we should call Him Lord,
faith - ful - ly He bore it, spot - less to the last,
to the throne of God - head, to the Fa - ther's breast;
He is God the Sav - ior, He is Christ the Lord,
crown Him as your Cap - tain in temp - ta - tion's hour;
For all wreaths of em - pire meet up - on His brow,

who from the be - gin - ning was the might - y Word.
brought it back vic - to - rious when from death He passed.
filled it with the glo - ry of that per - fect rest.
ev - er to be wor - shipped, trust - ed and a - dored.
let His will en - fold you in its light and pow'r.
and our hearts con - fess Him King of glo - ry now.

1. *bated: restrained*

WORDS: Caroline Maria Noel, 1870, alt.
MUSIC: *Wye Valley*, James Mountain, 1876   6.5.6.5 D
This tune in a lower key, No. 412.

At the Name of Jesus

At the name of Jesus everyone will bow down, those in heaven, on earth, and under the earth. – Philippians 2:10 CEV

1. At the name of Je - sus, ev - 'ry knee shall bow,
2. Hum - bled for a sea - son, to re - ceive a name
3. Bore it up tri - um - phant with its hu - man light,
4. Name Him, Chris - tians, name Him, with love strong as death,
5. In your hearts en - throne Him; there let Him sub - due
6. Chris - tians, this Lord Je - sus shall re - turn a - gain,

ev - 'ry tongue con - fess Him King of glo - ry now;
from the lips of sin - ners un - to whom He came,
through all ranks of crea - tures, to the cen - tral height,
but with awe and won - der, and with bat - ed[1] breath;
all that is not ho - ly, all that is not true;
with His Fa - ther's glo - ry, with His an - gel train;

'tis the Fa - ther's plea - sure we should call Him Lord,
faith - ful - ly He bore it, spot - less to the last,
to the throne of God - head, to the Fa - ther's breast;
He is God the Sav - ior, He is Christ the Lord,
crown Him as your Cap - tain in temp - ta - tion's hour;
For all wreaths of em - pire meet up - on His brow,

who from the be - gin - ning was the might - y Word.
brought it back vic - to - rious when from death He passed.
filled it with the glo - ry of that per - fect rest.
ev - er to be wor - shiped, trust - ed and a - dored.
let His will en - fold you in its light and pow'r.
and our hearts con - fess Him King of glo - ry now.

1. bated: restrained

WORDS: Caroline Maria Noel, 1870, alt.
MUSIC: *Belle Rive,* Eric Wyse, 2005
6.5.6.5 D

209 Ye Servants of God

Praise our God, all ye His servants, and ye that fear Him, both small and great. – Revelation 19:5 KJV

1. Ye ser-vants of God, your Mas-ter pro-claim,
2. God rul-eth on high, Al-might-y to save,
3. "Sal-va-tion to God, who sits on the throne!"
4. Then let us a-dore and give Him His right,

and pub-lish a-broad His won-der-ful name;
and still He is nigh, His pres-ence we have;
Let all cry a-loud and hon-or the Son;
all glo-ry and pow'r, all wis-dom and might;

the name all vic-to-rious of Je-sus ex-tol,
the great con-gre-ga-tion His tri-umph shall sing,
the prais-es of Je-sus the an-gels pro-claim,
all hon-or and bless-ing with an-gels a-bove,

His king-dom is glo-rious and rules o-ver all.
as-crib-ing sal-va-tion to Je-sus, our King.
fall down on their fac-es and wor-ship the Lamb.
and thanks nev-er ceas-ing and in-fi-nite love.

WORDS: Charles Wesley, 1744
MUSIC: *Hanover*, attr. William Croft, 1708

10.10.11.11

Lo! He Comes with Clouds Descending 210

They will see the Son of Man coming on the clouds of the sky, with power and great glory. – Matthew 24:30 NIV

1. Lo! He comes with clouds de-scend-ing, once for fa-vored
2. Ev - 'ry eye shall now be-hold Him robed in dread-ful
3. Those dear to-kens of His pas-sion still His daz-zling
4. Yea, A-men! Let all a-dore Thee, high on Thine e-

sin-ners slain; thou-sand thou-sand saints at-tend-ing,
maj - es - ty; those who set at naught and sold Him,
bod - y bears; cause of end-less ex - ul-ta - tion
ter - nal throne; Sav - ior, take the pow'r and glo - ry,

swell the tri - umph of His train: Al - le - lu - ia!
pierced and nailed Him to the tree, deep - ly wail-ing,
to His ran - somed wor - ship-ers; with what rap - ture,
claim the king - dom for Thine own; O come quick - ly!

Al - le - lu - ia! God ap - pears on earth to reign.
deep - ly wail - ing, shall the true Mes - si - ah see.
with what rap - ture, gaze we on those glo - rious scars!
O come quick - ly! Thou shalt reign and Thou a - lone!

WORDS: John Cennick, 1752; Charles Wesley, 1758, alt.; Martin Madan, 1760, alt.
MUSIC: *Regent Square*, Henry Thomas Smart, 1867
8.7.8.7.4.7 with Repeat
This tune in a lower key, No. 317.

211 Lo! He Comes with Clouds Descending

They will see the Son of Man coming on the clouds of the sky, with power and great glory. – Matthew 24:30 NIV

1. Lo! He comes with clouds de-scend - ing, once for fa - vored sin - ners slain; thou - sand thou - sand saints at - tend - ing, swell the tri - umph of His train: Al - le - lu - ia! Al - le - lu - ia!

2. Ev - 'ry eye shall now be - hold Him robed in dread - ful maj - es - ty; those who set at naught and sold Him, pierced and nailed Him to the tree, deep - ly wail - ing, deep - ly wail - ing,

3. Those dear to - kens of His pas - sion still His daz - zling bod - y bears; cause of end - less ex - ul - ta - tion to His ran - somed wor - ship - ers; with what rap - ture, with what rap - ture,

4. Yea, A - men! Let all a - dore Thee, high on Thine e - ter - nal throne; Sav - ior, take the pow'r and glo - ry, claim the king - dom for Thine own; O come quick - ly! O come quick - ly!

WORDS: John Cennick, 1752; Charles Wesley, 1758, alt.; Martin Madan, 1760, alt.
MUSIC: *Helmsley*, traditional English melody, 18th c.; harm. from *The English Hymnal*, 1906

8.7.8.7.4.7 with Repeat

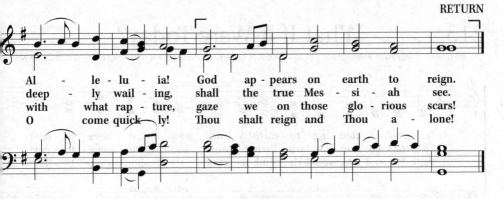

Al - le - lu - ia! God ap - pears on earth to reign.
deep - ly wail - ing, shall the true Mes - si - ah see.
with what rap - ture, gaze we on those glo - rious scars!
O come quick - ly! Thou shalt reign and Thou a - lone!

When He Cometh 212

"They shall be Mine," says the Lord of hosts, "On the day that I make them My jewels." – Malachi 3:17 NKJV

1. When He com - eth, when He com - eth to make up His
2. He will gath - er, He will gath - er the gems for His
3. Lit - tle chil - dren, lit - tle chil - dren, who love their Re -

jew - els, all His jew - els, pre - cious jew - els, His loved and His own.
king - dom; all the pure ones, all the bright ones, His loved and His own.
deem - er, are the jew - els, pre - cious jew - els, His loved and His own.

Refrain

Like the stars of the morn - ing, His bright crown a -

dorn - ing, they shall shine in their beau - ty, bright gems for His crown.

WORDS: William Orcutt Cushing, 1856
MUSIC: *Jewels,* George Frederick Root, 1866

8.6.8.5 with Refrain

213 What If It Were Today?

When these things begin to take place...lift up your heads, because your redemption is drawing near. – Luke 21:28 NIV

1. Je - sus is com - ing to earth a - gain; what if it were to - day?
2. Sa - tan's do - min - ion will then be o'er, oh, that it were to - day!
3. Faith - ful and true would He find us here if He should come to - day?

Com - ing in pow - er and love to reign; what if it were to - day?
Sor - row and sigh - ing shall be no more, oh, that it were to - day!
Watch - ing in glad - ness and not in fear, if He should come to - day?

Com - ing to claim His cho - sen Bride, all the re -
Then shall the dead in Christ a - rise, caught up to
Signs of His com - ing mul - ti - ply; morn - ing light

deemed and pu - ri - fied, o - ver this whole earth
meet Him in the skies, when shall these glo - ries
breaks in east - ern sky, watch, for the time is

WORDS: Leila Naylor Morris, 1912
MUSIC: *Second Coming,* Leila Naylor Morris, 1912

Irregular with Refrain

scat - tered wide; what if it were to - day?
meet our eyes? What if it were to - day?
draw - ing nigh, what if it were to - day?

Refrain

Glo - ry, glo - ry! Joy to my heart 'twill bring,
Joy to my heart 'twill bring,

glo - ry, glo - ry! When we shall crown Him King;
When we shall crown Him King;

glo - ry, glo - ry! Haste to pre - pare the way;
Haste to pre - pare the way;

glo - ry, glo - ry! Je - sus will come some day.

214 Is It the Crowning Day?

When the Son of Man comes in His glory...He will sit on His throne in heavenly glory. – Matthew 25:31 NIV

1. Je - sus may come to - day, glad day, glad day! And I would
2. I may go home to - day, glad day, glad day! It seems I
3. Why should I anx - ious be? Glad day, glad day! Lights ap - pear
4. Faith - ful I'll be to - day, glad day, glad day! And I will

see my Friend; dan - gers and trou - bles would end if Je - sus shoul
hear their song; hail to the ra - di - ant throng! If I should go
on the shore, storms will af - fright nev - er - more, for He is "at
free - ly tell why I should love Him so well, for He is my

Refrain

come to - day.
home to - day.
hand" to - day. Glad day, glad day! Is it the crown - ing
all to - day.

day? I'll live for to - day, nor anx - ious be, Je - sus, my Lord I

soon shall see; glad day, glad day! Is it the crown-ing day?

WORDS: George Walker Whitcomb, 1910
MUSIC: *Crowning Day,* Charles Howard Marsh, 1910

Irregular with Refrain

Christ Returneth!

Keep watch because you do not know when the owner of the house will come back. – Mark 13:35 NIV

1. It may be at morn, when the day is a-wak-ing, when
2. It may be at mid-day, it may be at twi-light, it
3. While hosts cry Ho-san-na, from heav-en de-scend-ing, with
4. O joy! O de-light! Should we go with-out dy-ing, no

sun-light through dark-ness and shad-ow is break-ing that Je-sus will
may be, per-chance, that the black-ness of mid-night will burst in-to
glo-ri-fied saints and the an-gels at-tend-ing, with grace on His
sick-ness, no sad-ness, no dread and no cry-ing, caught up through the

come in the full-ness of glo-ry to re-ceive from the world His own.
light in the blaze of His glo-ry, when Je-sus re-ceives His own.
brow, like a ha-lo of glo-ry, will Je-sus re-ceive His own.
clouds with our Lord in-to glo-ry, when Je-sus re-ceives His own.

Refrain

O Lord Je-sus, how long, how long ere we shout the glad song, "Christ re-

turn-eth! Hal-le-lu-jah! Hal-le-lu-jah! A-men. Hal-le-lu-jah! A-men."

WORDS: H. L. Turner, 1878
MUSIC: *Christ Returneth*, James McGranahan, 1906

Irregular with Refrain

216 Come Down, O Love Divine

Now that we are His children, God has sent the Spirit of His Son into our hearts. – Galatians 4:6 CEV

1. Come down, O Love di - vine, seek Thou this soul of mine,
2. O let it free - ly burn, till earth - ly pas - sions turn
3. And so the yearn - ing strong with which the soul will long

and vis - it it with Thine own ar - dor glow - ing;
to dust and ash - es in its heat con - sum - ing;
shall far out - pass the pow'r of hu - man tell - ing;

O Com - fort - er, draw near, with - in my heart ap - pear,
and let Thy glo - r'ous light shine ev - er on my sight,
for none can guess its grace, till He be - come the place

and kin - dle it, Thy ho - ly flame be - stow - ing.
and clothe me round, the while my path il - lum - ing.
where - in the Ho - ly Spir - it makes His dwell - ing.

WORDS: From *Discendi, Amor Santo*, Bianco of Sierra, 15th c.; tr. Richard Frederick Littledale, 1867
MUSIC: *Down Ampney*, Ralph Vaughan Williams, 1906

6.6.11 D

Spirit of God, Descend upon My Heart 217

If we live in the Spirit, let us also walk in the Spirit. – Galatians 5:25 NKJV

1. Spir - it of God, de - scend up - on my heart;
2. Hast Thou not bid us love Thee, God and King?
3. Teach me to feel that Thou art al - ways nigh;
4. Teach me to love Thee as Thine an - gels love,

wean it from earth, through all its puls - es move;
All, all Thine own soul, heart, and strength, and mind!
teach me the strug - gles of the soul to bear,
one ho - ly pas - sion fill - ing all my frame;

stoop to my weak - ness, might - y as Thou art,
I see Thy cross there teach my heart to cling;
to check the ris - ing doubt, the reb - el sigh;
the bap - tism of the heav'n - de - scend - ed Dove

and make me love Thee as I ought to love.
O let me seek Thee, and O let me find!
teach me the pa - tience of un - an - swered prayer.
my heart an al - tar, and Thy love the flame.

WORDS: George Croly, 1854
MUSIC: *Morecambe,* Frederick Cook Atkinson, 1870

10.10.10.10

218 Come, Holy Ghost, Our Souls Inspire

God's Spirit has given us life, and so we should follow the Spirit. – Galatians 5:25 CEV

Leader

1. Come, Ho - ly Ghost, our souls in - spire,
2. Thou the a - noint - ing Spir - it art,
3. Thy bless - ed unc - tion from a - bove
4. En - a - ble with per - pe - tual light,
5. A - noint and cheer our soil - ed face
6. Keep far our foes, give peace at home;
7. Teach us to know the Fa - ther, Son,
8. That, through the a - ges all a - long,

All

and light - en with ce - les - tial fire.
who dost Thy sev'n - fold gifts im - part
is com - fort, life, and fire of love.
the dull - ness of our blind - ed sight.
with the a - bun - dance of Thy grace.
where Thou art Guide, no ill can come.
and Thee of both to be but One,
— this may be our end - less song,

Leader

9. Praise to Thy e - ter - nal mer - it,

All

Fa - ther, Son, and Ho - ly Spir - it.

WORDS: 9th c. Latin hymn; John Cosin, 1627
MUSIC: *Veni Creator,* John Henry Hopkins, Jr., 1865

8.8

Fill Me Now

Be filled with the Spirit. – Ephesians 5:18 CEV

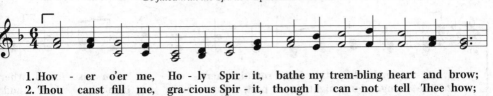

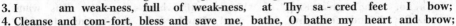

1. Hov - er o'er me, Ho - ly Spir - it, bathe my trem-bling heart and brow;
2. Thou canst fill me, gra-cious Spir - it, though I can-not tell Thee how;
3. I am weak-ness, full of weak-ness, at Thy sa - cred feet I bow;
4. Cleanse and com-fort, bless and save me, bathe, O bathe my heart and brow;

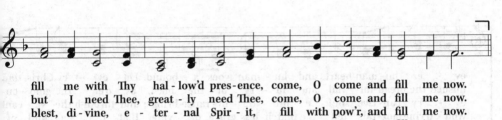

fill me with Thy hal - low'd pres-ence, come, O come and fill me now.
but I need Thee, great - ly need Thee, come, O come and fill me now.
blest, di - vine, e - ter - nal Spir - it, fill with pow'r, and fill me now.
Thou art com - fort - ing and sav - ing, Thou art sweet - ly fill - ing now.

Refrain

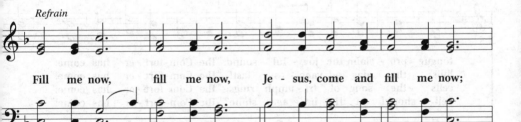

Fill me now, fill me now, Je - sus, come and fill me now;

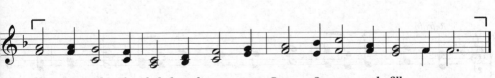

fill me with Thy hal - lowed pres - ence: Come, O come and fill me now.

WORDS: Elwood H. Stokes, 1879
MUSIC: *Fill Me Now*, John R. Sweney, 1879

8.7.8.7 with Refrain

220 The Comforter Has Come!

I will ask the Father to send you the Holy Spirit who will...always be with you. – John 14:16 CEV

1. O spread the tid-ings 'round, wher-ev-er man is found, wher-
2. The long, long night is past; the morn-ing breaks at last; and
3. Lo, the great King of kings, with heal-ing in His wings, to
4. O bound-less love di-vine! How shall this tongue of mine to

ev-er hu-man hearts and hu-man woes a-bound. Let ev-'ry Chris-tian
hushed the dread-ful wail and fu-ry of the blast, as o'er the gold-en
ev-'ry cap-tive soul a full de-liv-'rance brings; and through the va-cant
won-d'ring mor-tals tell the match-less grace di-vine: That I, a child of

tongue pro-claim the joy-ful sound: "The Com-fort-er has come!"
hills the day ad-vanc-es fast! "The Com-fort-er has come!"
cells the song of tri-umph rings: "The Com-fort-er has come!"
hell, should in His im-age shine? "The Com-fort-er has come!"

Refrain

The Com-fort-er has come! The Com-fort-er has come! The Ho-ly

WORDS: Frank Bottome, 1890
MUSIC: *Comforter*, William James Kirkpatrick, 1890

12.12.12.6 with Refrain

Ghost from heav'n, the Fa-ther's prom-ise giv'n, O spread the tid-ings 'round, wher-ev-er man is found: "The Com-fort-er has come!"

Spirit of the Living God

221

The Holy Spirit came on all who heard the message. – Acts 10:44 NIV

Spir-it of the liv-ing God, fall a-fresh on me. Spir-it of the liv-ing God, fall a-fresh on me. Melt me, mold me, fill me, use me. Spir-it of the liv-ing God, fall a-fresh on me.

WORDS: Daniel Iverson, 1926
MUSIC: *Iverson*, Daniel Iverson, 1926

Irregular

Pentecostal Power

All...were filled with the Holy Spirit and began to speak. – Acts 2:4 NIV

1. Lord, as of old at Pen - te - cost Thou didst Thy pow'r dis - play,
2. For might - y works for Thee, pre - pare and strength - en ev - 'ry heart;
3. All self con - sume, all sin de - stroy! With ear - nest zeal en - due
4. Speak, Lord! Be - fore Thy throne we wait, Thy prom - ise we be - lieve,

with cleans - ing, pu - ri - fy - ing flame, de - scend on us to - day.
come, take pos - ses - sion of Thine own, and nev - er - more de - part.
each wait - ing heart to work for Thee; O Lord, our faith re - new!
and will not let Thee go un - til the bless - ing we re - ceive.

Refrain

Lord, send the old - time pow - er, the Pen - te - cos - tal

pow - er! Thy flood - gates of bless - ing on us throw o - pen

wide! Lord, send the old - time pow - er, the Pen - te - cos - tal

WORDS: Charles Hutchinson Gabriel, ca. 1912
MUSIC: *Old-Time Power*, Charles Hutchinson Gabriel, ca. 1912

C.M. with Refrain

pow-er, that sin-ners be con-vert-ed and Thy name glo-ri-fied!

Holy Ghost, with Light Divine   223

"Not by might, nor by power, but by My Spirit," saith the Lord of hosts. – Zechariah 4:6 KJV

1. Ho - ly Ghost, with light di - vine, shine up -
2. Ho - ly Ghost, with pow'r di - vine, cleanse this
3. Ho - ly Ghost, with joy di - vine, cheer this
4. Ho - ly Spir - it, all di - vine, dwell with -

on this heart of mine; chase the shades of
guilt - y heart of mine; long hath sin with -
sad - dened heart of mine; bid my man - y
in this heart of mine; cast down ev - 'ry

night a - way, turn my dark - ness in - to day.
out con - trol held do - min - ion o'er my soul.
woes de - part, heal my wound - ed, bleed - ing heart.
i - dol - throne, reign su - preme and reign a - lone.

WORDS: Andrew Reed, 1817
MUSIC: *Mercy,* Louis Moreau Gottschalk, 1854; adapt. Hubert Platt Main, 1866   7.7.7.7

224 Bring Your Vessels, Not a Few

Go outside, borrow vessels from all your neighbors, empty vessels and not too few. – 2 Kings 4:3-4 ESV

1. Are you long-ing for the full-ness of the bless-ing of the Lord
2. Bring your emp-ty earth-en ves-sels, clean through Je-sus' pre-cious blood.
3. Like the jar of oil un-fail-ing is His grace for-ev-er-more,

in your heart and life to-day? Claim the prom-ise of your Fa-ther, come ac-
Come, ye need-y, one and all, and in hum-ble con-se-cra-tion wait be-
and His love un-chang-ing still, and ac-cord-ing to His prom-ise with the

cord-ing to His Word in the bless-ed old-time way.
fore the throne of God till the Ho-ly Ghost shall fall.
Ho-ly Ghost and pow'r, He will ev-'ry ves-sel fill.

Refrain

He will fill your heart to-day to o-ver-flow - ing, as the
He will fill your heart to o-ver-flow-ing.

Lord com-mand-eth you, "Bring your ves-sels, not a few," He will fill your heart to-
He will fill

WORDS: Lelia Naylor Morris, 1912
MUSIC: *Vessels*, Lelia Naylor Morris, 1912

8.7.7 D with Refrain

day to o-ver-flow - - ing with the Ho-ly Ghost and pow'r.
your heart to o-ver-flow-ing.

Breathe on Me, Breath of God 225

He breathed on them and said, "Receive the Holy Spirit." – John 20:22 NIV

1. Breathe on me, Breath of God, fill me with
2. Breathe on me, Breath of God, un - til my
3. Breathe on me, Breath of God, till I am
4. Breathe on me, Breath of God, so shall I

life a new, that I may love what
heart is pure, un - til with Thee I
whol - ly Thine, till all this earth - ly
nev - er die, but live with Thee the

Thou dost love, and do what Thou wouldst do.
will Thy will, to do and to en - dure.
part of me glows with Thy fire di - vine.
per - fect life of Thine e - ter - ni - ty.

WORDS: Edwin Hatch, 1878
MUSIC: *Trentham*, Robert Jackson, 1888

S.M.

226 Come! Every One Who Is Thirsty

Come, everyone who thirsts, come to the waters. – Isaiah 55:1 ESV

1. Come! Ev-'ry one who is thirst-y in spir-it, Come! Ev-'ry one who is wea-ry and sad, come to the foun-tain, there's full-ness in Je-sus, all that you're long-ing for, come and be glad.

2. Child of the world, are you tired of your bond-age? Wea-ry of earth-joys, so false, so un-true; thirst-ing for God, and His full-ness of bless-ing? List to the prom-ise: A mes-sage for you.

3. Child of the king-dom, be filled with the Spir-it, noth-ing but full-ness thy long-ing can meet, 'tis the en-due-ment for life and for ser-vice; Thine is the prom-ise, so cer-tain, so sweet.

Refrain

"I will pour wa-ter on him who is thirst-y, I will pour floods up-on the dry ground; o-pen your heart for the gift I am

WORDS: Lucy Jane Rider, 1884
MUSIC: *Rider*, Lucy Jane Rider, 1884

11.10.11.10 with Refrain

bring - ing, while you are seek - ing Me, I will be found."

Gracious Spirit, Dwell with Me   227

By the Holy Spirit who dwells within us, guard the good deposit entrusted to you. – 2 Timothy 1:14 ESV

1. Gra - cious Spir - it, dwell with me! I my - self would gra - cious be;
2. Truth - ful Spir - it, dwell with me! I my - self would truth - ful be;
3. Might - y Spir - it, dwell with me! I my - self would might - y be;
4. Ho - ly Spir - it, dwell with me! I my - self would ho - ly be;
5. Ten - der Spir - it, dwell with me! I my - self would ten - der be;

and with words that help me heal would Thy life in mine re - veal;
and with wis - dom kind and clear let Thy life in mine ap - pear;
might - y so as to pre - vail, where un - aid - ed I must fail;
sep - a - rate from sin, I would choose and cher - ish all things good,
shut my heart up like a flower in temp - ta - tion's dark - some hour,

and with ac - tions bold and meek would for Christ my Sav - ior speak.
and with ac - tions broth - er - ly speak my Lord's sin - cer - i - ty.
ev - er, by a migh - ty hope, press - ing on and bear - ing up.
and what - ev - er I can be, give to Him who gave me Thee!
o - pen it when shines the sun, and His love by fra - grance own.

WORDS: Thomas Toke Lynch, 1855
MUSIC: *Redhead 76 (Gethsemane),* from *Church Hymn Tunes, Ancient and Modern,* Richard Redhead, 1853   7.7.7.7.7.7
This tune in a lower key (D), No. 290; (C), No. 158.

228 Blessed Quietness

He shall give you another Comforter, that He may abide with you forever. – John 14:16 KJV

1. Joys are flow-ing like a riv-er, since the Com-fort-er has come;
2. Bring-ing life and health and glad-ness, all a-round this heav'n-ly Guest
3. Like the rain that falls from heav-en; like the sun-light from the sky;
4. See, a fruit-ful field is grow-ing, bless-ed fruit of right-eous-ness;
5. What a won-der-ful sal-va-tion, where we al-ways see His face!

He a-bides with us for-ev-er, makes the trust-ing heart His home.
ban-ished un-be-lief and sad-ness, changed our wea-ri-ness to rest.
so the Ho-ly Ghost is giv-en, com-ing on us from on high.
and the streams of life are flow-ing; in the lone-ly wil-der-ness.
What a per-fect hab-i-ta-tion, what a qui-et rest-ing place!

Refrain

Bless-ed qui-et-ness, ho-ly qui-et-ness, what as-sur-ance in my soul!

On the storm-y sea He speaks peace to me, how the bil-lows cease to roll!

WORDS: Manie Payne Ferguson, ca. 1897
MUSIC: *Blessed Quietness,* W. S. Marshall, ca. 1897; arr. James M. Kirk, 1900

8.7.8.7 with Refrain

Open My Eyes, That I May See

Open Thou mine eyes, that I may behold wondrous things. – Psalm 119:18 KJV

1. O - pen my eyes, that I may see glimps-es of truth Thou hast for me;
2. O - pen my ears, that I may hear voic-es of truth Thou send-est clear;
3. O - pen my mouth, and let me bear glad-ly thewarm truth ev - 'ry - where;

place in my hands the won-der - ful key that shall un - clasp and
and while the wave-notes fall on my ear, ev - 'ry - thing false will
o - pen my heart, and let me pre-pare love with Thy chil - dren,

set me free; si-lent-ly now I wait for Thee, read-y, my God, Thy
dis - ap-pear; si-lent-ly now I wait for Thee, read-y, my God, Thy
thus to share; si-lent-ly now I wait for Thee, read-y, my God, Thy

will to see; o-pen my eyes, il - lu - mine me, Spir - it di - vine!
will to see; o-pen my eyes, il - lu - mine me, Spir - it di - vine!
will to see; o-pen my eyes, il - lu - mine me, Spir - it di - vine!

WORDS: Clara H. Fiske Scott, ca. 1895
MUSIC: *Scott,* Clara H. Fiske Scott, ca. 1895

Irregular

230 O Word of God Incarnate

What God has said isn't only alive and active! It is sharper than any double-edged sword. – Hebrews 4:12 CEV

1. O Word of God in-car-nate, O wis-dom from on high,
2. The Church from You, dear Mas-ter, re-ceived the gift di-vine,
3. O make Your Church, dear Sav-ior, a lamp of bur-nished gold

O truth un-changed, un-chang-ing, O light of our dark sky;
and still that light is lif-ted o'er all the earth to shine.
to bear be-fore the na-tions Your true light, as of old;

we praise You for the ra-diance that from the hal-lowed page,
It is the chart and com-pass that o'er life's surg-ing sea,
O teach Your wan-d'ring pil-grims by this their path to trace,

a lan-tern to our foot-steps, shines on from age to age.
a-mid the rocks and quick-sands, still guides, O Christ, to Thee.
till clouds and dark-ness en-ded, they see You face to face.

WORDS: William Walsham How, 1866
MUSIC: *Munich*, from *Neuvermehrtes Gesangbuch*, Meiningen, 1693; arr. Felix Mendelssohn-Bartholdy, 1847   7.6.7.6 I

Break Thou the Bread of Life 231

Here is the bread that comes down from heaven, which a man may eat and not die. – John 6:50 NIV

1. Break Thou the bread of life, dear Lord, to me,
2. Bless Thou the truth, dear Lord, to me, to me,
3. Thou art the Bread of Life, O Lord, to me,
4. O send Thy Spir-it, Lord, now un-to me,

as Thou didst break the loaves be - side the sea;
as Thou didst bless the bread by Gal - i - lee;
Thy ho - ly Word the truth that sav - eth me;
that He may touch mine eyes, and make me see;

be - yond the sa - cred page I seek Thee, Lord;
then shall all bond - age cease, all fet - ters fall;
give me to eat and live with Thee a - bove;
show me the truth con - cealed with - in Thy Word,

my spir - it pants for Thee, O liv - ing Word.
and I shall find my peace, my all in all.
teach me to love Thy truth, for Thou art love.
and in Thy Book re - vealed I see Thee, Lord.

WORDS: Sts. 1, 2 Mary Artemesia Lathbury, 1877; Sts. 3, 4 Alexander Groves, 1913
MUSIC: *Bread of Life*, William Fiske Sherwin, 1877
This tune in a higher key, No. 327.

6.4.6.4 D

232 Thy Word Have I Hid in My Heart

Your word I have hidden in my heart, that I might not sin against You. – Psalm 119:11 NKJV

1. Thy Word is a lamp to my feet, a light to my path al-
2. For-ev-er, O Lord, is Thy Word es-tab-lished and fixed on
3. At morn-ing, at noon, and at night I ev-er will give Thee
4. Through Him whom Thy Word hath fore-told, the Sav-ior and Morn-ing

way, to guide and to save me from sin, and show me the
high; Thy faith-ful-ness un-to all men a-bid-eth for-
praise; for Thou art my por-tion, O Lord, and shall be through
Star, sal-va-tion and peace have been brought to those who have

Refrain

heav'n-ly way.
ev-er nigh. Thy Word have I hid in my heart, that
all my days! in my heart
strayed a-far.

I might not sin a-gainst Thee, that I might not
a-gainst Thee

WORDS: Adapt. Ernest Orlando Sellers, 1908
MUSIC: *Eola*, Ernest Orlando Sellers, 1908

8.7.8.7 with Refrain

sin, that I might not sin, Thy Word have I hid in my heart.

Holy Bible, Book Divine

233

And beginning with Moses…He explained what was said in all the Scriptures concerning Himself. – Luke 24:27 NIV

1. Ho - ly Bi - ble, Book di - vine, pre - cious
2. Mine to chide me when I rove, mine to
3. Mine to com - fort in dis - tress, suf - f'ring
4. Mine to tell of joys to come, and the

trea - sure, thou art mine; mine to tell me
show a Sav - ior's love; mine thou art to
in this wil - der - ness; mine to show, by
reb - el sin - ner's doom; O thou ho - ly

whence I came; mine to teach me what I am.
guide and guard; mine to pun - ish or re - ward.
liv - ing faith, we can tri - umph o - ver death.
Book di - vine, pre - cious trea - sure, thou art mine.

WORDS: John Burton, Sr., 1803
MUSIC: *Aletta*, William Batchelder Bradbury, 1858

7.7.7.7

234 Wonderful Words of Life

The words I have spoken to you are spirit and they are life. – John 6:63 NIV

1. Sing them o - ver a - gain to me, won - der - ful words of life;
2. Christ, the bless - ed One, gives to all won - der - ful words of life;
3. Sweet - ly ech - o the gos - pel call, won - der - ful words of life;

let me more of their beau - ty see, won - der - ful words of life;
sin - ner, list to the lov - ing call, won - der - ful words of life;
of - fer par - don and peace to all, won - der - ful words of life;

words of life and beau - ty, teach me faith and du - ty:
all so free - ly giv - en, woo - ing us to heav - en:
Je - sus, on - ly Sav - ior, sanc - ti - fy for - ev - er,

Refrain

Beau - ti - ful words, won - der - ful words, won - der - ful words of life;

beau - ti - ful words, won - der - ful words, won - der - ful words of life.

WORDS: Philip Paul Bliss, 1874
MUSIC: *Words of Life*, Philip Paul Bliss, 1874

8.6.8.6.6.6 with Refrain

Joyful, Joyful, We Adore Thee

My lips will shout for joy, when I sing praises to You. – Psalm 71:23 ESV

1. Joy - ful, joy - ful, we a - dore Thee, God of glo - ry Lord of love;
2. All Thy works with joy sur-round Thee, earth and heav'n re - flect Thy rays,
3. Thou art giv - ing and for - giv - ing, ev - er bless - ing, ev - er blest,
4. Mor - tals join the migh - ty cho - rus which the morn - ing stars be - gan;

hearts un - fold like flow'rs be - fore Thee, op'n - ing to the sun a - bove.
stars and an - gels sing a - round Thee, cen - ter of un - bro - ken praise.
well - spring of the joy of liv - ing, o - cean-depth of hap - py rest!
love di - vine is reign - ing o'er us, lead - ing us with mer - cy's hand.

Melt the clouds of sin and sad - ness; drive the dark of doubt a - way;
Field and for - est, vale and moun - tain, flow - 'ry mead - ow, flash - ing sea,
Thou our Fa - ther, Christ our Broth - er, all who live in love are Thine;
Ev - er sing - ing, march we on - ward, vic - tors in the midst of strife;

Giv - er of im - mor - tal glad - ness, fill us with the light of day!
chant - ing bird and flow - ing foun - tain call us to re - joice in Thee.
teach us how to love each oth - er, lift us to the joy di - vine.
joy - ful mu - sic leads us sun - ward in the tri - umph song of life.

WORDS: Henry Jackson Van Dyke, 1907
MUSIC: *Hymn to Joy,* Ludwig van Beethoven, 1824; adapt. Edward Hodges, 1864
This tune in a lower key, No. 190.

8.7.8.7 D

236 All Creatures of Our God and King

Let the heaven and earth praise Him, the seas, and every thing that moveth therein. – Psalm 69:34 KJV

1. All crea-tures of our God and King, lift up your voice and with us
2. Thou rush-ing wind that art so strong, ye clouds that sail in heav'n a-
3. Thou flow-ing wa-ter, pure and clear, make mu-sic for thy Lord to
4. All ye who are of ten-der heart, for-giv-ing oth-ers, take your
5. And Thou, most kind and gen-tle death, wait-ing to hush our lat-est
6. Let all things their Cre-a-tor bless and wor-ship Him in hum-ble-

sing, Al-le-lu-ia! Al-le-lu-ia! Thou burn-ing sun with
long, O praise Him, Al-le-lu-ia! Thou ris-ing morn, in
hear, Al-le-lu-ia! Al-le-lu-ia! Thou fire so mas-ter-
part. Al-le-lu-ia! Al-le-lu-ia! Ye who long pain and
breath, O praise Him, Al-le-lu-ia! Thou lead-est home the
ness! O praise Him, Al-le-lu-ia! Praise, praise the Fa-ther,

gold-en beam, thou sil-ver moon with soft-er gleam:
praise re-joice; ye lights of eve-ning, find a voice!
ful and bright, that giv-est us both warmth and light:
sor-row bear, praise God and on Him cast your care!
child of God, and Christ our Lord the way hath trod:
praise the Son, and praise the Spir-it, Three in One:

Refrain

O praise Him, O praise Him! Al-le-

WORDS: St. Francis of Assisi, ca. 1225; based on Psalm 148; tr. William Henry Draper, 1919
MUSIC: *Lasst Uns Erfreuen,* from *Geistliche Kirchengesäng,* 1623; harm. Ralph Vaughan Williams, 1906   L.M. with Alleluias
This tune in a higher key, No. 19.

lu - ia! Al - le - lu - ia! Al - le - lu - ia!

This Is My Father's World   237

For the world is Mine, and all its fullness. – Psalm 50:12 NKJV

1. This is my Fa - ther's world, and to my lis - t'ning ears, all
2. This is my Fa - ther's world, the birds their car - ols raise; the
3. This is my Fa - ther's world, O let me ne'er for - get that

na - ture sings, and 'round me rings the mu - sic of the spheres.
morn - ing light, the lil - y white de - clare their Mak - er's praise.
though the wrong seems oft so strong, God is the Rul - er yet.

This is my Fa - ther's world, I rest me in the thought of
This is my Fa - ther's world, He shines in all that's fair; in the
This is my Fa - ther's world, the bat - tle is not done; Je -

rocks and trees, of skies and seas; His hand the won - ders wrought.
rus - tling grass I hear Him pass, He speaks to me ev - 'ry - where.
sus who died shall be sat - is - fied, and earth and heav - en be one.

WORDS: Maltbie Davenport Babcock, 1901, alt.
MUSIC: *Tera Patris (Terra Beata),* Franklin Lawrence Sheppard, 1915   S.M.D.

238 Praise the Lord! Ye Heavens, Adore Him

Sing for joy, O heavens, and exult, O earth; break forth, O mountains, into singing! – Isaiah 49:13 ESV

1. Praise the Lord! Ye heav'ns, a- dore Him; praise Him, an- gels in the height. Sun and moon re- joice before Him; praise Him, all ye stars of light. Praise the Lord, for He hath spo- ken; worlds His might- y voice o- beyed. Laws which He hath spo- ken;

2. Praise the Lord, for He is glo- rious; nev- er shall His prom- ise fail. God hath made His saints vic- to- rious; sin and death shall not pre- vail. Praise the God of our sal- va- tion! Hosts on high, His pow'r pro- claim; heav'n and

3. Wor- ship, hon- or, glo- ry, bless- ing, Lord, we of- fer un- to Thee. Young and old, Thy praise ex- press- ing, in glad hom- age bend the knee. All the saints in heav'n a- dore Thee; we would bow before Thy throne. As Thine

WORDS: Sts. 1, 2 anon., *Psalms, Hymns and Anthems of the Foundling Hospital*, 1796; St. 3 Edward Osler, 1836
MUSIC: *Hyfrydol*, Rowland Hugh Prichard, 1830; harm. *The English Hymnal*, 1906

8.7.8.7 I

This tune in a lower key (E♭), No. 42; another harmonization, in a lower key (D), No. 248.

nev - er shall be bro - ken for their guid - ance He hath made.
earth and all cre - a - tion, laud and mag - ni - fy His name
an - gels serve be - fore Thee, so on earth Thy will be done.

For the Beauty of the Earth 239

Holy, holy, holy is the Lord of hosts; the whole earth is full of His glory. – Isaiah 6:3 ESV

1. For the beau - ty of the earth, for the glo - ry of the skies,
2. For the beau - ty of each hour of the day and of the night,
3. For the joy of hu - man love, broth - er, sis - ter, par - ent, child,
4. For each per - fect gift of Thine, to the world so free - ly giv'n,
5. For Thy Church, that ev - er - more lift - eth ho - ly hands a - bove,

for the love which from our birth o - ver and a - round us lies;
hill and vale, and tree and flow'r, sun and moon, and stars of light;
friends on earth and friends a - bove, for all gen - tle thoughts and mild;
grac - es hu - man and di - vine, flow'rs of earth and buds of heav'n;
of - f'ring up on ev - 'ry shore her pure sac - ri - fice of love;

Refrain

Lord of all, to Thee we raise this our hymn of grate - ful praise.

WORDS: *Lyra Eucharisticia,* Folliot Sandford Pierpoint, 1864, alt.
MUSIC: *Dix,* Conrad Kocher, 1838; arr. William Henry Monk, 1865   7.7.7.7 with Refrain
This tune in a higher key, No. 595.

240   The Spacious Firmament

The heavens declare the glory of God; and the firmament shows His handiwork. – Psalm 19:1 NKJV

1. The spacious firmament on high, with all the blue ethereal sky, and spangled heav'ns, a shining frame, their great Original pro-

2. Soon as the evening shades prevail, the moon takes up the wondrous tale; and nightly to the listening earth repeats the story of her

3. What though in solemn silence all move 'round the dark terrestrial ball? What though no real voice nor sound amid their radiant orbs be

WORDS: Joseph Addison, 1712; based on Psalm 19
MUSIC: *Creation,* from *The Creation,* Franz Joseph Haydn, 1798

L.M.D.

claim. th'un - wea - ried sun, from day to
birth; while all the stars that 'round her
found? In rea - son's ear they all re -

day, does his Cre - a - tor's pow'r dis -
burn, and all the plan - ets in their
joice, and ut - ter forth a glo - r'ous

play; and pub - lish - es to ev - 'ry
turn, con - firm the ti - dings as they
voice for - ev - er sing - ing as they

land the work of an Al - migh - ty hand.
roll, and spread the truth from pole to pole.
shine, "The hand that made us is di - vine."

241 I Sing the Mighty Power of God

For God is the King of all the earth; sing ye praises with understanding. – Psalm 47:7 KJV

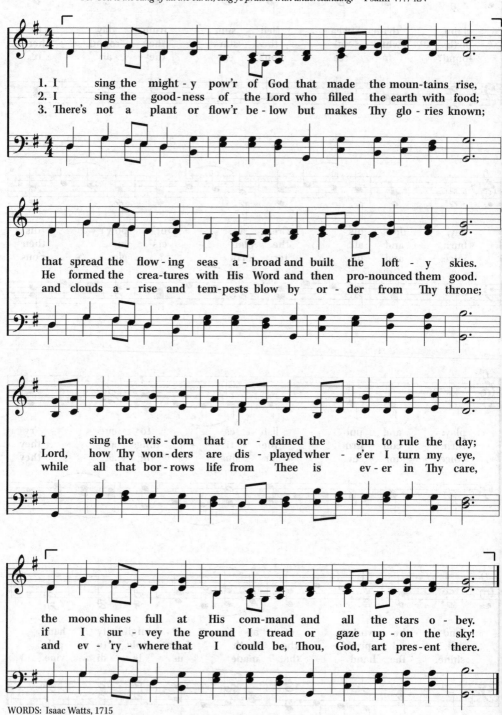

1. I sing the might-y pow'r of God that made the moun-tains rise,
2. I sing the good-ness of the Lord who filled the earth with food;
3. There's not a plant or flow'r be - low but makes Thy glo - ries known;

that spread the flow-ing seas a - broad and built the loft - y skies.
He formed the crea-tures with His Word and then pro-nounced them good.
and clouds a - rise and tem-pests blow by or - der from Thy throne;

I sing the wis - dom that or - dained the sun to rule the day;
Lord, how Thy won - ders are dis - played wher - e'er I turn my eye,
while all that bor - rows life from Thee is ev - er in Thy care,

the moon shines full at His com-mand and all the stars o - bey.
if I sur - vey the ground I tread or gaze up - on the sky!
and ev - 'ry - where that I could be, Thou, God, art pres-ent there.

WORDS: Isaac Watts, 1715
MUSIC: *Ellacombe,* from *Gesangbuch der H.W.K. Hofkapelle,* 1784; harm. William Henry Monk, 1868
This tune in a higher key, No. 186.

C.M.D.

I Sing the Mighty Power of God

For God is the King of all the earth; sing ye praises with understanding. – Psalm 47:7 KJV

1. I sing the might-y pow'r of God that made the moun-tains rise,
2. I sing the good-ness of the Lord who filled the earth with food;
3. There's not a plant or flow'r be - low but makes Thy glo - ries known;

that spread the flow - ing seas a - broad and built the loft - y skies.
He formed the crea - tures with His Word and then pro-nounced them good.
and clouds a - rise and tem - pests blow by or - der from Thy throne;

I sing the wis - dom that or-dained the sun to rule the day;
Lord, how Thy won - ders are dis-played wher - e'er I turn my eye,
while all that bor - rows life from Thee is ev - er in Thy care,

the moon shines full at His com-mand and all the stars o - bey.
if I sur - vey the ground I tread or gaze up - on the sky!
and ev - 'ry-where that I could be, Thou, God, art pres - ent there.

WORDS: Isaac Watts, 1715
MUSIC: *Forest Green*, traditional English melody, n.d.; arr. Ralph Vaughan Williams, 1906
This tune in a higher key, No. 96.

C.M.D.

243 All Things Bright and Beautiful

God saw everything that He had made, and behold, it was very good. – Genesis 1:31 ESV

Refrain

All things bright and beau - ti - ful, all crea - tures great and small,

all things wise and won - der - ful: The Lord God made them all. *Fine*

1. Each lit - tle flow'r that o - pens, each lit - tle bird that sings,
2. The pur - ple - head - ed moun - tain, the riv - er run - ning by,
3. The cold wind in the win - ter, the pleas - ant sum - mer sun,
4. The tall trees in the green-wood, the mead - ows where we play
5. He gave us eyes to see them, and lips that we might tell

D.C.

He made their glow - ing col - ors, He made their ti - ny wings.
the sun - set and the morn - ing, that bright - ens up the sky.
the ripe fruits in the gar - den: He made them ev - 'ry one.
the rush - es by the wa - ter we gath - er ev - 'ry day.
how great is God Al - might - y, who has made all things well.

WORDS: *Hymns for Little Children*, Cecil Frances Humphreys Alexander, 1848
MUSIC: *Royal Oak*, 17th c. English melody; arr. Martin Shaw, 1915

7.6.7.6 with Refrain

All Things Bright and Beautiful 244

God saw everything that He had made, and behold, it was very good. – Genesis 1:31 ESV

Refrain

All things bright and beau-ti-ful, all crea-tures great and small,

all things wise and won-der-ful: The Lord God made them all.

Fine

1. Each lit-tle flow'r that o - pens, each lit-tle bird that sings,
2. The pur-ple-head-ed moun - tain, the riv-er run-ning by,
3. The cold wind in the win - ter, the pleas-ant sum-mer sun,
4. The tall trees in the green - wood, the mead-ows where we play,
5. He gave us eyes to see them, and lips that we might tell

D.C.

He made their glow-ing col - ors, He made their ti-ny wings.
the sun-set and the morn - ing, that bright-ens up the sky.
the ripe fruits in the gar - den: He made them ev-'ry one.
the rush-es by the wa - ter we gath-er ev-'ry day.
how great is God Al-migh - ty, who has made all things well.

WORDS: *Hymns for Little Children*, Cecil Frances Humphreys Alexander, 1848
MUSIC: *All Things Bright and Beautiful*, William Henry Monk, 1868

7.6.7.6 with Refrain

245 Let the Whole Creation Cry

Let them praise the name of the Lord, for He commanded and they were created. – Psalm 148:5 NKJV

1. Let the whole cre - a - tion cry, Al - le - lu - ia!
2. Praise Him, all ye hosts a - bove, Al - le - lu - ia!
3. War - riors fight - ing for the Lord, Al - le - lu - ia!
4. Men and wom - en, young and old, Al - le - lu - ia!

Glo - ry to the Lord on high! Al - le - lu - ia!
Ev - er bright and fair in love! Al - le - lu - ia!
Proph - ets burn - ing with His Word, Al - le - lu - ia!
Raise the an - them man - i - fold; Al - le - lu - ia!

Heav'n and earth, a - wake and sing, Al - le - lu - ia!
Sun and moon, lift up your voice, Al - le - lu - ia!
Those to whom the arts be - long, Al - le - lu - ia!
And let chil - dren's hap - py hearts, Al - le - lu - ia!

God is God and there - fore King, Al - le - lu - ia!
Night and stars in God re - joice, Al - le - lu - ia!
Add their voic - es to the song, Al - le - lu - ia!
In this wor - ship bear their parts: Al - le - lu - ia!

WORDS: Stopford Augustus Brooke, 1881; based on Psalm 148
MUSIC: *Llanfair*, Robert Williams, 1817
Another harmonization of this tune, No. 25, and in a higher key, No. 193.

7.7.7.7 with Alleluias

Arise, My Soul, Arise!

He is able to save completely...because He always lives to intercede for them.. – Hebrews 7:25 NIV

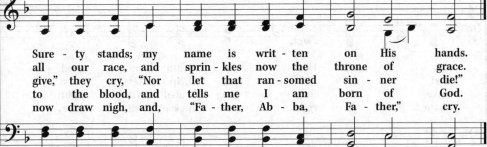

1. A - rise, my soul, a - rise! Shake off thy guilt - y fears.
2. He ev - er lives a - bove for me to in - ter - cede,
3. Five bleed - ing wounds He bears, re - ceived on Cal - va - ry.
4. The Fa - ther hears Him pray, His dear A - noint - ed One;
5. My God is rec - on - ciled; His par - d'ning voice I hear.

The bleed - ing Sac - ri - fice in my be - half ap - pears.
His all - re - deem - ing love, His pre - cious blood to plead.
They pour ef - fec - tual prayers; they strong - ly plead for me.
He can - not turn a - way the pres - ence of His Son.
He owns me for His child; I can no long - er fear.

Be - fore the throne my Sure - ty[1] stands, be - fore the throne my
His blood a - toned for all our race, His blood a - toned for
"For - give him, O, for - give," they cry, "For - give him, O, for -
His Spir - it an - swers to the blood, His Spir - it an - swers
With con - fi - dence I now draw nigh, with con - fi - dence I

Sure - ty stands; my name is writ - ten on His hands.
all our race, and sprin - kles now the throne of grace.
give," they cry, "Nor let that ran - somed sin - ner die!"
to the blood, and tells me I am born of God.
now draw nigh, and, "Fa - ther, Ab - ba, Fa - ther," cry.

1. Surety: One who becomes legally liable for another's debt

WORDS: *Hymns and Sacred Poems,* Charles Wesley, 1742
MUSIC: *Lenox,* from *The Chorister's Companion,* Lewis Edson, Sr., 1782

6.6.6.6.8.8 with Repeat

247 — And Can It Be?

God showed how much He loved us by having Christ die for us, even though we were sinful. – Romans 5:8 CEV

1. And can it be that I should gain an
   in-terest in the Sav-ior's blood!
   Died He for me who caused His pain! For
   me, who Him to death pur-sued?

2. He left His Fa-ther's throne a-bove, so
   free, so in-fi-nite His grace.
   Emp-tied Him-self of all but love, and
   bled for Ad-am's help-less race.

3. Long my im-pris-oned spir-it lay, fast
   bound in sin and na-ture's night;
   Thine eye dif-fused a quick-'ning ray;
   woke, the dun-geon flamed with light;

4. No con-dem-na-tion now I dread; Jesus, and all in Him, is mine;
   a-live in Him, my liv-ing Head, and
   clothed in right-eous-ness di-vine,

WORDS: *Psalms and Hymns*, Charles Wesley, 1739
MUSIC: *Sagina*, Thomas Campbell, 1825

8.8.8.8 D

A - maz - ing love! How can it be that
'Tis mer - cy all, im - mense and free, for
my chains fell off, my heart was free, I
bold I ap - proach the e - ter - nal throne, and

Thou, my God, shouldst die for me? A -
O my God, it found out me! 'Tis
rose, went forth, and fol - lowed Thee. My
claim the crown, through Christ, my own. Bold

maz - ing love! How can it be that
mer - cy all, im - mense and free, for
chains fell off, my heart was free, I
I ap - proach th'e - ter - nal throne, and

A - maz - ing love! How can it be
'Tis mer - cy all, im - mense and free,
My chains fell off, my heart was free,
Bold I ap - proach th'e - ter - nal throne,

Thou, my God, shouldst die for me?
O my God, it found out me!
rose, went forth, and fol - lowed Thee.
claim the crown, through Christ, my own.

that Thou, my God,
for O my God,
I rose, went forth,
and claim the crown,

Our Great Savior

Many..."sinners" came and ate with Him. – Matthew 9:10 NIV

1. Je - sus, what a Friend for sin - ners! Je - sus! Lov - er
2. Je - sus, what a strength in weak - ness! Let me hide my
3. Je - sus, what a help in sor - row! While the bil - low
4. Je - sus, what a Guide and Keep - er! While the tem - pest
5. Je - sus! I do now re - ceive Him, more than all in

of my soul; friends may fail me, foes as - sail me,
self in Him; tempt - ed, tried, and some - times fail - ing,
o'er me roll, e - ven when my heart is break - ing,
still is high, storms a - bout me, night o'er-takes me,
Him I find; He hath grant - ed me for - give - ness,

Refrain

He, my Sav - ior, makes me whole.
He, my strength, my vic - t'ry wins.
He, my com - fort, helps my soul. Hal - le - lu - jah! What a
He, my Pi - lot, hears my cry.
I am His, and He is mine.

Sav - ior! Hal - le - lu - jah! What a friend! Sav - ing, help - ing,

WORDS: John Wilbur Chapman, 1810
MUSIC: *Hyfrydol,* Rowland Hugh Prichard, ca. 1830; arr. Robert Harkness, 1910
Another harmonization of this tune in a higher key (E♭), No. 42 and (F) No. 238.

8.7.8.7 with Refrain

keep - ing, lov - ing, He is with me to the end.

There Is a Redeemer 249

Christ Jesus...is, our righteousness, holiness and redemption. – 1 Corinthians 1:30 NIV

1. There is a Re - deem - er: Je - sus, God's own Son;
2. Je - sus, my Re - deem - er: Name a - bove all names;
3. When I stand in glo - ry, I will see His face;

pre - cious Lamb of God, Mes - si - ah, Ho - ly One.
pre - cious Lamb of God, Mes - si - ah, Hope for sin - ners slain.
there I'll serve my King for - ev - er in that ho - ly place.

Refrain

Thank You, O my Fa - ther, for giv - ing us Your Son, and

leav - ing Your Spir - it till the work on earth is done.

WORDS: Melody Green, 1982
MUSIC: *There Is a Redeemer*, Melody Green, 1982
Irregular with Refrain

250 O Boundless Salvation

You also were included in Christ when you heard the word of truth, the gospel of your salvation. – Ephesians 1:13 NIV

1. O bound - less sal - va - tion, deep o - cean of love! O
2. My sins, they are man - y, their stains are so deep, and
3. The tide now is flow - ing; I'm touch - ing the wave, I
4. And now, Hal - le - lu - jah! The rest of my days shal

full - ness of mer - cy Christ brought from a - bove, the
bit - ter the tears of re - morse that I weep; but
hear the loud call of "the Might - y to save." My
glad - ly be spent in pro - mot - ing His praise, who

whole world re - deem - ing, so rich and so free, now
weep - ing is use - less Thou great crim - son sea, Thy
faith's grow - ing bold - er, de - liv - ered I'll be! I
o - pened His bos - om to pour out this sea of

flow - ing for sin - ners, now flow - ing for sin - ners, now
wa - ters can cleanse me, Thy wa - ters can cleanse me, Thy
plunge 'neath the wa - ters, I plunge 'neath the wa - ters, I
bound - less sal - va - tion, of bound - less sal - va - tion, of

WORDS: William Booth, 1893
MUSIC: *Boundless Salvation*, attr. J. Ellis, 19th c.

11.11.11.11 with Repe

flow - ing for sin - ners: Come, roll o - ver me!
wa - ters can cleanse me. Come, roll o - ver me!
plunge 'neath the wa - ters: They roll o - ver me!
bound - less sal - va - tion, for you and for me!

Jesus, Thy Blood and Righteousness 251

Christ offered His life's blood, so that by faith in Him we could come to God. – Romans 3:25 CEV

1. Je - sus, Thy blood and righ - teous - ness my beau - ty are, my
2. Bold shall I stand in Thy great day; for who aught to my
3. When from the dust of death I rise to claim my man - sion
4. Je - sus, be end - less praise to Thee, whose bound - less mer - cy
5. O let the dead now hear Thy voice; now bid Thy ban - ished

glo - r'ous dress; 'midst flam - ing worlds, in these ar -
charge shall lay? Ful - ly ab - solved through these I
in the skies, ev'n then this shall be all my
hath for me; for me a full a - tone - ment
ones re - joice; their beau - ty this, their glo - r'ous

rayed, with joy shall I lift up my head.
am from sin and fear, from guilt and shame.
plea, Je - sus hath lived, hath died, for me.
made, and ev - er - last - ing ran - som paid.
dress, Je - sus, Thy blood and righ - teous - ness.

WORDS: Nicholas Ludwig von Zinzendorf, 1739; *Hymns and Sacred Poems,* 1740; tr. John Wesley, 1740, alt.
MUSIC: *Germany (Gardiner),* from William Gardiner's *Sacred Melodies,* 1815   L.M.

Baruch Hashem Adonai

Blessed Be the Name of the Lord

Blessed be Your glorious name, which is exalted above all blessing and praise. – Nehemiah 9:5 ESV

1. Who am I to be part of Your peo-ple, the ones that are called by Your name? Could I be cho-sen as one of Your own, could it be that our blood is the same? How can a strang-er, a rem-nant of na-tions be-long to the roy - al line? You showed Your grace when the branch - es were bro-ken, and I graft-ed in - to the Vine.

2. How could You show me such boun-ti-ful mer-cy by tak-ing the life of the Lamb? Your love is great-er that I can i - mag-ine, I bless You with all that I am. Praise to You, Je - sus, the veil has been part-ed, and what once was se - cret is known. Now I can cry to you, Ab - ba, my Fa - ther, and praise You as one of Your own.

WORDS: Dawn Rodgers and Tricia Walker, 1982
MUSIC: *Finto*, Dawn Rodgers and Tricia Walker, 1982; arr. Eric Wyse, 2005

Irregular with Refrain

Bar - uch Ha-shem A-do - nai. Bar - uch Ha-shem A-do - nai.

Bless - ed be the name of the Lord. Bar - uch Ha - shem A-do - nai.

For God So Loved Us 253

For God so loved the world that He gave His one and only Son. – John 3:16 NIV

1. For God so loved us, He sent the Sav - ior; for God so
2. He sent the Sav - ior, the blest Re - deem - er; He sent the
3. He bade me wel - come, O Word of mer - cy; He bade me
4. Glo - ry and hon - or, O love e - ter - nal, to Thee be

Refrain

loved us, and loves me too.
Sav - ior to set me free.
wel - come, O voice di - vine. Love so un - end - ing! I'll
giv - en while life shall last.

sing Thy prais - es, God loves His chil - dren, loves e - ven me.

WORDS: August Rische, 1856; tr. Sts. 1-3 Esther Bergen, 1956; St. 4 and Refrain, *The Hymnbook*, 1960
MUSIC: *Gott Ist Die Liebe*, Thüringer melody, ca. 1840

5.5.5.4 with Refrain

254 Here Is Love, Vast As the Ocean

God gave Jesus to die for our sins, and He raised Him to life, so that we would be made acceptable to God. – Romans 4:25 CEV

1. Here is love, vast as the o-cean, lov-ing-kind-ness as the flood,
2. On the mount of cru-ci-fix-ion, foun-tains o-pened deep and wide;
3. Let me all Your love ac-cept-ing love You ev-er all my days.

when the Prince of life, our ran-som, shed for us His pre-cious blood.
through the flood-gates of God's mer-cy flowed a vast and gra-cious tide.
Let me seek Your king-dom on-ly, all my life be to Your praise.

Who His love will not re-mem-ber? Who can cease to sing His praise?
Grace and love, like might-y riv-ers, poured in-ces-sant from a-bove,
You a-lone shall be my glo-ry, noth-ing in the world I see.

He can nev-er be for-got-ten, through-out heav'n's e-ter-nal days.
and heav'n's peace and per-fect jus-tice kissed a guilt-y world in love.
You have cleansed and sanc-ti-fied me, You a-lone have set me free.

WORDS: Sts. 1-2 William Rees, 19th c.; St. 3 anon.; tr. William Edwards, 1900
MUSIC: *Cymraeg*, Robert Lowry, 1876

8.7.8.7 D

Nothing but the Blood

No sins can be forgiven unless blood is offered. – Hebrews 9:22 CEV

1. What can wash a - way my sin? Noth-ing but the blood of Je - sus;
2. For my par-don, this I see, noth-ing but the blood of Je - sus;
3. Noth - ing can for sin a - tone, noth-ing but the blood of Je - sus;
4. This is all my hope and peace, noth-ing but the blood of Je - sus;

what can make me whole a - gain? Noth-ing but the blood of Je - sus.
for my cleans-ing, this my plea, noth-ing but the blood of Je - sus.
naught of good that I have done, noth-ing but the blood of Je - sus.
this is all my righ - teous - ness, noth-ing but the blood of Je - sus.

Refrain

Oh! Pre - cious is the flow that makes me white as snow;

no oth - er fount I know, noth-ing but the blood of Je - sus.

WORDS: Robert Lowry, 1876
MUSIC: *Plainfield*, Robert Lowry, 1876

7.8.7.8 with Refrain

256   Are You Washed in the Blood?

They have washed their robes in the blood of the Lamb and have made them white. – Revelation 7:14 CEV

1. Have you been to Je-sus for the cleans-ing pow'r? Are you
2. Are you walk-ing dai-ly by the Sav-ior's side? Are you
3. When the Bride-groom com-eth will your robes be white? Are you
4. Lay a-side the gar-ments that are stained with sin, and be

washed in the blood of the Lamb?   Are you ful-ly trust-ing in His
washed in the blood of the Lamb?   Do you rest each mo-ment in the
washed in the blood of the Lamb?   Will your soul be read-y for the
washed in the blood of the Lamb;   there's a foun-tain flow-ing for the

grace this hour? Are you washed in the blood of the Lamb?
Cru-ci-fied? Are you washed in the blood of the Lamb?
man-sions bright, and be washed in the blood of the Lamb?
soul un-clean, O be washed in the blood of the Lamb.

Refrain

Are you washed in the blood,
Are you washed in the blood,   in the blood,   in the

soul-cleans-ing blood of the Lamb?   Are your gar-ments spot-less?
of the Lamb?

WORDS: Elisha Albright Hoffman, 1878
MUSIC: *Washed in the Blood*, Elisha Albright Hoffman, 1878

11.9.11.9 with Refrai

Are they white as snow? Are you washed in the blood of the Lamb?

What a Wonderful Savior! 257

God was in Christ, offering peace and forgiveness to the people of this world. – 2 Corinthians 5:19 CEV

1. Christ has for sin a - tone - ment made: What a won - der - ful Sav - ior!
2. I praise Him for the cleans - ing blood: What a won - der - ful Sav - ior!
3. He cleansed my heart from all its sin: What a won - der - ful Sav - ior!
4. He gives me o - ver - com - ing pow'r: What a won - der - ful Sav - ior!

We are re - deemed, the price is paid: What a won - der - ful Sav - ior!
That rec - on - ciled my soul to God: What a won - der - ful Sav - ior!
And now He reigns and rules there - in: What a won - der - ful Sav - ior!
And tri - umph in each try - ing hour: What a won - der - ful Sav - ior!

Refrain

What a won - der - ful Sav - ior is Je - sus, my Je - sus!

What a won - der - ful Sav - ior is Je - sus, my Lord!

WORDS: Elisha Albright Hoffman, 1891
MUSIC: *Benton Harbor,* Elisha Albright Hoffman, 1891

8.7.8.7 with Refrain

258 There Is Power in the Blood

They overcame him by the blood of the Lamb and by the word of their testimony. – Revelation 12:11 NIV

1. Would you be free from your bur-den of sin? There's pow'r in the blood,
2. Would you be free from your pas-sion and pride? There's pow'r in the blood,
3. Would you be whit-er, much whit-er than snow? There's pow'r in the blood,
4. Would you do ser-vice for Je-sus, your King? There's pow'r in the blood,

pow'r in the blood; would you o'er e-vil a vic-to-ry win? There's
pow'r in the blood; come for a cleans-ing to Cal-va-ry's tide. There's
pow'r in the blood; sin-stains are lost in its life-giv-ing flow. There's
pow'r in the blood; would you live dai-ly His prais-es to sing? There's

Refrain

won-der-ful pow'r in the blood.
won-der-ful pow'r in the blood. There is pow'r, pow'r, won-der-work-ing
won-der-ful pow'r in the blood. There is pow'r,
won-der-ful pow'r in the blood.

pow'r in the blood of the Lamb. There is pow'r, pow'r,
in the blood of the Lamb. There is pow'r,

won-der-work-ing pow'r in the pre-cious blood of the Lamb.

WORDS: Lewis Ellington Jones, 1899
MUSIC: *Power in the Blood*, Lewis Ellington Jones, 1899

10.9.10.8 with Refrain

There Is a Fountain

And God was pleased for Him to make peace by sacrificing His blood on the cross. – Colossians 1:20 CEV

1. There is a foun-tain filled with blood drawn from Em - man - uel's veins,
2. The dy - ing thief re - joiced to see that foun - tain in his day,
3. Dear dy - ing Lamb, Thy pre - cious blood shall nev - er lose its pow'r,
4. E'er since, by faith, I saw the stream Thy flow - ing wounds sup - ply,
5. When this poor lisp-ing, stam-m'ring tongue lies si - lent in the grave,

and sin - ners plunged be - neath that flood lose all their guilt - y stains;
and there may I, though vile as he, wash all my sins a - way;
till all the ran - somed Church of God be saved to sin no more;
re - deem - ing love has been my theme and shall be till I die;
then in a no - bler, sweet - er song I'll sing Thy pow'r to save;

lose all their guilt - y stains, lose all their guilt - y stains;
wash all my sins a - way, wash all my sins a - way;
be saved to sin no more, be saved to sin no more;
and shall be till I die, and shall be till I die;
I'll sing Thy pow'r to save, I'll sing Thy pow'r to save;

and sin - ners plunged be - neath that flood lose all their guilt - y stains.
and there may I, though vile as he, wash all my sins a - way.
till all the ran - somed Church of God be saved to sin no more.
re - deem - ing love has been my theme and shall be till I die.
then in a no - bler, sweet - er song I'll sing Thy pow'r to save.

WORDS: William Cowper, 1772
MUSIC: *Cleansing Fountain,* traditional American camp meeting melody, 19th c.; arr. Lowell Mason, 1830

C.M.D.

260 When I See the Blood

When I see the blood, I will pass over you. – Exodus 12:13 ESV

1. Christ our Re - deem - er died on the cross, died for the sin - ner,
2. Chief - est of sin - ners, Je - sus will save; all He has prom - ised,
3. Judg - ment is com - ing, all will be there, each one re - ceiv - ing
4. O great com - pas - sion! O bound - less love! O lov - ing kind - ness,

paid all his due; sprin - kle your soul with the blood of the Lamb,
that He will do; wash in the foun - tain o - pened for sin,
just - ly his due; hide in the sav - ing sin - cleans - ing blood,
faith - ful and true! Find peace and shel - ter un - der the blood,

Refrain

and I will pass, will pass o - ver you. When I see the
and I will pass, will pass o - ver you. When I
and I will pass, will pass o - ver you.
and I will pass, will pass o - ver you.

blood, when I see the blood, when I see the
see the blood, when I see the blood, when I

blood, I will pass, I will pass o - ver you.
see the blood, o - ver you.

WORDS: John G. Foote, 19th c.
MUSIC: *When I See the Blood*, John G. Foote, 19th c.

9.9.10.9 with Refrain

The Cleansing Wave

On that day there shall be a fountain...to cleanse them from sin and uncleanness. – Zechariah 13:1 ESV

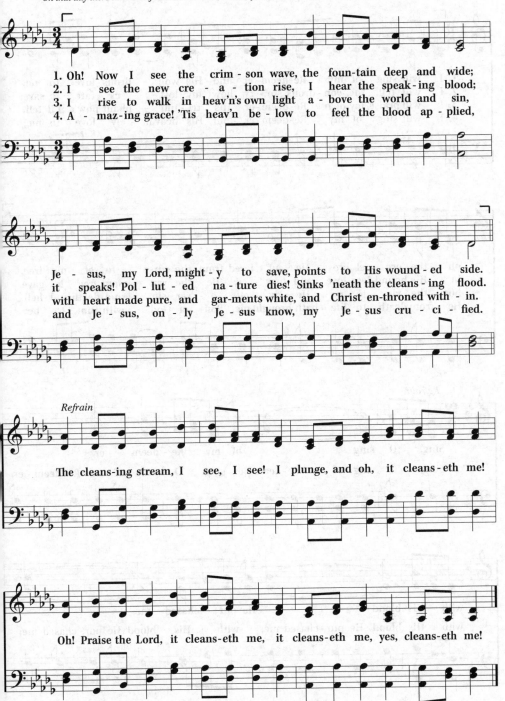

1. Oh! Now I see the crim-son wave, the foun-tain deep and wide;
2. I see the new cre - a - tion rise, I hear the speak-ing blood;
3. I rise to walk in heav'n's own light a - bove the world and sin,
4. A - maz-ing grace! 'Tis heav'n be - low to feel the blood ap - plied,

Je - sus, my Lord, might - y to save, points to His wound - ed side.
it speaks! Pol - lut - ed na - ture dies! Sinks 'neath the cleans - ing flood.
with heart made pure, and gar-ments white, and Christ en-throned with - in.
and Je - sus, on - ly Je - sus know, my Je - sus cru - ci - fied.

Refrain

The cleans-ing stream, I see, I see! I plunge, and oh, it cleans-eth me!

Oh! Praise the Lord, it cleans-eth me, it cleans-eth me, yes, cleans-eth me!

WORDS: Phoebe Worrell Palmer, 1871
MUSIC: *Knapp*, Phoebe Palmer Knapp, 1871

C. M. with Refrain

262 I Will Sing of My Redeemer

You, O Lord, are our Father, our Redeemer from of old is Your name. – Isaiah 63:16 ESV

1. I will sing of my Re-deem-er and His won - drous love to me;
2. I will tell the won-drous sto - ry, how my lost es - tate to save;
3. I will praise my dear Re-deem-er, His tri - um - phant pow'r I'll tell,
4. I will sing of my Re-deem-er, and His heav'n - ly love to me;

on the cru - el cross He suf - fered from the curse to set me free.
in His bound-less love and mer - cy, He the ran - som free-ly gave.
how the vic - to - ry He giv - eth o - ver sin and death and hell.
He from death to life hath brought me, Son of God, with Him to be.

Refrain

Sing, O sing of my Re-deem-er,
Sing, O sing of my Re-deem-er, sing, O sing of my Re-deem-er,

with His blood He pur - chased me;
with His blood He pur-chased me, with His blood He pur-chased me;

WORDS: Philip Paul Bliss, 1876
MUSIC: *My Redeemer,* James McGranahan, 1877

8.7.8.7 with Refrain

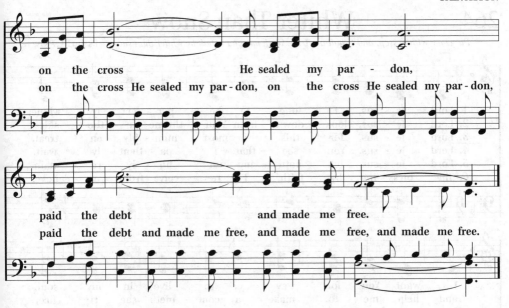

on the cross He sealed my par - don,
on the cross He sealed my par - don, on the cross He sealed my par - don,

paid the debt and made me free.
paid the debt and made me free, and made me free, and made me free.

I Am Not Skilled to Understand 263

Christ Jesus, who died...who was raised to life–is at the right hand of God and is also interceding for us. – Romans 8:34 NIV

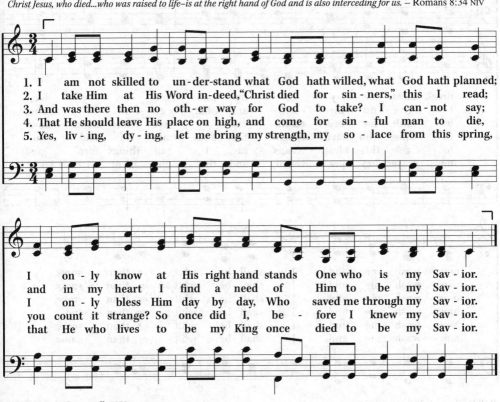

1. I am not skilled to un-der-stand what God hath willed, what God hath planned;
2. I take Him at His Word in-deed, "Christ died for sin - ners," this I read;
3. And was there then no oth-er way for God to take? I can-not say;
4. That He should leave His place on high, and come for sin - ful man to die,
5. Yes, liv - ing, dy - ing, let me bring my strength, my so - lace from this spring,

I on - ly know at His right hand stands One who is my Sav - ior.
and in my heart I find a need of Him to be my Sav - ior.
I on - ly bless Him day by day, Who saved me through my Sav - ior.
you count it strange? So once did I, be - fore I knew my Sav - ior.
that He who lives to be my King once died to be my Sav - ior.

WORDS: Dora Greenwell, 1873
MUSIC: *Greenwell*, William James Kirkpatrick, 1885

8.8.8.7

264 Whiter Than Snow

Purge me with hyssop, and I shall be clean. Wash me, and I shall be whiter than snow. – Psalm 51:7 KJV

1. Lord Je - sus, I long to be per - fect - ly whole;
2. Lord Je - sus, look down from Your throne in the skies,
3. Lord Je - sus, for this I most hum - bly en - treat,
4. Lord Je - sus, You see that I pa - tient - ly wait,
5. Lord Je - sus, let noth - ing un - ho - ly re - main,
6. The bless - ing by faith, I re - ceive from a - bove;

I want You for - ev - er to live in my soul,
and help me to make a com - plete sac - ri - fice;
I wait, bless - ed Lord, at Your cru - ci - fied feet;
come now, and with - in me a new heart cre - ate;
ap - ply Thine own blood and ex - tract ev - 'ry stain;
O glo - ry! My soul is made per - fect in love;

break down ev - 'ry i - dol, cast out ev - 'ry foe;
I give up my - self, and what - ev - er I know,
by faith, for my cleans - ing I see Your blood flow,
to those who have sought You, You nev - er said, "No,"
to get this blest cleans - ing, I all things fore - go:
my prayer has pre - vailed, and this mo - ment I know,

now wash me and I shall be whit - er than snow.
now wash me and I shall be whit - er than snow.
now wash me and I shall be whit - er than snow.
now wash me and I shall be whit - er than snow.
Now wash me and I shall be whit - er than snow.
now wash me and I shall be whit - er than snow.

WORDS: James L. Nicholson, 1872
MUSIC: *Fischer*, William Gustavus Fischer, n.d.

11.11.11.11 with Refrain

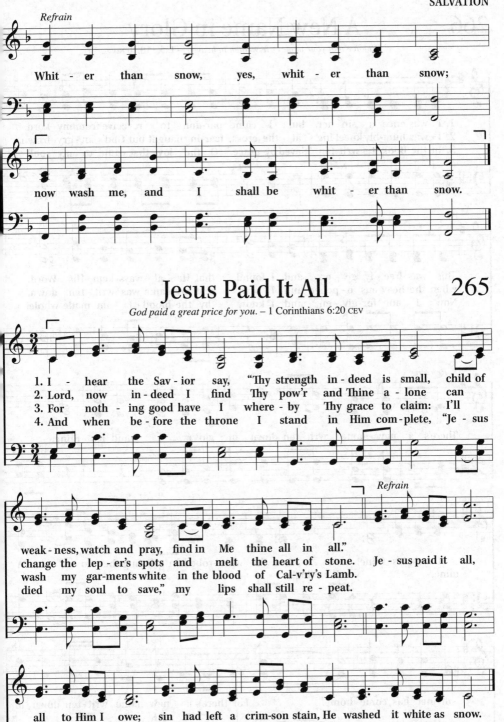

Refrain

Whit - er than snow, yes, whit - er than snow;
now wash me, and I shall be whit - er than snow.

Jesus Paid It All 265

God paid a great price for you. – 1 Corinthians 6:20 CEV

1. I - hear the Sav - ior say, "Thy strength in - deed is small, child of
2. Lord, now in - deed I find Thy pow'r and Thine a - lone can
3. For noth - ing good have I where - by Thy grace to claim: I'll
4. And when be - fore the throne I stand in Him com - plete, "Je - sus

weak - ness, watch and pray, find in Me thine all in all."
change the lep - er's spots and melt the heart of stone. Je - sus paid it all,
wash my gar - ments white in the blood of Cal - v'ry's Lamb.
died my soul to save," my lips shall still re - peat.

Refrain

all to Him I owe; sin had left a crim - son stain, He washed it white as snow.

WORDS: Elvina Mable Reynolds Hall, 1865
MUSIC: *All to Christ*, John Thomas Grape, 1868

6.6.7.7 with Refrain

266
A New Name in Glory

Rejoice that your names are written in heaven. – Luke 10:20 NIV

1. I was once a sin-ner, but I came par-don to re-ceive from my Lord.
2. I was hum-bly kneel-ing at the cross, fear-ing naught but God's an-gry frown,
3. In the Book 'tis writ-ten, "Saved by grace." O the joy that came to my soul!

This was free-ly giv-en, and I found that He al-ways kept His Word.
when the heav-ens o-pened and I saw that my name was writ-ten down.
Now I am for-giv-en, and I know by the blood I am made whole.

Refrain

There's a new name writ-ten down in glo-ry, and it's mine,
and it's

O yes, it's mine! And the white-robed an-gels sing the sto-ry, "A
mine, yes it's mine!

sin-ner has come home." For there's a new name writ-ten down in
has come home.

WORDS: Charles Austin Miles, ca. 1905
MUSIC: *New Name*, Charles Austin Miles, ca. 1905

Irregular with Refrain

glo - ry, and it's mine, O yes, it's mine! With my
and it's mine, yes, it's mine!

sins for - giv - en I am bound for heav - en, nev - er - more to roam.

I Know a Fount 267

I will freely give water from the life-giving fountain to everyone who is thirsty. – Revelation 21:6 CEV

I know a fount where sins are washed a - way, I know a

place where night is turned to day; bur - dens are lift - ed, blind eyes made to

see; there's a won - der - work - ing pow'r in the blood of Cal - va - ry.

WORDS: Oliver Cooke, ca. 1923
MUSIC: *I Know a Fount,* Oliver Cooke, ca. 1923 Irregular

268 Redeemed, How I Love to Proclaim It!

Because you were slain, and with Your blood You purchased men for God. – Revelation 5:9 NIV

1. Re - deemed, how I love to pro - claim it! Re - deemed by the blood of the Lamb; re - deemed through His in - fi - nite mer - cy, His child, and for - ev - er, I am.

2. Re - deemed, and so hap - py in Je - sus, no lan - guage my rap - ture can tell; I know that the light of His pres - ence with me doth con - tin - ual - ly dwell.

3. I think of my bless - ed Re - deem - er, I think of Him all the day long; I sing, for I can - not be si - lent; His love is the theme of my song.

4. I know I shall see in His beau - ty the King in whose law I de - light; Who lov - ing - ly guard - eth my foot - steps and giv - eth me songs in the night.

Refrain

Re - deemed, re - deemed, re - deemed by the blood of the Lamb; re - deemed, re - deemed, His child, and for - ev - er I am.

WORDS: Fanny Jane Crosby, 1882
MUSIC: *Redeemed*, William James Kirkpatrick, 1882

9.8.9.8 with Refrain

Ring the Bells of Heaven!

There is rejoicing in the presence of the angels of God over one sinner who repents. – Luke 15:10 NIV

1. Ring the bells of heav-en! There is joy to-day, for a soul, re-
2. Ring the bells of heav-en! There is joy to-day, for the wan-d'rer
3. Ring the bells of heav-en! Spread the feast to-day! An-gels, swell the

turn-ing from the wild! See, the Fa-ther meets him out up-on the way,
now is rec-on-ciled; yes, a soul is res-cued from his sin-ful way,
glad tri-um-phant strain! Tell the joy-ful tid-ings, bear it far a-way!

Refrain

wel-com-ing His wea-ry, wan-d'ring child.
and is born a-new a ran-somed child. Glo-ry! Glo-ry! How the
For a pre-cious soul is born a-gain.

an-gels sing; glo-ry! Glo-ry! How the loud harps ring! 'Tis the ran-somed

ar-my, like a might-y sea, peal-ing forth the an-them of the free.

WORDS: William Orcutt Cushing, 1866
MUSIC: *Ring the Bells*, George Frederick Root, 1866

11.9.11.9 with Refrain

270 The Way of the Cross Leads Home

If anyone would come after Me, he must deny himself, take up his cross and follow Me. – Matthew 16:24 NIV

1. I must needs go home by the way of the cross, there's
2. I must needs go on in the blood-sprin-kled way, the
3. Then I bid fare-well to the way of the world, to

no oth-er way but this; I shall ne'er get sight of the
path that the Sav-ior trod, if I ev-er climb to the
walk in it nev-er-more; for the Lord says, "Come," and I

gates of light, if the way of the cross I miss.
heights sub-lime, where the soul is at home with God.
seek my home, where He waits at the o-pen door.

Refrain

The way of the cross leads home, the way of the cross leads home;
leads home, leads home

it is sweet to know as I on-ward go, the way of the cross leads home.

WORDS: Jessie Brown Pounds, 1906
MUSIC: *Way of the Cross*, Charles Hutchinson Gabriel, n.d.

Irregular with Refrain

Ye Must Be Born Again

I tell you the truth, no one can see the kingdom of God unless he is born again. – John 3:3 NIV

1. A rul-er once came to Je-sus by night to ask Him the way of sal-
2. Ye chil-dren of men, at-tend to the Word so sol-emn-ly ut-tered by
3. O ye who would en-ter that glo-ri-ous rest, and sing with the ran-somed the

va-tion and light; the Mas-ter made an-swer in words true and plain,
Je-sus the Lord; and let not this mes-sage to you be in vain,
song of the blest; the life ev-er-last-ing if ye would ob-tain,

Refrain

"Ye must be born a-gain."
"Ye must be born a-gain." "Ye must be born a-
"Ye must be born a-gain." a-gain."

gain, Ye must be born a-gain; I ver-i-ly,
a-gain, a-gain;

ver-i-ly say un-to thee, Ye must be born a-gain."
a-gain."

WORDS: William True Sleeper, 1877
MUSIC: *Born Again*, George Coles Stebbins, 1877

Irregular with Refrain

272 O the Deep, Deep Love of Jesus

Stand firm and be deeply rooted in His love. – Ephesians 3:17 CEV

1. O the deep, deep love of Je - sus, vast, un - mea - sured,
2. O the deep, deep love of Je - sus; spread His praise from
3. O the deep, deep love of Je - sus, love of ev - 'ry

bound - less, free, roll - ing as a might - y o - cean
shore to shore! How He lov - eth, ev - er lov - eth,
love the best; 'tis an o - cean vast of bless - ing,

in its full - ness o - ver me. Un - der - neath me, all a -
chang - eth nev - er, nev - er - more. How He watch - es o'er His
'tis a ha - ven sweet of rest. O the deep, deep love of

round me, is the cur - rent of Thy love; lead - ing on - ward,
loved ones, died to call them all His own; how for them He
Je - sus, 'tis a heav'n of heav'ns to me; and it lifts me

WORDS: Samuel Trevor Francis, 1875
MUSIC: *Ebenezer (Ton-y-Botel)*, Thomas John Williams, 1890
This tune in a higher key, No. 321.

8.7.8.7 I

lead - ing home - ward to my glo - r'ous rest a - bove.
in - ter - ced - eth, watch - eth o'er them from the throne.
up to glo - ry, for it lifts me up to Thee.

There's a Wideness in God's Mercy   273

His mercy extends to those who fear Him, from generation to generation. – Luke 1:50 NIV

1. There's a wide - ness in God's mer - cy, like the
2. There is wel - come for the sin - ner, and more
3. But we make His love too nar - row by false
4. For the love of God is broad - er than the
5. If our love were but more sim - ple, we could

wide - ness of the sea; there's a kind - ness
grac - es for the good; there is mer - cy
lim - its of our own; and we mag - ni -
mea - sure of one's mind; and the heart of
take Him at His Word; and our lives would

in His jus - tice, which is more than lib - er - ty.
with the Sav - ior; there is heal - ing in His blood.
fy His strict - ness with a zeal He will not own.
the E - ter - nal is most won - der - ful - ly kind.
be more lov - ing in the like - ness of our Lord.

WORDS: Frederick William Faber, 1854
MUSIC: *Wellesley*, Lizzie Shove Tourjée, 1878

8.7.8.7

274 Jesus Loves Me!

Let love be your guide. Christ loved us and offered His life for us. – Ephesians 5:2 CEV

1. Je - sus loves me! This I know, for the Bi - ble tells me so;
2. Je - sus loves me! He who died heav - en's gates to o - pen wide!
3. Je - sus loves me! Loves me still, though I'm ve - ry weak and ill;
4. Je - sus loves me! He will stay close be - side me all the way;
5. Je - sus loves me! This I know, as He loved so long a - go,
6. Je - sus loves me still to - day, walk - ing with me on my way,

lit - tle ones to Him be - long; they are weak, but He is strong.
He will wash a - way my sin, let His lit - tle child come in.
from His shin - ing throne on high, comes to watch me where I lie.
if I love Him, when I die He will take me home on high.
tak - ing chil - dren on His knee, say - ing, "Let them come to me."
want - ing as a Friend to give, light and love to all who live.

Refrain

Yes, Je - sus loves me, yes, Je - sus loves me,

yes, Je - sus loves me, the Bi - ble tells me so.

WORDS: Anna Bartlett Warner, 1860
MUSIC: *China*, William Batchelder Bradbury, 1862

7.7.7.7 with Refrain

Jesus Loves Even Me!

Christ loved the church and gave His life for it. – Ephesians 5:25 CEV

1. I am so glad that our Fa-ther in heav'n tells of His
2. Though I for-get Him and wan-der a-way, still He doth
3. O if there's on-ly one song I can sing when in His

love in the Book He has giv'n. Won-der-ful things in the
love me wher-ev-er I stray. Back to His dear, lov-ing
beau-ty I see the great King. This shall my song in e-

Bi-ble I see, this is the dear-est, that Je-sus loves me.
arms would I flee when I re-mem-ber that Je-sus loves me.
ter-ni-ty be: "O what a won-der, that Je-sus loves me!"

Refrain

I am so glad that Je-sus loves me, Je-sus loves me, Je-sus loves me.

I am so glad that Je-sus loves me; Je-sus loves e-ven me!

WORDS: Philip Paul Bliss, 1870
MUSIC: *Gladness*, Philip Paul Bliss, 1870

10.10.10.10 with Refrain

276 The Love of God

I am sure that nothing can separate us from God's love. – Romans 8:38 CEV

1. The love of God is great-er far than tongue or pen can ev-er
2. When years of time shall pass a-way and earth-ly thrones and king-doms
3. Could we with ink the o-cean fill and were the skies of parch-ment

tell; it goes be-yond the high-est star, and reach-es to the low-est
fall, when men who here re-fuse to pray, on rocks and hills and moun-tains
made, were ev-'ry stalk on earth a quill and ev-'ry man a scribe by

hell; the guilt-y pair, bowed down with care, God gave His Son to
call, God's love so sure shall still en-dure, all mea-sure-less and
trade, to write the love of God a-bove would drain the o-cean

win; His err-ing child He rec-on-ciled, and par-doned from his sin.
strong; re-deem-ing grace to Ad-am's race the saints' and an-gels' song.
dry; nor could the scroll con-tain the whole, though stretched from sky to sky.

WORDS: Sts. 1, 2 Frederick Martin Lehman, 1917; St. 3 Meir Ben Isaac Nehorai, 1050;
     from the Jewish poem, *Haddamut*, 1050, Worms, Germany
MUSIC: *Love of God*, Frederick Martin Lehman, 1917; arr. Claudia Faustina Lehman Mays, 1917   8.8.8.8.8.8.6.8.6 with Refrain

O How He Loves You and Me   277

As the Father has loved Me, so have I loved you. – John 15:9 NIV

1. O how He loves you and me. O how He loves you and
2. Je - sus to Cal - v'ry did go, His love for man - kind to

me; He gave His life, what more could He give? O how He
show; what He did there brought hope from de - spair: O how He

loves you; O how He loves me; O how He loves you and me!
loves you; O how He loves me; O how He loves you and me!

WORDS: Kurt Kaiser, 1975
MUSIC: *Patricia*, Kurt Kaiser, 1975

Irregular

278 Love Is the Theme

God is love, and anyone who doesn't love others has never known Him. – 1 John 4:8 CEV

1. Of the themes that men have known, one su-preme-ly stands a-lone;
2. Let the bells of heav-en ring, let the saints their trib-ute bring;
3. Since the Lord my soul un-bound, I am tell-ing all a-round,
4. As of old when blind and lame to the bless-ed Mas-ter came,

through the a-ges it has shown, 'tis His won-der-ful, won-der-ful love.
let the world true prais-es sing for His won-der-ful, won-der-ful love.
par-don, peace, and joy are found in His won-der-ful, won-der-ful love.
sin-ners, call ye on His name, trust His won-der-ful, won-der-ful love.

Refrain
Descant

Love is the theme, love is su-preme; sweet-er it grows, glo-ry be-stows!

Love is the theme, love is su-preme; sweet-er it grows, glo-ry be-stows!

Bright as the sun ev-er it glows! Love is the theme, e-ter-nal theme!

Bright as the sun ev-er it glows! Love is the theme, e-ter-nal theme!

WORDS: Albert Christopher Fisher, 1912, alt.
MUSIC: *Fisher,* Albert Christopher Fisher, 1912

7.7.7.9 with Refrain

Grace Greater Than Our Sin

279

Yet where sin was powerful, God's kindness was even more powerful. – Romans 5:20 CEV

1. Mar-vel-ous grace of our lov-ing Lord, grace that ex-ceeds our
2. Dark is the stain that we can-not hide, what can a-vail to
3. Mar-vel-ous, in-fi-nite, match-less grace, free-ly be-stowed on

sin and our guilt, yon-der on Cal-va-ry's mount out-poured,
wash it a-way? Look! There is flow-ing a crim-son tide;
all who be-lieve; all who are long-ing to see His face.

Refrain

there where the blood of the Lamb was spilt. Grace, grace,
whit-er than snow you may be to-day. Mar-vel-ous grace,
Will you this mo-ment His grace re-ceive?

God's grace, grace that will par-don and cleanse with-in; grace,
in-fi-nite grace, mar-vel-ous

grace, God's grace, grace that is great-er than all our sin.
grace, in-fi-nite grace,

WORDS: *Hymns Tried and True,* Julia Harriette Johnston, 1910
MUSIC: *Moody,* Daniel Brink Towner, 1910

9.9.9.9 with Refrain

Amazing Grace!

God treats us much better than we deserve. – Romans 3:24 CEV

1. A - maz - ing grace! How sweet the sound that
2. 'Twas grace that taught my heart to fear, and
3. Through man - y dan - gers, toils, and snares, I
4. The Lord has prom - ised good to me, His
5. Yea, when this flesh and heart shall fail, and
6. When we've been there ten thou - sand years, bright

saved a wretch like me! I once was lost, but
grace my fears re - lieved; how pre - cious did that
have al - read - y come; 'tis grace hath brought me
Word my hope se - cures; He will my shield and
mor - tal life shall cease, I shall pos - sess, with
shin - ing as the sun, we've no less days to

now am found; was blind, but now I see.
grace ap - pear the hour I first be - lieved.
safe thus far, and grace will lead me home.
por - tion be, as long as life en - dures.
in the veil, a life of joy and peace.
sing God's praise than when we first be - gun.

WORDS: Sts. 1-5 John Newton, 1779; St. 6 John Rees, ca. 1859
MUSIC: *Amazing Grace (New Britain)*, from *Virginia Harmony*, 1831; early American folk hymn, 19th c.;
harm. Edwin Othello Excell, 1900

C.M.

Amazing Grace!

God treats us much better than we deserve. – Romans 3:24 CEV

1. A - maz - ing grace! How sweet the sound that
2. 'Twas grace that taught my heart to fear, and
3. Through man - y dan - gers, toils, and snares, I
4. The Lord has prom - ised good to me, His
5. Yea, when this flesh and heart shall fail, and
6. When we've been there ten thou - sand years, bright

saved a wretch like me! I once was lost, but
grace my fears re - lieved; how pre - cious did that
have al - read - y come; 'tis grace hath brought me
Word my hope se - cures; He will my shield and
mor - tal life shall cease, I shall pos - sess, with -
shin - ing as the sun, we've no less days to

now am found; was blind, but now I see.
grace ap - pear the hour I first be - lieved.
safe thus far, and grace will lead me home.
por - tion be, as long as life en - dures.
in the veil, a life of joy and peace.
sing God's praise than when we first be - gun.

WORDS: Sts. 1-5 John Newton, 1779; St. 6 John Rees, ca. 1859
MUSIC: *Land of Rest*, from *The Christian Harp*, 1836; early American folk hymn, 19th c.; arr. Eric Wyse, 2005

C.M.

This tune in a lower key, No. 570.

282 Wonderful Grace of Jesus

The grace of our Lord was poured out on me abundantly, along with the faith and love. – 1 Timothy 1:14 NIV

1. Won - der - ful grace of Je - sus, great - er than all my sin;
2. Won - der - ful grace of Je - sus, reach - ing to all the lost,
3. Won - der - ful grace of Je - sus, reach - ing the most de - filed,

how shall my tongue de - scribe it, where shall its praise be - gin?
by it I have been par - doned, saved to the ut - ter - most;
by its trans - form - ing pow - er mak - ing him God's dear child.

Tak - ing a - way my bur - den, set - ting my spir - it free,
chains have been torn a - sun - der, giv - ing me lib - er - ty,
Pur - chas - ing peace and heav - en for all e - ter - ni - ty:

for the won - der - ful grace of Je - sus reach - es me.
for the won - der - ful grace of Je - sus reach - es me.
And the won - der - ful grace of Je - sus reach - es me.

Refrain

Won - der - ful the match - less grace, the match - less grace of Je - sus,
Won - der - ful the match - less grace of Je - sus,

WORDS: Haldor Lillenas, 1918
MUSIC: *Wonderful Grace*, Haldor Lillenas, 1918

Irregular with Refrai

deep - er than the might - y roll - ing sea, the roll - ing sea;
deep - er than the might - y roll - ing sea;

won - der - ful grace, all - suf - fi -
high - er than the moun - tain, spark - ling like a foun - tain, all - suf - fi - cient

cient for me, for e - ven me. Broad - er than the scope of my trans-
grace for e - ven me. Broad - er than the scope of my trans-

gres - sions, great - er far than all my sin and shame; O
gres - sions, sing it! Great - er far than all my sin and shame, my sin and shame; O

mag - ni - fy the pre - cious name of Je - sus, praise His name!

283 Great God of Wonders!

The heavens shall praise Thy wonders, O Lord. – Psalm 89:5 KJV

1. Great God of won - ders! All Thy ways are match - less,
2. In won - der lost, with trem - bling joy, we take the
3. O may this strange, this match - less grace, this God - like

God - like, and di - vine; but the fair glo - ries
par - don of our God: Par - don for crimes of
mir - a - cle of love, fill the whole earth with

of Thy grace more God - like and un - ri - valed
deep - est dye, a par - don bought with Je - sus'
grate - ful praise, and all the an - gel - ic choirs a -

shine, more God - like and un - ri - valed shine.
blood, a par - don bought with Je - sus' blood.
bove, and all the an - gel - ic choirs a - bove.

Refrain (To be sung twice after last stanza)

Who is a par - d'ning God like Thee? Or who has grace so

WORDS: Samuel Davies, 1779
MUSIC: *Wonders,* John Newton, 19th c.

8.8.8.8 with Repeat & Refrain

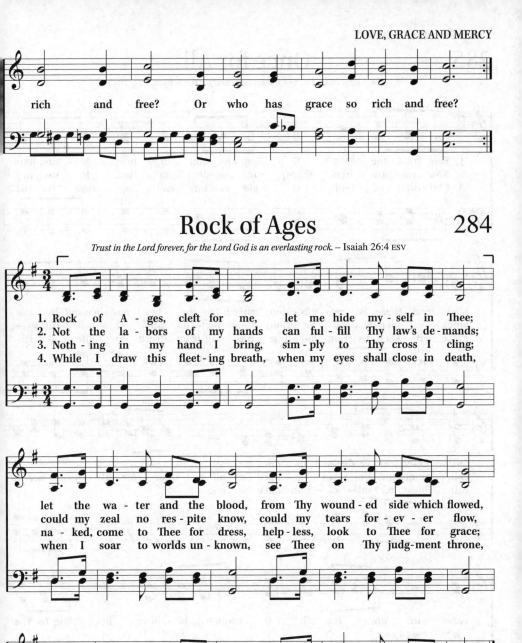

rich and free? Or who has grace so rich and free?

Rock of Ages

284

Trust in the Lord forever, for the Lord God is an everlasting rock. – Isaiah 26:4 ESV

1. Rock of A - ges, cleft for me, let me hide my - self in Thee;
2. Not the la - bors of my hands can ful - fill Thy law's de - mands;
3. Noth - ing in my hand I bring, sim - ply to Thy cross I cling;
4. While I draw this fleet - ing breath, when my eyes shall close in death,

let the wa - ter and the blood, from Thy wound - ed side which flowed,
could my zeal no res - pite know, could my tears for - ev - er flow,
na - ked, come to Thee for dress, help - less, look to Thee for grace;
when I soar to worlds un - known, see Thee on Thy judg-ment throne,

be of sin the dou - ble cure, save from wrath and make me pure.
all for sin could not a - tone; Thou must save and Thou a - lone.
foul, I to the foun-tain fly; wash me, Sav - ior, or I die!
Rock of A - ges, cleft for me, let me hide my - self in Thee.

WORDS: Augustus Montague Toplady, 1776
MUSIC: *Toplady*, Thomas Hastings, 1830

7.7.7.7.7.7

285 Once for All

When Christ died, He died for sin once and for all. – Romans 6:10 CEV

1. Free from the law, O happy con - di - tion, Je - sus hath
2. Now we are free there's no con - dem - na - tion, Je - sus pro -
3. Chil - dren of God, O glo - ri - ous call - ing, sure - ly His

bled, and there is re - mis - sion; cursed by the law and bruised by the
vides a per - fect sal - va - tion; "Come un - to Me," O hear His sweet
grace will keep us from fall - ing; pass - ing from death to life at His

Refrain

fall, grace hath re - deemed us once for all.
call, come, and He saves us once for all. Once for all, O sin - ner, re -
call, bless - ed sal - va - tion once for all.

ceive it; once for all, O broth - er, be - lieve it; cling to the

cross, the bur - den will fall, Christ hath re - deemed us once for all.

WORDS: Philip Paul Bliss, 1873
MUSIC: *Once for All*, Philip Paul Bliss, 1873

Irregular with Refrain

The Great Physician

On hearing this, Jesus said, "It is not the healthy who need a doctor, but the sick." – Matthew 9:12 NIV

1. The great Phy-si-cian now is near: The sym-pa-thiz-ing Je-sus;
2. Your man-y sins are all for-giv'n, O hear the voice of Je-sus;
3. All glo-ry to the dy-ing Lamb, I now be-lieve in Je-sus;
4. And when to that bright world a-bove we rise to be with Je-sus,

He speaks the droop-ing heart to cheer: O hear the voice of Je-sus!
go on your way in peace to heav'n and wear a crown with Je-sus.
I love the bless-ed Sav-ior's name, I love the name of Je-sus.
we'll sing a-round the throne of love His name, the name of Je-sus.

Refrain

Sweet-est note in ser-aph song, sweet-est name on mor-tal tongue,

sweet-est car-ol ev-er sung, Je-sus, bless-ed Je-sus!

WORDS: William Hunter, 1859; Ref., Richard Kempenfelt, 1777
MUSIC: *Great Physician*, John Hart Stockton, 1869

8.7.8.7 with Refrain

287 He Is Able to Deliver Thee

Our God whom we serve is able to deliver us. – Daniel 3:17 ESV

1. 'Tis the grand-est theme through the a - ges rung; 'tis the grand-est theme for a mor-tal tongue; 'tis the grand-est theme that the world e'er sung, "Our God is a - ble to de - liv - er thee."

2. 'Tis the grand-est theme in the earth or main; 'tis the grand-est theme for a mor-tal strain; 'tis the grand-est theme, tell the world a - gain, "Our God is a - ble to de - liv - er thee."

3. 'Tis the grand-est theme, let the ti - dings roll, to the guilt - y heart, to the sin - ful soul; look to God in faith, He will make thee whole, "Our God is a - ble to de - liv - er thee."

Refrain

He is a - ble to de - liv - er thee, He is a - ble to de - liv - er thee; though by sin op-pressed, go to

a - ble, He is a - ble a - ble, He is a - ble

WORDS: William Augustine Ogden, 1887
MUSIC: *Deliverance*, William Augustine Ogden, 1887

10.10.10.10 with Refrai

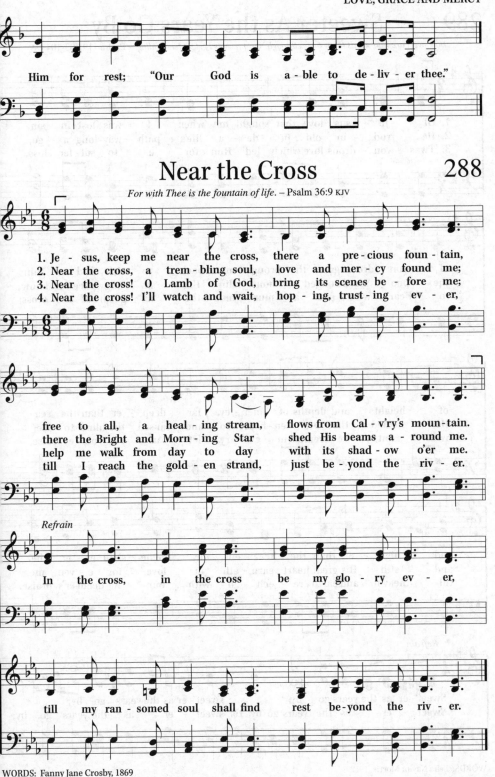

Him for rest; "Our God is a - ble to de - liv - er thee."

Near the Cross

288

For with Thee is the fountain of life. – Psalm 36:9 KJV

1. Je - sus, keep me near the cross, there a pre - cious foun - tain,
2. Near the cross, a trem - bling soul, love and mer - cy found me;
3. Near the cross! O Lamb of God, bring its scenes be - fore me;
4. Near the cross! I'll watch and wait, hop - ing, trust - ing ev - er,

free to all, a heal - ing stream, flows from Cal - v'ry's moun - tain.
there the Bright and Morn - ing Star shed His beams a - round me.
help me walk from day to day with its shad - ow o'er me.
till I reach the gold - en strand, just be - yond the riv - er.

Refrain

In the cross, in the cross be my glo - ry ev - er,

till my ran - somed soul shall find rest be - yond the riv - er.

WORDS: Fanny Jane Crosby, 1869
MUSIC: *Near the Cross*, William Howard Doane, 1869

7.6.7.6 with Refrain

289 Sweeter As the Years Go By

How sweet are Your words to my taste...through Your precepts I get understanding. – Psalm 119:103-104 ESV

1. Of Jesus' love that sought me when I was lost in sin,
2. He trod in old Judea life's pathway long ago,
3. 'Twas wondrous love which led Him for us to suffer loss,

of wondrous grace that brought me back to His fold again;
the people thronged about Him, His saving grace to know;
to bear without a murmur the anguish of the cross;

of heights and depths of mercy, far deeper than the sea
He healed the brokenhearted, and caused the blind to see;
with saints redeemed in glory, let us our voices raise,

and higher than the heavens, my theme shall ever be.
and still His great heart yearneth in love for even me.
till heav'n and earth reecho with our Redeemer's praise.

Refrain

Sweeter as the years go by, sweeter as the years go by;
Sweeter as the years go by, 'tis sweeter as the years go by;

WORDS: Lelia Naylor Morris, 1912
MUSIC: *Years Go By,* Lelia Naylor Morris, 1912

7.6.7.6 D with Refrain

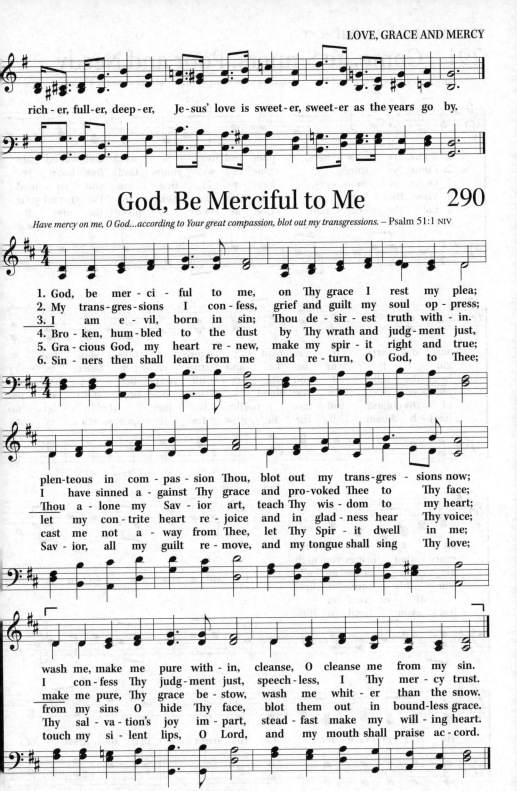

rich - er, full - er, deep - er, Je - sus' love is sweet - er, sweet - er as the years go by.

God, Be Merciful to Me   290

Have mercy on me, O God...according to Your great compassion, blot out my transgressions. – Psalm 51:1 NIV

1. God, be mer - ci - ful to me, on Thy grace I rest my plea;
2. My trans - gres - sions I con - fess, grief and guilt my soul op - press;
3. I am e - vil, born in sin; Thou de - sir - est truth with - in.
4. Bro - ken, hum - bled to the dust by Thy wrath and judg - ment just,
5. Gra - cious God, my heart re - new, make my spir - it right and true;
6. Sin - ners then shall learn from me and re - turn, O God, to Thee;

plen - teous in com - pas - sion Thou, blot out my trans - gres - sions now;
I have sinned a - gainst Thy grace and pro - voked Thee to Thy face;
Thou a - lone my Sav - ior art, teach Thy wis - dom to my heart;
let my con - trite heart re - joice and in glad - ness hear Thy voice;
cast me not a - way from Thee, let Thy Spir - it dwell in me;
Sav - ior, all my guilt re - move, and my tongue shall sing Thy love;

wash me, make me pure with - in, cleanse, O cleanse me from my sin.
I con - fess Thy judg - ment just, speech - less, I Thy mer - cy trust.
make me pure, Thy grace be - stow, wash me whit - er than the snow.
from my sins O hide Thy face, blot them out in bound - less grace.
Thy sal - va - tion's joy im - part, stead - fast make my will - ing heart.
touch my si - lent lips, O Lord, and my mouth shall praise ac - cord.

WORDS: Anon., 1912 from *The Psalter*, based on Psalm 51:1-12
MUSIC: *Redhead 76 (Gethsemane)*, from *Church Hymn Tunes, Ancient and Modern*, Richard Redhead, 1853   7.7.7.7.7.7
This tune in a lower key, No. 158 and in a higher key, No. 227.

291 Come, Ye Sinners, Poor and Needy

But if we confess our sins to God, He can always be trusted to forgive us and take our sins away. – 1 John 1:9 CEV

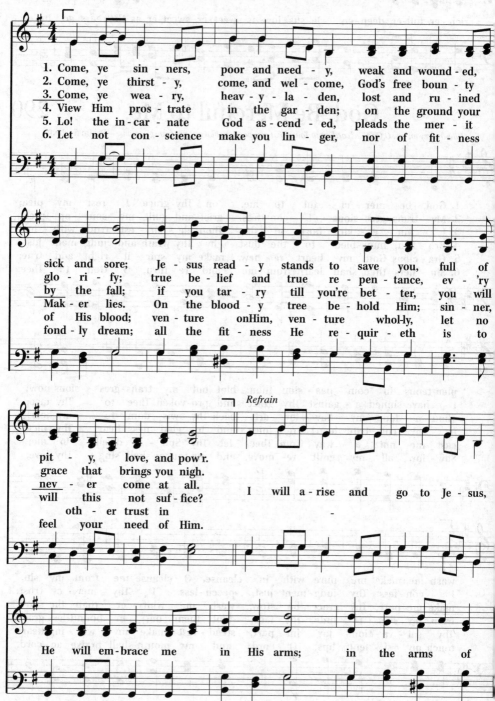

1. Come, ye sin - ners, poor and need - y, weak and wound - ed,
2. Come, ye thirst - y, come, and wel - come, God's free boun - ty
3. Come, ye wea - ry, heav - y - la - den, lost and ru - ined
4. View Him pros - trate in the gar - den; on the ground your
5. Lo! the in - car - nate God as - cend - ed, pleads the mer - it
6. Let not con - science make you lin - ger, nor of fit - ness

sick and sore; Je - sus read - y stands to save you, full of
glo - ri - fy; true be - lief and true re - pen - tance, ev - 'ry
by the fall; if you tar - ry till you're bet - ter, you will
Mak - er lies. On the blood - y tree be - hold Him; sin - ner,
of His blood; ven - ture on Him, ven - ture whol - ly, let no
fond - ly dream; all the fit - ness He re - quir - eth is to

Refrain

pit - y, love, and pow'r.
grace that brings you nigh.
nev - er come at all. I will a - rise and go to Je - sus,
will this not suf - fice?
oth - er trust in
feel your need of Him.

He will em - brace me in His arms; in the arms of

WORDS: Joseph Hart, 1759, alt.
MUSIC: *Restoration*, from *The Southern Harmony and Musical Companion*, William Walker, 1835   8.7.8.7 with Refrain

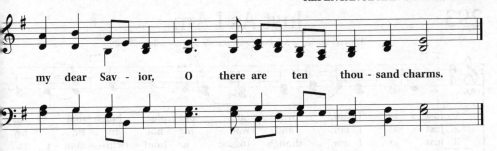

my dear Sav - ior, O there are ten thou - sand charms.

Depth of Mercy! Can There Be 292

He saved us because of His mercy, and not because of any good things that we have done. – Titus 3:5 CEV

1. Depth of mer - cy! Can there be mer - cy
2. I have long with - stood His grace; long pro -
3. Je - sus speaks, and pleads His blood! He dis -
4. There for me the Sav - ior stands, shows His
5. Now in - cline me to re - pent; let me

still re - served for me? Can my God His
voked Him to His face; would not heark - en
arms the wrath of God; now my Fa - ther's
wounds and spreads His hands. God is love! I
now my fall la - ment; deep - ly my re -

wrath for - bear, me, the chief of sin - ners, spare?
to His calls; grieved Him by a thou - sand falls.
mer - cies move, jus - tice lin - gers in - to love.
know, I feel; Je - sus weeps and loves me still.
volt de - plore, weep, be - lieve, and sin no more.

WORDS: Charles Wesley, 1740
MUSIC: *Seymour,* Carl Maria Friedrich Ernst von Weber, 1826

7.7.7.7

293

Just As I Am

Whoever comes to Me I will never drive away. – John 6:37 NIV

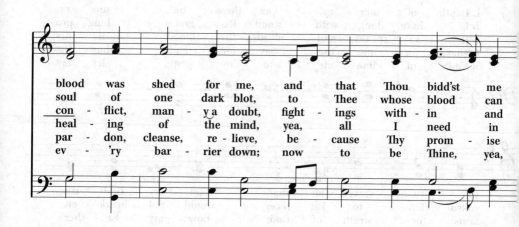

1. Just as I am, with-out one plea, but that Thy
2. Just as I am, and wait-ing not to rid my
3. Just as I am, though tossed a-bout with man-y a
4. Just as I am, poor, wretch-ed, blind; sight, rich-es,
5. Just as I am, Thou wilt re-ceive, wilt wel-come,
6. Just as I am, Thy love un-known hath bro-ken

blood was shed for me, and that Thou bidd'st me
soul of one dark blot, to Thee whose blood can
con-flict, man-y a doubt, fight-ings with-in and
heal-ing of the mind, yea, all I need in
par-don, cleanse, re-lieve, be-cause Thy prom-ise
ev-'ry bar-rier down; now to be Thine, yea,

come to Thee, O Lamb of God, I come! I come!
cleanse each spot, O Lamb of God, I come! I come!
fears with-out, O Lamb of God, I come! I come!
Thee to find, O Lamb of God, I come! I come!
I be-lieve, O Lamb of God, I come! I come!
Thine a-lone, O Lamb of God, I come! I come!

WORDS: Charlotte Elliot, 1834
MUSIC: *Woodworth*, William Batchelder Bradbury, ca. 1849

L.M.

I Lay My Sins on Jesus

294

Christ carried the burden of our sins. – 1 Peter 2:24 CEV

1. I lay my sins on Je - sus, the spot - less Lamb of God;
2. I lay my wants on Je - sus: All full - ness dwells in Him;
3. I long to be like Je - sus: Meek, lov - ing, low - ly, mild;

He bears them all, and frees us from the ac - curs - ed load.
He heals all my dis - eas - es, He doth my soul re - deem.
I long to be like Je - sus: The Fa - ther's ho - ly Child.

I bring my guilt to Je - sus, to wash my crim - son stains;
I lay my griefs on Je - sus, my bur - dens and my cares;
I long to be with Je - sus, a - mid the heav'n - ly throng,

white in His blood most pre - cious, till not a spot re - mains.
He from them all re - leas - es, He all my sor - rows shares.
to sing with saints His prais - es, to learn the an - gels' song.

WORDS: Horatius Bonar, 1843
MUSIC: *Crucifix*, traditional Greek melody, n.d.
Another harmonization of this tune in a higher key, No. 596.

7.6.7.6 D

295 Search Me, O God

O Lord, Thou hast searched me, and known me. – Psalm 139:1 KJV

1. Search me, O God, and know my heart to-day;
2. I praise Thee, Lord, for cleans-ing me from sin;
3. Lord, take my life and make it whol-ly Thine;
4. O Ho-ly Spir-it, re-viv-al comes from Thee;

try me, O Sav-ior, know my thoughts, I pray.
ful-fill Thy Word and make me pure with-in.
fill my poor heart with Thy great love di-vine.
send a re-viv-al; start the work in me.

See if there be some wick-ed way in me;
Fill me with fire where once I burned with shame;
Take all my will, my pas-sion, self and pride;
Thy Word de-clares Thou wilt sup-ply our need;

cleanse me from ev-'ry sin and set me free.
grant my de-sire to mag-ni-fy Thy name.
I now sur-ren-der, Lord: In me a-bide.
for bless-ings now, O Lord, I hum-bly plead.

WORDS: James Edwin Orr, 1936
MUSIC: *Maori*, traditional Maori melody, n.d.

10.10.10.10

Search Me, O God

O Lord, Thou hast searched me, and known me. – Psalm 139:1 KJV

1. Search me, O God, and know my heart to-day;
2. I praise You, Lord, for cleans-ing me from sin;
3. Lord, take my life, for I would live for You;
4. O Ho-ly Spir-it, re-viv-al comes from You;

try me, O Sav-ior, know my thoughts, I pray.
ful-fill Your Word and make me pure with-in.
fill my poor heart with Your great love so true.
send a re-viv-al, my own heart re-new.

See if there be some wick-ed way in me;
Fill me with fire where once I burned with shame;
Take all my will, my pas-sion, self, and pride;
Your Word de-clares You will sup-ply our need;

cleanse me from ev-'ry sin and set me free.
grant my de-sire to mag-ni-fy Your name.
I now sur-ren-der; Lord, in me a-bide.
for bless-ings now, O Lord, I hum-bly plead.

WORDS: James Edwin Orr, 1936
MUSIC: *Ellers*, Edward John Hopkins, 1869
Another harmonization of this tune, No. 588.

10.10.10.10

297 Turn Your Eyes upon Jesus

We must keep our eyes on Jesus. – Hebrews 12:2 CEV

1. O soul, are you wea-ry and trou-bled? No light in the
2. Through death in-to life ev-er-last-ing He passed, and we
3. His Word shall not fail you: He prom-ised; be-lieve Him, and

dark-ness you see? There's light for a look at the
fol-low Him there; o-ver us sin no more hath do-
all will be well; then go to a world that is

Sav-ior, and life more a-bun-dant and free!
min-ion: For more than con-qu'rors we are!
dy-ing, His per-fect sal-va-tion to tell!

Refrain

Turn your eyes up-on Je-sus, look full in His

won-der-ful face, and the things of earth will grow

WORDS: Helen Howarth Lemmel, 1922
MUSIC: *Lemmel*, Helen Howarth Lemmel, 1922

9.8.9.8 with Refrain

strange - ly dim in the light of His glo - ry and grace.

Have Thine Own Way, Lord! 298

O Lord, You are our Father; we are the clay, and You are our potter. – Isaiah 64:8 ESV

1. Have Thine own way, Lord! Have Thine own way! Thou art the
2. Have Thine own way, Lord! Have Thine own way! Search me and
3. Have Thine own way, Lord! Have Thine own way! Wound - ed and
4. Have Thine own way, Lord! Have Thine own way! Hold o'er my

pot - ter, I am the clay! Mold me and make me af - ter Thy
try me, Mas - ter, to - day! Whit - er than snow, Lord, wash me just
wea - ry, help me, I pray! Pow - er, all pow - er sure - ly is
be - ing ab - so - lute sway! Fill with Thy Spir - it till all shall

will, while I am wait - ing, yield - ed and still.
now, as in Thy pres - ence hum - bly I bow.
Thine! Touch me and heal me, Sav - ior di - vine.
see Christ on - ly, al - ways, liv - ing in me.

WORDS: Adelaide Addison Pollard, 1907
MUSIC: *Adelaide*, George Coles Stebbins, 1907

5.4.5.4 D

299

Jesus, I Come

Out of the depths have I cried unto Thee, O Lord. – Psalm 130:1 KJV

1. Out of my bond - age, sor - row and night, Je - sus, I come;
2. Out of my shame - ful fail - ure and loss, Je - sus, I come;
3. Out of un - rest and ar - ro - gant pride, Je - sus, I come;
4. Out of the fear and dread of the tomb, Je - sus, I come;

Je - sus, I come. In - to Thy free - dom, glad - ness and light,
Je - sus, I come. In - to the glo - r'ous gain of Thy cross,
Je - sus, I come. In - to Thy bless - ed will to a - bide,
Je - sus, I come. In - to the joy and light of Thy home,

Je - sus, I come to Thee. Out of my sick - ness in - to Thy
Je - sus, I come to Thee. Out of earth's sor - rows in - to Thy
Je - sus, I come to Thee. Out of my - self to dwell in Thy
Je - sus, I come to Thee. Out of the depths of ru - in un -

health, out of my want and in - to Thy wealth,
balm, out of life's storms and in - to Thy calm,
love, out of de - spair in - to rap - tures a - bove,
told, in - to the peace of Thy shel - ter - ing fold,

WORDS: William True Sleeper, 1887
MUSIC: *Jesus, I Come*, George Coles Stebbins, 1887

Irregular

out of my sin and in - to Thy - self, Je - sus, I come to Thee.
out of dis-tress to ju - bi - lant psalm, Je - sus, I come to Thee.
up - ward I rise on wings like a dove, Je - sus, I come to Thee.
ev - er Thy glo - r'ous face to be - hold, Je - sus, I come to Thee.

I Have Decided to Follow Jesus 300

Those who belong to Christ Jesus have crucified the sinful nature with its passions and desires. – Galatians 5:24 NIV

1. I have de - cid - ed to fol - low Je - sus, I have de -
2. Though none go with me, still I will fol - low; though none go
3. The cross be - fore me, the world be - hind me; the cross be -

cid - ed to fol - low Je - sus, I have de - cid - ed to fol - low
with me, still I will fol - low; though none go with me, still I will
fore me, the world be - hind me; the cross be - fore me, the world be -

Je - sus; no turn - ing back, no turn - ing back.
fol - low; no turn - ing back, no turn - ing back.
hind me; no turn - ing back, no turn - ing back.

WORDS: Indian folk song, n.d.
MUSIC: *Assam*, Indian folk song, n.d.; arr. Eric Wyse, 2005

10.10.10.8

301 Take My Life, and Let It Be

Who then will offer willingly, consecrating himself today to the Lord? – 1 Chronicles 29:5b ESV

1. Take my life and let it be con-se-crat-ed, Lord, to Thee. Take my mo-ments and my days; let them flow in cease-less praise.

2. Take my hands, and let them move at the im-pulse of Thy love. Take my feet, and let them be swift and beau-ti-ful for Thee.

3. Take my voice, and let me sing al-ways, on-ly, for my King. Take my lips, and let them be filled with mes-sag-es from Thee.

4. Take my sil-ver and my gold; not a mite would I with-hold. Take my in-tel-lect, and use ev-'ry pow'r as Thou shalt choose.

5. Take my will, and make it Thine; it shall be no long-er mine. Take my heart, it is Thine own; it shall be Thy roy-al throne.

6. Take my love, my Lord, I pour at Thy feet its trea-sure store. Take my-self, and I will be ev-er, on-ly, all for Thee.

Refrain

Lord, I give my life to Thee, Thine for-ev-er-more to be; Lord, I give my life to

WORDS: Frances Ridley Havergal, 1874
MUSIC: *Yarbrough*, William Batchelder Bradbury, 19th c.

7.7.7.7 with Refrain

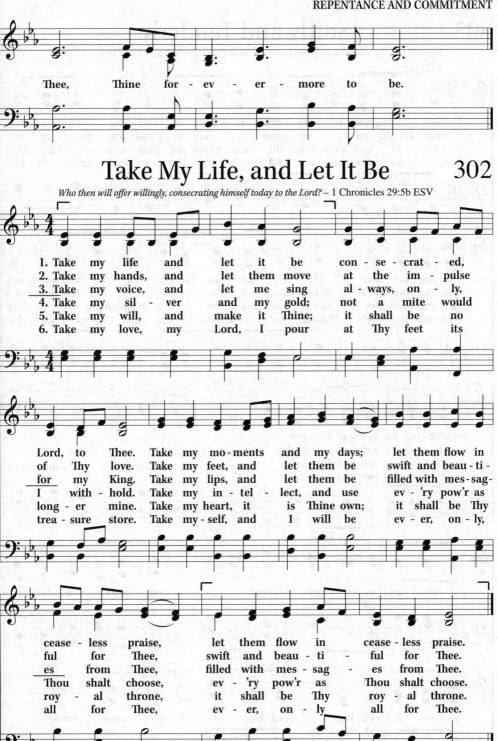

Take My Life, and Let It Be 302

Who then will offer willingly, consecrating himself today to the Lord? – 1 Chronicles 29:5b ESV

1. Take my life and let it be con-se-crat-ed, Lord, to Thee. Take my mo-ments and my days; let them flow in cease-less praise, let them flow in cease-less praise.
2. Take my hands, and let them move at the im-pulse of Thy love. Take my feet, and let them be swift and beau-ti-ful for Thee, swift and beau-ti-ful for Thee.
3. Take my voice, and let me sing al-ways, on-ly, for my King. Take my lips, and let them be filled with mes-sag-es from Thee, filled with mes-sag-es from Thee.
4. Take my sil-ver and my gold; not a mite would I with-hold. Take my in-tel-lect, and use ev-'ry pow'r as Thou shalt choose, ev-'ry pow'r as Thou shalt choose.
5. Take my will, and make it Thine; it shall be no long-er mine. Take my heart, it is Thine own; it shall be Thy roy-al throne, it shall be Thy roy-al throne.
6. Take my love, my Lord, I pour at Thy feet its trea-sure store. Take my-self, and I will be ev-er, on-ly, all for Thee, ev-er, on-ly, all for Thee.

WORDS: Frances Ridley Havergal, 1874
MUSIC: *Hendon,* Henri Abraham César Malan, 1827; harm. Lowell Mason, 1841
7.7.7.7 with Repeat

303 Softly and Tenderly

Then will I teach transgressors Thy ways; and sinners shall be converted unto Thee. – Psalm 51:13 KJV

1. Soft - ly and ten - der - ly Je - sus is call - ing, call - ing for
2. Why should we tar - ry when Je - sus is plead - ing, plead - ing for
3. Time is now fleet - ing, the mo - ments are pass - ing, pass - ing from
4. O for the won - der - ful love He has prom - ised, prom - ised for

you and for me; see, on the por - tals He's wait - ing and watch - ing,
you and for me? Why should we lin - ger and heed not His mer - cies,
you and from me; shad - ows are gath - er - ing, death's night is com - ing,
you and for me! Though we have sinned, He has mer - cy and par - don,

Refrain

watch - ing for you and for me.
mer - cies for you and for me? Come home, come home,
com - ing for you and for me. Come home, come home,
par - don for you and for me.

ye who are wea - ry, come home; ear - nest - ly, ten - der - ly,

Je - sus is call - ing, call - ing, O sin - ner, come home!

WORDS: Will Lamartine Thompson, 1880
MUSIC: *Thompson*, Will Lamartine Thompson, 1880

11.7.11.7 with Refrain

Jesus Is Calling

"Come, follow me," Jesus said, "and I will make you fishers of men." – Matthew 4:19 NIV

1. Je-sus is ten-der-ly call-ing thee home, call-ing to-day,
2. Je-sus is call-ing the wea-ry to rest, call-ing to-day,
3. Je-sus is wait-ing, O come to Him now, wait-ing to-day,
4. Je-sus is plead-ing, O list to His voice, hear Him to-day,

call-ing to-day. Why from the sun-shine of love wilt thou roam
call-ing to-day. Bring Him thy bur-den and thou shalt be blest;
wait-ing to-day. Come with thy sins, at His feet low-ly bow;
hear Him to-day. They who be-lieve on His name shall re-joice;

far-ther and far-ther a-way?
He will not turn thee a-way.
come and no long-er de-lay.
quick-ly a-rise and a-way.

Refrain

Call-ing to-
Call-ing, call-ing to-

day, call-ing to-day. Je-
day, to-day, call-ing, call-ing to-day, to-day. Je-sus is

-sus is call-ing, is ten-der-ly call-ing to-day.
ten-der-ly call-ing to-day,

WORDS: Fanny Jane Crosby, 1883
MUSIC: *Calling Today*, George Coles Stebbins, 1883

10.8.10.7 with Refrain

305 I Surrender All

Any of you who does not give up everything he has cannot be My disciple. – Luke 14:33 NIV

1. All to Je-sus I sur-ren-der, all to Him I free-ly give;
2. All to Je-sus I sur-ren-der, hum-bly at His feet I bow,
3. All to Je-sus I sur-ren-der, make me, Sav-ior, whol-ly Thine;
4. All to Je-sus I sur-ren-der, Lord, I give my-self to Thee;

1. I will ev-er love and trust Him, in His pres-ence dai-ly live.
2. world-ly plea-sures all for-sak-en, take me, Je-sus, take me now.
3. may Thy Ho-ly Spir-it fill me, may I know Thy pow'r di-vine.
4. fill me with Thy love and pow-er, let Thy bless-ing fall on me.

Refrain

I sur-ren-der all, I sur-ren-der all.

All to Thee, my bless-ed Sav-ior, I sur-ren-der all.

WORDS: Judson Wheeler Van DeVenter, 1896
MUSIC: *Surrender,* Winfield Scott Weeden, 1896

8.7.8.7 with Refrain

Only Trust Him

306

Some trust in chariots and some in horses, but we trust in the name of the Lord our God. – Psalm 20:7 ESV

1. Come, ev - 'ry soul by sin op - pressed, there's mer - cy with the Lord,
2. For Je - sus shed His pre - cious blood rich bless-ings to be - stow;
3. Yes, Je - sus is the truth, the way, that leads you in - to rest;
4. Come, then, and join this ho - ly band, and on to glo - ry go,

and He will sure - ly give you rest by trust-ing in His Word.
plunge now in - to the crim-son flood that wash - es white as snow.
be - lieve in Him with - out de - lay and you are ful - ly blest.
to dwell in that ce - les - tial land where joys im - mor - tal flow.

Refrain

On - ly trust Him, on - ly trust Him, on - ly trust Him now;

He will save you, He will save you, He will save you now.

WORDS: John Hart Stockton, 1874
MUSIC: *Stockton (Minerva)*, John Hart Stockton, 1869; Ref. Ira David Sankey, 1873

C.M. with Refrain

307 Lord, I'm Coming Home

I will set out and go back to my father. – Luke 15:18 NIV

1. I've wan-dered far a - way from God, now I'm com-ing home;
2. I've wast - ed man - y pre - cious years, now I'm com-ing home;
3. I've tired of sin and stray - ing, Lord, now I'm com-ing home;
4. My soul is sick, my heart is sore, now I'm com-ing home;

the paths of sin too long I've trod, Lord, I'm com-ing home.
I now re-pent with bit - ter tears, Lord, I'm com-ing home.
I'll trust Thy love, be - lieve Thy Word, Lord, I'm com-ing home.
my strength re-new, my hope re-store, Lord, I'm com-ing home.

Refrain

Com-ing home, com-ing home, nev-er-more to roam,

o - pen wide Thine arms of love, Lord, I'm com-ing home.

WORDS: William James Kirkpatrick, 1892
MUSIC: *Coming Home,* William James Kirkpatrick, 1892

8.5.8.5 with Refrain

Have You Any Room for Jesus? 308

I am the gate; whoever enters through Me will be saved. – John 10:9 NIV

1. Have you an - y room for Je - sus, He who bore your load of sin?
2. Room for plea-sure, room for busi - ness, but for Christ the Cru - ci - fied,
3. Have you an - y room for Je - sus, as in grace He calls a - gain?
4. Room and time now give to Je - sus, soon will pass God's day of grace;

As He knocks and asks ad - mis - sion, sin - ner, will you let Him in?
not a place that He can en - ter, in the heart for which He died?
O, to - day is time ac - cept - ed, you will nev - er call in vain.
soon your heart left cold and si - lent, and the Sav - ior's plead - ing cease.

Refrain

Room for Je - sus, King of glo - ry! Has - ten now, His Word o - bey;

swing the heart's door wide - ly o - pen, bid Him en - ter while you may.

WORDS: Anon.; adapt. Daniel Webster Whittle 1878, alt.
MUSIC: *Any Room,* C. C. Williams, 1878

8.7.8.7 with Refrain

309 Draw Me Nearer

Let's come near God with pure hearts and a confidence that comes from having faith. – Hebrews 10:22 CEV

1. I am Thine, O Lord, I have heard Thy voice, and it told Thy
2. Con - se - crate me now to Thy ser - vice, Lord, by the pow'r of
3. O, the pure de - light of a sin - gle hour that be - fore Thy
4. There are depths of love that I can - not know till I cross the

love to me; but I long to rise in the arms of faith,
grace di - vine; let my soul look up with a stead - fast hope,
throne I spend, when I kneel in prayer, and with Thee, my God,
nar - row sea; there are heights of joy that I may not reach

Refrain

and be clos - er drawn to Thee.
and my will be lost in Thine.
I com - mune as friend with friend! Draw me near - er,
till I rest in peace with Thee.

near - er, bless - ed Lord, to the cross where Thou hast died; draw me

near - er, near - er, near - er, bless - ed Lord, to Thy pre - cious, bleed - ing side.

WORDS: Fanny Jane Crosby, 1875
MUSIC: *I Am Thine*, William Howard Doane, 1875

10.7.10.7 with Refrain

Kneel at the Cross

I dwell...with Him also that is of a contrite and humble spirit. – Isaiah 57:15 KJV

1. Kneel at the cross, Christ will meet you there, come while He waits for you;
2. Kneel at the cross, there is room for all who would His glo - ry share;
3. Kneel at the cross, give your i - dols up, look un - to realms a - bove;

list to His voice, leave with Him your care and be - gin life a - new.
bliss there a - waits, harm can ne'er be - fall those who are an - chored there.
turn not a - way to life's spark - ling cup; trust on - ly in His love.

Refrain

Kneel at the cross, leave
Kneel at the cross, kneel at the cross, leave ev - 'ry care,

ev - 'ry care. Kneel at the
leave ev - 'ry care. Kneel at the cross,

cross, Je - sus will meet you there.
kneel at the cross, meet you there.

WORDS: Charles E. Moody, 20th c.
MUSIC: *Kneel at the Cross,* Charles E. Moody, 20th c.

9.6.9.6 with Refrain

311 Pass Me Not, O Gentle Savior

O Lord, if I have found favor in Your sight, do not pass by Your servant. – Genesis 18:3 ESV

1. Pass me not, O gen-tle Sav-ior; hear my hum-ble cry;
2. Let me at the throne of mer-cy find a sweet re-lief;
3. Trust-ing on-ly in Thy mer-it, would I seek Thy face.
4. Thou, the Spring of all my com-fort, more than life to me,

while on oth-ers Thou art call-ing, do not pass me by.
kneel-ing there in deep con-tri-tion, help my un-be-lief.
Heal my wound-ed, bro-ken spir-it; save me by Thy grace.
whom have I on earth be-side Thee? Whom in heav'n but Thee?

Refrain

Sav-ior, Sav-ior, hear my hum-ble cry;

while on oth-ers Thou art call-ing, do not pass me by.

WORDS: Fanny Jane Crosby, 1868
MUSIC: *Pass Me Not*, William Howard Doane, 1870

8.5.8.5 with Refrain

Not I, But Christ

For I resolved to know nothing while I was with you except Jesus Christ and Him crucified. – 1 Corinthians 2:2 NIV

1. Not I, but Christ, be hon-ored, loved, ex-alt-ed; not I, but Christ,
2. Not I, but Christ, to gent-ly soothe in sor-row; not I, but Christ,
3. Not I, but Christ, in low-ly, si-lent la-bor; not I, but Christ,
4. Christ, on-ly Christ, ere long will fill my vi-sion; glo-ry ex-cel-

be seen, be known, be heard; not I, but Christ, in ev-'ry look and
to wipe the fall-ing tear; not I, but Christ, to lift the wea-ry
in hum-ble, ear-nest toil; Christ, on-ly Christ! No show, no os-ten-
ling, soon, full soon, I'll see; Christ, on-ly Christ, my ev-'ry wish ful-

ac-tion; not I, but Christ, in ev-'ry thought and word.
bur-den! Not I, but Christ, to hush a-way all fear.
ta-tion! Christ, none but Christ, the gath-'rer of the spoil.
fill-ing; Christ, on-ly Christ, my All in all to be.

Refrain (Optionally to be sung after the last verse only)

Oh, to be saved from my-self, dear Lord, oh, to be lost in Thee;

oh, that it may be no more I, but Christ that lives in me.

WORDS: Ada A. Whiddington, ca. 1880
MUSIC: *Exaltation*, C. H. Forrest, ca. 19th c.

11.10.11.10 with Refrain

313 His Way with Thee

Listen! I am standing and knocking at your door. – Revelation 3:20a CEV

1. Would you live for Je - sus, and be al - ways pure and good?
2. Would you have Him make you free, and fol - low at His call?
3. Would you in His king - dom find a place of con - stant rest?

Would you walk with Him with - in the nar - row road? Would you have Him
Would you know the peace that comes by giv - ing all? Would you have Him
Would you prove Him true in prov - i - den - tial test? Would you in His

bear your bur - den, car - ry all your load? Let Him have His way with thee.
save you, so that you need nev - er fall? Let Him have His way with thee.
ser - vice la - bor al - ways at your best? Let Him have His way with thee.

Refrain

His pow'r can make you what you ought to be; His blood can

cleanse your heart and make you free; His love can fill your soul, and

WORDS: Cyrus Silvester Nusbaum, 1898
MUSIC: *Nusbaum*, Cyrus Silvester Nusbaum, 1898

13.11.13.7 with Refrai

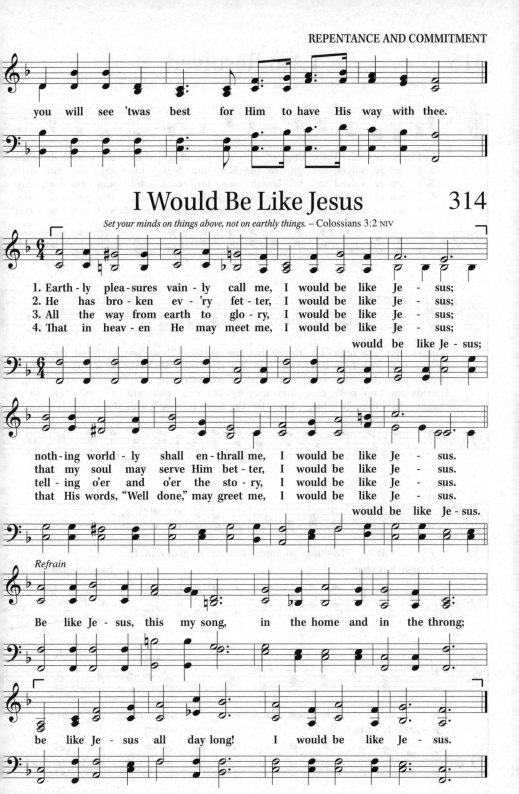

you will see 'twas best for Him to have His way with thee.

I Would Be Like Jesus 314

Set your minds on things above, not on earthly things. – Colossians 3:2 NIV

1. Earth-ly plea-sures vain-ly call me, I would be like Je - sus;
2. He has bro-ken ev-'ry fet-ter, I would be like Je - sus;
3. All the way from earth to glo-ry, I would be like Je - sus;
4. That in heav-en He may meet me, I would be like Je - sus;

would be like Je-sus;

noth-ing world-ly shall en-thrall me, I would be like Je - sus.
that my soul may serve Him bet-ter, I would be like Je - sus.
tell-ing o'er and o'er the sto-ry, I would be like Je - sus.
that His words, "Well done," may greet me, I would be like Je - sus.

would be like Je-sus.

Refrain

Be like Je-sus, this my song, in the home and in the throng;

be like Je-sus all day long! I would be like Je - sus.

WORDS: James Rowe, 1911
MUSIC: *Spring Hill*, Bentley DeForest Ackley , 20th c.

8.7.8.7 with Refrain

315   I Am Resolved

They must turn to God in repentance and have faith in our Lord Jesus. – Acts 20:21 NIV

1. I am re-solved no long-er to lin-ger, charmed by the world's de-light;
2. I am re-solved to go to the Sav-ior, leav-ing my sin and strife.
3. I am re-solved to fol-low the Sav-ior, faith-ful and true each day.
4. I am re-solved to en-ter the king-dom, leav-ing the paths of sin.
5. I am re-solved, and who will go with me? Come, friends with-out de-lay;

things that are high-er, things that are no-bler: These have al-lured my sight.
He is the true One; He is the just One; He hath the words of life.
Heed what He say-eth, do what He will-eth; He is the Liv-ing Way.
Friends may op-pose me, foes may be-set me; still will I en-ter in.
taught by the Bi-ble, led by the Spir-it, we'll walk the heav'n-ly way.

Refrain

I will has-ten to Him, has-ten so glad and free.
I will has-ten has-ten glad and free.

Je-sus, Great-est, High-est, I will come to Thee.
Je-sus, Je-sus,

WORDS: Palmer Hartsough, 1896
MUSIC: *Resolution*, James Henry Fillmore, 1896

10.6.10.6 with Refrain

The Church's One Foundation 316

Christ is the only foundation. – 1 Corinthians 3:11 CEV

1. The Church's one foun - da - tion is Je - sus Christ her Lord;
2. E - lect from ev - 'ry na - tion, yet one o'er all the earth,
3. Though with a scorn - ful won - der we see her sore op - pressed,
4. The Church shall nev - er per - ish! Her dear Lord to de - fend,
5. 'Mid toil and trib - u - la - tion, and tu - mult of her war,
6. Yet she on earth hath un - ion with God the Three in One,

she is His new cre - a - tion by wa - ter and the Word:
her char - ter of sal - va - tion, one Lord, one faith, one birth;
by schi - sms rent a - sun - der, by her - e - sies dis - tressed,
to guide, sus - tain and cher - ish, is with her to the end;
she waits the con - sum - ma - tion of peace for ev - er - more;
and mys - tic sweet com - mu - nion with those whose rest is won:

From heav'n He came and sought her to be His ho - ly bride;
one ho - ly name she bless - es, par - takes one ho - ly food,
yet saints their watch are keep - ing, their cry goes up, "How long?"
though there be those that hate her, and false sons in her pale,
till with the vi - sion glo - r'ous her long - ing eyes are blest,
O hap - py ones and ho - ly! Lord, give us grace that we,

with His own blood He bought her, and for her life He died.
and to one hope she press - es, with ev - 'ry grace en - dued.
And soon the night of weep - ing shall be the morn of song.
a - gainst the foe or trai - tor she ev - er shall pre - vail.
and the great Church vic - to - r'ous shall be the Church at rest.
like them, the meek and low - ly, on high may dwell with Thee.

WORDS: Samuel Johnson Stone, 1866, alt.
MUSIC: *Aurelia*, Samuel Sebastian Wesley, 1864

7.8.7.8 D

317 Christ Is Made the Sure Foundation

I am the one who has laid as a foundation in Zion...a sure foundation. – Isaiah 28:16a ESV

1. Christ is made the sure foun-da-tion, Christ the Head and Cor-ner-stone; Cho-sen of the Lord, and pre-cious, bind-ing all the Church in one, ho-ly Zi-on's help for-ev-er, and her con-fi-dence a-lone.

2. All that ded-i-cat-ed ci-ty, dear-ly loved of God on high, in ex-ul-tant ju-bi-la-tion, pours per-pet-ual mel-o-dy, God the One in Three a-dor-ing in glad hymns e-ter-nal-ly.

3. To this tem-ple, where we call Thee, come, O Lord of Hosts, to-day; with Thy wont-ed lov-ing kind-ness hear Thy ser-vants as they pray. And Thy full-est ben-e-dic-tion shed with-in its walls al-way.

4. Here vouch-safe to all Thy ser-vants what they ask of Thee to gain; what they gain from Thee for-ev-er with the bless-ed to re-tain, and here-af-ter in Thy glo-ry ev-er-more with Thee to reign.

5. Laud and hon-or to the Fa-ther, laud and hon-or to the Son, laud and hon-or to the Spir-it, ev-er Three and ev-er One; con-sub-stan-tial, co-e-ter-nal, while un-end-ing a-ges run.

WORDS: Latin, Anon. 7th c.; tr. John Mason Neale, 1851
MUSIC: *Regent Square*, Henry Thomas Smart, 1867

8.7.8.7.8.7

This tune in a higher key (A♭), No. 98; and (B♭) No. 210.

Christ Is Made the Sure Foundation 318

I am the one who has laid as a foundation in Zion...a sure foundation. – Isaiah 28:16a ESV

1. Christ is made the sure foun-da-tion, Christ the Head and
2. All that ded-i-cat-ed cit-y, dear-ly loved of
3. To this tem-ple, where we call Thee, come, O Lord of
4. Here vouch-safe to all Thy ser-vants what they ask of
5. Laud and hon-or to the Fa-ther, laud and hon-or

Cor-ner-stone; Cho-sen of the Lord, and pre-cious,
God on high, in ex-ul-tant ju-bi-la-tion,
Hosts, to-day; with Thy wont-ed lov-ing kind-ness
Thee to gain; what they gain from Thee for-ev-er
to the Son, laud and hon-or to the Spir-it,

bind-ing all the Church in one, ho-ly Zi-on's
pours per-pet-ual mel-o-dy, God the One in
hear Thy ser-vants as they pray. And Thy full-est
with the bless-ed to re-tain, and here-af-ter
ev-er Three and ev-er One; con-sub-stan-tial,[1]

help for-ev-er, and her con-fi-dence a-lone.
Three a-dor-ing in glad hymns e-ter-nal-ly.
ben-e-dic-tion shed with-in its walls al-way.
in Thy glo-ry ev-er-more with Thee to reign.
co-e-ter-nal, while un-end-ing a-ges run.

consubstantial: of the same essence

WORDS: Latin, Anon. 7th c.; tr. John Mason Neale, 1851
MUSIC: *Westminster Abbey*, Henry Purcell, ca. 1680

8.7.8.7.8.7

319 Glorious Things of Thee Are Spoken

Glorious things are spoken of thee, O city of God. – Psalm 87:3 KJV

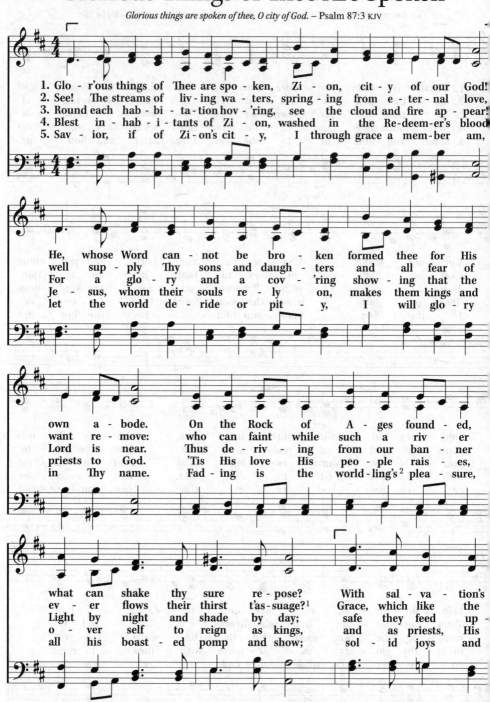

1. Glo - r'ous things of Thee are spo - ken, Zi - on, cit - y of our God!
2. See! The streams of liv - ing wa - ters, spring - ing from e - ter - nal love,
3. Round each hab - bi - ta - tion hov - 'ring, see the cloud and fire ap - pear!
4. Blest in - hab - i - tants of Zi - on, washed in the Re - deem - er's blood
5. Sav - ior, if of Zi - on's cit - y, I through grace a mem - ber am,

He, whose Word can - not be bro - ken formed thee for His
well sup - ply Thy sons and daugh - ters and all fear of
For a glo - ry and a cov - 'ring show - ing that the
Je - sus, whom their souls re - ly on, makes them kings and
let the world de - ride or pit - y, I will glo - ry

own a - bode. On the Rock of A - ges found - ed,
want re - move: who can faint while such a riv - er
Lord is near. Thus de - riv - ing from our ban - ner
priests to God. 'Tis His love His peo - ple rais - es,
in Thy name. Fad - ing is the world - ling's² plea - sure,

what can shake thy sure re - pose? With sal - va - tion's
ev - er flows their thirst t'as - suage?¹ Grace, which like the
Light by night and shade by day; safe they feed up -
o - ver self to reign as kings, and as priests, His
all his boast - ed pomp and show; sol - id joys and

1 assuage: to quench, satisfy

2 worldling: cosmopolitan or sophisticated person

WORDS: John Newton, 1779

MUSIC: *Austrian Hymn*, Franz Joseph Haydn, 1797

8.7.8.7

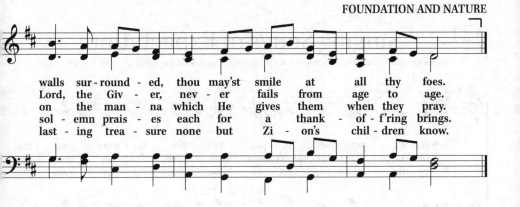

walls sur - round - ed, thou may'st smile at all thy foes.
Lord, the Giv - er, nev - er fails from age to age.
on the man - na which He gives them when they pray.
sol - emn prais - es each for a thank - of - f'ring brings.
last - ing trea - sure none but Zi - on's chil - dren know.

I Love Thy Kingdom, Lord　　320

Lord, I have loved the habitation of Your house, and the place where Your glory dwells. – Psalm 26:8 NKJV

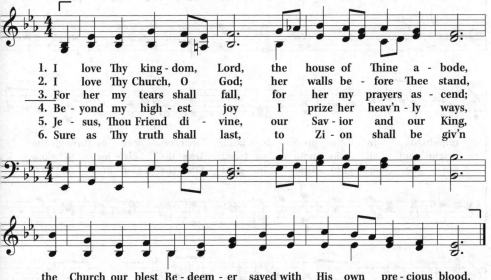

1. I love Thy king - dom, Lord, the house of Thine a - bode,
2. I love Thy Church, O God; her walls be - fore Thee stand,
3. For her my tears shall fall, for her my prayers as - cend;
4. Be - yond my high - est joy I prize her heav'n - ly ways,
5. Je - sus, Thou Friend di - vine, our Sav - ior and our King,
6. Sure as Thy truth shall last, to Zi - on shall be giv'n

the Church our blest Re - deem - er saved with His own pre - cious blood.
dear as the ap - ple of Thine eye, and grav - en on Thy hand.
to her my cares and toils be giv'n, till toils and cares shall end.
her sweet com - mu - nion, sol - emn vows, her hymns of love and praise.
Thy hand from ev - 'ry snare and foe shall great de - liv - 'rance bring.
the bright - est glo - ries earth can yield, and bright - er bliss of heav'n.

WORDS: Timothy Dwight, 1800
MUSIC: *St. Thomas*, Aaron Williams, 1762; arr. Lowell Mason, 19th c.　　　　S.M.
This tune in a higher key, No. 341.

321 Singing Songs of Expectation

I am with you and will keep you wherever you go, and will bring you back to this land. – Genesis 28:15 ESV

1. Sing-ing songs of ex-pec - ta - tion, on - ward goes the
2. One the light of God's own pres - ence, o'er His ran - somed
3. One the strain the lips of thou - sands lift as from the

pil - grim band, through the night of doubt and sor - row,
peo - ple shed, chas - ing far the gloom and ter - ror,
heart of one; one the con - flict, one the per - il,

march-ing to the prom - ised land. Clear be - fore us through the
bright-'ning all the path we tread. One the ob - ject of our
one the march in God be - gun: One the glad - ness of re -

dark - ness gleams and burns the guid - ing light; broth - er clasps the
jour - ney, one the faith which nev - er tires, one the ear - nest
joic - ing on the far e - ter - nal shore, where the one al -

WORDS: Bernard Severin Ingemann, 1826; tr. Sabine Baring-Gould, 1867, alt.
MUSIC: *Ebenezer (Ton-y-Botel)*, Thomas John Williams, 1890
This tune in a lower key, No. 272.

8.7.8.7 D

hand of broth - er, step - ping fear - less through the night.
look - ing for - ward, one the hope our God in - spires.
might - y Fa - ther reigns in love for - ev - er - more.

Faith of Our Fathers

322

Contend for the faith that was once for all delivered to the saints. – Jude 1:3 ESV

1. Faith of our fa - thers, liv - ing still, in spite of dun-geon, fire and sword;
2. Faith of our moth - ers, we will love both friend and foe in all our strife;
3. Faith of the mar - tyrs, who, though bound, were still in heart and con - science true.
4. Faith of our fa - thers, we will strive to win all na - tions un - to Thee;

O how our hearts beat high with joy when e'er we hear that glo - rious Word!
and preach Thee, too, as love knows how, by kind-ly words and vir - tuous life.
How blest would be their chil - dren's fate, if they, like them, should live for You!
and through the truth that comes from God, the earth shall then be tru - ly free.

Faith of our fa - thers, ho - ly faith, we will be true to Thee till death.
Faith of our moth - ers, ho - ly faith, we will be true to Thee till death.
Faith of the mar - tyrs, ho - ly faith, we will be true to Thee till death.
Faith of our fa - thers, ho - ly faith, we will be true to Thee till death.

WORDS: Frederick Williams Faber, 1849, alt.
MUSIC: *St. Catherine*, Henri F. Henry, 1864; arr. James George Walton, 1864

8.8.8.8.8.8

O Happy Day

They sought God eagerly, and He was found by them. – 2 Chronicles 15:15 NIV

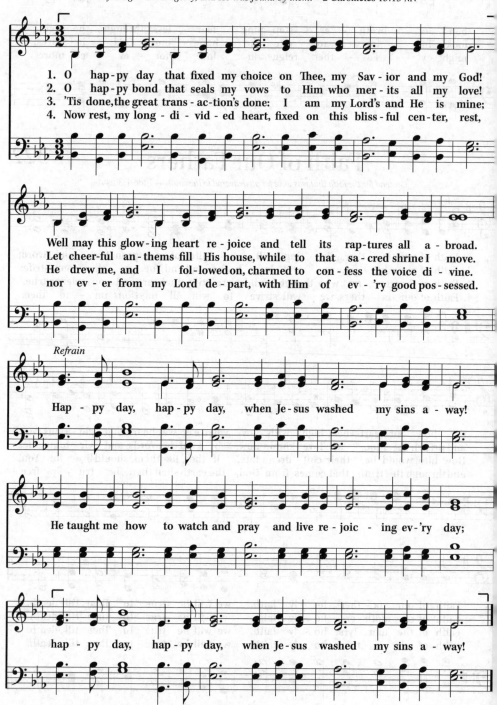

1. O hap-py day that fixed my choice on Thee, my Sav-ior and my God!
2. O hap-py bond that seals my vows to Him who mer-its all my love!
3. 'Tis done, the great trans-ac-tion's done: I am my Lord's and He is mine;
4. Now rest, my long-di-vid-ed heart, fixed on this bliss-ful cen-ter, rest,

Well may this glow-ing heart re-joice and tell its rap-tures all a-broad.
Let cheer-ful an-thems fill His house, while to that sa-cred shrine I move.
He drew me, and I fol-lowed on, charmed to con-fess the voice di-vine.
nor ev-er from my Lord de-part, with Him of ev-'ry good pos-sessed.

Refrain

Hap-py day, hap-py day, when Je-sus washed my sins a-way!

He taught me how to watch and pray and live re-joic-ing ev-'ry day;

hap-py day, hap-py day, when Je-sus washed my sins a-way!

WORDS: Philip Doddridge, 1755; Ref., attr. Edward Francis Rimbault, 1854
MUSIC: *Happy Day*, Anon.; Ref., attr. Edward Francis Rimbault, 1854

L.M. with Refrain

Come, Holy Spirit, Dove Divine 324

Jesus saw the Spirit of God descending like a dove and lighting on Him. – Matthew 3:16 NIV

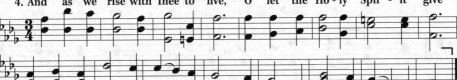

1. Come, Ho - ly Spir - it, Dove di - vine, on these bap - tis - mal wa - ters shine,
2. We love Thy name, we love Thy laws, and joy - ful - ly em - brace Thy cause;
3. We sink be - neath the wat - er's face; and thank Thee for Thy sav - ing grace;
4. And as we rise with Thee to live, O let the Ho - ly Spir - it give

and teach our hearts, in high - est strain, to praise the Lamb for sin - ners slain.
we love Thy cross, the shame, the pain, O Lamb of God, for sin - ners slain.
we die to sin, and seek a grave with Thee, be - neath the yield - ing wave.
the seal - ing unc - tion from a - bove, the joy of life, the fire of love.

WORDS: Adoniram Judson, ca. 1829, alt.
MUSIC: *Maryton*, Henry Percy Smith, 1874
This tune in a lower key, No. 485.

L.M.

Jesus, Our Lord and King 325

Present your bodies as a living sacrifice. – Romans 12:1 ESV

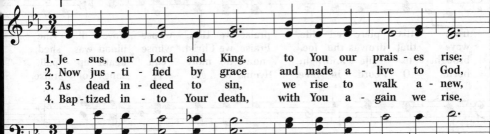

1. Je - sus, our Lord and King, to You our prais - es rise;
2. Now jus - ti - fied by grace and made a - live to God,
3. As dead in - deed to sin, we rise to walk a - new,
4. Bap - tized in - to Your death, with You a - gain we rise,

to You our bod - ies we pre - sent, a liv - ing sac - ri - fice.
formed for Your-self to show Your praise, we sound Your love a - broad.
hence - forth, as not our own, but Yours, we fol - low on - ly You.
to new - ness of a life of faith, to new and end - less joys.

WORDS: Anon., n.d.
MUSIC: *Trentham*, Robert Jackson, 1888

S.M.

326 At the Lamb's High Feast We Sing

Our Passover lamb is Christ, who has already been sacrificed. – 1 Corinthians 5:7 CEV

1. At the Lamb's high feast we sing, praise to our vic to - r'ous King, who hath washed us in the tide flow - ing from His pierc - ed side; praise we Him, whose love di - vine gives His sa - cred blood for wine, gives His bod - y

2. Where the Pas - chal blood is poured, death's dark an - gel sheathes his sword; Is - rael's hosts tri - um - phant go through the wave that drowns the foe. Praise we Christ, whose blood was shed, pas - chal Vic - tim, pas - chal Bread; with sin - cer - i -

3. Might - y Vic - tim from on high, hell's fierce pow'rs be - neath Thee lie; Thou hast con - quered in the fight, Thou has brought us life and light; now no more can death ap - pall, now no more the grave en - thrall; Thou hast o - pened

4. Eas - ter tri - umph, Eas - ter joy, on - ly sin can these de - stroy; from sin's pow'r do Thou set free souls new - born, O Lord, in Thee. Hymns of glo - ry songs of praise, Fa - ther, un - to Thee we raise; ris - en Lord, all

WORDS: *Ad regias Agni dapes*, ca. 6th c.; tr. Robert Campbell, 1849, alt.
MUSIC: *Salzburg*, Jacob Hintze, 1678; harm. Johann Sebastian Bach, 18th c.

7.7.7.7 D

for the feast, Christ the Vic - tim, Christ the Priest.
ty and love eat we man - na from a - bove.
par - a - dise, and in Thee Thy saints shall rise.
praise to Thee, with the Spir - it ev - er be.

Here at Thy Table, Lord 327

While they were eating, Jesus took bread, gave thanks and broke it, and gave it to His disciples. – Matthew 26:26 NIV

1. Here at Thy ta - ble, Lord, this sa - cred hour,
2. Come then, O ho - ly Christ, feed us, we pray;

O let us feel Thee near, in lov - ing pow'r;
touch with Thy pierc - ed hand each com - mon day,

call - ing our thoughts a - way from self and sin,
mak - ing this earth - ly life full of Thy grace,

as to Thy ban - quet hall we en - ter in.
till in the home of heav'n we find our place.

WORDS: May Pierpont Hoyt, 19th c.
MUSIC: *Bread of Life*, William Fiske Sherwin, 1877
This tune in a lower key, No. 231.

6.4.6.4 D

328 My God, Thy Table Now Is Spread

He took bread, gave thanks, broke it, and gave it to them, saying, "This is My body given for you." – Luke 22:19 NIV

1. My God, Thy ta - ble now is spread,
2. Hail, sa - cred feast, which Je - sus makes,
3. Let all ap - proach with hearts pre - pared,
4. Oh, let Thy ta - ble hon - ored be
5. Drawn by Thy quick - 'ning grace, O Lord,
6. Nor let Thy spread - ing gos - pel rest,

Thy cup with love doth o - ver - flow;
rich ban - quet of His flesh and blood!
with hearts in - flamed let all at - tend;
and fur - nished well with joy - ful guests;
in count - less num - bers let them come;
till through the world Thy truth has run;

may all Thy chil - dren there be led
Thrice hap - py he who here par - takes
nor, when we leave our Fa - ther's board,
and may each soul sal - va - tion see
and gath - er from their Fa - ther's board
till with this Bread shall all be blest,

and let them all its sweet - ness know.
that sa - cred stream, that heav'n - ly food!
the plea - sure or the prof - it end.
that here its sa - cred pledg - es tastes.
the Bread that lives be - yond the tomb.
who see the light or feel the sun.

WORDS: Sts. 1-5 Philip Doddridge, 1755; St. 6 Isaac Watts, 1719, alt.
MUSIC: *Rockingham*, Anon.; arr. Edward Miller, 1790

L.M.

Let Thy Blood in Mercy Poured   329

When we drink from the cup that we ask God to bless, isn't that sharing in the blood of Christ? – 1 Corinthians 10:16a CEV

1. Let Thy blood in mer - cy poured, let Thy gra - cious
2. Thou didst die that I might live; bless - ed Lord, Thou
3. By the thorns that crowned Thy brow, by the spear - wound
4. Wilt Thou own the gift I bring? All my pen - i -

Bod - y bro - ken, be to me, O gra - cious Lord,
cam'st to save me; all that love of God could give
and the nail - ing, by the pain and death, I now
tence I give Thee; Thou art my ex - alt - ed King,

of Thy bound - less love the to - ken.
Je - sus by His sor - rows gave me.
claim, O Christ, Thy love un - fail - ing.
of Thy match - less love for - give me.

Refrain

Thou didst give Thy - self for me, now I give my - self to thee.

WORDS: Greek hymn, anon., n.d.; tr. John Brownlie, 1907
MUSIC: *Jesu, Meine Zuversicht*, melody Johann Cruger, 1653; harm *The Chorale Book for England*, 1863   7.8.7.8 with Refrain

330

Let Us Break Bread Together

They also broke bread and prayed together. – Acts 2:42b CEV

1. Let us break bread to-geth-er on our knees, on our knees;
2. Let us *take the cup to-geth-er on our knees, on our knees;

let us break bread to-geth-er on our knees, on our knees.
let us *take the cup to-geth-er on our knees, on our knees.

Refrain

When I fall on my knees with my face to the ris-ing sun,

O Lord, have mer-cy on me, on me.

3. Let us praise God to-geth-er on our knees, on our knees;

*optional: drink wine

WORDS: Negro spiritual, n.d.
MUSIC: *Let Us Break Bread*, Negro spiritual, n.d.; arr. Eric Wyse, 2005

Irregular with Refrain

let us praise God to-geth-er on our knees, on our knees.

Refrain

When I fall on my knees with my face to the ris-ing sun,

O Lord, have mer-cy on me, on me.

Shepherd of Souls, Refresh and Bless 331

Man shall not live by bread alone, but by every word of God. – Luke 4:4 KJV

1. Shep-herd of souls, re-fresh and bless   Thy cho-sen pil-grim flock
2. We would not live by bread a-lone,   but by Thy Word of grace,
3. Be known to us in break-ing bread,   but do not then de-part;
4. There sup with us in love di-vine;   Your bod-y and Your blood,

with man-na in the wil-der-ness,   with wa-ter from the rock.
in strength of which we trav-el on   to our a-bid-ing place.
Sav-ior, a-bide with us, and spread   Your ta-ble in our heart.
that liv-ing bread, that heav'n-ly wine,   be our im-mor-tal food.

WORDS: James Montgomery, 1825, alt.
MUSIC: *St. Agnes,* John Bacchus Dykes, 1866
This tune in a higher key No. 55.

C.M.

332 According to Thy Gracious Word

This is My body, which is given for you. Eat this and remember Me. – 1 Corinthians 11:24 CEV

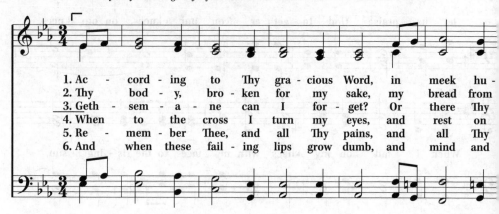

1. Ac - cord - ing to Thy gra - cious Word, in meek hu -
2. Thy bod - y, bro - ken for my sake, my bread from
3. Geth - sem - a - ne can I for - get? Or there Thy
4. When to the cross I turn my eyes, and rest on
5. Re - mem - ber Thee, and all Thy pains, and all Thy
6. And when these fail - ing lips grow dumb, and mind and

mil - i - ty, this will I do, my
heav'n shall be; Thy test - a - men - tal
con - flict see, Thine ag - o - ny and
Cal - va - ry, O Lamb of God, my
love to me: Yea, while a breath, a
mem - 'ry flee; when Thou shalt in Thy

dy - ing Lord, I will re - mem - ber Thee.
cup I take, and thus re - mem - ber Thee.
blood - y sweat, and not re - mem - ber Thee?
sac - ri - fice, I must re - mem - ber Thee.
pulse re - mains will I re - mem - ber Thee.
king - dom come, Je - sus, re - mem - ber me.

WORDS: James Montgomery, 1825
MUSIC: *Manoah*, from *A Collection of Psalm and Hymn Tunes*, Henry Wellington Greatorex, 1851
This tune in a higher key, No. 30.

C.M

Lift Up Your Hearts!

Let us lift up our hearts and hands to God in heaven.– Lamentations 3:41 ESV

1. "Lift up your hearts!" We lift them, Lord, to Thee;
   here at Thy feet none oth - er may we see.
   "Lift up your hearts!" E'en so, with one ac - cord,
   we lift them up, we lift them to the Lord.

2. A - bove the lev - el of the for - mer years,
   the mire of sin, the weight of guilt - y fears;
   the mist of doubt, the blight of love's de - cay,
   O Lord of Light, lift all our hearts to - day!

3. Lift ev - 'ry gift that Thou Thy - self hast giv'n;
   low lies the best till lift - ed up to heav'n:
   Low lie the bound - ing heart, the teem - ing brain,
   till, sent from God, they mount to God a - gain.

4. Then, as the trum - pet call, in af - ter years,
   "Lift up your hearts!" rings peal - ing in our ears.
   Still shall those hearts re - spond, with full ac - cord,
   "We lift them up, we lift them to the Lord!"

WORDS: Henry Montague Butler, 1881
MUSIC: *Woodlands,* Walter Greatorex, 1916

10.10.10.10

334 Blest Be the Tie

That they may be one as we are one. – John 17:11 NIV

1. Blest be the tie that binds our hearts in
2. Be - fore our Fa - ther's throne we pour our
3. We share our mu - tual woes, our mu - tual
4. When we a - sun - der part, it gives us

Chris - tian love; the fel - low - ship of
ar - dent pray'rs; our fears, our hopes, our
bur - dens bear and of - ten for each
in - ward pain but we shall still be

kin - dred minds is like to that a - bove.
aims are one, our com - forts and our cares.
oth - er flows the sym - pa - thiz - ing tear.
joined in heart, and hope to meet a - gain.

WORDS: John Fawcett, 1782
MUSIC: *Dennis*, Johann Georg Nageli, 19th c.; arr. Lowell Mason, 1845

S.M

335 In Christ There Is No East or West

Faith in Christ Jesus is what makes each of you equal with each other. – Galatians 3:28 CEV

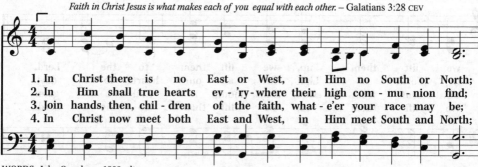

1. In Christ there is no East or West, in Him no South or North;
2. In Him shall true hearts ev - 'ry - where their high com - mu - nion find;
3. Join hands, then, chil - dren of the faith, what - e'er your race may be;
4. In Christ now meet both East and West, in Him meet South and North;

WORDS: John Oxenham, 1908, alt.
MUSIC: *St. Peter*, from *Song Tunes for the Voice and Pianoforte*; Alexander Robert Reinagle, 1836

C.M

but one great fel-low-ship of love through-out the whole wide earth.
His ser-vice is the gold-en chord, close bind-ing all man-kind.
who serves my Fa-ther as a child is sure-ly kin to me.
all Christ-ly souls are one in Him through-out the whole wide earth.

In Christ There Is No East or West   336

God does not show favoritism but accepts men from every nation. – Acts 10:34-35 NIV

1. In Christ there is no East or West, in
2. In Him shall true hearts ev-'ry-where their
3. Join hands, then, chil-dren of the faith, what-
4. In Christ now meet both East and West, in

Him no South or North; but one great fel-low-
high com-mu-nion find; His ser-vice is the
e'er your race may be; who serves my Fa-ther
Him meet South and North; all Christ-ly souls are

ship of love through-out the whole wide earth.
gold-en chord, close bind-ing all man-kind.
as a child is sure-ly kin to me.
one in Him through-out the whole wide earth.

WORDS: John Oxenham, 1908, alt.
MUSIC: *McKee*, Negro spiritual, arr. Harry Thacker Burleigh, early 20th c.

C.M.

337 God of Grace and God of Glory

The God of all grace called you to His eternal glory in Christ. — 1 Peter 5:10 NIV

1. God of grace and God of glo - ry, on Thy peo - ple pour Thy pow'r;
2. Lo! The hosts of e - vil round us scorn Thy Christ, as - sail His ways!
3. Cure Thy chil - dren's war - ring mad - ness, bend our pride to Thy con - trol;
4. Save us from weak res - ig - na - tion to the e - vils we de - plore;

crown Thine an - cient Church's sto - ry; bring Her bud to glo - r'ous flow'r.
Fears and doubts too long have bound us; free our hearts to work and praise.
shame our wan - ton, self - ish glad - ness, rich in things and poor in soul.
let the search for Thy sal - va - tion be our glo - ry ev - er - more.

Grant us wis - dom, grant us cour - age, for the fac - ing of this
Grant us wis - dom, grant us cour - age, for the liv - ing of these
Grant us wis - dom, grant us cour - age, lest we miss Thy king - dom's
Grant us wis - dom, grant us cour - age, serv - ing Thee whom we a -

hour, of this hour, for the fac - ing of this hour.
days, of these days, for the liv - ing of these days.
goal, king - dom's goal, lest we miss Thy king - dom's goal.
dore we a - dore, serv - ing Thee whom we a - dore.

WORDS: Harry Emerson Fosdick, 1930
MUSIC: *Cwm Rhondda*, John Hughes, 1907

8.7.8.7.8.7 with Repeat

Revive Us Again

Wilt Thou not revive us again; that Thy people may rejoice in Thee? – Psalm 85:6 KJV

1. We praise Thee, O God, for the Son of Thy love,
2. We praise Thee, O God, for Thy Spir - it of light,
3. All glo - ry and praise to the Lamb that was slain,
4. Re - vive us a - gain: fill each heart with Thy love;

for Je - sus who died and is now gone a - bove.
Who has shown us our Sav - ior and scat - tered our night.
Who has borne all our sins and has cleansed ev - 'ry stain.
may each soul be re - kin - dled with fire from a - bove.

Refrain

Hal - le - lu - jah, Thine the glo - ry! Hal - le - lu - jah, a - men!

Hal - le - lu - jah, Thine the glo - ry! Re - vive us a - gain.

WORDS: William Paton Mackay, 1863
MUSIC: *Revive Us Again,* John Jenkins Husband, ca. 1815

11.11 with Refrain

339 O Breath of Life

The Lord God formed the man of dust from the ground and breathed into his nostrils the breath of life. – Genesis 2:7 ESV

1. O Breath of Life, come sweep-ing through us,
2. O Wind of God, come bend us, break us,
3. O Breath of Love, come breathe with-in us,
4. O Heart of Christ, once bro-ken for us,
5. Re-vive us, Lord! Is zeal a-bat-ing

re-vive Your Church with life and pow'r;
till hum-bly we con-fess our need;
re-new-ing thought and will and heart;
'tis there we find our strength and rest;
while har-vest fields are vast and white?

O Breath of Life, come, cleanse, re-new us,
then in Your ten-der-ness re-make us,
come, love of Christ, a-fresh to win us,
our bro-ken, con-trite hearts now so-lace,
Re-vive us, Lord, the world is wait-ing,

and fit Your Church to meet this hour.
re-vive, re-store, for this we plead.
re-vive Your Church in ev-'ry part.
and let Your wait-ing Church be blest.
e-quip Your Church to spread the light.

WORDS: Elizabeth Ann Porter Head, ca. 1914
MUSIC: *Spiritus Vitae*, Mary Jane Hammond, ca. 1920

9.8.9.8

Rise Up, O Men of God! 340

We will serve the Lord our God and obey Him. – Joshua 24:24 NIV

1. Rise up, O men* of God! Have done with less-er things.
2. Rise up, O men of God! His king-dom tar-ries long.
3. Rise up, O men of God! The Church for you doth wait,
4. Lift high the cross of Christ! Tread where His feet have trod.

Give heart and mind and soul and strength to serve the King of kings.
Bring in the day of broth-er-hood and end the night of wrong.
her strength un-e-qual to her task; rise up, and make her great!
As fol-l'wers of the Son of Man, rise up, O men of God!

"Ye saints" may be substituted for "O men."
WORDS: William Pierson Merrill, 1911
MUSIC: *Festal Song*, William Henry Walter, 1894
This tune in a higher key, No. 583.

S.M.

Rise Up, O Men of God! 341

We will serve the Lord our God and obey Him. – Joshua 24:24 NIV

1. Rise up, O men* of God! Have done with less-er things.
2. Rise up, O men of God! His king-dom tar-ries long.
3. Rise up, O men of God! The Church for you doth wait,
4. Lift high the cross of Christ! Tread where His feet have trod.

Give heart and mind and soul and strength to serve the King of kings.
Bring in the day of broth-er-hood and end the night of wrong.
her strength un-e-qual to her task; rise up, and make her great!
As fol-l'wers of the Son of Man, rise up, O men of God!

"Ye saints" may be substituted for "O men."
WORDS: William Pierson Merrill, 1911
MUSIC: *St. Thomas*, Aaron Williams, 1762; harm. Lowell Mason, 19th c.
This tune in a lower key, No. 320.

S.M.

342 There Shall Be Showers of Blessing

I will send down showers...there will be showers of blessing. – Ezekiel 34:26 NIV

1. There shall be show-ers of bless-ing; this is the prom-ise of love;
2. There shall be show-ers of bless-ing, pre-cious re-viv-ing a-gain;
3. There shall be show-ers of bless-ing; send them up-on us, O Lord;
4. There shall be show-ers of bless-ing; oh, that to-day they might fall,

there shall be sea-sons re-fresh-ing, sent from the Sav-ior a-bove.
o-ver the hills and the val-leys, sound of a-bun-dance of rain.
grant to us now a re-fresh-ing, come, and now hon-or Thy Word.
now as to God we're con-fess-ing, now as on Je-sus we call!

Refrain

Show - ers of bless-ing,
Show-ers, show-ers of bless-ing, show-ers of bless-ing we need:

Mer-cy-drops round us are fall-ing, but for the show-ers we plead.

WORDS: Daniel Webster Whittle, 1883
MUSIC: *Showers of Blessing,* James McGranahan, 1883

8.7.8.7 with Refrain

O Zion, Haste

343

O Zion, herald of good news; lift up your voice with strength. – Isaiah 40:9 ESV

1. O Zi - on,¹ haste, thy mis - sion high ful - fill - ing, to tell to
2. Be - hold how man - y thou-sands still are ly - ing bound in the
3. Pro - claim to ev - 'ry peo - ple, tongue and na - tion that God, in
4. Send her - alds forth to bear the mes - sage glo - r'ous; give of thy

all the world that God is Light; that He who made all na - tions
dark - some pris - on - house of sin, with none to tell them of the
Whom they live and move, is love: Tell how He stoop'd to save His
wealth to speed them on their way; pour out thy soul for them in

is not will - ing one soul should per - ish, lost in shades of night.
Sav - ior's dy - ing, or of the life He died for them to win.
lost cre - a - tion, and died on earth that we might live a - bove.
pray'r vic - to - r'ous; and all thou spend - est Je - sus will re - pay.

Refrain

Pub - lish glad tid - ings, tid - ings of peace,

tid - ings of Je - sus, re - demp - tion and re - lease.

¹ *Zion: the Church*

WORDS: Mary Ann Faulkner Thomson, 1868, 1871
MUSIC: *Tidings*, James Walch, 1875

11.10.11.10 with Refrain

344 "Christ for the World!" We Sing

He said to them, "Go into all the world and preach the good news." – Mark 16:15 NIV

1. "Christ for the world!" we sing; the world to
2. "Christ for the world!" we sing; the world to
3. "Christ for the world!" we sing; the world to
4. "Christ for the world!" we sing; the world to

Christ we bring with loving zeal;
Christ we bring with fervent prayer;
Christ we bring with one accord;
Christ we bring with joyful song;

the poor, and them that mourn, the faint and over-borne,
the wayward and the lost, by restless passions tossed,
with us the work to share, with us reproach to dare,
the new-born souls, whose days, reclaimed from error's ways,

sin-sick and sorrow-worn, whom Christ doth heal.
redeemed at countless cost, from dark despair.
with us the cross to bear, for Christ our Lord.
inspired with hope and praise, to Christ belong.

WORDS: Samuel Wolcott, 1869
MUSIC: *Italian Hymn*, from *The Collection of Psalm and Hymn Tunes*
Sung at the *Chapel of the Lock Hospital*, Felice de Giardini, 1769
Another harmonization of this tune, No. 4.

6.6.4.6.6.6.4

Christ Receiveth Sinful Men

345

This man welcomes sinners and eats with them. – Luke 15:2 NIV

1. Sin - ners Je - sus will re - ceive; sound this word of grace to all
2. Come and He will give you rest; trust Him, for His Word is plain;
3. Now my heart con - demns me not, pure be - fore the law I stand;
4. Christ re - ceiv - eth sin - ful men, e - ven me with all my sin;

who the heav'n - ly path-way leave, all who lin - ger, all who fall.
He will take the sin - ful - est; Christ re - ceiv - eth sin - ful men.
He who cleansed me from all spot, sat - is - fied its last de - mand.
purged from ev - 'ry spot and stain, heav'n with Him I en - ter in.

Refrain

Sing it o'er and o'er a - gain, Christ re -
Sing it o'er and o'er a - gain,

ceiv - eth sin - ful men; make the mes - sage clear and
Christ re - ceiv - eth sin - ful men; make the mes - sage

plain, Christ re - ceiv - eth sin - ful men.
clear and plain,

WORDS: Erdmann Neumeister, 1718, from *Evangelischer Nachklang;* tr. Emma Frances Shuttleworth Bevan, 1858
MUSIC: *Neumeister,* From *The Gospel Male Choir,* James McGranahan, 1883

7.7.7.7 with Refrain

346 Jesus Saves!

Christ Jesus came into the world to save sinners. This...is true and it can be trusted. – 1 Timothy 1:15 CEV

1. We have heard the joy-ful sound: Je-sus saves! Je-sus saves!
2. Waft it on the roll-ing tide: Je-sus saves! Je-sus saves!
3. Sing a-bove the bat-tle strife: Je-sus saves! Je-sus saves!
4. Give the winds a might-y voice: Je-sus saves! Je-sus saves!

Spread the tid - ings all a - round: Je-sus saves! Je-sus saves!
Tell to sin - ners far and wide: Je-sus saves! Je-sus saves!
By His death and end - less life: Je-sus saves! Je-sus saves!
Let the na - tions now re - joice: Je-sus saves! Je-sus saves!

Bear the news to ev - 'ry land, climb the steeps and cross the waves;
Sing, ye is - lands of the sea; ech - o back, ye o - cean caves;
Sing it soft - ly through the gloom, when the heart for mer - cy craves;
Shout sal - va - tion full and free; high-est hills and deep-est caves;

on - ward! 'Tis our Lord's com - mand; Je-sus saves! Je-sus saves!
earth shall keep her ju - bi - lee: Je-sus saves! Je-sus saves!
sing in tri - umph o'er the tomb: Je-sus saves! Je-sus saves!
this our song of vic - to - ry: Je-sus saves! Je-sus saves!

WORDS: Priscilla Jane Owens, 1882
MUSIC: *Jesus Saves*, William James Kirkpatrick, 1882

7.6.7.6.7.7.7.6

Jesus Saves!

Christ Jesus came into the world to save sinners. This...is true and it can be trusted. – 1 Timothy 1:15 CEV

1. We have heard the joy - ful sound: Je - sus saves!
2. Waft it on the roll - ing tide: Je - sus saves!
3. Sing a - bove the bat - tle strife: Je - sus saves!
4. Give the winds a might - y voice: Je - sus saves!

Spread the tid - ings all a - round: Je - sus saves!
Tell to sin - ners far and wide: Je - sus saves!
By His death and end - less life: Je - sus saves!
Let the na - tions now re - joice: Je - sus saves!

Bear the news to ev - 'ry land, climb the steeps and cross the waves;
Sing, ye is - lands of the sea; ech - o back, ye o - cean caves;
Sing it soft - ly through the gloom, when the heart for mer - cy craves;
Shout sal - va - tion full and free; high - est hills and deep - est caves;

on - ward! 'Tis our Lord's com - mand; Je - sus saves!
earth shall keep her ju - bi - lee: Je - sus saves!
sing in tri - umph o'er the tomb: Je - sus saves!
this our song of vic - to - ry: Je - sus saves!

WORDS: Priscilla Jane Owens, 1882
MUSIC: *Limpsfield*, Josiah Booth, 1898

7.3.7.3.7.7.7.3

348 Shine, Jesus, Shine

I have come into the world as a light, so that no one who believes in Me should stay in darkness. – John 12:46 NIV

1. Lord, the light of Your love is shin - ing, in the midst of the
2. Lord, I come to Your awe - some pres - ence, from the shad - ows in -
3. As we gaze on Your king - ly bright - ness so our fac - es dis -

dark - ness shin - ing; Je - sus, Light of the World, shine up - on us,
to Your ra - diance; by the blood I may en - ter Your bright - ness,
play Your like - ness, ev - er chang - ing from glo - ry to glo - ry;

set us free by the truth You now bring us; shine on me,
search me, try me, con - sume all my dark - ness; shine on me,
mir - rored here, may our lives tell Your sto - ry; shine on me,

Refrain

shine on me. Shine, Je - sus, shine, fill this
shine on me.
shine on me.

land with the Fa - ther's glo - ry; blaze, Spir - it blaze; set our

WORDS: Graham Kendrick, 1987
MUSIC: *Shine, Jesus, Shine*, Graham Kendrick, 1987

Irregular with Refrain

hearts on fire; flow, riv-er, flow, flood the na-tions with

grace and mer-cy; send forth Your Word, Lord, and let there be light.

Lord, Lay Some Soul upon My Heart 349

Yet I have made myself a servant unto all. that I might gain the more. – 1 Corinthians 9:19 KJV

Lord, lay some soul up-on my heart and

love that soul through me; and may I ev-er

do my part to win that soul for Thee.

WORDS: Leon Tucker, 19th c.
MUSIC: *Ira,* Ira David Sanky, 19th c.

C.M.

350 Hark, the Voice of Jesus Calling

I heard the voice of the Lord saying, "Whom shall I send?" – Isaiah 6:8 ESV

1. Hark, the voice of Je-sus call-ing, "Who will go and work to-day?
2. If you can-not cross the o-cean, and the dis-tant lands ex-plore.
3. Let none hear you i-dly say-ing, "There is noth-ing I can do."

Fields are white, and har-vests wait-ing, who will bear the sheaves a-way?"
You can find the lost a-round you, you can help them at your door.
While the lost of earth are dy-ing, and the Mas-ter calls for you;

Loud and long the Mas-ter calls us, rich re-ward He of-fers free;
If you can-not give your thou-sands, you can give the wid-ows's mite;
take the task He gives you glad-ly, let His work your plea-sure be;

who will an-swer, glad-ly say-ing, "Here am I, send me, send me"?
what you tru-ly give for Je-sus will be pre-cious in His sight.
an-swer quick-ly when He calls you, "Here am I, send me, send me."

WORDS: Daniel March, 1868, alt.
MUSIC: *Ellesdie,* attr. Wolfgang Amadeus Mozart, 18th c.; from Leavitt's *The Christian Lyre,* 1831;
arr. Hubert Platt Main, 1868

8.7.8.7.D

This tune in a lower key, No. 483.

Throw Out the Life-Line!

If one of you should wander from the truth, someone should bring him back. – James 5:19 NIV

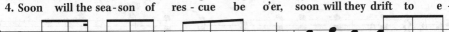

1. Throw out the Life-Line a - cross the dark wave, there is a broth - er whom
2. Throw out the Life-Line with hand quick and strong; why do you tar - ry, why
3. Throw out the Life-Line to dan - ger-fraught men, sink - ing in an - guish where
4. Soon will the sea-son of res - cue be o'er, soon will they drift to e -

some - one should save; some - bod - y's broth - er! Oh, who then will dare to
lin - ger so long? See! He is sink - ing; oh, has - ten to - day and
you've nev - er been: Winds of temp - ta - tion and bil - lows of woe will
ter - ni - ty's shore, haste then, my broth - er, no time for de - lay, but

Refrain

throw out the Life - Line, his per - il to share?
out with the Life - Boat! A - way, then, a - way! Throw out the Life - Line!
soon hurl them out where the dark wa - ters flow.
throw out the Life - Line and save them to - day.

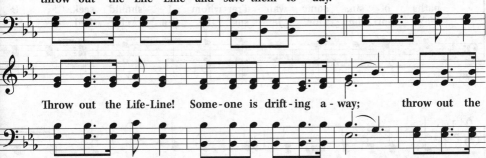

Throw out the Life-Line! Some - one is drift - ing a - way; throw out the

Life - Line! Throw out the Life - Line! Some - one is sink - ing to - day.

WORDS: Edward Smith Ufford, 1888
MUSIC: *Lifeline,* Edward Smith Ufford, 1888; arr. George Coles Stebbins, 1890

10.10.10.11 with Refrain

352 I'll Go Where You Want Me to Go

You must go to everyone I send you to and say whatever I command you. – Jeremiah 1:7 NIV

1. It may not be on the moun-tain's height or
2. Per-haps to-day there are lov-ing words which
3. There's sure-ly some-where a low-ly place in

o-ver the storm-y sea; it may not be at the
Je-sus would have me speak; there may be now, in the
earth's har-vest fields so wide, where I may la-bor through

bat-tle's front my Lord will have need of me. But
paths of sin, some wan-d'rer whom I should seek. O
life's short day for Je-sus, the Cru-ci-fied. So,

if by a still, small voice He calls to paths that I
Sav-ior, if Thou wilt be my Guide, though dark and
trust-ing my all to Thy ten-der care, and know-ing Thou

WORDS: St. 1 Mary Brown, 1899; Sts. 2, 3 Charles Edwin Prior, 1894
MUSIC: *Manchester,* Carrie Esther Parker Rounsefell, 1894

Irregular with Refrain

do not know, I'll an - swer dear Lord with my
rug - ged the way, my voice shall ech - o the
lov - est me, I'll do Thy will with a

hand in Thine, "I'll go where You want me to go."
mes - sage sweet. I'll say what You want me to say.
heart sin - cere. I'll be what You want me to be.

Refrain

I'll go where You want me to go, dear Lord, o - ver

moun - tain, or plain, or sea. I'll say what You want me to

say, dear Lord. I'll be what You want me to be.

353 We've a Story to Tell

Therefore go and make disciples of all nations. – Matthew 28:19 NIV

1. We've a sto-ry to tell to the na - tions, that shall turn their hearts
2. We've a song to be sung to the na - tions, that shall lift their hearts
3. We've a mes-sage to give to the na - tions, that the Lord who reign -
4. We've a Sav-ior to show to the na - tions, Who the path of sor -

to the right, a sto-ry of truth and mer - cy, a sto-ry of
to the Lord, a song that shall con - quer e - vil, and shat-ter the
eth a - bove hath sent us His Son to save us, and show us that
row hath trod, that all of the world's great peo - ples may come to the

peace and light, a sto-ry of peace and light.
spear and sword, and shat-ter the spear and sword.
God is love, and show us that God is love.
truth of God, may come to the truth of God.

Refrain

For the

dark-ness shall turn to dawn - ing, and the dawn-ing to noon-day bright, and

WORDS: Henry Ernest Nichol, 1896
MUSIC: *Message*, Henry Ernest Nichol, 1896

Irregular with Refrain

Christ's great king-dom shall come on earth, the king-dom of love and light.

Come, Labor On

354

His master replied, "Well done, good and faithful servant!" – Matthew 25:23 NIV

Unison

1. Come, la - bor on. Who dares stand i - dle on the har - vest plain,
2. Come, la - bor on. The en - e - my is watch - ing night and day,
3. Come, la - bor on. A - way with gloom-y doubts and faith-less fear!
4. Come, la - bor on. Claim the high call - ing an - gels can - not share
5. Come, la - bor on. No time for rest, till glows the west - ern sky

while all a - round Him waves the gold - en grain? And to each
to sow the tares, to snatch the seed a - way; while we in
No arm so weak but may do ser - vice here; by fee - blest
to young and old the gos - pel glad - ness bear: Re - deem the
till the long shad - ows o'er our path - way lie, and a glad

ser - vant does the Mas - ter say, "Go work to - day."
sleep our du - ty have for - got, He slum - ber'd not.
a - gents may our God ful - fill His righ - teous will.
time; its hours too swift - ly fly. The night draws nigh.
sound comes with the set - ting sun, "Well done, well done."

WORDS: Jane Laurie Borthwick, 1859, alt.
MUSIC: *Ora Labora*, Thomas Tertius Noble, 1918

4.10.10.10.4

355 If Jesus Goes with Me, I'll Go

The steps of a good man are ordered by the Lord: And he delighteth in His way. – Psalm 37:23 KJV

1. It may be in the val-ley, where count-less dan-gers hide;
2. It may be I must car-ry the bless-ed Word of life
3. But if it be my por-tion to bear my cross at home,
4. It is not mine to ques-tion the judg-ments of my Lord,

it may be in the sun-shine that I, in peace a-bide;
a-cross the burn-ing des-erts to those in sin-ful strife;
while oth-ers bear their bur-dens be-yond the bil-low's foam,
it is but mine to fol-low the lead-ings of His Word;

but this one thing I know: If it be dark or fair,
and though it be my lot to bear my col-ors there,
I'll prove my faith in Him: Con-fess His judg-ments fair,
but if to go or stay, or wheth-er here or there,

if Je-sus is with me, I'll go an-y-where!
if Je-sus goes with me, I'll go an-y-where!
and, if He stays with me, I'll stay an-y-where!
I'll be, with my Sav-ior, con-tent an-y-where!

WORDS: Charles Austin Miles, 1908
MUSIC: *If Jesus Goes,* Charles Austin Miles, 1908

Irregular with Refrain

Refrain

If Je-sus goes with me, I'll go an-y-

I'll go

where! 'Tis heav-en to me, wher-e'er I may be, if

He is there! I count it a priv-i-lege

here His cross to bear; if

His cross, His cross, His cross to bear;

Je-sus goes with me, I'll go an-y-where!

356
Send the Light!

O send out Thy light and Thy truth: let them lead me. – Psalm 43:3 KJV

1. There's a call comes ring-ing o'er the rest - less wave, "Send the
2. We have heard the Mac - e - do - nian call to - day, "Send the
3. Let us pray that grace may ev - 'ry - where a - bound, "Send the
4. Let us not grow wea - ry in the work of love, "Send the

light! Send the light!" There are souls to res - cue, there are
light! Send the light!" And a gold - en of - f'ring at the
light! Send the light!" And a Christ-like spir - it ev - 'ry-
light! Send the light!" Let us gath - er jew - els for a

"Send the light! Send the light!"

souls to save, Send the light! Send the light!
cross we lay, Send the light! Send the light!
where be found, Send the light! Send the light!
crown a - bove, Send the light! Send the light!

Send the light! Send the light!

Refrain

Send the light, the bless - ed gos - pel light; let it

Send the light, the bless - ed gos - pel light;

shine from shore to shore! Send the light, the

let it shine from shore to shore! Send the light,

WORDS: Charles Hutchison Gabriel, 1890
MUSIC: *McCabe*, Charles Hutchison Gabriel, 1890

11.6.11.6 with Refrain

bless-ed gos - pel light; let it shine for-ev-er-more!
the bless-ed gos-pel light; let it shine for-ev-er-more!

Let the Lower Lights Be Burning   357

Walk while you have the light, before darkness overtakes you. – John 12:35 NIV

1. Bright - ly beams our Fa - ther's mer - cy from His light-house ev - er - more,
2. Dark the night of sin has set-tled, loud the an - gry bil-lows roar;
3. Trim your fee - ble lamp, my broth-er! Some poor sail - or, tem-pest-tossed,

but to us He gives the keep-ing of the lights a - long the shore.
ea - ger eyes are watch-ing, long-ing, for the lights a - long the shore.
try - ing now to make the har - bor, in the dark-ness may be lost.

Refrain

Let the low - er lights be burn-ing! Send a gleam a-cross the wave!

Some poor faint - ing, strug-gling sea-man you may res-cue, you may save.

WORDS: Philip Paul Bliss, 1871
MUSIC: *Lower Lights,* Philip Paul Bliss, 1871

8.7.8.7 with Refrain

358
The Call for Reapers

Open your eyes and look at the fields! They are ripe for harvest. – John 4:35 NIV

1. Far and near the fields are teem - ing with the waves of
2. Send them forth with morn's first beam - ing; send them in the
3. O thou, whom thy Lord is send - ing, gath - er now the

rip - ened grain; far and near their gold is gleam - ing
noon - tide's glare; when the sun's last rays are gleam - ing,
sheaves of gold; heav'n - ward then at eve - ning wend - ing,[1]

Refrain

o'er the sun - ny slope and plain.
bid them gath - er ev - 'ry - where. Lord of har - vest, send forth
Thou shalt come with joy un - told.

reap - ers! Hear us, Lord, to Thee we cry; send them now the

sheaves to gath - er, ere the har - vest - time pass by.

1. wending: traveling on one's way

WORDS: James Oren Thompson, 1885
MUSIC: *Call for Reapers*, James Bowman Overton Clem, 19th c.

8.7.8.7 with Refrain

Rescue the Perishing

359

If someone is trapped in sin, you should gently lead that person back to the right path. – Galatians 6:1 CEV

1. Res - cue the per - ish - ing, care for the dy - ing, snatch them in pit - y from
2. Though they are slight-ing Him, still He is wait - ing, wait - ing the pen - i - tent
3. Down in the hu - man heart, crushed by the tempt-er, feel - ings lie bur-ied that
4. Res - cue the per - ish - ing, du - ty de-mands it; strength for thy la - bor the

sin and the grave; weep o'er the err-ing one, lift up the fall - en,
child to re - ceive; plead with them ear-nest-ly, plead with them gent - ly,
grace can re - store; touched by a lov-ing heart, wak-ened by kind-ness,
Lord will pro - vide; back to the nar-row way pa - tient - ly win them,

Refrain

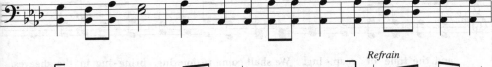

tell them of Je - sus the might - y to save.
He will for - give if they on - ly be - lieve.
chords that are bro - ken will vi - brate once more. Res-cue the per-ish-ing,
tell the poor wan-d'rer a Sav - ior has died.

care for the dy - ing; Je - sus is mer-ci - ful, Je - sus will save.

WORDS: Fanny Jane Crosby, 1869
MUSIC: *Rescue*, William Howard Doane, 1870

11.10.11.10 with Refrain

360 Bringing in the Sheaves

He who goes out weeping...shall come home with shouts of joy, bringing his sheaves with him. – Psalm 126:6 ESV

1. Sow-ing in the morn-ing, sow-ing seeds of kind-ness, sow-ing in the
2. Sow-ing in the sun-shine, sow-ing in the shad-ows, fear-ing nei-ther
3. Go-ing forth with weep-ing, sow-ing for the Mas-ter, though the loss sus-

noon-tide and the dew-y eve, wait-ing for the har-vest
clouds nor win-ter's chill-ing breeze; by and by the har-vest
tained our spir-it of-ten grieves; when our weep-ing's o-ver

and the time of reap-ing: We shall come re-joic-ing, bring-ing in the sheaves.
and the la-bor end-ed: We shall come re-joic-ing, bring-ing in the sheaves.
He will bid us wel-come: We shall come re-joic-ing, bring-ing in the sheaves.

Refrain

Bring-ing in the sheaves, bring-ing in the sheaves, we shall come re-

joic-ing, bring-ing in the sheaves. Bring-ing in the sheaves,

WORDS: Knowles Shaw, 1874
MUSIC: *Harvest*, George Austin Minor, 1880

12.11.12.11 with Refrain

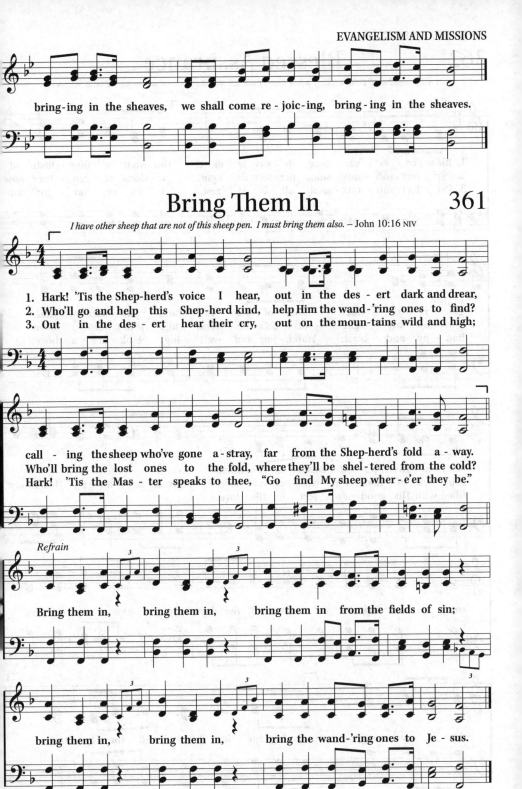

bring-ing in the sheaves, we shall come re-joic-ing, bring-ing in the sheaves.

Bring Them In

361

I have other sheep that are not of this sheep pen. I must bring them also. – John 10:16 NIV

1. Hark! 'Tis the Shep-herd's voice I hear, out in the des - ert dark and drear,
2. Who'll go and help this Shep-herd kind, help Him the wand-'ring ones to find?
3. Out in the des - ert hear their cry, out on the moun-tains wild and high;

call - ing the sheep who've gone a-stray, far from the Shep-herd's fold a - way.
Who'll bring the lost ones to the fold, where they'll be shel-tered from the cold?
Hark! 'Tis the Mas - ter speaks to thee, "Go find My sheep wher-e'er they be."

Refrain

Bring them in, bring them in, bring them in from the fields of sin;

bring them in, bring them in, bring the wand-'ring ones to Je - sus.

WORDS: Alexcenah Thomas, 1885
MUSIC: *Bring Them In,* William Augustine Ogden, 1885

L.M. with Refrain

362 Blessed Assurance

I will praise You, O Lord, with my whole heart; I will tell of all Your marvelous works. – Psalm 9:1 NKJV

1. Bless-ed as-sur-ance, Je-sus is mine! Oh, what a fore-taste of
2. Per-fect sub-mis-sion, per-fect de-light, vi-sions of rap-ture now
3. Per-fect sub-mis-sion, all is at rest, I in my Sav-ior am

glo-ry di-vine! Heir of sal-va-tion, pur-chase of God,
burst on my sight: An-gels de-scend-ing bring from a-bove
hap-py and blest: Watch-ing and wait-ing, look-ing a-bove,

born of His Spir-it, washed in His blood.
ech-oes of mer-cy, whis-pers of love. This is my sto-ry, this is my
filled with His good-ness, lost in His love.

Refrain

song, prais-ing my Sav-ior all the day long; this is my sto-ry,

this is my song, prais-ing my Sav-ior all the day long.

WORDS: Fanny Jane Crosby, 1873
MUSIC: *Assurance*, Phoebe Palmer Knapp, 1873

9.10.9.9 with Refrain

It Is Well with My Soul

I pray that...your soul is...well. – 3 John 2 NIV

1. When peace like a riv-er at-tend-eth my way, when sor-rows like
2. Though Sa-tan should buf-fet, though tri-als should come, let this blest as-
3. My sin: O, the bliss of this glo-ri-ous thought: My sin: Not in
4. And, Lord, haste the day when the faith shall be sight, the clouds be rolled

sea bil-lows roll; what-ev-er my lot, Thou hast taught me to say,
sur-ance con-trol, that Christ hath re-gard-ed my help-less es-tate,
part, but the whole, is nailed to the cross, and I bear it no more,
back as a scroll, the trump shall re-sound and the Lord shall de-scend,

Refrain

"It is well, it is well with my soul."   It is well   with my
and hath shed His own blood for my soul.   It is well
praise the Lord, praise the Lord, O my soul!
"E-ven so": It is well with my soul.

soul,   with my soul,   it is well, it is well with my soul.

WORDS: Horatio Gates Spafford, 1873
MUSIC: *Ville Du Havre*, Philip Paul Bliss, 1876

11.8.11.9 with Refrain

364
Be Still, My Soul!

My soul is in anguish. How long, O Lord, how long? – Psalm 6:3 NKJV

1. Be still, my soul! The Lord is on thy side; bear pa-tient-
2. Be still, my soul! Thy God doth un-der-take to guide the
3. Be still, my soul! The hour is has-t'ning on when we shall

ly the cross of grief or pain. Leave to thy God to
fu- ture as He has the past. Thy hope, thy con - fi -
be for - ev - er with the Lord, when dis - ap - point - ment,

or - der and pro - vide; in ev -'ry change He faith-ful
dence let noth-ing shake; all now mys - te - r'ous shall be
grief, and fear are gone, sor - row for - got, love's pur - est

will re - main. Be still, my soul! Thy best, thy heav'n - ly
bright at last. Be still, my soul! The waves and winds still
joys re - stored. Be still, my soul! When change and tears are

WORDS: Katharina Amalia Dorothea von Schlegel, 1752; *Hymns from the Land of Luther*, tr. Jane Laurie Borthwick, 1855
MUSIC: *Finlandia*, Jean Sibelius, 1899; arr. Paul Nelson, 2005

10.10.10.10.10.10

This tune in a lower key, No. 444.

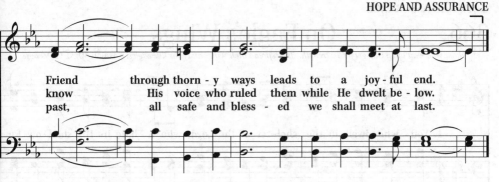

Friend   through thorn - y ways   leads   to   a   joy - ful   end.
know   His   voice who ruled   them while He   dwelt be - low.
past,   all   safe and bless - ed   we   shall meet at   last.

Be Still and Know

I am the Lord that healeth thee. – Exodus 15:26 KJV

365

1. Be   still   and   know   that   I   am
2. I   am   the   Lord   that   heal - eth
3. In   Thee,   O   Lord, I   put   my

God;   be   still   and   know   that   I   am
thee; I   am   the   Lord   that   heal - eth
trust; in   Thee,   O Lord, I   put   my

God;   be   still   and   know   that   I   am   God.
thee; I   am   the   Lord   that   heal - eth   thee.
trust; in   Thee,   O Lord, I   put   my   trust.

WORDS: Adapt. from Psalm 46:10; Exodus 15:26, Psalm 71:1
MUSIC: *Be Still and Know*, anon.; arr. Eric Wyse, 2005

8.8.8

366 On Eagle's Wings

Those who wait upon God get fresh strength. They spread their wings and soar like eagles. – Isaiah 40:31 The Message

1. You who dwell in the shel-ter of the Lord, who a-bide in His shad-ow for life, say to the Lord: "My ref-uge, my rock in whom I trust!"

Refrain

And He will raise you up on ea-gle's wings, bear you on the breath of dawn, make you to shine like the sun, and hold you in the palm of His hand.

Fine

2. The snare of the fowl-er will nev-er cap-ture you, and fam-ine will bring you no

WORDS: Based on Psalm 91; Michael Joncas, 1979, alt.
MUSIC: *On Eagle's Wings*, Michael Joncas, 1979; arr. Eric Wyse, 2005

Irregular with Refrain

fear;   un-der His wings your ref-uge, His   faith-ful-ness your shield.

3. You need not fear the ter-ror of the night, nor the ar-row that flies by

day;   though thou-sands fall a-round you,   near you it shall not come.

4. For to His an-gels is giv-en a com-mand to guard you in all of your ways;   up-

on their hands they will bear you up lest you dash your foot a-gainst a stone.

367 Jesus, I Am Resting, Resting

The promise of entering His rest still stands. – Hebrews 4:1 NIV

1. Je - sus, I am rest - ing, rest - ing in the joy of what Thou art;
2. O, how great Thy lov - ing kind - ness, vast - er, broad - er than the sea!
3. Sim - ply trust - ing Thee, Lord Je - sus, I be - hold Thee as Thou art,
4. Ev - er lift Thy face up - on me as I work and wait for Thee;

I am find - ing out the great - ness of Thy lov - ing heart.
O, how mar - vel - ous Thy good - ness, lav - ished all on me!
and Thy love, so pure, so change - less, sat - is - fies my heart;
rest - ing 'neath Thy smile, Lord Je - sus, earth's dark shad - ows flee.

Thou hast bid me gaze up - on Thee, and Thy beau - ty fills my soul,
Yes, I rest in Thee, Be - lov - ed, know what wealth of grace is Thine,
sat - is - fies its deep - est long - ings, meets, sup - plies its ev - 'ry need,
Bright - ness of my Fa - ther's glo - ry, sun - shine of my Fa - ther's face,

for by Thy trans - form - ing pow - er, Thou hast made me whole.
know Thy cer - tain - ty of prom - ise, and have made it mine.
com - pass - eth me round with bless - ings: Thine is love in - deed!
keep me ev - er trust - ing, rest - ing, fill me with Thy grace.

WORDS: Jean Sophia Pigott, 1876
MUSIC: *Tranquility*, James Mountain, 1876

8.7.8.5 D with Refrain

Refrain

Je-sus, I am rest-ing, rest-ing in the joy of what Thou art;

I am find-ing out the great-ness of Thy lov-ing heart.

As Longs the Deer for Cooling Streams 368

As the deer pants for the water brooks, so pants my soul for You, O God. – Psalm 42:1-2 NKJV

1. As longs the deer for cool - ing streams in
2. For Thee, my God, the liv - ing God, my
3. Why rest - less, why cast down, my soul? Hope
4. To Fa - ther, Son, and Ho - ly Ghost, the

parched and bar - ren ways, so longs my soul, O
thirst - y soul doth pine: O when shall I be -
still, and thou shalt sing the praise of Him who
God, whom we a - dore, be glo - ry, as it

God, for Thee and Thy re - fresh - ing grace.
hold Thy face, Thou Maj - es - ty di - vine?
is thy God, thy health's e - ter - nal spring.
was, is now, and shall be ev - er - more.

WORDS: *New Version of the Psalms of David*, Nahum Tate and Nicholas Brady, 1696; based on Psalm 42.
MUSIC: *Martyrdom*, melody and bass attr. Hugh Wilson, ca. 1800; adapt. and harm. Robert Smith, 1825
Another harmonization of this tune, No. 177.

C.M.

369 The Lord's My Shepherd, I'll Not Want

The Lord is my shepherd; I shall not want. – Psalm 23:1 KJV

1. The Lord's my Shep-herd, I'll not want; He makes me
2. My soul He doth re - store a - gain, and me to
3. Yea, though I walk in death's dark vale, yet will I
4. My ta - ble Thou hast fur - nish-ed in pres - ence
5. Good - ness and mer - cy all my life shall sure - ly

down to lie in pas - tures green; He
walk doth make with - in the paths of
fear no ill; for Thou art with me,
of my foes: My head Thou dost with
fol - low me, and in God's house for -

lead - eth me the qui - et wa - ters by.
righ - teous - ness, e'en for His own name's sake.
and Thy rod and staff me com - fort still.
oil a - noint, and my cup o - ver - flows.
ev - er - more my dwell - ing place shall be.

WORDS: Based on Psalm 23; metrical version from *The Scottish Psalter*, 1650
MUSIC: *Crimond*, Jessie Seymour Irvine, 1872

C.M.

370 The King of Love My Shepherd Is

I am the good shepherd; I know My sheep and My sheep know Me. – John 10:14 NIV

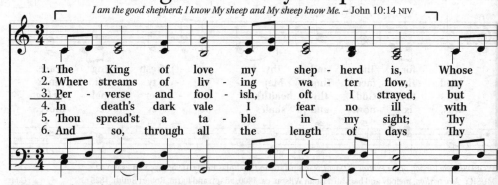

1. The King of love my shep - herd is, Whose
2. Where streams of liv - ing wa - ter flow, my
3. Per - verse and fool - ish, oft I strayed, but
4. In death's dark vale I fear no ill with
5. Thou spread'st a ta - ble in my sight; Thy
6. And so, through all the length of days Thy

WORDS: Paraphrase of Psalm 23; Henry Williams Baker, 1868
MUSIC: *St. Columba*, traditional Irish melody; harm. Charles Villiers Stanford, 1906

8.7.8.7

good - ness fail - eth nev - er; I noth - ing lack if
ran - somed soul He lead - eth, and where the ver - dant
yet in love He sought me, and on His shoul - der
Thee, dear Lord, be - side me; Thy rod and staff my
unc - tion grace be - stow - eth: And oh, what trans - port
good - ness fail - eth nev - er; Good Shep - herd, may I

I am His, and He is mine for - ev - er.
pas - tures grow, with food ce - les - tial feed - eth.
gent - ly laid, and home, re - joic - ing, brought me.
com - fort still, Thy cross be - fore to guide me.
of de - light from Thy pure chal - ice flow - eth!
sing Thy praise with - in Thy house for - ev - er.

The King of Love My Shepherd Is 371

I am the good shepherd; I know My sheep and My sheep know Me. – John 10:14 NIV

1. The King of love my shep-herd is, Whose good-ness fail-eth nev - er;
2. Where streams of liv-ing wa - ter flow, my ran-somed soul He lead - eth,
3. Per - verse and fool-ish, oft I strayed, but yet in love He sought me,
4. In death's dark vale I fear no ill with Thee, dear Lord, be - side me;
5. Thou spread'st a ta - ble in my sight; Thy unc - tion grace be - stow - eth:
6. And so, through all the length of days Thy good-ness fail-eth nev - er;

I noth - ing lack if I am His, and He is mine for - ev - er.
and where the ver - dant pas-tures grow, with food ce - les - tial feed - eth.
and on His shoul - der gent - ly laid, and home, re - joic-ing, brought me.
Thy rod and staff my com-fort still, Thy cross be - fore to guide me.
And oh, what trans-port of de - light from Thy pure chal-ice flow - eth!
Good Shep-herd, may I sing Thy praise with - in Thy house for - ev - er.

WORDS: Paraphrase of Psalm 23; Henry Williams Baker, 1868
MUSIC: *Dominus Regit Me*, John Bacchus Dykes, 1868

8.7.8.7

372 My Shepherd Will Supply My Need

He restoreth my soul: He leadeth me in the paths of righteousness for His name's sake. – Psalm 23:3 KJV

1. My Shepherd will supply my need; Jehovah is His name:
2. When I walk through the shades of death Thy presence is my stay;
3. The sure provisions of my God attend me all my days;

in pastures fresh He makes me feed, beside the living stream.
one word of Thy supporting grace drives all my fears away.
O may Thy house be my abode, and all my work be praise.

He brings my wand'ring spirit back, when I forsake His ways;
Thy hand, in sight of all my foes, doth still my table spread;
There would I find a settled rest, while others go and come;

and leads me, for His mercy's sake, in paths of truth and grace.
my cup with blessings overflows, Thine oil anoints my head.
no more a stranger, nor a guest, but like a child at home.

WORDS: Isaac Watts, 1719; based on Psalm 23
MUSIC: *Resignation*, from *Southern Harmony*, 1855; traditional American melody   C.M.D

Savior, Like a Shepherd Lead Us   373

He makes me to lie down in green pastures. – Psalm 23:2 KJV

1. Sav - ior, like a shep-herd lead us, much we need Thy ten - der care;
2. We are Thine; do Thou be-friend us, be the guard-ian of our way;
3. Thou hast prom-ised to re - ceive us, poor and sin - ful though we be;
4. Ear - ly let us seek Thy fa - vor; ear - ly let us do Thy will;

in Thy pleas - ant pas-tures feed us, for our use Thy folds pre - pare:
keep Thy flock, from sin de - fend us, seek us when we go a - stray;
Thou hast mer - cy to re - lieve us, grace to cleanse, and pow'r to free:
bless - ed Lord and on - ly Sav - ior, with Thy love our be - ings fill:

Bless - ed Je - sus, bless - ed Je - sus, Thou has bought us, Thine we are;
Bless - ed Je - sus, bless - ed Je - sus, hear, O hear us when we pray;
Bless - ed Je - sus, bless - ed Je - sus, ear - ly let us turn to Thee;
Bless - ed Je - sus, bless - ed Je - sus, Thou hast loved us, love us still;

bless - ed Je - sus, bless - ed Je - sus, Thou hast bought us, Thine we are.
bless - ed Je - sus, bless - ed Je - sus, hear, O hear us when we pray.
bless - ed Je - sus, bless - ed Je - sus, ear - ly let us turn to Thee.
bless - ed Je - sus, bless - ed Je - sus, Thou hast loved us, love us still.

WORDS: Attr. Dorothy Ann Thrupp, 1836; from *Hymns for the Young*, 1836,
MUSIC: *Bradbury,* William Batchelder Bradbury, 1859

8.7.8.7 D

374　He Leadeth Me! O Blessed Thought

Lead me in Your truth and teach me, for You are the God of my salvation. – Psalm 25:5 NKJV

1. He leadeth me! O blessed thought! O words with heav'nly
2. Sometimes 'mid scenes of deepest gloom, sometimes where Eden's
3. Lord, I would clasp Thy hand in mine, nor ever murmur
4. And when my task on earth is done, when, by Thy grace, the

com - fort fraught! What-e'er I do, wher-e'er I be, still
bow - ers₁ bloom, by wa - ters still, o'er trou - bled sea, still
nor re - pine,₂ con - tent, what-ev - er lot I see, since
vic - t'ry's won, e'en death's cold wave I will not flee, since

'tis God's hand that lead-eth me.
'tis His hand that lead-eth me.　He lead-eth me, He lead-eth me,
'tis Thy hand that lead-eth me.
God through Jor - dan lead-eth me.

by His own hand He lead-eth me: His faith-ful fol-l'wer

I would be, for by His hand He lead-eth me.

Refrain

1. *bowers: a pleasant shady place under trees of foliage*
2. *repine: to express discontent; fret or complain*

WORDS: Joseph Henry Gilmore, 1862
MUSIC: *He Leadeth Me,* William Batchelder Bradbury, 1864

L.M. with Refrain

Anywhere with Jesus I Can Safely Go 375

The Lord has promised that He will not leave us or desert us. – Hebrews 13:5 CEV

1. An-y-where with Je-sus I can safe-ly go; an-y-where He
2. An-y-where with Je-sus I am not a-lone, oth-er friends may
3. An-y-where with Je-sus o-ver land and sea, tell-ing souls in

leads me in this world be-low; an-y-where with-out Him dear-est
fail me, He is still my own; though His hand may lead me o-ver
dark-ness of sal-va-tion free; read-y as He sum-mons me to

joys would fade; an-y-where with Je-sus I am not a-fraid.
drea-ry ways, an-y-where with Je-sus is a house of praise.
go or stay, an-y-where with Je-sus when He points the way.

Refrain

An-y-where! An-y-where! Fear I can-not know;

an-y-where with Je-sus I can safe-ly go.

WORDS: Sts. 1, 2 Jessie Brown Pounds, 1887; St. 3 Helen Cadbury Alexander Dixon, ca. 1915
MUSIC: *I Can Safely Go*, Daniel Brink Towner, 1887

11.11.11.11 with Refrain

376 Moment by Moment

I will instruct you and teach you...counsel you and watch over you. – Psalm 32:8 NIV

1. Dy - ing with Je - sus, by death reck-oned mine; liv - ing with Je - sus a
2. Nev - er a tri - al that He is not there, nev - er a bur - den that
3. Nev - er a weak-ness that He doth not feel, nev - er a sick-ness that

new life di - vine; look-ing to Je - sus till glo - ry doth shine, mo-ment by
He doth not bear, nev - er a sor-row that He doth not share, mo-ment by
He can-not heal; nev - er a mo-ment, His grace doth not fill, Je - sus my

Refrain

mo-ment, O Lord, I am Thine.
mo-ment, I'm un - der His care. Mo-ment by mo-ment I'm kept in His love;
Sav - ior a - bides with me still.

mo-ment by mo-ment I've life from a - bove; look-ing to Je - sus till

glo - ry doth shine; mo-ment by mo-ment, O Lord, I am Thine.

WORDS: Daniel Webster Whittle, 1893, alt.
MUSIC: *Whittle*, May Whittle Moody, 1893

10.10.10.10 with Refrain

Take the Name of Jesus with You 377

Whatever you say or do should be done in the name of the Lord Jesus. – Colossians 3:17 CEV

1. Take the name of Je-sus with you, child of sor-row and of woe;
2. Take the name of Je-sus ev-er as a shield from ev-'ry snare;
3. O the pre-cious name of Je-sus! How it thrills our souls with joy,
4. At the name of Je-sus bow-ing, fall-ing pros-trate at His feet,

it will joy and com-fort give you, take it then wher-e'er you go.
when temp-ta-tions round you gath-er, breathe that ho-ly name in pray'r.
when His lov-ing arms re-ceive us, and His songs our tongues em-ploy.
King of kings in heav'n we'll crown Him, when our jour-ney is com-plete.

Refrain

Pre-cious name, O how sweet! Hope of earth and joy of heav'n;
Pre-cious name, O how sweet!

pre-cious name, O how sweet! Hope of earth and joy of heav'n.
Pre-cious name, O how sweet, how sweet!

WORDS: Lydia Odell Baxter, 1870
MUSIC: *Precious Name*, William Howard Doane, 1871

8.7.8.7 with Refrain

378 His Eye Is on the Sparrow

Are not five sparrows sold for two pennies? Yet not one of them is forgotten by God. – Luke 12:6 NIV

1. Why should I feel dis-cour-aged? Why should the shad-ows come?
2. "Let not your heart be trou-bled," His ten-der words I hear;
3. When-ev-er I am tempt-ed, when-ev-er clouds a-rise,

Why should my heart be lone-ly and long for heav'n and home
and rest-ing on His good-ness, I lose my doubt and fear.
when songs give place to sigh-ing, when hope with-in me dies,

when Je-sus is my por-tion? My con-stant Friend is He:
Though by the path He lead-eth but one step I may see:
I draw the clos-er to Him; from care He sets me free:

His eye is on the spar-row, and I know He watch-es me.
His eye is on the spar-row, and I know He watch-es me.
His eye is on the spar-row, and I know He watch-es me.

His eye is on the spar-row, and I know He watch-es me.
His eye is on the spar-row, and I know He watch-es me.
His eye is on the spar-row, and I know He watch-es me.

WORDS: Civilla Durfee Martin, 1905
MUSIC: *Sparrow,* Charles Hutchinson Gabriel, 1905

Irregular with Refrain

Refrain

I sing be-cause I'm hap-py, I sing be-cause I'm free; for His

eye is on the spar-row, and I know He watch-es me.

Children of the Heavenly Father 379

Let the little children come to me,...for the kingdom of God belongs to such as these. – Mark 10:14 NIV

1. Chil - dren of the heav'n - ly Fa - ther, safe - ly in His bos - om gath - er;
2. God His own doth tend and nour-ish; in His ho - ly courts they flour-ish.
3. Nei - ther life nor death shall ev - er from the Lord His chil - dren sev - er;
4. Though He giv - eth or He tak-eth, God His chil - dren ne'er for - sak-eth;

nes - tling bird nor star in heav - en such a ref - uge e'er was giv - en.
From all e - vil things He spares them; in His might - y arms He bears them.
un - to them His grace He show-eth, and their sor - rows all He know-eth.
His the lov - ing pur-pose sole - ly to pre - serve them pure and ho - ly.

WORDS: Karolina Wilhelmina Sandell-Berg, 1855; tr. Ernest William Olson, 1925
MUSIC: *Tryggare Kan Ingen Vara*, traditional Swedish melody, n.d.; from *The Hymnal*, arr. Oskar Ahnfelt, 1925 L.M.

380 Nearer, Still Nearer

Draw near to God, and He will draw near to you. – James 4:8 ESV

1. Near - er, still near - er, close to Thy heart, draw me, my
2. Near - er, still near - er, noth - ing I bring, naught as an
3. Near - er, still near - er, Lord, to be Thine! Sin, with its
4. Near - er, still near - er, while life shall last, till safe in

Sav - ior: So pre - cious Thou art! Fold me, O fold me
of - f'ring to Je - sus, my King: On - ly my sin - ful,
fol - lies, I glad - ly re - sign, all of its plea - sures,
glo - ry my an - chor is cast; through end - less a - ges

close to Thy breast. Shel - ter me safe in that ha - ven of
now con - trite heart. Grant me the cleans - ing Thy blood doth im -
pomp and its pride. Give me but Je - sus, my Lord, cru - ci -
ev - er to be near - er, my Sav - ior, still near - er to

rest; shel - ter me safe in that ha - ven of rest.
part; grant me the cleans - ing Thy blood doth im - part.
fied; give me but Je - sus, my Lord, cru - ci - fied.
Thee; near - er my Sav - ior, still near - er to Thee.

WORDS: Lelia Naylor Morris, 1898
MUSIC: *Morris,* Lelia Naylor Morris, 1898

9.10.9.10 with Repeat

Hiding in Thee

You are my hiding place; You shall preserve me from trouble. – Psalm 32:7 NKJV

1. O safe to the Rock that is high - er than I,
2. In the calm of the noon - tide, in sor - row's lone hour,
3. How oft in the con - flict, when press'd by the foe,

my soul in its con - flicts and sor - rows would fly;
in times when temp - ta - tion casts o'er me its pow'r;
I have fled to my ref - uge and breathed out my woe;

so sin - ful, so wea - ry, Thine own would I be; Thou
in the tem - pests of life, on its wide, heav - ing sea, Thou
how of - ten, when tri - als like sea bil - lows roll, have I

Refrain

blest "Rock of A - ges," I'm hid - ing in Thee.
blest "Rock of A - ges," I'm hid - ing in Thee. Hid - ing in Thee,
hid - den in Thee, O Thou Rock of my soul.

hid - ing in Thee, Thou blest "Rock of A - ges," I'm hid - ing in Thee.

WORDS: William Orcutt Cushing, 1876
MUSIC: *Hiding in Thee*, Ira David Sankey, 1877

11.11.11.11 with Refrain

382 He Hideth My Soul

He shall hide me; He shall set me high upon a rock. – Psalm 27:5 NKJV

1. A won-der-ful Sav-ior is Je-sus my Lord, a won-der-ful
2. A won-der-ful Sav-ior is Je-sus my Lord: He tak-eth my
3. With num-ber-less bless-ings each mo-ment He crowns, and, filled with His
4. When clothed in His bright-ness trans-port-ed I rise to meet Him in

Sav-ior to me; He hid-eth my soul in the cleft of the rock, where
bur-den a-way; He hold-eth me up and I shall not be moved, He
full-ness di-vine, I sing in my rap-ture, "O glo-ry to God for
clouds of the sky, His per-fect sal-va-tion, His won-der-ful love, I'll

Refrain

riv-ers of plea-sure I see.
giv-eth me strength as my day.
such a Re-deem-er as mine!"
shout with the mil-lions on high.

He hid-eth my soul in the cleft of the rock

that shad-ows a dry, thirst-y land; He hid-eth my life in the depths of His love,

WORDS: Fanny Jane Crosby, 1890
MUSIC: *Kirkpatrick*, William James Kirkpatrick, n.d.

11.8.11.8 with Refrain

and cov-ers me there with His hand, and cov-ers me there with His hand.

There Is a Balm in Gilead 383

Is there no balm in Gilead? Is there no physician there? – Jeremiah 8:22 ESV

Refrain

There is a balm in Gil-e-ad to make the wound-ed whole;

there is a balm in Gil-e-ad to heal the sin-sick soul.

Fine

1. Some-times I feel dis-cour-aged, and think my work's in vain,
2. If you can't preach like Pe-ter, if you can't pray like Paul,

but then the Ho-ly Spir-it re-vives my soul a-gain.
just tell the love of Je-sus, and say He died for all.

D.C.

WORDS: Negro spiritual, n.d.
MUSIC: *Balm in Gilead*, Negro spiritual, n.d.

7.6.7.6 with Refrain

384
Under His Wings

Yea, in the shadow of Thy wings will I make my refuge. – Psalm 57:1 KJV

1. Un-der His wings   I am safe-ly a-bid-ing.   Though the night
2. Un-der His wings: What a   ref-uge in sor-row!   How the heart
3. Un-der His wings: O what pre-cious en-joy-ment! There will I

deep-ens and   tem-pests are wild,   still I   can trust Him; I
yearn-ing-ly   turns to His rest!   Of-ten when earth has no
hide till life's   tri-als are o'er;   shel-tered, pro-tect-ed, no

know He will keep me.   He has re-deemed me, and   I   am His child.
balm for my heal-ing,   there I find com-fort, and there I am blest.
e-vil can harm me.   Rest-ing in Je-sus, I'm safe ev-er-more.

Refrain

Un-der His wings,   un-der His wings,   who from His love   can sev-er?

Un-der His wings my soul shall a-bide,   safe-ly a-bide   for-ev-er.

WORDS: William Orcutt Cushing, ca. 1896
MUSIC: *Hingham*, Ira David Sankey, 1896

11.10.11.10 with Refrain

Give Me Jesus

What good is it for a man to gain the whole world, yet forfeit his soul? – Mark 8:36 NIV

1. Take the world, but give me Je-sus, all its joys are but a name,
2. Take the world, but give me Je-sus; sweet-est com-fort of my soul.
3. Take the world, but give me Je-sus; let me view His con-stant smile.
4. Take the world, but give me Je-sus; in His cross my trust shall be,

but His love a-bid-eth ev-er, through e-ter-nal years the same.
With my Sav-ior watch-ing o'er me, I can sing though bil-lows roll.
Then through-out my pil-grim jour-ney light will cheer me all the while.
till, with clear-er, bright-er vi-sion, face to face my Lord I see.

Refrain

O the height and depth of mer-cy! O the length and breadth of love!

O the full-ness of re-demp-tion, pledge of end-less life a-bove!

WORDS: Fanny Jane Crosby, 1879
MUSIC: *Give Me Jesus (Sweney)*, John Robson Sweney, 1879

8.7.8.7.D. with Refrain

386 Be Thou My Vision

Not that we are sufficient in ourselves...our sufficiency is from God. – 2 Corinthians 3:5 NKJV

1. Be Thou my vi - sion, O Lord of my heart;
2. Be Thou my vi - sion, and Thou my true Word;
3. Rich - es I heed not, nor man's emp - ty praise,
4. High King of heav - en, my vic - to - ry won,

naught be all else to me, save that Thou art;
I ev - er with Thee and Thou with me Lord;
Thou mine in - her - i - tance, now and al - ways:
may I reach heav - en's joys, bright heav - en's Sun!

Thou my best thought, by day or by night,
Thou my great Fa - ther, and I Thy true son;
Thou and Thou on - ly, first in my heart,
Heart of my own heart what - ev - er be - fall,

wak - ing or sleep - ing, Thy pres - ence my light.
I in Thee dwell - ing, and I with Thee one.
High King of heav - en, my trea - sure Thou art.
still be my vi - sion, O Rul - er of all.

WORDS: Attr. Dallan Forgaill, 8th c.; tr. Mary Elizabeth Byrne, 1905; versified Eleanor Henrietta Hull, 1912
MUSIC: *Slane*, traditional Irish melody, n.d.; harm. Eric Wyse, 2005

10.10.10.10

If Thou but Trust in God to Guide Thee 387

I have had God's help to this very day, and so I stand here and testify. – Acts 26:22 NIV

1. If thou but trust in God to guide thee, and hope in
Him through all thy ways, He'll give thee strength, what-
e'er be - tide thee, to bear thee through the e - vil
days; who trusts in God's un - chang - ing love
builds on the rock that naught can move.

2. On - ly be still, and wait His lei - sure in cheer - ful
hope, with heart con - tent to take what - e'er thy
Fa - ther's plea - sure and all dis - cern - ing love hath
sent; nor doubt our in - most wants are known
to Him who chose us for His own.

3. Sing, pray, and keep His ways un - swerv - ing; so do thine
own part faith - ful - ly; and trust His Word, though
un - der - serv - ing, thou yet shalt find it true for
thee; God nev - er yet for - sook at need,
the soul that trust - ed Him in - deed.

WORDS: Georg Neumark, 1641; tr. Catherine Winkworth, 1855, alt.
MUSIC: *Neumark*, Georg Neumark, 1641

9.8.9.8.8.8

388 Jesus, Priceless Treasure

You are followers of the Lord, and that cornerstone is precious to you. – 1 Peter 2:7 CEV

1. Je - sus, price - less trea - sure, source of pur - est plea - sure, tru - est friend to me: Ah, how long I've pant - ed, and my heart has faint - ed, thirst - ing, Lord, for Thee! Thine I am, O spot - less Lamb; I will suf - fer

2. In thine arms I rest me; foes who would mo - lest me can - not reach me here. Though the earth be shak - ing, ev - 'ry heart be quak - ing, Je - sus calms my fear. Sin and hell in con - flict fell with their bit - ter

3. Hence, all fears and sad - ness, for the Lord of glad - ness, Je - sus, en - ters in. Those who love the Fa - ther, though the storms may gath - er, still have peace with - in. Yea, what - e'er I here must bear, still in Thee lies

WORDS: Johann Franck, 1653; tr. Catherine Winkworth, 1863, alt.
MUSIC: *Jesu, Meine Freude*, from *Praxis Pietatis Melica*, 1653; harm. Johann Sebastian Bach, 1723

Irregular

nought to hide Thee, nought I ask be - side Thee.
storms as - sail me, Je - sus will not fail me.
pur - est plea - sure, Je - sus, price - less trea - sure!

O Love That Will Not Let Me Go 389

I have loved you with an everlasting love. – Jeremiah 31:3 ESV

1. O Love that will not let me go, I rest my wea - ry
2. O Light that fol - low'st all my way, I yield my flick - 'ring
3. O Joy that seek - est me through pain, I can - not close my
4. O Cross that lift - est up my head, I dare not ask to

soul in Thee. I give Thee back the life I owe, that
torch to Thee. My heart re - stores its bor - rowed ray, that
heart to Thee. I trace the rain - bow through the rain, and
fly from Thee. I lay in dust life's glo - ry dead, and

in Thine o - cean depths its flow may rich - er, full - er be.
in Thy sun - shine's blaze its day may bright - er, fair - er be.
feel the prom - ise is not vain that morn shall tear - less be.
from the ground there blos - soms red life that shall end - less be.

WORDS: George Matheson, 1882
MUSIC: *St. Margaret,* Albert Lister Peace, 1884

8.8.8.8.6

390
In Christ Alone

On Him we have set our hope that He will continue to deliver us. – 2 Corinthians 1:10 NIV

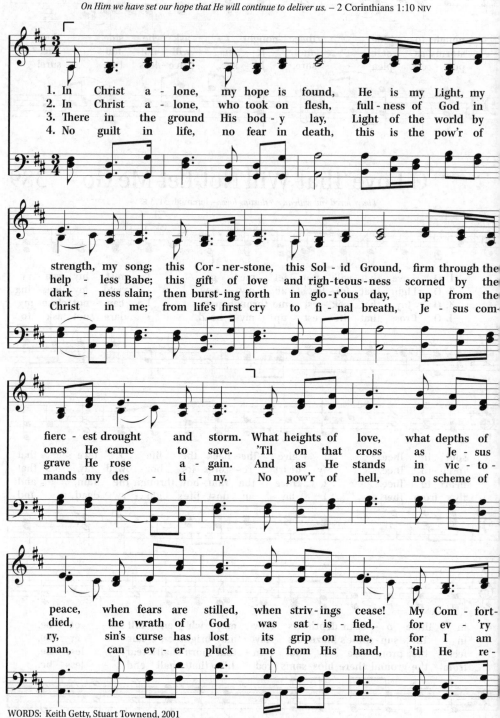

1. In Christ a - lone, my hope is found, He is my Light, my
2. In Christ a - lone, who took on flesh, full - ness of God in
3. There in the ground His bod - y lay, Light of the world by
4. No guilt in life, no fear in death, this is the pow'r of

strength, my song; this Cor - ner-stone, this Sol - id Ground, firm through the
help - less Babe; this gift of love and righ-teous-ness scorned by the
dark - ness slain; then burst-ing forth in glo - r'ous day, up from the
Christ in me; from life's first cry to fi - nal breath, Je - sus com-

fierc - est drought and storm. What heights of love, what depths of
ones He came to save. 'Til on that cross as Je - sus
grave He rose a - gain. And as He stands in vic - to -
mands my des - ti - ny. No pow'r of hell, no scheme of

peace, when fears are stilled, when striv - ings cease! My Com - fort-
died, the wrath of God was sat - is - fied, for ev - 'ry
ry, sin's curse has lost its grip on me, for I am
man, can ev - er pluck me from His hand, 'til He re-

WORDS: Keith Getty, Stuart Townend, 2001
MUSIC: *In Christ Alone*, Keith Getty, Stuart Townend, 2001; arr. Eric Wyse, 2005

L.M.D

er, my all - in - all; here in the love of Christ I stand.
sin on Him was laid; here in the death of Christ I live.
His and He is mine; bought with the pre-cious blood of Christ.
turns or calls me home; here in the pow'r of Christ I'll stand.

Jesus, Savior, Pilot Me   391

The wind died down...then those in the boat worshipped Him, saying, "Truly you are the Son of God." – Matthew 14:32-33 NIV

1. Je - sus, Sav - ior, pi - lot me o - ver life's tem - pes - tuous sea;
2. As a moth - er stills her child, Thou canst hush the o - cean wild;
3. When at last I near the shore, and the fear - ful break - ers roar

un - known waves be - fore me roll, hid - ing rock and treach - 'rous
bois - t'rous waves o - bey Thy will when Thou say'st to them, "Be
'twixt me and the peace - ful rest, then, while lean - ing on Thy

shoal; chart and com - pass came from Thee: Je - sus, Sav - ior, pi - lot me.
still!" Won - drous Sov - 'reign of the sea, Je - sus, Sav - ior, pi - lot me.
breast, may I hear Thee say to me, "Fear not, I will pi - lot thee."

WORDS: Edward Hopper, 1871
MUSIC: *Pilot,* John Edgar Gould, 1871   7.7.7.7.7.7

392 How Firm a Foundation

But the foundation that God has laid is solid. – 2 Timothy 2:19 CEV

1. How firm a foun-da-tion, ye saints of the Lord,
is laid for your faith in His ex-cel-lent Word!
What more can He say than to you He hath said,
to you who for ref-uge to Je-sus have fled?

2. "Fear not, I am with thee, O be not dis-mayed,
for I am thy God, and will still give thee aid;
I'll strength-en thee, help thee, and cause thee to stand,
up-held by my righ-teous, om-nip-o-tent hand.

3. "When through the deep wa-ters I call thee to go,
the riv-ers of sor-row shall not o-ver-flow;
for I will be with thee, thy trou-bles to bless,
and sanc-ti-fy to thee thy deep-est dis-tress.

4. "When through fier-y tri-als thy path-way shall lie,
My grace, all-suf-fi-cient, shall be thy sup-ply:
The flame shall not hurt thee; I on-ly de-sign
thy dross to con-sume, and thy gold to re-fine.

5. "The soul that on Je-sus hath leaned for re-pose,
I will not, I will not de-sert to its foes;
that soul, though all hell should en-deav-or to shake,
I'll nev-er, no, nev-er, no, nev-er for-sake!"

WORDS: *A Selection of Hymns*, John Rippon, 1787
MUSIC: *Foundation*, from *Genuine Church Music*, Joseph Funk, 1832

11.11.11.11

God Will Take Care of You

I will do whatever you ask in My name, so that the Son may bring glory to the Father. — John 14:13 NIV

1. Be not dis-mayed what-e'er be-tide, God will take care of you;
2. Through days of toil when heart doth fail, God will take care of you;
3. No mat-ter what may be the test, God will take care of you;

be-neath His wings of love a-bide, God will take care of you.
when dan-gers fierce your path as-sail, God will take care of you.
lean, wea-ry one, up-on His breast, God will take care of you.

Refrain

God will take care of you, through ev-'ry day, o'er all the way;

He will take care of you, God will take care of you.

WORDS: Civilla Durfee Martin, 1904
MUSIC: *God Cares*, Walter Stillman Martin, 1904

C.M. with Refrain

394 Jesus, Lover of My Soul

God will redeem my soul from the power of the grave, for He shall receive me. – Psalm 49:15 KJV

1. Je - sus, lov - er of my soul, let me to Thy bos - om fly,
2. Oth - er ref - uge have I none, hangs my help-less soul on Thee;
3. Thou, O Christ, art all I want, more than all in Thee I find;
4. Plen - t'ous grace with Thee is found, grace to cov - er all my sin;

while the near - er wa - ters roll, while the tem-pest still is high.
leave, ah! Leave me not a - lone, still sup-port and com - fort me.
raise the fall - en, cheer the faint, heal the sick, and lead the blind
let the heal - ing streams a - bound, make and keep me pure with - in.

Hide me, O my Sav - ior, hide, till the storm of life is past;
All my trust on Thee is stayed, all my help from Thee I bring;
Just and ho - ly is Thy name, I am all un - righ-teous - ness;
Thou of life the foun-tain art, free - ly let me take of Thee;

safe in - to the ha - ven guide; O re - ceive my soul at last.
cov - er my de - fense-less head with the shad - ow of Thy wing.
false and full of sin I am; Thou art full of truth and grace.
spring Thou up with - in my heart; rise to all e - ter - ni - ty.

WORDS: Charles Wesley, 1740
MUSIC: *Martyn*, Simeon Butler Marsh, 1834; arr. Rhys Thomas, 1916

7.7.7.7 D

Jesus, Lover of My Soul

God will redeem my soul from the power of the grave, for He shall receive me. – Psalm 49:15 KJV

1. Je - sus, lov - er of my soul, let me to Thy bos - om fly,
2. Oth - er ref - uge have I none, hangs my help - less soul on Thee;
3. Thou, O Christ, art all I want, more than all in Thee I find;
4. Plen - t'ous grace with Thee is found, grace to cov - er all my sin;

while the near - er wa - ters roll, while the tem - pest still is high.
leave, ah! Leave me not a - lone, still sup - port and com - fort me.
raise the fall - en, cheer the faint, heal the sick, and lead the blind.
let the heal - ing streams a - bound, make and keep me pure with - in.

Hide me, O my Sav - ior, hide, till the storm of life is past;
All my trust on Thee is stayed, all my help from Thee I bring;
Just and ho - ly is Thy name, I am all un - righ - teous - ness;
Thou of life the foun - tain art, free - ly let me take of Thee;

safe in - to the ha - ven guide; O re - ceive my soul at last.
cov - er my de - fense - less head with the shad - ow of Thy wing.
false and full of sin I am; Thou art full of truth and grace.
spring Thou up with - in my heart; rise to all e - ter - ni - ty.

WORDS: Charles Wesley, 1740
MUSIC: *Aberystwyth*, Joseph Parry, 1879

7.7.7.7 D

396 A Shelter in the Time of Storm

Thou hast been a shelter for me, and a strong tower from the enemy. – Psalm 61:3 KJV

1. The Lord's our rock; in Him we hide, a shel-ter in the time of storm;
2. A shade by day, de-fense by night, a shel-ter in the time of storm;
3. The rag-ing storms may round us beat, a shel-ter in the time of storm;
4. O Rock di-vine, O ref-uge dear, a shel-ter in the time of storm;

se-cure what-ev-er ill be-tide, a shel-ter in the time of storm.
no fears a-larm, no foes af-fright, a shel-ter in the time of storm.
we'll nev-er leave our safe re-treat, a shel-ter in the time of storm.
be Thou our Help-er ev-er near, a shel-ter in the time of storm.

Refrain

O Je-sus is a rock in a wea-ry land, a wea-ry land, a wea-ry land;

O Je-sus is a rock in a wea-ry land: A shel-ter in the time of storm.

WORDS: Vernon John Charlesworth, ca. 1880; adapt. Ira David Sankey, 1885
MUSIC: *Shelter*, Ira David Sankey, 1885

L.M. with Refrain

Leaning on the Everlasting Arms 397

The eternal God is your dwelling place, and underneath are the everlasting arms. – Deuteronomy 33:27 ESV

1. What a fel-low-ship, what a joy di-vine, lean-ing on the ev-er-
2. Oh, how sweet to walk in this pil-grim way, lean-ing on the ev-er-
3. What have I to dread, what have I to fear, lean-ing on the ev-er-

last-ing arms; what a bless-ed-ness, what a peace is mine,
last-ing arms; oh, how bright the path grows from day to day,
last-ing arms? I have bless-ed peace with my Lord so near,

Refrain

lean-ing on the ev-er-last-ing arms.
lean-ing on the ev-er-last-ing arms. Lean - ing,
lean-ing on the ev-er-last-ing arms. Lean-ing on Je-sus,

lean - ing, safe and se-cure from all a-larms; lean -
lean-ing on Je-sus, lean-ing on

ing, lean - ing, lean-ing on the ev-er-last-ing arms.
Je-sus, lean-ing on Je-sus,

WORDS: Elisha Albright Hoffman, 1887
MUSIC: *Showalter*, Anthony Johnson Showalter, 1887

10.9.10.9 with Refrain

398 I Am His, and He Is Mine

Everything belongs to you, and you belong to Christ, and Christ belongs to God. – 1 Corinthians 3:22-23 CEV

1. Loved with ev-er-last-ing love, led by grace that love to know;
2. Heav'n a-bove is soft-er blue, earth a-round is sweet-er green!
3. Things that once were wild a-larms can-not now dis-turb my rest;
4. His for-ev-er, on-ly His; who the Lord and me shall part?

gra-cious Spir-it from a-bove, Thou hast taught me it is so!
Some-thing lives in ev-'ry hue Christ-less eyes have nev-er seen:
closed in ev-er-last-ing arms, pil-lowed on the lov-ing breast.
Ah, with what a rest of bliss Christ can fill the lov-ing heart!

O this full and per-fect peace! O this trans-port all di-vine!
Birds with glad-der songs o'er-flow, flow'rs with deep-er beau-ties shine,
O to lie for-ev-er here, doubt and care and self re-sign,
Heav'n and earth may fade and flee, first-born light in gloom de-cline;

In a love which can-not cease, I am His, and He is mine.
Since I know, as now I know, I am His, and He is mine.
While He whis-pers in my ear, I am His, and He is mine.
But while God and I shall be, I am His, and He is mine.

WORDS: George Wade Robinson, 1876
MUSIC: *Everlasting Love*, James Mountain, 1876

7.7.7.7 D with Repeat

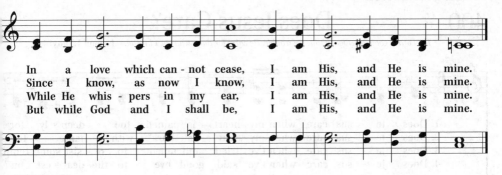

In a love which can-not cease, I am His, and He is mine.
Since I know, as now I know, I am His, and He is mine.
While He whis - pers in my ear, I am His, and He is mine.
But while God and I shall be, I am His, and He is mine.

How Sweet the Name of Jesus Sounds! 399

Then God gave Christ the highest place and honored His name above all others. – Philippians 2:9 CEV

1. How sweet the name of Je - sus sounds in
2. It makes the wound - ed spir - it whole, and
3. Dear name! The rock on which I build, my
4. Je - sus, my Shep - herd, Guard - 'an, Friend, my
5. Weak is the ef - fort of my heart, and
6. Till then I would Thy love pro - claim with

a be - liev - er's ear! It soothes my sor - rows,
calms the trou - bled breast; 'tis man - na to the
shield and hid - ing place; my nev - er - fail - ing
Proph - et, Priest, and King, my Lord, my life, my
cold my warm - est thought; but when I see Thee
ev - 'ry fleet - ing breath; and may the mu - sic

heals my wounds, and drives a - way my fear.
hun - gry soul, and to the wea - ry rest.
trea - s'ry filled with bound - less stores of grace.
way, my end, ac - cept the praise I bring.
as Thou art, I'll praise Thee as I ought.
of Thy name re - fresh my soul in death.

WORDS: John Newton, 1779, alt.
MUSIC: *St. Peter*, from *Song Tunes for the Voice and Pianoforte*, Alexander Robert Reinagle, 1836   C.M.

400 Does Jesus Care?

The Lord is good, a refuge in times of trouble. He cares for those who trust in Him. – Nahum 1:7 NIV

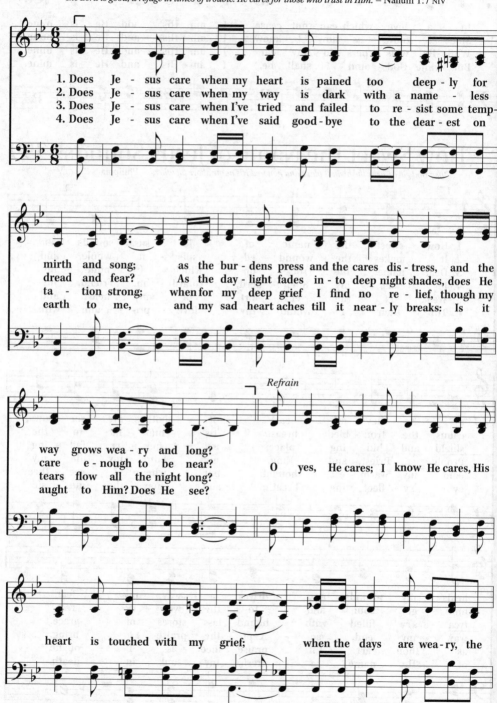

1. Does Je - sus care when my heart is pained too deep - ly for
2. Does Je - sus care when my way is dark with a name - less
3. Does Je - sus care when I've tried and failed to re - sist some temp-
4. Does Je - sus care when I've said good-bye to the dear - est on

mirth and song; as the bur - dens press and the cares dis - tress, and the
dread and fear? As the day - light fades in - to deep night shades, does He
ta - tion strong; when for my deep grief I find no re - lief, though my
earth to me, and my sad heart aches till it near - ly breaks: Is it

Refrain

way grows wea - ry and long?
care e - nough to be near?
tears flow all the night long?
aught to Him? Does He see?

O yes, He cares; I know He cares, His

heart is touched with my grief; when the days are wea - ry, the

WORDS: Frank E. Graeff, 1901
MUSIC: *My Savior Cares,* Joseph Lincoln Hall, 1901

Irregular with Refrain

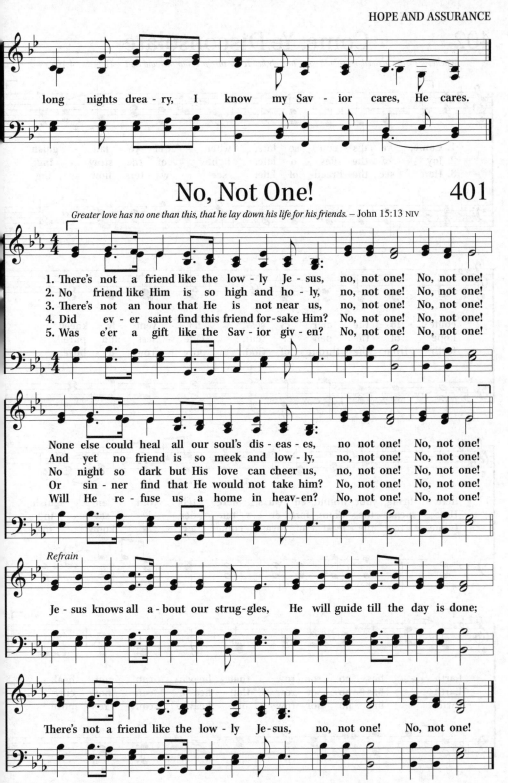

long nights drea-ry, I know my Sav-ior cares, He cares.

No, Not One! 401

Greater love has no one than this, that he lay down his life for his friends. – John 15:13 NIV

1. There's not a friend like the low-ly Je-sus, no, not one! No, not one!
2. No friend like Him is so high and ho-ly, no, not one! No, not one!
3. There's not an hour that He is not near us, no, not one! No, not one!
4. Did ev-er saint find this friend for-sake Him? No, not one! No, not one!
5. Was e'er a gift like the Sav-ior giv-en? No, not one! No, not one!

None else could heal all our soul's dis-eas-es, no not one! No, not one!
And yet no friend is so meek and low-ly, no, not one! No, not one!
No night so dark but His love can cheer us, no, not one! No, not one!
Or sin-ner find that He would not take him? No, not one! No, not one!
Will He re-fuse us a home in heav-en? No, not one! No, not one!

Refrain

Je-sus knows all a-bout our strug-gles, He will guide till the day is done;

There's not a friend like the low-ly Je-sus, no, not one! No, not one!

WORDS: Johnson Oatman, Jr., 1890
MUSIC: *Harper Memorial (No, Not One),* George Crawford Hugg, 1890

10.6.10.6 with Refrain

402 Come, Ye Disconsolate

Whenever we are in need, we should come bravely before the throne of our merciful God. – Hebrews 4:16 CEV

1. Come, ye dis-con-so-late, wher-e'er ye lan-guish,
come to the mer-cy seat, fer-vent-ly kneel;
here bring your wound-ed hearts, here tell your an-guish:
Earth has no sor-row that heav'n can-not heal.

2. Joy of the des-o-late, light of the stray-ing,
hope of the pen-i-tent, fade-less and pure!
Here speaks the Com-fort-er, ten-der-ly say-ing,
"Earth has no sor-row that heav'n can-not cure."

3. Here see the Bread of Life; see wa-ters flow-ing
forth from the throne of God, pure from a-bove:
Come to the feast of love; come, ev-er know-ing
earth has no sor-row but heav'n can re-move.

WORDS: Thomas Moore, 1816; Thomas Hastings, 1831, alt.
MUSIC: *Consolator*, from *Collection of Motetts or Antiphons*, Samuel Webbe, 1792

11.10.11.10

A Child of the King

403

If we are children, then we are...heirs of God and co-heirs with Christ. – Romans 8:17 NIV

1. My Fa-ther is rich in hous-es and lands, He hold-eth the
2. My Fa-ther's own Son, the Sav-ior of men, once wan-dered on
3. I once was an out-cast strang-er on earth, a sin-ner by
4. A tent or a cot-tage, why should I care? They're build-ing a

wealth of the world in His hands! Of ru-bies and dia-monds, of
earth as the poor-est of them; but now He is reign-ing for-
choice, and an a-lien by birth; but I've been a-dopt-ed, my
pal-ace for me o-ver there; though ex-iled from home, yet

sil-ver and gold, His cof-fers are full, He has rich-es un-told.
ev-er on high, and will give me a home in heav'n by and by.
name's writ-ten down, an heir to a man-sion, a robe, and a crown.
still may I sing: All glo-ry to God, I'm a child of the King.

Refrain

I'm a child of the King, a child of the King:

With Je-sus my Sav-ior, I'm a child of the King.

WORDS: Harriet Eugenia Buell, 1877
MUSIC: *Binghampton*, John Bunnell Sumner, 1877

10.11.11.11 with Refrain

404 Wonderful Peace

The Lord will bless His people with peace. – Psalm 29:11 NKJV

1. Far a - way in the depths of my spir - it to - night rolls a
2. What a trea - sure I have in this won - der - ful peace, bur - ied
3. I am rest - ing to - day in this won - der - ful peace, rest - ing
4. And I know when I rise to that cit - y of peace, where the
5. O soul, are you here with - out com - fort or rest, walk - ing

mel - o - dy sweet - er than psalm; in ce - les - tial - like strains it un -
deep in the heart of my soul; so se - cure that no pow - er can
sweet - ly in Je - sus' con - trol; and I'm kept from all dan - ger by
Au - thor of peace I shall see. That one of the an - thems the
down the rough path - way of time? Make Je - sus your friend ere the

ceas - ing - ly falls o'er my soul like an in - fi - nite calm.
mine it a - way, while the years of e - ter - ni - ty roll.
night and by day, now His glo - ry is flood - ing my soul.
ran - somed will sing, in that heav - en - ly king - dom shall be:
shad - ows grow dark; O ac - cept this sweet peace so sub - lime.

Refrain

Peace! Peace! Won - der - ful peace, com - ing down from the Fa - ther a - bove; sweep

WORDS: Warren D. Cornell, 1889, alt.
MUSIC: *Wonderful Peace*, W. George Cooper, 1889

12.9.12.9 with Refrain

o - ver my spir - it for - ev - er, I pray, in fath - om - less bil - lows of love.

Peace, Perfect Peace

405

You keep him in perfect peace whose mind is stayed on You, because he trusts in You. – Isaiah 26:3 ESV

1. Peace, per - fect peace, in this dark world of sin?
2. Peace, per - fect peace, by throng - ing du - ties pressed?
3. Peace, per - fect peace, with sor - rows surg - ing round?
4. Peace, per - fect peace, with loved ones far a - way?
5. Peace, per - fect peace, our fu - ture all un - known?
6. Peace, per - fect peace, death shad - 'wing us and ours?
7. It is e - nough: Earth's strug - gles soon shall cease,

The blood of Je - sus whis - pers peace with - in.
To do the will of Je - sus, this is rest.
On Je - sus' bos - om naught but calm is found.
In Je - sus' keep - ing we are safe and they.
Je - sus we know, and He is on the throne.
Je - sus has van - quished death and all its pow'rs.
and Je - sus call us to heav'n's per - fect peace.

WORDS: Edward Henry Bickersteth, Jr., 1875
MUSIC: *Pax Tecum*, George Thomas Caldbeck, 1877; arr. Charles J. Vincent, 1877

10.10

406 Whispering Hope

Be of good courage, and He shall strengthen your heart, all ye that hope in the Lord. – Psalm 31:24 KJV

1. Soft as the voice of an an - gel, breath-ing a les-son un-heard,
2. If in the dusk of the twi - light, dim be the re-gion a - far,
3. Hope, as an an-chor so stead - fast rends the dark veil for the soul,

hope with a gen-tle per - sua - sion, whis-pers her com-fort-ing word.
will not the deep-en-ing dark - ness bright-en the glim-mer-ing star?
whith-er the Mas-ter has en - tered, rob-bing the grave of its goal.

Wait till the dark - ness is o - ver, wait till the tem-pest is
Then when the night is up - on us, why should the heart sink a -
Come then, O come, glad fru - i - tion, come to my sad, wea - ry

done, hope for the sun-shine to - mor - row,
way? When the dark mid-night is o - ver,
heart; come, O Thou blest hope of glo - ry,

Refrain

af - ter the show - er is gone. Whis - per-ing hope,
watch for the break-ing of day. Whis-per-ing hope,
nev - er, O nev - er de-part. whis-per-ing

WORDS: Alice Hawthorne, 1868
MUSIC: *Whispering Hope*, Alice Hawthorne, 1868

8.7.8.7 D with Refrain

O how wel - come thy voice; mak -
hope, wel-come thy voice, O how wel-come thy voice; mak-ing my

ing my heart, in its sor - row re - joice.
heart, mak-ing my heart in its sor-row, its sor-row re - joice.

Thou Wilt Keep Him in Perfect Peace 407

Thou wilt keep him in perfect peace, whose mind is stayed on Thee. – Iasiah 26:3 KJV

1. Thou wilt keep him in per - fect peace,
2. They that wait up - on the Lord,

Thou wilt keep him in per - fect peace, Thou wilt keep him in
they that wait up - on the Lord, they that wait up -

per - fect peace, whose mind is staid on Thee.
on the Lord, they shall re - new their strength.

WORDS: Isaiah 26:3; 40:31
MUSIC: *Fürchte Dich Nicht,* Robert Witty n.d.; arr. Eric Wyse, 2005   8.8.8.6

408 Peace Like a River

Then your peace would have been like a river, and your righteousness like the waves of the sea. – Isaiah 48:18 NKJV

1. I've got peace like a riv-er, I've got peace like a
2. I've got love like an o-cean, I've got love like an
3. I've got joy like a foun-tain, I've got joy like a

riv-er, I've got peace like a riv-er in my soul;
o-cean, I've got love like an o-cean, in my soul;
foun-tain, I've got joy like a foun-tain in my soul;

I've got peace like a riv-er, I've got peace like a
I've got love like an o-cean, I've got love like an
I've got joy like a foun-tain, I've got joy like a

riv-er, I've got peace like a riv-er in my soul.
o-cean, I've got love like an o-cean in my soul.
foun-tain, I've got joy like a foun-tain in my soul.

WORDS: Traditional American melody, n.d.
MUSIC: *Peace Like a River*, traditional American melody, n.d.

7.7.10 D

He's Got the Whole World in His Hands 409

In His hand is the life of every living thing and the breath of all mankind. – Job 12:10 ESV

1. He's got the whole wide world in His hands,
2. He's got the wind and the rain in His hands,
3. He's got the ti - ny lit - tle ba - by in His hands,
4. He's got you and me, broth - er, in His hands,
5. He's got ev - 'ry - bod - y here in His hands,

He's got the whole wide world in His hands,
He's got the wind and the rain in His hands,
He's got the ti - ny lit - tle ba - by in His hands,
He's got you and me, broth - er, in His hands,
He's got ev - 'ry - bod - y here in His hands,

He's got the whole wide world in His hands,
He's got the wind and the rain in His hands,
He's got the ti - ny lit - tle ba - by in His hands,
He's got you and me, broth - er, in His hands,
He's got ev - 'ry - bod - y here in His hands,

He's got the whole world in His hands.
He's got the whole world in His hands.
He's got the whole world in His hands.
He's got the whole world in His hands.
He's got the whole world in His hands.

WORDS: Negro spiritual, n.d.
MUSIC: *Whole World,* Negro spiritual, n.d.; arr. Eric Wyse, 2005

Irregular

410 The Solid Rock

Anyone who hears and obeys...is like a wise person who built a house on solid rock. – Matthew 7:24 CEV

1. My hope is built on noth-ing less than Je-sus' blood and
2. When dark-ness seems to hide His face, I rest on His un-
3. His oath, His cov-e-nant, His blood sup-port me in the
4. When He shall come with trum-pet sound, oh, may I then in

righ-teous-ness; I dare not trust the sweet-est frame but
chang-ing grace; in ev-'ry high and storm-y gale, my
whelm-ing flood; when all a-round my soul gives way, He
Him be found; dressed in His righ-teous-ness a-lone, fault-

Refrain

whol-ly lean on Je-sus' name.
an-chor holds with-in the veil.
then is all my hope and stay.   On Christ the sol-id Rock I stand;
less to stand be-fore the throne.

all oth-er ground is sink-ing sand, all oth-er ground is sink-ing sand.

WORDS: Edward Mote, 1834
MUSIC: *Solid Rock*, William Batchelder Bradbury, 1863

L.M. with Refrain

The Solid Rock

Anyone who hears and obeys...is like a wise person who built a house on solid rock. – Matthew 7:24 CEV

1. My hope is built on noth - ing less than Je - sus' blood and
2. When dark - ness veils His love - ly face, I rest on His un -
3. His oath, His cov - e - nant, His blood, sup - port me in the
4. When He shall come with trum - pet sound, O may I then in

righ - teous - ness; I dare not trust the sweet - est frame, but
chang - ing grace; in ev - 'ry high and storm - y gale, my
whelm - ing flood; when all a - round my soul gives way, He
Him be found; dressed in His righ - teous - ness a - lone, fault -

whol - ly lean on Je - sus' name. On Christ, the sol - id
an - chor holds with - in the veil. On Christ, the sol - id
then is all my hope and stay. On Christ, the sol - id
less to stand be - fore the throne. On Christ, the sol - id

Rock I stand; all oth - er ground is sink - ing sand.
Rock I stand; all oth - er ground is sink - ing sand.
Rock I stand; all oth - er ground is sink - ing sand.
Rock I stand; all oth - er ground is sink - ing sand.

WORDS: Edward Mote, 1834
MUSIC: *Melita,* John Bacchus Dykes, 1861
This tune in a higher key, No. 600.

8.8.8.8.8.8

412 Like a River Glorious

I will extend peace...like a river, and the glory of the nations like an overflowing stream. – Isaiah 66:12 ESV

1. Like a riv-er glo-rious is God's per-fect peace, o-ver all vic-to-rious in its bright in-crease; per-fect, yet it flow-eth full-er ev-'ry day; per-fect, yet it grow-eth deep-er all the way.

2. Hid-den in the hol-low of His bless-ed hand, nev-er foe can fol-low, nev-er trai-tor stand; not a surge of wor-ry, not a shade of care, not a blast of hur-ry touch the spir-it there.

3. Ev-'ry joy or tri-al fall-eth from a-bove, traced up-on our di-al by the Sun of Love; we may trust Him ful-ly all for us to do; they who trust Him whol-ly find Him whol-ly true.

Refrain

Stayed up-on Je-ho-vah, hearts are ful-ly blessed; find-ing, as He prom-ised, per-fect peace and rest.

WORDS: Frances Ridley Havergal, 1876
MUSIC: *Wye Valley*, James Mountain, 1876
This tune (without the refrain) in a higher key, No. 207.

6.5.6.5 D with Refrain

Guide Me, O Thou Great Jehovah   413

And the Lord will guide you continually and satisfy your desire in scorched places. – Isaiah 58:11 ESV

1. Guide me, O Thou great Je - ho - vah, pil - grim through this
2. O - pen now the crys - tal foun - tain, whence the heal - ing
3. When I tread the verge of Jor - dan, bid my anx - ious

bar - ren land. I am weak, but Thou art might - y; hold me with Thy
stream doth flow; let the fire and cloud - y pil - lar lead me all my
fears sub - side; death of death and hell's de - struc - tion, land me safe on

pow'r - ful hand. Bread of Heav - en, Bread of Heav - en, feed me till I
jour - ney through. Strong De - liv - 'rer, Strong De - liv - 'rer, be Thou still my
Ca - nann's side. Songs of prais - es, songs of prais - es, I will ev - er

want no more, want no more; feed me till I want no more.
strength and shield, strength and shield; be Thou still my strength and shield.
give to Thee, give to Thee; I will ev - er give to Thee.

WORDS: William Williams, 1745; tr. Peter Williams, 1771
MUSIC: *Cwm Rhondda,* John Hughes, 1907

8.7.8.7.4.7 with Repeat

414 'Tis So Sweet to Trust in Jesus

In You our fathers trusted; they trusted, and You delivered them. – Psalm 22:4 ESV

1. 'Tis so sweet to trust in Je-sus, just to take Him at His Word; just to rest up-on His prom-ise, just to know "Thus saith the Lord."
2. O how sweet to trust in Je-sus, just to trust His cleans-ing blood; just in sim-ple faith to plunge me neath the heal-ing, cleans-ing flood!
3. Yes, 'tis sweet to trust in Je-sus, just from sin and self to cease; just from Je-sus sim-ply tak-ing life and rest, and joy and peace.
4. I'm so glad I learned to trust Him, pre-cious Je-sus, Sav-ior, Friend; and I know that He is with me, will be with me to the end.

Refrain

Je-sus, Je-sus, how I trust Him! How I've proved Him o'er and o'er! Je-sus, Je-sus, pre-cious Je-sus! O for grace to trust Him more!

WORDS: Louisa M. R. Stead, 1882
MUSIC: *Trust in Jesus,* William James Kirkpatrick, 1882

8.7.8.7 with Refrain

Trusting Jesus

Do not let your hearts be troubled. Trust in God; trust also in Me. – John 14:1 NIV

1. Sim - ply trust - ing ev - 'ry day, trust - ing through a
2. Bright - ly doth His Spir - it shine in - to this poor
3. Sing - ing if my way is clear, pray - ing if the
4. Trust - ing Him while life shall last, trust - ing Him till

storm - y way; e - ven when my faith is small,
heart of mine; while He leads I can - not fall,
path be drear; if in dan - ger, for Him call,
earth be past; till with - in the jas - per wall,

Refrain

trust - ing Je - sus, that is all.
trust - ing Je - sus, that is all.
trust - ing Je - sus, that is all. Trust - ing as the
trust - ing Je - sus, that is all.

mo - ments fly, trust - ing as the days go by;

trust - ing Him what - e'er be - fall, trust - ing Je - sus, that is all.

WORDS: Edgar Page Stites, 1876
MUSIC: *Trusting Jesus,* Ira David Sankey, 19th c.

7.7.7.7 with Refrain

416
Day by Day

Blessed be the Lord, who daily loads us with benefits. – Psalm 68:19 NKJV

1. Day by day and with each pass-ing mo-ment, strength I find to
2. Ev - 'ry day the Lord Him-self is near me with a spe-cial
3. Help me then in ev-'ry trib-u - la - tion so to trust Your

meet my tri - als here; trust-ing in my Fa-ther's wise be - stow-ment,
mer - cy for each hour; all my cares He fain would bear, and cheer me,
prom - is - es, O Lord, that I lose not faith's sweet con - so - la - tion

I've no cause for wor - ry or for fear. He whose heart is kind be-
He whose name is Coun-sel - or and Pow'r. The pro - tec - tion of His
of - fered me with - in Your ho - ly Word. Help me, Lord, when toil and

yond all mea - sure gives un - to each day what He deems best— lov-ing-
child and trea - sure is a charge that on Him-self He laid; "As your
trou - ble meet - ing, e're to take, as from a fath - er's hand, one by

WORDS: Carolina Wilhelmina Sandell-Berg, 1865; tr. Andrew L. Skoog, 1931
MUSIC: *Blott En Dag*, Oscar Ahnfelt, 1872

Irregular

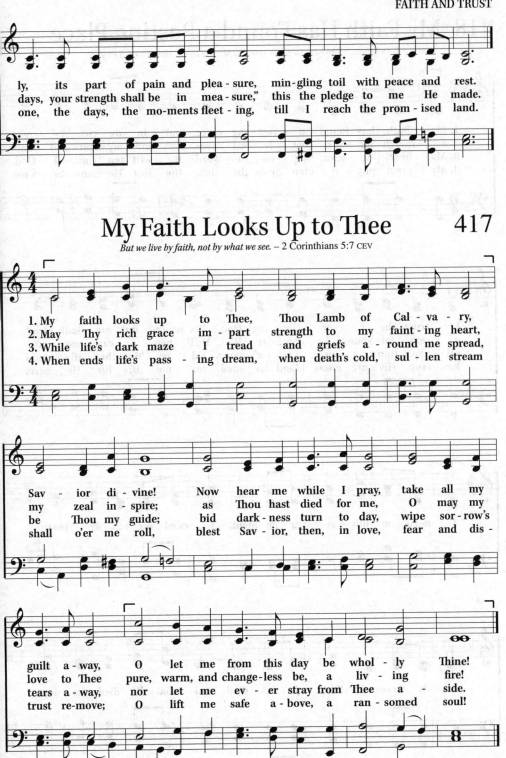

ly,   its   part   of   pain and plea - sure,   min - gling toil with peace and   rest.
days, your strength shall be   in   mea - sure,"   this   the pledge to   me   He   made.
one,   the   days,   the mo - ments fleet - ing,   till   I   reach the prom - ised   land.

My Faith Looks Up to Thee   417

But we live by faith, not by what we see. – 2 Corinthians 5:7 CEV

1. My   faith   looks   up   to   Thee,   Thou Lamb   of   Cal - va - ry,
2. May   Thy   rich   grace   im - part   strength   to   my   faint - ing heart,
3. While   life's   dark   maze   I   tread   and   griefs   a - round me spread,
4. When   ends   life's   pass - ing   dream,   when death's cold,   sul - len   stream

Sav - ior di - vine!   Now   hear me while   I   pray,   take   all   my
my   zeal in - spire;   as   Thou hast died   for me,   O   may my
be   Thou my guide;   bid   dark - ness turn   to day,   wipe   sor - row's
shall   o'er me   roll,   blest   Sav - ior,   then,   in love,   fear   and dis -

guilt   a - way,   O   let   me from this day   be   whol - ly   Thine!
love   to Thee   pure, warm, and change - less be,   a   liv - ing   fire!
tears   a - way,   nor   let   me   ev - er stray from Thee   a - side.
trust   re - move;   O   lift   me   safe   a - bove,   a   ran - somed   soul!

WORDS: Ray Palmer, 1830
MUSIC: *Olivet*, Lowell Mason, 1832

6.6.4.6.6.6.4

418 My Faith Has Found a Resting Place

Only people who have faith will enter the place of rest. – Hebrews 4:3 CEV

1. My faith has found a rest-ing place, not in de-vice or creed;
2. E-nough for me that Je-sus saves, this ends my fear and doubt;
3. My heart is lean-ing on the Word, the writ-ten Word of God;
4. My great phy-si-cian heals the sick, the lost He came to save;

I trust the Ev-er-liv-ing One, His wounds for me shall plead.
a sin-ful soul, I come to Him, He'll nev-er cast me out.
sal-va-tion by my Sav-ior's name, sal-va-tion thro' His blood.
for me His pre-cious blood He shed, for me His life He gave.

Refrain

I need no oth-er ar-gu-ment, I need no oth-er plea;

it is e-nough that Je-sus died, and that He died for me.

WORDS: Lidie H. Edmunds, 1891
MUSIC: *Landas,* Norwegian folk melody, n.d.; arr. William James Kirkpatrick, 1891

C.M. with Refrain

Savior, More Than Life to Me

419

You will receive a rich welcome into the eternal kingdom of our Lord and Savior Jesus Christ. – 2 Peter 1:11 NIV

1. Sav - ior, more than life to me, I am cling-ing, cling-ing close to Thee;
2. Through this chang - ing world be - low, lead me gent - ly, gent - ly, as I go;
3. Let me love Thee more and more till this fleet-ing, fleet-ing life is o'er;

let Thy pre - cious blood, ap - plied, keep me ev - er, ev - er near Thy side.
trust - ing Thee, I can - not stray– I can nev - er, nev - er lose my way.
till my soul is lost in love in a bright-er, bright-er world a - bove.

Refrain

Ev - 'ry day, ev - 'ry hour, let me feel Thy cleans-ing pow'r;
Ev - 'ry day and hour, ev - 'ry day and hour,

may Thy ten - der love to me bind me clos - er, clos - er, Lord, to Thee.

WORDS: Fanny Jane Crosby, 1875
MUSIC: *Every Day*, William Howard Doane, 1875

7.9.7.9 with Refrain

420 Wonderful, Wonderful Jesus

Let all who take refuge in You...sing for joy. – Psalm 5:11 NIV

1. There is nev-er a day so drea-ry, there is nev-er a night so
2. There is nev-er a cross so heav-y, there is nev-er a weight of
3. There is nev-er a care or bur-den, there is nev-er a grief or
4. There is nev-er a guilt-y sin-ner, there is nev-er a wan-d'ring

long, but the soul that is trust-ing Je-sus will some-where
woe, but that Je-sus will help to car-ry be-cause He
loss, but that Je-sus in love will light-en when car-ried
one, but that God can in mer-cy par-don through Je-sus

Refrain

find a song.
lov-eth so.   Won-der-ful, won-der-ful Je-sus, in the
to the cross.
Christ, His Son.

heart He im-plant-eth a song; a song of de-liv-'rance, of

cour-age, of strength; in the heart He im-plant-eth a song.

WORDS: Anna Belle Russell, 1921
MUSIC: *New Orleans,* Ernest Orlando Sellers, 1921

Irregular with Refrain

All the Way My Savior Leads Me 421

Our God...will be our guide even unto death. – Psalm 48:14 KJV

1. All the way my Sav-ior leads me; what have I to ask be-side?
2. All the way my Sav-ior leads me; cheers each wind-ing path I tread,
3. All the way my Sav-ior leads me; O, the full-ness of His love!

Can I doubt His ten-der mer-cy, who through life has been my guide?
Gives me grace for ev-'ry tri-al, feeds me with the liv-ing bread:
Per-fect rest to me is prom-ised in my Fa-ther's house a-bove:

Heav'n-ly peace, di-vin-est com-fort, here by faith in Him to dwell!
Though my wea-ry steps may fal-ter, and my soul a-thirst may be,
When my spir-it, cloth'd im-mor-tal, wings its flight to realms of day,

For I know what-e'er be-fall me, Je-sus do-eth all things well;
gush-ing from the Rock be-fore me, lo, a spring of joy I see;
this my song through end-less a-ges: Je-sus led me all the way;

For I know what-e'er be-fall me, Je-sus do-eth all things well.
gush-ing from the Rock be-fore me, lo, a spring of joy I see.
this my song through end-less a-ges: Je-sus led me all the way.

WORDS: Fanny Jane Crosby, 1875
MUSIC: *All the Way*, Robert Lowry, 1875

8.7.8.7 with Repeat

422 God Leads Us Along

When you pass through the waters, I will be with you. – Isaiah 43:2 ESV

1. In shad-y, green pas-tures, so rich and so sweet, God leads His dear
2. Some-times on the mount where the sun shines so bright, God leads His dear
3. Though sor-rows be-fall us and Sa-tan op-pose, God leads His dear

chil-dren a-long. Where the wa-ter's cool flow bathes the wea-ry one's feet,
chil-dren a-long. Some-times in the val-ley, in dark-est of night,
chil-dren a-long. Through grace we can con-quer, de-feat all our foes;

Refrain

God leads His dear chil-dren a-long.
God leads His dear chil-dren a-long. Some through the wa-ters, some through the
God leads His dear chil-dren a-long.

flood, some through the fire, but all through the blood. Some through great

sor-row, but God gives a song in the night sea-son and all the day long.

WORDS: George A. Young, 1903
MUSIC: *God Leads Us*, George A. Young, 1903

11.8.11.8 with Refrain

We Have an Anchor

423

This hope is like a firm and steady anchor for our souls. – Hebrews 6:19 CEV

1. Will your an-chor hold in the storms of life, when the clouds un - fold
2. It is safe - ly moored, 'twill the storms with-stand, for 'tis well se - cured
3. It will firm - ly hold in the straits of fear, when the break-ers have told
4. When our eyes be - hold through the gath - 'ring night the cit - y of gold,

their wings of strife? When the strong tides lift, and the ca - bles strain,
by the Sav - ior's hand; and the ca - bles passed from His heart to mine,
the reef is near; though the tem - pest rave and the wild winds blow,
our har - bor bright, we shall an - chor fast by the heav'n - ly shore,

Refrain

will your an - chor drift, or firm re - main?
can de - fy that blast through strength di - vine.
not an an - gry wave shall our bark o'er - flow.
with the storms all past for - ev - er - more.

We have an an-chor that

keeps the soul stead-fast and sure while the bil - lows roll, fas-tened to the

Rock which can - not move, ground-ed firm and deep in the Sav - ior's love.

WORDS: Priscilla Jane Owens, 1882
MUSIC: *Anchor,* William James Kirkpatrick, 1882

10.9.10.9 with Refrain

424 Master, the Tempest Is Raging!

He got up, rebuked the wind and said to the waves, "Quiet! Be still!" – Mark 4:39 NIV

1. Mas-ter, the tem-pest is rag-ing! The bil-lows are toss-ing high!
2. Mas-ter, with an-guish of spir-it I bow in my grief to-day;
3. Mas-ter, the ter-ror is o-ver, the el-e-ments sweet-ly rest;

The sky is o'er-sha-dowed with black-ness, no shel-ter of help is nigh:
the depths of my sad heart are trou-bled; O wak-en and save, I pray!
earth's sun in the calm lake is mir-rored, and heav-en's with-in my breast.

"Car-est Thou not that we per-ish?" How canst Thou lie a-sleep,
Tor-rents of sin and of an-guish sweep o'er my sink-ing soul!
Lin-ger, O bless-ed Re-deem-er, leave me a-lone no more;

when each mo-ment go mad-ly is threat-'ning a grave in the an-gry deep.
And I per-ish! I per-ish, dear Mas-ter; O has-ten, and take con-trol!
and with joy I shall make the blest har-bor, and rest on the bliss-ful shore.

WORDS: Mary Ann Baker, 1874
MUSIC: *Peace Be Still,* Horatio Richmond Palmer, 1874

Irregular with Refrain

Refrain

"The winds and the waves shall o-bey My will, peace, be still!"
peace, be still! peace, be still!

Wheth-er the wrath of the storm-tossed sea, or de-mons, or men, or what-

ev-er it be, no wa-ter can swal-low the ship where lies the

Mas-ter of o-cean and earth and skies; they all shall sweet-ly o-

bey my will; peace, be still! Peace, be still! They

all shall sweet-ly o-bey my will; peace, peace, be still!

425 Stepping in the Light

Jesus told us that God is light and doesn't have any darkness in Him. Now we are telling you. – 1 John 1:5 CEV

1. Try - ing to walk in the steps of the Sav - ior, try - ing to fol - low our
2. Press-ing more close - ly to Him who is lead-ing– when we are tempt - ed to
3. Walk-ing in foot-steps of gen - tle for-bear-ance, foot-steps of faith - ful - ness,
4. Try - ing to walk in the steps of the Sav - ior, up - ward, still up - ward we'll

Sav - ior and King, shap - ing our lives by His bless - ed ex - am - ple,
turn from the way, trust - ing the arm that is strong to de - fend us,
mer - cy and love, look - ing to Him for the grace free - ly prom - ised,
fol - low our Guide; when we shall see Him, the King in His beau - ty,

Refrain

hap - py, how hap - py, the songs that we bring.
hap - py, how hap - py, our prais - es each day. How beau-ti-ful to walk in the
hap - py, how hap - py, our jour - ney a - bove.
hap - py, how hap - py, our place at His side.

steps of the Sav - ior, step-ping in the light, step - ping in the light; how

beau - ti - ful to walk in the steps of the Sav - ior, led in paths of light.

WORDS: Eliza Edmunds Hewitt, ca. 1890
MUSIC: *Beautiful to Walk*, William James Kirkpatrick, 1890

11.10.11.10 with Refrain

Nearer, My God, to Thee

426

It is good for me to draw near to God; I have put my trust in the Lord God. – Psalm 73:28 KJV

1. Near - er, my God, to Thee, near - er to Thee!
2. Though like the wan - der - er, the sun gone down,
3. There let the way ap - pear steps un - to heav'n;
4. Then, with my wak - ing thoughts bright with Thy praise,
5. Or if on joy - ful wing, cleav - ing the sky,

E'en though it be a cross that rais - eth me;
dark - ness be o - ver me, my rest a stone;
all that thou send - est me in mer - cy giv'n;
out of my ston - y griefs, Beth - el I'll raise;
sun, moon, and stars for - got, up - ward I fly,

still all my song shall be, near - er, my God, to Thee,
yet in my dreams I'd be, near - er, my God, to Thee,
an - gels to beck - on me, near - er, my God, to Thee,
so by my woes to be, near - er my God, to Thee,
still all my song shall be, near - er my God, to Thee,

near - er, my God, to Thee, near - er to Thee.
near - er, my God, to Thee, near - er to Thee.
near - er, my God, to Thee, near - er to Thee.
near - er, my God, to Thee, near - er to Thee.
near - er, my God, to Thee, near - er to Thee.

WORDS: Sarah Fuller Flower Adams, 1841
MUSIC: *Bethany*, Lowell Mason, 1856

6.4.6.4.6.6.6.4

427 Yesterday, Today, and Forever

Jesus Christ never changes! He is the same yesterday, today, and forever. – Hebrews 13:8 CEV

1. O how sweet the glorious message simple faith may
2. He, who was the Friend of sinners, seeks the lost one
3. Oft on earth He healed the suff'rer by His mighty
4. As of old He walked t'Emmaus, with them to a-

claim; yesterday, today, forever
now; sinner come, and at His footstool
hand; still our sicknesses and sorrows
bide; so, through all life's way He walketh

Jesus is the same. Still He loves to
penitently bow. He who said, "I'll
go at His command. He who gave His
ever near our side. Soon again we

save the sinful, heal the sick and lame,
not condemn thee, go and sin no more."
healing virtue to a woman's touch,
shall behold Him, hasten, Lord, the day;

WORDS: Albert Benjamin Simpson, 1890; based on Hebrews 13:8
MUSIC: *Nyack*, James H. Burke, 19th c.

8.5.8.5 D with Refrain

cheer the mourn - er, still the tem - pest, glo - ry to His name.
Speaks to thee that word of par - don as in days of yore.
to the faith that claims His full - ness still will give as much.
but t'will still be this same Je - sus as He went a - way.

Refrain

Yes - ter - day, to - day, for - ev - er, Je - sus is the same.

All may change, but Je - sus nev - er! Glo - ry to His name!

Glo - ry to His name! Glo - ry to His name!

All may change, but Je - sus nev - er! Glo - ry to His name!

428 Dwelling in Beulah Land

Until I come and take you away to a land like your own land, a land of corn and wine. – Isaiah 36:17 KJV

1. Far a-way the noise of strife up-on my ear is fall-ing,
2. Far be-low the storm of doubt up-on the world is beat-ing,
3. Let the storm-y breez-es blow, their cry can-not a-larm me;
4. View-ing here the works of God, I sink in con-tem-pla-tion,

then I know the sins of earth be-set on ev-ery hand;
sons of men in bat-tle long the en-e-my with-stand;
I am safe-ly shel-tered here, pro-tect-ed by God's hand;
hear-ing now His bless-ed voice, I see the way He planned;

doubt and fear and things of earth in vain to me are call-ing,
safe am I with-in the cas-tle of God's Word re-treat-ing,
here the sun is al-ways shin-ing, here there's naught can harm me,
dwell-ing in the Spir-it, here I learn of full sal-va-tion,

none of these shall move me from Beu-lah Land.
noth-ing then can reach me, 'tis Beu-lah Land.
I am safe for-ev-er in Beu-lah Land.
glad-ly I will tar-ry in Beu-lah Land.

Refrain

I'm liv-ing on the moun-tain, un-der-neath a cloud-less

WORDS: Charles Austin Miles, 1911
MUSIC: *Beulah Land*, Charles Austin Miles, 1911

14.13.14.10 with Refrain

sky, I'm drink-ing at the foun-tain that nev-er shall run
praise God!

dry; O yes! I'm feast-ing on the man-na from a

boun-ti-ful sup-ply, for I am dwell-ing in Beu-lah Land.

I Am Trusting Thee, Lord Jesus 429

We are sure about all this. Christ makes us sure in the very presence of God. – 2 Corinthians 3:4 CEV

1. I am trust-ing Thee, Lord Je-sus, trust-ing on-ly Thee;
2. I am trust-ing Thee to guide me, Thou a-lone shalt lead,
3. I am trust-ing Thee for pow-er, Thine can nev-er fail;
4. I am trust-ing Thee, Lord Je-sus, nev-er let me fall;

trust-ing Thee for full sal-va-tion, great and free.
ev-ery day and hour sup-ply-ing all my need.
words which Thou Thy-self shalt give me must pre-vail.
I am trust-ing Thee for-ev-er, and for all.

WORDS: Frances Ridley Havergal, 1874
MUSIC: *Bullinger,* Ethelbert William Bullinger, 1874

8.5.8.3

430 Standing on the Promises

God made great and marvelous promises, so that His nature would become part of us. – 2 Peter 1:4 CEV

1. Stand-ing on the prom-is-es of Christ, my King! Through e-ter-nal
2. Stand-ing on the prom-is-es that can-not fail, when the howl-ing
3. Stand-ing on the prom-is-es, I now can see per-fect, pres-ent
4. Stand-ing on the prom-is-es of Christ, the Lord, bound to Him e-
5. Stand-ing on the prom-is-es, I can-not fall, lis-t'ning ev-ery

a - ges let His prais-es ring; "Glo-ry in the high-est!" I will
storms of doubt and fear as-sail, by the liv-ing Word of God I
cleans-ing in the blood for me; stand-ing in the lib-er-ty where
ter-nal-ly by love's strong cord, o-ver-com-ing dai-ly with the
mo-ment to the Spir-it's call, rest-ing in my Sav-ior as my

shout and sing, stand-ing on the prom-is-es of God.
shall pre-vail, stand-ing on the prom-is-es of God.
Christ makes free, stand-ing on the prom-is-es of God.
Spir-it's Sword, stand-ing on the prom-is-es of God.
all in all, stand-ing on the prom-is-es of God.

Refrain

Stand - ing, stand - ing,
stand-ing on the prom-is-es, stand-ing on the prom-is-es, stand-ing on the

WORDS: Russell Kelso Carter, 1886
MUSIC: *Promises*, Russell Kelso Carter, 1886

11.11.11.9. with Refrain

prom - is - es   of   God,   my   Sav - ior;   stand - - - ing,
standing on the prom - is - es,

stand - - - ing,   I'm   stand - ing   on   the   prom - is - es   of   God.
stand-ing   on   the   prom - is - es,

God Is My Strong Salvation   431

The salvation...comes from the Lord; He is their stronghold in time of trouble. – Psalm 37:39 NIV

1. God   is   my strong sal - va - tion, what   foe   have I   to   fear?
2. Though hosts en - camp   a - round   me,   firm   to   the fight I   stand;
3. Place   on   the   Lord   re - li - ance,   my   soul, with cour-age   wait;
4. His   might thy heart shall strength - en,   His   love thy joy in - crease;

In   dark-ness and temp - ta - tion   my   light, my help,   is   near.
what   ter - ror can con - found   me,   with   God   at   my right   hand?
His   truth be thine af - fi - ance,[1] when   faint and des - o - late.
mer - cy thy days shall length - en;   the   Lord will give thee   peace.

1. *affiance: trust, confidence*

WORDS: James Montgomery, 1817
MUSIC: *Christus Der Ist Mein Leben*, Melchior Vulpius, 1609   7.6.7.6

Only Believe

Everything is possible for him who believes. – Mark 9:23 NIV

1. Fear not, lit-tle flock, from the cross to the throne, from death in-to
2. Fear not, lit-tle flock, He go-eth a-head, your Shep-herd se-
3. Fear not, lit-tle flock, what - ev - er your lot; He en-ters all

life He went for His own; all pow-er in earth, all pow-er a-
lect - ed the path you must tread; the wa-ters of Ma - rah He'll sweet-en for
rooms, "the doors be-ing shut." He nev - er for-sakes, He nev-er is

Refrain

bove, is giv-en to Him for the flock of His love. On - ly be-lieve,
thee, He drank all the bit - ter in Geth-sem-a - ne. On - ly be-lieve,
gone, So count on His pres-ence in dark-ness and dawn.

on - ly be-lieve; all things are pos-si-ble, on - ly be-lieve. On - ly be-

lieve, on - ly be-lieve; all things are pos-si-ble, on - ly be - lieve.

WORDS: Paul Rader, 1921
MUSIC: *Only Believe*, Paul Rader, 1921

Irregular with Refrain

Lead, Kindly Light

Thy word is a lamp unto my feet, and a light unto my path. – Psalm 119:105 KJV

1. Lead, kind-ly Light, a-mid th'en-cir-cling gloom lead Thou me on; the night is dark, and I am far from home; lead Thou me on; keep Thou my feet; I do not ask to see the dis-tant scene, one step e-nough for me.

2. I was not ev-er thus, nor prayed that Thou shouldst lead me on; I loved to choose and see my path; but now lead Thou me on; I loved the gar-ish day, and, spite of fears, pride ruled my will; re-mem-ber not past years.

3. So long Thy pow'r hath blest me, sure it still will lead me on; o'er moor and fen,[1] o'er crag and tor-rent, till the night is gone; and with the morn those an-gel fac-es smile, which I have loved long since, and lost a-while.

1. fen: *flooded marshland*

WORDS: John Henry Newman, 1833
MUSIC: *Lux Benigna*, John Bacchus Dykes, 1865

10.4.10.4.10.10

434 Faith Is the Victory

Every child of God can defeat the world, and our faith is what gives us this victory. – 1 John 5:4 CEV

1. En - camped a - long the hills of light, ye Chris - tian sol - diers, rise
2. His ban - ner o - ver us is love, our sword the Word of God;
3. On ev - ery hand the foe we find drawn up in dread ar - ray;
4. To him who o - ver-comes the foe white rai - ment shall be giv'n;

and press the bat - tle ere the night shall veil the glow - ing skies.
we tread the road the saints a - bove with shouts of tri - umph trod.
let tents of ease be left be - hind and on - ward to the fray.
be - fore the an - gels he shall know His name con - fessed in heav'n.

A - gainst the foe in vales be - low let all our strength be hurled;
By faith they, like a whirl-wind's breath swept on o'er ev - ery field
Sal - va - tion's hel - met on each head, with truth all girt a - bout,
Then on - ward from the hills of light, our hearts with love a - flame,

faith is the vic - to - ry, we know, that o - ver-comes the world.
the faith by which they con - quered death is still our shin - ing shield.
the earth shall trem - ble 'neath our tread and ech - o with our shout.
we'll van - quish all the hosts of night in Je - sus' con - qu'ring name.

WORDS: John Henry Yates, 1891
MUSIC: *Sankey,* Ira David Sankey, 1891

C.M.D. with Refrain

Refrain

Faith is the vic - to - ry! Faith is the vic - to - ry!

O glo - ri - ous vic - to - ry that o - ver-comes the world!

Give Me Jesus 435

What good will it be for a man if he gains the whole world, yet forfeits his soul? – Matthew 16:26 NIV

1. In the morn - ing when I rise, in the morn - ing when I rise, in the
2. Dark mid - night was my cry, dark mid - night was my cry, dark
3. Just a - bout the break of day, just a - bout the break of day, just a -
4. O when I am a - lone, O when I am a - lone, O
5. O when I come to die, O when I come to die, O

Refrain

morn - ing when I rise, give me Je - sus.
mid - night was my cry, give me Je - sus.
bout the break of day, give me Je - sus. Give me Je - sus, give me
when I am a - lone, give me Je - sus.
when I come to die, give me Je - sus.

Je - sus, you can have all this world, but give me Je - sus.

WORDS: Negro spiritual, n.d.
MUSIC: *Give Me Jesus (Spiritual)*, Negro spiritual, n.d.; arr. Eric Wyse, 2005

Irregular with Refrain

436 Who Is on the Lord's Side?

The Lord our God we will serve, and His voice we will obey. – Joshua 24:24 ESV

1. Who is on the Lord's side? Who will serve the King? Who will be His helpers, other lives to bring? Who will leave the world's side? Who will face the foe? Who is on the Lord's side? Who for Him will go? By Thy call of mercy, by Thy grace divine.

2. Not for weight of glory, not for crown and palm, enter we the army, raise the warrior psalm; but for love that claimeth lives for whom He died; he whom Jesus nameth must be on His side. By Thy love constraining, by Thy grace divine.

3. Jesus, Thou hast bought us, not with gold or gem, but with Thine own lifeblood, for Thy diadem. With Thy blessing filling each who comes to Thee, Thou hast made us willing, Thou hast made us free. By Thy grand redemption, by Thy grace divine.

4. Fierce may be the conflict, strong may be the foe, but the King's own army none can overthrow. Round His standard ranging vict'ry is secure; for His truth unchanging makes the triumph sure. Joyfully enlisting by Thy grace divine.

Refrain

We are on the Lord's side, Savior, we are Thine.

WORDS: Frances Ridley Havergal, 1877
MUSIC: *Armageddon*, C. Luise Reichardt, 1853; arr. John Goss, 1871

6.5.6.5 D with Refrain

Go Foward, Christian Soldier

Soldiers on duty don't work at outside jobs. They try only to please their commanding officer. – 2 Timothy 2:4 CEV

1. Go for-ward, Chris-tian sol - dier, be - neath His ban - ner true:
2. Go for-ward, Chris-tian sol - dier, fear not the se - cret foe;
3. Go for-ward, Chris-tian sol - dier, nor dream of peace-ful rest,
4. Go for-ward, Chris-tian sol - dier, fear not the gath - 'ring night:

The Lord Him-self, thy Lead - er, shall all thy foes sub - due.
for more o'er thee are watch - ing than hu - man eyes can know:
till Sa - tan's host is van - quished and heav'n is all pos - sessed;
The Lord has been thy shel - ter; the Lord will be thy light.

His love fore-tells thy tri - al; He knows thine hour - ly need;
trust on - ly Christ, thy Cap - tain; cease not to watch and pray;
till Christ Him - self shall call thee to lay thine ar - mor by,
When morn His face re - veal - eth thy dan - gers all are past:

He can with bread of heav - en thy faint - ing spir - it feed.
heed not the treach-'rous voic - es that lure thy soul a - stray.
and wear in end - less glo - ry the crown of vic - to - ry.
O pray that faith and vir - tue may keep thee to the last!

WORDS: Lawrence Tuttiett, 1861
MUSIC: *Lancashire*, Henry Thomas Smart, 1835
This tune in a lower key, No. 451.

7.6.7.6 D

438 Onward, Christian Soldiers

Fight a good fight for the faith and claim eternal life. – 1 Timothy 6:12 CEV

1. On - ward, Chris - tian sol - diers, march - ing as to war,
2. At the sign of tri - umph Sa - tan's host doth flee;
3. Like a might - y ar - my moves the Church of God,
4. Crowns and thrones may per - ish, king - doms rise and wane,
5. On - ward, then, ye peo - ple, join our hap - py throng,

with the cross of Je - sus go - ing on be - fore.
on then, Chris - tian sol - diers, on to vic - to - ry!
Chris - tians, we are tread - ing where the saints have trod,
but the Church of Je - sus con - stant will re - main;
blend with ours your voic - es in the tri - umph song;

Christ, the roy - al Mas - ter, leads a - gainst the foe,
Hell's foun - da - tions quiv - er at the shout of praise;
we are not di - vid - ed, all one bod - y we,
gates of hell can nev - er 'gainst that Church pre - vail,
glo - ry, laud, and hon - or un - to Christ the King,

for - ward in - to bat - tle, see His ban - ners go.
Chris - tians lift your voic - es, loud your an - thems raise.
one in hope and doc - trine, one in char - i - ty.
we have Christ's own prom - ise, and that can - not fail.
this through count - less a - ges saints and an - gels sing.

WORDS: Sabine Baring-Gould, 1865, alt.
MUSIC: *St. Gertrude*, Arthur Seymour Sullivan, 1871

6.5.6.5 D with Refrain

Refrain

On - ward, Chris - tian sol - diers, march - ing as to war,

with the cross of Je - sus go - ing on be - fore.

Am I a Soldier of the Cross? 439

As a good soldier of Christ Jesus you must endure your share of suffering. – 2 Timothy 2:3 CEV

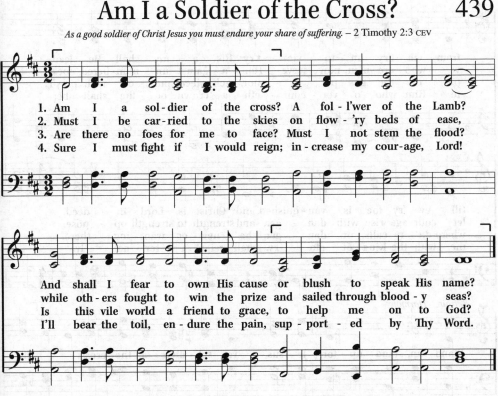

1. Am I a sol - dier of the cross? A fol - l'wer of the Lamb?
2. Must I be car - ried to the skies on flow - 'ry beds of ease,
3. Are there no foes for me to face? Must I not stem the flood?
4. Sure I must fight if I would reign; in - crease my cour - age, Lord!

And shall I fear to own His cause or blush to speak His name?
while oth - ers fought to win the prize and sailed through blood - y seas?
Is this vile world a friend to grace, to help me on to God?
I'll bear the toil, en - dure the pain, sup - port - ed by Thy Word.

WORDS: Isaac Watts, 1724
MUSIC: *Arlington*, Thomas Augustine Arne, 1762

C.M.

440 Stand Up, Stand Up for Jesus

Keep alert. Be firm in your faith. Stay brave and strong. – 1 Corinthians 16:13 CEV

1. Stand up, stand up for Je - sus, we sol - diers of the cross;
2. Stand up, stand up for Je - sus, the trum - pet call o - bey;
3. Stand up, stand up for Je - sus, stand in His strength a - lone;
4. Stand up, stand up for Je - sus, the strife will not be long;

lift high His roy - al ban - ner, it must not suf - fer loss;
forth to the might - y con - flict, in this His glo - rious day;
the arm of flesh will fail you, ye dare not trust your own;
this day the noise of bat - tle, the next, the vic - tor's song;

from vic - t'ry un - to vic - t'ry His ar - my shall He lead,
ye who are men, now serve Him a - gainst un - num - bered foes;
put on the gos - pel ar - mor, each piece put on with pray'r;
to Him who o - ver - com - eth a crown of life shall be;

till ev - 'ry foe is van - quished, and Christ is Lord in - deed.
let cour - age rise with dan - ger, and strength to strength op - pose.
where du - ty calls, or dan - ger, be nev - er want - ing there.
me, with the King of glo - ry, shall reign e - ter - nal - ly.

Refrain *Harmony*

Stand up, stand up for Je - sus, ye sol - diers of the cross; lift

WORDS: George Duffield, Jr., 1858
MUSIC: *Geibel*, Adam Geibel, 1901

7.6.7.6 D with Refrain

high His roy-al ban-ner, it must not, it must not suf-fer loss.

Stand Up, Stand Up for Jesus 441

Keep alert. Be firm in your faith. Stay brave and strong. – 1 Corinthians 16:13 CEV

1. Stand up, stand up for Je-sus, ye sol-diers of the cross;
2. Stand up, stand up for Je-sus, the trum-pet call o - bey;
3. Stand up, stand up for Je-sus, stand in His strength a - lone;
4. Stand up, stand up for Je-sus, the strife will not be long;

lift high His roy - al ban - ner, it must not suf - fer loss.
forth to the might - y con - flict, in this His glo - rious day.
the arm of flesh will fail you, ye dare not trust your own.
this day the noise of bat - tle, the next, the vic - tor's song.

From vic - t'ry un - to vic - t'ry His ar - my shall He lead,
Ye that are men, now serve Him a - gainst un - num - bered foes;
Put on the gos - pel ar - mor, each piece put on with prayer;
To him who o - ver - com - eth a crown of life shall be;

till ev - 'ry foe is van - quished and Christ is Lord in - deed.
let cour - age rise with dan - ger and strength to strength op - pose.
where du - ty calls or dan - ger, be nev - er want - ing there.
he, with the King of glo - ry, shall reign e - ter - nal - ly.

WORDS: George Duffield, Jr., 1858
MUSIC: *Webb*, George James Webb, 1830

7.6.7.6 D

442 The Son of God Goes Forth to War

They did not love their lives so much as to shrink from death. – Revelation 12:11 NIV

1. The Son of God goes forth to war, a king-ly crown to gain;
2. The mar-tyr first, whose ea-gle eye could pierce be-yond the grave,
3. A glo-rious band, the cho-sen few on whom the Spir-it came,
4. A no-ble ar-my, men and boys, the ma-tron and the maid,

His blood-red ban-ner streams a-far; who fol-lows in His train.
who saw his Mas-ter in the sky, and called on Him to save;
twelve val-iant saints, their hope they knew, and mocked the cross and flame,
a-round the Sav-ior's throne re-joice, in robes of light ar-rayed;

Who best can drink His cup of woe, tri-um-phant o-ver pain,
like Him, with par-don on his tongue in midst of mor-tal pain,
they met the ty-rant's bran-dished steel, the li-on's gor-y mane;
they climbed the steep as-cent of heav'n through per-il, toil, and pain;

who pa-tient bears his cross be-low, he fol-lows in His train.
he prayed for them that did the wrong; who fol-lows in his train?
they bowed their necks the death to feel; who fol-lows in their train?
O God, to us may grace be giv'n to fol-low in their train!

WORDS: Reginald Heber, 1827
MUSIC: *All Saints New*, Henry Stephen Cutler, 1872

C.M.D

The Banner of the Cross

443

Set up a banner and proclaim. – Jeremiah 50:2 ESV

1. There's a roy-al ban-ner giv-en for dis-play to the sol-diers
2. Though the foe may rage and gath-er as the flood, let the stan-dard
3. O - ver land and sea, wher-ev-er peo-ple dwell, make the glo-r'ous
4. When the glo-ry dawns, 'tis draw-ing ver-y near, it is has-t'ning

of the King; as an en-sign fair we lift it up to-day,
be dis-played; and be-neath its folds, as sol-diers of the Lord,
ti - dings known; of the crim-son ban-ner now the sto-ry tell,
day by day; then be-fore our King the foe shall dis-ap-pear,

Refrain

while as ran-somed ones we sing.
for the truth be not dis-mayed!
while the Lord shall claim His own!
and the cross the world shall sway!

March-ing on, march-ing
on, on,

on, for Christ count ev-'ry-thing but loss! And to
on, on, ev-'ry-thing, ev-'ry-thing but loss!

crown Him King, toil and sing 'neath the ban-ner of the cross!
we'll be - neath

WORDS: Daniel Webster Whittle, 1887
MUSIC: *Royal Banner,* James McGranahan, 1887

11.7.11.7 with Refrain

444 We Rest on Thee

Learn from me, for I am gentle and humble in heart, and you will find rest for your souls. – Matthew 11:29 NIV

1. We rest on Thee, our shield and our de-fend-er! We go not
2. Yea, in Thy name, O Cap-tain of sal-va-tion! In Thy dear
3. We go in faith, our own great weak-ness feel-ing, and need-ing
4. We rest on Thee, our shield and our de-fend-er! Thine is the

forth a-lone a-gainst the foe; strong in Thy strength, safe
name, all oth-er names a-bove; Je-sus our righ-teous-
more each day Thy grace to know; yet from our hearts a
bat-tle, Thine shall be the praise when pass-ing through the

in Thy keep-ing ten-der, We rest on Thee, and in Thy name we
ness, our sure foun-da-tion, our Prince of glo-ry and our King of
song of tri-umph peal-ing, "We rest on Thee, and in Thy name we
gates of pearl-y splen-dor, vic-tors, we rest with Thee, through end-less

go. Strong in Thy strength, safe in Thy keep-ing ten-der,
love, Je-sus our righ-teous-ness, our sure foun-da-tion,
go." Yet from our hearts a song of tri-umph peal-ing,
days, when pass-ing through the gates of pearl-y splen-dor,

WORDS: Edith Gilling Cherry, ca. 1895
MUSIC: *Finlandia*, Jean Sibelius, 1899; arr. Paul Nelson, 2005

11.10.11.10.11.10

This tune in a higher key, No. 364.

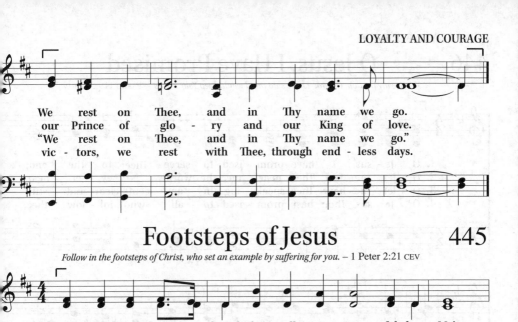

We rest on Thee, and in Thy name we go.
our Prince of glo - ry and our King of love.
"We rest on Thee, and in Thy name we go."
vic - tors, we rest with Thee, through end - less days.

Footsteps of Jesus

445

Follow in the footsteps of Christ, who set an example by suffering for you. – 1 Peter 2:21 CEV

1. Sweet - ly, Lord, have we heard Thee call - ing, come, fol - low Me!
2. Though they lead o'er the cold, dark moun - tains, seek - ing His sheep;
3. If they lead through the tem - ple ho - ly, preach - ing the Word;
4. Then at last, when on high He sees us, our jour - ney done,

And we see where Thy foot - prints fall - ing lead us to Thee.
or a - long by Si - lo - am's foun - tains, help - ing the weak:
or in homes of the poor and low - ly, serv - ing the Lord:
we will rest where the steps of Je - sus end at His throne.

Refrain

Foot - prints of Je - sus, that make the path - way glow;

we will fol - low the steps of Je - sus wher - e'er they go.

WORDS: Mary Bridges Brown Baker Canedy Slade, 1871
MUSIC: *Footsteps,* Asa Brooks Everett, 1871

9.4.9.4 with Refrain

446 O Jesus, I Have Promised

You are my portion, O Lord; I have said that I would keep Your words. – Psalm 119:57 NKJV

1. O Je-sus, I have prom-ised to serve Thee to the end;
2. O let me feel Thee near me, the world is ev-er near;
3. O let me hear Thee speak-ing in ac-cents clear and still,
4. O Je-sus, Thou hast prom-ised to all who fol-low Thee,

be Thou for-ev-er near me, my Mas-ter and my Friend;
I see the sights that daz-zle, the tempt-ing sounds I hear;
a-bove the storms of pas-sion, the mur-murs of self-will.
that where Thou art in glo-ry, there shall Thy ser-vant be;

I shall not fear the bat-tle if Thou art by my side,
my foes are ev-er near me, a-round me and with-in;
O speak to re-as-sure me, to has-ten or con-trol;
and Je-sus, I have prom-ised to serve Thee to the end;

nor wan-der from the path-way if Thou wilt be my guide.
but, Je-sus, draw Thou near-er, and shield my soul from sin.
O speak, and make me lis-ten, Thou guard-ian of my soul.
O give me grace to fol-low, my Mas-ter and my Friend.

WORDS: John Ernest Bode, 1868
MUSIC: *Angel's Story*, Arthur Henry Mann, 1881

7.6.7.6

Higher Ground

I run toward the goal, so that I can win the prize of being called to heaven. – Philippians 3:14 CEV

1. I'm press-ing on the up-ward way, new heights I'm
2. My heart has no de-sire to stay where doubts a-
3. I want to live a-bove the world, though Sa-tan's
4. I want to scale the ut-most height and catch a

gain-ing ev-'ry day; still pray-ing as I on-ward
rise and fears dis-may; though some may dwell where these a-
darts at me are hurled; for faith has caught the joy-ful
gleam of glo-ry bright; but still I'll pray till heav'n I've

Refrain

bound, "Lord, plant my feet on high-er ground."
bound, my prayer, my aim is high-er ground.
sound, the song of saints on high-er ground.
found, "Lord, lead me on to high-er ground." Lord, lift me

up and let me stand, by faith, on heav-en's ta-ble-land, a high-er

plane than I have found; Lord, plant my feet on high-er ground.

WORDS: Johnson Oatman, Jr., 1898
MUSIC: *Higher Ground*, Charles Hutchinson Gabriel, 1898

L.M. with Refrain

448 True-Hearted, Whole-Hearted

Be strong in the Lord and in His mighty power. – Ephesians 6:10 NIV

1. True-heart-ed, whole-heart-ed, faith-ful and loy-al, King of our lives, by Thy grace we will be; un-der the stan-dard ex-alt-ed and roy-al, strong in Thy strength we will bat-tle for Thee.

2. True-heart-ed, whole-heart-ed, full-est al-le-giance yield-ing hence-forth to our glo-ri-ous King; val-iant en-deav-or and lov-ing o-be-dience, free-ly and joy-ous-ly now would we bring.

3. True-heart-ed, whole-heart-ed, Sav-ior all glo-rious! Take Thy great pow-er and reign there a-lone, o-ver our wills and af-fec-tions vic-to-rious free-ly sur-ren-dered and whol-ly Thine own.

Refrain

Peal out the watch-word! Si-lence it nev-er! Song of our spir-its, re-joic-ing and free. Peal out the watch-word!

WORDS: Frances Ridley Havergal, 1878
MUSIC: *Truehearted,* George Coles Stebbins, 1878

11.10.11.10 with Refrain

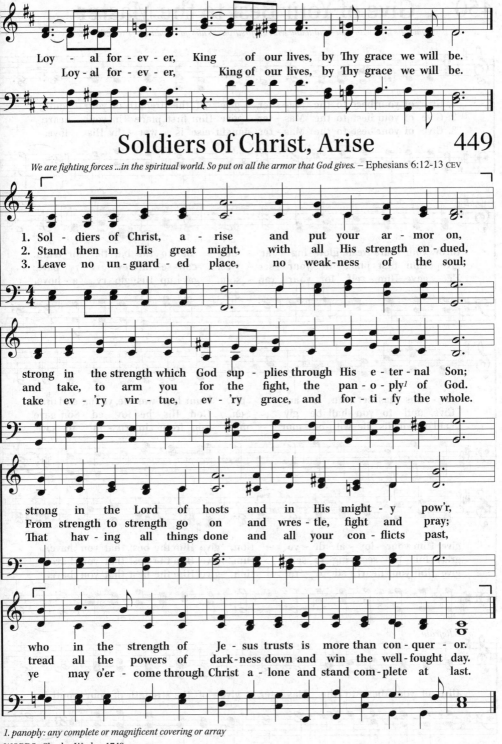

Loy - al for - ev - er, King of our lives, by Thy grace we will be.
Loy - al for - ev - er, King of our lives, by Thy grace we will be.

Soldiers of Christ, Arise

449

We are fighting forces ...in the spiritual world. So put on all the armor that God gives. – Ephesians 6:12-13 CEV

1. Sol - diers of Christ, a - rise and put your ar - mor on,
2. Stand then in His great might, with all His strength en - dued,
3. Leave no un - guard - ed place, no weak - ness of the soul;

strong in the strength which God sup - plies through His e - ter - nal Son;
and take, to arm you for the fight, the pan - o - ply[1] of God.
take ev - 'ry vir - tue, ev - 'ry grace, and for - ti - fy the whole.

strong in the Lord of hosts and in His might - y pow'r,
From strength to strength go on and wres - tle, fight and pray;
That hav - ing all things done and all your con - flicts past,

who in the strength of Je - sus trusts is more than con - quer - or.
tread all the powers of dark - ness down and win the well - fought day.
ye may o'er - come through Christ a - lone and stand com - plete at last.

1. panoply: any complete or magnificent covering or array

WORDS: Charles Wesley, 1749
MUSIC: *Diademata*, George Job Elvey, 1868
This tune in a higher key, No. 46; another harmonization of this tune, No. 488.

S.M.D.

450 Give of Your Best to the Master

Honor the Lord with your wealth and with the firstfruits of all your produce. – Proverbs 3:9 ESV

1. Give of your best to the Mas - ter, give of the strength of your youth;
2. Give of your best to the Mas - ter, give Him first place in your heart;
3. Give of your best to the Mas - ter, naught else is wor - thy His love;

throw your soul's fresh, glow-ing ar - dor in-to the bat-tle for truth.
give Him first place in your ser - vice, con-se-crate ev - 'ry part.
He gave Him-self for your ran - som, gave up His glo-ry a - bove.

Je - sus has set the ex - am - ple, daunt-less was He, young and brave;
Give, and to you shall be giv - en, God His be - lov - ed Son gave;
Laid down His life with-out mur - mur, you from sin's ru - in to save;

give Him your loy - al de - vo - tion, give Him the best that you have.
grate-ful - ly seek-ing to serve Him, give Him the best that you have.
give Him your heart's ad - o - ra - tion, give Him the best that you have.

Refrain

Give of your best to the Mas - ter, give of the strength of your youth;

WORDS: Howard Benjamin Grose, 19th c.
MUSIC: *Barnard*, Charlotte Alington Pye Barnard, 19th c.

8.7.8.7 D with Refrain

clad in sal - va - tion's full ar - mor, join in the bat - tle for truth.

Lead On, O King Eternal 451

He is...the eternal King. – Jeremiah 10:10 NIV

1. Lead on, O King e - ter - nal, the day of march has come;
2. Lead on, O King e - ter - nal, till sin's fierce war shall cease,
3. Lead on, O King e - ter - nal; we fol - low, not with fears;

hence - forth in fields of con - quest Thy tents shall be our home;
and ho - li - ness shall whis - per the sweet "A - men" of peace;
for glad - ness breaks like morn - ing wher - e'er Thy face ap - pears.

through days of prep - a - ra - tion Thy grace has made us strong,
for not with swords loud clash - ing, nor roll of stir - ring drums,
Thy cross is lift - ed o'er us; we jour - ney in its light;

and now, O King e - ter - nal, we lift our bat - tle song.
but deeds of love and mer - cy, the heav'n - ly king - dom comes.
the crown a - waits the con - quest; lead on, O God of might!

WORDS: Ernest Warburton Shurtleff, 1888
MUSIC: *Lancashire*, Henry Thomas Smart, 1835
This tune in a higher key, No. 437.

7.6.7.6 D

452

Follow On

They left everything and went with Jesus. – Luke 5:11 CEV

1. Down in the val-ley with my Sav-ior I would go, where the flow'rs are
2. Down in the val-ley with my Sav-ior I would go, where the storms are
3. Down in the val-ley or up-on the moun-tain steep, close be-side my

bloom-ing and the sweet wa-ters flow; ev-'ry-where He leads me I would
sweep-ing and the dark wa-ters flow; with His hand to lead me I will
Sav-ior would my soul ev-er keep; He will lead me safe-ly in the

fol-low, fol-low on, walk-ing in His foot-steps till the crown be won.
nev-er, nev-er fear, dan-ger can-not fright me if my Lord is near.
path that He has trod, up to where they gath-er on the hills of God.

Refrain

Fol-low! Fol-low! I would fol-low Je-sus! An-y-where, ev-'ry-where,

I would fol-low on! Fol-low! Fol-low! I would fol-low Je-sus!

WORDS: William Orcutt Cushing, 1880
MUSIC: *Follow On*, Robert Lowry, 1880

Irregular with Refrain

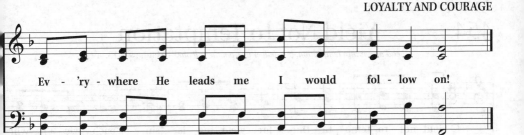

Ev - 'ry - where He leads me I would fol - low on!

He Who Would Valiant Be 453

Thanks be to God! He gives us the victory through our Lord Jesus Christ. – 1 Corinthians 15:57 NIV

1. He who would val - iant be 'gainst all dis - as - ter,
2. Who so be - set him round with dis - mal sto - ries,
3. Since, Lord, Thou dost de - fend us with Thy Spir - it,

let him in con - stan - cy fol - low the Mas - ter.
do but them - selves con - found, his strength the more is.
we know we at the end shall life in - her - it.

There's no dis - cour - age - ment shall make him once re - lent
No foes shall stay his might, though he with gi - ants fight;
Then fan - cies flee a - way! I'll fear not what men say,

his first a - vowed in - tent to be a pil - grim.
he will make good his right to be a pil - grim.
I'll la - bor night and day to be a pil - grim.

WORDS: John Bunyan, 1684; Percy Dearmer, 1906, alt.
MUSIC: *St. Dunstans,* Charles Winfred Douglas, 1917

6.5.6.5.6.6.6.5

454 Yield Not to Temptation

Lead us not into temptation, but deliver us from the evil one. – Matthew 6:13 NIV

1. Yield not to temp-ta-tion, for yield-ing is sin, each vic-t'ry will
2. Shun e-vil com-pan-ions, bad lan-guage dis-dain, God's name hold in
3. To him that o'er-com-eth God giv-eth a crown, through faith we shall

help you some oth-er to win; fight man-ful-ly on-ward, dark
rev-'rence, nor take it in vain; be thought-ful and ear-nest, kind
con-quer, though of-ten cast down; He, who is our Sav-ior, our

pas-sions sub-due, look ev-er to Je-sus, He'll car-ry you through.
heart-ed and true, look ev-er to Je-sus, He'll car-ry you through.
strength will re-new, look ev-er to Je-sus, He'll car-ry you through.

Refrain

Ask the Sav-ior to help you, com-fort, strength-en, and keep you,

He is will-ing to aid you, He will car-ry you through.

WORDS: Horatio Richmond Palmer, 1868
MUSIC: *Fortitude*, Horatio Richmond Palmer, 1868

6.5.6.5 D with Refrain

The Beautiful Garden of Prayer 455

He was walking in the garden in the cool of the day. – Genesis 3:8 NIV

1. There's a gar-den where Je-sus is wait-ing, there's a place that is
2. There's a gar-den where Je-sus is wait-ing, and I go with my
3. There's a gar-den where Je-sus is wait-ing, and He bids you to

won-drous-ly fair; for it glows with the light of His pres-ence,
bur-den and care; just to learn from His lips words of com-fort,
come meet Him there; just to bow, and re-ceive a new bless-ing,

Refrain

'tis the beau-ti-ful gar-den of prayer.
in the beau-ti-ful gar-den of prayer.
in the beau-ti-ful gar-den of prayer. O the beau-ti-ful gar-den, the

gar-den of prayer, O the beau-ti-ful gar-den of prayer; there my Sav-ior a-

waits, and He o-pens the gates to the beau-ti-ful gar-den of prayer.

WORDS: Eleanor Allen Schroll, 1920
MUSIC: *Garden of Prayer,* anon.; adapt. James Henry Fillmore, 20th c.

10.9.10.9 with Refrain

456 In the Garden

Coming out, He went to the Mount of Olives, as He was accustomed, and His disciples also followed Him. – Luke 22:39 NJKV

1. I come to the gar-den a-lone, while the dew is
2. He speaks, and the sound of His voice is so sweet the
3. I'd stay in the gar-den with Him though the night a-

still on the ros-es; and the voice I hear, fall-ing on my ear,
birds hush their sing-ing; and the mel-o-dy that He gave to me
round me be fall-ing; but He bids me go, through the voice of woe;

Refrain

the Son of God dis-clos-es.
with-in my heart is ring-ing. And He walks with me, and He
His voice to me is call-ing.

talks with me, and He tells me I am His own; and the joy we

WORDS: Charles Austin Miles, 1912
MUSIC: *Garden*, Charles Austin Miles, 1912

Irregular with Refrain

share as we tar - ry there none oth - er has ev - er known.

Near to the Heart of God 457

It is good for me to draw near to God. – Psalm 73:28 KJV

1. There is a place of qui - et rest, near to the heart of God;
2. There is a place of com - fort sweet, near to the heart of God;
3. There is a place of full re - lease, near to the heart of God;

a place where sin can - not mo - lest, near to the heart of God.
a place where we our Sav - ior meet, near to the heart of God.
a place where all is joy and peace, near to the heart of God.

Refrain

O Je - sus, blest Re - deem - er, sent from the heart of God,

hold us, who wait be - fore Thee, near to the heart of God.

WORDS: Cleland Boyd McAfee, 1903
MUSIC: *McAfee*, Cleland Boyd McAfee, 1903

C.M. with Refrain

458

Sweet Hour of Prayer

They all joined together constantly in prayer. – Acts 1:14 NIV

1. Sweet hour of prayer, sweet hour of prayer, that calls me from a
2. Sweet hour of prayer, sweet hour of prayer, Thy wings shall my pe-
3. Sweet hour of prayer, sweet hour of prayer, may I Thy con-so-

world of care and bids me at my Fa-ther's throne make all my
ti-tion bear to Him whose truth and faith-ful-ness en-gage the
la-tion share, till, from Mount Pis-gah's loft-y height, I view my

wants and wish-es known! In sea-sons of dis-tress and grief,
wait-ing soul to bless; and since He bids me seek His face,
home and take my flight; this robe of flesh I'll drop and rise

my soul has of-ten found re-lief, and oft es-caped the
be-lieve His Word and trust His grace, I'll cast on Him my
to seize the ev-er-last-ing prize; and shout, while pass-ing

WORDS: William Walford, 1845
MUSIC: *Sweet Hour*, William Batchelder Bradbury, 1861

L.M.D.

tempt - er's snare by Thy re - turn, sweet hour of prayer.
ev - 'ry care, and wait for Thee, sweet hour of prayer.
through the air, "Fare - well, fare - well, sweet hour of prayer!"

I Need Thee Every Hour

459

Bow down Thine ear, O Lord, hear me: for I am poor and needy. – Psalm 86:1 KJV

1. I need Thee ev - 'ry hour, most gra - cious Lord;
2. I need Thee ev - 'ry hour, stay Thou near by;
3. I need Thee ev - 'ry hour, in joy or pain;
4. I need Thee ev - 'ry hour, most Ho - ly One;

no ten - der voice like Thine can peace af - ford.
temp - ta - tions lose their pow'r when Thou art nigh.
come quick - ly and a - bide or life is vain.
oh, make me Thine in - deed, Thou bless - ed Son!

Refrain

I need Thee, oh, I need Thee; ev - 'ry hour I need Thee;

oh, bless me now, my Sav - ior, I come to Thee!

WORDS: Annie Sherwood Hawks, 1872
MUSIC: *Need*, Robert Lowry, 1872

6.4.6.4 with Refrain

460 What a Friend We Have in Jesus

I no longer call you servants...Instead I have called you friends. – John 15:15 NIV

1. What a Friend we have in Je - sus, all our sins and griefs to bear!
2. Have we tri - als and temp - ta - tions? Is there trou - ble an - y - where?
3. Are we weak and heav - y - lad - en, cum - bered with a load of care?

What a priv - i - lege to car - ry ev - 'ry-thing to God in prayer!
We should nev - er be dis - cour - aged; take it to the Lord in prayer.
Pre - cious Sav - ior, still our ref - uge; take it to the Lord in prayer.

Oh, what peace we of - ten for - feit, oh, what need-less pain we bear,
Can we find a Friend so faith - ful Who will all our sor - rows share?
Do thy friends de-spise, for - sake thee? Take it to the Lord in prayer;

all be - cause we do not car - ry ev - 'ry-thing to God in prayer!
Je - sus knows our ev - ery weak - ness; take it to the Lord in prayer.
in His arms He'll take and shield thee; thou wilt find a so - lace there.

WORDS: Joseph Medlicott Scriven, 1855
MUSIC: *Converse*, Charles Crozat Converse, 1868

8.7.8.7 D

Just a Closer Walk with Thee

461

I can do everything through Him who gives me strength. – Philippians 4:13 NIV

1. I am weak but Thou art strong; Je-sus, keep me from all wrong.
2. Through this world of toil and snares, if I fal-ter, Lord, who cares?
3. When my fee-ble life is o'er, time for me will be no more;

I'll be sat-is-fied as long as I walk, let me walk close to Thee.
Who with me my bur-den shares? None but Thee, dear Lord, none but Thee.
guide me gent-ly, safe-ly o'er to Thy king-dom shore, to Thy shore.

Refrain

Just a clos-er walk with Thee, grant it, Je-sus, is my plea.

Dai-ly walk-ing close to Thee, let it be, dear Lord, let it be.

WORDS: Anon., n.d.
MUSIC: *Closer Walk*, traditional folk song, n.d.

Irregular with Refrain

462   I Must Tell Jesus!

Now that Jesus has suffered and was tempted, He can help anyone else who is tempted. – Hebrews 2:18   CEV

1. I must tell Je - sus all of my tri - als; I can - not bear these
2. I must tell Je - sus all of my trou - bles; He is a kind, com -
3. Tempt - ed and tried, I need a great Sav - ior, One who can help my
4. O how the world to e - vil al - lures me! O how my heart is

bur - dens a - lone;   in my dis - tress He kind - ly will help me;
pas - sion - ate Friend;   if I but ask Him, He will de - liv - er,
bur - dens to bear;   I must tell Je - sus, I must tell Je - sus;
tempt - ed to sin!   I must tell Je - sus, and He will help me

Refrain

He ev - er loves and cares for His own.
make of my trou - bles quick - ly an end.
He all my cares and sor - rows will share.
o - ver the world the vic - t'ry to win.

I must tell Je - sus!

I must tell Je - sus! I can - not bear my bur - dens a - lone; I must tell

WORDS: Elisha Albright Hoffman, 1893
MUSIC: *Orwigsburg*, Elisha Albright Hoffman, 1893

10.9.10.9 with Refrain

Je - sus, I must tell Je - sus! Je - sus can help me, Je - sus a - lone.

More Love to Thee, O Christ 463

This is my prayer: that your love may abound more and more. – Philippians 1:9 NIV

1. More love to Thee, O Christ, more love to Thee! Hear Thou the
2. Once earth - ly joy I craved, sought peace and rest; now Thee a -
3. Then shall my lat - est breath whis - per Thy praise; this be the

prayer I make on bend - ed knee. This is my ear - nest plea:
lone I seek; give what is best. This all my prayer shall be:
part - ing cry my heart shall raise. This still its prayer shall be:

More love, O Christ, to Thee, more love to Thee, more love to Thee!
More love, O Christ, to Thee, more love to Thee, more love to Thee!
More love, O Christ, to Thee, more love to Thee, more love to Thee!

WORDS: Elizabeth Payson Prentiss, 1856
MUSIC: *More Love to Thee,* William Howard Doane, 1870

6.4.6.4.6.6.4.4

464
I Am Praying for You

Please help us by praying for us. – 2 Corinthians 1:11 CEV

1. I have a Savior, He's pleading in glory, a dear, loving Savior though earth-friends be few; and now He is watching in tenderness o'er me, but oh, that my Savior were your Savior too!
2. I have a Father; to me He has given a hope for eternity, blessed and true; and soon He will call me to meet Him in heaven, but oh, that He'd let me bring you with me too!
3. I have a robe; 'tis resplendent in whiteness, awaiting in glory my wondering view; oh, when I receive it all shining in brightness, dear friend, could I see you receiving one too?
4. When He has found you, tell others the story, that my loving Savior is your Savior, too; then pray that your Savior may bring them to glory, and prayer will be answered, 'twas answered for you!

Refrain

For you I am praying, for you I am

WORDS: Samuel O'Malley Gore Cluff, 1860
MUSIC: *Praying for You,* Ira David Sankey, 1874

11.11.11.11. with Refrain

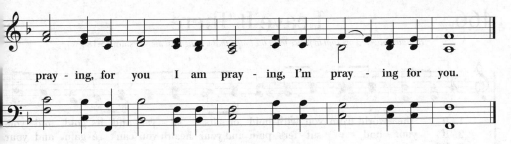

pray - ing, for you I am pray - ing, I'm pray - ing for you.

Lord, Speak to Me, That I May Speak 465

Now I want you to tell these same things to followers who can be trusted to tell others. – 2 Timothy 2:2 CEV

1. Lord, speak to me, that I may speak in liv - ing
2. O teach me, Lord, that I may teach the pre - cious
3. O fill me with Thy full - ness, Lord, un - til my
4. O use me, Lord, use e - ven me, just as Thou

ech - oes of Thy tone; as Thou hast sought, so
things Thou dost im - part; and wing my words that
ve - ry heart o'er - flow in kin - dling thought and
wilt, and when, and where, un - til Thy bless - ed

let me seek Thy err - ing chil - dren lost and lone.
they may reach the hid - den depths of man - y a heart.
glow - ing word, Thy love to tell, Thy praise to show.
face I see; Thy rest, Thy joy, Thy glo - ry share.

WORDS: Frances Ridley Havergal, 1872
MUSIC: *Canonbury,* adapt. Robert Alexander Schumann, 1839

L.M.

466 Leave It There

He hath delivered my soul in peace from the battle that was against me. – Psalm 55:18 KJV

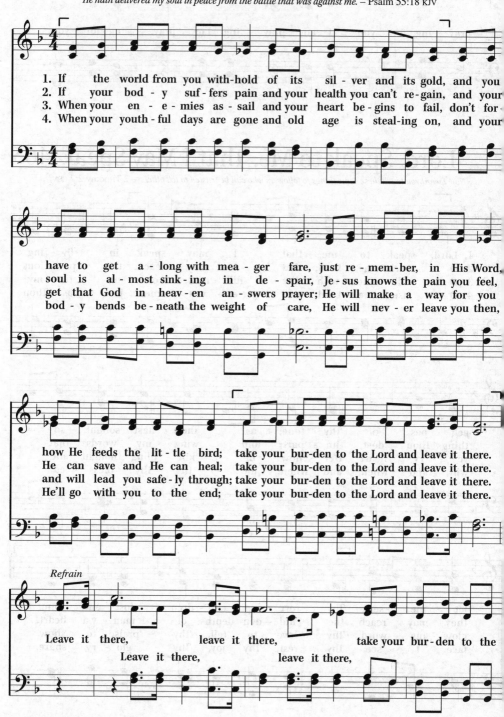

1. If the world from you with-hold of its sil - ver and its gold, and you
2. If your bod - y suf - fers pain and your health you can't re - gain, and your
3. When your en - e - mies as - sail and your heart be - gins to fail, don't for
4. When your youth - ful days are gone and old age is steal-ing on, and your

have to get a - long with mea - ger fare, just re - mem - ber, in His Word,
soul is al - most sink - ing in de - spair, Je - sus knows the pain you feel,
get that God in heav - en an - swers prayer; He will make a way for you
bod - y bends be - neath the weight of care, He will nev - er leave you then,

how He feeds the lit - tle bird; take your bur-den to the Lord and leave it there.
He can save and He can heal; take your bur-den to the Lord and leave it there.
and will lead you safe - ly through; take your bur-den to the Lord and leave it there.
He'll go with you to the end; take your bur-den to the Lord and leave it there.

Refrain

Leave it there, leave it there, take your bur - den to the
Leave it there, leave it there,

WORDS: Charles Albert Tindley, 1916
MUSIC: *Leave It There,* Charles Albert Tindley, 1916

14.11.14.11 with Refrain

Lord and leave it there; if you trust and nev-er doubt, He will leave it there; sure-ly bring you out; take your bur-den to the Lord and leave it there.

Lord Jesus, Think on Me 467

Order my steps in Thy word: and let not any iniquity have dominion over me. – Psalm 119:133 KJV

1. Lord Je-sus, think on me, and purge a-way my sin;
2. Lord Je-sus, think on me, nor let me go a-stray;
3. Lord Je-sus, think on me, when flows the tem-pest high;
4. Lord Je-sus, think on me, that, when the flood is past,
5. Lord Je-sus, think on me, that I may sing a-bove

from earth-borne pas-sions set me free, and make me pure with-in.
through dark-ness and per-plex-i-ty point Thou the heav'n-ly way.
when on doth rush the en-e-my, O Sav-ior be Thou nigh.
I may th'e-ter-nal bright-ness see, and share Thy joy at last.
to Fa-ther, Spir-it, and to Thee the strains of praise and love.

WORDS: Greek poem, Synesius of Cyrene, ca. 430; tr. Allen William Chatfield, 1876
MUSIC: *Southwell*, William Daman, 1579   S.M.

468 From Every Stormy Wind That Blows

I will commune with thee from above the mercy seat. – Exodus 25:22 KJV

1. From ev - 'ry storm - y wind that blows, from
2. There is a place where Je - sus sheds the
3. There is a spot where spir - its blend, where
4. Ah, whith - er could we flee for aid, when
5. There, there on ea - gle wings we soar, and
6. O may my hand for - get her skill, my

ev - 'ry swell - ing tide of woes, there is a calm, a
oil of glad - ness on our heads, a place than all be -
friend holds fel - low - ship with friend, though sun - dered[1] far; by
temp - ted, des - o - late, dis - mayed, or how the hosts of
time and sense seem all no more, and heav'n comes down our
tongue be si - lent, cold, and still, this bound - ing[2] heart for -

sure re - treat; 'tis found be - neath the mer - cy seat.
sides more sweet; it is the blood - stained mer - cy seat.
faith they meet a - round the com - mon mer - cy seat.
hell de - feat, had suf - f'ring saints no mer - cy seat?
souls to greet, and glo - ry crowns the mer - cy seat.
get to beat, if I for - get the mer - cy seat.

1. sundered: spread out
2. bounding: leaping, running

WORDS: Hugh Stowell, 1828, 1831
MUSIC: *Retreat*, Thomas Hastings, 1842; arr. Rhys Thomas, 1916

L. M.

All Your Anxiety

God cares for you, so turn all your worries over to Him. – 1 Peter 5:7 CEV

1. Is there a heart o'er-come by sor-row? Is there a life weighed
2. No oth-er friend so swift to help you; no oth-er friend so
3. Come then at once; de-lay no long-er! Heed His en-treat-y

down by care? Come to the cross, each bur-den bear-ing;
quick to hear. No oth-er place to leave your bur-den;
kind and sweet. You need not fear a dis-ap-point-ment;

Refrain

all your anx-i-e-ty– leave it there.
no oth-er one to hear your prayer. All your anx-i-e-ty,
you shall find peace at the mer-cy seat.

all your care, bring to the mer-cy seat; leave it there. Nev-er a

bur-den He can-not bear; nev-er a friend like Je-sus!

WORDS: Edward Henry Joy, 1920
MUSIC: *All Your Anxiety*, Edward Henry Joy, 1920

Irregular with Refrain

470
O to Be Like Thee!

I follow the example of Christ. – 1 Corinthians 11:1 CEV

1. O to be like Thee! Bless-ed Re - deem - er, this is my con - stant
2. O to be like Thee! Full of com - pas - sion, lov - ing, for - giv - ing,
3. O to be like Thee! While I am plead - ing, pour out Thy Spir - it;

long - ing and prayer. Glad - ly I'll for - feit all of earth's trea - sures,
ten - der and kind. Help-ing the help - less, cheer-ing the faint - ing,
fill with Thy love. Make me a tem - ple meet for Thy dwell - ing;

Refrain

Je - sus, Thy per - fect like - ness to wear.
seek - ing the wan - d'ring sin - ner to find.   O to be like Thee!
fit me for life and heav - en a - bove.

O to be like Thee, bless - ed Re - deem - er, pure as Thou art! Come in Thy

WORDS: Thomas Obediah Chisholm, 1897
MUSIC: *Rondinella*, William James Kirkpatrick, 1897

10.9.10.9. with Refrain

sweet-ness, come in Thy full-ness; stamp Thine own im-age deep on my heart.

O for a Closer Walk with God   471

If we walk in the light, as He is in the light...the blood of Jesus...purifies us from all sin. – 1 John 1:7 NIV

1. O for a clos-er walk with God,
2. Where is the bless-ed-ness I knew
3. Re-turn, O ho-ly Dove, re-turn,
4. The dear-est i-dol I have known,
5. So shall my walk be close with God,

a calm and heav'n-ly frame, a light to shine up-
when first I saw the Lord? Where is the soul-re-
sweet mes-sen-ger of rest; I hate the sins that
what-e'er that i-dol be, help me to tear it
calm and se-rene my frame; so pur-er light shall

on the road that leads me to the Lamb!
fresh-ing view of Je-sus and His Word?
made Thee mourn, and drove Thee from my breast.
from Thy throne, and wor-ship on-ly Thee.
mark the road that leads me to the Lamb.

WORDS: William Cowper, 1779
MUSIC: *Beatitudo,* John Bacchus Dykes, 1875

C.M.

472 Take Time to Be Holy

Always live as God's holy people should, because God is the one who chose you, and He is holy. – 1 Peter 1:15 CEV

1. Take time to be ho - ly, speak oft with Thy Lord;
2. Take time to be ho - ly, the world rush - es on;
3. Take time to be ho - ly, let Him be thy guide,
4. Take time to be ho - ly, be calm in thy soul;

a - bide in Him al - ways and feed on His Word.
spend much time in se - cret with Je - sus a - lone.
and run not be - fore Him, what - ev - er be - tide.
each thought and each mo - tive be - neath His con - trol.

Make friends with God's chil - dren, help those who are weak;
By look - ing to Je - sus, like Him thou shalt be;
In joy or in sor - row still fol - low thy Lord,
Thus led by His Spir - it to foun - tains of love,

for - get - ting in noth - ing His bless - ing to seek.
thy friends in thy con - duct His like - ness shall see.
and, look - ing to Je - sus, still trust in His Word.
thou soon shall be fit - ted for ser - vice a - bove.

WORDS: William Dunn Longstaff, 1882
MUSIC: *Holiness*, George Coles Stebbins, 1890

6.5.6.5 D

"Are Ye Able," Said the Master 473

Can you drink the cup I drink or be baptized with the baptism I am baptized with? – Mark 10:38 NIV

1. "Are ye a - ble," said the Mas - ter, "to be cru - ci - fied with Me?"
2. "Are ye a - ble," to re - mem - ber, when a thief lifts up his eyes,
3. "Are ye a - ble," when the shad - ows close a - round you with the sod,
4. "Are ye a - ble," still the Mas - ter whis - pers down e - ter - ni - ty,

"Yea," the stur - dy dream - ers an - swered, "to the death we fol - low Thee."
that his par - doned soul is wor - thy of a place in par - a - dise?
to be - lieve that spir - it tri - umphs, to com - mend your soul to God?
and he - ro - ic spir - its an - swer, now, as then in Gal - i - lee.

Refrain

"Lord, we are a - ble!" Our spir - its are Thine, re - mold them,

make us like Thee, di - vine; Thy guid - ing ra - diance a - bove

us shall be a bea - con to God, to faith and loy - al - ty.

WORDS: Earl Bowman Marlatt, 1925
MUSIC: *Beacon Hill*, Harry Silverdale Mason, 1924

8.7.8.7 with Refrain

474 Dear Lord and Father of Mankind

We have only one God, and He is the Father. He created everything, and we live for Him. – 1 Corinthians 8:6 CEV

1. Dear Lord and Father of mankind, for-
2. In simple trust like theirs who heard, be-
3. O Sabbath rest by Galilee! O
4. Drop Thy still dews of quietness, till
5. Breathe through the heats of our desire Thy

give our foolish ways! Re-clothe us in our
side the Syrian Sea, the gracious calling
calm of hills above, where Jesus knelt to
all our strivings cease; take from our souls the
coolness and Thy balm; let sense be dumb, let

rightful mind; in purer lives Thy
of the Lord, let us, like them, with-
share with thee the silence of e-
strain and stress, and let our or-dered
flesh retire; speak through the earthquake,

service find, in deeper reverence, praise.
out a word, rise up and follow Thee.
ternity, interpreted by love!
lives confess the beauty of Thy peace.
wind and fire, O still small voice of calm!

WORDS: John Greenleaf Whittier, 1872
MUSIC: *Rest (Elton),* Frederick Charles Maker, 1887

8.6.8.8.6

Dear Lord and Father of Mankind 475

We have only one God, and He is the Father. He created everything, and we live for Him. – 1 Corinthians 8:6 CEV

1. Dear Lord and Fa - ther of man - kind, for-
2. In sim - ple trust like theirs who heard, be-
3. O sab - bath rest by Gal - i - lee! O
4. Drop Thy still dews of qui - et - ness, till
5. Breathe through the heats of our de - sire Thy

give our fool - ish ways! Re - clothe us in our
side the Syr - ian Sea, the gra - cious call - ing
calm of hills a - bove, where Je - sus knelt to
all our striv - ings cease; take from our souls the
cool - ness and Thy balm; let sense be dumb, let

right - ful mind, in pur - er lives Thy ser - vice find, in
of the Lord, let us, like them, with - out a word, rise
share with thee the si - lence of e - ter - ni - ty, in -
strain and stress, and let our or - dered lives con - fess the
flesh re - tire; speak through the earth - quake, wind and fire, O

deep - er rev - 'rence, praise, in deep - er rev - 'rence, praise.
up and fol - low Thee, rise up and fol - low Thee.
ter - pret - ed by love, in - ter - pret - ed by love!
beau - ty of Thy peace, the beau - ty of Thy peace.
still, small voice of calm, O still, small voice of calm!

WORDS: John Greenleaf Whittier, 1872
MUSIC: *Repton*, Charles Hubert Hastings Parry, 1888

8.6.8.8.6 with Repeat

476 Teach Me Your Way, O Lord

Show me Your ways, O Lord; teach me Your paths. – Psalm 25:4 NKJV

1. Teach me Your way, O Lord, teach me Your way!
2. When I am sad at heart, teach me Your way!
3. When doubts and fears a - rise, teach me Your way!
4. Long as my life shall last, teach me Your way!

Your guid - ing grace af - ford, teach me Your way!
When earth - ly joys de - part, teach me Your way!
When storm-clouds fill the skies, teach me Your way!
Wher - e'er my lot be cast, teach me Your way!

Help me to walk a - right, more by faith, less by sight;
In hours of lone - li - ness, in times of dire dis - tress,
Shine through the wind and rain, through sor - row, toil and pain;
Un - til the race is run, un - til the jour - ney's done,

lead me with heav'n - ly light, teach me Your way!
in fail - ure or suc - cess, teach me Your way!
make now my path - way plain, teach me Your way!
un - til the crown is won, teach me Your way!

WORDS: Benjamin Mansell Ramsey, 1919, alt.
MUSIC: *Camacha;* Benjamin Mansell Ramsey, 1919

6.4.6.4.6.6.6.4

Where He Leads Me

My sheep listen to My voice; I know them, and they follow Me. – John 10:27 NIV

1. I can hear my Sav - ior call - ing, I can hear my Sav - ior
2. I'll go with Him through the gar - den, I'll go with Him through the
3. I'll go with Him through the judg - ment, I'll go with Him through the
4. He will give me grace and glo - ry, He will give me grace and

call - ing, I can hear my Sav - ior call - ing, "Take thy
gar - den, I'll go with Him through the gar - den, I'll go
judg - ment, I'll go with Him through the judg - ment, I'll go
glo - ry, He will give me grace and glo - ry, and go

Refrain

cross and fol - low, fol - low Me." Where He leads me I will
with Him, with Him all the way.
with Him, with Him all the way.
with me, with me all the way.

fol - low, where He leads me I will fol - low, where He leads me

I will fol - low, I'll go with Him, with Him all the way.

WORDS: Ernest W. Blandy, 1890
MUSIC: *Norris,* John Samuel Norris, 1890

8.8.8.9 with Refrain

478 Jesus Calls Us

"Come, follow Me," Jesus said, "and I will make you fishers of men." – Mark 1:17 NIV

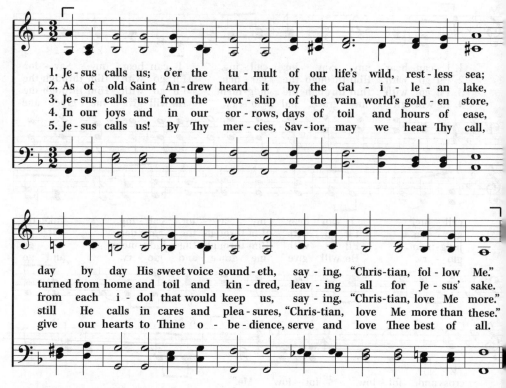

1. Je-sus calls us; o'er the tu-mult of our life's wild, rest-less sea;
2. As of old Saint An-drew heard it by the Gal - i - le-an lake,
3. Je-sus calls us from the wor-ship of the vain world's gold-en store,
4. In our joys and in our sor-rows, days of toil and hours of ease,
5. Je-sus calls us! By Thy mer-cies, Sav-ior, may we hear Thy call,

day by day His sweet voice sound-eth, say - ing, "Chris-tian, fol - low Me."
turned from home and toil and kin-dred, leav - ing all for Je - sus' sake.
from each i - dol that would keep us, say - ing, "Chris-tian, love Me more."
still He calls in cares and plea-sures, "Chris-tian, love Me more than these."
give our hearts to Thine o - be - dience, serve and love Thee best of all.

WORDS: Cecil Frances Humphreys Alexander, 1852
MUSIC: *Galilee*, William Herbert Jude, 1874

8.7.8.7

479 Jesus Calls Us

"Come, follow Me," Jesus said, "and I will make you fishers of men." – Mark 1:17 NIV

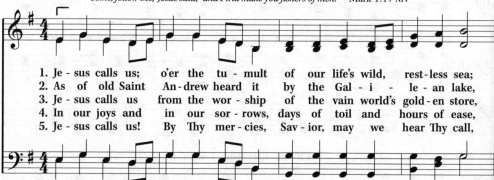

1. Je - sus calls us; o'er the tu - mult of our life's wild, rest-less sea;
2. As of old Saint An-drew heard it by the Gal - i - le-an lake,
3. Je - sus calls us from the wor - ship of the vain world's gold-en store,
4. In our joys and in our sor-rows, days of toil and hours of ease,
5. Je - sus calls us! By Thy mer-cies, Sav - ior, may we hear Thy call,

WORDS: Cecil Frances Humphreys Alexander, 1852
MUSIC: *Restoration*, from *The Southern Harmony and Musical Companion*, William Walker, 1835

8.7.8.7

day   by   day   His   sweet voice sound - eth,   say - ing, "Chris - tian,   fol - low Me."
turned from home and   toil   and   kin - dred, leav - ing   all   for   Je - sus' sake.
from   each   i - dol   that would keep   us,   say - ing, "Chris - tian,   love Me more."
still   He   calls in   cares and plea - sures, "Chris-tian, love   Me   more than these."
give   our hearts to   Thine   o - be - dience, serve and love Thee best of   all.

All for Jesus! All for Jesus!   480

He taught us to give up our wicked ways and our worldly desires and to live decent and honest lives. — Titus 2:12 CEV

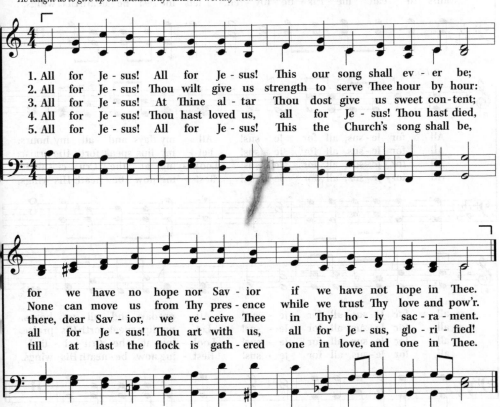

1. All   for   Je - sus!   All   for   Je - sus!   This   our song shall ev - er   be;
2. All   for   Je - sus! Thou wilt give   us strength to serve Thee hour by hour:
3. All   for   Je - sus!   At Thine al - tar Thou dost give us sweet con - tent;
4. All   for   Je - sus! Thou hast loved us,   all   for   Je - sus! Thou hast died,
5. All   for   Je - sus!   All   for   Je - sus!   This   the Church's song shall be,

for   we   have   no   hope nor Sav - ior   if   we have not hope in   Thee.
None   can move us   from Thy pres - ence while we trust Thy love and pow'r.
there, dear Sav - ior, we   re - ceive Thee   in   Thy ho - ly   sac - ra - ment.
all   for   Je - sus! Thou art with us,   all   for   Je - sus, glo - ri - fied!
till   at   last the flock is gath - ered one   in love, and one in   Thee.

WORDS: William John Sparrow-Simpson, 1887
MUSIC: *All for Jesus,* John Stainer, 1887   8.7.8.7

481

All for Jesus

We have left all we had to follow You! – Luke 18:28 NIV

1. All for Je-sus, all for Je-sus! All my be-ing's ran-somed pow'rs:
2. Let my hands per-form His bid-ding, let my feet run in His ways.
3. Since my eyes were fixed on Je-sus, I've lost sight of all be-side,
4. O what won-der! How a-maz-ing! Je-sus, glo-rious King of kings,

All my thoughts and words and do-ings, all my days and all my hours.
Let my eyes see Je-sus on-ly, let my lips speak forth His praise.
so en-chained my spir-it's vi-sion, look-ing at the Cru-ci-fied.
wants to call me His be-lov-ed, lets me rest be-neath His wings.

Refrain

All for Je-sus, all for Je-sus! All my days and all my hours;
All for Je-sus, all for Je-sus! Let my lips speak forth His praise;
All for Je-sus, all for Je-sus! Look-ing at the Cru-ci-fied;
All for Je-sus, all for Je-sus! Rest-ing now be-neath His wings;

all for Je-sus, all for Je-sus! All my days and all my hours.
all for Je-sus, all for Je-sus! Let my lips speak forth His praise.
all for Je-sus, all for Je-sus! Look-ing at the Cru-ci-fied.
all for Je-sus, all for Je-sus! Rest-ing now be-neath His wings.

WORDS: Mary Dagworthy James, 1889
MUSIC: *Constancy,* Asa Hull, 1889

8.7.8.7. with Refrain

I Gave My Life for Thee

482

I am the Good Shepherd. The good shepherd lays down his life for the sheep. – John 10:11 NIV

1. I gave My life for thee, My pre - cious blood I shed,
2. My Fa - ther's house of light, My glo - ry - cir - cled throne,
3. I suf - fered much for thee, more than thy tongue can tell,
4. And I have brought to thee, down from My home a - bove,

that thou might'st ran - somed be, and quick - ened from the dead;
I left, for earth - ly night, for wan - d'rings sad and lone;
of bit - t'rest ag - o - ny, to res - cue thee from hell;
sal - va - tion full and free, My par - don and My love;

I gave, I gave My life for thee, what hast thou giv'n for Me?
I left, I left it all for thee, hast thou left aught for Me?
I've borne, I've borne it all for thee, what hast thou borne for Me?
I bring, I bring rich gifts to thee, what hast thou brought to Me?

I gave, I gave My life for thee, what hast thou giv'n for Me?
I left, I left it all for thee, hast thou left aught for Me?
I've borne, I've borne it all for thee, what hast thou borne for Me?
I bring, I bring rich gifts to thee, what hast thou brought to Me?

WORDS: Frances Ridley Havergal, 1858
MUSIC: *Kenosis,* Philip Paul Bliss, 1873

6.6.6.6.8.6 with Repeat

483 Jesus, I My Cross Have Taken

Anyone who does not take his cross and follow Me is not worthy of Me. – Matthew 10:38 NIV

1. Je - sus, I my cross have tak - en, all to leave and
2. Let the world de - spise and leave me, they have left my
3. Man may trou - ble and dis - tress me, 'twill but drive me
4. Has - ten on from grace to glo - ry, armed by faith and

fol - low Thee; des - ti - tute, de - spised, for - sak - en,
Sav - ior too; hu - man hearts and looks de - ceive me;
to Thy breast; life with tri - als hard may press me,
winged by prayer; heav'n's e - ter - nal day's be - fore me,

Thou from hence my all shalt be: Per - ish ev - 'ry fond am -
Thou art not, like man, un - true; and, while Thou shalt smile up -
heav'n will bring me sweet - er rest. O 'tis not in grief to
God's own hand shall guide me there. Soon shall close my earth - ly

bi - tion, all I've sought, and hoped, and known; yet how rich is
on me, God of wis - dom, love, and might, foes may hate and
harm me, while Thy love is left to me; O 'twere not in
mis - sion, swift shall pass my pil - grim days, hope shall change to

WORDS: Henry Francis Lyte, 1833
MUSIC: *Ellesdie,* attr. Wolfgang Amadeus Mozart, 18th c.;
from Leavitt's *The Christian Lyre,* 1831; arr. Hubert Platt Main, 1868
This tune in a higher key, No. 350.

8.7.8.7.D

my   con-di-tion,   God   and heav'n   are   still   my   own!
friends   may   shun   me;   show Thy face,   and   all   is   bright.
joy   to   charm   me,   were that joy   un-   mixed with Thee.
glad   fru-i-tion,   faith to   sight,   and   prayer to praise.

"Take Up Thy Cross," the Savior Said 484

If anyone would come after Me, he must...take up his cross and follow Me. – Mark 8:34 NIV

1. "Take up   thy cross,"   the   Sav-ior said,   "If   thou wouldst
2. Take up   thy cross;   let   not   its   weight   fill   thy weak
3. Take up   thy cross,   nor   heed the   shame,   and   let   thy
4. Take up   thy cross,   then, in   His   strength,   and   calm-ly
5. Take up   thy cross,   and   fol-low Christ,   nor   think till

My   dis-ci-ple   be;   de-ny thy-self,   the
soul   with vain   a-larm;   His strength shall bear   thy
fool-ish pride   be   still: Thy Lord re-fused   not
ev-'ry   dan-ger brave;   twill guide thee   to   a
death   to   lay   it   down;   for   on-ly   one   who

world   for-sake,   and   hum-bly fol-low   af-ter   Me."
spir-it   up,   and   brace thy   heart   and nerve   thine arm.
e'en   to   die   up-on a   cross   on   Cal-v'ry's hill.
bet-ter   home,   and   lead   to   vic-t'ry o'er   the   grave.
bears   the   cross   may   hope   to   wear   the   glo-r'ous crown.

WORDS: Charles William Everest, 1833, alt.
MUSIC: *Quebec*, Henry Williams Baker, 1862

L.M.

485 O Master, Let Me Walk with Thee

You have accepted Christ Jesus as your Lord. Now keep on following Him. – Colossians 2:6 CEV

1. O Master, let me walk with Thee, in lowly
paths of service free. Tell me Thy secret;
help me bear the strain of toil, the fret of care.

2. Help me the slow of heart to move by some clear,
winning word of love. Teach me the wayward
feet to stay, and guide them in the homeward way.

3. Teach me Thy patience; still with Thee in closer,
dearer, companiony, in work that keeps faith
sweet and strong, in trust that triumphs over wrong.

4. In hope that sends a shining ray far down the
future's broadening way, in peace that only
Thou canst give, with Thee, O Master, let me live.

WORDS: Washington Gladden, 1879
MUSIC: *Maryton*, Henry Percy Smith, 1874
This tune in a higher key, No. 324.

L.M.

486 Must Jesus Bear the Cross Alone?

If anyone would come after Me, he must deny himself and take up his cross daily and follow Me. – Luke 9:23 NIV

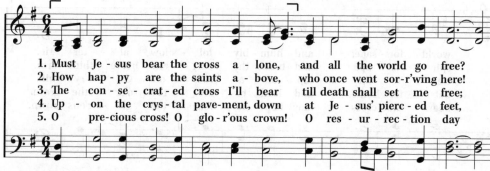

1. Must Jesus bear the cross alone, and all the world go free?

2. How happy are the saints above, who once went sorrowing here!

3. The consecrated cross I'll bear till death shall set me free;

4. Upon the crystal pavement, down at Jesus' pierced feet,

5. O precious cross! O glorious crown! O resurrection day

WORDS: Thomas Shepherd, and others, 1693 alt.
MUSIC: *Maitland*, George Nelson Allen, 1844

C.M.

No,   there's a cross for ev - 'ry - one,   and there's a cross for me.
But   now they taste un - min - gled love   and joy with - out a tear.
and   then go home my crown to wear,   for there's a crown for me.
joy - ful I'll cast my gold - en crown   and His dear name re - peat.
when   Christ the Lord from heav'n comes down   and bears my soul a - way.

Something for Thee   487

Do your best to present yourself to God as one approved. – 2 Timothy 2:15 NIV

1. Sav - ior, Thy dy - ing love   Thou gav - est me,   nor should I
2. Give me a faith - ful heart,   guid - ed by Thee,   that each de -
3. All that I am and have,   Thy gifts so free,   ev - er in

aught with - hold, dear Lord, from Thee;   in love my soul would bow, my
part - ing day hence - forth may see   some work of love be - gun, some
joy or grief, my Lord, for Thee;   and when Thy face I see, my

heart ful - fill its vow, some of - f'ring bring Thee now, some - thing for Thee.
deed of kind - ness done, some wan - d'rer sought and won, some - thing for Thee.
ran - somed soul shall be, through all e - ter - ni - ty, some - thing for Thee.

WORDS: Sylvanus Dryden Phelps, 1862
MUSIC: *Something for Jesus*, Robert Lowry, 1871   6.4.6.4.6.6.6.4

488 Make Me a Captive, Lord

It has become clear...to everyone...that I am in chains for Christ. – Philippians 1:13 NIV

1. Make me a cap-tive, Lord, and then I shall be free;
2. My heart is weak and poor un-til its mas-ter finds;
3. My pow'r is faint and low till I have learned to serve;
4. My will is not my own till Thou hast made it Thine;

force me to ren-der up my sword, and I shall con-qu'ror be.
it has no spring of ac-tion sure, it var-ies with the wind.
it wants the need-ed fire to glow, it wants the breeze to nerve;
if it would reach a mon-arch's throne, it must its crown re-sign;

I sink in life's a-larms when by my-self I stand;
It can-not free-ly move till Thou hast wrought its chain;
it can-not drive the world un-til it-self be driv'n;
it on-ly stands un-bent a-mid the clash-ing strife,

im-pris-on me with-in Thine arms and strong shall be my hand.
en-slave it with Thy match-less love and death-less it shall reign.
its flag can on-ly be un-furled when Thou shalt breathe from heav'n.
when on Thy bos-om it has leaned, and found in Thee its life.

WORDS: George Matheson, 1890
MUSIC: *Diademata*, George Job Elvey, 1868
Another harmonization of this tune, No. 449; another harmonization in a higher key, No. 46.

S.M.D.

"Give Me Thy Heart"

For where your treasure is, there your heart will be also. – Matthew 6:21 NIV

1. "Give Me thy heart," says the Fa-ther a - bove, no gift so pre-cious to
2. "Give Me thy heart," says the Sav-ior to - day, call-ing in mer - cy His
3. "Give Me thy heart," says the Spir-it di - vine, "All that thou hast, to My

Him as our love; soft - ly He whis-pers, wher - ev - er thou art,
sweet voice o - bey; "Turn now from sin, and from e - vil de - part,
keep-ing re - sign; grace more a - bound-ing is Mine to im - part,

Refrain

"Grate-ful-ly trust Me, and give Me thy heart." "Give Me thy heart,
have I not died for thee? give Me thy heart."
make full sur - ren - der and give Me thy heart."

give Me thy heart." Hear the soft whis-per, wher - ev - er thou art: From this dark

world He would draw thee a - part; speak-ing so ten-der-ly, "Give Me thy heart."

WORDS: Eliza Edmunds Hewitt, 1898, alt.
MUSIC: *Bourne*, William James Kirkpatrick, 1898, alt.

10.10.10.10. with Refrain

490 Little Is Much When God Is in It

They said, "We have only five small loaves of bread and two fish."– Matthew 14:17 NIV

1. In the har-vest field now rip-ened there's a work for all to do;
2. Does the place you're called to la-bor seem too small and lit-tle known?
3. When the con-flict here is end-ed and our race on earth is run,

hark! the voice of God is call-ing to the har-vest call-ing you.
It is great if God is in it, and He'll not for-get His own.
He will say, if we are faith-ful, "Wel-come home, My child, well done!"

Refrain

Lit-tle is much when God is in it! La-bor not for wealth or fame.

There's a crown, and you can win it, if you go in Je-sus' name.

WORDS: Kittie Louise Suffield, ca. 1924
MUSIC: *Little Is Much*, Kittie Louise Suffield, ca. 1924

8.7.8.7. with Refrain

I'll Live for Him

491

Whether we are at home with the Lord or away from Him, we still try our best to please Him. – 2 Corinthians 5:9 CEV

1. My life, my love I give to Thee, Thou Lamb of God who died for me;
2. I now be-lieve Thou dost re-ceive, for Thou hast died that I might live;
3. O Thou who died on Cal-va-ry, to save my soul and make me free;

O may I ev-er faith-ful be, my Sav-ior and my God!
and now hence-forth I'll trust in Thee, my Sav-ior and my God!
I'll con-se-crate my life to Thee, my Sav-ior and my God!

Refrain

I'll live for Him who died for me, how hap-py then my life shall be!

I'll live for Him who died for me, my Sav-ior and my God!

WORDS: Ralph Erskine Hudson, 1882
MUSIC: *Dunbar*, C. R. Dunbar, 1882

8.8.8.6. with Refrain

492 Living for Jesus

Those who live should no longer live for themselves but for Him who died for them. – 2 Corinthians 5:15 NIV

1. Liv-ing for Je-sus, a life that is true, striv-ing to
2. Liv-ing for Je-sus who died in my place, bear-ing on
3. Liv-ing for Je-sus, wher-ev-er I am, do-ing each
4. Liv-ing for Je-sus through earth's lit-tle while, my dear-est

please Him in all that I do; yield-ing al-le-giance, glad-
Cal-v'ry my sin and dis-grace; such love con-strains me to
du-ty in His ho-ly name; will-ing to suf-fer af-
trea-sure, the light of His smile; seek-ing the lost ones He

heart-ed and free, this is the path-way of bless-ing for me.
an-swer His call, fol-low His lead-ing and give Him my all.
flic-tion or loss, deem-ing each tri-al a part of my cross.
died to re-deem, bring-ing the wea-ry to find rest in Him.

Refrain

O Je-sus, Lord and Sav-ior, I give my-self to Thee; for Thou, in Thy a-

tone-ment, didst give Thy-self for me. I own no oth-er mas-ter, my heart shall

WORDS: Thomas Obediah Chisholm, 1917
MUSIC: *Living,* Carl Harold Lowdon, 1915

10.10.10.10 with Refrain

be Thy throne. My life I give, hence-forth to live, O Christ, for Thee a - lone.

Close to Thee

493

Come near to God, and He will come near to you. – James 4:8 CEV

1. Thou, my ev - er - last - ing por - tion, more than friend or life to me;
2. Not for ease or world - ly plea - sure, nor for fame my prayer shall be;
3. Lead me through the vale of shad - ows, bear me o'er life's fit - ful sea;

all a - long my pil - grim jour - ney, Sav - ior, let me walk with Thee.
glad - ly will I toil and suf - fer, on - ly let me walk with Thee.
then the gate of life e - ter - nal may I en - ter, Lord, with Thee.

Refrain

Close to Thee, close to Thee, close to Thee, close to Thee;

all a - long my pil - grim jour - ney, Sav - ior, let me walk with Thee.
glad - ly will I toil and suf - fer, on - ly let me walk with Thee.
then the gate of life e - ter - nal may I en - ter, Lord, with Thee.

WORDS: Fanny Jane Crosby, 1874
MUSIC: *Close to Thee*, Silas Jones Vail, 1874

8.7.8.7 with Refrain

494 Open the Wells of Salvation

It is to us that this message of salvation has been sent. – Acts 13:26 NIV

1. Lord, I am fond-ly, ear-nest-ly long-ing, in-to Thy
2. Dead to the world would I be, O Fa-ther! Dead un-to
3. I would be Thine, and serve Thee for-ev-er, filled with Thy

ho-ly like-ness to grow; thirst-ing for more and deep-er com-
sin, a-live un-to Thee; cru-ci-fy all the earth-ly with-
Spir-it, lost in Thy love; come to my heart, Lord come with a-

mu-nion, yearn-ing Thy love more ful-ly to know.
in me, emp-tied of sin and self may I be.
noint-ing, show-ers of grace send down from a-bove.

Refrain

O-pen the wells of grace and sal-va-tion,
O-pen the wells of grace and sal-va-tion,

pour the rich streams deep in-to my heart;
pour the rich streams deep in-to my heart;

WORDS: Elisha Albright Hoffman, ca. 1902
MUSIC: *Open the Wells,* Charles Edward Pollock, 1853

10.9.10.9 with Refrain

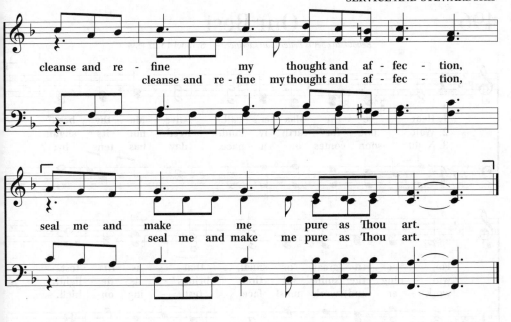

cleanse and re - fine   my   thought and   af - fec - tion,
cleanse and re - fine   my thought and   af - fec - tion,

seal me and   make   me   pure as Thou   art.
seal me and make   me pure as Thou   art.

A Charge to Keep I Have   495

Those who have been given a trust must prove faithful. – 1 Corinthians 4:2 NIV

1. A   charge to   keep   I   have,   a   God to   glo - ri - fy,
2. To   serve   the pres - ent   age,   my   call - ing   to   ful - fill;
3. Arm   me   with jeal - ous   care,   as   in Thy sight   to   live;

who   gave His Son   my   soul to save, and   fit   it   for   the   sky.
O   may it   all   my   pow'rs en - gage   to   do   my Mas - ter's   will!
and   O Thy ser - vant,   Lord, pre - pare   a   strict ac - count   to   give!

WORDS: Charles Wesley, 1762
MUSIC: *Boylston*, Lowell Mason, 1832

S.M.

496 Our Best

Behold, to obey is better than sacrifice. – 1 Samuel 15:22 ESV

1. Hear ye the Mas-ter's call, "Give Me thy best!"
2. Wait not for earth-ly laud, heed not its slight;
3. Night soon comes on a-pace, day has-tens by;

For, be it great or small, that is His test.
win-ning the smile of God brings its de-light!
work-er and work must face test-ing on high.

Do then your ver-y best, not for re-ward,
Aid-ing the good and true ne'er goes un-blest,
Oh, may we in that day find rest, sweet rest,

not for vain praise ex-pressed, but for the Lord.
all that we think or do, be it the best.
which God has prom-ised those who do their best.

Refrain

Ev-'ry work for Je-sus will be blest, but He

WORDS: S. C. Kirk, ca. 1912
MUSIC: *Tullar,* Grant Colfax Tullar, ca. 1912

10.10.10.10 with Refrain

asks from ev - 'ry - one their best. Our tal - ents may be few,

these may be small, but un - to Him is due our best, our all.

May the Mind of Christ, My Savior 497

Let the word of Christ dwell in you richly. – Colossians 3:16 NIV

1. May the mind of Christ, my Sav - ior, live in me from day to day,
2. May the Word of God dwell rich - ly in my heart from hour to hour,
3. May the peace of God, my Fa - ther, rule my life in ev - 'ry - thing,
4. May the love of Je - sus fill me, as the wa - ters fill the sea;
5. May I run the race be - fore me, strong and brave to face the foe,
6. May His beau - ty rest up - on me as I seek the lost to win;

by His love and pow'r con - trol - ling all I do and say.
so that all may see I tri - umph on - ly through His pow'r.
that I may be calm to com - fort sick and sor - row - ing.
Him ex - alt - ing, self a - bas - ing, this is vic - to - ry.
look - ing on - ly un - to Je - sus as I on - ward go.
and may they for - get the chan - nel, see - ing on - ly Him.

WORDS: Kate Barclay Wilkinson, 1925
MUSIC: *St. Leonards,* Arthur Gyril Barham-Gould, 1925

8.7.8.5

498 Channels Only

If a man cleanses himself...he will be an instrument for noble purposes...useful to the Master. – 2 Timothy 2:21 NIV

1. How I praise Thee, pre-cious Sav-ior, that Thy love laid hold of me;
2. Emp-tied that Thou should-est fill me, a clean ves-sel in Thy hand;
3. Wit-ness-ing Thy pow'r to save me, set-ting free from self and sin;
4. Je-sus, fill now with Thy Spir-it hearts that full sur-ren-der know;

Thou has saved and cleansed and filled me that I might Thy chan-nel be.
with no pow'r but as Thou giv-est gra-cious-ly with each com-mand.
Thou who bought me to pos-sess me, in Thy full-ness, Lord, come in.
that the streams of liv-ing wa-ter from our in-ner man may flow.

Refrain

Chan-nels on-ly, bless-ed Mas-ter, but with all Thy won-drous pow'r
flow-ing through us, Thou canst use us ev-'ry day and ev-'ry hour.

WORDS: Mary E. Maxwell, 1910
MUSIC: *Channels*, Ada Rose Gibbs, 1900

8.7.8.7 with Refrain

More About Jesus

I want to know Christ and the power of His resurrection. – Philippians 3:10 NIV

1. More a-bout Je-sus would I know, more of His grace to oth-ers show;
2. More a-bout Je-sus let me learn, more of His ho-ly will dis-cern;
3. More a-bout Je-sus in His Word, hold-ing com-mu-nion with my Lord;
4. More a-bout Je-sus; on His throne, rich-es in glo-ry all His own;

more of His sav-ing full-ness see, more of His love who died for me.
Spir-it of God, my teach-er be, show-ing the things of Christ to me.
hear-ing His voice in ev-'ry line, mak-ing each faith-ful say-ing mine.
more of His king-dom's sure in-crease; more of His com-ing, Prince of Peace.

Refrain

More, more a-bout Je-sus, more, more a-bout Je-sus;

more of His sav-ing full-ness see, more of His love who died for me.

WORDS: Eliza Edmunds Hewitt, 1887
MUSIC: *Sweney,* John Robson Sweney, 1887

L.M. with Refrain

500 I Would Be True

Be faithful unto death, and I will give you the crown of life. – Revelation 2:10 ESV

1. I would be true, for there are those who trust me; I would be
2. I would be friend of all, the foe, the friend - less; I would be
3. I would be learn - ing day by day the les - sons my heav'n - ly
4. I would be prayer - ful through each bus - y mo - ment; I would be

pure, for there are those who care: I would be strong, for there is
giv - ing, and for - get the gift; I would be hum - ble, for I
Fa - ther gives me in His Word; I would be quick to hear His
con - stant - ly in touch with God; I would be tuned to hear His

much to suf - fer; I would be brave, for there is much to
know my weak - ness; I would look up, and laugh, and love, and
light - est whis - per, and prompt and glad to do the things I've
slight - est whis - per, I would have faith to keep the path Christ

dare; I would be brave, for there is much to dare.
lift; I would look up and laugh, and love, and lift.
heard; and prompt and glad to do the things I've heard.
trod; I would have faith to keep the path Christ trod.

WORDS: Sts. 1-3, Howard Arnold Walter, 1907; St. 4, Samuel Ralph Harlow, ca. 1918
MUSIC: *Peek*, Joseh Yates Peek, 1909

11.10.11.10 with Repeat

Nothing Between

501

You shall have no other gods before Me. – Exodus 20:3 ESV

1. Noth-ing be-tween my soul and the Sav-ior, naught of this world's de-
2. Noth-ing be-tween, like world-ly plea-sure; hab-its of life, though
3. Noth-ing be-tween, like pride or sta-tion; self or friends shall
4. Noth-ing be-tween, e'en man-y hard tri-als, Through the whole world a-

lu - sive dream; I have re-nounced all sin - ful plea-sure;
harm-less they seem, must not my heart from Him e'er sev-er;
not in-ter-vene, tho' it may cost me much trib-u - la-tion,
gainst me con-vene; watch-ing with pray'r and much self-de-ni-al,

Je - sus is mine; there's noth-ing be-tween.
He is my all, there's noth-ing be-tween.
I am re-solved, there's noth-ing be-tween.
tri-umph at last, there's noth-ing be-tween.

Refrain

Noth-ing be-tween my

soul and the Sav-ior, so that His bless-ed face may be seen; noth-ing pre-

vent-ing the least of His fa-vor, keep the way clear! Let noth-ing be-tween.

WORDS: Charles Albert Tindley, 1905
MUSIC: *Nothing Between*, Charles Albert Tindley, 1905; arr. F. A. Clark, 1905

Irregular with Refrain

502 Deeper and Deeper

For who has known the mind of the Lord that He may instruct him? But we have the mind of Christ. – 1 Corinthians 2:16 NIV

1. In - to the heart of Je - sus, deep-er and deep-er I go,
2. In - to the will of Je - sus, deep-er and deep-er I go,
3. In - to the cross of Je - sus, deep-er and deep-er I go,
4. In - to the joy of Je - sus, deep-er and deep-er I go,
5. In - to the love of Je - sus, deep-er and deep-er I go,

seek - ing to know the rea - son why He should love me so;
pray - ing for grace to fol - low, seek - ing His way to know;
fol - low - ing through the gar - den, fac - ing the dread - ed foe;
ris - ing, with soul en - rap - tured far from the world be - low.
prais - ing the One who brought me out of my sin and woe;

Why He should stoop to lift me up from the mir - y clay,
bow - ing in full sur - ren - der low at His bless - ed feet,
Drink - ing the cup of sor - row, sob - bing with bro - ken heart,
Joy in the place of sor - row, peace in the midst of pain,
and through e - ter - nal a - ges grate - ful - ly I shall sing,

sav - ing my soul, mak - ing me whole, though I had wan-dered a - way.
bid - ding Him take, break me and make, till I am mold - ed, com - plete.
"O Sav - ior, help! Dear Sav - ior, help! Grace for my weak-ness im - part."
Je - sus will give, Je - sus will give, He will up-hold and sus - tain.
"O how He loved! O how He loved! Je - sus, my Lord and my King!"

WORDS: Oswald Jeffrey Smith, 1914
MUSIC: *Deeper and Deeper*, Oswald Jeffrey Smith, 1914

Irregular

Deeper, Deeper

503

The Spirit searches all things, even the deep things of God. – 1 Corinthians 2:10 NIV

1. Deep-er, deep-er in the love of Je-sus, dai-ly let me go;
2. Deep-er, deep-er! Bless-ed Ho-ly Spir-it, take me deep-er still,
3. Deep-er, deep-er! Though it cost hard tri-als, deep-er let me go!
4. Deep-er, deep-er, ev-'ry day in Je-sus, till all con-flict past,

high-er, high-er in the school of wis-dom, more of grace to know.
till my life is whol-ly lost in Je-sus and His per-fect will.
Root-ed in the ho-ly love of Je-sus, let me fruit-ful grow.
finds me con-qu'ror, and in His own im-age per-fect-ed at last.

Refrain

O deep - er yet, I pray, and
O deep-er yet, I pray, deep-er yet, I pray, and

high - er ev-'ry day; and wis - er,
high-er ev-'ry day, high-er ev-'ry day; and wis-er, bless-ed Lord,

bless-ed Lord, in Thy pre-cious, ho-ly Word.
wis-er, bless-ed Lord,

WORDS: Charles Price Jones, 1900
MUSIC: *Deeper, Deeper*, Charles Price Jones, 1900

10.5.10.5 with Refrain

504 Trust and Obey

He became the source of eternal salvation for all who obey Him. — Hebrews 5:9 NIV

1. When we walk with the Lord in the light of His Word, what a glo - ry He
2. Not a shad - ow can rise, not a cloud in the skies, but His smile quick - ly
3. Not a bur - den we bear, not a sor - row we share, but our toil He doth
4. But we nev - er can prove the de-lights of His love un - til all on the
5. Then in fel - low-ship sweet we will sit at His feet, or we'll walk by His

sheds on our way! While we do His good will, He a - bides with us still,
drives it a - way; not a doubt nor a fear, not a sigh nor a tear,
rich - ly re - pay; not a grief nor a loss, not a frown nor a cross,
al - tar we lay; for the fa - vor He shows, for the joy He be - stows,
side in the way; what He says we will do, where He sends we will go;

Refrain

And with all who will trust and o - bey.
can a - bide while we trust and o - bey.
but is blessed if we trust and o - bey. Trust and o - bey, for there's
are for them who will trust and o - bey.
nev - er fear, on - ly trust and o - bey.

no oth - er way to be hap - py in Je - sus, but to trust and o - bey.

WORDS: John Henry Sammis, ca. 1887
MUSIC: *Trust and Obey,* Daniel Brink Towner, ca. 1887

12.9.12.9 with Refrain

We'll Work Till Jesus Comes

505

Don't get tired of helping others. You will be rewarded when the time is right, if you don't give up. – Galatians 6:9 CEV

1. O land of rest, for thee I sigh! When will the mo-ment come
2. To Je-sus Christ I fled for rest; He bade me cease to roam,
3. I sought at once my Sav-ior's side, no more my steps to roam:

when I shall lay my ar-mor by and dwell in peace at home?
and lean for com-fort on His breast till He con-ducts me home.
With Him I'll brave death's chill-ing tide and reach my heav'n-ly home.

Refrain

We'll work till Je-sus comes, we'll work till Je-sus comes;
We'll work we'll work

we'll work till Je-sus comes, and we'll be gath-ered home.
we'll work

WORDS: Elizabeth Mills, 19th c.
MUSIC: *O Land of Rest*, William Miller, 19th c.

C.M. with Refrain

506 Work, for the Night Is Coming

We must work...while it is day; night is coming, when no one can work. – John 9:4 ESV

1. Work, for the night is com-ing, work through the morn-ing hours;
2. Work, for the night is com-ing, work through the sun-ny noon;
3. Work, for the night is com-ing, un-der the sun-set skies;

work while the dew is spar-kling, work 'mid spring-ing flow'rs.
fill bright-est hours with la-bor, rest comes sure and soon.
while their bright tints are glow-ing, work, for day-light flies.

Work when the day grows bright-er, work in the glow-ing sun;
Give ev-'ry fly-ing min-ute, some-thing to keep in store;
Work till the last beam fad-eth, fad-eth to shine no more;

work, for the night is com-ing, when our work is done.
work, for the night is com-ing, when we work no more.
work, while the night is dark-'ning, when our work is o'er.

WORDS: Annie Louisa Coghill, 1854, alt.
MUSIC: *Work Song*, Lowell Mason, 1864

7.6.7.5. D

I Will Sing the Wondrous Story

They were singing, "Lord God All-Powerful, You have done great and marvelous things." – Revelation 15:2-3 CEV

1. I will sing the won-drous sto - ry of the Christ who died for me;
2. I was lost, but Je - sus found me, found the sheep that went a - stray;
3. Days of dark - ness still come o'er me; sor - row's paths I of - ten tread,
4. He will keep me till the riv - er rolls its wa - ters at my feet;

how He left His home in glo - ry for the cross of Cal - va - ry.
threw His lov - ing arms a - round me, drew me back in - to His way.
but the Sav - ior still is with me; by His hand I'm safe - ly led.
then He'll bear me safe - ly o - ver, where the loved ones I shall meet.

Refrain

Yes, I'll sing the won-drous sto - ry of the Christ who died for me;

sing it with the saints in glo - ry, gath-ered by the crys - tal sea.

WORDS: Francis Harold Rowley, 1886
MUSIC: *Wondrous Story*, Peter Philip Bilhorn, 1886

8.7.8.7 with Refrain

508 He Keeps Me Singing

Sing unto the Lord; for He hath done excellent things. – Isaiah 12:5 KJV

1. There's with-in my heart a mel-o-dy Je-sus whis-pers
2. All my life was wrecked by sin and strife, dis-cord filled my
3. Feast-ing on the rich-es of His grace, rest-ing 'neath His
4. Though some-times He leads through wa-ters deep, tri-als fall a-
5. Soon He's com-ing back to wel-come me, far be-yond the

sweet and low, "Fear not, I am with thee, peace, be still,"
heart with pain, Je-sus swept a-cross the bro-ken strings,
shel-t'ring wing, al-ways look-ing on His smil-ing face,
cross the way, though some-times the path seems rough and steep,
star-ry sky; I shall wing my flight to worlds un-known,

in all of life's ebb and flow.
stirred the slum-b'ring chords a-gain.
that is why I shout and sing.
see His foot-prints all the way.
I shall reign with Him on high.

Refrain

Je-sus, Je-sus, Je-sus, sweet-est name I know, fills my ev-'ry long-ing, keeps me sing-ing as I go.

WORDS: Luther Burgess Bridgers, 1910
MUSIC: *Sweetest Name,* Luther Burgess Bridgers, 1910

9.7.9.7 with Refrain

How Can I Keep from Singing?

Every day will I bless Thee; and I will praise Thy name for ever and ever. – Psalm 145:2 KJV

1. My life flows on in end-less song; a-bove earth's lam-en-
2. Through all the tu-mult and the strife, I hear that mu-sic
3. What though my joys and com-forts die? The Lord my Sav-ior
4. The peace of Christ makes fresh my heart, a foun-tain ev-er

ta - tion, I catch the sweet, though far-off hymn that
ring - ing. It finds an ech - o in my soul. How
liv - eth. What though the dark-ness gath-er round? Songs
spring-ing! All things are mine since I am His! How

Refrain

hails a new cre - a - tion.
can I keep from sing-ing? No storm can shake my
in the night He giv - eth.
can I keep from sing-ing?

in-most calm while to that ref-uge cling-ing; since Christ is

Lord of heav-en and earth, how can I keep from sing-ing?

WORDS: Robert Lowry, 1860, alt.
MUSIC: *Endless Song*, Robert Lowry, 1860

8.7.8.7 with Refrain

510

I Will Praise Him!

I will greatly praise the Lord with my mouth; yea, I will praise Him among the multitude. – Psalm 109:30 KJV

1. When I saw the cleans-ing foun-tain, o - pen wide for all my sin,
2. Though the way seems straight and nar-row, all I claimed was swept a-way;
3. Then God's fire up-on the al-tar of my heart was set a-flame;
4. Bless-ed be the name of Je-sus! I'm so glad He took me in;
5. Glo-ry, glo-ry to the Fath-er! Glo-ry, glo-ry to the Son!

I o-beyed the Spir-it's woo-ing, when He said, "Wilt thou be clean?"
my am-bi-tions, plans and wish-es, at my feet in ash-es lay.
I shall nev-er cease to praise Him glo-ry, glo-ry to His name!
He's for-giv-en my trans-gres-sions, He has cleansed my heart from sin.
Glo-ry, glo-ry to the Spir-it! Glo-ry to the Three in One!

Refrain

I will praise Him! I will praise Him! Praise the Lamb for sin-ners slain.

Give Him glo-ry, all ye peo-ple, for His blood can wash a-way each stain.

WORDS: Margaret Jenkins Harris, 1898
MUSIC: *I Will Praise Him*, Margaret Jenkins Harris, 1898

8.7.8.7 with Refrain

Since I Have Been Redeemed

Whereby ye are sealed unto the day of redemption. – Ephesians 4:30 KJV

1. I have a song I love to sing, since I have been re-deemed,
2. I have a Christ who sat-is-fies, since I have been re-deemed,
3. I have a wit-ness bright and clear, since I have been re-deemed,
4. I have a home pre-pared for me, since I have been re-deemed,

of my Re-deem-er, Sav-ior King, since I have been re-deemed.
to do His will— my high-est prize, since I have been re-deemed.
dis-pel-ling ev-'ry doubt and fear, since I have been re-deemed.
where I shall dwell e-ter-nal-ly, since I have been re-deemed.

Refrain

Since I have been re-deemed, since
Since I have been re-deemed, since I have been re-deemed, since

I have been re-deemed, I will glo-ry in His name; since
I have been re-

have been re-deemed, I will glo-ry in my Sav-ior's name.
deemed, since I have been re-deemed,

WORDS: Edwin Othello Excell, ca. 1884
MUSIC: *Othello*, Edwin Othello Excell, ca. 1884

C.M. with Refrain

512 Saved, Saved!

Everyone who calls on the name of the Lord will be saved. – Acts 2:21 NIV

Unison

1. I've found a Friend, who is all to me; His
2. He saves me from ev-'ry sin and harm, se-
3. When poor and need-y and all a-lone, in

love is ev-er true. I
cures my soul each day. I'm
love He said to me, "Come

love to tell how He lift-ed me and
lean-ing strong on His might-y arm; I
un-to Me and I'll lead you home, to

what His grace can do for you.
know He'll guide me all the way.
live with Me et-er-nal-ly."

WORDS: Jack P. Scholfield, 1911
MUSIC: *Rapture*, Jack P. Scholfield, 1911

9.6.9.8 with Refrain

Refrain Harmony

Saved by His pow'r di-vine! Saved to new life sub-lime!
Saved by His pow'r, Saved to new life,

Life now is sweet and my joy is com-plete, for I'm saved, saved, saved!

Immortal Love, Forever Full   513

God so loved the world. – John 3:16 KJV

1. Im - mor - tal Love, for - ev - er full, for - ev - er flow - ing free,
2. We may not climb the heav'n - ly steeps to bring the Lord Christ down;
3. The heal - ing of His seam - less dress is by our beds of pain;
4. O Lord and Mas - ter of us all, what - e'er our name or sign,

for - ev - er shared, for - ev - er whole, a nev - er - ebb - ing sea!
in vain we search the low - est deeps, for Him no depths can drown.
we touch Him in life's throng and press, and we are whole a - gain.
we own Thy sway, we hear Thy call, we test our lives by Thine.

WORDS: John Greenleaf Whittier, 1856
MUSIC: *Serenity,* William Vincent Wallace, 1836; Uzziah Christopher Burnap, 1856, adapt.   C.M.

514 Since Jesus Came into My Heart

Anyone who belongs to Christ is a new person. The past is forgotten, and everything is new. – 2 Corinthians 5:17 CEV

1. What a won-der-ful change in my life has been wrought since Je-sus came
2. I have ceased from my wan-d'ring and go-ing a-stray, since Je-sus came
3. I shall go there to dwell in that ci-ty, I know, since Je-sus came

in-to my heart! I have light in my soul for which long I had sought,
in-to my heart! And my sins, which were man-y, are all washed a-way,
in-to my heart! And I'm hap-py, so hap-py, as on-ward I go,

Refrain

since Je-sus came in-to my heart!
Since Je-sus came in-to my heart! Since Je-sus came in-to my
since Je-sus came in-to my heart!

heart, since Je-sus came in-to my heart, floods of joy o'er my

soul like the sea bil-lows roll, since Je-sus came in-to my heart.

WORDS: Rufus Henry McDaniel, 1914
MUSIC: *McDaniel*, Charles Hutchinson Gabriel, 1914

12.8.12.8 with Refrain

I've Found a Friend

There is a friend who sticks closer than a brother. – Proverbs 18:24 ESV

1. I've found a Friend, oh, such a friend! He loved me ere I knew Him;
2. I've found a Friend, oh, such a friend! He bled, He died to save me;
3. I've found a Friend, oh, such a friend! So kind and true and ten - der,

He drew me with the cords of love, and thus He bound me to Him.
and not a - lone the gift of life, but His own self He gave me!
so wise a Coun - sel - or and Guide, so might - y a De - fend - er!

And round my heart still close-ly twine those ties which naught can sev - er,
Naught that I have mine own I call, I'll hold it for the Giv - er,
From Him who loves me now so well what pow'r my soul can sev - er?

for I am His, and He is mine, for - ev - er and for - ev - er.
my heart, my strength, my life, my all are His, and His for - ev - er.
Shall life or death, shall earth or hell? No! I am His for - ev - er.

WORDS: James Grindlay Small, 1863
MUSIC: *Friend*, George Coles Stebbins, 1878

8.7.8.7 D

Love Lifted Me!

I will exalt you, O Lord, for you lifted me out of the depths. – Psalm 30:1 NIV

1. I was sink - ing deep in sin, far from the peace - ful shore,
2. All my heart to Him I give, ev - er to Him I'll cling
3. Souls in dan - ger look a - bove, Je - sus com - plete - ly saves;

ve - ry deep - ly stained with - in, sink - ing to rise no more;
in His bless - ed pres - ence live, ev - er His prais - es sing;
He will lift you by His love, out of the an - gry waves;

but the Mas - ter of the sea, heard my de - spair - ing cry,
love so might - y and so true, mer - its my soul's best songs;
He's the Mas - ter of the sea, bil - lows His will o - bey;

from the wa - ters lift - ed me, now safe am I.
faith - ful, lov - ing ser - vice too, to Him be - longs.
He your Sav - ior wants to be, be saved to - day.

Refrain

Love lift - ed me! Love lift - ed me!
e - ven me! e - ven me!

WORDS: James Rowe, 1912
MUSIC: *Safety,* Howard E. Smith, 1912

7.6.7.6.7.6.7.4 with Refrain

When noth - ing else could help, love lift - ed me!

Love lift - ed me! Love lift - ed me!
e - ven me! e - ven me!

When noth - ing else could help, love lift - ed me!

God Is So Good 517

Oh give thanks to the Lord, for He is good. – 1 Chronicles 16:34 ESV

1. God is so good, God is so good,
2. He an - swers prayer, He an - swers prayer,
3. He cares for me, He cares for me,
4. I love Him so, I love Him so,

God is so good, He's so good to me!
He an - swers prayer, He's so good to me!
He cares for me, He's so good to me!
I love Him so, He's so good to me!

WORDS: Traditional, n.d.
MUSIC: *God Is So Good*, traditional, n.d.

4.4.4.5

518 My Savior's Love

Nothing in all creation can separate us from God's love for us in Christ Jesus our Lord. – Romans 8:39 CEV

1. I stand a-mazed in the pres-ence of Je - sus the Naz-a-rene,
2. For me it was in the gar-den He prayed, "Not My will, but Thine."
3. He took my sins and my sor-rows, He made them His ve-ry own;
4. When with the ran-somed in glo-ry His face I at last shall see,

and won-der how He could love me, a sin-ner, con-demned, un-clean.
He had no tears for His own griefs, but sweat drops of blood for mine.
He bore the bur-den to Cal-v'ry, and suf-fered and died a-lone.
'twill be my joy through the a-ges to sing of His love for me.

Refrain

How mar-vel-ous! How won-der-ful!
Oh, how mar-vel-ous! Oh, how won-der-ful!
And my song shall ev-er be;

how mar-vel-ous! How won-der-ful!
oh, how mar-vel-ous! Oh, how won-der-ful!
Is my Sav-ior's love for me!

WORDS: Charles Hutchinson Gabriel, 1905
MUSIC: *My Savior's Love*, Charles Hutchinson Gabriel, 1905

8.7.8.7 with Refrain

He Lifted Me!

He also brought me up out of a horrible pit, out of the miry clay, and set my feet upon a rock. – Psalm 40:2 NKJV

1. In lov-ing-kind-ness Je-sus came, my soul in mer-cy
2. He called me long be-fore I heard, be-fore my sin-ful
3. His brow was pierced with many a thorn; His hands by cru-el
4. Now on a high-er plane I dwell, and with my soul I

to re-claim; and from the depths of sin and shame, through
heart was stirred; but when I took Him at His Word, for-
nails were torn when from my guilt and grief, for-lorn, in
know 'tis well; yet how or why, I can-not tell, He

Refrain

grace He lift-ed me, He lift-ed me.
giv'n, He lift-ed me, He lift-ed me.
love He lift-ed me, He lift-ed me. From sink-ing sand He
should have lift-ed me, He lift-ed me.

lift-ed me, with ten-der hand He lift-ed me; from

shades of night to planes of light, oh, praise His name, He lift-ed me!

WORDS: Charles Hutchinson Gabriel, 1905
MUSIC: *He Lifted Me*, Charles Hutchinson Gabriel, 1905

8.8.8.6 with Refrain

520 Love Found a Way

In His love and in His pity He redeemed them; He lifted them up and carried them. – Isaiah 63:9 ESV

1. Won-der-ful love that res-cued me, sunk deep in sin,
2. Love brought my Sav-ior here to die on Cal-va-ry,
3. Love o-pened wide the gates of light to heav'n's do-main,

guil-ty and vile as I could be, no hope with-in;
for such a sin-ful wretch as I, how can it be?
where in e-ter-nal pow'r and might Je-sus shall reign.

when ev-'ry ray of light had fled, O glo-rious day!
Love bridged the gulf 'twixt me and heav'n, taught me to pray,
Love lift-ed me from depths of woe to end-less day,

Refrain

Rais-ing my soul from out the dead, love found a way.
I am re-deemed, set free, for-giv'n, love found a way. Love found a
there was no help in earth be-low; love found a way.

way to re-deem my soul, love found a way, that could
a way to re-deem my soul, a way

WORDS: Avis Marguerite Burgeson Christiansen, 1915
MUSIC: *Love Found a Way*, Harry Dixon Loes, 1921

8.4.8.4 D with Refrain

make me whole. Love sent my Lord to the cross of
could make me whole; my Lord to the cross, to the

shame, love found a way, O praise His ho-ly name!
cross of shame,

Ask Ye What Great Thing I Know? 521

Always be ready to give an answer when someone asks you about your hope. — 1 Peter 3:15 CEV

1. Ask ye what great thing I know, that de-lights and
2. Who de-feats my fierc-est foes? Who con-soles my
3. Who is life in life to me? Who the death of
4. This is that great thing I know; this de-lights and

stirs me so? What the high re-ward I win? Whose the name I
sad-dest woes? Who re-vives my faint-ing heart, heal-ing all its
death will be? Who will place me on His right, with the count-less
stirs me so: Faith in Him who died to save, Him who tri-umphed

glo-ry in? Je-sus Christ, the cru-ci-fied.
hid-den smart? Je-sus Christ, the cru-ci-fied.
hosts of light? Je-sus Christ, the cru-ci-fied.
o'er the grave: Je-sus Christ, the cru-ci-fied.

WORDS: Johann Christoph Schwedler, 1741; tr. Benjamin Hall Kennedy, 1863
MUSIC: *Hendon*, Henri Abraham César Malan, 1827; harm. Lowell Mason, 1841
This tune in a higher key, No. 302.

7.7.7.7.7

522
I Love to Tell the Story

Those who had been scattered preached the word wherever they went. – Acts 8:4 NIV

1. I love to tell the sto - ry of un - seen things a -
2. I love to tell the sto - ry; more won - der - ful it
3. I love to tell the sto - ry, 'tis plea - sant to re -
4. I love to tell the sto - ry, for those who know it

bove, of Je - sus and His glo - ry, of Je - sus and His
seems than all the gold - en fan - cies of all our gold - en
peat what seems, each time I tell it, more won - der - ful - ly
best seem hun - ger - ing and thirst - ing to hear it like the

love. I love to tell the sto - ry, be - cause I know 'tis
dreams. I love to tell the sto - ry, it did so much for
sweet. I love to tell the sto - ry, for some have nev - er
rest. And when, in scenes of glo - ry, I sing the new, new

true; it sat - is - fies my long - ings as noth - ing else can do.
me; and that is just the rea - son I tell it now to thee.
heard the mes - sage of sal - va - tion from God's own ho - ly Word.
song, 'twill be the old, old sto - ry that I have loved so long.

Refrain

I love to tell the sto - ry, 'twill be my theme in glo - ry,

WORDS: Arabella Catherine Hankey, 1886
MUSIC: *Hankey*, William Gustavus Fischer, 1869

7.6.7.6 D with Refrain

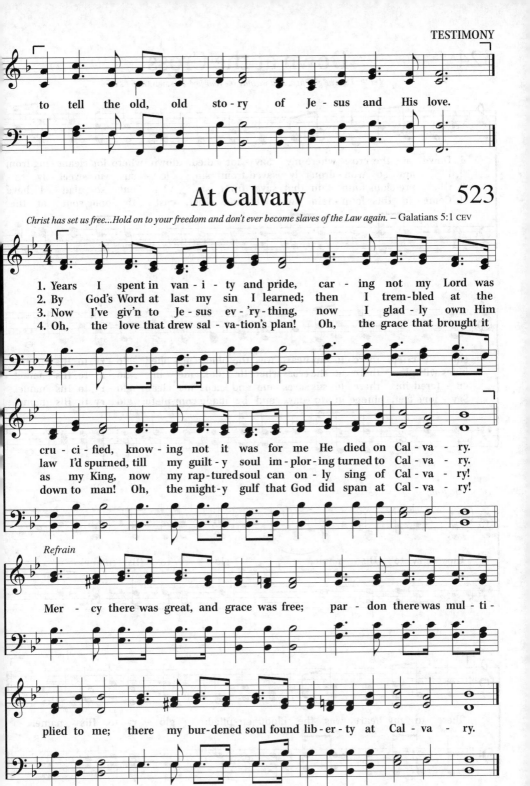

to tell the old, old sto - ry of Je - sus and His love.

At Calvary

523

Christ has set us free...Hold on to your freedom and don't ever become slaves of the Law again. – Galatians 5:1 CEV

1. Years I spent in van - i - ty and pride, car - ing not my Lord was
2. By God's Word at last my sin I learned; then I trem - bled at the
3. Now I've giv'n to Je - sus ev - 'ry - thing, now I glad - ly own Him
4. Oh, the love that drew sal - va - tion's plan! Oh, the grace that brought it

cru - ci - fied, know - ing not it was for me He died on Cal - va - ry.
law I'd spurned, till my guilt - y soul im - plor - ing turned to Cal - va - ry.
as my King, now my rap - tured soul can on - ly sing of Cal - va - ry!
down to man! Oh, the might - y gulf that God did span at Cal - va - ry!

Refrain

Mer - cy there was great, and grace was free; par - don there was mul - ti -

plied to me; there my bur - dened soul found lib - er - ty at Cal - va - ry.

WORDS: William Reed Newell, 1895
MUSIC: *Calvary*, Daniel Brink Towner, 1895

9.9.9.4 with Refrain

524 Down at the Cross

Let the Lord be glorified, that we may see your joy! – Isaiah 66:5 ESV

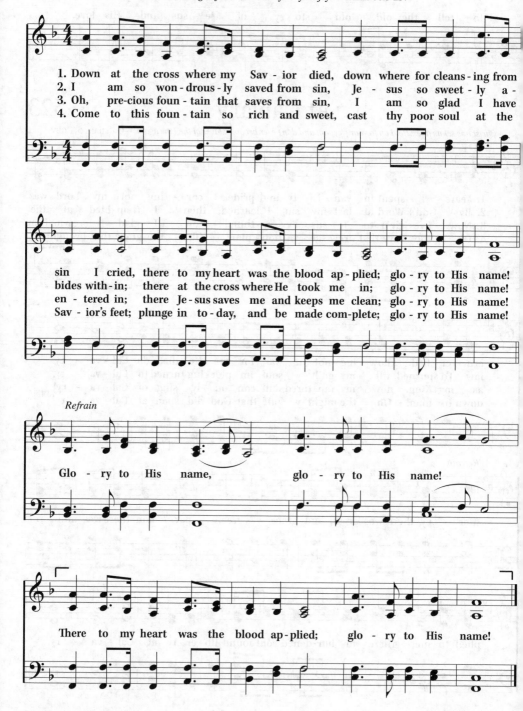

1. Down at the cross where my Sav-ior died, down where for cleans-ing from
2. I am so won-drous-ly saved from sin, Je-sus so sweet-ly a-
3. Oh, pre-cious foun-tain that saves from sin, I am so glad I have
4. Come to this foun-tain so rich and sweet, cast thy poor soul at the

sin I cried, there to my heart was the blood ap-plied; glo-ry to His name!
bides with-in; there at the cross where He took me in; glo-ry to His name!
en-tered in; there Je-sus saves me and keeps me clean; glo-ry to His name!
Sav-ior's feet; plunge in to-day, and be made com-plete; glo-ry to His name!

Refrain

Glo-ry to His name, glo-ry to His name!

There to my heart was the blood ap-plied; glo-ry to His name!

WORDS: Elisha Albright Hoffman, 1878
MUSIC: *Glory to His Name,* John Hart Stockton, 1878

9.9.9.5 with Refrain

At the Cross

Carrying His own cross, He went out to the place of the Skull. – John 19:17 NIV

1. A - las! And did my Sav - ior bleed and did my Sov - 'reign die?
2. Was it for crimes that I had done He groaned up - on the tree?
3. Well might the sun in dark-ness hide and shut his glo - ries in,
4. Thus might I hide my blush-ing face while His dear cross ap - pears,
5. But drops of grief can ne'er re - pay the debt of love I owe:

Would He de - vote that sa - cred head for sin - ners such as I?
A - maz - ing pit - y, grace un-known; and love be - yond de - gree!
when Christ, the might - y Mak - er died, for man, the crea - ture's sin.
dis - solve my heart in thank - ful - ness, and melt mine eyes to tears.
Here, Lord, I give my - self a - way, 'tis all that I can do.

Refrain

At the cross, at the cross where I first saw the light, and the

bur - den of my heart rolled a - way; rolled a - way, it was there by faith

I re - ceived my sight, and now I am hap - py all the day!

WORDS: Isaac Watts, 1707; Ref., Ralph Erskine Hudson, 1885
MUSIC: *Hudson*, Ralph Erskine Hudson, 1885

C.M. with Refrain

526

He Lives

The angel spoke to the women...He is not here. He was raised, just as He said. – Matthew 28:5-6 The Message

1. I serve a ris-en Sav-ior, He's in the world to-day;
2. In all the world a-round me I see His lov-ing care;
3. Re-joice, re-joice, O Chris-tian, lift up your voice and sing

I know that He is liv-ing what-ev-er men may say.
and though my heart grows wea-ry I nev-er will de-spair;
e-ter-nal Hal-le-lu-jahs to Je-sus Christ the King!

I see His hand of mer-cy, I hear His voice of cheer,
I know that He is lead-ing through all the storm-y blast,
The hope of all who seek Him, the help of all who find,

and just the time I need Him, He's al-ways near.
the day of His ap-pear-ing will come at last.
none oth-er is so lov-ing, so good and kind.

Refrain

He lives, He lives, Christ Je-sus lives to-day!
He lives, He lives,

He walks with me and talks with me a-long life's

WORDS: Alfred Henry Ackley, 1933
MUSIC: *Ackley*, Alfred Henry Ackley, 1933

7.6.7.6.7.6.7.4 with Refrain

nar - row way. He lives, He lives, sal - va - tion to im - part!

He lives, He lives,

You ask me how I know He lives? He lives with - in my heart.

I Know Not How That Bethlehem's Babe 527

For in Him dwelleth all the fullness of the Godhead bodily. – Colossians 2:9 KJV

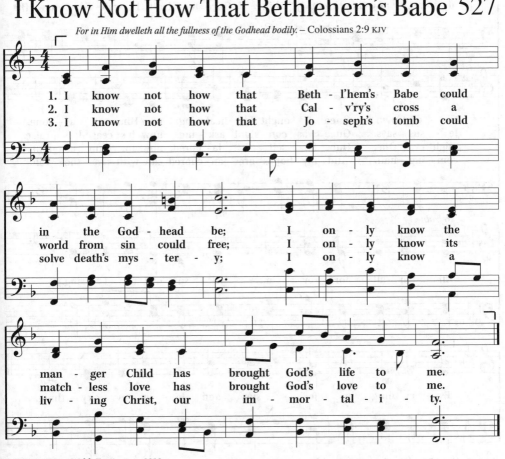

1. I know not how that Beth - l'hem's Babe could
2. I know not how that Cal - v'ry's cross a
3. I know not how that Jo - seph's tomb could

in the God - head be; I on - ly know the
world from sin could free; I on - ly know its
solve death's mys - ter - y; I on - ly know a

man - ger Child has brought God's life to me.
match - less love has brought God's love to me.
liv - ing Christ, our im - mor - tal - i - ty.

WORDS: Harry Webb Farrington, 1910
MUSIC: *St. Magnus,* attr. Jeremiah Clark, 1707; harm. William Henry Monk, 1868

C.M.

528

Himself

Yield yourselves unto God. – Romans 6:13 KJV

1. Once it was the bless-ing, now it is the Lord. Once it was the
2. Once 'twas bus-y plan-ning, now it's trust-ful prayer. Once 'twas anx-ious
3. Once it was my work-ing, His it hence shall be. Once I tried to
4. Once I hoped for Je-sus, now I know He's mine. Once my lamps were

feel-ing, now it is His Word. Once His gifts I want-ed, now the
car-ing, now He has the care. Once 'twas what I want-ed, now what
use Him, now He us-es me. Once the power I want-ed, now the
dy-ing, now they bright-ly shine. Once for death I wait-ed, now His

Giv-er own. Once I sought for heal-ing, now Him-self a-lone.
Je-sus says. Once 'twas con-stant ask-ing, now it's cease-less praise.
might-y One. Once for self I la-bored, now for Him a-lone.
com-ing hail. And my hopes are an-chored safe with-in the veil.

Refrain

All in all for-ev-er, Je-sus will I sing.

Ev-'ry-thing in Je-sus, and Je-sus ev-'ry-thing.

WORDS: Albert Benjamin Simpson, 19th c., alt.
MUSIC: *Himself,* Albert Benjamin Simpson, 19th c.

6.5.6.5 D with Refrain

Jesus Is the Sweetest Name I Know 529

Christ is all that matters, and He lives in all of us. – Colossians 3:11 CEV

1. There have been names that I have loved to hear, but nev-er has there
2. There is no name in earth or heav'n a-bove, that we should give such
3. And some day I shall see Him face to face to thank and praise Him

been a name so dear to this heart of mine, as the name di-vine, the
hon-or and such love as the bless-ed name, let us all ac-claim, that
for His won-drous grace, which He gave to me, when He made me free, the

Refrain

pre-cious, pre-cious name of Je-sus.
won-drous, glo-rious name of Je-sus. Je-sus is the sweet-est name I
bless-ed Son of God called Je-sus.

know, and He's just the same as His love-ly name, and that's the rea-son

why I love Him so; oh, Je-sus is the sweet-est name I know.

WORDS: Lela B. Long, 20th c.
MUSIC: *Lovely Name*, Lela B. Long, 20th c.

10.10.10.9 with Refrain

530 I Heard the Voice of Jesus Say

Come to me, all you who are weary and burdened, and I will give you rest. – Matthew 11:28 NIV

1. I heard the voice of Je - sus say, "Come un - to Me and rest;
2. I heard the voice of Je - sus say, "Be - hold, I free - ly give
3. I heard the voice of Je - sus say, "I am this dark world's light;

lay down, thou wea - ry one, lay down thy head up - on My breast."
the liv - ing wa - ter; thirst - y one, stoop down, and drink, and live."
look un - to Me, thy morn shall rise, and all thy day be bright."

I came to Je - sus, as I was, wea - ry and worn and sad;
I came to Je - sus, and I drank of that life - giv - ing stream;
I looked to Je - sus, and I found in Him my star, my sun;

I found in Him a rest - ing place, and He has made me glad.
my thirst was quenched, my soul re - vived, and now I live in Him.
and in that light of life I'll walk, till trav - 'ling days are done.

WORDS: Horatius Bonar, 1846
MUSIC: *Kingsfold;* from *English Country Songs,* 1893; traditional English melody collected by Lucy Broadwood;
    arr. and harm. Ralph Vaughan Williams, 1906

C.M.D.

This tune in a higher key, No. 146.

I Heard the Voice of Jesus Say 531

Come to me, all you who are weary and burdened, and I will give you rest. – Matthew 11:28 NIV

1. I heard the voice of Je - sus say, "Come un - to Me and rest;
2. I heard the voice of Je - sus say, "Be - hold, I free - ly give
3. I heard the voice of Je - sus say, "I am this dark world's light;

lay down, thou wea - ry one, lay down thy head up - on My breast."
the liv - ing wa - ter; thirst - y one, stoop down, and drink, and live."
look un - to Me, thy morn shall rise, and all thy day be bright."

I came to Je - sus, as I was, wea - ry and worn and sad;
I came to Je - sus, and I drank of that life - giv - ing stream;
I looked to Je - sus, and I found in Him my star, my sun;

I found in Him a rest - ing place, and He has made me glad.
my thirst was quenched, my soul re - vived, and now I live in Him.
and in that light of life I'll walk, till trav - 'ling days are done.

WORDS: Horatius Bonar, 1846
MUSIC: *Vox Dilecti*, John Bacchus Dykes, 1868

C.M.D.

532 Tell Me the Old, Old Story

So that you may know the certainty of the things you have been taught. – Luke 1:4 NIV

1. Tell me the old, old story of un-seen things a - bove, of
2. Tell me the sto - ry slow - ly, that I may take it in; that
3. Tell me the same old sto - ry when you have cause to fear that

Je - sus and His glo - ry, of Je - sus and His love.
won - der - ful re - demp - tion, God's rem - e - dy for sin.
this world's emp - ty glo - ry is cost - ing me too dear.

Tell me the sto - ry sim - ply, as to a lit - tle child, for
Tell me the sto - ry of - ten, for I for - get so soon; the
Tell me the sto - ry al - ways, if you would real - ly be, in

I am weak and wea - ry, and help - less and de - filed.
ear - ly dew of morn - ing has passed a - way at noon.
an - y time of trou - ble, a com - fort - er to me.

Refrain

Tell me the old, old sto - ry, tell me the old, old sto - ry.

WORDS: Arabella Catherine Hankey, 1866
MUSIC: *Evangel*, William Howard Doane, 1867

7.6.7.6 D with Refrain

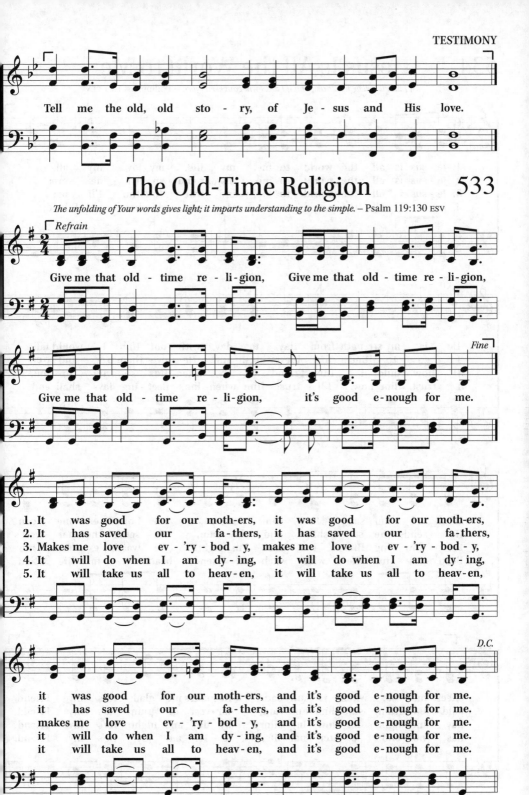

Tell me the old, old sto - ry, of Je - sus and His love.

The Old-Time Religion 533

The unfolding of Your words gives light; it imparts understanding to the simple. – Psalm 119:130 ESV

Refrain

Give me that old - time re - li - gion, Give me that old - time re - li - gion,

Fine

Give me that old - time re - li - gion, it's good e-nough for me.

1. It was good for our moth-ers, it was good for our moth-ers,
2. It has saved our fa-thers, it has saved our fa-thers,
3. Makes me love ev - 'ry - bod - y, makes me love ev - 'ry - bod - y,
4. It will do when I am dy - ing, it will do when I am dy - ing,
5. It will take us all to heav-en, it will take us all to heav-en,

D.C.

it was good for our moth-ers, and it's good e-nough for me.
it has saved our fa-thers, and it's good e-nough for me.
makes me love ev - 'ry - bod - y, and it's good e-nough for me.
it will do when I am dy - ing, and it's good e-nough for me.
it will take us all to heav-en, and it's good e-nough for me.

WORDS: Negro spiritual, 19th c.
MUSIC: *Old-Time Religion,* Negro spiritual, 19th c.

Irregular with Refrain

534 Jesus Is All the World to Me

If I live, it will be for Christ, and if I die, I will gain even more. – Philippians 1:21 CEV

1. Je-sus is all the world to me, my life, my joy, my all;
2. Je-sus is all the world to me, my Friend in tri-als sore;
3. Je-sus is all the world to me, and true to Him I'll be;
4. Je-sus is all the world to me, I want no bet-ter Friend;

He is my strength from day to day, with-out Him I would fall.
I go to Him for bless-ings, and He gives them o'er and o'er.
O how could I this Friend de-ny, when He's so true to me?
I trust Him now, I'll trust Him when life's fleet-ing days shall end.

When I am sad, to Him I go, no oth-er one can
He sends the sun-shine and the rain, He sends the har-vest's
Fol-low-ing Him I know I'm right, He watch-es o'er me
Beau-ti-ful life with such a Friend, beau-ti-ful life that

cheer me so; when I am sad, He makes me glad; He's my Friend.
gold-en grain; sun-shine and rain, har-vest of grain; He's my Friend.
day and night; fol-low-ing Him by day and night; He's my Friend.
has no end; e-ter-nal life, e-ter-nal joy; He's my Friend.

WORDS: Will Lamartine Thompson, 1904
MUSIC: *Elizabeth*, Will Lamartine Thompson, 1904

Irregular

I Know Whom I Have Believed

535

I know whom I have believed, and am convinced that He is able to guard what I have entrusted to Him. – 2 Timothy 1:12 NIV

1. I know not why God's won-drous grace to me He hath made known,
2. I know not how this sav - ing faith to me He did im - part,
3. I know not how the Spir - it moves, con-vinc - ing me of sin,
4. I know not when my Lord may come, at night or noon - day fair,

nor why, un-wor - thy, Christ in love re - deemed me for His own.
nor how be - liev - ing in His Word wrought peace with - in my heart.
re - veal - ing Je - sus through the Word, cre - a - ting faith in Him.
nor if I'll walk the vale with Him, or meet Him in the air.

Refrain

But "I know whom I have be - liev - ed, and am per - suad - ed that He is

a - ble to keep that which I've com - mit - ted un-to Him a - gainst that day."

WORDS: Daniel Webster Whittle, 1883
MUSIC: *El Nathan*, James McGranahan, 1883

C.M. with Refrain

536 There Is Sunshine in My Soul

Blessed are the people...who walk, O Lord, in the light of Your face. – Psalm 89:15 ESV

1. There is sun-shine in my soul to-day; more glo-ri-ous and bright
2. There is mu-sic in my soul to-day; a car-ol to my King,
3. There is spring-time in my soul to-day; for when the Lord is near,
4. There is glad-ness in my soul to-day; and hope and love and praise,

than glows in an-y earth-ly sky, for Je-sus is my light.
and Je-sus, lis-ten-ing, can hear the songs I can-not sing.
the dove of peace sings in my heart, the flow'rs of grace ap-pear.
for bless-ings which He gives me now, for joys in fu-ture days.

Refrain

O there's sun-shine, bless-ed sun-shine, when the peace-ful, hap-py mo-ments roll; when Je-sus shows His smil-ing face, there is sun-shine in my soul.

WORDS: Eliza Edmunds Hewitt, 1887
MUSIC: *Sunshine*, John Robson Sweney, 1887

9.6.8.6 with Refrain

Sunlight

His brightness was like the light; rays flashed from His hand; and there He veiled His power. — Habakkuk 3:4 ESV

1. I wan - dered in the shades of night, till Je - sus came to me,
2. Though clouds may gath - er in the sky, and bil - lows round me roll,
3. While walk - ing in the light of God, I sweet com - mu - nion find;
4. I cross the wide ex - tend - ed fields, I jour - ney o'er the plain,
5. Soon I shall see Him as He is, the light that came to me;

and with the sun - light of His love bid all my dark-ness flee.
how ev - er dark the world may be I've sun - light in my soul.
I press with ho - ly vig - or on, and leave the world be-hind.
and in the sun - light of His love I reap the gold - en grain.
be - hold the bright-ness of His face, through - out e - ter - ni - ty.

Refrain

Sun - light, sun - light in my soul to - day, sun - light, sun - light

all a - long the way; since the Sav - ior found me, took a - way my

sin, I have had the sun - light of His love with - in.

WORDS; Judson Wheeler Van DeVenter, 1897
MUSIC: *Sunlight in My Soul,* Winfield Scott Weeden, 19th c.

C.M. with Refrain

538

The Lily of the Valley

I am a rose of Sharon, a lily of the valleys. – Song of Solomon 2:1 ESV

1. I have found a friend in Je-sus, He's ev-'ry-thing to me, He's the
2. He all my grief has tak-en, and all my sor-rows borne; in temp-
3. He will nev-er, nev-er leave me, nor yet for-sake me here, while I

fair-est of ten thou-sand to my soul; the Lil-y of the Val-ley, in
ta-tion He's my strong and might-y tow'r; I have all for Him for-sak-en, and
live by faith and do His bless-ed will; a wall of fire a-bout me, I've

Him a-lone I see all I need to cleanse and make me ful-ly whole.
all my i-dols torn from my heart and now He keeps me by His pow'r.
noth-ing now to fear, with His man-na He my hun-gry soul shall fill.

In sor-row He's my com-fort, in trou-ble He's my stay; He tells me
Though all the world for-sake me, and Sa-tan tempt me sore, through Je-sus
Then sweep-ing up to glo-ry to see His bless-ed face, where riv-ers

Refrain

ev-'ry care on Him to roll.
I shall safe-ly reach the goal.
of de-light shall ev-er roll.

He's the Lil-y of the Val-ley, the

Hal-le-lu-jah!

WORDS: Charles William Fry, 1881
MUSIC: *Salvationist*, William Shakespeare Hays, 1881; adapt. Charles William Fry, 1881

Irregular with Refrain

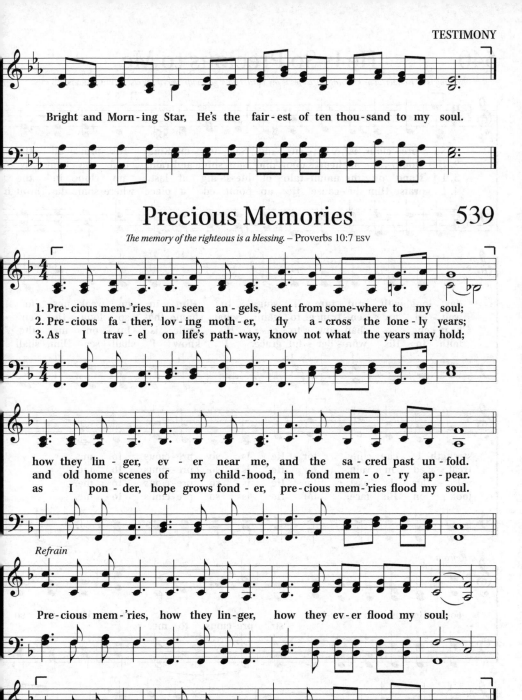

Bright and Morn-ing Star, He's the fair-est of ten thou-sand to my soul.

Precious Memories

539

The memory of the righteous is a blessing. – Proverbs 10:7 ESV

1. Pre-cious mem-'ries, un-seen an-gels, sent from some-where to my soul;
2. Pre-cious fa-ther, lov-ing moth-er, fly a-cross the lone-ly years;
3. As I trav-el on life's path-way, know not what the years may hold;

how they lin-ger, ev-er near me, and the sa-cred past un-fold.
and old home scenes of my child-hood, in fond mem-o-ry ap-pear.
as I pon-der, hope grows fond-er, pre-cious mem-'ries flood my soul.

Refrain

Pre-cious mem-'ries, how they lin-ger, how they ev-er flood my soul;

in the still-ness of the mid-night, pre-cious, sa-cred scenes un-fold.

WORDS: attr. J. B. F. Wright and Lonnie B. Combs, ca. 1923
MUSIC: *Precious Memories*, attr. J. B. F. Wright, ca. 1923

8.7.8.7 with Refrain

540 He Is So Precious to Me

Nothing is as wonderful as knowing Christ Jesus my Lord. I have given up everything else. – Philippians 3:8 CEV

1. So pre-cious is Je-sus, my Sav-ior, my King, His praise all the
2. He stood at my heart's door 'mid sun-shine and rain, and pa-tient-ly
3. I stand on the moun-tain of bless-ing at last, no cloud in the
4. I praise Him be-cause He ap-point-ed a place where some day, through

day long with rap-ture I sing; to Him in my weak-ness for
wait-ed an en-trance to gain; what shame that so long He en-
heav-ens a shad-ow to cast; His smile is up-on me, the
faith in His won-der-ful grace, I know I shall see Him, shall

strength I can cling, for He is so pre-cious to me.
treat-ed in vain, for He is so pre-cious to me.
val-ley is past, for He is so pre-cious to me.
look on His face, for He is so pre-cious to me.

Refrain

For He is so prec-ious to me;
so pre-cious to me,
for He is so
pre-cious to me.
so pre-cious to me;
'Tis heav-en be-low, my Re-

WORDS: Charles Hutchinson Gabriel, 1902
MUSIC: *Precious to Me*, Charles Hutchinson Gabriel, 1902

11.11.11.8 with Refrain

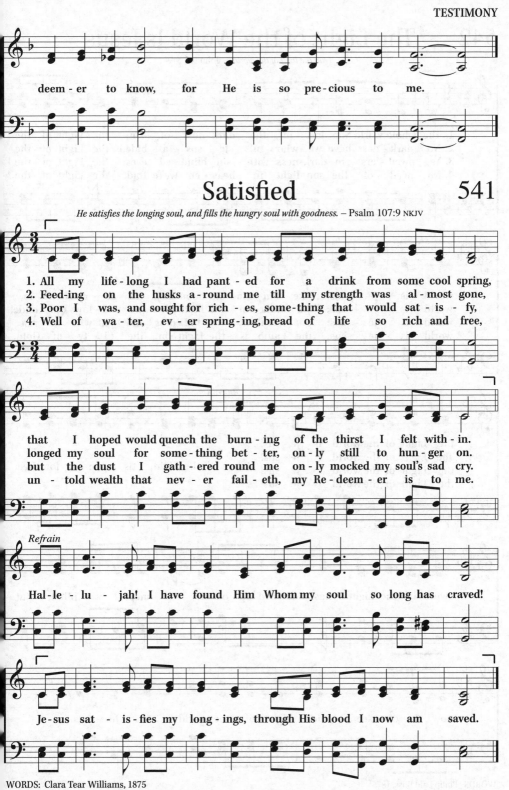

deem - er to know, for He is so pre-cious to me.

Satisfied

541

He satisfies the longing soul, and fills the hungry soul with goodness. – Psalm 107:9 NKJV

1. All my life-long I had pant-ed for a drink from some cool spring,
2. Feed-ing on the husks a-round me till my strength was al-most gone,
3. Poor I was, and sought for rich - es, some-thing that would sat - is - fy,
4. Well of wa - ter, ev - er spring-ing, bread of life so rich and free,

that I hoped would quench the burn - ing of the thirst I felt with - in.
longed my soul for some - thing bet - ter, on - ly still to hun - ger on.
but the dust I gath - ered round me on - ly mocked my soul's sad cry.
un - told wealth that nev - er fail - eth, my Re - deem - er is to me.

Refrain

Hal - le - lu - jah! I have found Him Whom my soul so long has craved!

Je - sus sat - is - fies my long - ings, through His blood I now am saved.

WORDS: Clara Tear Williams, 1875
MUSIC: *Satisfied,* Ralph Erskine Hudson, 1875

8.7.8.7 with Refrain

542 The Light of the World Is Jesus

I am the light of the world. – John 9:5 NIV

1. The whole world was lost in the dark-ness of sin; the Light of the
2. No dark-ness have we who in Je-sus a-bide, the Light of the
3. Ye dwell-ers in dark-ness with sin-blind-ed eyes, the Light of the
4. No need of the sun-light in heav-en we're told, the Light of the

world is Je-sus! Like sun-shine at noon-day, His glo-ry shone in,
world is Je-sus; we walk in the light when we fol-low our Guide!
world is Je-sus; go, wash, at His bid-ding, and light will a-rise,
world is Je-sus; the Lamb is the Light in the Ci-ty of Gold,

Refrain

the Light of the world is Je-sus!
The Light of the world is Je-sus!
the Light of the world is Je-sus! Come to the Light, 'tis shin-ing for thee;
the Light of the world is Je-sus!

sweet-ly the Light has dawned up-on me; once I was blind, but

now I can see; the Light of the world is Je-sus.

WORDS: Philip Paul Bliss, 1875
MUSIC: *Light of the World,* Philip Paul Bliss, 1875

11.8.11.8. with Refrain

I'm So Glad Jesus Lifted Me

I will extol Thee, O Lord, for Thou hast lifted me up. – Psalm 30:1 KJV

1. I'm so glad, Jesus lift-ed me,
2. Sa-tan had me bound, Jesus lift-ed me,
3. When I was in trou-ble, Jesus lift-ed me,
4. Glo-ry, hal-le-lu-jah! Jesus lift-ed me,

I'm so glad, Jesus lift-ed me,
Sa-tan had me bound, Jesus lift-ed me,
when I was in trou-ble, Jesus lift-ed me,
glo-ry, hal-le-lu-jah! Jesus lift-ed me,

I'm so glad, Jesus lift-ed me, sing-ing,
Sa-tan had me bound, Jesus lift-ed me, sing-ing,
when I was in trou-ble, Jesus lift-ed me, sing-ing,
glo-ry, hal-le-lu-jah! Jesus lift-ed me, sing-ing,

"Glo-ry, hal-le-lu-jah, Jesus lift-ed me."
"Glo-ry, hal-le-lu-jah, Jesus lift-ed me."
"Glo-ry, hal-le-lu-jah, Jesus lift-ed me."
"Glo-ry, hal-le-lu-jah, Jesus lift-ed me."

WORDS: Negro spiritual, n.d.
MUSIC: *I'm So Glad*, Negro spiritual, n.d.

Irregular

544 Be Present at Our Table, Lord

Give us today our daily bread. – Matthew 6:11 NIV

1. Be pres-ent at our ta-ble, Lord; be here and ev-'ry-
2. We thank Thee, Lord, for this our food, for life and health and
3. We thank Thee, Lord, for this our food, but more be-cause of

where a-dored; Thy crea-tures bless, and grant that
ev-'ry good; by Thine own hand may we be
Je-sus' blood; let man-na to our souls be

we may feast in par-a-dise with Thee.
fed; give us each day our dai-ly bread.
giv'n, the bread of life sent down from heav'n.

WORDS: Sts. 1,3 John Cennick; St. 2 alt.
MUSIC: *Old 100th,* (original) from *Genevan Psalter,* attr. Louis Bourgeois, 1551
Other harmonizations of this tune, No. 21; and in a higher key, No. 622.

L.M.

545 Father, We Thank Thee

I will give thanks unto Thee, O Lord...and I will sing praises unto Thy name. – 2 Samuel 22:50 KJV

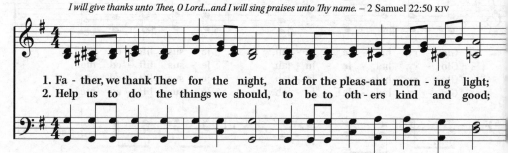

1. Fa-ther, we thank Thee for the night, and for the pleas-ant morn-ing light;
2. Help us to do the things we should, to be to oth-ers kind and good;

WORDS: Rebecca J. Weston, 1885
MUSIC: *Batchellor (Onslow),* Daniel J. Batchellor, 1885

L.M.

for rest and food and lov-ing care, and all that makes the world so fair.
in all we do, in work or play, to grow more lov-ing ev-'ry day.

O Perfect Love

546

There is no fear in love. But perfect love drives out fear. — 1 John 4:18 NIV

1. O per-fect love, all hu-man thought tran-scend-ing,
2. O per-fect life, be Thou their full as-sur-ance,
3. Grant them the joy which bright-ens earth-ly sor-row;

low-ly we kneel in prayer be-fore Thy throne,
of ten-der char-i-ty and stead-fast faith,
grant them the peace which calms all earth-ly strife,

that theirs may be the love which knows no end-ing,
of pa-tient hope and qui-et, brave en-dur-ance,
and to life's day the glo-rious un-known mor-row

whom Thou for-ev-er-more dost join in one.
with child-like trust that fears not pain nor death.
that dawns up-on e-ter-nal love and life.

WORDS: Dorothy Frances Blomfield Gurney, 1883
MUSIC: *O Perfect Love*, Joseph Barnby, 1889; arr. John Stainer, 1898

11.10.11.10

547 For All the Saints

Such a large crowd of witnesses is all around us! We must get rid of everything that slows us down. – Hebrews 12:1 CEV

Unison

1. For all the saints who from their la-bors rest,
2. Thou wast their rock, their for-tress, and their might;
6. But lo! There breaks a yet more glo-r'ous day;
7. From earth's wide bounds, from o-cean's far-thest coast,

who Thee by faith be - fore the world con - fessed,
Thou, Lord, their Cap - tain in the well-fought fight;
the saints tri - um - phant rise in bright ar - ray;
through gates of pearl stream in the count - less host,

Thy name, O Je - sus, be for - ev - er blest.
Thou, in the dark - ness drear, their one true Light.
the King of glo - ry pass - es on His way.
sing - ing to Fa - ther, Son, and Ho - ly Ghost.

Al - le - lu - ia! Al - le - lu - ia!

WORDS: William Walsham How, 1867, alt.
MUSIC: *Sine Nomine*, Ralph Vaughan Williams, 1906

10.10.10 with Alleluias

Harmony

3. O blest com - mu - nion, fel - low - ship di - vine!
4. And when the strife is fierce, the war - fare long,
5. The gold - en eve - ning bright - ens in the west;

We fee - bly strug - gle; they in glo - ry shine.
steals on the ear the dis - tant tri - umph song;
soon, soon to faith - ful war - riors com - eth rest;

Yet all are one in Thee, for all are Thine.
and hearts are brave a - gain and arms are strong.
and sweet the calm of par - a - dise, the blest.

D.C. stanzas 6 and 7

Al - le - lu - ia!

Al - le - lu - ia! Al - le - lu - ia!

548 O What Their Joy and Their Glory Must Be

I will write on each...the name of my God and the name of His city...the new Jerusalem. – Revelation 3:12 CEV

1. O what their joy and their glory must be,
those end-less Sab-baths the bless-ed ones see;
crown for the val-iant, to wea-ry ones rest;

2. What are the Mon-arch, His court, and His throne?
What are the peace and the joy that they own?
O that the blest ones, who in it have share,

3. Tru-ly Je-ru-sa-lem name we that shore,
vi-sion of peace, that brings joy ev-er-more;
wish and ful-fill-ment can sev-ered be ne'er,

4. There, where no trou-bles dis-trac-tion can bring,
we the sweet an-thems of Zi-on shall sing;
while for Thy grace, Lord, their voic-es of praise,

5. There dawns no Sab-bath, no Sab-bath is o'er,
those Sab-bath-keep-ers have one ev-er-more;
one and un-end-ing is that tri-umph-song,

6. Now, in the mean-while, with hearts raised on high,
we for that coun-try must yearn and must sigh;
seek-ing Je-ru-sa-lem, dear na-tive land,

7. Low be-fore Him with our prais-es we fall,
of Whom, and in Whom, and through Whom are all;
of Whom, the Fa-ther; and in Whom, the Son;

WORDS: Peter Abelard, 12th c.; tr. John Mason Neale, 1854
MUSIC: *O Quanta Qualia*, from *Paris Antiphoner*; harm. John Bacchus Dykes, 1868
Another harmonization of this tune, in a higher key, No. 194.

10.10.10.10

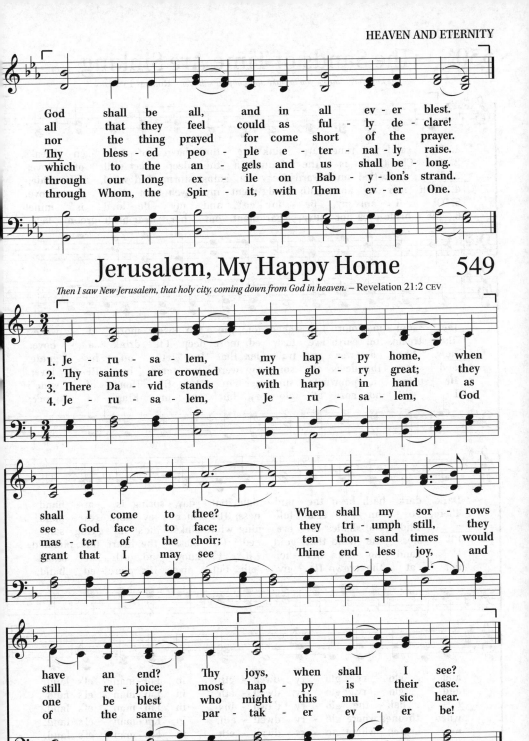

God shall be all, and in all ev - er blest.
all that they feel could as ful - ly de - clare!
nor the thing prayed for come short of the prayer.
Thy bless - ed peo - ple e - ter - nal - ly raise.
which to the an - gels and us shall be - long.
through our long ex - ile on Bab - y - lon's strand.
through Whom, the Spir - it, with Them ev - er One.

Jerusalem, My Happy Home   549

Then I saw New Jerusalem, that holy city, coming down from God in heaven. – Revelation 21:2 CEV

1. Je - ru - sa - lem, my hap - py home, when
2. Thy saints are crowned with glo - ry great; they
3. There Da - vid stands with harp in hand as
4. Je - ru - sa - lem, Je - ru - sa - lem, God

shall I come to thee? When shall my sor - rows
see God face to face; they tri - umph still, they
mas - ter of the choir; ten thou - sand times would
grant that I may see Thine end - less joy, and

have an end? Thy joys, when shall I see?
still re - joice; most hap - py is their case.
one be blest who might this mu - sic hear.
of the same par - tak - er ev - er be!

WORDS: Joseph Bromehead, 1795, alt.
MUSIC: *Land of Rest*, from *The Christian Harp*, 1836; Early American folk hymn, 19th c.; arr. Eric Wyse, 2005   C.M.
This tune in a lower key, No. 570.

550 The Sands of Time Are Sinking

The hour has come for you to wake up from your slumber. – Romans 13:11 NIV

1. The sands of time are sink-ing, the dawn of heav-en breaks,
2. O Christ! He is the foun-tain the deep sweet well of love!
3. I've wres-tled on towards heav-en, 'gainst storm, and wind, and tide;
4. With mer-cy and with judg-ment my web of time He wove,
5. O! I am my Be-lov-ed's, and my Be-lov'd is mine!
6. The bride eyes not her gar-ment, but her dear bride-groom's face;

the sum-mer morn I've sighed for, the fair sweet morn a-wakes:
The streams on earth I've tast-ed, more deep I'll drink a-bove:
now, like a wea-ry trav-'ler, that lean-eth on his guide,
and yes, the dews of sor-row were lus-tered by His love;
He brings a poor vile sin-ner in-to His "House of wine":
I will not gaze at glo-ry, but on my King of grace;

Dark, dark hath been the mid-night, but day-spring is at hand,
There, to an o-cean full-ness, His mer-cy doth ex-pand,
a-mid the shades of eve-ning, while sinks life's lin-g'ring sand,
I'll bless the hand that guid-ed, I'll bless the heart that planned,
I stand up-on His mer-it, I know no oth-er stand,
not at the crown He giv-eth, but on His pierc-ed hand;

and glo-ry, glo-ry dwell-eth in Em-man-'el's land.
and glo-ry, glo-ry dwell-eth in Em-man-'el's land.
I hail the glo-ry dawn-ing in Em-man-'el's land.
when throned where glo-ry dwell-eth, in Em-man-'el's land.
now e'en where glo-ry dwell-eth, in Em-man-'el's land.
the Lamb is all the glo-ry of Em-man-'el's land.

WORDS: Anne Ross Cousin, 1857
MUSIC: *Rutherford*, Chrétien d' Urhan, 1734; arr. Edward Francis Rimbault, 1867

7.6.7.6.7.6.7.5

When I Can Read My Title Clear 551

Now we are children of God, and what we will be has not yet been made known. – 1 John 3:2 NIV

1. When   I   can read   my   ti - tle clear to man - sions in the skies,
2. Should earth a - gainst my   soul en - gage, and   fi - ery darts be hurled,
3. Let   cares like a   wild   del - uge come, and storms of sor - row fall!
4. There shall I bathe my   wea - ry soul   in seas of heav'n - ly rest,

I'll   bid fare - well to   ev - 'ry fear, and wipe my   weep - ing   eyes;
then   I   can smile at   Sa - tan's rage, and face a   frown - ing   world;
May   I   but safe - ly   reach my home, my God, my   heav'n, my   all;
and   not a wave of   trou - ble roll a - cross my   peace - ful breast,

and wipe my weep - ing   eyes,   and wipe my weep - ing eyes,
and face a frown - ing   world,   and face a frown - ing world,
my God, my heav'n, my   all,   my God, my heav'n, my   all,
a - cross my peace - ful   breast,   a - cross my peace - ful breast,

I'll   bid fare - well to   ev - 'ry fear, and wipe my   weep - ing   eyes.
then   I   can smile at   Sa - tan's rage, and face a   frown - ing   world.
may   I   but safe - ly   reach my home, my God, my   heav'n, my   all.
and   not a wave of   trou - ble roll a - cross my   peace - ful breast.

WORDS: Isaac Watts, 1707
MUSIC: *Pisgah,* traditional American melody, 1817

8.6.8.6.6.6.8.6

552 When the Roll Is Called Up Yonder

The Lord will return...then those who had faith in Christ before they died will be raised to life. – 1 Thessalonians 4:16 CEV

1. When the trum-pet of the Lord shall sound, and time shall be no more,
2. On that bright and cloud-less morn-ing when the dead in Christ shall rise,
3. Let us la-bor for the Mas-ter from the dawn till set-ting sun;

and the morn-ing breaks, e-ter-nal, bright and fair; when the saved of earth shall
and the glo-ry of His res-ur-rec-tion share; when His cho-sen ones shall
let us talk of all His won-drous love and care. Then when all of life is

gath-er o-ver on the oth-er shore, and the roll is called up yon-der, I'll be
gath-er to their home be-yond the skies, and the roll is called up yon-der, I'll be
o-ver, and our work on earth is done, and the roll is called up yon-der, I'll be

Refrain

there. When the roll is called up yon - der, when the
there.
there. When the roll is called up yon-der, I'll be there.

roll is called up yon - der, when the roll is called up
When the roll is called up yon-der, I'll be there. When the roll is called up

WORDS: James Milton Black, 1893
MUSIC: *Roll Call*, James Milton Black, 1893

15.11.15.11 with Refrain

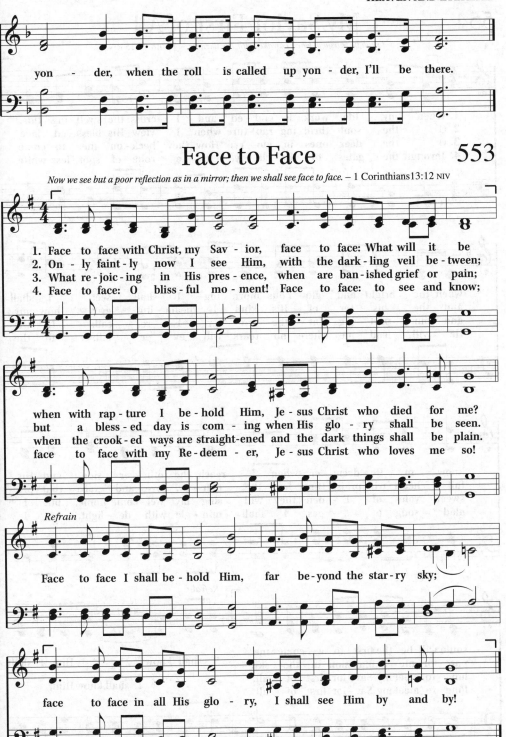

yon - der, when the roll is called up yon - der, I'll be there.

Face to Face 553

Now we see but a poor reflection as in a mirror; then we shall see face to face. – 1 Corinthians 13:12 NIV

1. Face to face with Christ, my Sav - ior, face to face: What will it be
2. On - ly faint - ly now I see Him, with the dark - ling veil be - tween;
3. What re - joic - ing in His pres - ence, when are ban - ished grief or pain;
4. Face to face: O bliss - ful mo - ment! Face to face: to see and know;

when with rap - ture I be - hold Him, Je - sus Christ who died for me?
but a bless - ed day is com - ing when His glo - ry shall be seen.
when the crook - ed ways are straight-ened and the dark things shall be plain.
face to face with my Re - deem - er, Je - sus Christ who loves me so!

Refrain

Face to face I shall be - hold Him, far be - yond the star - ry sky;

face to face in all His glo - ry, I shall see Him by and by!

WORDS: Carrie Elizabeth Breck, 1898
MUSIC: *Face to Face*, Grant Colfax Tullar, 1898

8.7.8.7 with Refrain

554 My Savior First of All

I shall be satisfied, when I awake, with Thy likeness. – Psalm 17:15 KJV

1. When my life-work is end-ed and I cross the swell-ing tide,
2. O the soul-thrill-ing rap-ture when I view His bless-ed face
3. O the dear ones in glo-ry: How they beck-on me to come,
4. Through the gates to the cit-y in a robe of spot-less white,

when the bright and glo-r'ous morn-ing I shall see; I shall
and the lus-ter of His kind-ly beam-ing eye; how my
and our part-ing at the riv-er I re-call; to the
He will lead me where no tears will ev-er fall; in the

know my Re-deem-er when I reach the oth-er side, and His
full heart will praise Him for the mer-cy, love and grace that pre-
sweet vales of E-den they will sing my wel-come home, but I
glad song of a-ges I shall min-gle with de-light, but I

Refrain

smile will be the first to wel-come me.
pare for me a man-sion in the sky.
long to meet my Sav-ior first of all.
long to meet my Sav-ior first of all.

I shall know Him, I shall
I shall know Him,

WORDS: Fanny Jane Crosby, 1894
MUSIC: *I Shall Know Him,* John Robson Sweney, 1894

14.11.14.11 with Refrain

know Him, and re-deemed by His side   I shall stand;   I shall know Him,

I shall know Him,

I shall know   Him, by the prints   of the nails   in His   hand.

Deep River

555

I pray, let me cross over and see the good land beyond the Jordan. – Deuteronomy 3:25 NKJV

Deep   river - er,   my   home   is   o - ver

Jor - dan,   deep   riv - er, Lord;   I

want   to   cross   o - ver   in - to   camp - ground.

WORDS: Negro spiritual, 19th c.
MUSIC: *Deep River,* Negro spiritual, 19th c.; arr. Eric Wyse, 2006
Arr. © 2006 Vine Ridge Music BMI (admin. by Integrated Copyright Group). All rights reserved. Used by permission.

Irregular

556 Saved by Grace

For it is by grace you have been saved, through faith—and this not from yourselves, it is the gift of God. – Ephesians 2:8 NIV

1. Some day the sil - ver cord will break, and I no more as now shall sing;
2. Some day my earth - ly house will fall, I can - not tell how soon 'twill be;
3. Some day, when fades the gold - en sun be-neath the ro - sy - tint - ed west,
4. Some day, till then I'll watch and wait, my lamp all trimmed and burn-ing bright,

but oh, the joy when I shall wake with - in the pal - ace of the King!
but this I know: My All in All has now a place in heav'n for me.
my bless - ed Lord will say, "Well done!" And I shall en - ter in - to rest.
that when my Sav - ior opes the gate, my soul to Him may take its flight.

Refrain

And I shall see Him face to face, and tell the sto-ry: Saved by grace;
shall see to face,

and I shall see Him face to face, and tell the sto-ry: Saved by grace.
shall see to face,

WORDS: Fanny Jane Crosby, 1891
MUSIC: *Saved by Grace*, George Coles Stebbins, 1894

L.M. with Refrain

When We All Get to Heaven

557

But in keeping with His promise, we are looking forward to a new heaven and a new earth. – 2 Peter 3:13 NIV

1. Sing the won-drous love of Je - sus, sing His mer - cy and His grace;
2. While we walk the pil - grim path-way, clouds will o - ver - spread the sky;
3. Let us then be true and faith - ful, trust-ing, serv - ing ev - 'ry day;
4. On - ward to the prize be - fore us! Soon His beau - ty we'll be - hold;

in the man-sions bright and bless-ed, He'll pre-pare for us a place.
He'll pre - pare for us a place.

but when trav - 'ling days are o - ver, not a shad-ow, not a sigh.
not a shad - ow, not a sigh.

just one glimpse of Him in glo - ry will the toils of life re - pay.
will the toils of life re - pay.

soon the pearl - y gates will o - pen; we shall tread the streets of gold.
we shall tread the streets of gold.

Refrain

When we all get to heav - en, what a day of re -
When we all get to heav - en, what a

joic - ing that will be! When we all see
day of re - joic - ing that will be! When we all see

Je - sus, we'll sing and shout the vic - to - ry.
Je - sus, we'll sing and shout, and shout the vic - to - ry.

WORDS: Eliza Edmunds Hewitt, ca. 1898
MUSIC: *Heaven*, Emily Divine Wilson, ca. 1898

8.7.8.7 with Refrain

558 Just Over in the Glory-Land

So our faces are not covered. They show the bright glory of the Lord. – 2 Corinthians 3:18 CEV

1. I've a home pre-pared where the saints a-bide, just o-ver in the glo-ry-land; and I long to be by my Sav-ior's side, just o-ver in the glo-ry-land.
2. I am on my way to those man-sions fair, just o-ver in the glo-ry-land; there to sing God's praise, and His glo-ry share, just o-ver in the glo-ry-land.
3. What a joy-ful thought that my Lord I'll see, just o-ver in the glo-ry-land; and with kin-dred saved, there for-ev-er be, just o-ver in the glo-ry-land.
4. With the blood-washed throng I will shout and sing, just o-ver in the glo-ry-land; glad ho-san-nas to Christ, the Lord and King, just o-ver in the glo-ry-land.

Refrain

Just o-ver in the glo-ry-land, I'll join the hap-py an-gel band, just o-ver in the glo-ry-land; just o-ver in the glo-ry-land, there

o-ver, o-ver join yes, join o-ver, o-ver

WORDS: , 1906
MUSIC: *Glory-Land*, Emmett Sidney Dean, 1906

10.8.10.8 with Refrain

with the might-y host I'll stand, just o-ver in the glo-ry land.
with yes, with

Shall We Gather at the River? 559

The angel showed me the river of the water of life...flowing from the throne of God. – Revelation 22:1 NIV

1. Shall we gath-er at the riv-er, where bright an-gel feet have trod;
2. On the mar-gin of the riv-er wash-ing up its sil-ver spray,
3. Ere we reach the shin-ing riv-er, lay we ev-'ry bur-den down;
4. Soon we'll reach the shin-ing riv-er, soon our pil-grim-age will cease;

with its crys-tal tide for-ev-er flow-ing by the throne of God?
we will walk and wor-ship ev-er, all the hap-py gold-en day.
grace our spir-its will de-liv-er, and pro-vide a robe and crown.
soon our hap-py hearts will quiv-er with the mel-o-dy of peace.

Refrain

Yes, we'll gath-er at the riv-er, the beau-ti-ful, the beau-ti-ful riv-er;

gath-er with the saints at the riv-er that flows by the throne of God.

WORDS: Robert Lowry, 1864
MUSIC: *Hanson Place*, Robert Lowry, 1864

8.7.8.7 with Refrain

560 In the Sweet By and By

On this earth we don't have a city that lasts forever, but we are waiting for such a city. – Hebrews 13:14 CEV

1. There's a land that is fair-er than day, and by faith we can
2. We shall sing on that beau-ti-ful shore the me-lo-di-ous
3. To our boun-ti-ful Fa-ther a-bove, we will of-fer the

see it a-far; for the Fa-ther waits o-ver the way to pre-
songs of the blest, and our spir-its shall sor-row no more, not a
trib-ute of praise for the glo-ri-ous gift of His love, and the

pare us a dwell-ing place there.
sigh for the bless-ing of rest.
bless-ings that hal-low our days.

Refrain

In the sweet by and
In the sweet

by, we shall meet on that beau-ti-ful shore; in the
by and by, by and by;

sweet by and by, we shall meet on that beau-ti-ful shore.
in the sweet by and by,

WORDS: Sanford Fillmore Bennett, 1868
MUSIC: *Sweet By and By,* Joseph Philbrick Webster, 1868

9.9.9.9 with Refrain

I Belong to the King

561

The Father...loves us so much that He lets us be called His children. – 1 John 3:1 CEV

1. I be - long to the King, I'm a child of His love. I shall dwell in His
2. I be - long to the King, and He loves me, I know, for His mer - cy and
3. I be - long to the King, and His prom - ise is sure, that we all shall be

pal - ace so fair; for He tells of its bliss in yon heav - en a - bove, and His
kind - ness, so free, are un - ceas - ing - ly mine where - so - ev - er I go, and my
gath - ered at last in His king - dom a - bove, by life's wa - ters so pure, when this

Refrain

chil - dren its splen - dors shall share.
ref - uge un - fail - ing is He. I be - long to the King, I'm a
life with its tri - als is past.

child of His love, and He nev - er for - sak - eth His own; He will call me some

day to His pal - ace a - bove, I shall dwell by His glo - ri - fied throne.

WORDS: Ida Reed Smith, 1896
MUSIC: *Clifton,* Joseph Lincoln Hall, 1896

12.9.12.9 with Refrain

562 If We Never Meet Again

I will create new heavens and a new earth.
The former things will not be remembered, nor will they come to mind. – Isaiah 65:17 NIV

1. Soon we'll come to the end of life's jour-ney and per-
2. Oh, so of-ten we're part-ed with sor-row, ben-e-
3. Oh, they say we shall meet by the riv-er, where no

haps we'll nev-er meet an-y more, till we gath-er in
dic-tions of-ten quick-en our pain, but we nev-er shall
storm-clouds ev-er dark-en the sky, and they say we'll be

heav-en's bright cit-y far a-way on that beau-ti-ful shore.
sor-row in heav-en God be with you till we meet a-gain.
hap-py in heav-en in the won-der-ful sweet by and by.

Refrain

If we nev-er meet a-gain this side of heav-en,
Nev-er meet this side of heav-en,

as we strug-gle through this world and its strife; there's an-
strug-gle through this world and its strife;

WORDS: Albert Edward Brumley, 1945
MUSIC: *Meet Again*, Albert Edward Brumley, 1945

10.10.10.9 with Refrain

563 The Unclouded Day

On each side of the river stood the tree of life...the leaves of the tree are for the healing of the nations. – Revelation 22:2 NIV

1. O they tell me of a home far be-yond the skies, O they
2. O they tell me of a home where my friends have gone, O they
3. O they tell me of a King in His beau-ty there, and they
4. O they tell me that He smiles on His chil-dren there, and His

tell me of a home far a-way; O they tell me of a home where no
tell me of that land far a-way, where the tree of life in e-
tell me that mine eyes shall be-hold where He sits on the throne that is
smile drives their sor-rows all a-way; and they tell me that no tears ev-er

storm-clouds rise, O they tell me of an un-cloud-ed day.
ter-nal bloom sheds its fra-grance through the un-cloud-ed day.
whit-er than snow, in the cit-y that is made of gold.
come a-gain, in that love-ly land of un-cloud-ed day.

Refrain

O the land of cloud-less day, O the land of an un-cloud-ed

WORDS: Josiah Kelley Alwood, ca. 1880
MUSIC: *The Unclouded Day,* Josiah Kelley Alwood, ca. 1880

12.10.12.10 with Refrain

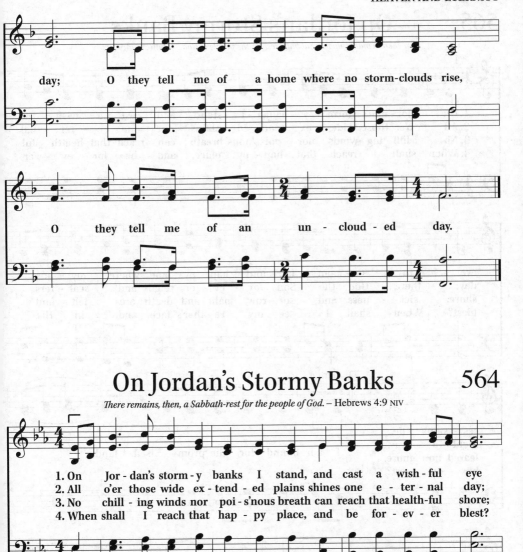

day; O they tell me of a home where no storm-clouds rise,

O they tell me of an un-cloud-ed day.

On Jordan's Stormy Banks 564

There remains, then, a Sabbath-rest for the people of God. – Hebrews 4:9 NIV

1. On Jor - dan's storm - y banks I stand, and cast a wish - ful eye
2. All o'er those wide ex - tend - ed plains shines one e - ter - nal day;
3. No chill - ing winds nor poi - s'nous breath can reach that health - ful shore;
4. When shall I reach that hap - py place, and be for - ev - er blest?

to Ca - naan's fair and hap - py land, where my pos - ses - sions lie.
there God the Son for - ev - er reigns and scat - ters night a - way.
sick - ness and sor - row, pain and death are felt and feared no more.
When shall I see my Fa - ther's face, and in His bos - om rest?

WORDS: Samuel Stennett, 1787
MUSIC: *Evergreen Shore*, Tullius Clinton O'Kane, 1877   C.M.

565 On Jordan's Stormy Banks

There remains, then, a Sabbath-rest for the people of God. – Hebrews 4:9 NIV

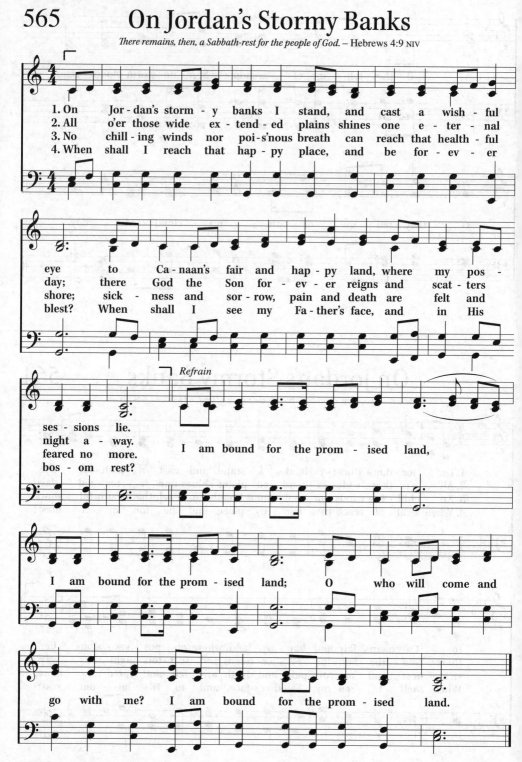

1. On Jor - dan's storm - y banks I stand, and cast a wish - ful
2. All o'er those wide ex - tend - ed plains shines one e - ter - nal
3. No chill - ing winds nor poi - s'nous breath can reach that health - ful
4. When shall I reach that hap - py place, and be for - ev - er

eye to Ca - naan's fair and hap - py land, where my pos -
day; there God the Son for - ev - er reigns and scat - ters
shore; sick - ness and sor - row, pain and death are felt and
blest? When shall I see my Fa - ther's face, and in His

ses - sions lie.
night a - way.
feared no more.   I am bound for the prom - ised land,
bos - om rest?

Refrain

I am bound for the prom - ised land; O who will come and

go with me? I am bound for the prom - ised land.

WORDS: Samuel Stennett, 1787
MUSIC: *Promised Land,* American folk hymn, 19th c.; arr. Regdon McCoy McIntosh, 1895

C. M. with Refrain

O That Will Be Glory for Me

566

The mystery is that Christ lives in you, and He is your hope of sharing in God's glory. – Colossians 1:27 CEV

1. When all my la-bors and tri-als are o'er, and I am safe on that beau-ti-ful shore, just to be near the dear Lord I a-dore, will through the a-ges be glo-ry for me.

2. When, by the gift of His in-fi-nite grace, I am ac-cord-ed in heav-en a place, just to be there and to look on His face will through the a-ges be glo-ry for me.

3. Friends will be there I have loved long a-go; joy like a riv-er a-round me will flow. Yet, just a smile from my Sav-ior, I know, will through the a-ges be glo-ry for me.

Refrain

O that will be glo-ry for me, glo-ry for me, glo-ry for me! When by His grace I shall look on His face, that will be glo-ry, be glo-ry for me!

O that will be glo-ry for me, be glo-ry for me, glo-ry for me, glo-ry for me!

WORDS: Charles Hutchinson Gabriel, 1900
MUSIC: *Glory Song,* Charles Hutchinson Gabriel, 1900

10.10.10.10 with Refrain

Beulah Land

Thou shalt be called Hephzibah, and thy land Beulah: for the Lord delighteth in thee. – Isaiah 62:4 KJV

1. I've reached the land of joy di - vine, and all its beau - ty
2. The Sav - ior comes and walks with me, and sweet com - mu - nion
3. A sweet per-fume up - on the breeze, is borne from spring's bright
4. The breez - es seem to float to me, sweet sounds of heav - en's

now is mine. Here shines un - dimmed one bliss - ful day, for
here have we; He gent - ly leads me with His hand, for
leaf - y trees; and flow'rs that nev - er fad - ing grow, where
mel - o - dy; as an - gels, with the white-robed throng, join

all my night has passed a - way.
this is heav - en's bor - der - land.
streams of life for - ev - er flow.
in the sweet re - demp - tion song.

Refrain

O Beu - lah land, sweet Beu - lah land, as on the high-est mount I stand; I look a - way a - cross the sea, where man - sions are pre - pared for me; and

WORDS: Edgar Page Stites, 1876
MUSIC: *Sweet Beulah Land*, John Robson Sweney, 1876

L.M. with Refrain

view the shin-ing glo-ry shore, my heav'n, my home for-ev-er-more.

He the Pearly Gates Will Open   568

Its gates are always open during the day, and night never comes. – Revelation 21:25 CEV

1. Love di-vine, so great and won-drous, deep and might-y, pure, sub-lime;
2. Like a dove when hunt-ed, fright-ened, as a wound-ed fawn was I,
3. Love di-vine, so great and won-drous: All my sins He then for-gave,
4. In life's e-ven-tide, at twi-light, at His door I'll knock and wait;

com-ing from the heart of Je-sus: Just the same through test of time.
bro-ken heart-ed, yet He healed me: He will heed the sin-ner's cry.
I will sing His praise for-ev-er, for His blood, His pow'r to save.
by the pre-cious love of Je-sus, I shall en-ter heav-en's gate.

Refrain

He the pearl-y gates will o-pen, so that I may en-ter in;

for He pur-chased my re-demp-tion, and for-gave me all my sin.

WORDS: Fredrick Arvid Blom, 1917; tr. Nathaniel Carlson, ca. 1935
MUSIC: *Pearly Gates,* Elsie Rebekah Ahlwen, 1930

8.7.8.7 with Refrain

569 We'll Understand It Better By and By

Faith makes us sure of what we hope for and gives us proof of what we cannot see. – Hebrews 11:1 CEV

1. We are oft-en tossed and driv'n on the rest-less sea of time,
2. We are oft-en des-ti-tute of the things that life de-mands,
3. Tri-als dark on ev-'ry hand, and we can-not un-der-stand
4. Temp-ta-tions, hid-den snares of-ten take us un-a-wares,

som-bre skies and howl-ing tem-pests oft suc-ceed a bright sun-shine,
want of food and want of shel-ter, thirst-y hills and bar-ren lands,
all the ways that God would lead us to that bless-ed Prom-ised Land;
and our hearts are made to bleed for some thought-less word or deed,

in the land of per-fect day, when the mists have rolled a-way, we will
we are trust-ing in the Lord, and ac-cord-ing to His Word, we will
but He guides us with His eye, and we'll fol-low till we die; for we'll
and we won-der why the test when we try to do our best, but we'll

Refrain

un-der-stand it bet-ter by and by.
un-der-stand it bet-ter by and by.
un-der-stand it bet-ter by and by.
un-der-stand it bet-ter by and by.

By and by, when the morn-ing comes,

when the saints of God are gath-ered home; we will tell the sto-ry

WORDS: Charles Albert Tindley, 1906
MUSIC: *By and By,* Charles Albert Tindley, 1906, arr F. A. Clark, 1906

Irregular with Refrain

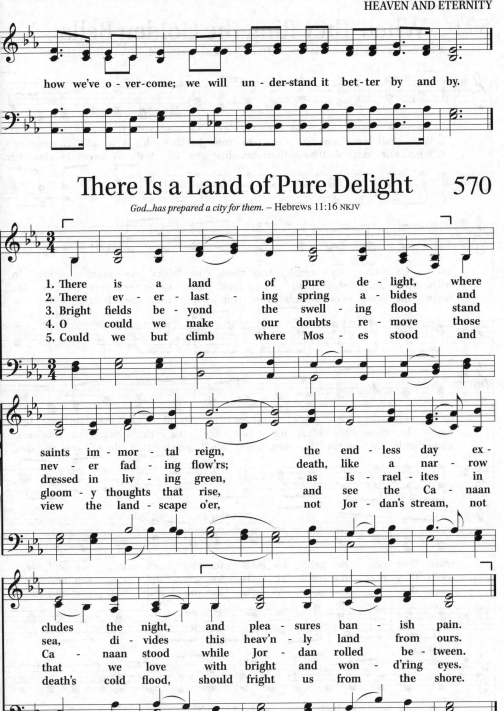

how we've o - ver - come; we will un - der - stand it bet - ter by and by.

There Is a Land of Pure Delight 570

God...has prepared a city for them. – Hebrews 11:16 NKJV

1. There is a land of pure de - light, where
2. There ev - er - last - ing spring a - bides and
3. Bright fields be - yond the swell - ing flood stand
4. O could we make our doubts re - move those
5. Could we but climb where Mos - es stood and

saints im - mor - tal reign, the end - less day ex -
nev - er fad - ing flow'rs; death, like a nar - row
dressed in liv - ing green, as Is - rael - ites in
gloom - y thoughts that rise, and see the Ca - naan
view the land - scape o'er, not Jor - dan's stream, not

cludes the night, and plea - sures ban - ish pain.
sea, di - vides this heav'n - ly land from ours.
Ca - naan stood while Jor - dan rolled be - tween.
that we love with bright and won - d'ring eyes.
death's cold flood, should fright us from the shore.

WORDS: From *Hymns and Spiritual Songs,* Isaac Watts, 1707
MUSIC: *Land of Rest,* from *The Christian Lyre,* 1836, early American folk hymn, 19th c.; arr. Eric Wyse, 2005   C.M.

This tune in a higher key, No. 549.

571 When They Ring the Golden Bells

He will swallow up death forever; and the Lord God will wipe away tears from all faces. – Isaiah 25:8 ESV

1. There's a land be-yond the riv-er, that we call the sweet for-ev-er,
2. We shall know no sin or sor-row, in that ha-ven of to-mor-row,
3. When our days shall know their num-ber, and in death we sweet-ly slum-ber,

and we on-ly reach that shore by faith's de-cree; one by
when our ship shall sail be-yond the sil-ver sea; we shall
when the King com-mands the spir-it to be free; nev-er-

one we'll gain the por-tals, there to dwell with the im-mor-tals,
on-ly know the bless-ing of our Fa-ther's sweet ca-ress-ing,
more with an-guish la-den, we shall reach that love-ly ai-den,

when they ring the gold-en bells for you and me, you and me.
when they ring the gold-en bells for you and me, you and me.
when they ring the gold-en bells for you and me, you and me.

Refrain

Don't you hear the bells now ring-ing? Don't you hear the an-gels sing-ing?

WORDS: Daniel De Marbelle, 1887
MUSIC: *Golden Bells,* Daniel De Marbelle, 1887

8.8.11.8.8.11 with Refrain

'Tis the glo-ry hal-le-lu-jah ju-bi-lee, ju-bi-lee. In that

far-off sweet for-ev-er, just be-yond the shin-ing riv-er,

when they ring the gold-en bells for you and me, you and me.

Will the Circle Be Unbroken? 572

In My Father's house are many mansions...I go to prepare a place for you. – John 14:2 NKJV

Will the cir-cle be un-bro-ken, by and by, Lord, by and by?

There's a bet-ter home a-wait-ing in the sky, Lord, in the sky.

WORDS: Ada Ruth Habershon, 1907, alt.
MUSIC: *Unbroken Circle*, traditional, n.d.; arr. Eric Wyse, 2006 8.7.8.7

573 Christ, Whose Glory Fills the Skies

The Sun of Righteousness shall rise with healing in its wings. – Malachi 4:2 ESV

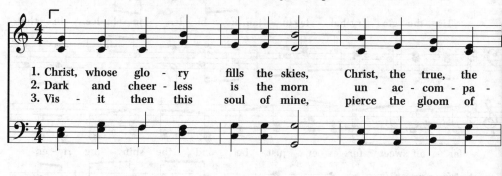

1. Christ, whose glo - ry fills the skies, Christ, the true, the
2. Dark and cheer - less is the morn un - ac - com - pa -
3. Vis - it then this soul of mine, pierce the gloom of

on - ly Light, Sun of Righ - teous - ness, a - rise,
nied by Thee; joy - less is the day's re - turn
sin and grief; fill me, Ra - d'an - cy di - vine,

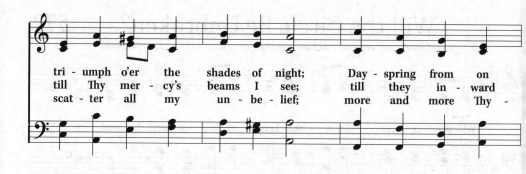

tri - umph o'er the shades of night; Day - spring from on
till Thy mer - cy's beams I see; till they in - ward
scat - ter all my un - be - lief; more and more Thy -

high be near; Day - star, in my heart ap - pear.
light im - part, glad my eyes, and warm my heart.
self dis - play, shin - ing to the per - fect day.

WORDS: Charles Wesley, 1740
MUSIC: *Ratisbon*, from Johann Gottlob Werner's *Choralbuch*, 1815; harm. William Henry Havergal, 1861   7.7.7.7.7.7

Still, Still with Thee

Thy thoughts...are more in number than the sand: when I awake, I am still with Thee. — Psalm 139:17-18 KJV

1. Still, still with Thee, when pur - ple morn - ing break - eth,
2. A - lone with Thee, a - mid the mys - tic shad - ows,
3. Still, still with Thee! As to each new - born morn - ing,
4. When sinks the soul, sub - dued by toil, to slum - ber,
5. So shall it be at last, in that bright morn - ing,

when the bird wak - eth, and the shad - ows flee;
the sol - emn hush of na - ture new - ly born;
a fresh and sol - emn splen - dor still is giv'n,
its clos - ing eyes look up to Thee in prayer;
when the soul wak - eth and life's shad - ows flee;

fair - er than morn - ing, love - li - er than day - light,
a - lone with Thee in breath - less ad - o - ra - tion,
so does this bless - ed con - scious - ness, a - wak - ing,
sweet the re - pose be - neath Thy wings o'er - shad - ing,
O in that hour, fair - er than day - light dawn - ing,

dawns the sweet con - scious - ness, I am with Thee.
in the calm dew and fresh - ness of the morn.
breathe each day near - ness un - to Thee and heav'n.
but sweet - er still to wake and find Thee there.
shall rise the glo - rious thought, I am with Thee.

WORDS: Harriet Beecher Stowe, 1853
MUSIC: *Consolation,* Felix Mendelssohn-Bartholdy, 1834

11.10.11.10

575

Abide with Me

It is the Lord your God who goes with you. He will not leave you or forsake you. – Deuteronomy 31:6 ESV

1. A - bide with me, fast falls the e - ven-tide, the dark - ness
2. Swift to its close ebbs out life's lit - tle day, earth's joys grow
3. I need Thy pres - ence ev - 'ry pass-ing hour; what but Thy
4. I fear no foe, with Thee at hand to bless; ills have no
5. Hold Thou Thy cross be - fore my clos-ing eyes; shine through the

deep - ens; Lord, with me a - bide! When oth - er help - ers
dim, its glo - ries pass a - way; change and de - cay in
grace can foil the tempt-er's pow'r? Who, like Thy - self, my
weight, and tears no bit - ter - ness. Where is death's sting? Where,
gloom and point me to the skies. Heav'n's morn - ing breaks, and

fail, and com-forts flee, Help of the help - less, O a - bide with me.
all a - round I see: O Thou, who chang-est not, a - bide with me.
guide and stay can be? Through cloud and sun-shine, O a - bide with me.
grave, thy vic - to - ry? I tri - umph still, if Thou a - bide with me.
earth's vain shad-ows flee; in life, in death, O Lord, a - bide with me.

WORDS: Henry Francis Lyte, 1847
MUSIC: *Eventide,* William Henry Monk, 1861

10.10.10.10

576

Now the Day Is Over

Stay with us, for it is nearly evening; the day is almost over. – Luke 24:29 NIV

1. Now the day is o - ver, night is draw-ing nigh,
2. Je - sus, give the wea - ry calm and sweet re - pose;
3. Through the long night watch - es may Thine an - gels spread
4. When the morn - ing wak - ens, then may I a - rise

WORDS: Sabine Baring-Gould, 1865
MUSIC: *Merrial,* Joseph Barnby, 1868

6.5.6.5

shad - ows of the eve - ning steal a - cross the sky.
with Thy ten - d'rest bless - ing may mine eye - lids close.
their white wings a - bove me, watch - ing round my bed.
pure, and fresh, and sin - less, in Thy ho - ly eyes.

1. eve - ning steal a - cross the sky.
2. bless-ing may mine eye - lids close.
3. bove me, watch-ing round my bed.
4. sin - less, in Thy ho - ly eyes.

Sun of My Soul

577

Now God is shining in our hearts to let you know that His glory is seen in Jesus Christ. – 2 Corinthians 4:6 CEV

1. Sun of my soul, Thou Sav - ior dear, it is not
2. When the soft dews of kind - ly sleep my wea - ry
3. A - bide with me from morn till eve, for with - out
4. Be near and bless me when I wake, ere through the

night if Thou be near; O may no earth - born
eye - lids gent - ly steep, be my last thought, how
Thee I can - not live; a - bide with me when
world my way I take; a - bide with me till

cloud a - rise to hide Thee from Thy ser - vant's eyes.
sweet to rest for - ev - er on my Sav - ior's breast.
night is nigh, for with - out Thee I dare not die.
in Thy love I lose my - self in heav'n a - bove.

WORDS: John Keble, 1827
MUSIC: *Hursley,* anon., from *Katholisches Gesangbuch,* Vienna, ca. 1774

L.M.

578 The Day Thou Gavest, Lord, Is Ended

The Lord of hosts is with us; the God of Jacob is our fortress. – Psalm 46:7 ESV

1. The day Thou gav - est, Lord, is end - ed; the
2. We thank Thee that Thy church, un - sleep - ing while
3. As o'er each con - ti - nent and is - land the
4. The sun that bids us rest is wak - ing be -
5. So be it, Lord; Thy throne shall nev - er, like

dark - ness falls at Thy be - hest;[1] to
earth rolls on - ward in - to light, through
dawn leads on an - oth - er day, the
liev - ers 'neath the west - ern sky, and
earth's proud em - pires, pass a - way: Thy

Thee our morn - ing hymns as - cend - ed, Thy
all the world her watch is keep - ing, and
voice of prayer is nev - er si - lent, nor
hour by hour fresh lips are mak - ing Thy
king - dom stands, and grows for - ev - er, till

praise shall hal - low now our rest.
rests not now by day or night.
dies the strain of praise a - way.
won - drous do - ings heard on high.
all Thy crea - tures own Thy sway.

1. behest: command

WORDS: John Ellerton, 1870
MUSIC: *St. Clement,* Clement Cotterill Scholefield, 1874

9.8.9.8

Day Is Dying in the West

God said, "Let there be lights in the expanse of the heavens to separate the day from the night." – Genesis 1:14 ESV

1. Day is dy - ing in the west; heav'n is touch - ing
2. Lord of life, be - neath the dome of the u - ni -
3. While the deep - 'ning shad - ows fall, heart of love en -
4. When for - ev - er from our sight pass the stars, the

earth with rest; wait and wor - ship while the night sets her eve - ning
verse, Thy home, gath - er us who seek Thy face to the fold of
fold - ing all, through the glo - ry and the grace of the stars that
day, the night, Lord of an - gels, on our eyes let e - ter - nal

Refrain

lamps a - light through all the sky.
Thy em - brace, for Thou art nigh. Ho - ly, ho - ly,
veil Thy face, our hearts as - cend.
morn - ing rise and shad - ows end.

ho - ly, Lord God of Hosts! Heav'n and earth are full of Thee!

Heav'n and earth are prais - ing Thee, O Lord most high!

WORDS: Mary Artemesia Lathbury, 1877
MUSIC: *Chautauqua*, William Fiske Sherwin, 1877

7.7.7.7.4 with Refrain

580   A Peaceful Night

Thou shalt not be afraid for the terror by night. – Psalm 91:5 KJV

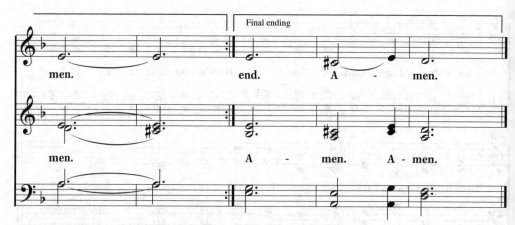

WORDS: From *The Service of Compline,* adapt. Darrell A. Harris and Eric Wyse, 2005
MUSIC: *Quietude,* Darrell A. Harris and Eric Wyse, 2005

4.4.4.4 with Amens

Brethren, We Have Met to Worship 581

Behold, I will rain bread from heaven for you. – Exodus 16:4 KJV

1. Breth-ren, we have met to wor-ship and a-dore the Lord our God;
2. Breth-ren, see poor sin-ners round you slum-b'ring on the brink of woe;
3. Sis-ters, will you join and help us? Mo-ses' sis-ter aid-ed him;
4. Let us love our God su-preme-ly, let us love each oth-er too;

will you pray with all your pow-er, while we try to preach the Word?
death is com-ing, hell is mov-ing: can you bear to let them go?
will you help the trem-bling mourn-ers who are strug-gling hard with sin?
let us love and pray for sin-ners till our God makes all things new.

All is vain un-less the Spir-it of the Ho-ly One comes down;
See our fa-thers and our moth-ers and our chil-dren sink-ing down;
Tell them all a-bout the Sav-ior: Tell them that He will be found;
Then He'll call us home to heav-en, at His ta-ble we'll sit down;

breth-ren, pray, and ho-ly man-na will be show-ered all a-round.
breth-ren, pray, and ho-ly man-na will be show-ered all a-round.
sis-ters, pray, and ho-ly man-na will be show-ered all a-round.
Christ will gird Him-self and serve us with sweet man-na all a-round.

WORDS: George Atkins, 1819; from *Spiritual Songster*, 1819
MUSIC: *Holy Manna*, 1825; attr. William Moore, 19th c.

8.7.8.7 D

582 The Church in the Wildwood

The church of the living God is the strong foundation of truth. – 1 Timothy 3:15 CEV

1. There's a church in the val-ley by the wild-wood, no
2. Oh, come to the church in the wild-wood, to the
3. How sweet on a clear Sab-bath morn-ing, to
4. From the church in the val-ley by the wild-wood, when

love-li-er spot in the dale; no place is so dear to my
trees where the wild flow-ers bloom; where the part-ing hymn will be
list to the clear ring-ing bell; its tones so sweet-ly are
day fades a-way in-to night; I would fain from this spot of my

Refrain

child-hood as the lit-tle brown church in the vale.
chant-ed, we will weep by the side of the tomb.
call-ing, oh, come to the church in the vale. Oh,
child-hood, wing my way to the man-sions of light.

Come to the church in the wild - wood, oh,
come, come, come, come, come, come, come, come, come, come, come, come,

WORDS: William Savage Pitts, 1857
MUSIC: *Wildwood,* William Savage Pitts, 1857

Irregular with Refrain

come to the church in the vale;   no   spot   is so dear to my
come, come,   come, come,   come, come, come.

child - hood   as   the   lit - tle brown church   in   the vale.

Come, We That Love the Lord   583

And the ransomed of the Lord shall return and come to Zion with singing. – Isaiah 35:10 ESV

1. Come, we that love the Lord,   and let our joys be known;
2. Let   those re - fuse to sing   who nev - er knew our God;
3. The   hill of Zi - on yields a   thou - sand sa - cred sweets,
4. Then let   our songs a - bound, and ev - 'ry tear be   dry;

join in a   song with sweet ac - cord, and thus sur - round the throne.
but chil - dren of the heav'n - ly King may speak their joys a - broad.
be - fore we   reach the heav'n - ly fields or walk the gold - en streets.
we're march-ing through Em - man - uel's ground to fair - er worlds on high.

WORDS: Isaac Watts, 1707
MUSIC: *Festal Song*, William Henry Walter, 1894
This tune in a lower key, No. 340.

S.M.

584 We're Marching to Zion

And the ransomed of the Lord shall return and come to Zion with singing. – Isaiah 35:10 ESV

1. Come, we that love the Lord, and let our joys be known. Join
2. Let those re-fuse to sing who nev-er knew our God; but
3. The hill of Zi-on yields a thou-sand sa-cred sweets be-
4. Then let our songs a-bound, and ev-'ry tear be dry. We're

in a song with sweet ac-cord, join in a song with sweet ac-
chil-dren of the heav'n-ly King, but chil-dren of the heav'n-ly
fore we reach the heav'n-ly fields, be-fore we reach the heav'n-ly
march-ing through Em-man-uel's ground, we're march-ing through Em-man-uel's

cord, and thus sur-round the throne, and thus sur-round the throne.
King may speak their joys a-broad, may speak their joys a-broad.
fields or walk the gold-en streets, or walk the gold-en streets.
ground to fair-er worlds on high, to fair-er worlds on high.

Refrain

We're march-ing to Zi-on, beau-ti-ful, beau-ti-ful Zi-on. We're
We're march-ing on to Zi-on,

march-ing up-ward to Zi-on, the beau-ti-ful cit-y of God.
Zi-on, Zi-on,

WORDS: Isaac Watts, 1707; Ref., Robert Lowry, 1867
MUSIC: *Marching to Zion*, Robert Lowry, 1867

6.6.8.8.6.6 with Refrain

Lord, Dismiss Us with Thy Blessing 585

May Your blessing be on Your people. – Psalm 3:8 NIV

1. Lord, dis-miss us with Thy bless-ing; fill our hearts with
2. Thanks we give and ad-o-ra-tion for Thy gos-pel's
3. So that when Thy love shall call us, Sav-ior, from the

joy and peace; let us each, Thy love pos-sess-ing,
joy-ful sound: May the fruits of Thy sal-va-tion
world a-way, let no fear of death ap-pall us,

tri-umph in re-deem-ing grace: O re-fresh us,
in our hearts and lives a-bound: Ev-er faith-ful,
glad Thy sum-mons to o-bey: May we ev-er,

O re-fresh us, trav-'ling through this wil-der-ness.
ev-er faith-ful to the truth may we be found;
may we ev-er reign with Thee in end-less day.

WORDS: Sts. 1, 2 attr. John Fawcett, 1773; St. 3 Godfrey Thring, 1773
MUSIC: *Sicilian Mariners*, Tattersall's *Psalmody*, 1794

8.7.8.7.8.7

586 God Be with You Till We Meet Again

May the Lord keep watch between you and me when we are away from each other. – Genesis 31:49 NIV

1. God be with you till we meet a-gain, by His coun-sels guide, up - hold you,
2. God be with you till we meet a-gain, 'neath His wings pro - tect - ing hide you,
3. God be with you till we meet a-gain, when life's per - ils thick con - found you,
4. God be with you till we meet a-gain, keep love's ban - ner float - ing o'er you;

with His sheep se - cure - ly fold you; God be with you till we meet a-gain.
dai - ly man - na still pro - vide you; God be with you till we meet a-gain.
put His arms un - fail - ing round you; God be with you till we meet a-gain.
smite death's threat-'ning wave be - fore you; God be with you till we meet a-gain.

Refrain (optional)

Till we meet, till we meet, till we
Till we meet, till we meet,

meet at Je - sus' feet; till we meet,
till we meet; till we meet,

till we meet, God be with you till we meet a - gain.
till we meet,

WORDS: Jeremiah Eames Rankin, 1880
MUSIC: *Endeavor,* William Gould Tomer, 1880

9.8.8.9 with Refrain

God Be with You Till We Meet Again 587

May the Lord keep watch between you and me when we are away from each other. – Genesis 31:49 NIV

Unison

1. God be with you till we meet a - gain,
2. God be with you till we meet a - gain,
3. God be with you till we meet a - gain,
4. God be with you till we meet a - gain,

Harmony

by His coun - sels guide, up - hold you,
'neath His wings pro - tect - ing hide you,
when life's per - ils thick con - found you,
keep love's ban - ner float - ing o'er you;

with His sheep se - cure - ly fold you;
dai - ly man - na still pro - vide you;
put His arms un - fail - ing round you;
smite death's threat - 'ning wave be - fore you;

Unison

God be with you till we meet a - gain.
God be with you till we meet a - gain.
God be with you till we meet a - gain.
God be with you till we meet a - gain.

WORDS: Jeremiah Eames Rankin, 1880
MUSIC: *Randolph*, Ralph Vaughan Williams, 1906

9.8.8.9

588 Savior, Again to Thy Dear Name We Raise

I pray that the Lord, who gives peace, will always bless you with peace. – 2 Thessalonians 3:16 CEV

1. Sav - ior, a - gain to Thy dear name we raise
2. Grant us Thy peace up - on our home - ward way;
3. Grant us Thy peace through - out our earth - ly life;
4. Thy peace in life, the balm of ev - 'ry pain;

with one ac - cord our part - ing hymn of praise;
with Thee be - gan, with Thee shall end the day;
peace to Thy Church from er - ror and from strife;
Thy peace in death, the hope to rise a - gain;

guard Thou the lips from sin, the hearts from shame,
from harm and dan - ger keep Thy chil - dren free,
peace to our land, the fruit of truth and love;
then, when Thy voice shall bid our con - flict cease,

that in this house have called up - on Thy name.
for dark and light are both a - like to Thee.
peace in each heart, Thy Spir - it from a - bove.
call us, O Lord, to Thine e - ter - nal peace.

WORDS: John Ellerton, 1866, alt.
MUSIC: *Ellers,* Edward John Hopkins, 1869
Another harmonization of this tune, No. 296.

10.10.10.10

Now Thank We All Our God 589

So let the peace that comes from Christ control your thoughts. And be grateful. – Colossians 3:15 CEV

1. Now thank we all our God with heart and hands and voic - es,
2. O may this boun-t'ous God through all our life be near us,
3. All praise and thanks to God the Fa - ther now be giv - en,

who won-drous things hath done, in whom this world re - joic - es;
with ev - er joy - ful hearts and bless - ed peace to cheer us;
the Son, and Him who reigns with them in high - est heav - en,

who, from our moth - ers' arms hath bless'd us on our way
and keep us in His grace, and guide us when per - plexed,
the one e - ter - nal God, whom heav'n and earth a - dore;

with count - less gifts of love, and still is ours to - day.
and free us from all ills in this world and the next.
for thus it was, is now, and shall be ev - er - more.

WORDS: Martin Rinkart, 1636; tr. Catherine Winkworth, 1858
MUSIC: *Nun Danket*, attr. Johann Crüger, ca. 1636; harm. Felix Mendelssohn-Bartholdy, 1840
6.7.6.7.6.6.6.6

590 We Gather Together

For where two or three come together in My name, there am I with them. – Matthew 18:20 NIV

1. We gath - er to - geth - er to ask the Lord's bless - ing,
2. Be - side us to guide us, our God with us join - ing,
3. We all do ex - tol Thee, Thou lead - er in bat - tle,

He chas - tens and has - tens His will to make known;
or - dain - ing, main - tain - ing His king - dom di - vine;
and pray that Thou still our de - fend - er wilt be.

the wick - ed op - press - ing now cease from dis - tress - ing,
so from the be - gin - ning the fight we were win - ning,
Let Thy con - gre - ga - tion es - cape trib - u - la - tion;

sing prais - es to His name, He for - gets not His own.
Thou, Lord wast at our side: The glo - ry be Thine!
Thy name be ev - er praised: O Lord, make us free!

WORDS: Attr. Adrianus Valerius, 1597; tr. Theodore Baker, 1894
MUSIC: *Kremser*, attr. Adrianus Valerius, 1625; arr. Edward Kremser, 1877

12.11.12.12

Come, Ye Thankful People, Come 591

Come before His presence with thanksgiving, and make a joyful noise unto Him with psalms. – Psalm 95:2 KJV

1. Come, ye thank-ful peo-ple, come; raise the song of har-vest home;
2. All the world is God's own field, fruit un-to His praise to yield;
3. For the Lord our God shall come, and shall take His har-vest home;
4. E-ven so, Lord, quick-ly come to Thy fi-nal har-vest-home;

all is safe-ly gath-ered in ere the win-ter storms be-gin.
wheat and tares to-geth-er sown, un-to joy or sor-row grown.
from His field shall in that day all of-fens-es purge a-way.
gath-er Thou Thy peo-ple in, free from sor-row, free from sin.

God, our Mak-er, doth pro-vide for our wants to be sup-plied.
First the blade, and then the ear, then the full corn shall ap-pear;
Give His an-gels charge at last in the fire the tares to cast,
There for-ev-er pu-ri-fied, in Thy pres-ence to a-bide.

Come to God's own tem-ple, come; raise the song of har-vest home.
Lord of har-vest, grant that we whole-some grain and pure may be.
but the fruit-ful ears to store in His gar-ner ev-er-more.
Come, with all Thine an-gels come; raise the glo-r'ous har-vest home.

WORDS: Henry Alford, 1844
MUSIC: *St. George's Windsor*, George Job Elvy, 1858

7.7.7.7 D

592 We Plow the Fields and Scatter

The field is the world, and the good seed stands for the sons of the kingdom. – Matthew 13:38 NIV

1. We plow the fields and scat - ter the good seed on the land,
2. You on - ly are the Mak - er of all things near and far;
3. We thank You, then, Cre - a - tor, for all things bright and good,

but it is fed and wa - tered by God's al - might - y hand;
You paint the way - side flow - er, You light the eve - ning star;
the seed - time and the har - vest, our life, our health, our food;

God sends the snow in win - ter, the warmth to swell the grain,
the winds and waves o - bey You, by You the birds are fed;
ac - cept the gifts we of - fer, for all Your love im - parts,

the breez - es and the sun - shine, and soft, re - fresh - ing rain.
much more to us, Your chil - dren, You give our dai - ly bread.
and what You most would wel - come, our hum - ble, thank-ful hearts.

WORDS: Claudius Matthias, 1782; tr. Jane Montgomery Campbell, 1861, alt.
MUSIC: *Es Flog Ein Kleins Waldvögelein*, 19th c. German folk song; harm. Henry Walford Davies, 1923

7.6.7.6 D

Sing to the Lord of Harvest

Praise the Lord for His goodness, and for His wonderful works. – Psalm 107:8 KJV

1. Sing to the Lord of har - vest, sing songs of love and praise;
2. God makes the clouds rain good - ness, the des - erts bloom and spring,
3. Bring to this sa - cred al - tar the gifts His good-ness gave,

with joy - ful hearts and voic - es your al - le - lu - ias raise.
the hills leap up in glad - ness, the val - leys laugh and sing.
the gold - en sheaves of har - vest, the souls Christ died to save.

By Him the roll-ing sea - sons in fruit - ful or - der move;
God fills them with His full - ness, all things with large in - crease;
Your hearts lay down be - fore Him when at His feet you fall,

sing to the Lord of har - vest a joy - ous song of love.
He crowns the year with bless - ing, with plen - ty and with peace.
and with your lives a - dore Him who gave His life for all.

WORDS: John Samuel Bewley Monsell, 1866 alt.
MUSIC: *Wie Lieblich Ist Der Maien (Steurlein),* Johann Steuerlein, ca. 1581

7.6.7.6 D

594

Count Your Blessings

Many, O Lord my God, are Thy wonderful works which Thou hast done. – Psalm 40:5 KJV

1. When up-on life's bil-lows you are tem-pest tossed, when you are dis-
2. Are you ev-er bur-dened with a load of care? Does the cross seem
3. When you look at oth-ers with their lands and gold, think that Christ has
4. So, a-mid the con-flict, wheth-er great or small, do not be dis-

cour-aged, think-ing all is lost, count your man-y bless-ings, name them
heav-y you are called to bear: Count your man-y bless-ings, ev-'ry
prom-ised you His wealth un-told; count your man-y bless-ings, mon-ey
cour-aged, God is o-ver all; count your man-y bless-ings, an-gels

one by one, and it will sur-prise you what the Lord hath done.
doubt will fly, and you will be sing-ing as the days go by.
can-not buy your re-ward in heav-en, nor your home on high.
will at-tend, help and com-fort give you to your jour-ney's end.

Refrain

Count your bless-ings, name them one by one; count your
Count your man-y bless-ings, name them one by one; count your man-y

WORDS: Johnson Oatman, Jr., 1897
MUSIC: *Blessings*, Edwin Othello Excell, 1897

11.11.11.11 with Refrain

bless-ings, see what God hath done; count your bless-ings,
bless-ings, see what God hath done; count your man - y bless-ings,

name them one by one; count your man - y bless-ings, see what God hath done.

Praise to God, Immortal Praise 595

Let the people praise Thee, O God; let all the people praise Thee. – Psalm 67:3 KJV

1. Praise to God, im - mor - tal praise, for the love that crowns our days;
2. All the plen - ty sum - mer pours; au - tumn's rich o'er flow - ing stores;
3. As Thy pros - p'ring hand hath blessed, may we give Thee of our best;

boun - t'ous source of ev - 'ry joy, let Thy praise our tongues em - ploy:
flocks that whit - en all the plain; yel - low sheaves of rip - ened grain;
and by deeds of kind - ly love for Thy mer - cies grate - ful prove;

All to Thee, our God, we owe, source whence all our bless-ings flow.
Lord, for these our souls shall raise grate - ful vows and sol - emn praise.
sing - ing thus through all our days praise to God, im - mor - tal praise.

WORDS: Anna Laetitia Aikin Barbauld, 1772
MUSIC: *Dix*, Conrad Kocher, 1838; arr. William Henry Monk, 1865
This tune in a lower key, No. 239.

7.7.7.7.7.7

596 Another Year Is Dawning

Teach us to number our days, that we may apply our hearts unto wisdom. – Psalm 90:12 KJV

1. An - oth - er year is dawn - ing, dear Fa - ther, let it be,
2. An - oth - er year of mer - cies, of faith - ful - ness and grace,
3. An - oth - er year of ser - vice, of wit - ness for Thy love,

in work - ing or in wait - ing, an - oth - er year with Thee;
an - oth - er year of glad - ness, the glo - ry of Thy face;
an - oth - er year of train - ing for ho - l'er work a - bove;

an - oth - er year of prog - ress, an - oth - er year of praise,
an - oth - er year of lean - ing up - on Thy lov - ing breast,
an - oth - er year is dawn - ing, dear Fa - ther, let it be,

an - oth - er year of prov - ing Thy pres - ence all the days.
an - oth - er year of trust - ing, of qui - et, hap - py rest.
on earth, or else in heav - en, an - oth - er year for Thee.

WORDS: Frances Ridley Havergal, 1874
MUSIC: *Crucifix*, traditional Greek melody, n.d.
Another harmonization of this tune in a lower key, No. 294.

7.6.7.6 D

God of Our Fathers

597

O Lord God of our fathers...rulest not Thou over all the kingdoms? – 2 Chronicles 20:6 KJV

1. God of our fathers, whose almighty hand leads forth in beauty all the starry band of shining worlds in splendor through the skies, our grateful songs before Thy throne arise.

2. Thy love divine hath led us in the past, in this free land by Thee our lot is cast; be Thou our Ruler, Guardian, Guide and Stay, Thy Word our law, Thy paths our chosen way.

3. From war's alarms, from deadly pestilence, be Thy strong arm our ever sure defense; Thy true religion in our hearts increase, Thy bounteous goodness nourish us in peace.

4. Refresh Thy people on their toilsome way, lead us from night to never-ending day; fill all our lives with love and grace divine, and glory, laud and praise be ever Thine!

WORDS: Daniel Crane Roberts, 1876
MUSIC: *National Hymn,* George William Warren, 1888

10.10.10.10

598 Once to Every Man and Nation

Choose this day whom you will serve...as for me and my house, we will serve the Lord. – Joshua 24:15 ESV

1. Once to ev-'ry man and na - tion comes the mo - ment
2. Then to side with truth is no - ble, when we share her
3. By the light of burn-ing mar-tyrs, Christ, Thy bleed-ing
4. Though the cause of e - vil pros - per, yet the truth a -

to de - cide, in the strife of truth with false-hood,
wretch - ed crust, ere her cause bring fame and prof - it,
feet we track; toil-ing up new Cal-v'ries ev - er
lone is strong; though her por - tion be the scaf - fold,

for the good or e - vil side; some great cause, some great de -
and 'tis pros - p'rous to be just; then it is the brave man
with the cross that turns not back. new oc - ca-sions teach new
and up - on the throne be wrong, yet that scaf-fold sways the

ci - sion, of-f'ring each the bloom or blight, and the choice goes
choos - es while the cow - ard stands a - side, till the mul - ti
du - ties; time makes an - cient good un - couth; they must up - ward
fu - ture, and, be - hind the dim un - known, stand-eth God, with-

WORDS: James Russell Lowell, 1845
MUSIC: *Ebenezer (Ton-y-Botel)*, Thomas John Williams, 1890
This tune in a lower key, No. 272.

8.7.8.7 D

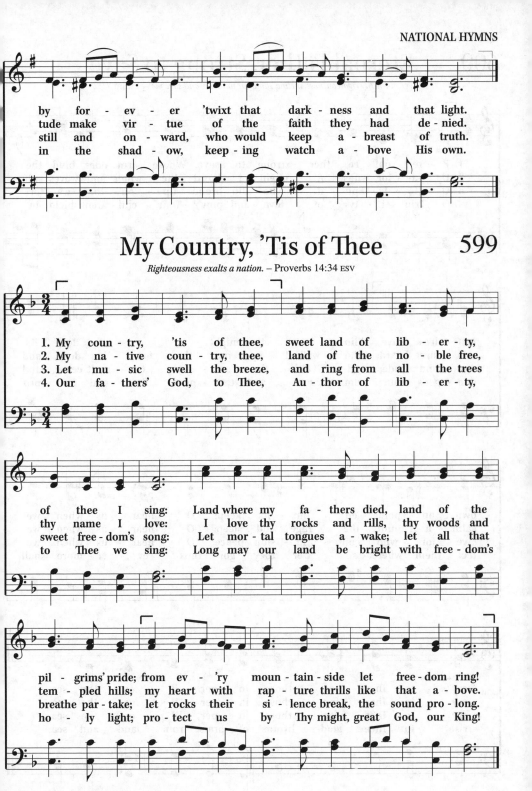

by for - ev - er 'twixt that dark - ness and that light.
tude make vir - tue of the faith they had de - nied.
still and on - ward, who would keep a - breast of truth.
in the shad - ow, keep - ing watch a - bove His own.

My Country, 'Tis of Thee 599

Righteousness exalts a nation. – Proverbs 14:34 ESV

1. My coun - try, 'tis of thee, sweet land of lib - er - ty,
2. My na - tive coun - try, thee, land of the no - ble free,
3. Let mu - sic swell the breeze, and ring from all the trees
4. Our fa - thers' God, to Thee, Au - thor of lib - er - ty,

of thee I sing: Land where my fa - thers died, land of the
thy name I love: I love thy rocks and rills, thy woods and
sweet free - dom's song: Let mor - tal tongues a - wake; let all that
to Thee we sing: Long may our land be bright with free - dom's

pil - grims' pride; from ev - 'ry moun - tain - side let free - dom ring!
tem - pled hills; my heart with rap - ture thrills like that a - bove.
breathe par - take; let rocks their si - lence break, the sound pro - long.
ho - ly light; pro - tect us by Thy might, great God, our King!

WORDS: Samuel Francis Smith, 1832
MUSIC: *America, (Thesaurus Musicus),* anon., 1744
Another harmonization of this tune, in a higher key, No. 607.

6.6.4.6.6.6.4

600 Eternal Father, Strong to Save

Deliver me in Thy righteousness, incline Thine ear unto me, and save me. – Psalm 71:2 KJV

1. E - ter - nal Fa - ther, strong to save, Whose arm does bind the restless wave, Who bids the might - y o - cean deep its own ap - point - ed lim - its keep: O hear us when we cry to Thee for those in per - il on the sea.

2. O Sav - ior, whose Al - might - y Word the winds and waves sub - missive heard; Who walked up - on the foam - ing deep, and calm a - mid the rage did sleep; O hear us when we cry to Thee for those in per - il on the sea.

3. O Ho - ly Spir - it, who did brood up - on the wa - ters dark and rude; and bid their an - gry tu - mult cease, and give for wild con - fu - sion peace; O hear us when we cry to Thee for those in per - il on the sea.

4. O Trin - i - ty of love and pow'r, Your chil - dren shield in dan - ger's hour; from rock and tem - pest, fire and foe, pro - tect them where - so - e'er they go; thus ev - er - more shall rise to Thee glad hymns of praise from land and sea.

WORDS: William Whiting, 1860
MUSIC: *Melita,* John Bacchus Dykes, 1861
This tune in a lower key, No. 411.

8.8.8.8.8.8

America the Beautiful

Give ear to Me, My nation...and I will set My justice for a light to the peoples. – Isaiah 51:4 ESV

1. O beau - ti - ful for spa - cious skies, for am - ber waves of grain,
2. O beau - ti - ful for pil - grim feet, whose stern, im - pas-sioned stress
3. O beau - ti - ful for he - roes proved in lib - er - at - ing strife,
4. O beau - ti - ful for pa - triot dream that sees be - yond the years

for pur - ple moun - tain maj - es - ties a - bove the fruit - ed plain!
a thor - ough - fare for free - dom beat a - cross the wil - der - ness!
who more than self their coun - try loved and mer - cy more than life!
thine al - a - bas - ter cit - ies gleam, un - dimmed by hu - man tears!

A - mer - i - ca! A - mer - i - ca! God shed His grace on thee,
A - mer - i - ca! A - mer - i - ca! God mend thine ev - ery flaw,
A - mer - i - ca! A - mer - i - ca! May God thy gold re - fine
A - mer - i - ca! A - mer - i - ca! God shed His grace on thee,

and crown thy good with broth - er - hood from sea to shin - ing sea!
con - firm thy soul in self - con - trol, thy lib - er - ty in law!
till all suc - cess be no - ble - ness, and ev - ery gain di - vine!
and crown thy good with broth - er - hood from sea to shin - ing sea!

WORDS: Katherine Lee Bates, 1893
MUSIC: *Materna*, Samuel Augustus Ward, 1882

C.M.D.

602 Lift Every Voice and Sing

Sing to Him, sing praises to Him; tell of all His wondrous works. – Psalm 105:2 ESV

1. Lift ev - 'ry voice and sing, till earth and heav - en ring,
2. Ston - y the road we trod, bit - ter the chas - t'ning rod,
3. God of our wea - ry years, God of our si - lent tears,

ring with the har - mo - nies of lib - er - ty;
felt in the days when hope un - born had died;
Thou who hast brought us thus far on the way;

let our re - joic - ing rise, high as the lis - t'ning skies,
yet with a stead - y beat, have not our wea - ry feet,
Thou who hast by Thy might, led us in - to the light,

let it re - sound loud as the roll - ing sea.
come to the place for which our fa - thers sighed?
keep us for - ev - er in the path, we pray.

WORDS: James Weldon Johnson, 1899
MUSIC: *Lift Every Voice*, John Rosamond Johnson, 1899

Irregular

Unison

Sing a song full of the faith that the dark past has taught us,
We have come o - ver a way that with tears has been wa - tered,
Lest our feet stray from the plac - es, our God, where we met Thee.

Harmony

sing a song full of the hope that the pres - ent has brought
we have come, tread - ing our path through the blood of the slaugh -
Lest our hearts, drunk with the wine of the world, we for - get

us; fac - ing the ris - ing sun of our new day be - gun,
tered; out from the gloom - y past, till now we stand at last
Thee; shad - owed be - neath Thy hand, may we for - ev - er stand

let us march on till vic - to - ry is won.
where the white gleam of our bright star is cast.
true to our God, true to our na - tive land.

603 Battle Hymn of the Republic

The Lord will roar from on high and shout...against the inhabitants of earth. – Jeremiah 25:30 ESV

1. Mine eyes have seen the glo - ry of the com - ing of the Lord,
2. I have seen Him in the watch - fires of a hun - dred cir - cling camps;
3. He has sound - ed forth the trum - pet that shall nev - er sound re - treat,
4. In the beau - ty of the lil - ies Christ was born a - cross the sea,
5. He is com - ing like the glo - ry of the morn - ing on the wave;

He is tram - pling out the vin - tage where the grapes of wrath are
they have build - ed Him an al - tar in the eve - ning dews and
He is sift - ing out the hearts of men be - fore His judg - ment
with a glo - ry in His bos - om that trans - fig - ures you and
He is wis - dom to the might - y, He is hon - or to the

stored; He hath loosed the fate - ful light - ning of His
damps; I can read His righ - teous sen - tence by the
seat; O be swift, my soul, to an - swer Him; be
me; as He died to make men ho - ly, let us
brave; so the world shall be His foot - stool, and the

ter - ri - ble, swift sword; His truth is march - ing on.
dim and flar - ing lamps. His day is march - ing on.
ju - bi - lant, my feet! Our God is march - ing on.
live to make men free, while God is march - ing on.
soul of wrong His slave, our God is march - ing on.

WORDS: Julia Ward Howe, 1861, alt.
MUSIC: *Battle Hymn,* American folk song, 19th c.; attr. John William Steffe, 1856

Irregular with Refrain

Refrain

Glo - ry! Glo - ry, hal - le - lu - jah! Glo - ry! Glo - ry, hal - le - lu - jah!

Glo - ry! Glo - ry, hal - le - lu - jah! Our God is march - ing on.

God Bless Our Native Land 604

Blessed is the nation whose God is the Lord. – Psalm 33:12 KJV

1. God bless our na - tive land; firm may she ev - er stand
2. For her our prayers shall rise to God, a - bove the skies;

through storm and night. When the wild tem - pests rave, ru - ler of
on Him we wait. Thou who art ev - er nigh, guard - ing with

wind and wave, do thou our coun - try save by Thy great might.
watch - ful eye, to Thee a - loud we cry, God save the State!

WORDS: Seigfried A. Mahlmann, 1815; tr. Charles Timothy Brooks, 1833
MUSIC: *America (Thesaurus Musicus)*, anon. 1744
Another harmonization of this tune, in a higher key, No. 607.

6.6.4.6.6.6.4

605 The Star-Spangled Banner

It is better to take refuge in the Lord than to trust in princes. – Psalm 118:9 NIV

1. O say, can you see, by the dawn's ear - ly light,
2. O thus be it ev - er, when free men shall stand

what so proud - ly we hailed at the twi - light's last gleam - ing,
be - tween their loved homes and the war's des - o - la - tion;

whose broad stripes and bright stars, through the per - il - ous fight,
blest with vic - t'ry and peace, may the heav'n - res - cued land

o'er the ram - parts we watched, were so gal - lant - ly stream - ing?
praise the Pow'r that hath made and pre - served us a na - tion!

WORDS: Frances Scott Key, 1814
MUSIC: *National Anthem*(USA), Anon., 18th c.; attr. John Stafford Smith, ca. 1775

Irregular with Refrain

And the rock - ets' red glare, the bombs burst - ing in air,
Then con - quer we must, when our cause it is just;

gave proof through the night that our flag was still there.
and this be our mot - to: "In God is our trust!"

Refrain

O say, does that star - span - gled ban - ner yet
And the star - span - gled ban - ner in tri - umph shall

wave o'er the land of the free and the home of the brave?
wave o'er the land of the free and the home of the brave.

606 O Canada!

For the kingdom is the Lord's: and He is the governor among the nations. – Psalm 22:28 KJV

1. O Can - a - da! Our home and na - tive land!
2. Al - might - y Love, by Thy mys - te - r'ous pow'r,

True pa - triot love in all thy sons com - mand.
in wis - dom guide, with faith and free - dom dow'r;

With glow-ing hearts we see thee rise, the true north, strong and free.
be ours a na - tion ev - er-more that no op - pres - sion blights,

From far and wide, O Can - a - da, we stand on guard for
where jus - tice rules from shore to shore, from lakes to north - ern

Refrain

thee. God keep our land glo - r'ous and free!
lights. May love a - lone for wrong a - tone;

WORDS: St. 1 Robert Stanley Weir, 1908; St. 2 Albert Durrant Watson, 1917
MUSIC: *O Canada*, Calixa Lavallée, 1880; arr. Frederick Caton Silvester, 20th c.

Irregular with Refrain

O Can - a - da, we stand on guard for thee.
Lord of the lands, make Can - a - da Thine own!

O Can - a - da, we stand on guard for thee.
Lord of the lands, make Can - a - da Thine own!

God Save the Queen 607

The authorities that exist have been established by God. – Romans 13:1 NIV

1. God save our gra - cious Queen! Long live our no - ble Queen!
2. Thy choic - est gifts in store, on her be pleased to pour,

God save the Queen! Send her vic - to - ri - ous, hap - py and
long may she reign. May she de - fend our laws and ev - er

glo - ri - ous, long to reign o - ver us: God save the Queen.
give us cause to sing with heart and voice, God save the Queen.

WORDS: Anon., ca. 18th c.
MUSIC: *National Anthem* (British Commonwealth), 1744
Another harmonization of this tune, in a lower key, No. 604.

6.6.4.6.6.6.4

608 The Lord Is in His Holy Temple

The Lord is in His holy temple; let all the earth keep silence before Him. – Habakkuk 2:20 ESV

The Lord is in His ho-ly tem - ple, the Lord is in His ho-ly tem - ple; let all the earth keep si - lence, let all the earth keep si - lence be - fore Him, keep si - lence, keep si - lence, be - fore Him.

WORDS: Habakkuk 2:20
MUSIC: *Quam Dilecta*, George Frederick Root, 1872

Irregular

609 Be Still

Be still, and know that I am God. – Psalm 46:10 NIV

Be still, be still; know that I am God.

WORDS: Darrell A. Harris and Eric Wyse, 2004; based on Psalm 46:10a
MUSIC: *Be Still*, Darrell A. Harris and Eric Wyse, 2004

Irregular

Bless the Lord

Praise the Lord, O my soul. – Psalm 103:1 NIV

LEADER: Behold the tabernacle of God is with men, and He shall dwell with them,
and they shall be His people, and God Himself shall be with them and be their God.

Bless the Lord, O my soul, bless-ed art Thou, O Lord.

LEADER: The Lord is nigh unto all that call upon Him, to all that call upon Him in truth,
He will hear their cry and will save them.

Bless the Lord, O my soul and all that

is with-in me bless His ho - ly Name.

Bless the Lord, O my soul.

The responses may be used separately or together.

WORDS: Psalm 103:1
MUSIC: *Ivanoff*, Mikhail Ippolitoff-Ivanoff, 19th-20th c.

Irregular

611 Kyrie Eleison (Lord, Have Mercy)

Hear me, O Lord...turn unto me according to the multitude of Thy tender mercies. – Psalm 69:16 KJV

Ky - ri - e e - le - i - son. Chris - te e -
le - i - son. Ky - ri - e e - le - i - son.
Lord, have mer - cy. Christ, have
mer - cy. Lord, have mer - cy.

WORDS: Traditional, n.d.
MUSIC: *Brentwood,* Eric Wyse, 2003

Irregular

612 Holy God

TRISAGION

Are you not from everlasting, O Lord my God, my Holy One? – Habakkuk 1:12 ESV

Ho - ly God, ho - ly and might - y, ho - ly im - mor - tal

WORDS: Traditional, n.d.
MUSIC: *Belmont Park,* Eric Wyse, 2001

Irregular

613 Glory Be to God on High

Give glory to the Lord your God. – Jeremiah 13:16 ESV

1. Glory be to God on high, and on earth peace good will towards men.

2. We praise Thee, we bless Thee, we wor - ship Thee, we glorify Thee, we give

thanks to Thee for Thy great glo - ry: 3. O Lord God, heaven - ly King,

God the Fa - ther Al - might - y. 4. O Lord, the only begotten Son,

Je - sus Christ; O Lord God, Lamb of God, Son of the Fa - ther,

WORDS: Anon., ca. 5th c.
MUSIC: *Gloria in Excelsis*, Anon., ca. 16th c.

Irregular

5. Thou that takest away the sins of the world, have mercy up - on us.

6. Thou that takest away the sins of the world, re - ceive our prayer.

7. Thou that sittest at the right hand of God, the Father, have mercy up - on us.

8. For Thou on - ly art holy; Thou on - ly art the Lord; 9. Thou only, O Christ,

with the Ho-ly Ghost, art most high in the glory of God, the Fa - ther. A - men.

614

Glory Be to the Father

Give unto the Lord the glory due unto His name. – Psalm 96:8 KJV

Glo-ry be to the Fa-ther, and to the Son and to the Ho-ly Ghost; as it was in the be-gin-ning, is now, and ev-er shall be, world with-out end. A-men, A-men.

WORDS: *Gloria Patri*, traditional, 2nd c.
MUSIC: *Greatorex*, Henry Wellington Greatorex, 1851

Irregular

615

Glory Be to the Father

GLORIA PATRI
TRADITIONAL LANGUAGE

Give unto the Lord the glory due unto His name. – Psalm 96:8 KJV

Glo-ry be to the Fa-ther, and to the Son and to the Ho-ly Ghost; as it was in the be-gin-ning, is now, and ev-er

WORDS: *Gloria Patri*, traditional, 2nd c.
MUSIC: *Meineke*, Christopher Meineke, 1844

Irregular

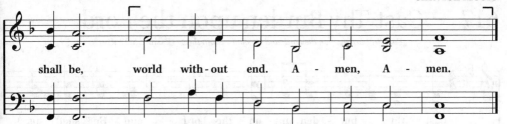

shall be, world with-out end. A-men, A-men.

GLORIA PATRI
CONTEMPORARY LANGUAGE

Glory to the Father

616

Give unto the Lord the glory due unto His name. – Psalm 96:8 KJV

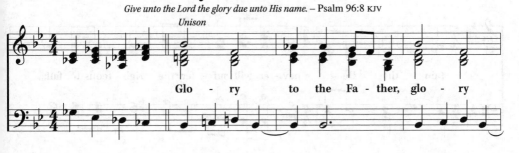

Unison

Glo - ry to the Fa - ther, glo - ry

to the Son, glo - ry to the Ho - ly Spir - it.

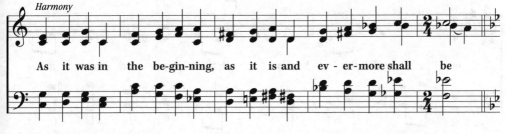

Harmony

As it was in the be-gin-ning, as it is and ev - er-more shall be

Unison

world with - out end. A - men. A - men.

WORDS: *International Consultation on English Texts*, 1975
MUSIC: *Cedar Lane*, Eric Wyse, 1993

Irregular

617 Cast Thy Burden upon the Lord

Cast thy burden upon the Lord, and He shall sustain thee. – Psalm 55:22 KJV

Cast thy bur-den up-on the Lord, and He shall sus-tain thee. He nev-er will suf-fer the righ-teous to fall; He is at thy right hand. Thy mer-cy, Lord, is great and far a-bove the heav'ns; let none be made a-sham-ed that wait up-on Thee.

WORDS: Based on Psalm 55:22 and Psalm 16:8
MUSIC: *Birmingham,* from *Elijah,* Felix Mendelssohn,, 1846

Irregular

Hear Our Prayer, O Lord

Hear my prayer, O Lord, give ear to my supplications. – Psalm 143:1 KJV

Hear our prayer, O Lord, hear our prayer, O Lord; in-cline Thine ear to us, and grant us Thy peace.

WORDS: Based on Psalm 143:1
MUSIC: *Whelpton,* George Whelpton, 1897

Irregular

Let the Words of My Mouth

619

Let the words of my mouth, and the meditation of my heart, be acceptable in Thy sight. – Psalm 19:14 KJV

Let the words of my mouth and the med-i-ta-tion of my heart be ac-cept-a-ble in Thy sight, O Lord, my strength, and my Re-deem-er.

WORDS: Psalm 19:14
MUSIC: *Baumbach,* Adolph Baumbach, 1862

Irregular

620 Lead Me, Lord

Teach me Thy way, O Lord, and lead me in a plain path. – Psalm 27:11 KJV

Lead me, Lord, lead me in Thy righ-teous-ness;
make Thy way plain be-fore my face.
For it is Thou, Lord, Thou, Lord, on - ly, that
mak - est me dwell in safe - ty.

WORDS: Based on Psalm 5:8 and Psalm 4:8
MUSIC: *Lead Me, Lord,* Samuel Sebastian Wesley, 1861

Irregular

PRESENTATION OF OFFERING

621 Praise God, from Whom All Blessings Flow

Let every thing that hath breath praise the Lord. Praise ye the Lord! – Psalm 150:6 KJV

Praise God, from whom all bless-ings flow; praise Him all crea-

WORDS: Thomas Ken, 1709
MUSIC: *Old 100th,* (altered); attr. Louis Bourgeois, 1551

L.M.

tures here be - low; praise Him a - bove, ye, heav'n - ly

host; praise Fa - ther, Son, and Ho - ly Ghost. A - men.

PRESENTATION OF OFFERING

Praise God, from Whom All Blessings Flow 622

Let every thing that hath breath praise the Lord. Praise ye the Lord! – Psalm 150:6 KJV

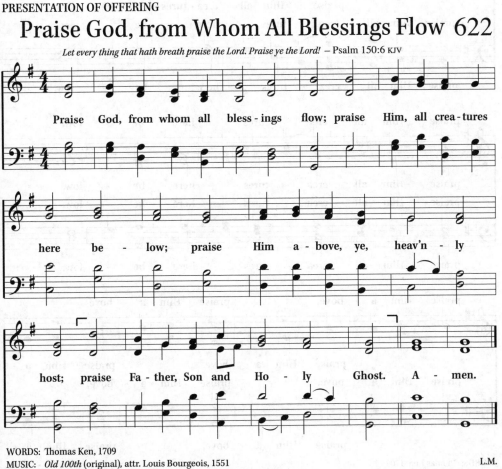

Praise God, from whom all bless - ings flow; praise Him, all crea - tures

here be - low; praise Him a - bove, ye, heav'n - ly

host; praise Fa - ther, Son and Ho - ly Ghost. A - men.

WORDS: Thomas Ken, 1709
MUSIC: *Old 100th* (original), attr. Louis Bourgeois, 1551
Other harmonizations of this tune, in a lower key, No. 21 and No. 544.

L.M.

623 Praise God, from Whom All Blessings Flow

Let every thing that hath breath praise the Lord. Praise ye the Lord! – Psalm 150:6 KJV

Praise God from whom all bless - ings flow,
Praise God from whom all bless - ings flow,
Praise God from whom all bless - ings flow,
Praise God from whom all bless - ings flow,

praise Him all crea - tures here be - low,
praise Him all crea - tures here be - low,
praise Him all crea - tures here be - low,
praise Him all crea - tures here be - low,

praise Him all crea - tures here be - low,
praise Him all crea - tures here be - low,
praise Him all crea - tures here be - low,

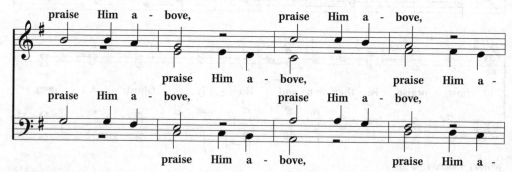

praise Him a - bove, praise Him a - bove,
praise Him a - bove, praise Him a -
praise Him a - bove, praise Him a - bove,
praise Him a - bove, praise Him a -

WORDS: Thomas Ken, 1709
MUSIC: *Dedication Anthem (606),* attr. Samuel Stanley, 19th c.

L. M. with Hallelujahs

praise Him a - bove, ye heav'n - ly host.
bove, praise Him a - bove ye heav'n - ly host.
praise Him a - bove, ye heav'n - ly host.
bove, praise Him a - bove, ye heav'n - ly host.
Praise Him a - bove, praise Him a - bove,
Praise
praise Him a - bove, ye heav'n - ly host. Praise
Fa - ther, Son, and Ho - ly Ghost. Praise
Praise Fa - ther, Son, and Ho - ly Ghost. Praise
Fa - ther, Son, and Ho - ly Ghost, praise
Praise Fa - ther, Son, and Ho - ly Ghost. Praise
Fa - ther, Son, and Ho - ly Ghost, praise

Praise God, from Whom All Blessings Flow 624

Let every thing that hath breath praise the Lord. Praise ye the Lord! – Psalm 150:6 KJV

Praise God, from whom all bless-ings flow. Praise Him, all crea-tures here be-low. Al - le - lu - ia! Al - le - lu - ia! Praise Him a - bove, ye heav'n-ly host. Praise Fa - ther, Son, and Ho - ly Ghost. Al - le - lu - ia! Al - le - lu - ia! Al - le - lu - ia! Al - le - lu - ia! Al - le - lu - ia! A - men.

WORDS: Thomas Ken, 1709, alt.
MUSIC: *Lasst Uns Erfreuen*, from *Geistliche Kirchengesäng*, 1623; harm. Ralph Vaughan Williams, 1906   L.M. with Alleluias
This tune in a lower key, No. 236.

625 Bless Thou the Gifts

As the Lord your God has blessed you, you shall give to Him. – Deuteronomy 15:14 ESV

Bless Thou the gifts our hands have brought; bless Thou the work our hearts have planned; ours is the faith, the will, the thought, the rest, O God, is in Thy hand.

WORDS: Samuel Longfellow, 1886
MUSIC: *Canonbury,* adapt. Robert Alexander Schumann, 1839

L.M.

626 All Things Come of Thee, O Lord

Through Him all things were made; without Him nothing was made that has been made. – John 1:3 NIV

All things come of Thee, O Lord, and of Thine own have we giv-en Thee.

WORDS: Based on 1 Chronicles 29:14
MUSIC: *Montgomery Lands,* Eric Wyse, 2001

Irregular

Holy, Holy, Holy

"Holy, holy, holy is the Lord Almighty; the whole earth is full of His glory." – Isaiah 6:3 NIV

WORDS: Based on Matthew 21:9 and Isaiah 6:3; *International Consultation on English Texts*, 1975
MUSIC: *Darnell,* Brian Darnell, 2003

Irregular

628 Holy, Holy, Holy

"Holy, holy, holy is the Lord Almighty; the whole earth is full of His glory." — Isaiah 6:3 NIV

WORDS: Based on Matthew 21:9 and Isaiah 6:3; *International Consultation on English Texts,* 1975
MUSIC: *Heilig Ist Der Herr,* Franz Peter Schubert, 1826, alt.

Irregular

629

It Is Finished

God paid a great price for you. – 1 Corinthians 7:23 CEV

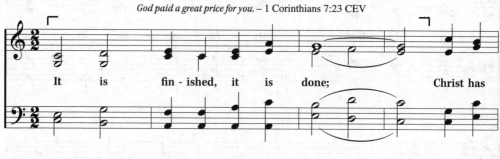

It is fin - ished, it is done; Christ has

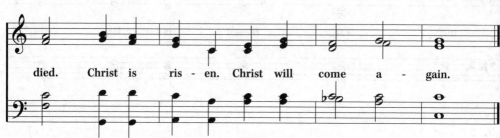

died. Christ is ris - en. Christ will come a - gain.

WORDS: Darrell A. Harris and Tom Howard, 2005; *International Commission on English in the Liturgy,* 1973
MUSIC: *Anamnesis,* Darrell A. Harris and Tom Howard, 2005
Irregular

630

We Remember His Death

Christ died...He was raised...and...He appeared. – 1 Corinthians 15:3-5 NIV

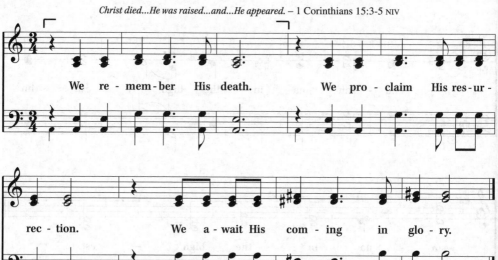

We re - mem - ber His death. We pro - claim His res - ur -

rec - tion. We a - wait His com - ing in glo - ry.

WORDS: *International Commission on English in the Liturgy,* 1973
MUSIC: *Tyne,* Eric Wyse, 2002
Irregular

The Lord's Prayer

Our Father in heaven, hallowed be Your name. – Matthew 6:9 NIV

Unison

Our Fa - ther, who art in heav'n, hal - lowed be Thy name.

Thy king-dom come. Thy will be done, on earth as it is in heav'n.

Give us this day or dai-ly bread. For-give us our debts as we for-give our debt-ors.

And lead us not in-to temp-ta-tion, but de-liv-er us from e-vil.

For Thine is the king-dom, the pow-er and the glo-ry

for-ev-er and for-ev-er. A-men.

WORDS: Based on Matthew 6:9-13,
MUSIC: *Conditor Alme Siderum*, Sarum plainsong, Mode IV, arr. Eric Wyse, 2005

Irregular

632

The Lord's Prayer

Our Father in heaven, hallowed be Your name. – Matthew 6:9 NIV

Our Fa - ther, which art in heav - en, hal - low - ed be Thy name. Thy king - dom come, Thy will be done on earth as it is in heav - en. Give us this day our dai - ly bread, and for -

WORDS: Based on Matthew 6:9 -13
MUSIC: *Malotte*, Albert Hay Malotte, 1935; arr. Eric Wyse, 2005

Irregular

LORD'S PRAYER
CONTEMPORARY LANGUAGE

633 Our Father in Heaven

Our Father in heaven, hallowed be Your name. – Matthew 6:9 NIV

Our Fa - ther in heav - en, hal - lowed be Your name, Your king - dom come, Your will be done on earth as in heav'n. Give us to - day our dai - ly bread. For - give us our sins as we for - give those who sin a - gainst us.

WORDS: Based on Matthew 6:9-13; *International Consultation on English Texts,* 1975
MUSIC: *Wildgrove,* Eric Wyse, 1999, alt.

Irregular

634

Lamb of God

Look, the Lamb of God, who takes away the sin of the world!. – John 1:29 NIV

Lamb of God, You take a-way the sins of the world; have mer-cy on us, have mer-cy on us. Lamb of God, You take a-way the sins of the world; have mer-cy on us, have mer-cy on us. Lamb of God, You take a-way the sins of the world; grant us peace.

WORDS: *International Consultation on English Texts,* 1975
MUSIC: *Nancarrow,* Eric Wyse, 1998

Irregular

God Be in My Head

635

God has chosen to make known...Christ in you, the hope of glory. – Colossians 1:27 NIV

God be in my head, and in my un-der-stand-ing.

God be in mine eyes and in my look-ing. God be in my

mouth and in my speak-ing. God be in my

heart, and in my think-ing. God be at mine end,

Optional

A - men.

and at my de-part-ing. A - men. A - men.
A - men. A - men.

A - men.

WORDS: From *Book of Hours*, 1514
MUSIC: *God Be in My Head*, Henry Walford Davies, 1910, alt.

Irregular

636 The Lord Bless You and Keep You

The Lord lift up His countenance upon you and give you peace. – Numbers 6:26 KJV

The Lord bless you and keep you; the Lord lift His coun-te-nance up-

on You, and give you peace, and give you peace,

and give you peace, and give you peace;

the Lord make His face to shine up-on you,

the Lord make His face to shine up-on you,

and be gra - cious un-to you, be gra-cious,

and be gra-cious, and be gra-cious,

the Lord be gra-cious, gra-cious un-to you.

WORDS: Based on Numbers 6:24-26
MUSIC: *Benediction*, Peter C. Lutkin, 1900

Irregular

637 Twofold Amen   Twofold Amen 638

A - men. A - men.

MUSIC: *Twofold*, Dresden

A - men. A - men.

MUSIC: *Twofold*, Greek

Threefold Amen

A - men.   A - men.   A -   men.

MUSIC: *Threefold*, Danish

640 Fourfold Amen

Blessed be the Lord for evermore. Amen, and Amen. – Psalm 89:52 KJV

A - men. A - men. A - men. A - men.

MUSIC: *Fourfold*, John Stainer, ca. 1870

641 Sevenfold Amen

Blessed be the Lord for evermore. Amen, and Amen. – Psalm 89:52 KJV

MUSIC: *Sevenfold*, John Stainer, ca. 1870

The Christian Life Hymnal – A Guide to the Indexes

Each index in the hymnal has been developed and designed to aid worshippers in quickly finding specific titles and to learn more about the hymns they sing. This brief guide provides a description of each index to help the user better understand the index and how to gain the most from it.

Scriptural Allusion Index (pp. 644-648)— This index provides scriptural references and allusions for each title. Some references may relate to a specific key word, thought, phrase, stanza or thought within the hymn; other references may allude to the overall content of the hymn or the topic under which it is found.

Hymn Tune Index (pp. 648-651)— Each title in a hymnal is given an identifying tune name by its composer or hymnal editor. The tune name may be of personal or family significance, relate to the hymn's history or usage, or something else entirely. This index lists tunes alphabetically for easy reference, along with the meter of the hymn.

Metrical Tune Index (pp. 651-654)— Just as every title in the hymnal has a tune name, each title has a metrical designation, or meter, as well. This numeric or alpha-numeric naming indicates and directly relates to the poetic meter or pulses, accents and cadences of the hymn lyrics. There are many different hymn meters in the hymnal. As a general rule, hymns having a meter identical to those of other hymns may be sung to those tunes. Hymns with "Irregular" meters have non-recurring pulses and accents in the lyrics and cannot be used with any other tune.

To further illustrate, let's look at "Amazing Grace" (No. 280), and "O God, Our Help in Ages Past" (No. 28), Both hymns have an 8.6.8.6 (C.M.) meter. Try singing the lyrics of "Amazing Grace" to the tune of "O God, Our Help in Ages Past". Now, try singing these hymns the other way, swapping text and tune. You will immediately notice how easily this can be done. The secret is in counting the number of words or syllables in each phrase of the lyrics. Here's how. Look again at the lyrics of "Amazing Grace", phrase by phrase:

1 2   3   4   5   6   7   8
A-maz-ing grace! How sweet the sound

1   2   3   4   5 6
that saved a wretch like me!

1 2   3   4   5   6   7   8
I once was lost, but now am found;

1   2   3   4 5 6
was blind, but now I see.

We can now indicate the meter of the hymn by writing the number of words and syllables of each phrase: 8.6.8.6 (C.M.). (The C.M. indicates Common Meter, the most common of the named hymn meters used to pair hymn lyrics with melodies.) C.M. is used as shorthand for 8.6.8.6. This index indicates the meter for every hymn. Take some time to discover other lyrics and tunes which can be used interchangeably. Doing so often brings new energy to the hymn singing.

Authors Composers, and Sources Index (pp. 654-659)— Basic information related to the people who wrote the hymns you sing is located directly beneath each hymn, including the name of the author and translator of the hymn text, composer and arranger of the music, and if applicable, information on the source of lyrics or music. All dates related to the hymn lyrics and music is contained on the hymn page. This index contains more complete information related to people and sources associated with the hymns, including birth and death dates or dates of sources from which they derived.

Church Year Index (pp. 659-661)— Time is generally measured by hour and day, month and season. Our activities generally are grouped according to time and season. The Church Year, or Christian Calendar, offers recurring times and opportunities for remembering and celebrating significant events of the Christian faith during times of worship. This index groups hymns appropriate for various seasons and events of the Church Year.

Topical Index (pp. 662-677)— Use this index to find hymns listed under a common topic or theme. You'll notice that many hymns are appropriate to use for different themes or topics. The index is cross-referenced for even easier use.

Hymn Titles and First Lines with Key (pp. 678-684)— This index is the most used of any hymnal, helping you to quickly find any title, along with its key. It also is useful when creating same-key or related key medleys.

GENESIS

1:1	237
1:14	579
1:16	76
1:31	241, 242, 243, 244
2:7	339
3:8	455
5:24	504
12:2	604
17:4-6	604
18:3	311
28:15	321
28:17	562
31:49	586, 587

EXODUS

3:5	67
3:6	16, 25
3:8	563
12:13	260
12:20	326
15:1	56, 181
15:2	11
15:11	27
15:13	374
15:26	365
16:4	581
16:32-34	548
19:05	378
20:3	501
20:11	241, 242
25:22	468
30:6	401
33:22	382
36:26	436

LEVITICUS

11:44	301, 302
14:4	264
17:11	255
26:11-12	246

NUMBERS

6:26	636
7:89	468

DEUTERONOMY

2:29	555
3:25	555
4:19	76
7:6	212
7:7-8	520
10:17	68
11:13-14	342
15:14	625
28:12	342
31:3	575
31:6	422, 575
31:8	422
32:3	29
32:12	421, 612
32:29	596
33:25	416
33:27	397

JOSHUA

1:6-7	575
1:9 3	37

RUTH

5:15	67, 68
24:15	598
24:24	340, 341, 436

RUTH

2:12	384

1 SAMUEL

2:9	355
2:10	78
6:11-13	14
6:12	13
15:22	496

2 SAMUEL

17:22	565
22:50	31, 545

1 KINGS

5:7	187
8:30	618
18:21	598
19:8	151

2 KINGS

4:3-4	224

1 CHRONICLES

16:8	19, 20
16:25	9
16:29	581
16:30-31	35
16:34	517
29:5	301, 302
29:11	10, 197
29:13	38
29:14	625, 626

2 CHRONICLES

15:15	323
19:9	448
20:6	597
29:13	38
29:30	70

NEHEMIAH

3:16	266
9:5	34, 252
12:46	144
13:22	467

JOB

9:8	528
11:7	502, 503
12:10	409
22:26	11
33:4	409
38:7	142

PSALMS

2:7	80
3:8	585
4:8	620
5:3	51
5:8	620
5:11	420
6:3	364, 365
9:1	31, 362

9:2	12
9:9	578
9:11	113
15:15	25
16:6	601
16:8	617
16:11	433, 557
17:8	385, 387, 388
17:15	554
18:1	60
18:2	78
18:16	516
18:30-32	13
19	240
19:1	238, 283
19:7	33
19:10	289
19:14	55, 619
20:7	306, 605
22:4	414, 597
22:27	26
22:28	606
23	369, 370, 371, 372
23:2	373
23:3	372
24	77
24:1	237
24:7	77, 193
25:1	333
25:4	303, 476
25:5	374
25:7	467
25:20	406
26:2	295, 296
26:7	545
26:8	320
27:1	425
27:5	382
27:11	476, 620
28:7	52
29:2	143
29:10	4
29:11	404, 588
30:1	516, 543
30:4	32, 47, 90, 610
31:20	381, 382
31:21	174
31:24	406
32:7	381
32:8	376, 421
32:11	24
33:6	245
33:7	420
33:9	245
33:12	599, 601, 604
33:20	387
34:18	457
35:28	30, 49, 50
36:9	288
37:5	313, 415, 474, 475
37:23	355
37:24	469
37:31	232
37:39	431
38:15	333
40:2	516, 519
40:3	508

40:5	594
40:8	232
41:13	640, 641
42	368
42:1	52
42:1-2	226
42:11	368
43:3	356
44:20-21	295, 296
45:1-2	53, 54
45:17	595
46	22, 23, 365
46:4	412
46:7	578, 597
46:10	364, 365, 609
47:6	29, 583, 584
47:7	241, 242
48:1-2	64
48:14	416, 421
49:15	394, 395
50:11	378
50:12	237
51:1-12	290
51:2	293
51:7	256, 261, 264
51:13	303, 351
55:17	458
55:18	363, 466
55:22	469, 539, 617
56:2	466
57:1	384
59:16	574
60:4	443
61:2-3	381
61:3	396
62:7	396
63:4	509
63:8	376
65:11	591
66:1	71
66:4	595
66:9	355, 356
66:16	507
67:1	590
67:3	595
68:4	29
68:18	181
68:19	416
68:35	27
69:2	299, 519
69:16	611
69:30	56, 545
69:34	236
71:1	365
71:1-2	406
71:2	600
71:20	338, 339
71:23	235
71:23-24	511
72	39, 79
72:17	19
72:19	37, 43
72:19-20	640, 641
73:25	386
73:28	426, 457
79:9	615
80:18	338, 339
84:11	577

(PSALMS)

85:6	338, 339
86:1	459
86:9	79
86:11	298
86:12	25, 111
87:3	319
88:13	51
89:1	33, 522
89:5	283
89:7	64
89:15	425, 536
89:52	640, 641
90:1	28
90:2	18
90:12	577, 596
91	366
91:1	381, 382, 387, 388
91:4	6, 384, 385
91:5	580
94:22	284
95:2	591
95:3	63
95:6	581
96:2	346, 347
96:3	602
96:4	9, 63
96:8	614, 615, 616
96:9	143
96:11	236
97	240, 603
97:6	283
97:9	63
97:12	610
98	92
98:3	26
98:4	71, 114
98:6	36
100	21
100:1	71
100:2	70
100:3	364, 365
100:4	591
100:5	273
102:26-27	428
103:1	36, 610, 627
103:2	363
103:4	466
103:11	273, 276
103:13	379
104:1	10, 35
104:2	528
104:33	29
104:34	55
105:1	33, 113
105:2	602
105:1-5	19, 20
106:1	517
107:1-2	268
107:8	593
107:9	541
107:22	545
107:30-31	600
107:31	594
109:21	611
109:30	510
112:6	539
113:4	606
116:1	61
117:1	595
118:1	517
118:9	605, 606
118:19-20	77
119:11	232, 233
119:17	5
119:18	229, 234
119:57	446
119:71	463
119:89	392
119:103-104	289
119:105	433
119:130	533
119:133	467
119:142	250
119:151	426, 457
119:172	30
121	15
121:7	636
122:2	549
126:6	360
130:1	299
130:20	8
134:1	144
136:7-8	76
138:1-2	8
138:4	79
139:1	295, 296
139:14	235
139:17-18	574
143:1	618
145:1	3
145:2	509
145:18	457
146:2	509
148	26, 236, 245
148:1	7, 238
148:13	25
149:25	83, 584
150	25, 26, 150
150:6	621, 622, 623, 624

PROVERBS

3:9	450
3:24	576
6:23	33
10:7	539
14:34	599
17:17	515
18:24	515
19:17	148
23:26	489, 490, 493
24:13	289

ECCLESIASTES

3:11	243, 244

SONG OF SOLOMON

2:1	538
5:10-16	200
5:13	538
5:38	538
6:10	53, 54

ISAIAH

1:18	257, 258, 259, 261, 264, 265
5:26	443, 444
6:3	1, 239, 579, 627, 628
6:8	350
6:9	2
7:14	72, 85, 87, 102, 110
9:6	69, 87, 110
9:7	83, 84
11:10	84
12:1	510
12:2	414
12:3	117
12:4	113, 589
12:5	508
18:3	443, 444
19:20	109
25:4	383, 394, 395
25:8	571
25:9	306
26:2	77
26:3	405, 407
26:4	284
26:9	439
28:16	316, 317, 318
30:29	89
32:2	170, 396
33:17	13
35:10	571, 583, 584
36:17	428
39:5	5
40:1	81
40:9	343
40:10	73, 74
40:11	370, 371, 373
40:22	528
40:26	76
40:31	366
41:17	227, 229
42:1	80
42:6	88
42:11-12	132
43:2	422, 600
43:25	260, 263, 290
44:3	228
44:22	260, 263
44:23	114, 236, 240
45:22	297, 417
48:17	408, 451
48:18	408, 412
49:6	88
49:13	81, 235, 238, 240
49:23	128
50:8	457
51:3	81
51:4	601
51:11	571
51:12	81
52:7	132
53:3	176, 178, 201
53:5	177, 525
53:6	294
53:11	354
55:1	226
57:15	310
57:19	426
58:8	573
58:11	413
60:2-3	4
60:3	88
60:16	128
60:20	431
61:1	75, 299, 343
61:10	251
62:4	567
62:11	73
63:9	520
63:16	262, 298
64:8	298
65:17	562
66:5	524
66:12	408, 412
70:14	72

JEREMIAH

1:7	352
1:8	422
6:16	380
8:22	383
10:10	451
13:16	613
15:20	287
23:5	136
23:29	230
25:30	603
31:3	276, 389
31:25	530, 531
32:18-19	27
50:2	443

LAMENTATIONS

3:22-23	33
3:41	333

EZEKIEL

34:26	342
36:25	309
36:26-27	217

DANIEL

12:3	351, 352
3:17	287

HOSEA

1:7	223

JOEL

3:10	461
3:16	78

MICAH

5:2	92, 95, 96, 117
5:5	126
6:8	471
7:8	431

NAHUM

1:7	3, 93, 400

HABAKKUK

1:12	612
2:20	608, 609
3:2	338
3:4	537

ZEPHANIAH

1:7	89, 608, 609

HAGGAI

2:4-5	224

ZECHARIAH

2:13	82
4:6	223
9:9	156
13:1	259, 261

MALACHI

2:6	252
3:16	266
3:17	212
4:2	573

MATTHEW
1:2 — 131
1:9-10 — 142
1:16 — 116
1:18 — 85, 97
1:20-21 — 129
1:21 — 95, 96, 102, 130
1:23 — 72, 87, 108
2:1-2 — 136
2:2 — 47, 140, 141
2:6 — 98
2:10 — 141
2:11 — 127, 134
3:16 — 324
3:17 — 80, 86
4:2 — 151
4:18-22 — 479
4:19 — 304
4:20 — 445
5:6 — 512, 541
5:16 — 506
6:9-13 — 631, 632, 633
6:11 — 544
6:13 — 454
6:21 — 489
6:24 — 598, 599
7:24 — 410, 411
8:19 — 300, 452, 477
9:10 — 248
9:12 — 286
9:21 — 513
9:36 — 8
9:37-38 — 593
10:32 — 207
10:38 — 270, 483
10:39 — 488
10:42 — 149
11:28 — 303, 462
11:28-29 — 530, 531
11:29 — 383, 444
12:37 — 619
13:34 — 152
13:38 — 592
13:39 — 591
14:14 — 149
14:17 — 490
14:32-33 — 391
16:24 — 270, 484
16:26 — 435
16:31 — 214
17:20 — 432
17:23 — 187
18:20 — 375, 590
21:5 — 156
21:9 — 153, 154, 155, 627
21:15 — 153
22:9 — 149
22:37 — 480
24:14 — 353
24:30 — 210, 211, 212
24:35 — 324
24:44 — 213
25:6 — 550
25:13 — 213, 354
25:23 — 354
25:31 — 214
25:40 — 148
26:25-27 — 330
26:26 — 327
26:28 — 177
26:30 — 159, 327
26:36 — 158, 159, 455
26:38 — 158
27:29 — 169
28:1 — 185, 186
28:5-7 — 526
28:6-7 — 184
28:8 — 182
28:9 — 185, 186
28:16-20 — 344
28:19 — 353
28:20 — 375

MARK
1:9 — 555
1:15 — 194
1:17 — 478, 479
2:6 — 98
2:12 — 518
2:17 — 286
4:39 — 424
8:31 — 201
8:34 — 477, 484, 486
8:36 — 385, 435
9:23 — 432
9:31 — 193
10:14 — 103, 106, 379
10:28 — 483
10:35-40 — 473
10:45 — 484
11:9 — 153, 154, 155
11:10 — 66
13:35 — 215
14:22-25 — 327
14:32 — 455
14:32-42 — 159
15:17 — 169
15:25 — 161
16:6 — 183
16:12 — 485
16:15 — 344

LUKE
1:4 — 532
1:16 — 353, 354
1:27 — 83, 85
1:28 — 90
1:30-33 — 108, 145
1:31 — 72, 102
1:32 — 141
1:35 — 129
1:42 — 135
1:47 — 94
1:49 — 310
1:50 — 273
1:69 — 78
2:4 — 83
2:6 — 102, 107
2:7 — 109, 119, 122, 123, 142, 308
2:7-8 — 89
2:7-11 — 104, 105, 107
2:8 — 97, 124, 125
2:8-11 — 120
2:8-14 — 111, 112
2:9 — 88, 100
2:9-11 — 103, 133
2:10 — 98, 100, 269
2:10-11 — 101, 121
2:11 — 83, 94, 95, 96, 97, 124, 125
2:12 — 104, 105, 135
2:13 — 93, 120
2:13-14 — 19, 99, 127
2:14 — 100, 126
2:15 — 90, 106
2:15-18 — 134
2:16 — 89, 115
2:17 — 92, 132
2:17-18 — 110
2:18 — 112
2:19 — 122, 123
2:20 — 97, 131
2:21 — 99
2:29-30 — 110
2:32 — 101
4:4 — 331
4:18 — 286
4:22 — 200
5:11 — 445, 452, 481
5:30 — 345
5:31 — 287
6:47-49 — 411
7:34 — 248
7:39 — 345
8:25 — 391
8:35 — 474, 475
9:10 — 359
9:22 — 176
9:23 — 483, 486
9:32 — 567
9:35 — 80
9:57 — 452
10:2 — 350, 593
10:20 — 266
11:2-4 — 631, 632, 633
12:6 — 378
12:48 — 450
14:13-14 — 139
14:21 — 139
14:27 — 270, 486
14:33 — 305, 450
15:2 — 345
15:10 — 269
15:18 — 307
18:16 — 103
18:28 — 305, 446, 481
19:9 — 323
21:28 — 213
22:13-15 — 330
22:17-20 — 328, 329, 331, 332
22:19 — 328
22:20 — 630
22:39-46 — 160, 164, 455, 456, 459
22:40 — 454
22:44 — 518
23:33 — 135, 167, 523
24:4-7 — 145, 146, 185, 186
24:6 — 184
24:27 — 233
24:29 — 575, 576, 580
24:34 — 188, 189
24:47 — 377
24:49 — 220
25:26 — 183
38:39 — 311

JOHN
1:1 — 86
1:3 — 243, 244, 626
1:4 — 41
1:7 — 173
1:9 — 348
1:11 — 137
1:14 — 44, 65
1:16-17 — 279
1:19 — 175
1:29 — 634
1:33 — 225
1:36 — 175, 634
2:11 — 173
3:3 — 271
3:16 — 91, 253, 513
4:14 — 229, 288, 413
4:21, 23-24 — 2
4:35 — 358, 593
4:42 — 178, 257
5:17 — 506
5:19 — 453
6:37 — 293
6:50 — 231
6:63 — 234
6:68 — 34
7:33 — 192
7:37 — 230, 532
8:12 — 348, 481, 542
8:33 — 335, 336
8:51 — 231, 390, 391, 397
8:58 — 400, 427, 429
9:4 — 357, 505, 506
9:5 — 542
10:3 — 373
10:9 — 308
10:11 — 157, 482
10:14 — 69, 370, 371, 372
10:15 — 373, 374
10:16 — 361
10:27 — 476
11:4 — 56
11:25 — 552
11:26 — 231
11:28 — 304
11:40 — 432, 433, 434
11:50-52 — 334
12:12-13 — 147
12:13 — 48, 154, 155
12:26 — 300, 446
12:27 — 158
12:28 — 80
12:32 — 162, 163, 203
12:35 — 357
12:46 — 348, 357, 358, 360, 361
13:1 — 376
14:1 — 414, 415
14:2 — 551, 557, 560, 572
14:3 — 557
14:6 — 251, 252
14:13 — 393
14:14 — 227
14:16 — 220, 228
14:19 — 192
14:26 — 222
14:27 — 405, 407
15:5 — 459
15:9 — 277, 278, 294, 295
15:10-11 — 62
15:13 — 157, 277, 401, 460, 482, 515
15:15 — 401, 460, 534
16:16 — 192
17:3 5 — 40, 572
17:11 — 334, 376
17:24 — 434, 558
19:2 — 169
19:17 — 167, 525
19:18 — 160
19:25 — 170
19:30 — 629
19:37 — 171, 172
20:14 — 187

(JOHN)

20:14-20	456
20:22	225
21:4	187
21:15	61

ACTS

1:3	190
1:8	222, 349
1:14	458
2:4	217, 222
2:21	512
2:23	161
2:24	182
2:36	196, 204, 205
2:42	330
3:1	458
3:19	292, 294
4:12	494
4:31	221
5:20	494
5:42	75, 76, 138
7:33	67, 68
8:4	522
8:16	561
8:35	152
10:34-35	335, 336
10:36	152
10:44	221
11:3	345
13:23	84
13:26	494
13:32	138, 343
13:32-33	74, 75
13:33	86
15:11	279
16:9	356
16:31	306
17:24	325
18:10	377
20:21	315
20:32	403
26:22	387

ROMANS

2:11	335, 336
3:24	280, 281
3:25	251
4:16	280, 281
4:25	254
5:5	218
5:6	150, 254
5:8	174, 247, 418, 525
5:11	91, 101
5:18	254
5:20	279
6:4	324
6:10	285
6:13	305, 528
8:9	314, 389
8:17	403
8:22	344
8:24	569, 570
8:29	470
8:31	590
8:34	263
8:35	275
8:37	362, 603
8:38	276
8:38-39	398
8:39	501, 518
9:4	430

10:9	196, 346, 347
11:33	292, 502, 503
12:1	301, 302, 325, 480
12:2	481, 635
13:1	607
13:11	550, 572
14:7	465
14:7-9	534
14:8	492
14:12	495
14:17	320
15:8	430
15:11	25
15:20	316, 317, 319, 321
15:33	404
16:26	504

1 CORINTHIANS

1:2-3	399
1:17	166
1:17-18	203
1:18	168, 177, 525
1:23-24	312
1:30	249
2:2	165, 312, 521
2:10	502, 503
2:16	502, 503
3:11	316, 317, 318
3:16	582
3:22-23	398
4:2	495, 496
5:7	326
5:8	326
6:20	265, 301, 302
7:23	629
8:6	474, 475
9:19	349
10:16	329, 630
11:1	470
11:16-18	330
11:23-25	328, 329, 331
11:24	332
13:12	553, 554, 559
15:3-5	630
15:4-5	189
15:20	184, 190
15:54	191
15:54-55	188
15:57	453
16:13	340, 341, 440, 441

2 CORINTHIANS

1:10	390
1:11	464
2:14	438
3:4	429
3:5	386
3:11	410
3:18	297, 558, 562
4:4-6	558, 561
4:6	356, 536, 537, 541, 542, 577
4:11	553
4:18	570
5:1	39
5:7	417, 461
5:8	563
5:9	491, 492
5:14	389
5:15	256, 482, 491, 492
5:17	514
5:18-20	91, 93
5:19	257

6:2	308
6:16	582
7:1	430
8:5	123
8:9	113, 147, 282, 556
9:8	490, 498
10:4	410
10:16	319, 320, 321, 322
12:9	416, 461
13:4	147

GALATIANS

1:3-5	31
2:19-20	535
2:20	165, 253, 394, 395, 513, 514, 518, 524
3:13	174, 179, 285, 511
3:28	334, 335, 336
3:29	403
4:4-5	150
4:6	216
4:8-9	541, 542, 544
4:19	470
5:1	523
5:16	221
5:24	300
5:25	217, 218
6:1	359
6:9	505, 506
6:14	162, 163, 171, 172, 288, 312, 314, 315

EPHESIANS

1:3	51, 594, 621, 622, 623, 624
1:5	420
1:6	64, 65
1:7	262, 282
1:13	250, 252, 487
1:21	43
2:6	447, 448, 449
2:7	247
2:8	281, 512, 556
2:13	258
2:20	318
3:12	417
3:16	462, 463, 466
3:17-18	272
3:17-19	546
3:19	164
3:20	498
4:1	495
4:8	193
4:30	511
5:2	274
5:8	337, 504
5:8-14	471
5:18	219
5:18-20	219
5:19	45
5:20	239, 583, 584
5:25	275
5:31	546
6:10	448
6:10-11	449
6:12-13	449
6:13	436
6:13-14	440, 441

PHILIPPIANS

1:3	331
1:9	463

1:11	535
1:13	488
1:15	447, 543
1:21	218, 380, 534
2:2-10	166
2:3	540
2:5	497
2:5-7	137
2:5-8	44
2:6	527
2:7	147
2:8	137, 167, 168
2:9	202, 399
2:9-11	49, 50, 57, 58, 59, 130, 196
2:10	39, 207, 208
2:15	473, 476
3:7	171, 172, 386, 432, 437, 439, 440, 441, 442
3:8	540
3:10	190, 397, 499
3:13-14	315
3:14	447
4:4	94
4:6	460
4:7	408
4:13	461

COLOSSIANS

1:10	492
1:11	462, 463, 465
1:12-14	471, 473, 476
1:13	253, 419
1:15	250, 487
1:20	259, 524
1:22	418
1:27	566, 635
2:2	198, 543, 544, 566,
2:5	415
2:6	485
2:9	527
2:15	204
3:2	314
3:3	398
3:11	529
3:15	363, 589
3:16	497
3:17	377

1 THESSALONIANS

4:16	552
4:17	191, 557
5:10	554
5:23	404
5:28	586, 587

2 THESSALONIANS

1:7	216
2:13	274
3:13	505
3:16	404, 588
4:18	422

1 TIMOTHY

1:12	464
1:14	282, 283
1:15	246, 346, 347
1:17	18
2:1-2	607
2:3-4	464
2:5	177
3:15	582

(1 TIMOTHY)
3:16 — 146, 150
4:12 — 500
6:12 — 438, 451
6:15 — 206, 208, 209

2 TIMOTHY
1:7 — 405, 406
1:12 — 535
1:14 — 227
2:2 — 465
2:3 — 438, 439
2:4 — 437
2:15 — 487
2:19 — 392, 423
2:21 — 498
3:16 — 233
4:12 — 424
4:17 — 464
4:18 — 194, 419
6:12 — 439

TITUS
2:4 — 546
2:12 — 480, 491
2:13 — 248, 554
2:13-14 — 179, 198, 262
2:14 — 274
3:4-5 — 519
3:5 — 292, 512

HEBREWS
1:5 — 86
1:6 — 98
1:12 — 427, 428
2:9 — 206
2:9-10 — 202
2:12 — 3
2:18 — 454, 462
2:20 — 82
4:1 — 367
4:3 — 418
4:7 — 304
4:9 — 228, 367, 564, 565
4:11 — 564, 565
4:12 — 230
4:16 — 402
5:9 — 504
6:19 — 423

7:19 — 380
7:25 — 246, 307
7:27-28 — 285
9:14 — 309, 310
9:20 — 627, 628
9:22 — 255, 524
9:28 — 185, 214
10:19 — 468
10:22 — 309, 362
10:37 — 340, 341
11:1 — 569
11:6 — 322, 559
11:10 — 549, 550, 552
11:13 — 547
11:16 — 564, 565, 567, 570
12:1 — 547
12:2 — 162, 163, 170, 297, 367, 417
12:3 — 55
12:14 — 472
13:5 — 375
13:8 — 427, 429, 529
13:12 — 160
13:14 — 560
13:15 — 66, 589

JAMES
1:17 — 13, 14, 239, 592, 621, 622, 623, 624
1:18 — 489, 490, 493
1:22-25 — 411
2:17 — 487
4:8 — 380, 493
5:19 — 351

1 PETER
1:3 — 7, 271
1:8 — 62, 94
1:15 — 472
1:15-16 — 472
1:18-19 — 268
1:23 — 392
2:7 — 388, 399
2:9 — 537
2:16 — 605
2:21 — 445
2:24 — 265, 285, 294
3:15 — 521
3:18 — 168

4:7 — 573
4:11 — 51
5:4 — 553
5:7 — 393, 400, 469, 617
5:10 — 337
5:14 — 447

2 PETER
1:4 — 430
1:11 — 419
1:17 — 197
3:9 — 311
3:13 — 558
3:18 — 499, 562

1 JOHN
1:5 — 425
1:7 — 255, 267, 471
1:9 — 291, 293
2:6 — 485
2:8 — 358, 360, 361
2:28 — 219
2:29 — 271, 272
3:1 — 7, 379, 561
3:2 — 210, 211, 551, 553
3:14 — 508, 556
3:16 — 157
4:4 — 521
4:8-9 — 278
4:10 — 174
4:16 — 40, 41, 42, 50
4:18 — 546
4:19 — 60, 61, 62, 532
5:4 — 434
5:5 — 453
5:20 — 277, 278, 279

3 JOHN
2 — 363, 364

JUDE
1:3 — 322
2:3 — 359

REVELATION
1:5-6 — 510
1:6 — 73, 613, 614, 616
1:7 — 210, 211, 216
1:8 — 4, 80, 86

1:16 — 53
1:18 — 526
2:10 — 500
2:17 — 548
3:12 — 548, 549, 551, 552
3:20 — 313
4:1 — 199
4:8 — 1, 58
4:11 — 9, 57, 58, 59
5:9 — 64, 268, 507
5:12 — 180
5:13 — 66
7:9 — 195
7:10 — 209
7:11 — 68
7:14 — 256
11:15 — 204, 205
12:11 — 258, 442
14:13 — 547
14:15 — 350
15:2-3 — 507
15:3-4 — 4
15:4 — 66, 70
15:5 — 199
16:15 — 215
17:14 — 119, 145, 207, 208, 325
19:1 — 190, 195, 585
19:5 — 209
19:6 — 17, 195
19:11 — 199
19:12 — 46
19:16 — 119, 206
21:2 — 549
21:3 — 246
21:5 — 596
21:6 — 267
21:23 — 559, 560
21:24 — 89
21:25 — 568
22:1 — 307, 559
22:2 — 563
22:12 — 73
22:13 — 86
22:14 — 568
22:16 — 118
22:17 — 291
22:20 — 73

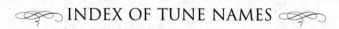

INDEX OF TUNE NAMES

Aberystwyth, 7.7.7.7 D — 395
Acclaim, 8.8.8.5 — 65
Ackley, 7.6.7.6.7.6.7.4 with Refrain — 526
Adelaide, 5.4.5.4 D — 98
Adeste Fideles, Irregular with Refrain — 90
Adeste Fideles (Refrain only), 7.7.10 — 47
Adore Thee, Irregular — 180
Aletta, 7.7.7.7 — 233
All for Jesus, 8.7.8.7 — 480
All Saint New, 8.6.8.6 D (C.M.D.) — 442
All the Way, 8.7.8.7 D with Repeat — 421
All Things Bright and Beautiful,
  7.6.7.6 with Refrain — 244
All to Christ, 6.6.7.7 with Refrain — 265

All Your Anxiety, Irregular with Refrain — 469
Amazing Grace (New Britain), 8.6.8.6 (C.M.) — 280
America (Thesaurus Musicus),
  6.6.4.6.6.6.4 — 599, 604
Anamnesis, Irregular — 29
Anchor, 10.9.10.9 with Refrain — 423
Angel's Story, 7.6.7.6 D — 446
Antioch, 8.6.8.6 (C.M.) with Repeat — 92
Any Room, 8.7.8.7 with Refrain — 308
Ariel, 8.8.6.8.8.6 with Repeat — 44
Arlington, 8.6.8.6 (C.M.) — 439
Armageddon, 6.5.6.5 D with Refrain — 436
As the Deer, Irregular with Refrain — 52
Assam, 10.10.10.8 — 300

Assurance, 9.10.9.9.9 with Refrain — 362
Aurelia, 7.8.7.8 D — 315
Austrian Hymn, 8.7.8.7 D — 319
Away in a Manger (Mueller), 11.11.11.11 — 105
Azmon, 8.6.8.6 (C.M.) — 49

Balm in Gilead, 7.6.7.6 with Refrain — 383
Barnard, 8.7.8.7 D with Refrain — 450
Batchellor (Onslow), 8.8.8.8 (L.M.) — 545
Battle Hymn, Irregular with Refrain — 603
Baumbach, Irregular — 619
Be Still, Irregular — 609
Be Still and Know, 8.8.8 — 365
Beacon Hill, 8.7.8.7 with Refrain — 473

Beatitudo, 8.6.8.6 (C.M.) 471
Beatty, Irregular 67
Beautiful Name, Irregular with Refrain 130
Beautiful to Walk, 11.10.11.10 with Refrain 425
Beecher, 8.7.8.7 D 2, 40
Belle Rive, 6.5.6.5 D 208
Belmont Park, Irregular 612
Benediction, Irregular 636
Benton Harbor, 8.7.8.7 with Refrain 257
Bethany, 6.4.6.4.6.6.6.4 426
Beulah Land, 14.13.14.10 with Refrain 428
Binghampton, 10.11.11.11 with Refrain 403
Birmingham, Irregular 617
Blaenwern, 8.7.8.7 D 41
Bless the Lord, Irregular 36
Blessed Name, 8.8.8.8 (L.M.) with Refrain 37
Blessed Quietness, 8.7.8.7 with Refrain 228
Blessings, 11.11.11.11 with Refrain 594
Blott En Dag, Irregular 416
Born Again, Irregular with Refrain 271
Boundless Salvation,
    11.11.11.11 with Repeat 250
Bourne, 10.10.10.10 with Refrain 489
Boylston, 6.6.8.6 (S.M.) 495
Bradbury, 8.7.8.7 D 373
Branle de l'Officiel, 7.7.7.7 with Refrain 120
Bread of Life, 6.4.6.4 D 231, 327
Brentwood, Irregular 611
Bring a Torch, Irregular 134
Bring Them In, 8.8.8.8 (L.M.) with Refrain 361
Bryn Calfaria, 8.7.8.7.4.7 with Repeat 205
Bullinger, 8.5.8.3 429
Bunessan, 5.5.5.3 D 115
By and By, Irregular with Refrain 569

Call for Reapers, 8.7.8.7 with Refrain 358
Calling Today, 10.8.10.7 with Refrain 304
Calvary, 9.9.9.4 with Refrain 523
Camacha, 6.4.6.4.6.6.6.4 476
Canonbury, 8.8.8.8 (L.M.) 465, 625
Cantique De Noel, Irregular 129
Carol, 8.6.8.6 D (C.M.D.) 100
Castle, Irregular 123
Cedar Lane, Irregular 616
Channels, 8.7.8.7 with Refrain 498
Chautauqua, 7.7.7.7.4 with Refrain 579
China, 7.7.7.7 with Refrain 274
Christ Arose, 6.5.6.4 with Refrain 182
Christ Returneth, Irregular with Refrain 215
Christmas, 8.6.8.6 (C.M.) with Repeat 125
Christmas Song, 6.6.6.6.12.12 135
Christus Der Ist Mein Leben, 7.6.7.6 431
Cleansing Fountain, 8.6.8.6 D (C.M.D.) 259
Clifton, 12.9.12.9 with Refrain 561
Cloninger, 8.8.10.8 106
Close to Thee, 8.7.8.7 with Refrain 493
Closer Walk, Irregular with Refrain 461
Comforter, 12.12.12.6 with Refrain 220
Coming Home, 8.5.8.5 with Refrain 307
Conditor Alme Siderum, 8.8.8.8 (L.M.) 76
Conditor Alme Siderum, Irregular 631
Consolation, 11.10.11.10 574
Consolator, 11.10.11.10 402
Constancy, 8.7.8.7 with Refrain 481
Converse, 8.7.8.7 D 460
Coronation, 8.6.8.6 (CM) with Repeat 57
Cradle Song, 11.11.11.11 104
Cranham, Irregular 122
Creation, 8.8.8.8 D (L.M.D.) 240
Crimond, 8.6.8.6 (C.M.) 369
Cross of Jesus, 8.7.8.7 168

Crowning Day, Irregular with Refrain 214
Crucifer, 10.10 with Refrain 203
Crucifix, 7.6.7.6 D 294, 596
Crucifixion, 8.7.8.7 162
Crusader's Hymn (St. Elizabeth), Irregular 53
Cwm Rhondda, 8.7.8.7.4.7 with Repeat 413
Cwm Rhondda, 8.7.8.7.8.7. with Repeat 337
Cymraeg, 8.7.8.7 D 254

Darnell, Irregular 627
Darwall's 148th, 6.6.6.6.8.8 43, 206
Dedication Anthem
    8.8.8.8 (L.M.) with Hallelujahs 23
Deep River, Irregular 555
Deeper and Deeper, Irregular 502
Deeper, Deeper, 10.5.10.5 with Refrain 503
Deirdre 8.8.8.8 D (L.M.D.) 6
Deliverance, 10.10.10.10 with Refrain 287
Dennis, 6.6.8.6 (S.M.) 334
Diadem, 8.6.8 (C.M.) with Repeat & Refrain 58
Diademata, 6.6.8.6 D (S.M.D.) 46, 449, 488
Divinum Mysterium, 8.7.8.7.8.7.7 80, 86
Dix, 7.7.7.7 with Refrain 141, 595
Dix, 7.7.7.7.7.7 141, 595
Dominus Regit Me, 8.7.8.7 371
Down Ampney, 6.6.11 D 216
Duke Street, 8.8.8.8 (L.M.) 20, 39
Dunbar, 8.8.8.6 with Refrain 491
Duncannon, 8.6.8.6 (C.M.) with Refrain 165

Easter Hymn, 7.7.7.7 with Alleluias 183, 184
Ebenezer (Ton-y-Botel), 8.7.8.7 D 272, 321, 598
Ein' Feste Burg (Isometric), Irregular 22
Ein' Feste Burg (Rhythmic), Irregular 23
El Nathan, 8.6.8.6 (C.M.) with Refrain 535
Elizabeth, Irregular 534
Ellacombe, 7.6.7.6 D 153
Ellacombe, 8.6.8.6 D (C.M.D.) 186, 241
Ellers, 10.10.10.10 296, 588
Ellesdie, 8.7.8.7 D 350, 483
Endeavor, 9.8.8.9 with Refrain 586
Endless Song, 8.7.8.7 with Refrain 509
Engleberg, 10.10.10 with Alleluias 56
Eola, 8.7.8.7 with Refrain 232
Ermuntre Dich Mein Schwacher,
    8.7.8.7.8.8.7.7 88
Es Flog Ein Kleins Waldvögelein, 7.6.7.6 D 79, 592
Es Ist Ein Ros', 7.6.7.6.6.7.6 84
Es Ist Ein Ros', 7.6.7.6 with Refrain 85
Evangel, 7.6.7.6 D with Refrain 532
Eventide, 10.10.10.10 575
Evergreen Shore, 8.6.8.6 (C.M.) 564
Everlasting Love, 7.7.7.7 D with Repeat 398
Every Day, 7.9.7.9 with Refrain 419
Exaltation, 11.10.11.10 with Refrain 312

Face to Face, 8.7.8.7 with Refrain 553
Faithfulness, 11.10.11.10 with Refrain 33
Father's Love, Irregular 157
Festal Song, 6.6.8.6 (S.M.) 340, 583
Fill Me Now, 8.7.8.7 with Refrain 219
Finlandia, 10.10.10.10.10.10 364
Finlandia, 11.10.11.10.11.10 444
Finto, Irregular with Refrain 252
Fischer, 11.11.11.11 with Refrain 264
Fisher, 7.7.7.9 with Refrain 278
Flemming, 11.11.11.6 8
Follow, 10.7.10.7 with Refrain 133
Follow On, Irregular with Refrain 452
Footsteps, 9.4.9.4 with Refrain 445
Forest Green, 8.6.8.6 D (C.M.D.) 96, 242

Fortitude, 6.5.6.5 D with Refrain 454
Foundation, 11.11.11.11 392
Fourfold Amen 640
Friend, 8.7.8.7 D 515
Fürchte Dich Nicht, 8.8.8.6 407

Galilee, 8.7.8.7 478
Garden, Irregular with Refrain 456
Garden of Prayer, 10.9.10.9 with Refrain 455
Garton, 6.7.6.7 91
Geibel, 7.6.7.6 D with Refrain 440
Germany (Gardiner), 8.8.8.8 (L.M.) 149, 251
Give Me Jesus (Spiritual),
    Irregular with Refrain 435
Give Me Jesus (Sweney),
    8.7.8.7 D with Refrain 385
Gladness, 10.10.10.10 with Refrain 275
Gloria, 7.7.7.7 with Refrain 99
Gloria in Excelsis, Irregular 613
Glorious Name, 8.7.8.7 with Refrain 38
Glory Song, 10.10.10.10 with Refrain 566
Glory to His Name, 9.9.9.5 with Refrain 524
Glory-Land, 10.8.10.8 with Refrain 558
Go Tell It, 7.6.7.6 with Refrain 132
God Be in My Head, Irregular 635
God Cares, 8.6.8.6 (C.M.) with Refrain 393
God Is So Good, 4.4.4.5 517
God Leads Us, 11.8.11.8 with Refrain 422
God Rest Ye Merry, Irregular with Refrain 116
Golden Bells, 8.8.11 D with Refrain 571
Gordon, 11.11.11.11 61
Gott Ist Die Liebe, 5.5.5.4 with Refrain 253
Great Physician, 8.7.8.7 with Refrain 286
Greatorex, Irregular 614
Greensleeves, 8.7.8.7.6.8.6.7 with Refrain 110
Greenwell, 8.8.8.7 263
Grosser Gott, Wir Loben Dich, 7.8.7.8.7.7 3

Hagen, 7.7.7.7 with Repeat 118
Hamburg, 8.8.8.8 (L.M.) 171
Hankey, 7.6.7.6 D with Refrain 522
Hanover, 10.10.11.11 209
Hanson Place, 8.7.8.7 with Refrain 559
Happy Day, 8.8.8.8 (L.M.) with Refrain 323
Harper Memorial (No, Not One),
    10.6.10.6 with Refrain 401
Harvest, 12.11.12.11 with Refrain 360
He Is Exalted, Irregular 63
He Is Lord, Irregular 196
He Leadeth Me, 8.8.8.8 (L.M.) with Refrain 374
He Lifted Me, 8.8.8.6 with Refrain 519
Heaven, 8.7.8.7 with Refrain 557
Heilig Ist Der Herr, Irregular 628
Helmsley, 8.7.8.7.4.7 with Repeat 211
Hendon, 7.7.7.7.7 521
Hendon, 7.7.7.7 with Repeat 302
Herzliebster Jesu, 11.11.11.5 176
Hiding in Thee, 11.11.11.11 with Refrain 381
Higher Ground, 8.8.8.8 (L.M.) with Refrain 447
Himself, 6.5.6.5 D with Refrain 528
Hingham, 11.10.11.10 with Refrain 384
Holiness, 6.5.6.5 D 472
Holy Ground, Irregular 68
Holy Manna, 8.7.8.7 D 581
Horsley, 8.6.8.6 (C.M.) 160, 200
Hosanna, 8.8.8.8 (L.M.) with Refrain 48
Hudson, 8.6.8.6 (C.M.) with Refrain 525
Humility (Oxford), 7.7.7.7 with Refrain 121
Hursley, 8.8.8.8 (L.M.) 577
Hyfrydol, 8.7.8.7 D 42, 74, 195, 238
Hyfrydol, 8.7.8.7 with Refrain 248

Hymn to Joy, 8.7.8.7 D — 190, 235

I Am Thine, 10.7.10.7 with Refrain — 309
I Can Safely Go, 11.11.11.11 with Refrain — 375
I Know a Fount, Irregular — 267
I Love Thee, 11.11.11.11 — 60
I Shall Know Him, 14.11.14.11 with Refrain — 554
I Will Praise Him, 8.7.8.7 with Refrain — 510
If Jesus Goes, Irregular with Refrain — 355
Il Est Né, 7.8.7.7 with Refrain — 102
I'm So Glad, Irregular — 543
In Babilone, 8.7.8.7 D — 199, 201
In Christ Alone, 8.8.8.8 D (L.M.D.) — 390
In Dulci Jubilo, Irregular — 94
Ira, 8.6.8.6 (C.M.) — 349
Irby, 8.7.8.7.7.7 — 83
Italian Hymn, 6.6.4.6.6.6.4 — 4, 344
Ivanoff, Irregular — 610
Iverson, Irregular — 221

Jesu, Meine Freude, Irregular — 388
Jesu, Meine Zuversicht, 7.8.7.8 with Refrain — 329
Jesus Saves, 7.6.7.6.7.7.7.6 — 346
Jesus, I Come, Irregular — 299
Jewels, 8.6.8.5 with Refrain — 212
Joy Has Dawned, 7.6.7.6 D — 101
Joyful Song, Irregular with Refrain — 64
Judson, Irregular with Refrain — 9
Jüngst, Irregular with Refrain — 117

Kenosis, 6.6.6.6.8.6 with Repeat — 482
Kings of Orient, 8.8.8.6 with Refrain — 140
Kingsfold, 8.6.8.6 D (C.M.D.) — 146, 147, 530
Kirkpatrick, 11.8.11.8 with Refrain — 382
Knapp, 8.6.8.6 (C.M.) with Refrain — 261
Kneel at the Cross, 9.6.9.6 with Refrain — 310
Kremser, 12.11.12.11 — 32
Kremser, 12.11.12.12 — 590

Lamb of God, 8.8.8.8 (L.M.) with Refrain — 175
Lancashire 7.6.7.6 D — 185, 437, 451
Land of Rest, 8.6.8.6 (C.M.) — 281, 549, 570
Landas, 8.6.8.6 (C.M.) with Refrain — 418
Lasst Uns Erfreuen,
    8.8.8.8 (L.M.) with Alleluias — 19, 236, 624
Lauda Anima, 8.7.8.7.8.7 — 12
Laudate Dominum (Parry), 10.10.11.11 — 26
Laudes Domini, 6.6.6.6.6.6 — 51
Lead Me, Lord, Irregular — 620
Leave It There, 14.11.14.11 with Refrain — 466
Lemmel, 9.8.9.8 with Refrain — 297
Lenox, 6.6.6.6.8.8 with Repeat — 246
Leoni, 6.6.8.4 D — 16
Let Us Break Bread, Irregular with Refrain — 330
Lifeline, 10.10.10.11 with Refrain — 351
Lift Every Voice, Irregular — 602
Light of the World, 11.8.11.8 with Refrain — 42
Limpsfield 7.3.7.3.7.7.7.3 — 347
Little Is Much, 8.7.8.7 with Refrain — 490
Living, 10.10.10.10 with Refrain — 492
Llanfair, 7.7.7.7 with Alleluias — 25, 193, 245
Lobe Den Herren, Irregular — 11
Love Found a Way, 8.4.8.4 D with Refrain — 520
Love of God, 8.8.8.8.8.6.8.6 with Refrain — 276
Lovely Name, 10.10.10.9 with Refrain — 529
Lower Lights, 8.7.8.7 with Refrain — 357
Lowliness, 7.7.7.7 with Refrain — 145
Lux Benigna, 10.4.10.4.10.10 — 433
Lyngham, 8.6.8.6 (C.M.) with Repeat — 50
Lyons, 10.10.11.11 — 10

Maccabaeus, 10.11.11.11 with Refrain — 188

Madrid, 6.6.6.6 D — 45
Maitland, 8.6.8.6 (C.M.) — 486
Majesty, Irregular — 197
Malotte, Irregular — 632
Man of Sorrows, 7.7.7.8 — 178
Manchester, Irregular with Refrain — 352
Manoah, 8.6.8.6 (C.M.) — 30, 332
Maori, 10.10.10.10 — 295
Marching to Zion,
    6.6.8.6 with Repeat & Refrain — 584
Margaret, Irregular with Refrain — 137
Marion, 6.6.8.6 (S.M.) with Refrain — 24
Martingale, Irregular with Refrain — 108
Martyn, 7.7.7.7 D — 394
Martyrdom, 8.6.8.6 (C.M.) — 177, 368
Maryton, 8.8.8.8 (L.M.) — 324, 485
Materna, 8.6.8.6 D (C.M.D.) — 601
McAfee, 8.6.8.6 (C.M.) with Refrain — 457
McCabe, 11.6.11.6 with Refrain — 356
McDaniel, 12.8.12.8 with Refrain — 514
McKee, 8.6.8.6 (C.M.) — 336
Meet Again, 10.10.10.9 with Refrain — 562
Meineke, Irregular — 615
Melita, 8.8.8.8 (L.M.) with Refrain — 411
Melita, 8.8.8.8.8.8 — 600
Mendelssohn, 7.7.7.7 D with Refrain — 93
Mercy, 7.7.7.7 — 223
Merrial, 6.5.6.5 — 576
Message, Irregular with Refrain — 353
Mieir, Irregular — 69
Miles Lane, 8.6.8 with Refrain — 59
Mit Freuden Zart, 8.7.8.7.8.8.7 — 29
Montgomery Lands, Irregular — 626
Moody, 9.9.9.9 with Refrain — 279
More Love to Thee, 6.4.6.4.6.6.4.4 — 463
Morecambe, 10.10.10.10 — 217
Morning Star, 11.10.11.10 — 142
Morris, 9.10.9.10 with Repeat — 380
Moscow, 6.6.4.6.6.6.4 — 5
Munich, 7.6.7.6 D — 230
My Redeemer, 8.7.8.7 with Refrain — 262
My Savior Cares, Irregular with Refrain — 400
My Savior's Love, 8.7.8.7 with Refrain — 518

Nancarrow, Irregular — 634
National Anthem, (British Commonwealth),
    6.6.4.6.6.6.4 — 607
National Anthem (USA),
    Irregular with Refrain — 605
National Hymn, 10.10.10.10 — 597
Near the Cross, 7.6.7.6 with Refrain — 288
Need, 6.4.6.4 with Refrain — 459
Neidlinger, 10.6.10.7 with Refrain — 136
Nettleton, 8.7.8.7 D — 13
Neumark, 9.8.9.8.8.8 — 387
Neumeister, 7.7.7.7 with Refrain — 345
New Name, Irregular with Refrain — 266
New Orleans, Irregular with Refrain — 420
Nicaea, 11.12.12.10 — 1
Noel Nouvelet, 6.5.6.5 with Refrain — 127
Norris, 8.8.8.9 with Refrain — 477
Nothing Between, Irregular — 501
Nun Danket, 6.7.6.7.6.6.6.6 — 589
Nusbaum, 13.11.13.7 with Refrain — 313
Nyack, 8.5.8.5 D with Refrain — 427

O Canada, Irregular with Refrain — 606
O Come, Little Children, 11.11.11.11 — 103
O Land of Rest, 8.6.8.6 (C.M.) — 505
O Perfect Love, 11.10.11.10 — 46
O Quanta Qualia, 10.10.10.10 — 194, 548
O Sanctissima, Irregular — 113

O Store Gud, 11.10.11.10 with Refrain — 27
Oh How I Love Jesus,
    8.6.8.6 (C.M.) with Refrain — 62
Old 100th (Altered), 8.8.8.8 (L.M.) — 621
Old 100th (Original), 8.8.8.8 (L.M.) — 21, 544, 622
Old Rugged Cross, Irregular with Refrain — 167
Old-Time Power, 8.6.8.6 (C.M.) with Refrain — 222
Old-Time Religion, Irregular with Refrain — 533
Olive's Brow, 8.8.8.8 (L.M.) — 159
Olivet, 6.6.4.6.6.6.4 — 417
On Eagle's Wings, Irregular with Refrain — 366
Once for All, Irregular with Refrain — 285
One Day, 11.10.11.10 with Refrain — 150
Only Believe, Irregular with Refrain — 432
Open the Wells, 10.9.10.9 with Refrain — 494
Ora Labora, 4.10.10.10.4 — 354
Orwigsburg, 10.9.10.9 with Refrain — 462
Othello, 8.6.8.6 (C.M.) with Refrain — 511

Pass Me Not, 8.5.8.5 with Refrain — 311
Passion Chorale, 7.6.7.6 D — 169
Patricia, Irregular — 277
Pax Tecum, 10.10 — 405
Peace Be Still, Irregular with Refrain — 424
Peace Like a River, 7.7.10 D — 408
Pearly Gates, 8.7.8.7 with Refrain — 568
Peek, 11.10.11.10 with Repeat — 500
Personent Hodie, 6.6.6.6.6.6 with Refrain — 114
Picardy, 8.7.8.7.8.7 — 82
Pilot, 7.7.7.7.7.7 — 391
Pisgah, 8.6.8.6 (C.M.) with Repeat — 551
Plainfield, 7.8.7.8 with Refrain — 255
Pleading Savior, 8.7.8.7 D — 148
Power in the Blood, 10.9.10.8 with Refrain — 258
Power of the Cross, 5.5.8.5.5.6 with Refrain — 166
Praying for You, 11.11.11.11 with Refrain — 464
Precious Memories, 8.7.8.7 with Refrain — 539
Precious Name, 8.7.8.7 with Refrain — 377
Precious to Me, 11.11.11.8 with Refrain — 540
Promised Land, 8.6.8.6 (C.M.) with Refrain — 565
Promises, 11.11.11.9 with Refrain — 430
Psalm 42, 8.7.8.7.7.7.8.8 — 81
Puer Nobis Nascitur, 7.6.7.7 with Repeat — 87

Quam Dilecta, Irregular — 608
Quebec, 8.8.8.8 (L.M.) — 484
Quietude, 4.4.4.4 with Amens — 580

Randolph, 9.8.8.9 — 587
Rapture, 9.6.9.8 with Refrain — 512
Rathbun, 8.7.8.7 — 163
Ratisbon, 7.7.7.7.7.7 — 573
Redeemed, 9.8.9.8 with Refrain — 268
Redeemer, 9.9.9.9 with Refrain — 179
Redhead 76 (Gethsemane)
    7.7.7.7.7.7 — 158, 227, 290
Regent Square, 8.7.8.7.8.7 — 317
Regent Square, 8.7.8.7 with Refrain — 98
Regent Square, 8.7.8.7.4.7 with Repeat — 204, 210
Repton, 8.6.8.8.6 with Repeat — 475
Rescue, 11.10.11.10 with Refrain — 359
Resignation, 8.6.8.6 D (C.M.D.) — 372
Resolution, 10.6.10.6 with Refrain — 315
Rest (Elton), 8.6.8.8.6 — 474
Restoration, 8.7.8.7 — 479
Restoration, 8.7.8.7 with Refrain — 291
Resurrection, Irregular with Refrain — 192
Retreat, 8.8.8.8 (L.M.) — 468
Revive Us Again, 11.11 with Refrain — 338
Rhosymedre, 6.6.6.6.8.8 with Repeat — 164
Richmond, 8.6.8.6 (C.M.) — 78
Rider, 11.10.11.10 with Refrain — 226

Ring the Bells, 11.9.11.9 with Refrain 269
Risen Christ, 8.8.8.8 (L.M.) 189
Rockingham, 8.8.8.8 (L.M.) 172, 328
Roll Call, 15.11.15.11 with Refrain 552
Rondinella, 10.9.10.9 with Refrain 470
Royal Banner, 11.7.11.7 with Refrain 443
Royal Oak, 7.6.7.6 with Refrain 243
Russian Hymn, 11.10.11.9 17
Rutherford, 7.6.7.6.7.6.7.5 550

Safety, 7.6.7.6.7.6.7.4 with Refrain 516
Sagina, 8.8.8.8 D (L.M.D.) 247
Salvationist, Irregular with Refrain 538
Salve Festa Dies, Irregular with Refrain 187
Salzburg, 7.7.7.7 D 144, 326
Sandon, 10.4.10.4.10.10 15
Sankey, 8.6.8.6 D (C.M.D.) with Refrain 434
Satisfied, 8.7.8.7 with Refrain 541
Saved By Grace, 8.8.8.8 (L.M.) with Refrain 556
Schönster Herr Jesu, Irregular 54
Scott, Irregular 229
Second Coming, Irregular with Refrain 213
Serenity, 8.6.8.6 (C.M.) 513
Sevenfold Amen 641
Seymour, 7.7.7.7 292
Shelter, 8.8.8.8 (L.M.) with Refrain 396
Shine, Jesus, Shine, Irregular with Refrain 348
Shout to the Lord, Irregular with Refrain 71
Showalter, 10.9.10.9 with Refrain 397
Showers of Blessing, 8.7.8.7 with Refrain 342
Sicilian Mariners, 8.7.8.7.8.7 585
Sine Nomine, 10.10.10 with Alleluias 547
Slane, 10.10.10.10 386
Solid Rock, 8.8.8.8 (L.M.) with Refrain 410
Something for Jesus, 6.4.6.4.6.6.6.4 487
Southwell, 6.6.8.6 (S.M.) 467
Sparrow, Irregular with Refrain 378
Spiritus Vitae, 9.8.9.8 339
Spring Hill, 8.7.8.7 with Refrain 314
St. Agnes, 8.6.8.6 (C.M.) 55, 331
St. Anne, 8.6.8.6 (C.M.) 28, 198
St. Catherine, 8.8.8.8.8.8 322
St. Christopher, Irregular 170
St. Clement, 9.8.9.8 578
St. Columba, 8.7.8.7 70
St. Denio, 11.11.11.11 18
St. Dunstans, 6.5.6.5.6.6.6.5 453
St. Flavian, 8.6.8.6 (C.M.) 151
St. George's Windsor, 7.7.7.7 D 591
St. Gertrude, 6.5.6.5 D with Refrain 438
St. Kevin, 7.6.7.6 D 181
St. Leonards, 8.7.8.5 97
St. Louis, 8.6.8.6 D (C.M.D.) 95
St. Magnus, 8.6.8.6 (C.M.) 202, 527

St. Margaret, 8.8.8.8.6 389
St. Michael (Old 134th), 6.6.8.6 (S.M.) 34
St. Patrick's Breastplate, 8.8.8.8 D (L.M.D.) 6
St. Peter, 8.6.8.6 (C.M.) 335, 399
St. Theodulph, 7.6.7.6D 154
St. Theodulph 7.6.7.6 with Refrain 155
St. Thomas, 6.6.8.6 (S.M.) 35, 320, 341
Still, Still, Still, 9.9.8.9 107
Stille Nacht, Irregular 89
Stockport (Yorkshire) 10.10.10.10.10.10 112
Stockton (Minerva),
    8.6.8.6 (C.M.) with Refrain 306
Stories of Jesus, 12.12.9.9 152
Stuttgart, 8.7.8.7 75
Sunlight in My Soul,
    8.6.8.6 (C.M.) with Refrain 537
Sunshine, 9.6.8.6 with Refrain 536
Surrender, 8.7.8.7 with Refrain 305
Sussex Carol, 8.8.8.8 (L.M.) with Repeat 128
Sweet Beulah Land,
    8.8.8.8 (L.M.) with Refrain 567
Sweet By and By, 9.9.9.9 with Refrain 560
Sweet Hour, 8.8.8.8 D (L.M.D.) 458
Sweetest Name, 9.7.9.7 with Refrain 508
Sweney, 8.8.8.8 (L.M.) with Refrain 499

Tempus Adest Floridum, 7.6.7.6 D 109, 139
Terra Patris (Terra Beata), 6.6.8.6 D (S.M.D.) 237
The First Noel, Irregular with Refrain 97
The Unclouded Day,
    12.10.12.10 with Refrain 563
There Is a Redeemer, Irregular with Refrain 249
Thompson, 11.7.11.7 with Refrain 303
Threefold Amen (Danish) 639
Tidings, 11.10.11.10 with Refrain 343
To God Be the Glory,
    11.11.11.11 with Refrain 31
Toplady, 7.7.7.7.7.7 284
Tranquility, 8.7.8.5 D with Refrain 367
Trentham, 6.6.8.6 (S.M.) 225, 325
Truehearted, 11.10.11.10 with Refrain 448
Truro, 8.8.8.8 (L.M.) 77
Trust and Obey, 12.9.12.9 with Refrain 504
Trust in Jesus, 8.7.8.7 with Refrain 414
Trusting Jesus, 7.7.7.7 with Refrain 415
Tryggare Kan Ingen Vara, 8.8.8.8 (L.M.) 379
Tullar, 10.10.10.10 with Refrain 496
Twofold Amen (Dresden) 637
Twofold Amen (Greek) 638
Tyne, Irregular 30

Unbroken Circle, 8.7.8.7 572

Veni Creator, 8.8 218

Veni Emmanuel, 8.8.8.8 (L.M.) with Refrain 72
Vessels, 8.7.7 D with Refrain 224
Victory, 8.8.8 with Alleluias 191
Ville Du Havre, 11.8.11.9 with Refrain 363
Vine Ridge, Irregular with Refrain 7
Vox Dilecti, 8.6.8.6 D (C.M.D.) 531

W Zlobie Lezy, 8.7.8.7.8.7.7 with Repeat 119
Waiting, 6.6.8.6 (S.M.) 73, 131
Waltham, 8.8.8.8 (L.M.) 126
Warrenton, 8.7.8.7 with Refrain 14
Warum Sollt' Ich Mich Denn Grämen,
    8.3.3.6 D 111
Was Lebet, Was Schwebet,
    12.10.12.10 143
Washed in the Blood,
    11.9.11.9 with Refrain 256
Way of the Cross, Irregular with Refrain 270
We Will Glorify, 9.7.9.6 66
We Wish You a Merry Christmas,
    Irregular with Refrain 138
Webb, 7.6.7.6 D 441
Wellesley, 8.7.8.7 273
Wem In Leidenstagen, 6.5.6.5 173
Were You There, Irregular 161
Westminster Abbey, 8.7.8.7.8.7 318
Whelpton, Irregular 618
When I See the Blood,
    9.9.10.9 with Refrain 260
Whispering Hope, 8.7.8.7 D with Refrain 406
Whittle, 10.10.10.10 with Refrain 376
Whole World, Irregular 409
Wie Lieblich Ist Der Maien (Steurlein)
    7.6.7.6 D 593
Wildgrove, Irregular 633
Wildwood, Irregular 582
Winchester New, 8.8.8.8 (L.M.) 156
Winchester Old, 8.6.8.6 (C.M.) 124
Wonderful Grace, Irregular with Refrain 282
Wonderful Peace, 12.9.12.9 with Refrain 404
Wonders, 8.8.8.8 with Repeat & Refrain 283
Wondrous Love, Irregular 174
Wondrous Story, 8.7.8.7 with Refrain 507
Woodlands, 10.10.10.10 333
Woodworth, 8.8.8.8 (L.M.) 293
Words of Life, 8.6.8.6.6.6.6 with Refrain 234
Work Song, 7.6.7.5 D with Refrain 506
Worship and Adore, Irregular with Refrain 70
Wye Valley, 6.5.6.5 D 207
Wye Valley, 6.5.6.5 D with Refrain 412

Yarbrough, 7.7.7.7 with Refrain 301
Years Go By, 7.6.7.6 D with Refrain 289

 ## METRICAL INDEX OF TUNES

SM = Short Meter (6.6.6.8)   CM = Common Meter (8.6.8.6)   LM = Long Meter (8.8.8.8)   D = Doubled

4.4.4.4 with Amens
Quietude, 580

4.4.4.5
God Is So Good, 517

4.10.10.10.4
Ora Labora, 354

5.4.5.4 D
Adelaide, 298

5.5.5.3 D
Bunessan, 115

5.5.5.4 with Refrain
Gott Ist Die Liebe, 253

5.5.8.5.5.6 with Refrain
Power of the Cross, 166

6.4.6.4 with Refrain
Need, 459

6.4.6.4 D
Bread of Life, 231, 327

6.4.6.4.6.6.4.4
More Love to Thee, 463

6.4.6.4.6.6.6.4
Bethany, 426
Camacha, 476
Something for Jesus, 487

6.5.6.4 with Refrain
Christ Arose, 182

6.5.6.5
Merrial, 576
Wem In Leidenstagen,
    173

6.5.6.5 with Refrain
Noel Nouvelet, 127

6.5.6.5 D
Belle Rive, 208
Holiness, 472
Wye Valley, 207

6.5.6.5 D with Refrain
Armageddon, 436
Fortitude, 454
Himself, 528
St. Gertrude, 438
Wye Valley, 412

6.5.6.5.6.6.6.5
St. Dunstans, 453

6.6.4.6.6.6.6.4
America (Thesaurus
   Musicus), 599, 604
Italian Hymn, 4, 344
Moscow, 5
National Anthem
   (British Common-
   wealth), 607
Olivet, 417

6.6.6.6 D
Madrid, 45

6.6.6.6.6 with Refrain
Personent Hodie, 114

6.6.6.6.6.6
Laudes Domini, 51

6.6.6.6.8.6 with Repeat
Kenosis, 482

6.6.6.6.8.8
Darwall's 148th, 43, 206

6.6.6.6.8.8 with Repeat
Lenox, 246
Rhosymedre, 164

6.6.6.6.12.12
Christmas Song, 135

6.6.7.7 with Refrain
All to Christ, 265

6.6.8.4 D
Leoni, 16

6.6.8.6 (S.M.)
Boylston, 495
Dennis, 334
Festal Song, 340, 583
Southwell, 467
St. Michael (Old 134th),
   34
St. Thomas, 35, 320, 341
Trentham, 225, 325
Waiting, 73, 131

**6.6.8.6 with Repeat &
Refrain**
Marching to Zion, 584

**6.6.8.6 (S.M.) with
   Refrain**
Marion, 24

6.6.8.6 D (S.M.D.)
Diademata, 46, 449, 488
Terra Patris (Terra
   Beata), 237

6.6.11 D
Down Ampney, 216

6.7.6.7
Gartan, 91

6.7.6.7.6.6.6.6
Nun Danket, 589

7.3.7.3.7.7.7.3
Limpsfield, 347

7.6.7.5 D
Work Song, 506

7.6.7.6
Christus Der Ist Mein
   Leben, 431

7.6.7.6 with Refrain
All Things Bright and
   Beautiful, 244
Balm in Gilead, 383
Es Ist Ein Ros', 85
Go Tell It, 132
Near the Cross, 288
Royal Oak, 243
St. Theodulph, 155

7.6.7.6 D
Angel's Story, 446
Crucifix, 294, 596
Ellacombe, 153, 186
Es Flog Ein Kleins
   Waldvögelein, 79, 592
Joy Has Dawned, 101
Lancashire, 185, 437, 451
Munich, 230
Passion Chorale, 169
St. Kevin, 181
St. Theodulph, 154
Tempus Adest
   Floridum, 109, 139
Webb, 441
Wie Lieblich Ist Der
   Maien (Steurlein),
   593

7.6.7.6 D with Refrain
Evangel, 532
Geibel, 440
Hankey, 522
Years Go By, 289

7.6.7.6.6.6.7.6
Es Ist Ein Ros', 84

**7.6.7.6.7.6.7.4 with
Refrain**
Ackley, 526
Safety, 516

7.6.7.6.7.6.7.5
Rutherford, 550

7.6.7.6.7.7.7.6
Jesus Saves, 346

7.6.7.7 with Repeat
Puer Nobis Nascitur, 87

7.7.7.7
Aletta, 233
Mercy, 223
Seymour, 292

7.7.7.7 with Alleluias
Easter Hymn, 183, 184
Llanfair, 25, 193, 245,

7.7.7.7 with Repeat
Hagan, 118
Hendon, 302

7.7.7.7 with Refrain
Branle de l'Officiel, 120
China, 274

Dix, 239
Gloria, 99
Humility (Oxford), 121
Lowliness, 145
Neumeister, 345
Trusting Jesus, 415
Yarbrough, 301

7.7.7.7 D
Aberystwyth, 395
Martyn, 394
Salzburg, 144, 326
St. George's Windsor,
   591

7.7.7.7 D with Repeat
Everlasting Love, 398

7.7.7.7 D with Refrain
Mendelssohn, 93

7.7.7.7.4 with Refrain
Chautauqua, 579

7.7.7.7.7
Hendon, 521

7.7.7.7.7.7
Dix, 141, 595
Pilot, 391
Ratisbon, 573
Redhead 76
   (Gethsemane),
   158, 227, 290
Toplady, 284

7.7.7.8
Man of Sorrows, 178

7.7.7.9 with Refrain
Fisher, 278

7.7.10
Adeste Fideles
   (Refrain only), 47

7.7.10 D
Peace Like a River, 408

7.8.7.7 with Refrain
Il Est Né, 102

7.8.7.8 with Refrain
Jesu, Meine Zuversicht,
   329
Plainfield, 255

7.8.7.8 D
Aurelia, 316

7.8.7.8.7.7
Grosser Gott, Wir Loben
   Dich, 3

7.9.7.9 with Refrain
Every Day, 419

8.3.3.3.6 D
Warum Sollt' Ich Mich
   Denn Gramen, 111

8.4.8.4 D with Refrain
Love Found a Way, 5, 20

8.5.8.3
Bullinger, 429

8.5.8.5 with Refrain
Coming Home, 307
Pass Me Not, 311

8.5.8.5 D with Refrain
Nyack, 427

**8.6.8 with Repeat
& Refrain**
Diadem, 58

8.6.8 with Refrain
Miles Lane, 59

8.6.8.5 with Refrain
Jewels, 212

8.6.8.6 (C.M.)
Amazing Grace
   (New Britain), 280
Arlington, 439
Azmon, 49
Beatitudo, 471
Crimond, 369
Evergreen Shore, 564
Horsley, 160, 200
Ira, 349
Land of Rest,
   281, 549, 570
Maitland, 486
Manoah, 30, 332
Martyrdom, 177, 368
McKee, 336
Richmond, 78
Serenity, 513
St. Agnes, 55, 331
St. Anne, 28, 198
St. Flavian, 151
St. Magnus, 202, 527
St. Peter, 335, 399
Winchester Old, 124

8.6.8.6 (C.M.) with Repeat
Antioch, 92
Christmas, 125
Coronation, 57
Lyngham, 50
Pisgah, 551

**8.6.8.6 (C.M.) with
Refrain**
Duncannon, 165
El Nathan, 535
God Cares, 393
Hudson, 525
Knapp, 261
Landas, 418
McAfee, 457
O Land of Rest, 505
Oh How I Love Jesus, 62
Old-Time Power, 222
Othello, 511
Promised Land, 565
Stockton (Minerva), 306
Sunlight in My Soul, 537

8.6.8.6 D (C.M.D.)
All Saints New, 442
Carol, 100
Cleansing Fountain, 259
Ellacombe, 241
Forest Green, 96, 242
Kingsfold, 146, 147, 530
Materna, 601

Resignation, 372
St. Louis, 95
Vox Dilecti, 531

**8.6.8.6. D (C.M.D.) with
Refrain**
Sankey, 434

8.6.8.6.6.6 with Refrain
Words of Life, 234

8.6.8.8.6
Rest (Elton), 474

8.6.8.8.6. with Repeat
Repton, 475

8.7.7 D with Refrain
Vessels, 224

8.7.8.5
St. Leonards, 497

8.7.8.5 D with Refrain
Tranquility, 367

8.7.8.7
All for Jesus, 480
Cross of Jesus, 168
Crucifixion, 162
Dominus Regit Me, 371
Galilee, 478
Rathbun, 163
Restoration, 479
St. Columba, 370
Stuttgart, 75
Unbroken Circle, 572
Wellesley, 273

8.7.8.7 with Refrain
Any Room, 308
Beacon Hill, 473
Benton Harbor, 257
Blessed Quietness, 228
Call for Reapers, 358
Channels, 498
Close to Thee, 493
Constancy, 481
Endless Song, 509
Eola, 232
Face to Face, 553
Fill Me Now, 219
Glorious Name, 38
Great Physician, 286
Hanson Place, 559
Heaven, 557
Hyfrydol, 248
I Will Praise Him, 510
Little Is Much, 490
Lower Lights, 357
My Redeemer, 262
My Savior's Love, 518
Pearly Gates, 568
Precious Memories, 539
Precious Name, 377
Regent Square, 98
Restoration, 291
Satisfied, 541
Showers of Blessing, 342
Spring Hill, 314
Surrender, 305
Trust in Jesus, 414
Warrenton, 14
Wondrous Story, 507

8.7.8.7 D
Austrian Hymn, 319
Beecher, 2, 40
Blaenwern, 41
Bradbury, 373
Converse, 460
Cymraeg, 254
Ebenezer (Ton-y-Botel),
    272, 321, 598
Ellesdie, 350, 483
Friend, 515
Holy Manna, 581
Hyfrydol,
    42, 74, 195, 238,
Hymn to Joy, 190, 235
In Babilone, 199, 201
Nettleton, 13
Pleading Savior, 148

8.7.8.7 D with Repeat
All the Way, 421

8.7.8.7 D with Refrain
Barnard, 450
Give Me Jesus (Sweney),
    385
Whispering Hope, 406

8.7.8.7.4.7 with Repeat
Bryn Calfaria, 205
Cwm Rhondda, 413
Helmsley, 211
Regent Square, 204, 210

8.7.8.7.6.8.6.7
Greensleeves, 110

8.7.8.7.7.7
Irby, 83

8.7.8.7.7.7.7.8.8
Psalm 42, 81

8.7.8.7.8.7
Lauda Anima, 12
Picardy, 82
Regent Square, 317
Sicilian Mariners, 585
Westminster Abbey, 318

8.7.8.7.8.7 with Repeat
Cwm Rhondda, 337

8.7.8.7.8.7.7
Divinum Mysterium, 80,
    86

8.7.8.7.8.8.7
Mit Freuden Zart, 29

8.7.8.7.8.8.7 with Repeat
W Zlobie Lezy, 119

8.7.8.7.8.8.7.7
Ermuntre Dich Mein
    Schwacher, 88

8.8.6.8.8.6. with Repeat
Ariel, 44

8.8
Veni Creator, 218

8.8.8
Be Still and Know, 365

8.8.8 with Alleluias
Victory, 191
8.8.8.5
Acclaim, 65

8.8.8.6
Fürchte Dich Nicht, 407

8.8.8.6 with Refrain
Dunbar, 491
He Lifted Me, 519
Kings of Orient, 140

8.8.8.7
Greenwell, 263

8.8.8.8 (L.M.)
Batchellor (Onslow), 545
Canonbury, 465, 625
Conditor Alme Siderum,
    76
Duke Street, 20, 39
Germany (Gardiner),
    149, 251
Hamburg, 171
Hursley, 577
Maryton, 324, 485
Old 100th (Altered), 621
Old 100th (Original),
    21, 544, 622
Olive's Brow, 159
Quebec, 484
Retreat, 468
Risen Christ, 189
Rockingham, 172, 328
Truro, 77
Tryggare Kan Ingen
    Vara, 379
Waltham, 126
Winchester New, 156
Woodworth, 293

**8.8.8.8 (L.M.) with
Alleluias/Hallelujahs**
Dedication Anthem, 623
Lasst Uns Erfreuen,
    19, 236, 624

8.8.8.8 (L.M.) with Repeat
Sussex Carol, 128

**8.8.8.8 (L.M.) with Repeat
& Refrain**
Wonders, 283

8.8.8.8 (L.M.) with Refrain
Blessed Name, 37
Bring Them In, 361
Happy Day, 323
He Leadeth Me, 374
Higher Ground, 447
Hosanna, 48
Lamb of God, 175
Melita, 411
Saved By Grace, 556
Shelter, 396
Solid Rock, 410
Sweet Beulah Land, 567
Sweney, 499
Veni Emmanuel, 72

8.8.8.8 D (L.M.D.)
Creation, 240
Deirdre, 6
In Christ Alone, 390
Sagina, 27

St. Patrick's Breastplate,
    6
Sweet Hour, 458

8.8.8.8.6.
St. Margaret, 389

8.8.8.8.8.6.8.6.
Love of God, 276

8.8.8.8.8.8
Melita, 600
St. Catherine, 322

8.8.8.8.9 with Refrain
Norris, 477

8.8.10.8
Cloninger, 106

8.8.11 D with Refrain
Golden Bells, 571

9.4.9.4 with Refrain
Footsteps, 445

9.6.8.6 with Refrain
Sunshine, 536

9.6.9.6 with Refrain
Kneel at the Cross, 310

9.6.9.8 with Refrain
Rapture, 512

9.7.9.6
We Will Glorify, 66

9.7.9.7 with Refrain
Sweetest Name, 508

9.8.8.9
Randolph, 587

9.8.8.9 with Refrain
Endeavor, 586

9.8.9.8
Spiritus Vitae, 339
St. Clement, 578

9.8.9.8 with Refrain
Lemmel, 297
Redeemed, 268

9.8.9.8.8.8
Neumark, 387

9.9.8.9
Still, Still, Still, 107

9.9.9.4 with Refrain
Calvary, 523

9.9.9.5 with Refrain
Glory to His Name, 524

9.9.9.9 with Refrain
Moody, 279
Redeemer, 179
Sweet By and By, 560

9.9.10.9 with Refrain
When I See the Blood,
    260
9.9.11.11 with Refrain

Praying for You, 464

9.10.9.9 with Refrain
Assurance, 362

9.10.9.10 with Repeat
Morris, 380

10.4.10.4.10.10
Lux Benigna, 433

10.5.10.5 with Refrain
Deeper, Deeper, 503

10.6.10.6 with Refrain
Harper Memorial
    (No, Not One), 401
Resolution, 315

10.6.10.7 with Refrain
Neidlinger, 136

10.7.10.7 with Refrain
Follow, 133
I Am Thine, 309

10.8.10.7 with Refrain
Calling Today, 304

10.8.10.8 with Refrain
Glory-Land, 558

10.9.10.8 with Refrain
Power in the Blood, 258

10.9.10.9 with Refrain
Anchor, 423
Garden of Prayer, 455
Open the Wells, 494
Orwigsburg, 462
Rondinella, 470
Showalter, 397

10.10
Pax Tecum, 405

10.10 with Refrain
Crucifer, 203

10.10.10 with Alleluias
Engleberg, 56
Sine Nomine, 547

10.10.10.8
Assam, 300

10.10.10.9 with Refrain
Lovely Name, 529
Meet Again, 562

10.10.10.10
Ellers, 296, 588
Eventide, 575
Maori, 295
Morecambe, 217
National Hymn, 597
O Quanta Qualia,
    194, 548
Slane, 386
Woodlands, 333

10.10.10.10 with Refrain
Bourne, 489
Deliverance, 287
Gladness, 275

Glory Song, 566
Living, 492
Tullar, 496
Whittle, 376

10.10.10.10.10.10
Finlandia, 364
Stockport (Yorkshire),
    112

10.10.10.11 with Refrain
Lifeline, 351

10.10.11.11
Hanover, 209
Laudate Dominum
    (Parry), 26
Lyons, 10

10.11.11.11 with Refrain
Binghampton, 403
Maccabaeus, 188

11.6.11.6 with Refrain
McCabe, 356

11.7.11.7 with Refrain
Royal Banner, 443
Thompson, 303

11.8.11.8 with Refrain
God Leads Us, 422
Kirkpatrick, 382
Light of the World, 542

11.8.11.9 with Refrain
Ville Du Havre, 363

11.9.11.9 with Refrain
Ring the Bells, 269
Washed in the Blood,
    256

11.10.11.9
Russian Hymn, 17

11.10.11.10
Consolation, 574
Consolator, 402
Morning Star, 142
O Perfect Love, 546

11.10.11.10 with Repeat
Peek, 500

11.10.11.10 with Refrain
Beautiful to Walk, 425
Exaltation, 312
Faithfulness, 33
Hingham, 384
O Store Gud, 27
One Day, 150
Rescue, 359
Rider, 226
Tidings, 343
Truehearted, 448

11.10.11.10.11.10
Finlandia, 444

11.11 with Refrain
Revive Us Again, 338

11.11.11.5
Herzliebster Jesu, 176
11.11.11.6

Flemming, 8

11.11.11.8 with Refrain
Precious to Me, 540

11.11.11.9 with Refrain
Promises, 430

11.11.11.11
Away in a Manger
  (Mueller), 105
Cradle Song, 104
Foundation, 392
Gordon, 61
I Love Thee, 60
O Come, Little Children,
  103
St. Denio, 18

11.11.11.11 with Repeat
Boundless Salvation, 250

11.11.11.11 with Refrain
Blessings, 594
Fischer, 264
Hiding in Thee, 381
I Can Safely Go, 375
Praying for You, 464
To God Be the Glory, 31

11.12.12.10
Nicaea, 1

12.8.12.8 with Refrain
McDaniel, 514

12.9.12.9 with Refrain
Clifton, 561
Trust and Obey, 504
Wonderful Peace, 404

12.10.12.10
Was Lebet, Was
  Schwebet, 143

12.10.12.10 with Refrain
The Unclouded Day, 563

12.11.12.11
Kremser, 32

12.11.12.11 with Refrain
Harvest, 360

12.11.12.12
Kremser, 590

12.12.9.9
Stories of Jesus, 152

12.12.12.6 with Refrain
Comforter, 220

13.11.13.7 with Refrain
Nusbaum, 313

14.11.14.11 with Refrain
I Shall Know Him, 554
Leave It There, 466

14.13.14.10 with Refrain
Beulah Land, 428

15.11.15.11 with Refrain
Roll Call, 552

Irregular
Adore Thee, 180
Anamnesis, 629
Baumbach, 619
Be Still, 609
Beatty, 67

Belmont Park, 612
Benediction, 636
Birmingham, 617
Bless the Lord, 36
Blott En Dag, 416
Brentwood, 611
Bring a Torch, 134
Cantique De Noel, 129
Castle, 123
Cedar Lane, 616
Conditor Alme
  Siderum, 631
Cranham, 122
Crusader's Hymn (St.
  Elizabeth), 53
Darnell, 627
Deep River, 555
Deeper and Deeper, 502
Ein' Feste Burg
  (Isometric), 22
Ein' Feste Burg
  (Rhythmic), 23
Elizabeth, 534
Father's Love, 157
Gloria in Excelsis, 613
God Be in My Head, 635
Greatorex, 614
He Is Exalted, 63
He Is Lord, 196
Heilig Ist Der Herr, 628
Holy Ground, 68
I Know a Fount, 267
I'm So Glad, 543
In Dulci Jubilo, 94
Ivanoff, 610
Iverson, 221
Jesu, Meine Freude, 388
Jesus, I Come, 299
Lead Me, Lord, 620
Lift Every Voice, 602
Lobe Den Herren, 11

Majesty, 197
Malotte, 632
Meineke, 615
Mieir, 69
Montgomery Lands, 626
Nancarrow, 634
O Sanctissima, 113
Patricia, 277
Quam Dilecta, 608
Schönster Herr Jesu, 54
Scott, 229
St. Christopher, 170
Stille Nacht, 89
Tyne, 630
Were You There, 161
Whelpton, 618
Whole World, 409
Wildgrove, 633
Wondrous Love, 174

Irregular with Refrain
Adeste Fideles, 90
All Your Anxiety, 469
As the Deer, 52
Battle Hymn, 603
Beautiful Name, 130
Born Again, 271
By and By, 569
Christ Returneth, 215
Closer Walk, 461
Crowning Day, 214
Finto, 252
Follow On, 452
Garden, 456
Give Me Jesus
  (Spiritual), 435
God Rest Ye Merry, 116
If Jesus Goes, 355
Joyful Song, 64
Judson, 9
Jüngst, 117

Let Us Break Bread, 330
Manchester, 352
Margaret, 137
Martingale, 108
Message, 353
My Savior Cares, 400
National Anthem (USA),
  605
New Name, 266
New Orleans, 420
Nothing Between, 501
O Canada, 606
Old Rugged Cross, 167
Old-Time Religion, 533
On Eagle's Wings, 366
Once for All, 285
Only Believe, 432
Peace Be Still, 424
Resurrection, 192
Salvationist, 538
Salve Festa Dies, 187
Second Coming, 213
Shine, Jesus, Shine, 348
Shout to the Lord, 71
Sparrow, 378
The First Noel, 97
There Is a Redeemer,
  249
Vine Ridge, 7
Way of the Cross, 270
We Wish You a Merry
  Christmas, 138
Wildwood, 582
Wonderful Grace, 282
Worship and Adore, 70

INDEX OF AUTHORS · COMPOSERS · SOURCE

A Collection of Psalm and Hymn Tunes (1851) 332
A New Version of the Psalms of David (1696) 368
A Selection of Hymns (1787) 392
A Supplement to the New Version, probably by
  William Croft (ca. 1708) 28
Abelard, Peter (1079-1142) 548
Ackley, Alfred Henry (1887-1960) 526
Ackley, Bentley DeForest (1872-1958) 314
Acuff, James W. (1864-1937) 558
Ad regias Agni dapes (ca. 6th c.) 326
Adam, Adolphe-Charles (1803-1856) 129
Adams, Sarah Fuller Flower (1803-1848) 426
Addison, Joseph (1672-1719) 240
Adoramus Te (n.d.) 180
Ahlwen, Elsie Rebekah (1905-1986) 568
Ahnfelt, Oscar (1813-1882) 379, 416
Alexander, Cecil Frances Humphreys (1818-1895)
  6, 83, 160, 243, 244, 478, 479
Alexander, James Waddel (1804-1859) 169
Alfonso, S. (18th c.) 173
Alford, Henry (1810-1871) 591
Allen, Chester G. (1838-1878) 64
Allen, George Nelson (1812-1877) 486
Alte Catholische Geistliche Kirchengesäng (1599) 85
Alwood, Josiah Kelly, (1828-1909) 563

Anonymous 3, 4, 11, 19, 32, 36, 45, 51, 53, 54, 60,
  76, 77, 82, 109, 113, 124, 139, 143, 148, 151,
  153, 156, 172, 183, 184, 186, 194, 230, 236, 241,
  290, 308, 317, 318, 323, 325, 326, 328, 365, 461,
  533, 548, 577, 585, 599, 604, 605, 607, 613, 624
Antiphoner (Anon.) (1681) 194
Arbeau, Thoinot (1519-1591) 120
Arne, Thomas Augustine (1710-1778) 439
Atkins, George (19th c.) 581
Atkinson, Frederick Cook (1841-1896) 217

Babcock, Maltbie Davenport (1858-1901) 237
Bach, Johann Sebastian (1685-1750) 88, 144, 169,
  326, 388
Baker, Henry Williams (1821-1877) 26, 86, 370,
  371, 484
Baker, Mary Ann (1831-1921) 424
Baker, Theodore (1851-1934) 84, 117, 180, 590
Bakewell, John (1721-1819) 201
Barbauld, Anna Laetitia Aikin (1743-1825) 595
Barham-Gould, Arthur Cyril (1891-1953) 497
Baring-Gould, Sabine (1834-1924) 321, 438, 576
Barnard, Charlotte Alington Pye (1830-1869) 450
Barnby, Joseph (1838-1896) 51, 546, 576
Batchellor, Daniel J. (1845-1934) 545

Bateman, Christian Henry (1813-1889) 45
Bates, Katherine Lee (1859-1929) 601
Baumbach, Adolph (1830-1880) 619
Baxter, Lydia Odell (1809-1874) 377
Beatty, Christopher (1944-) 67
Beethoven, Ludwig van (1770-1827) 190, 235
Bell, Maurice Frederick (1862-1931) 187
Bennard, George (1873-1960) 167
Bennett, Sanford Fillmore (1836-1889) 560
Bennett, W. Sterndale (1816-1875) 11
Benson, Louis Fitzgerald (1855-1930) 146
Bergen, Esther C. (1921-) 253
Bernard of Clairvaux (1091-1153) 55, 169
Bevan, Emma Frances Shuttleworth (1827-1909)
  345
Bianco of Siena (?-1434) 216
Bickersteth, Jr., Edward Henry (1825-1906) 405
Bilhorn, Peter Philip (1865-1936) 507
Black, James Milton (1856-1938) 552
Blandy, Ernest W. (19th c.) 477
Blankenship, Mark (1943-) 9
Blémont, Émile (1839-1927) 134
Bliss, Philip Paul (1838-1876) 178, 234, 262, 275,
  285, 357, 363, 482, 542
Blom, Frederick Arvid (1867-1927) 568

Boberg, Carl (1859-1940) 27
Bode, John Ernest (1816-1874) 446
Bonar, Horatius (1809-1889) 194, 294, 530, 531
Book of Hours (1514) 635
Booth, Josiah (1852-1930) 347
Booth, William (1829-1912) 250
Borthwick, Jane Laurie (1813-1897) 354, 364
Bottome, Frank (1823-1894) 220
Bourgeois, Louis (1510-1561) 21, 34, 81, 544, 621, 622
Bowring, John (1792-1872) 162, 163
Bradbury, William Batchelder (1816-1868) 159, 233, 274, 293, 301, 373, 374, 410, 458
Brady, Nicholas (1659-1726) 368
Breck, Carrie Elizabeth Ellis (1855-1934) 553
Bridgers, Luther Burgess (1884-1948) 508
Bridges, Matthew (1800-1894) 46
Bridges, Robert Seymour (1844-1930) 51, 169, 176
Bristol Tune Book (1881) 170
Broadwood, Lucy (1858-1929) 146, 147, 530
Bromehead, Joseph (1747-1826) 549
Brooke, Stopford Augustus (1832-1916) 245
Brooks, Charles Timothy (1813-1883) 604
Brooks, Phillips (1835-1893) 95, 96
Brown, Mary (19th c.) 352
Brownlie, John (1857-1925) 329
Brumley, Albert Edward (1905-1977) 562
Budry, Edmond Louis (1854-1932) 188
Buell, Harriet Eugenia (1834-1910) 403
Bullinger, Ethelbert William (1837-1913) 429
Bunyan, John (1628-1688) 453
Burke, James H. (1858-1901) 427
Burleigh, Harry Thacker (1866-1949) 336
Burnap, Uzziah Christopher (1834-1900) 513
Burton, Sr., John (1773-1822) 233
Butler, Henry Montague (1833-1918) 333
Byrne, Mary Elizabeth (1880-1931) 386
Byrom, John (1691-1763) 112

Caldbeck, George Thomas (1852-1918) 405
Calkin, John Baptiste (1827-1905) 126
Camp, Mabel Johnston (1871-1937) 130
Campbell, Jane Montgomery (1817-1878) 592
Campbell, John Douglas Southerland (1845-1914) 15
Campbell, Robert (1814-1868) 326
Campbell, Thomas (1777-1844) 247
Canaidau y Cyssegr (1839) 18
Cappeau, Placide (1808-1877) 129
Carlson, Nathaniel 1879-1957) 568
Carter, Russell Kelso (1849-1928) 430
Cason, Don (1954-) 73, 123, 131
Caswall, Edward (1814-1878) 55, 121, 173
Cennick, John (1718-1755) 210, 211, 544
Chadwick, James (1813-1882) 99
Challinor, Frederick Arthur (1866-1952) 152
Chandler, John (1806-1876) 198
Chapman, John Wilbur (1859-1918) 150, 248
Charles, Elizabeth Rundle (1828-1896) 8
Charlesworth, Vernon John (1839-1915) 396
Chatfield, Allen William (1808-1896) 467
Cherry, Edith Gilling (1872-1897) 444
Chisholm, Thomas Obediah (1866-1960) 33, 470, 492
Choral-Buch vor Johann Heinrich Reinhardt, Uttingen, Germany (1754) 143
Choralbuch (Werner, 1815) 573
Choralbuch zu den neuen protestantischen Gesangbüchern (1815) 573
Chorley, Henry Fothergill (1808-1872) 17
Christiansen, Avis Marguerite Burgeson

(1895-1985) 179, 520
Christmas Carols Old and New, (Bramley & Stainer) (1871) 94, 116, 139
Church Hymn Tunes, Ancient and Modern (1853) 158, 227, 290
Church Hymns with Tunes (1874) 324
Clark, F. A. (20th c.) 501, 569
Clark, Jeremiah (1670-1707) 202, 527
Clem, James Bowman Overton (1855-1927) 358
Clephane, Elizabeth Cecelia Douglas (1830-1869) 170
Cloninger, Claire (1942-) 73, 106, 131
Cluff, Samuel O'Malley Gore (1837-1910) 464
Coffin, Henry Sloane (1877-1654) 72
Coghill, Annie Louisa Walker (1836-1907) 506
Collections of Motetts or Antiphons (1792) 90, 402
Columbian Harmony (1825) 581
Combs, Lonnie B. (n.d.) 539
Conkey, Ithamar (1815-1867) 163
Converse, Charles Crozat (1832-1918) 460
Cook, Joseph Simpson (1859-1933) 109
Cooke, Oliver (1873-1945) 267
Cooper, W. G. (19th c.) 404
Cornell, W. D. (19th c.) 404
Cory, Julia Bulkley Cady (1882-1963) 32
Cosin, John (1594-1672) 218
Cousin, Anne Ross Cundle (1824-1906) 550
Cowper, William (1731-1800) 259, 471
Cox, Frances Elizabeth (1812-1897) 29
Croft, William (1678-1727) 28, 198, 209
Croly, George (1780-1860) 217
Crosby, Fanny Jane (1820-1915) 31, 64, 268, 288, 304, 309, 311, 359, 362, 382, 385, 419, 421, 493, 554, 556
Crossman, Samuel (1623-1683) 164
Crotch, William (1775-1847) 34
Crüger, Johann (1598-1662) 176, 329, 589
Cummings, William Hayman (1831-1915) 93
Cushing, William Orcutt (1823-1902) 212, 269, 381, 384, 452
Cutler, Henry Stephen (1825-1902) 442

Daman, William (ca. 1550-1593) 467
Darnell, Brian (1964-) 627
Darwall, John (1731-1789) 43, 206
Davies, Henry Walford (1869-1941) 79, 592, 635
Davies, Samuel (1723-1761) 283
Davis, Geron (1960-) 68
Davis, Roby Furley (1866-1937) 80
Day's *Psalter* (1562) 151
De Marbelle, Daniel (Dion) (1818-1903) 571
Dean, Emmet Sidney (1876-1951) 558
Dearmer, Percy (1867-1936) 453
Deutsche Messe (Franz Schubert) (1826) 628
DeVenter, Judson Wheeler Van (1855-1939) 305, 537
Devoti Musica Cordis (1630) 176
Die Schöpfung (The Creation) Franz Joseph Haydn) (1798) 240
Discendi amor santo (Bianco of Siena) (?-1434) 216
Dix, William Chatterton (1837-1898) 110, 141, 195
Dixon, Helen Cadbury Alexander (1877-1969) 375
Doane, William Howard (1832-1915) 31, 288, 309, 311, 359, 377, 419, 463, 532
Doddridge, Philip (1702-1751) 78, 323, 328
Douglas, Charles Winfred (1867-1944) 199, 453
Draper, William Henry (1855-1933) 236
Dubois, Theodore (1837-1924) 180
Duffield, Jr., George (1818-1888) 440, 441

Dunbar, C. R. (n.d.) 491
Dwight, John Sullivan (1812-1893) 129
Dwight, Timothy (1752-1817) 320
Dyke, Henry Jackson van (1852-1933) 148, 235
Dykes, John Bacchus (1823-1876) 1, 48, 55, 331, 371, 411, 433, 471, 531, 548, 600

Ebeling, Johann Georg (1637-1676) 111
Edmunds, Lidie H. (1851-1920) 418
Edson, Lewis (1748-1820) 246
Edwards, John David (1806-1885) 164
Edwards, William (1842-1929) 254
Ein andächtiges Gebet (1615) 154, 155
Elijah (Felix Mendelssohn) (1846) 617
Ellerton, John (1826-1893) 17, 578, 588
Elliott, Charlotte (1789-1871) 293
Elliott, Emily Elizabeth Steele (1836-1897) 137
Ellis, J. (19th c.) 250
Ellor, James (1819-1899) 58
Elvey, George Job (1816-1896) 46, 449, 488, 591
English Country Songs (1893) 146, 147, 530
Este's Psalter (1592) 124
Evangelischer Nachklang (1718) 345
Everest, Charles William (1814-1877) 484
Everett, Asa Brooks (1828-1875) 445
Excell, Edwin Othello (1851-1921) 280, 511, 594

Faber, Frederick William (1814-1863) 273, 322
Falk, Johannes Daniel (1768-1826) 113
Farrington, Harry Webb (1879-1930) 527
Fawcett, John (1740-1817) 334, 585
Featherstone, William Ralph (1846-1873) 61
Ferguson, Manie Payne (1850-1932) 228
Festgesang (1840) 93
Filitz, Friedrich (1816-1873) 173
Fillmore, James Henry (1849-1936) 315, 455
Finlandia, (Jean Sibelius) (1899) 364, 444
Fischer, William Gustavus (1835-1912) 264, 522
Fisher, Albert Christopher (1886-1946) 278
Flemming, Friedrich Ferdinand (1778-1813) 8
Foote, John G. (19th c.) 260
Forgaill, Dallan (8th c.) 386
Forrest, C. H. (ca. 19th c.) 312
Fortunatus, Venantius Honorius Clementianus (ca. 530-609) 187
Fosdick, Harry Emerson (1878-1969) 337
Four Score and Seven Psalms of David (1551) 544
Francis, Samuel Trevor (1834-1925) 272
Franck, Johann (1618-1677) 388
Franz, Ignaz (1719-1790) 3
Frazer, George West (1830-1896) 2
Fröhlich Sollmein Herze Springen (1653) 111
Fry, Charles William (1837-1882) 538
Funk, Joseph (1778-1862) 392

Gabriel, Charles Hutchinson (1856-1932) 222, 270, 356, 378, 447, 514, 518, 519, 540, 566
Gaither, Gloria (1942-) 192
Gaither, William J. (1936-) 192
Gardiner, William (1770-1853) 10, 149, 251
Gauntlett, Henry John (1805-1876) 75, 83
Geibel, Adam (1855-1933) 440
Geistliche Kirchengesäng (Anon.) (1623) 19, 84, 85, 236, 624
Genevan Psalter (Louis Bourgeois) (1551) 34, 544
Genuine Church Music (Joseph Funk) (1832) 392
Gerhardt, Paulus (1607-1676) 111, 169
German Jesuits, 54
Gesangbuch (Wittenberg) (1784) 153, 241
Gesangbuch der H. W. K Hofkapelle (1784) 186
Getty, Keith (1974-) 101, 166, 189, 390

Giardini, Felice de (1716-1796) 4, 5, 344
Gibbs, Ada Rose (1864-1905) 498
Gilmore, Joseph Henry (1834-1918) 374
Gladden, Washington (1836-1918) 485
Gläser, Carl Gotthelf (1784-1829) 49
Gordon, Adoniram Judson (1836-1895) 61
Goss, John (1800-1880) 12, 121, 436
Gottschalk, Louis Moreau (1829-1869) 223
Goudimel, Claude (1514-1572) 81
Gould, John Edgar (1821-1875) 391
Graeff, Frank E. 1860-1919) 400
Grant, Robert (1778-1838) 10
Grape, John Thomas (1835-1915) 265
Greatorex, Henry Wellington (1813-1858)
    30, 332, 614
Greatorex, Walter (1877-1949) 333
Green, Fred Pratt (1903-2000) 56
Green, Melody (1946-) 249
Greenwell, Dora (1821-1882) 263
Grose, Howard Benjamin (1851-1939) 450
Groves, Alexander (1842-1909) 231
Grüber, Franz Xaver (1787-1863) 89
Gurney, Dorothy Frances Blomfield (1858-1932)
    546

Haddamuf (fr. Jewish poem) (Meir Ben Isaac
    Nehorai) (1050) 276
Hagen, Francis Florentine (1818-1907) 118
Hall, Elvina Mable Reynolds (1820-1889) 265
Hall, Joseph Lincoln (1866-1930) 400, 561
Hammond, Mary J. (1878-1964) 339
Hanby, Benjamin Russell (1833-1867) 145
Handel, George Frederick (1685-1759) 125, 188
Hankey, Arabella Katherine (1834-1911) 522, 532
Harding, James Proctor (1850-1911) 142
Harkness, Robert (1880-1961) 248
Harlow, Samuel Ralph (1885-1972) 500
Harrington, Karl Pomeroy (1861-1953) 135
Harris, Darrell A. (1949-) 580, 609, 629
Harris, Margaret Jenkins (1865-1919) 510
Hart, Joseph (1712-1768) 291, 479
Hartsough, Palmer (1844-1932) 315
Harvey, Jr., Bennet (1829-1894) 118
Hassler, Hans Leo (1564-1612) 169
Hastings, Thomas (1784-1872) 284, 402, 468
Hatch, Edwin (1835-1889) 225
Hatton, John (ca. 1710-1793) 20, 39
Havergal, Frances Ridley (1836-1879) 301, 302,
    412, 429, 436, 448, 465, 596
Havergal, William Henry (1793-1820) 573
Havershon, Ada Ruth (1861-1918) 572
Haweis, Thomas (1734-1820) 78
Hawks, Annie Sherwood (1835-1919) 459
Hawthorne, Alice (1827-1902) 406
Haydn, Franz Joseph (1732-1809) 240, 319
Haydn, Johann Michael (1737-1806) 10
Hayford, Jack Williams (1934-) 197
Hays, William Shakespeare (1837-1907) 538
Head, Elizabeth Ann Porter (1850-1936) 339
Heber, Reginald (1783-1826) 1, 48, 142, 442
Hedge, Frederic Henry (1805-1890) 22, 23
Heermann, Johann (1585-1647) 176
Helmore, Thomas (1811-1890) 72
Henry, Henri F. (1818-1888) 322
Hernaman, Claudia Frances Ibotson (1838-1898)
    151
Hewitt, Eliza Edmunds (1851-1920)
    418, 425, 489, 499, 536, 557
Himmlische Lieder (1641) 88
Hine, Stuart K. (1899-1989) 27
Hintze, Jacob (1622-1702) 144, 326

Hodges, Edward (1796-1867) 190, 235
Hoffman, Elisha Albright (1839-1929)
    256, 257, 397, 462, 494, 524
Holden, Oliver (1765-1844) 57
Holford, William (19th c.) 92
Holland, Josiah Gilbert (1819-1881) 135
Holst, Gustav Theodore (1874-1934) 114, 122
Hopkins, Edward John (1818-1901) 296, 588
Hopkins, Jr., John Henry (1820-1891) 140, 218
Hopper, Edward (1816-1888) 391
Horsley, William (1774-1858) 160, 200
How, William Walsham (1823-1897) 230, 547
Howard, Tom (1950-) 629
Howe, Julia Ward (1819-1910) 603
Hoyle, Richard birch (1875-1939) 188
Hoyt, May Pierpont (19th c.) 327
Hudson, Ralph Erskine (1843-1901) 37, 491, 525,
    541
Hugg, George Crawford (1848-1907) 401
Hughes, John (1873-1932) 337, 413
Hull, Asa (1828-?) 481
Hull, Eleanor Henrietta (1860-1935) 386
Hunter, William (1811-1877) 286
Husband, John Jenkins (1760-1825) 338
Hussey, Jennie Evelyn (1874-1958) 165
Hymns Ancient and Modern (1861) 1, 600
Hymns Ancient and Modern (1875) 5
Hymns and Sacred Lyrics (1874) 46
Hymns and Sacred Poems (1739) 1
Hymns and Sacred Poems (1740) 251
Hymns and Sacred Poems (1742) 246
Hymns and Sacred Songs (1707) 30, 177, 525
Hymns and Spiritual Songs (Isaac Watts) (1707)
    570
Hymns for Little Children (1848) 243, 244
Hymns for the Nativity of Our Lord (1744) 74, 75
Hymns for the Young (1836) 373
Hymns from the Land of Luther (1855) 364
Hymns of Grace and Truth (1904) 2
Hymns Original and Selected (1846) 530, 531
Hymns Tried and True (1910) 279

Ingalls, Jeremiah (Christian Harmony), 1805
Ingemann, Bernard Severin (1789-1862) 321
International Consultation on English Texts (1975)
    616, 627, 628, 633, 634
International Commission on English in the
    Liturgy (1973) 629, 630
Ippolitoff-Ivanoff, Mikhail (1859-1935) 610
Irvine, Jessie Seymour (1836-1887) 369
Iverson, Daniel (1890-1977) 221

Jackson, Robert (1840-1914) 225, 325
James, Mary Dagworthy (1810-1883) 481
Jarman, Thomas (1776-1861) 50
Jeremiah Ingalls' Christian Harmony (1805) 60
Jesu, Meine Freude (fr. Praxis Pietatis Melica)
    (1653) 388
John of Damascus (675-749) 181, 185, 186
Johnson, James Weldon (1871-1938) 602
Johnson, John Rosamond (1873-1954) 602
Johnston, Julia Harriette (1849-1919) 279
Joncas, Michael (1951-) 366
Jones, Charles Price (1865-1949) 503
Jones, Danny R. (1949-) 70, 138, 196
Jones, Lewis Ellington (1865-1936) 258
Joseph, Jane M. (ca. 1894-1929) 114
Joy, Edward Henry (1871-1949) 469
Judah, Daniel ben (ca. 1400) 16
Judas Maccabaeus, (George Frederick Handel)
    (1747) 188

Jude, William Herbert (1851-1922) 478
Judson, Adoniram (1788-1850) 324
Jüngst, Hugo (1853-1923) 117

Kaiser, Kurt (1934-) 277
Katholisches Gesangbuch (1686) 3, 51, 577
Katterjohn, Henry (1869-1931) 113
Keble,John (1792-1866) 577
Kelly, Thomas (1769-1855) 65, 202, 204, 205
Kempenfelt, Richard (1718-1782) 286
Ken, Thomas (1637-1711) 621, 622, 623, 624
Kendrick, Graham (1950-) 348
Kennedy, Benjamin Hall (1804-1889) 521
Kentucky Harmony (1817) 551
Kethe, William (?-1594) 21
Key, Francis Scott (1779-1834) 605
Kirchengesänge (Bohemian Brethren) (1566) 29
Kirk, James M. (1854-1945) 228
Kirk, S. C. (n.d.) 496
Kirkpatrick, William James (1838-1921) 104, 165,
    220, 263, 268, 307, 346, 382, 414, 418, 423, 425,
    470, 489
Kitchin, George William (1871-1938) 203
Knapp, Phoebe Palmer (1839-1908) 261, 362
Kocher, Conrad (1786-1872) 141, 239, 595
Kremser, Edward (1838-1914) 32, 590

Lathbury, Mary Artemesia (1841-1913) 231, 579
Lavallee, Calixa (1842-1891) 606
Leavitt's The Christian Lyre (1831) 350, 483
Lehman, Frederick Ma (1868-1953) 276
Lemmel, Helen Howarth (1864-1961) 297
Lillenas, Haldor (1885-1959) 282
Littledale, Richard Frederick (1833-1890) 216
Loes, Harry Dixon (1892-1965) 179, 520
Loizeaux, Alfred Samuel (1877-1962) 2
Long, Lela B. (20th c.) 529
Longfellow, Henry Wadsworth (1807-1892) 126
Longfellow, Samuel (1819-1892) 625
Longstaff, William Dunn (1822-1894) 472
Lowden, Carl Harold (1883-1963) 492
Lowell, James Russell (1819-1891) 598
Lowry, Robert (1826-1899) 182, 254, 255, 421, 452,
    459, 487, 509, 559, 584
Luther, Martin (1483-1546) 22, 23
Lutkin, Peter Christian (1858-1931) 636
Lvov, Alexis Fyodorovich (1798-1870) 17
Lynch, Thomas Toke (1818-1871) 227
Lyon, Meyer (1751-1797) 16
Lyra Davidica (fr. The Compleat Psalmodist)
    (1708) 183, 184
Lyra Eucharisticia (1864) 239
Lyte, Henry Francis (1793-1847) 12, 25, 483, 575

MacDonald of Mull, Mary MacDougal
    (1789-1872) 115
Mackay, William Paton (1839-1885) 338
Madan, Martin (1725-1790) 210, 211
Madeira, Phil (1952-) 189
Mahlmann, Seigfried A. (1771-1826) 604
Main, Hubert Platt (1839-1925) 350, 483
Maker, Frederick Charles (1844-1927) 170, 474
Malan, Henri Abraham César (1787-1864) 302, 521
Malotte, Albert Hay (1895-1964) 632
Mann, Arthur Henry (1850-1929) 83, 446
March, Daniel (1816-1909) 350
Marlatt, Earl Bowman (1892-1976) 473
Marriott, John (1780-1825) 5
Marsh, Charles Howard (1886-1956) 150, 214
Marsh, Simeon Butler (1789-1875) 394
Marshall. W. S. (n.d.) 228

Martin, Civilla Durfee (1866-1948) 378, 393
Martin, Walter Stillman (1862-1935) 393
Mason, Harry Silverdale (1881-1964) 473
Mason, Lowell (1792-1872) 5, 35, 44, 49, 92, 125,171, 259, 302, 320, 334, 341, 417, 426, 495, 506, 521
Matheson, George (1842-1906) 389, 488
Matthews, Timothy Richard (1826-1910) 137
Matthias Claudius (1740-1815) 592
Maxwell, Mary E. (20th c.) 498
Mays, Claudia Faustina Lehman (1892-1973) 276
McAfee, Cleland Boyd (1866-1944) 457
McBean, Lachlan (1853-1931) 115
McDaniel, Rufus Henry (1850-1940) 514
McFarland, John Thomas (1851-1913) 104, 105
McGranahan, James (1840-1907) 215, 262, 342, 345, 443, 535
McIntosh, Rigdon McCoy (1836-1899) 565
McKinney, Baylus Benjamin (1886-1952) 38
Medley, Samuel (1738-1799) 44
Meineke, Christopher (1782-1850) 615
Mendelssohn-Bartholdy, Felix (1809-1847) 93, 230, 574, 589, 617
Merrill, William Pierson (1867-1954) 340, 341
Messiter, Arthur Henry (1834-1916) 24
Mieir, Audrey (1916-1996) 69
Miles, Charles Austin (1868-1946) 266, 355, 428, 456
Miller, Edward (1731-1807) 172, 328
Miller, William (19th c.) 505
Mills, Elizabeth (1805-1829) 505
Milman, Henry Hart (1791-1868) 156
Minor, George Austin (1845-1904) 360
Mohr, Joseph (1792-1848) 89
Monk, William Henry (1823-1889) 141, 154, 155, 156, 186, 191, 202, 239, 244, 527, 575, 595
Monsell, John Samuel Bewley (1811-1875) 143, 593
Montgomery, James (1771-1854) 34, 35, 79, 98, 147, 158, 331, 332, 431
Moody, Charles E. (20th c.) 310
Moody, May Whittle (1870-1963) 376
Moore, Thomas (1779-1852) 402
Moore, William (19th c.) 581
Morris, Leila Naylor (1862-1929) 213, 224, 289, 380
Mote, Edward (1797-1874) 410, 411
Moultrie, Gerald (1829-1885) 82
Mountain, James (1844-1933) 207, 367, 398, 412
Mozart, Wolfgang Amadeus (1756-1791) 44, 350, 483
Mühster Gesangbuch (1677) 53, 54
Murray, James Ramsey (1841-1905) 105
Musikalisch Handbuck (Georg Rebenlein) (1690) 156

Nachstück, Op. 23, No. 4 (Robert Schumann) (1839) 465, 625
Nägeli, Johann Georg (1773-1836) 334
Neale, John Mason (1818-1866) 72, 76, 85, 86, 94, 139, 154, 155, 181, 185, 186, 317, 318, 548
Neander, Joachim (1650-1680) 11
Nehorai, Meir Ben Isaac (?-1096) 276
Neidlinger, William Harold (1863-1924) 136
Nelson, Paul (1979-) 364, 444
Neumark, Georg (1621-1681) 387
Neumeister, Erdmann (1671-1756) 345
Neuvermehrtes Gesangbuch, Meiningen (1693) 230
New Version of the Psalms of David (1696) 368
Newbolt, Michael R. (1874-1956) 203
Newell, William Reed (1868-1956) 523

Newes Vollkömliches Gesangbuch Augsburgischer Confession (1640) 176
Newman, John Henry (1801-1890) 433
Newton, John (1725-1807) 280, 281, 283, 319, 399
Nichol, Henry Ernest (1862-1926) 353
Nicholson, James L. (ca. 1828-1876) 264
Nicholson, Sydney Hugo (1875-1947) 203
Noble, Thomas Tertius (1867-1953) 53, 354
Noel, Caroline Maria (1817-1877) 207, 208
Norris, John Samuel (1844-1907) 477
North, Frank Mason (1850-1935) 149
Nunn, Edward Cuthbart (1868-1914) 134
Nusbaum, Cyrus Silvester (1861-1937) 313
Nystrom, Martin (1956-) 52

Oakeley, Frederick (1802-1880) 90
Oatman, Jr., Johnson (1856-1922) 401, 447, 594
Orchesographie (Thoinot Arbeau) (1588) 120
Ogden, William Augustine (1841-1897) 287, 361
O'Kane, Tullius Clinton (1830-1912) 564
Olearius, Johannes G. (1611-1684) 81
Olivers, Thomas (1725-1799) 16
Olson, Ernest William (1870-1958) 379
Orr, James Edwin (1912-1987) 295, 296
Osler, Edward (1798-1863) 238
Owen, William (1813-1893) 205
Owens, Priscilla Jane (1829-1907) 346, 347, 423
Oxenham, John (1852-1941) 335, 336

Palestrina, Giovanni Pierluigi da (1525-1594) 191
Palmer, Horatio Richmond (1834-1907) 424, 454
Palmer, Phoebe Worrell (1807-1874) 261
Palmer, Ray (1808-1887) 417
Paris Antiphoner (1681) 548
Paris, Twila (1958-) 63, 66, 175
Parker, Edwin Pond (1836-1925) 223
Parker, William Henry (1845-1929) 152
Parry, Charles Hubert Hastings (1848-1918) 26, 475
Parry, Joseph (1841-1903) 395
Peace, Albert Lister (1844-1912) 389
Peek, Joseph Yates (1843-1911) 500
Perronet, Edward (1726-1792) 57, 58, 59
Perry, Jean (1865-1935) 130
Phelps, Sylvanus Dryden (1816-1895) 487
Piae Cantiones (1582) 87, 80, 109, 114, 139
Pierpoint, Folliot Sandford (1835-1917) 239
Pigott, Jean Sophia (1845-1882) 367
Pitts, William Savage (1830-1918) 582
Playford's Divine Companion (1709) 527
Plumptre, Edward Hayes (1821-1891) 24
Pollard, Adelaide Addison (1862-1934) 298
Pollock, Charles Edward (n.d.) 494
Pope, Robert Martin (1865-1944) 80
Pott, Francis (1832-1909) 191
Pounds, Jessie Brown (1861-1921) 270, 375
Praetorius, Michael (1571-1621) 84, 85
Praxis Pietatis Melica (1653) 388
Prentiss, Elizabeth Payson (1818-1878) 463
Prichard, Rowland Hugh (1811-1887) 42, 74, 195, 238, 248
Prior, Charles Edwin (1856-1927) 352
Prudentius, Marcus Aurelius Clemens (348-413) 80, 86
Psalmes of David in English Meter (1579) 467
Psalmodia Evangelica (Thomas Williams) (1789) 77
Psalms and Hymns (1739) 247
Psalms and Hymns (1844) 591
Psalms and Hymns for Divine Worship (1867) 98, 317

Psalms of David (1800) 320
Psalms, Hymns and Anthems of the Foundling Hospital (1796) 238
Pseaumes Octante Trois de David (1551) 21
Purcell, Henry (ca. 1659-1695) 318
Purday, Charles Henry (1799-1885) 15

Rader, Paul (1878-1938) 432
Ramsey, Benjamin Mansell (1849-1923) 476
Rankin, Jeremiah Eames (1828-1904) 586, 587
Rebenlein, Georg (Musikalisch Handback) (1690) 156
Redhead, Richard (1820-1901) 158, 227, 290
Redner, Lewis Henry (1830-1908) 95
Reed, Andrew (1787-1862) 223
Reed, Edith Margaret Gellibrand (1885-1933) 119
Rees, John (1828-1900) 280, 281
Rees, William (1802-1883) 254
Reichardt, C. Luise (1779-1826) 436
Reimann, Henrich (1850-1906) 29
Reinagle, Alexander Robert (1799-1877) 335, 399
Reinhardt Manuscript (1754) 143
Rider, Charles (19th c.) 92
Rider, Lucy Jane (1849-1922) 226
Rimbault, Edward Francis (1816-1876) 323, 550
Rinkart, Martin (1586-1649) 589
Rippon, John (1751-1836) 57, 58, 59, 392
Rische, August (?-1906) 253
Rist, Johann (1607-1667) 88
Roberts, Daniel Crane (1841-1907) 597
Roberts, John (1822-1877) 18, 25, 193
Robinson, George Wade (1838-1877) 398
Robinson, Robert (1735-1790) 13, 14
Rodgers, Dawn (1957-) 7, 106, 107, 108, 252
Rowlands, William Penfro (1860-1937) 41
Röntgen, Julius (1855-1932) 201
Root, George Frederick (1820-1895) 212, 269, 608
Rossetti, Christina Georgina (1830-1894) 91, 122, 123
Rounsefell, Carrie Esther Parker (1861-1930) 352
Rowe, James (1865-1933) 314, 516
Rowley, Francis Harold (1854-1952) 507
Runyan, William Marion (1870-1957) 33
Russell, Anna Belle (1862-1954) 420
Russell, Arthur Tozer (1806-1874) 88

Sacred Melodies (1815) 149
Sammis, John Henry (1846-1919) 504
Sandell-Berg, Carolina Wilhelmina (1832-1903) 379, 416
Sankey, Ira David (1840-1908) 306, 349, 381, 384, 396, 415, 434, 464
Sarum plainsong, Mode IV, 76, 631
Scheffler, Johann (1624-1677) 118
Schlegel, Katharina Amalia Dorothea von (1697-1768) 364
Schleische Volkslieder (1842) 53
Schofield, Jack P. (1882-1972) 512
Scholefield, Clement Cotterill (1839-1904) 578
Schop, Johann (1590-1664) 88
Schraid, Christian von (1768-1854) 103
Schroll, Eleanor Allen (20th c.) 455
Schubert, Franz Peter (1797-1828) 628
Schultz, Johann Abraham Peter (1747-1800) 103
Schumann, Robert Alexander (1810-1856) 465, 625
Schütz, Johann Jacob (1640-1690) 29
Schwedler, Johann Christoph (1672-1730) 521
Scott, Clara H. Fiske (1841-1897) 229
Scriven, Joseph Medlicott (1819-1886) 460
Sears, Edmund Hamilton (1810-1876) 100

Second Supplement to Psalmody in Miniature (ca. 1780) 328
Seiss, Joseph August (1823-1904) 53, 54
Sellers, Ernest Orlando (1869-1952) 232, 420
Shaw, Knowles (1834-1878) 360
Shaw, Martin (1875-1958) 243
Shepherd, Thomas (1665-1739) 486
Sheppard, Franklin Lawrence (1852-1930) 237
Sherwin, William Fiske (1826-1888) 231, 327, 579
Showalter, Anthony Johnson (1858-1924) 397
Shrubsole, William (1760-1806) 59
Shurtleff, Ernest Warburton (1862-1917) 451
Sibelius, Jean (1865-1957) 364, 444
Silvester, Frederick C. (1901-1966) 606
Simpson, Albert Benjamin (1843-1919) 427, 528
Siroe (George Frederick Handel) (1728) 125
Skoog, Andrew L. (1856-1934) 416
Slade, Mary Bridges Brown Baker Canedy (1826-1882) 445
Sleeper, William True (1819-1904) 271, 299
Small, James Grindlay (1817-1888) 515
Smart, Henry Thomas (1813-1879) 98, 185, 204, 210, 317, 437, 451
Smith, Henry Percy (1825-1898) 324, 485
Smith, Howard E. (1863-1918) 516
Smith, Ida Reed (1865-1951) 561
Smith, John Stafford (1750-1836) 605
Smith, Oswald Jeffrey (1889-1986) 502
Smith, Robert (1780-1829) 368
Smith, Samuel Francis (1808-1895) 599
Smith, Walter Chalmers (1824-1908) 18
Song Tunes for the Voice and Pianoforte (1836) 335, 399
Songs and Hymns of the Gael (1888) 115
Songs of Salvation and Service (1923) 33
Songs without Words (Felix Mendelssohn-Bartholdy) (1834) 574
Southern Harmony (1855) 174, 372
Spaeth, Harriet Reynolds Krauth (1845-1925) 84
Spafford, Horatio Gates (1828-1888) 363
Sparrow-Simpson, William John (1859-1952) 168, 480
Spiritual Songs for Gospel Meetings and the Sunday School (1878) 256
Spiritual Songster (1819) 581
St. Bernard of Clairvaux (1091-1153) 169
St. Francis of Assisi (1182-1226) 236
St. Germanus (ca. 639-734) 85
St. Patrick (ca. 386-460) 6
Stainer, John (1840-1901) 97, 109, 116, 139, 162, 168, 480, 546, 640, 641
Stanford, Charles Villiers (1852-1924) 6, 56, 370
Stanley, Samuel (1767-1822) 623
Stead, Louisa M. R. (ca. 1850-1917) 414
Stebbins, George Coles (1846-1945) 271, 298, 299, 304, 351, 448, 472, 515, 556
Steffe, John Williams (ca. 1830-1890) 603
Stennett, Samuel (1727-1795) 200, 564, 565
Steuerlein, Johann (1546-1613) 593
Stites, Edgar Page (1836-1921) 415, 567
Stockton, John Hart (1813-1877) 286, 306, 524
Stokes, Elwood Haines (1815-1895) 219
Stone, Samuel Johnson (1839-1900) 316
Stowe, Harriet Beecher (1812-1896) 574
Stowell, Hugh (1799-1865) 468
Stralsund Gesangbuch (1665), 11
Suffield, Kittie Louise (1884-1972) 490
Sullivan, Arthur Seymour (1842-1900) 181, 438
Sumner, John Bunnell (1838-1918) 403
Sweney, John Robson (1837-1899) 219, 385, 499, 536, 554, 567

Symphony No. 9, 4th Movement, Opus 125, "Choral" (Ludwig van Beethoven) (1824) 190, 235
Synesius of Cyrene (ca. 430) 467

Tappan, William Bingham (1794-1849) 159
Tate, Nahum (1652-1715) 124, 125, 368
Tattersall's Psalmody (1794) 113, 585
Te Deum (ca. 4th c.) 3
Teschner, Melchior (1584-1635) 154, 155
The Chorale Book for England (1863) 329
The Chorister's Companion (1782) 246
The Christian Harp (1836) 281, 549
The Christian Lyre (1831) 148, 350, 570
The Christmas Box (1825) 98
The Collection of Psalm and Hymn Tunes Sung at the Chapel of the Lock Hospital (1769) 4, 344
The Compleat Psalmodist (1719) 183, 184
The Creation (Franz. Joseph Haydn) (1798) 240
The Crucifixion (John Stainer) (1887) 168, 480
The English Hymnal (1906) 54, 96, 187, 195, 211, 238, 242
The Gospel Male Choir (1883) 345
The Hymnal (Oscar Ahnfelt) (1925) 379
The Moosburg Gradual (ca. 1360) 87
The Name of Jesus, and Other Verses for the Sick and Lonely (1870) 207
The New Hymnal (1916) 5
The New Universal Psalmodist (1770) 320
The Passion of Jesus (1852) 46
The Pilgrim's Progress (1684) 453
The Psalms of David (1719) 19, 20, 39
The Psalter (1912) 290, 393
The Psaltry (1845) 334
The Sacred Harp (1844) 14
The Scottish Psalter (1650) 369
The Service of Compline (n.d.) 580
The Seven Last Words of Christ (Theodore Dubois) (1867) 180
The Southern Harmony and Musical Companion (1835) 291, 479
Theodulph of Orleans (760-821) 154, 155
Thesaurus Musicus (Anon.) (1744) 599, 604,
Thomas, Alexcenah (19th c.) 361
Thomas, Rhys (n.d.) 394, 468
Thompson, James Oren (1834-1917) 358
Thompson, Will Lamartine (1847-1909) 303, 534
Thomson, Mary Ann Faulkner (1834-1923) 343
Threlfall, Jeanette (1821-1880) 153
Thring, Godfrey (1823-1903) 46, 585
Thrupp, Dorothy Ann (1779-1847) 373
Tindley, Charles Albert (1851-1933) 466, 501, 569
Tomer, William Gould (1833-1896) 586
Toplady, Augustus Montague (1740-1778) 284
Tourjée, Lizzie Shove (1858-1913) 273
Townend, Stuart (1963-) 101, 157, 166, 390
Towner, Daniel Brink (1850-1919) 279, 375, 504, 523
Traditional: 47, 70, 104, 105, 196, 461, 517, 543, 572, 611, 612, 614, 615, 616, 634
  American: 13, 14, 37, 62, 259, 280, 281, 372, 408, 549, 551, 565, 570, 603
  Appalachian: 174
  Austrian: 107, 319
  Dutch: 199, 201
  English: 96, 97, 110, 116, 128, 138, 146, 147, 211, 242, 243, 530
  French: 82, 99, 102, 127, 134
  German: 51, 54, 65, 79, 84, 94, 117, 253, 592
  Greek: 82, 185, 186, 294, 329, 467, 596
  Gregorian Chant: 171

  Hebrew: 16
  Hebridean: 115
  Indian: 300
  Irish: 6, 91, 370, 386
  Italian: 334
  Latin: 72, 76, 87, 94, 191, 198, 218, 317, 318
  Maori: 295
  Negro Spiritual: 132, 133, 161, 330, 336, 383, 408, 409, 435, 533, 543, 555
  Norwegian: 418
  Plainsong: 72, 76, 80, 86, 631
  Polish; 119
  Selisian: 53
  Spanish: 45
  Swedish: 27, 379
  Welsh: 18
Troutbeck, John (1832-1899) 88
Tucker, Leon (19th c.) 349
Tullar, Grant Colfax (1869-1950) 496, 553
Turner, H. L. (n.d.) 215
Tuttiett, Lawrence (1825-1897) 437
Twenty-Four Gems of Sacred Song (1900) 498

Ufford, Edward Smith (1851-1929) 351
d' Urhan, Chrétien (1790-1845), 550

Vail, Silas Jones (1818-1884) 493
Valerius, Adrianus (1575-1620) 32, 590
Vaughan Williams, Ralph (1872-1958) 19, 82, 96, 128, 146, 147, 187, 216, 236, 242, 530, 547, 587, 624
Venantius Honorius Fortunatus (from The English Hymnal, 1906) 187
Veni Creator Spiritus (para.) (9th c.) 218
Vincent, Charles J. (1852-1918) 405
Virginia Harmony (1831) 280
Vulpius, Melchior (ca. 1560-1615) 431

Wadding, Luke (1588-1657) 128
Wade, John Francis (ca. 1711-1786) 47, 90
Wade's *Cantus Diversi* (1751) 47
Wainwright, John (1723-1768) 112
Walch, James (1837-1901) 343
Walford, William (1772-1850) 458
Walker, Tricia (1953-) 252
Walker, William (1809-1875) 291, 479
Wallace, William Vincent (1812-1865) 513
Walter, Harold Arnold (1883-1918) 500
Walter, William Henry (1823-1893) 340, 583
Walton, James George (1821-1905) 322
Walworth, Clarence Alphonsus (1820-1900) 3
Ward, Samuel Augustus (1847-1903) 601
Warner, Anna Bartlett (1820-1915) 274
Warren, George William (1828-1902) 597
Watson, Albert C. (n.d.) 606
Watts, Isaac (1674-1748) 19, 20, 28, 30, 39, 43, 92, 171, 172, 177, 241, 242, 328, 372, 439, 525, 551, 570, 583, 584
Webb, George James (1803-1887) 441
Webbe, Samuel (1740-1816) 402
Weber, Carl Maria Friedrich Ernst von (1786-1826) 292
Webster, Joseph Philbrick (1819-1875) 560
Weeden, Winfield Scott (1847-1908) 305, 537
Weir, Robert Stanley (1856-1926) 606
Weissel, Georg (1590-1635) 77
Werner, Johann Gottlob (n.d.) 573
Wesley, Charles (1707-1788) 37, 40, 41, 42, 49, 50, 74, 75, 93, 183, 184, 193, 206, 209, 210, 211, 246, 247, 292, 394, 395, 449, 495, 573
Wesley, John (1703-1791) 251

Wesley, Samuel Sebastian (1810-1876) 316, 620
Wesleyan Sacred Harp, (William McDonald) (1854) 323
Weston, Rebecca J. (n.d.) 545
Whelpton, George (1847-1930) 618
Whiddington, Ada A. (19th c.) 312
Whitcomb, George Walker (1862-1941) 214
Whitfield, Frederick (1829-1904) 62
Whitfield, George (1714-1770) 93
Whiting, William (1825-1878) 600
Whittier, John Greenleaf (1807-1892) 474, 475, 513
Whittle, Daniel Webster (1840-1901) 308, 342, 376, 443, 535
Wilkinson, Kate Barclay (1859-1928) 497
William Gardiner's Sacred Melodies (1815) 10, 149, 251
Williams, Aaron (1731-1776) 35, 320, 341
Williams, C. C. (?-1892) 308

Williams, Clara Tear (1858-1937) 541
Williams, Peter (1723-1796) 413
Williams, Robert (1782-1818) 25, 193, 245
Williams, Thomas John (1869-1944) 272, 321, 598
Williams, William (1717-1791) 413
Willis, Richard Storrs (1819-1900) 53, 100
Wilson, Emily Divine (1865-1942) 557
Wilson, Hugh (1764-1824) 177, 368
Winkworth, Catherine (1827-1878) 11, 77, 81, 111, 387, 388, 589
Witt, Christian Friedrich (ca. 1660-1716) 75
Witty, Robert (n.d.) 407
Wolcott, Samuel (1813-1886) 344
Wood, Charles (1866-1926) 120
Woodward, George Ratcliffe (1848-1934) 87, 120
Wordsworth, Christopher (1807-1885) 144, 190, 199, 326
Work, Jr., John Wesley (1871-1925) 132
Wright, J. B. F. (1877-1959) 539

Württemberg Gesangbuch (1784) 153
Wyeth's *Repository of Sacred Music, Part Second* (1813) 13
Wyse, Eric Lee (1959-) 7, 14, 66, 71, 80, 87, 101, 102, 106, 107, 120, 127, 138, 157, 166, 189, 196, 208, 252, 281, 300, 330, 365, 366, 386, 390, 407, 409, 435, 549, 555, 570, 572, 580, 609, 611, 612, 616, 626, 630, 631, 632, 633, 634

Yates, John Henry (1837-1900) 434
York, Terry W. (1949-) 9
Young, George A. (1903-?) 422
Young, John Freeman (1820-1885) 89

Zinzendorf, Nikolaus Ludwig von (1700-1760) 251
Zschech, Darlene Joyce (1965-) 71
Zundel, John (1815-1882) 2, 40

CHURCH YEAR INDEX

ADVENT
Christ, Whose Glory Fills the Skies, 573
Come, Thou Long-Expected Jesus (*Hyfrydol*), 74
Come, Thou Long-Expected Jesus (*Stuttgart*), 75
Comfort, Comfort Ye My People, 81
Creator of the Stars of Night, 76
Hail to the Lord's Anointed, 79
Hark the Glad Sound! The Savior Comes, 78
Hosanna to the Living Lord, 48
Let All Mortal Flesh Keep Silence, 82
Lift Up Your Heads, Ye Mighty Gates! 77
Lo, How a Rose E'er Blooming, 84
O Come, O Come, Emmanuel, 72
Of the Father's Heart Begotten, 80
While We Are Waiting, Come, 73

CHRISTMAS
A Great and Mighty Wonder, 85
All My Heart This Night Rejoices, 111
Angels We Have Heard on High, 99
Angels, from the Realms of Glory, 98
Away in a Manger (*Away in a Manger*), 105
Away in a Manger (*Cradle Song*), 104
Break Forth, O Beauteous Heavenly Light, 88
Bring a Torch, Jeannette, Isabella! 134
Child in the Manger, 115
Christians, Awake! 112
Come as a Child, 106
Ding! Dong! Merrily on High, 120
Gentle Mary Laid Her Child, 109
Go, Tell It on the Mountain, 132
God Rest Ye Merry, Gentlemen, 116
Good Christian Friends, Rejoice, 94
Hark! The Herald Angels Sing, 93
He Is Born! 102
How Great Our Joy! 117

I Heard the Bells on Christmas Day, 126
In the Bleak Midwinter, 122
Infant Holy, Infant Lowly, 119
It Came upon the Midnight Clear, 100
Joy Has Dawned, 101
Joy to the World! The Lord Is Come, 92
Lo, How a Rose E'er Blooming, 84
Love Came Down at Christmas, 91
Morning Star, O Cheering Sight, 118
O Come, All Ye Faithful, 90
O Come, Little Children, 103
O Holy Night! 129
O Little Town of Bethlehem (*Forest Green*), 96
O Little Town of Bethlehem (*St. Louis*), 95
O Thou Joyful, O Thou Wonderful, 113
Of the Father's Love Begotten, 86
On Christmas Night All Christians Sing, 128
Once in David's Royal City, 83
Rise Up, Shepherd, and Follow, 133
Savior's Lullaby, 108
See, Amid the Winter's Snow, 121
Silent Night! 89
Sing We Now of Christmas, 127
Still, Still, Still, 107
That Beautiful Name, 130
The Birthday of a King, 136
The First Noel, 97
There's a Song in the Air! 135
Thou Didst Leave Thy Throne, 137
Unto Us Is Born a Son, 87
We Wish You a Merry Christmas, 138
What Can I Give Him? 123
What Child Is This? 110
While Shepherds Watched Their Flocks (*Christmas*), 125
While Shepherds Watched Their Flocks (*Winchester Old*), 124

NEW YEAR
All the Way My Savior Leads Me, 421
Another Year Is Dawning, 596
Day by Day, 416
Guide Me, O Thou Great Jehovah, 413
If Thou but Trust in God to Guide Thee, 387
Lead On, O King Eternal, 451
Now Thank We All Our God, 589
O God, Our Help in Ages Past, 28
Savior, Like a Shepherd Lead Us, 373
The Sands of Time Are Sinking, 550
We Rest on Thee, 444
Yesterday, Today, Forever, 427

EPIPHANY
As with Gladness Men of Old, 141
Brightest and Best of the Stars, 142
"Christ for the World!" We Sing, 344
Christ, Whose Glory Fills the Skies, 573
Good King Wenceslas, 139
Hail to the Lord's Anointed, 79
Joy Has Dawned, 101
Shine, Jesus, Shine, 348
Songs of Thankfulness and Praise, 144
The Light of the World Is Jesus, 542
We Three Kings of Orient Are, 140
Worship the Lord in the Beauty of Holiness, 143

BAPTISM OF JESUS
I Bind Unto Myself Today, 6
Hail to the Lord's Anointed, 79
Songs of Thankfulness and Praise, 144

LIFE & MINISTRY OF JESUS
"Christ for the World!" We Sing, 344
Christ, Whose Glory Fills the Skies, 573

Dear Lord and Father of Mankind *(Repton)*, 475

Dear Lord and Father of Mankind *(Rest)*, 474

Hail to the Lord's Anointed, 79

I Heard the Voice of Jesus Say *(Kingsfold)*, 530

I Heard the Voice of Jesus Say *(Vox Dilecti)*, 531

Jesus Calls Us *(Galilee)*, 478

Jesus Calls Us *(Restoration)*, 479

Jesus, Priceless Treasure, 388

O Jesus, I Have Promised, 446

Shine, Jesus, Shine, 348

Songs of Thankfulness and Praise, 144

"Take Up Thy Cross", the Savior Said, 484

When Jesus Left His Father's Throne, 147

TRANSFIGURATION SUNDAY

Hail to the Lord's Anointed, 79

He Is Exalted, 63

He Is Lord, 196

Holy God, We Praise Thy Name, 3

Holy Ground *(Beatty)*, 67

Holy Ground *(Holy Ground)*, 68

Immortal, Invisible, God Only Wise, 18

Jesus Shall Reign, 39

O Worship the King, 10

Open My Eyes, That I May See, 229

Songs of Thankfulness and Praise, 144

Spirit of God, Descend upon My Heart, 217

Spirit of the Living God, 221

Sun of My Soul, 577

The God of Abraham Praise, 16

Turn Your Eyes upon Jesus, 297

We Will Glorify, 66

We Worship and Adore You, 70

Worthy of Worship, 9

ASH WEDNESDAY

Come, Ye Sinners, Poor and Needy, 291

Dear Lord and Father of Mankind *(Repton)*, 475

Dear Lord and Father of Mankind *(Rest)*, 474

God, Be Merciful to Me, 290

I Know a Fount, 267

I Lay My Sins on Jesus, 294

Just As I Am, 293

Kyrie Eleison (Lord, Have Mercy), 611

Lord Jesus, Think on Me, 467

Lord, Who Throughout These Forty Days, 151

Search Me, O God *(Ellers)*, 296

Search Me, O God *(Maori)*, 295

Take My Life, and Let It Be Consecrated
(Hendon), 302

Take My Life, and Let It Be Consecrated
(Yarbrough), 301

Take Time to Be Holy, 472

There's a Wideness in God's Mercy, 273

LENT

Ah, Holy Jesus, 176

Alas! And Did My Savior Bleed, 177

Amazing Grace! *(Land of Rest)*, 281

Amazing Grace! *(New Britain)*, 280

As Longs the Deer for Cooling Streams, 368

At the Cross, 525

Be Still and Know, 365

Breathe on Me, Breath of God, 225

Come, Ye Sinners, Poor and Needy, 291

Dear Lord and Father of Mankind *(Repton)*, 475

Dear Lord and Father of Mankind *(Rest)*, 474

God, Be Merciful to Me, 290

Have Thine Own Way, Lord! 298

I Know a Fount, 267

I Lay My Sins on Jesus, 294

I Surrender All, 305

Just As I Am, 293

Kyrie Eleison (Lord, Have Mercy), 611

Lord Jesus, Think on Me, 467

Lord, Who Throughout These Forty Days, 151

Not I, But Christ, 312

Search Me, O God *(Ellers)*, 296

Search Me, O God *(Maori)*, 295

Take My Life, and Let It Be Consecrated
(Hendon), 302

Take My Life, and Let It Be Consecrated
(Yarbrough), 301

Take Time to Be Holy, 472

Teach Me Your Way, O Lord, 476

There's a Wideness in God's Mercy, 273

Where Cross the Crowded Ways of Life, 149

Wonderful, Merciful Savior, 7

PALM SUNDAY/PASSION SUNDAY

All Glory, Laud, and Honor, 154

All Glory, Laud, and Honor (with Refrain), 155

All Hail the Power of Jesus' Name! *(Coronation)*, 57

All Hail the Power of Jesus' Name! *(Diadem)*, 58

All Hail the Power of Jesus' Name! *(Miles Lane)*, 59

Glorious Is Thy Name, 38

Glory Be to Jesus, 173

Hallelujah! What a Savior! 178

Hark the Glad Sound! The Savior Comes, 78

He Is Exalted, 63

Hosanna to the Living Lord, 48

Hosanna, Loud Hosanna, 153

Lift Up Your Heads, Ye Mighty Gates! 77

Majesty, 197

My Savior's Love, 518

My Song Is Love Unknown, 164

Rejoice, the Lord Is King! 206

Ride On! Ride On in Majesty! 156

The Old Rugged Cross, 167

Were You There? 161

What Wondrous Love Is This, 174

When I Survey the Wondrous Cross
(Hamburg), 171

When I Survey the Wondrous Cross
(Rockingham), 172

When Jesus Left His Father's Throne, 147

**MAUNDY THURSDAY/
TENNEBRAE**

According to Thy Gracious Word, 332

At the Lamb's High Feast We Sing, 326

Go to Dark Gethsemane, 158

Lead Me to Calvary, 165

Let Thy Blood in Mercy Poured, 329

Let Us Break Bread Together, 330

My God, Thy Table Now Is Spread, 328

There Is a Fountain, 259

'Tis Midnight, and on Olive's Brow, 159

**GOOD FRIDAY/STATIONS
OF THE CROSS**

Ah, Holy Jesus, 176

Alas! And Did My Savior Bleed? 177

At the Cross, 525

Beneath the Cross of Jesus, 170

Blessed Redeemer! 179

Christ, We Do All Adore Thee, 180

Cross of Jesus, 168

Glory Be to Jesus, 173

Holy God - Trisagion, 612

How Deep the Father's Love for Us, 157

I Gave My Life for Thee, 482

I Have Decide to Follow Jesus, 300

In the Cross of Christ I Glory *(Crucifixion)*, 162

In the Cross of Christ I Glory *(Rathbun)*, 163

Lamb of God - Agnus Dei *(Nancarrow)*, 634

Lamb of God *(Lamb of God)*, 175

Must Jesus Bear the Cross Alone? 486

O Sacred Head Now Wounded, 169

Tell Me the Stories of Jesus, 152

The Old Rugged Cross, 167

The Power of the Cross, 166

There Is a Green Hill Far Away, 160

There Is a Redeemer, 249

Were You There? 161

What Wondrous Love Is This, 174

When I Survey the Wondrous Cross
(Hamburg), 171

When I Survey the Wondrous Cross
(Rockingham), 172

Where He Leads Me, 477

EASTER

Alleluia, Alleluia! Hearts to Heaven, 190

Ask Ye What Great Thing I Know? 521

At the Name of Jesus *(Belle Rive)*, 208

At the Name of Jesus *(Wye Valley)*, 207

Because He Lives, 192

Christ Arose! 182

"Christ the Lord Is Risen Today", 184

Christ, Whose Glory Fills the Skies, 573

Come, Ye Faithful, Raise the Strain! 181

Crown Him with Many Crowns, 46

Hail Thee, Festival Day! 187

He Lives, 526

Hosanna to the Living Lord, 48

I Will Sing of My Redeemer, 262

In Christ Alone, 390

Jesus Christ Is Risen Today, 183

Lift High the Cross, 203

One Day, 150

The Day of Resurrection! *(Ellacombe)*, 186

The Day of Resurrection! *(Lancashire)*, 185

The Power of the Cross, 166

The Risen Christ, 189

The Strife Is O'er, 191

Thine Be the Glory, 188

To God Be the Glory, 31

ROGATION SUNDAY

All Things Bright and Beautiful
    (All Things Bright and Beautiful), 244
All Things Bright and Beautiful *(Royal Oak)*, 243
Great Is Thy Faithfulness, 33
I Sing the Mighty Power of God *(Ellacombe)*, 241
I Sing the Mighty Power of God *(Forest Green)*, 242
This Is My Father's World, 237
We Plow the Fields and Scatter, 592

ASCENSION

All Hail the Power of Jesus' Name! *(Coronation)*, 57
All Hail the Power of Jesus' Name! *(Diadem)*, 58
All Hail the Power of Jesus' Name! *(Miles Lane)*, 59
Alleluia! Sing to Jesus, 195
Alleluia, Alleluia! Hearts to Heaven, 190
At the Name of Jesus *(Belle Rive)*, 208
At the Name of Jesus *(Wye Valley)*, 207
Blessing and Honor and Glory and Power, 194
Crown Him with Many Crowns, 46
Hail the Day That Sees Him Rise, 193
Hail Thee, Festival Day! 187
Hail, Thou Once-Despised Jesus, 201
Hallelujah! What a Savior! 178
He Is Exalted, 63
He Is Lord, 196
Holy God, We Praise Thy Name, 3
Jesus Shall Reign, 39
Lift High the Cross, 203
Look, Ye Saints! The Sight Is Glorious
    (Bryn Calfaria), 205
Look, Ye Saints! The Sight Is Glorious
    (Regent Square), 204
Majestic Sweetness Sits Enthroned, 200
Majesty, 197
Praise Him! Praise Him! 64
Rejoice, the Lord Is King! 206
See the Conqueror Mounts in Triumph, 199
The God of Abraham Praise, 16
The Head That Once Was Crowned, 202
We Will Glorify, 66
Ye Servants of God, 209

PENTECOST

Breathe on Me, Breath of God, 225
Bring Your Vessels, Not a Few, 224
Channels Only, 498
Come Down, O Love Divine, 216
Come, Everyone That Is Thirsty, 226
Come, Holy Ghost, Our Souls Inspire, 218
Fill Me Now, 219
God of Grace and God of Glory, 337
Gracious Spirit, Dwell with Me, 227
Hail Thee, Festival Day! 187
His Way with Thee, 313
Holy Ghost, with Light Divine, 223
O Breath of Life, 339
O to Be Like Thee! 470
Open My Eyes, That I May See, 229
Open the Wells of Salvation, 494
Pentecostal Power, 222
Revive Us Again, 338
Shine, Jesus, Shine, 348
Spirit of God, Descend upon My Heart, 217

Spirit of the Living God, 221
The Comforter Has Come! 220
There Shall Be Showers of Blessing, 342

TRINITY SUNDAY

All Creatures of Our God and King, 236
All People That on Earth Do Dwell, 21
Arise, My Soul, Arise! 246
At the Lamb's High Feast We Sing, 326
Christ Is Made the Sure Foundation
    (Regent Square), 317
Christ Is Made the Sure Foundation
    (Westminster Abbey), 318
Come, Thou Almighty King! 4
Eternal Father, Strong to Save, 600
Glory Be to the Father - Gloria Patri
    (Greatorex), 614
Glory Be to the Father - Gloria Patri *(Meineke)*, 615
Glory to the Father - Gloria Patri, 616
God, Our Father, We Adore Thee! 2
Holy God, We Praise Thy Name, 3
Holy, Holy, Holy! *(Nicaea)*, 1
I Bind Unto Myself Today, 6
I Will Praise Him! 510
Jesus Christ Is Risen Today, 183
Join All the Glorious Names, 43
Now Thank We All Our God, 589
Of the Father's Love Begotten, 86
Praise God, from Whom All Blessings Flow
    (Dedication Anthem), 623
Praise God, from Whom All Blessings Flow
    (Lasst Uns Erfreuen), 624
Praise God, from Whom All Blessings Flow
    (Old 100th Altered), 621
Praise God, from Whom All Blessings Flow
    (Old 100th Original), 622
Praise Ye the Triune God! 8
See the Conqueror Mounts in Triumph, 199
Shout to the Lord, 71
The God of Abraham Praise, 16
The Risen Christ, 189
There Is a Redeemer, 149
Thou, Whose Almighty Word, 5
Wonderful, Merciful Savior, 7
Worthy of Worship, 9

ALL SAINTS DAY

Faith of Our Fathers, 322
For All the Saints, 547
Glorious Things of Thee Are Spoken, 319
Holy God, We Praise Thy Name, 3
Holy, Holy, Holy! *(Nicaea)*, 1
If We Never Meet Again, 562
Jerusalem, My Happy Home, 549
O What the Joy and the Glory Must Be, 548
Rejoice, Ye Pure in Heart, 24
Shall We Gather at the River? 559
The Church's One Foundation, 316
The Day Thou Gavest, Lord, Is Ended, 578

REFORMATION SUNDAY

A Mighty Fortress (Isometric), 22
A Mighty Fortress (Rhythmic), 23
For All the Saints, 547
God of Our Fathers, 597

Holy God, We Praise Thy Name, 3
How Firm a Foundation, 392
I Love Thy Kingdom, Lord, 320
O God, Our Help in Ages Past, 28
Onward, Christian Soldiers, 438
The Church's One Foundation, 316

THANKSGIVING

All Things Come of Thee, O Lord, 626
Come, Ye Thankful People, Come, 591
Count Your Blessings, 594
Father, We Thank Thee, 545
For the Beauty of the Earth, 239
From All That Dwell Below the Skies
    (Duke Street), 20
From All That Dwell Below the Skies
    (Lasst Uns Erfreuen), 19
Great Is Thy Faithfulness, 33
Now Thank We All Our God , 589
Praise God, from Whom All Blessings Flow
    (Dedication Anthem), 623
Praise God, from Whom All Blessings Flow
    (Lasst Uns Erfreuen), 624
Praise God, from Whom All Blessings Flow
    (Old 100th Altered), 621
Praise God, from Whom All Blessings Flow
    (Old 100th Original), 622
Praise to God, Immortal Praise, 595
Sing to the Lord of Harvest, 593
Songs of Thankfulness and Praise, 144
There Is a Redeemer, 249
We Gather Together, 590
We Plow the Fields and Scatter, 592

CHRIST THE KING SUNDAY

All Hail the Power of Jesus' Name! *(Coronation)*, 57
All Hail the Power of Jesus' Name! *(Diadem)*, 58
All Hail the Power of Jesus' Name! *(Miles Lane)*, 59
Alleluia! Sing to Jesus, 195
Begin, My Tongue, Some Heavenly Theme, 30
Come, Thou Almighty King! 4
Crown Him with Many Crowns, 46
Hail to the Lord's Anointed, 79
Hallelujah! What a Savior! 178
He Is Exalted, 63
His Name Is Wonderful, 69
Holy God, We Praise Thy Name, 3
I Love Thy Kingdom, Lord, 320
Jesus Shall Reign, 39
Lead On, O King Eternal, 451
Lift Up Your Heads, Ye Mighty Gates! 77
Majesty, 197
O Worship the King, 10
Praise, My Soul, the King of Heaven, 12
Rejoice! The Lord Is King, 206
Shout to the Lord, 71
Sing Praise to God Who Reigns Above, 29
The Head That Once Was Crowned, 202
Thine Be the Glory, 188
Ye Servants of God, 209

ALLELUIAS & HALLELUJAHS
All Creatures of Our God and King, 236
Alleluia, Sing to Jesus, 195
Alleluia, Alleluia! Hearts to Heaven, 190
"Christ the Lord Is Risen Today", 184
Come, Christians, Join to Sing, 45
Come, Ye Faithful, Raise the Strain, 181
For All the Saints, 547
From All That Dwell Below the Skies
(Lasst Uns Erfreuen), 19
Hail the Day That Sees Him Rise, 193
Jesus Christ Is Risen Today, 183
Let the Whole Creation Cry, 245
Praise God from Whom All Blessings Flow
(Dedication Anthem), 623
Praise God from Whom All Blessings Flow
(Lasst Uns Erfreuen), 624
Praise the Lord! His Glories Show, 25
Praise, My Soul, the King of Heaven, 12
Savior's Lullaby, 108
The Strife Is O'er, 191
We Worship and Adore You, 70
When in Our Music God Is Glorified, 56

AMENS
Amen - Onefold (final 2 measures), 635
Amen - Twofold *(Dresden)*, 637
Amen - Twofold *(Greek)*, 638
Amen - Threefold *(Danish)*, 639
Amen - Fourfold, 640
Amen - Sevenfold, 641
Amen - Sevenfold (final 10 measures), 636

ANTHEMS (See Chorales and Anthems)

ASPIRATION & CONSECRATION
A Charge to Keep I Have, 495
Alas! And Did My Savior Bleed? 177
All for Jesus, 481
Am I a Soldier of the Cross? 439
At the Cross, 525
Be Thou My Vision, 386
Breathe On Me, Breath of God, 225
Deeper, Deeper, 503
Draw Me Nearer, 309
God, Be Merciful to Me, 290
He Leadeth Me! O Blessed Thought, 374
Himself, 528
I Gave My Life for Thee, 482
I Need Thee Every Hour, 459
I Surrender All, 305
I Would Be Like Jesus, 314
I Would Be True, 500
I'll Live for Him, 491
Jesus, I My Cross Have Taken, 483
Jesus, Priceless Treasure, 388
Little Is Much, When God Is in It, 490
May the Mind of Christ, My Savior, 497
Must Jesus Bear the Cross Alone? 486
Not I, But Christ, 312
O Breath of Life, 339
O Love That Will Not Let Me Go, 389
O Master, Let Me Walk with Thee, 485
O to Be Like Thee! 470
Open My Eyes, That I May See, 229
Open the Wells of Salvation, 494
Search Me, O God *(Ellers)*, 296
Search Me, O God *(Maori)*, 295
Something for Thee, 487

Spirit of God, Descend upon My Heart, 217
Spirit of the Living God, 221
Take My Life and Let It Be *(Hendon)*, 302
Take My Life and Let It Be *(Yarbrough)*, 301
Tell Me the Old, Old Story, 532
"Take Up Thy Cross", the Savior Said, 484
Trust and Obey, 504
When I Survey the Wondrous Cross
(Hamburg), 171
When I Survey the Wondrous Cross
(Rockingham), 172

ASSURANCE (See Hope and Assurance)

ATONEMENT
Ah, Holy Jesus, 176
Alas! And Did My Savior Bleed? 177
Alleluia! Sing to Jesus, 195
And Can It Be? 247
Arise, My Soul, Arise, 246
At the Cross, 525
At the Lamb's High Feast We Sing, 326
Baruch Hashem Adonai, 252
Beneath the Cross of Jesus, 170
Christ, We Do All Adore Thee, 180
Cross of Jesus, 168
Crown Him with Many Crowns, 46
Depth of Mercy! Can There Be? 292
Glory Be to Jesus, 173
God, Be Merciful to Me, 290
Great God of Wonders! 283
Hail, Thou Once-Despised Jesus, 201
Hallelujah! What a Savior! 178
Here Is Love, Vast as the Ocean, 254
How Deep the Father's Love for Us, 157
How Great Our Joy! 117
I Am Not Skilled to Understand, 263
Jesus, Thy Blood and Righteousness, 251
Join All the Glorious Names, 43
Just a Closer Walk with Thee, 461
Lamb of God - Agnus Dei, 634
Lamb of God, 175
Lead Me to Calvary, 165
Let Thy Blood in Mercy Poured, 329
My Savior's Love, 518
O Boundless Salvation, 250
O Happy Day, 323
O Sacred Head Now Wounded, 169
Rock of Ages, 284
The Head That Once Was Crowned, 202
The Old Rugged Cross, 167
The Power of the Cross, 166
There Is a Redeemer, 249
To God Be the Glory, 3
What a Wonderful Savior, 257
What Wondrous Love Is This? 174

BAPTISM
Come, Holy Spirit, Dove Divine, 324
Come, Thou Fount of Every Blessing
(Nettleton), 13
Come, Thou Fount of Every Blessing
(Warrenton), 14
I Bind Unto Myself Today, 6
I Have Decided to Follow Jesus, 300
Jesus, Our Lord and King, 325
Just a Closer Walk with Thee, 461
Moment by Moment, 376
O Happy Day, 323

O the Deep, Deep Love of Jesus, 272
Songs of Thankfulness and Praise, 144
Spirit of God, Descend upon My Heart, 217
Trust and Obey, 504

BENEDICTIONS
A Peaceful Night, 580
Amen - Twofold *(Dresden)*, 637
Amen - Twofold *(Greek)*, 638
Amen - Threefold *(Danish)*, 639
Amen - Fourfold, 640
Amen - Sevenfold, 641
Christ Be with Me, 6 (second part)
God Be in My Head, 635
God Be with You Till We Meet Again
(Endeavor), 586
God Be with You Till We Meet Again
(Randolph), 587
O for a Closer Walk with God, 471
The Lord Bless You and Keep You, 636
Thou Wilt Keep Him in Perfect Peace, 407
Will the Circle Be Unbroken, 572

BIBLE (See Word of God)

CALLS TO WORSHIP & INTROITS
All Glory, Laud and Honor, 154
All Glory, Laud and Honor (with Refrain), 155
Be Still, 609
Be Still and Know, 365
Bless the Lord, 610
Bless the Lord, O My Soul, 36
Brethren, We Have Met to Worship, 581
Christ, Whose Glory Fills the Skies, 573
Come, Christians, Join to Sing, 45
Come, Thou Fount of Every Blessing
(Nettleton), 13
Come, Thou Fount of Every Blessing
(Warrenton), 14
Come, We That Love the Lord, 583
Glorious Is Thy Name, 38
He Is Exalted, 63
Lead Me, Lord, 620
Let the Whole Creation Cry, 245
Majesty, 197
O for a Thousand Tongues to Sing *(Azmon)*, 49
O for a Thousand Tongues to Sing
(Lyngham), 50
Praise to the Lord, the Almighty, 11
The Lord Is in His Holy Temple, 608
The Strife Is O'er (Refrain), 191
We're Marching to Zion, 584

CHILD DEDICATION
Be Thou My Vision, 386
Children of the Heavenly Father, 379
He's Got the Whole World in His Hands,
409
Jesus Loves Me! 274
When He Cometh, 212
When Jesus Left His Father's Throne, 147

CHILDREN'S HYMNS
All Creatures of Our God and King, 236
All Glory, Laud and Honor, 154
All Glory, Laud and Honor
(with Refrain), 155
All Things Bright and Beautiful
(All Things Bright and Beautiful), 244

All Things Bright and Beautiful
(Royal Oak), 243
Away in a Manger *(Away in a Manger)*, 105
Away in a Manger *(Cradle Song)*, 104
Bring a Torch, Jeannette, Isabella! 134
Child in the Manger, 115
Children of the Heavenly Father, 379
Come as a Child, 106
Fairest Lord Jesus, 53
Father, We Thank Thee, 545
For God So Loved Us, 253
God Is So Good, 517
He Is Born, 102
He's Got the Whole World in His Hands, 409
Hosanna, Loud Hosanna, 153
I Belong to the King, 561
I Have Decided to Follow Jesus, 300
I Love Thee, 60
Jesus Loves Even Me! 275
Jesus Loves Me! 274
O Come, Little Children, 103
O Sing a Song of Bethlehem, 146
Once in Royal David's City, 83
Peace Like a River, 408
Praise, My Soul, the King of Heaven, 12
Savior's Lullaby, 108
Still, Still, Still, 107
Tell Me the Stories of Jesus, 152
The King of Love My Shepherd Is
(St. Columba), 370
There Is a Green Hill Far Away, 160
This Is My Father's World, 237
Trust and Obey, 504
When He Cometh, 212
When Jesus Left His Father's Throne,147
Wonderful, Merciful Savior, 7

CHOIR SELECTIONS
Ah, Holy Jesus, 176
Beautiful Savior, 54
Bless the Lord, 610
Break Forth, O Beauteous Heavenly Light, 88
Cast Thy Burden upon the Lord, 617
Christ, We Do All Adore Thee, 180
Come, Thou Fount of Every Blessing
(Warrenton), 14
Ding! Dong! Merrily on High, 120
For All the Saints, 547
God Be in My Head, 635
Hail Thee, Festival Day!187
His Eye Is on the Sparrow, 378
I Bind Unto Myself Today, 6
If Thou But Trust in God to Guide Thee, 387
Jesus, Priceless Treasure, 388
Lift Every Voice and Sing, 602
Majesty, 197
Master, the Tempest is Raging, 424
Morning Star, O Cheering Sight, 118
O Could I Speak the Matchless Worth, 44
O for a Thousand Tongues to Sing
(Lyngham), 50
O Sacred Head Now Wounded, 169
On This Day, Earth Shall Ring, 114
Open the Wells of Salvation, 494
Praise God, from Whom All Blessings
Flow *(Dedication Anthem)*, 623
The Power of the Cross, 166
The Spacious Firmament, 240
What Can I Give Him? 123
When I Can Read My Title Clear, 551

CHORALES & ANTHEMS
A Great and Mighty Wonder, 85
A Mighty Fortress Is Our God (Isometric), 22
A Mighty Fortress Is Our God (Rhythmic), 23
Ah, Holy Jesus, 176
Be Still, My Soul! 364
Break Forth, O Beauteous Heavenly Light, 88
Cast Thy Burden upon the Lord, 617
Christ, We Do All Adore Thee, 180
Come Down, O Love Divine, 216
Cross of Jesus, 168
If Thou but Trust in God to Guide Thee, 387
Jesus, Priceless Treasure, 388
Lo, How a Rose E'er Blooming, 84
Now Thank We All Our God, 589
O for a Thousand Tongues to Sing
(Lyngham), 50
O Sacred Head Now Wounded, 169
Praise God from Whom All Blessings Flow
(Dedication Anthem), 623
We Rest On Thee, 444

CHRISTIAN HERITAGE
America, the Beautiful, 601
Battle Hymn of the Republic, 603
Faith of Our Fathers, 322
Holy God, We Praise Thy Name, 3
Once to Every Man and Nation, 598
The God of Abraham Praise, 16
The Old-Time Religion, 533
The Son of God Goes Forth to War, 442
We Praise Thee, O God *(Kremser)*, 32

CHRISTMAS HYMNS & CAROLS
(See Jesus, Birth of)

CHURCH
Baruch Hashem Adonai, 252
Christ Is Made the Sure Foundation
(Regent Square), 317
Christ Is Made the Sure Foundation
(Westminster Abbey), 318
Faith of Our Fathers, 322
Glorious Things of Thee Are Spoken, 319
God of Grace and God of Glory, 337
I Love Thy Kingdom, Lord, 320
In Christ There Is No East or West
(McKee), 336
In Christ There Is No East or West
(St. Peter), 335
Lift High the Cross, 203
Onward, Christian Soldiers, 438
Rise Up, O Men of God! *(Festal Song)*, 340
Rise Up, O Men of God! *(St. Thomas)*, 341
Singing Songs of Expectation, 321
The Church's One Foundation, 316
The Risen Christ, 189
When in Our Music God Is Glorified, 56

CHURCH HISTORY
(see Reformation Sunday & Church History)

CLOSING HYMNS
A Peaceful Night, 580
Be Thou My Vision, 386
Lord, Dismiss Us with Thy Blessing, 585
Now the Day Is Over, 576
Savior, Again to Thy Dear Name We Raise, 588

COMFORT & CONSOLATION
A Mighty Fortress Is Our God (Isometric), 22
A Mighty Fortress Is Our God (Rhythmic), 23

Abide with Me, 575
All the Way My Savior Leads Me, 421
All Your Anxiety, 469
Amazing Grace! *(Land of Rest)*, 281
Amazing Grace! *(New Britain)*, 280
As Longs the Deer for Cooling Streams, 368
As the Deer, 52
Be Still, My Soul! 364
Be Thou My Vision, 386
Blest Be the Tie, 334
Cast Thy Burden upon the Lord, 617
Christ Be with Me, 6 (second part)
Come, Holy Spirit, Dove Divine, 324
Come, Ye Disconsolate, 402
Day by Day, 416
Does Jesus Care? 400
God Will Take Care of You, 393
He Leadeth Me! O Blessed Thought, 374
His Eye Is on the Sparrow, 378
How Sweet the Name of Jesus Sounds, 399
In Christ Alone, 390
It Is Well with My Soul, 363
Jesus Is All the World to Me, 534
Jesus, Lover of My Soul *(Aberystwyth)*, 395
Jesus, Lover of My Soul *(Martyn)*, 394
Near to the Heart of God, 457
O Master, Let Me Walk with Thee, 485
O Love That Wilt Not Let Me Go, 389
On Eagle's Wings, 366
Our Great Savior, 248
Tell Me the Old, Old Story, 532
Trust and Obey, 504
Under His Wings, 384
What a Friend We Have in Jesus, 460

COMMITMENT
(See Repentance & Commitment)

COMMUNION (See Lord's Supper)

COMMUNION OF SAINTS
Faith of Our Fathers, 322
For All the Saints, 547
Glorious Things of Thee Are Spoken, 319
Holy God, We Praise Thy Name, 3
Holy, Holy, Holy! *(Nicaea)*, 1
Hosanna to the Living Lord, 48
If We Never Meet Again, 562
Jerusalem, My Happy Home, 549
Must Jesus Bear the Cross Alone? 486
O for a Thousand Tongues to Sing
(Azmon), 49
O for a Thousand Tongues to Sing
(Lyngham), 50
O What Their Joy and Their Glory Must Be, 548
Rejoice, Ye Pure in Heart, 24
Shall We Gather at the River? 559
The Church's One Foundation, 316
The Day Thou Gavest, Lord, Is Ended, 578
The Son of God Goes Forth to War, 442

CONFESSION (See Repentance & Commitment)

CONFIRMATION
A Charge to Keep I Have, 495
Be Thou My Vision, 386
Blessed Assurance, 362
I Have Decided to Follow Jesus, 300

I Love Thee, 60
I Would Be True, 500
May the Mind of Christ, My Savior, 497
My Jesus, I Love Thee, 61
O Jesus, I Have Promised, 446
O Master, Let Me Walk with Thee, 485
"Take Up Thy Cross", the Savior Said, 484

CONSECRATION (See Aspiration & Consecration)

CONSOLATION (See Comfort and Consolation)

COURAGE (See Loyalty & Courage)

CREATION
All Creatures of Our God and King, 236
All Things Bright and Beautiful
   (All Things Bright and Beautiful), 244
All Things Bright and Beautiful
   (Royal Oak), 243
Beautiful Savior, 54
Fairest Lord Jesus, 53
For the Beauty of the Earth, 239
Great Is Thy Faithfulness, 33
He's Got the Whole World in His Hands, 409
How Great Thou Art! 27
I Bind Unto Myself Today, 6
I Sing the Mighty Power of God
   (Ellacombe), 241
I Sing the Mighty Power of God
   (Forest Green), 242
Joyful, Joyful, We Adore Thee, 235
Let the Whole Creation Cry, 245
May Jesus Christ Be Praised! 51
Praise, My Soul, the King of Heaven, 12
Praise the Lord! Ye Heavens, Adore Him, 238
Praise to the Lord, the Almighty, 11
Shout to the Lord, 71
Sing to the Lord of Harvest, 539
The Spacious Firmament, 240
This Is My Father's World, 237

CROSS OF JESUS CHRIST (See Jesus, His Passion & Death)

CRUCIFIXION (See Jesus, His Passion & Death)

DEATH (See Jesus, His Passion & Death)

DEDICATION OF BUILDING
Bless Thou the Gifts, 625
Christ Is Made the Sure Foundation
   (Regent Square), 317
Christ Is Made the Sure Foundation
   (Westminster Abbey), 318
Glorious Things of Thee Are Spoken, 319
God of Grace, and God of Glory, 337
O God, Our Help in Ages Past, 28

DEDICATION OF MUSIC INSTRUMENTS
O Praise Ye the Lord! 26
Praise the Lord! His Glories Show, 25
When in Our Music God Is Glorified, 56

DISCIPLESHIP
A Charge to Keep I Have, 495
Am I a Soldier of the Cross, 439

Dear Lord and Father of Mankind
   (Repton), 475
Dear Lord and Father of Mankind (Rest), 474
Give of Your Best to the Master, 450
Go Forward, Christian Soldier, 437
He Who Would Valiant Be, 453
I Gave My Life for Thee, 482
I Have Decided to Follow Jesus, 300
Jesus Calls Us (Restoration), 479
Jesus Calls Us (Galilee), 478
O Master, Let Me Walk with Thee, 485
O Jesus, I Have Promised, 446
Once to Every Man and Nation, 598
"Take Up Thy Cross", The Savior Said, 484
The Son of God Goes Forth to War, 442
True-Hearted, Whole-Hearted, 448

DOXOLOGIES (Last Stanza)
All Creatures of Our God and King, 236
All People That on Earth Do Dwell, 21
Alleluia, Alleluia! Hearts to Heaven, 190
As Longs the Deer for Cooling Streams, 368
Christ Is Made the Sure Foundation
   (Regent Square), 317
Christ Is Made the Sure Foundation
   (Westminster Abbey), 318
Come, Ye Faithful, Raise the Strain, 181
Creator of the Stars of Night, 76
God, Our Father, We Adore Thee! 2
Holy God, We Praise Thy Name, 3
I Will Praise Him, 510
Now Thank We All Our God, 598
O Christ, Our Hope, 198
O What the Joy and the Glory Must Be, 548
Of the Father's Love Begotten, 86
Praise God, from Whom All Blessings Flow
   (Dedication Anthem), 623
Praise God, from Whom All Blessings Flow
   (Lasst Uns Erfreuen), 624
Praise God, from Whom All Blessings Flow
   (Old 100th Altered), 621
Praise God, from Whom All Blessings Flow
   (Old 100th Original), 622
See the Conqueror Mounts in Triumph, 199
The Risen Christ, 189

EASTER (See Jesus, Resurrection of)

EPIPHANY
As with Gladness Men of Old, 141
Break Forth, O Beauteous Heavenly Light, 88
Brightest and Best, 142
"Christ for the World!" We Sing, 344
Christ, Whose Glory Fills the Skies, 573
Hail to the Lord's Anointed, 79
Immortal, Invisible, God Only Wise, 18
Joy Has Dawned, 101
Morning Star, O Cheering Sight, 118
Shine, Jesus, Shine, 348
Songs of Thankfulness and Praise, 144
The God of Abraham Praise, 16
The Light of the World Is Jesus, 542
Thou, Whose Almighty Word, 4
We Three Kings of Orient Are, 140
We've a Story to Tell, 353
Worship the Lord in the Beauty of Holiness, 143

ETERNITY (See Heaven & Eternity)

EUCHARIST (See Lord's Supper)

EVANGELISM & MISSIONS
A Charge to Keep I Have, 495
Bring Them In, 361
Bringing in the Sheaves, 360
"Christ for the World!" We Sing, 344
Christ Receiveth Sinful Men, 345
Come, Labor On, 354
Go, Tell It on the Mountain, 132
I Love to Tell the Story, 522
I Will Sing of My Redeemer, 262
I Will Sing the Wondrous Story, 507
If Jesus Goes with Me, I'll Go, 355
I'll Go Where You Want Me to Go, 352
Jesus Saves (Jesus Saves), 346
Jesus Saves (Limpsfield), 347
Let the Lower Lights Be Burning, 357
Lift High the Cross, 203
Lord, Lay Some Soul upon My Heart, 349
Lord, Speak to Me, that I May Speak, 465
O Breath of Life, 339
O for a Thousand Tongues to Sing
   (Azmon), 49
O for a Thousand Tongues to Sing
   (Lyngham), 50
O Happy Day, 323
O Master, Let Me Walk with Thee, 485
O Zion Haste, 343
Rescue the Perishing, 359
Ring the Bells of Heaven! 269
Send the Light! 356
Shine, Jesus, Shine, 348
Take My Life and Let It Be (Hendon), 302
Take My Life and Let It Be (Yarbrough), 301
The Call for Reapers, 358
Throw Out the Life-Line! 351
Thou, Whose Almighty Word, 4
We're Marching to Zion, 584
We've a Story to Tell, 353
Work, for the Night Is Coming, 506
Ye Servants of God, 209

EVENING
Abide with Me, 575
Be Thou My Vision, 386
Day Is Dying in the West, 579
Now the Day Is Over, 576
Sun of My Soul, 577
The Day Thou Gavest, Lord, Is Ended, 578

FAITH & TRUST
A Charge to Keep I Have, 495
A Shelter in the Time of Storm, 396
Abide with Me, 575
All the Way My Savior Leads Me, 421
As Longs the Deer for Cooling Streams, 368
Be Still and Know, 365
Day by Day, 416
Dwelling in Beulah Land, 428
Faith Is the Victory, 434
Faith of Our Fathers, 322
Give Me Jesus (Give Me Jesus/Spiritual), 435
Give Me Jesus (Sweney), 385
God Leads Us Along, 422
God Will Take Care of You, 393
Great Is Thy Faithfulness, 33
He Who Would Valiant Be, 453
He's Got the Whole World in His Hands, 409
I Am His, and He Is Mine, 398
I Am Trusting Thee, Lord Jesus, 429
I Know Whom I have Believed, 535

If Thou But Trust in God to Guide Thee, 387
In Christ Alone, 390
Jesus, Lover of My Soul *(Aberystwyth)*, 395
Jesus, Lover of My Soul *(Martyn)*, 394
Lead Kindly Light, 433
Leaning on the Everlasting Arms, 397
Like a River Glorious, 412
Make Me a Captive, Lord, 488
Master, the Tempest Is Raging! 424
Moment by Moment, 376
My Faith Has Found a Resting Place, 418
My Faith Looks Up to Thee, 417
Near the Cross, 288
Nearer, My God, to Thee, 426
O Master, Let Me Walk with Thee, 485
Only Believe, 432
Only Trust Him, 306
Savior, Like a Shepherd Lead Us, 373
Savior, More Than Life to Me, 419
Stand Up, Stand Up for Jesus *(Geibel)*, 440
Stand Up, Stand Up for Jesus *(Webb)*, 441
Standing on the Promises, 430
Stepping in the Light, 425
The Solid Rock *(Melita)*, 411
The Solid Rock *(The Solid Rock)*, 410
Tis So Sweet to Trust in Jesus, 414
Trust and Obey, 504
Trusting Jesus, 415
We Have an Anchor, 423
Wonderful, Wonderful Jesus, 420
Yesterday, Today, Forever, 427

FAMILY (See Marriage & Family)

FELLOWSHIP OF BELIEVERS
Blest Be the Tie, 334
Brethren, We Have Met to Worship, 581
From Every Stormy Wind That Blows, 468
In Christ There Is No East or West
    (McKee), 336
In Christ There Is No East or West
    (St. Peter), 335
The Church's One Foundation, 316
Will the Circle Be Unbroken, 572

FORGIVENESS
Arise, My Soul, Arise, 246
Because He Lives, 192
Grace Greater than Our Sin, 279
He Lifted Me! 519
Just As I Am, 293
Let Thy Blood in Mercy Poured, 329
My Faith Looks Up to Thee, 417
My Savior First of All, 554
Our Great Savior, 248
Search Me, O God *(Ellers)*, 296
Search Me, O God *(Maori)*, 295

FREEDOM & LIBERTY
And Can It Be? 247
Hark the Glad Sound! The Savior Comes, 78
He Is Able to Deliver Thee, 287
Jesus Shall Reign, 39
Lift Every Voice and Sing, 602
O for a Thousand Tongues to Sing
    (Azmon), 49
Once for All, 285
Ring the Bells of Heaven! 269
Wonderful Grace of Jesus, 282

FUNERAL & MEMORIAL HYMNS
A Mighty Fortress Is Our God (Isometric), 22
A Mighty Fortress Is Our God (Rhythmic), 23
Abide with Me, 575
All the Way My Savior Leads Me, 421
Amazing Grace *(New Britain)*, 280
Amazing Grace! *(Land of Rest)* 281
Be Still, My Soul! 364
Be Thou My Vision, 386
Because He Lives, 192
Children of the Heavenly Father, 379
Come, Ye Disconsolate, 402
Does Jesus Care? 400
Eternal Father, Strong to Save, 600
Face to Face, 553
For All the Saints, 547
Glorious Things of Thee Are Spoken, 319
Great Is Thy Faithfulness, 33
Guide Me, O Thou Great Jehovah, 413
How Great Thou Art! 27
In Christ Alone, 390
It Is Well with My Soul, 36
Joyful, Joyful, We Adore Thee,
    235
My Shepherd Will Supply My Need, 372
O God, Our Help in Ages Past, 28
O What Their Joy and Their Glory Must Be,
    548
On Eagle's Wings, 366
Peace, Perfect Peace, 405
Rock of Ages, 284
Shall We Gather at the River? 559
The King of Love My Shepherd Is
    (Dominus Regit Me), 371
The King of Love My Shepherd Is
    (St. Columba), 370
The Lord's My Shepherd, I'll Not Want, 369
What a Friend We Have in Jesus, 460

GLORIA
Angels We Have Heard on High - Refrain, 99
Ding Dong! Merrily on High - Refrain, 120
Glorious Is Thy Name - Refrain, 38
Glory Be to God on High, 613

GLORIA PATRI
Glory Be to the Father - Gloria Patri
    (Greatorex), 614
Glory Be to the Father - Gloria Patri
    (Meineke), 615
Glory to the Father - Gloria Patri, 616

GOD, FAITHFULNESS OF
Abide with Me, 575
Begin, My Tongue, Some Heavenly Theme, 30
Children of the Heavenly Father, 379
Great Is Thy Faithfulness, 33
How Firm a Foundation, 392
If Thou but Trust in God to Guide Thee, 387
Like a River Glorious, 412
On Eagle's Wings, 366
Praise, My Soul, the King of Heaven, 12
Standing on the Promises, 430
We Have an Anchor, 421
Wonderful, Merciful Savior, 7
Yesterday, Today, Forever, 427

GOD, GLORY OF
Beautiful Savior, 54
Blessing and Honor and Glory and Power, 194
Christ, Whose Glory Fills the Skies, 573

"Comfort, Comfort Ye My People", 81
Face to Face, 553
Fairest Lord Jesus, 53
Great God of Wonders! 283
Holy God, We Praise Thy Name, 3
Holy Ground *(Beatty)*, 68
Holy Ground *(Holy Ground)*, 69
Holy, Holy, Holy! *(Nicaea)*, 1
Holy, Holy, Holy - Sanctus *(Darnell)*, 627
Holy, Holy, Holy - Sanctus
    (Heilig Ist Der Herr), 628
Immortal, Invisible, God Only Wise, 18
Let the Whole Creation Cry, 245
O Could I Speak the Matchless Worth, 44
Praise Him! Praise Him! 64
Praise the Lord, Ye Heavens, Adore Him 238
Shine, Jesus, Shine, 348
Thine Be the Glory, 188

GOD, GUIDANCE & CARE
A Mighty Fortress Is Our God (Isometric), 22
A Mighty Fortress Is Our God (Rhythmic), 23
A Peaceful Night, 580
All the Way My Savior Leads Me, 421
Amazing Grace *(New Britain)*, 280
Amazing Grace! e! *(Land of Rest)*, 280
Be Still, My Soul! 364
Day by Day, 416
God Be with You Till We Meet Again
    (Endeavor), 586
God Be with You Till We Meet Again
    (Randolph), 587
Guide Me, O Thou Great Jehovah, 413
He Leadeth Me! O Blessed Thought, 374
I Bind Unto Myself Today, 6
If Thou But Trust in God to Guide Thee, 387
O God, Our Help in Ages Past, 28
Our Great Savior, 248
We Gather Together, 590
We Praise Thee, O God *(Kremser)*, 32

GOD, HOLINESS OF
Cross of Jesus, 168
Day Is Dying in the West, 579
Holy God, We Praise Thy Name, 3
Holy, Holy, Holy! *(Nicaea)*, 1
Holy, Holy, Holy - Sanctus *(Darnell)*, 627
Holy, Holy, Holy - Sanctus
    (Heilig Ist Der Herr), 628
O Could I Speak the Matchless Worth, 44
The God of Abraham Praise, 16

GOD, KINGDOM OF
A Mighty Fortress Is Our God (Isometric), 22
A Mighty Fortress Is Our God (Rhythmic), 23
Blessing and Honor and Glory and Power,
    194
Hail to the Lord's Anointed, 79
I Love Thy Kingdom, Lord, 320
Jesus Shall Reign, 39
Lead On, O King Eternal, 451
Our Father in Heaven - The Lord's Prayer, 633
Rejoice! The Lord Is King, 206
The Day Thou Gavest, Lord, Is Ended, 578
The Lord's Prayer *(Malotte)*, 632
The Lord's Prayer
    (Conditor Alme Siderum), 631
Ye Servants of God, 209

GOD, MYSTERY OF
And Can It Be? 247
Cross of Jesus, 168

Great God of Wonders! 283
I Know Not How That Bethlehem's Babe, 527
I Know Whom I Have Believed, 535
Joy Has Dawned, 101
Let All Mortal Flesh Keep Silence, 82

GOD, OUR FATHER
A Child of the King, 403
A Mighty Fortress Is Our God (Isometric), 22
A Mighty Fortress Is Our God (Rhythmic), 23
All People That on Earth Do Dwell, 21
All the Way My Savior Leads Me, 421
Begin, My Tongue, Some Heavenly Theme, 30
Children of the Heavenly Father, 379
Come, Thou Almighty King, 4
Come, Thou Fount of Every Blessing
    (Nettleton), 13
Come, Thou Fount of Every Blessing
    (Warrenton), 14
Day by Day, 416
Dear Lord and Father of Mankind
    (Repton), 475
Dear Lord and Father of Mankind (Rest), 474
Eternal Father, Strong to Save, 600
From All That Dwell Below the Skies
    (Duke Street), 20
From All That Dwell Below the Skies
    (Lasst Uns Erfreuen), 19
God, the Omnipotent, 17
Immortal, Invisible, God Only Wise, 18
O Bless the Lord, My Soul! 35
O God, Our Help in Ages Past, 28
O Praise Ye the Lord! 26
O Worship the King, 10
Praise the Lord! His Glories Show, 25
Praise to the Lord, the Almighty, 11
Praise, My Soul, the King of Heaven, 12
Rejoice, Ye Pure in Heart, 24
Sing Praise to God Who Reigns Above, 29
Stand Up, and Bless the Lord, 34
The God of Abraham Praise, 16
This Is My Father's World, 237
To God Be the Glory, 31
Unto the Hills, 15
We Praise Thee, O God (Kremser), 32
We Worship and Adore You, 70

GOD, PRESENCE OF
Abide with Me, 575
Be Thou My Vision, 386
Day by Day, 416
Close to Thee, 493
Great Is Thy Faithfulness, 33
God Be with You Till We Meet Again
    (Endeavor), 586
God Be with You Till We Meet Again
    (Randolph), 587
Holy Ground (Beatty), 68
Holy Ground (Holy Ground), 69
How Firm a Foundation, 392
In the Garden, 456
Just a Closer Walk with Thee, 461
Near to the Heart of God, 457
On Eagle's Wings, 366
Our Great Savior, 248
Still, Still with Thee, 574
The Beautiful Garden of Prayer, 455

GOD, PROVIDENCE OF
A Shelter in the Time of Storm, 396
Children of the Heavenly Father, 379
Be Still, My Soul! 364

Children of the Heavenly Father, 379
Come, Ye Thankful People, Come, 591
Day by Day, 416
Eternal Father, Strong to Save, 600
God, the Omnipotent! 17
He Hideth My Soul, 382
His Eye Is on the Sparrow, 378
I Sing the Mighty Power of God
    (Ellacombe), 241
I Sing the Mighty Power of God
    (Forest Green), 242
If Thou but Trust in God to Guide Thee, 387
Like a River Glorious, 412
Now Thank We All Our God, 589
My Shepherd Will Supply My Need, 372
O God, Our Help in Ages Past, 28
On Eagle's Wings, 366
Praise the Lord, His Glories Show, 25
Praise to the Lord, the Almighty, 11
Sing Praise to God Who Reigns Above, 29
Sing to the Lord of Harvest, 593
The King of Love My Shepherd Is
    (Dominus Regit Me), 371
The King of Love My Shepherd Is
    (St. Columba), 370
The Lord's My Shepherd, I'll Not Want, 369
This Is My Father's World, 237
Under His Wings, 384
Unto the Hills, 15
We Gather Together, 590
We Praise Thee, O God, 32

GOD, SOVEREIGNTY OF
A Child of the King, 403
Be Still, My Soul! 364
Come, Thou Almighty King, 4
Crown Him with Many Crowns, 46
God, the Omnipotent, 17
He's Got the Whole World in His Hands, 409
I Know Whom I Have Believed, 535
I Sing the Mighty Power of God
    (Ellacombe), 241
I Sing the Mighty Power of God
    (Forest Green), 242
Immortal, Invisible, God Only Wise, 18
Lift Up Your Heads, Ye Mighty Gates! 77
Master, the Tempest Is Raging! 424
Now Thank We All Our God, 589
O God, Our Help in Ages Past, 28
Praise to the Lord, the Almighty 11
The Spacious Firmament, 240
This Is My Father's World, 237
Unto the Hills, 15

GOOD FRIDAY
Ah, Holy Jesus, 176
Alas! And Did My Savior Bleed? 177
At the Cross, 525
Beneath the Cross of Jesus, 170
Blessed Redeemer! 179
Christ, We Do All Adore Thee, 180
Cross of Jesus, 168
Draw Me Nearer, 309
Glory Be to Jesus, 173
Hallelujah! What a Savior! 178
Holy God - Trisagion, 612
How Deep the Father's Love for Us, 157
I Gave My Life for Thee, 482
In the Cross of Christ I Glory
    (Crucifixion), 162
In the Cross of Christ I Glory (Rathbun) 163
Lamb of God, 175

Lamb of God - Agnus Dei, 634
Let Thy Blood in Mercy Poured, 329
Lord Jesus, Think on Me, 467
Must Jesus Bear the Cross Alone? 486
My Faith Looks Up to Thee, 417
My Savior's Love, 518
O Sacred Head Now Wounded, 169
Tell Me the Stories of Jesus, 152
The Old Rugged Cross, 167
The Power of the Cross, 166
There Is a Green Hill Far Away, 160
There Is a Redeem! redeemer, 249
Were You There? 161
What Wondrous Love Is This 174
When I Survey the Wondrous Cross
    (Hamburg), 171
When I Survey the Wondrous Cross
    (Lasst Uns Erfreuen), 172
Where He Leads Me, 477

GRACE (See Love, Grace & Mercy)

HARVEST & THANKSGIVING
All Things Come of Thee, O Lord, 626
Come, Ye Thankful People, Come, 591
Count Your Blessings, 594
Father, We Thank Thee, 545
For the Beauty of the Earth, 239
From All That Dwell Below the Skies
    (Duke Street), 20
From All That Dwell Below the Skies
    (Lasst Uns Erfreuen), 19
Great Is Thy Faithfulness, 33
Jesus Is All the World to Me, 534
Now Thank We All Our God, 589
Praise God, from Whom All Blessings Flow
    (Dedication Anthem), 623
Praise God, from Whom All Blessings Flow
    (Lasst Uns Erfreuen), 624
Praise God, from Whom All Blessings Flow
    (Old 100th, altered), 621
Praise God, from Whom All Blessings Flow
    (Old 100th, original), 622
Praise to God, Immortal Praise, 595
Rejoice, the Lord Is King! 206
Sing to the Lord of Harvest, 593
Songs of Thankfulness and Praise, 144
There Is a Redeemer, 249
We Gather Together, 590
We Plow the Fields and Scatter, 592
We Praise Thee, O God (Kremser), 32
Ye Servants of God, 209

HEALING
Be Still and Know, 365
Come, Ye Disconsolate, 402
How Sweet the Name of Jesus Sounds! 399
Jesus, Lover of My Soul (Aberystwyth), 395
Jesus, Lover of My Soul (Martyn), 394
I Heard the Voice of Jesus Say
    (Kingsfold), 530
I Heard the Voice of Jesus Say
    (Vox Dilecti), 531
I Lay My Sins on Jesus, 294
Immortal Love, Forever Full, 513
Jesus, I Come, 299
Jesus, Lover of My Soul (Aberystwyth), 395
Jesus, Lover of My Soul (Martyn), 394
Leave It There, 466
My Faith Has Found a Resting Place, 418
O Bless the Lord, My Soul! 35
The Great Physician, 286

There Is a Balm in Gilead, 383
Under His Wings, 384
Yesterday, Today, Forever, 427

HEAVEN & ETERNITY
A Child of the King, 403
Abide with Me, 575
All the Way My Savior Leads Me, 421
Amazing Grace *(New Britain)*, 280
Amazing Grace! *(Land of Rest)*, 281
At the Lamb's High Feast We Sing, 326
Be Still, My Soul! 364
Be Thou My Vision, 386
Because He Lives, 192
Beulah Land, 567
Breathe On Me, Breath of God, 225
Dwelling in Beulah Land, 428
Face to Face, 553
For All the Saints, 547
Glorious Things of Thee Are Spoken, 319
Hail the Day That Sees Him Rise, 193
He the Pearly Gates Will Open, 568
I Belong to the King, 561
I Would Be Like Jesus, 314
If We Never Meet Again, 562
In the Sweet By and By, 560
I've Found a Friend, 515
Jerusalem, My Happy Home, 549
Jesus Is All the World to Me, 534
Jesus Loves Even Me! 275
Just Over in the Glory Land, 558
My Savior First of All, 554
O Love That Will Not Let Me Go, 389
O That Will Be Glory for Me, 566
O the Deep, Deep Love of Jesus, 272
O What the Joy and the Glory Must Be, 548
On Jordan's Stormy Banks
    (Evergreen Shore), 564
On Jordan's Stormy Banks
    (Promised Land), 565
Saved by Grace, 556
Saved, Saved, 512
Shall We Gather at the River? 559
Sunlight, 537
The Day of Resurrection! *(Ellacombe)*, 186
The Day of Resurrection! *(Lancashire)*, 185
The Sands of Time Are Sinking, 550
The Unclouded Day, 563
We'll Work Till Jesus Comes, 505
We'll Understand It Better By and By, 569
We're Marching to Zion, 584
When I Can Read My Title Clear, 551
When the Roll Is Called Up Yonder, 552
When They Ring the Golden Bells, 571
When We All Get to Heaven, 557
Will the Circle Be Unbroken? 572

HOLY SPIRIT
Blessed Quietness, 228
Break Thou the Bread of Life, 231
Breathe On Me, Breath of God, 225
Bring Your Vessels, Not a Few, 224
Channels Only, 498
Come Down, O Love Divine, 216
Come! Everyone Who Is Thirsty, 226
Come, Holy Ghost, Our Souls Inspire, 218
Come, Holy Spirit, Dove Divine, 324
Fill Me Now, 219
Gracious Spirit, Dwell with Me, 227
Holy Ghost, with Light Divine, 223
I Will Praise Him! 510
Love Divine, All Loves Excelling

    (Beecher), 40
Love Divine, All Loves Excelling
    (Blaenwern), 41
Love Divine, All Loves Excelling
    (Hyfrydol), 42
O Breath of Life, 339
O for a Closer Walk with God, 471
Open My Eyes, That I May See, 229
Pentecostal Power, 222
Search Me, O God *(Ellers)*, 296
Search Me, O God *(Maori)*, 295
Shine, Jesus, Shine, 348
Spirit of God, Descend upon My Heart, 217
Spirit of the Living God, 221
The Comforter Has Come! 220

HOPE & ASSURANCE
A Child of the King, 403
A Mighty Fortress Is Our God (Isometric), 22
A Mighty Fortress Is Our God (Rhythmic), 23
A Shelter in the Time of Storm, 396
Abide with Me, 575
All for Jesus! All for Jesus! 480
All People That on Earth Do Dwell, 21
Amazing Grace *(New Britain)*, 280
Amazing Grace! *(Land of Rest)*, 281
Anywhere with Jesus, 375
Arise, My Soul, Arise, 246
As Longs the Deer for Cooling Streams, 368
As Ye What Great Thing I Know? 521
Be Still and Know, 365
Be Still, My Soul! 364
Be Thou My Vision, 386
Because He Lives, 192
Blessed Assurance! 362
Blessed Be the Name, 37
Children of the Heavenly Father, 379
"Christ for the World!" We Sing, 344
Come, Ye Disconsolate, 402
Day by Day, 416
Does Jesus Care? 400
For All the Saints, 547
Give Me Jesus *(Give Me Jesus/Spiritual)*, 435
Give Me Jesus *(Give Me Jesus/Sweney)*, 385
God Is So Good, 517
Grace Greater than Our Sin, 279
He Hideth My Soul, 382
He Leadeth Me! O Blessed Thought, 374
He's Got the Whole World in His Hands, 409
Hiding in Thee, 381
His Eye Is on the Sparrow, 378
How Firm a Foundation, 392
How Sweet the Name of Jesus Sounds, 399
I Am His, and He Is Mine, 398
I Bind Unto Myself Today, 6
I Know Whom I Have Believed, 535
If Thou But Trust in God to Guide Thee, 387
In Christ Alone, 390
In the Garden, 456
It Is Well with My Soul, 363
Jesus, I Am Resting, Resting, 367
Jesus, Lover of My Soul *(Aberystwyth)*, 395
Jesus, Lover of My Soul *(Martyn)*, 394
Jesus, Priceless Treasure, 388
Jesus, Savior, Pilot Me, 391
Jesus, the Very Thought of Thee, 55
Just a Closer Walk with Thee, 461
Leaning on the Everlasting Arms, 397
Moment by Moment, 376
My Shepherd Will Supply My Need, 372
Near the Cross, 288
Nearer, Still Nearer, 380

No, Not One! 401
O Love That Will Not Let Me Go, 389
O Master, Let Me Walk with Thee, 485
On Eagle's Wings, 366
Peace Like a River, 408
Peace, Perfect Peace, 405
Savior, Like a Shepherd Lead Us, 373
Standing on the Promises, 430
Sunlight, 537
Take the Name of Jesus with You, 377
The King of Love My Shepherd Is
    (Dominus Regit Me), 371
The King of Love My Shepherd Is
    (St. Columba), 372
The Lord's My Shepherd, I'll Not Want, 369
The Solid Rock *(Melita)*, 411
The Solid Rock *(The Solid Rock)*, 410
There Is a Balm in Gilead, 383
There Shall Be There Shall Be Showers of
    Blessing, 342
Under His Wings, 385
Whispering Hope, 406
Wonderful Peace, 404

INCARNATION
A Great and Mighty Wonder, 85
Ah, Holy Jesus, 176
All My Heart This Night Rejoices, 111
And Can It Be? 247
At the Name of Jesus *(Belle Rive)*, 208
At the Name of Jesus *(Wye Valley)*, 207
Break Forth, O Beauteous Heavenly Light, 88
Brightest and Best of the Stars, 142
Christians, Awake! 112
Come Down, O Love Divine, 216
Come, Thou Long-Expected Jesus
    (Hyfrydol), 74
Come, Thou Long-Expected Jesus
    (Stuttgart), 75
Creator of the Stars of Night, 76
For God So Loved Us, 253
Hark! The He! herald Angels Sing, 93
I Bind Unto Myself Today, 6
In Christ Alone, 390
Joy Has Dawned, 101
Lamb of God *(Lamb of God)*, 175
Let All Mortal Flesh Keep Silence, 82
My Song Is Love Unknown, 164
O Word of God Incarnate, 230
Of the Father's Heart Begotten, 80
Of the Father's Love Begotten, 86
One Day, 150
Songs of Thankfulness and Praise, 144
When Jesus Left His Father's Throne, 147
While We Are Waiting, Come, 73
Worship the Newborn King, 131

INTROITS (See Calls to Worship & Introits)

INVITATION
(See Repentance & Commitment)

JESUS, FRIENDSHIP WITH
Alleluia! Sing to Jesus, 195
As the Deer, 52
His Eye Is on the Sparrow, 378
I've Found a Friend, 515
Jesus Is All the World to Me, 534
Jesus, Priceless Treasure, 388
My Song Is Love Unknown, 164
O Jesus, I Have Promised, 446
Saved, Saved, 512

Savior, Like a Shepherd Lead Us, 373
The Lily of the Valley, 538
Tis So Sweet to Trust in Jesus, 414
What a Friend We Have in Jesus, 460

JESUS, HIS ADVENT
Come, Thou Long-Expected Jesus
   (Hyfrydol), 74
Come, Thou Long-Expected Jesus
   (Stuttgart), 75
"Comfort, Comfort Ye My People", 81
Creator of the Stars of Night, 76
Hail to the Lord's Anointed, 79
Hark the Glad Sound! The Savior Comes, 78
Let All Mortal Flesh Keep Silence, 82
Lift Up Your Heads, Ye Mighty Gates! 77
Lo! He Comes with Clouds Descending
   (Helmsley), 211
Lo! He Comes with Clouds Descending
   (Regent Square), 210
Lo, How a Rose E'er Blooming, 84
O Come, O Come, Emmanuel, 72
Of the Father's Heart Begotten, 80
While We Are Waiting, Come, 73

JESUS, HIS ASCENSION & REIGN
All Hail the Power of Jesus' Name!
   (Coronation), 57
All Hail the Power of Jesus' Name!
   (Diadem), 58
All Hail the Power of Jesus' Name!
   (Miles Lane), 59
Alleluia! Sing to Jesus, 195
Alleluia, Alleluia! Hearts to Heaven, 190
At the Name of Jesus *(Belle Rive)*, 208
At the Name of Jesus *(Wye Valley)*, 207
Beautiful Savior, 54
Blessing and Honor and Glory and Power,
   194
Christ, Whose Glory Fills the Skies, 573
Crown Him with Many Crowns, 46
Hail the Day That Sees Him Rise, 193
Hail Thee, Festival Day! 187
Hail to the Lord's Anointed, 79
Hail, Thou Once-Despised Jesus, 201
Hallelujah! What a Savior! 178
He Is Exalted, 63
He Is Lord, 196
Holy God, We Praise Thy Name, 3
Jesus Shall Reign, 39
Lift High the Cross, 203
Look, Ye Saints! The Sound Is Glorious
   (Bryn Calfaria), 205
Look, Ye Saints! The Sound Is Glorious
   (Regent Square), 204
Majestic Sweetness Sits Enthroned, 200
Majesty, 197
O Christ, Our Hope, 198
Praise Him! Praise Him! 64
Rejoice, the Lord Is King! 206
See the Conqueror Mounts in Triumph, 199
The God of Abraham Praise, 16
The Head That Once Was Crowned, 202
Thine Be the Glory, 188
We Will Glorify, 66
Ye Servants of God, 209

JESUS, HIS BIRTH
A Great and Mighty Wonder, 85
All My Heart This Night Rejoices, 111
Angels We Have Heard on High, 99
Angels, from the Realms of Glory, 98

Away in a Manger *(Cradle Song)*, 104
Away in a Manger *(Away in a Manger)*, 105
Break Forth, O Beauteous Heavenly Light, 88
Bring a Torch, Jeannette, Isabella! 134
Child in the Manger, 115
Christians, Awake! 112
Come as a Child, 106
Ding! Dong! Merrily on High, 120
Gentle Mary Laid Her Child, 109
Go, Tell It on the Mountain, 132
God Rest Ye Merry, Gentlemen, 116
Good Christian Friends, Rejoice, 94
Hark! The Herald Angels Sing, 93
He Is Born! 102
How Great Our Joy! 117
I Heard the Bells on Christmas Day, 126
In the Bleak Midwinter *(Cranham)*, 122
Infant Holy, Infant Lowly, 119
It Came upon the Midnight Clear, 100
Joy Has Dawned, 101
Joy to the World! The Lord Is Come, 92
Lo, How a Rose E'er Blooming, 84
Love Came Down at Christmas, 91
Morning Star, O Cheering Sight, 118
O Come, All Ye Faithful, 90
O Come, Little Children, 103
O Holy Night! 129
O Little Town of Bethlehem *(Forest Green)*, 96
O Little Town of Bethlehem *(St. Louis)*, 95
O Thou Joyful, O Thou Wonderful, 113
Of the Father's Love Begotten, 86
On Christmas Night All Christians Sing, 128
On This Day Earth Shall Ring, 114
Once in David's Royal City, 83
Rise Up, Shepherd, and Follow, 133
Savior's Lullaby, 108
See, Amid the Winter's Snow, 121
Silent Night! 89
Sing We Now of Christmas, 127
Still, Still, Still, 107
That Beautiful Name, 130
The Birthday of a King, 136
The First Noel, 97
There's a Song in the Air! 135
Thou Didst Leave Thy Throne, 137
Unto Us Is Born a Son, 87
We Wish You a Merry Christmas, 138
What Can I Give Him? *(Castle)*, 123
What Child Is This? 110
While Shepherds Watched Their Flocks
   (Christmas), 125
While Shepherds Watched Their Flocks
   (Winchester Old), 124

JESUS, HIS BLOOD
A New Name in Glory, 266
According to Thy Gracious Word, 332
Alas! And Did My Savior Bleed? 177
Alleluia! Sing to Jesus, 195
And Can It Be? 247
Are You Washed in the Blood? 256
Arise, My Soul, Arise, 246
At Calvary, 523
At the Cross, 525
At the Lamb's High Feast We Sing, 326
Beneath the Cross of Jesus, 170
Blessed Assurance, 362
Blessed Be the Name, 37
Blessed Redeemer! 179
Come Thou Fount of Every Blessing
   (Nettleton), 13
Come, Ye Sinners, Poor and Needy, 291

Cross of Jesus, 168
Depth of Mercy! Can There Be? 292
Draw Me Nearer, 309
Glory Be to Jesus, 173
Grace Greater than Our Sin, 279
Hail, Thou Once Despised Jesus, 201
Hallelujah! What a Savior! 178
Here Is Love, Vast as the Ocean, 254
I Know a Fount, 267
I Lay My Sins on Jesus, 294
I Will Sing of My Redeemer, 262
Jesus Paid It All, 265
Jesus, Thy Blood and Righteousness, 251
Just As I Am, 293
Join All the Glorious Names, 43
Lamb of God, 175
Let All Mortal Flesh Keep Silence, 82
Let Thy Blood in Mercy Poured, 329
My God, the Table Now Is Spread, 328
Nearer, Still Nearer, 380
Nothing but the Blood, 255
O Boundless Salvation, 250
O Could I Speak the Matchless Worth, 44
O For a Thousand Tongues to Sing, 49
Oh, How I Love Jesus, 62
Only Trust Him, 306
Peace, Perfect Peace, 405
Praise Him! Praise Him! 64
Redeemed, How I Love to Proclaim It! 268
The Cleansing Wave, 261
The Old Rugged Cross, 167
The Power of the Cross, 166
The Solid Rock *(Melita)*, 411
The Solid Rock *(The Solid Rock)*, 410
The Way of the Cross Leads Home, 270
There Is a Fountain, 259
There Is a Green Hill Far Away, 160
There Is Power in the Blood, 258
There's a Wideness in God's Mercy, 273
Tis Midnight and on Olive's Brow, 159
To God Be the Glory, 31
When I See the Blood, 260
When I Survey the Wondrous Cross
   (Hamburg), 171
When I Survey the Wondrous Cross
   (Rockingham), 172
Whiter Than Snow, 264

JESUS, HIS CROSS
(See Jesus, His Passion & Death)

JESUS, HIS DEATH
(See Jesus, His Passion & Death)

JESUS, HIS KINGSHIP
All Hail the Power of Jesus' Name!
   (Coronation), 57
All Hail the Power of Jesus' Name!
   (Diadem), 58
All Hail the Power of Jesus' Name!
   (Miles Lane), 59
Alleluia! Sing to Jesus, 195
Alleluia, Alleluia! Hearts to Heaven, 190
At the Name of Jesus *(Belle Rive)*, 208
At the Name of Jesus *(Wye Valley)*, 207
Christ Is Made the Sure Foundation
   (Regent Square), 318
Christ Is Made the Sure Foundation
   (Westminster Abbey), 318
Come, Thou Almighty King! 4
Crown Him with Many Crowns, 46
Fairest Lord Jesus, 53

Hail the Day That Sees Him Rise, 193
Hail to the Lord's Anointed, 79
Hail, Thou Once-Despised Jesus, 201
Hallelujah! What a Savior! 178
He Is Exalted, 63
I Love Thy Kingdom, Lord, 320
Jesus Shall Reign, 39
Lead On, O King Eternal, 451
Join All the Glorious Names, 43
Lift Up Your Heads, Ye Mighty Gates! 77
Look, Ye Saints! The Sound Is Glorious
    (Bryn Calfaria), 205
Look, Ye Saints! The Sound Is Glorious
    (Regent Square), 204
Majesty, 197
O Worship the King, 10
Praise, My Soul, the King of Heaven, 12
Rejoice! The Lord Is King, 206
Rejoice, Ye Pure in Heart, 24
Sing Praise to God Who Reigns Above, 29
The Head That Once Was Crowned, 202
Thine Be the Glory, 188
Ye Servants of God, 209

JESUS, HIS LIFE & MINISTRY
Break Thou the Bread of Life, 231
Dear Lord and Father of Mankind
    (Repton), 475
Dear Lord and Father of Mankind (Rest), 474
Hark the Glad Sound! The Savior Comes, 78
In Christ Alone, 390
Jesus Calls Us (Restoration), 479
Jesus Calls Us (Galilee), 478
Jesus, Thou Divine Companion, 148
Lord, Who Throughout These Forty Days,
    151
O Sing a Song of Bethlehem, 146
One Day, 150
Songs of Thankfulness and Praise, 144
Tell Me the Stories of Jesus, 152
That Beautiful Name130
When Jesus Left His Father's Throne, 147
Where Cross the Crowded Ways of Life, 149
Who Is He in Yonder Stall? 145

JESUS, HIS LORDSHIP
A Child of the King, 403
All Hail the Power of Jesus' Name!
    (Coronation), 57
All Hail the Power of Jesus' Name!
    (Diadem), 58
All Hail the Power of Jesus' Name!
    (Miles Lane), 59
Crown Him with Many Crowns, 46
Fairest Lord Jesus, 53
God the Omnipotent! 17
He Is Lord, 196
Himself, 528
His Name is Wonderful, 69
Lead Me to Calvary, 165
Living for Jesus,492
Not I, But Christ, 312
Praise the Lord, Ye Heavens, Adore Him, 238
Worthy of Worship, 9

JESUS, HIS MINISTRY
(See Jesus, Life & Ministry)

JESUS, HIS MIRACLES & WONDERS
Hark, the Glad Sound! The Savior Comes, 78
Love Is the Theme, 278
Master, the Tempest Is Raging! 424

O for a Thousand Tongues to Sing
    (Azmon), 49
Praise the Lord, His Glories Show, 25
Songs of Thankfulness and Praise, 144
Who Is He in Yonder Stall? 145

JESUS, HIS NAME
All Hail the Power of Jesus' Name!
    (Coronation), 57
All Hail the Power of Jesus' Name!
    (Diadem), 58
All Hail the Power of Jesus' Name!
    (Miles Lane), 59
All People That on Earth Do Dwell, 21
As Ye What Great Thing I Know? 521
At the Name of Jesus (Belle Rive), 208
At the Name of Jesus (Wye Valley), 207
Beautiful Savior, 54
Bless the Lord, O My Soul, 36
Blessed Be the Name, 37
Come, Thou Almighty King, 4
Fairest Lord Jesus, 53
Glorious Is Thy Name, 38
His Name Is Wonderful, 69
Holy God, We Praise Thy Name, 3
How Sweet the Name of Jesus Sounds! 399
Jesus Is the Sweetest Name I Know, 529
Jesus Shall Reign, 39
Join All the Glorious Names, 43
O for a Thousand Tongues to Sing
    (Azmon), 49
O for a Thousand Tongues to Sing
    (Lyngham), 50
Stand Up, and Bless the Lord, 34
Take the Name of Jesus with You, 377
That Beautiful Name, 130
The Solid Rock (Melita), 411
The Solid Rock (Solid Rock), 410
Ye Servants of God, 209

JESUS, HIS PASSION & DEATH
Ah, Holy Jesus, 176
According to Thy Gracious Word, 332
Alas! And Did My Savior Bleed? 177
And Can It Be? 247
Arise, My Soul, Arise, 246
At Calvary, 523
At the Cross, 525
At the Lamb's High Feast We Sing, 326
Beneath the Cross of Jesus, 170
Blessed Redeemer! 179
Christ, We Do All Adore Thee, 180
Cross of Jesus, 168
Depth of Mercy! Can There Be? 292
Glory Be to Jesus, 173
Go to Dark Gethsemane, 158
Grace Greater than Our Sin, 279
Hallelujah! What a Savior! 178
Here Is Love, Vast as the Ocean, 254
How Deep the Father's Love for Us, 157
How Great Thou Art! 27
I Gave My Life for Thee, 482
I Have Decided to Follow Jesus, 300
I Will Sing of My Redeemer, 262
In the Cross of Christ I Glory (Rathbun), 163
In the Cross of Christ I Glory
    (Crucifixion), 162
Jesus, Thy Blood and Righteousness, 251
Lamb of God - Agnus Dei (Nancarrow), 634
Lamb of God (Lamb of God), 175
Lead Me to Calvary, 165
Let Thy Blood in Mercy Poured, 329

Lift High the Cross, 203
Lift Up Your Heads, Ye Mighty Gates! 77
My Song Is Love Unknown, 164
Near the Cross, 288
Nothing but the Blood, 255
O How He Loves You and Me, 277
O Sacred Head Now Wounded, 169
O Sing a Song of Bethlehem, 146
Ride On! Ride On in Majesty! 156
Rock of Ages, 284
Take Up Thy Cross, 484
The Old Rugged Cross, 167
The Power of the Cross, 166
There Is a Fountain, 259
There Is a Green Hill Far Away, 160
There's a Wideness in God's Mercy, 273
Tis Midnight, and on Olive's Brow, 159
Were You There? 161
What Wondrous Love Is This, 174
When I Survey the Wondrous Cross
    (Hamburg), 171
When I Survey the Wondrous Cross
    (Rockingham), 172

JESUS, HIS REIGN
(See Jesus, His Ascension & Reign)

JESUS, HIS RESURRECTION
Alleluia, Alleluia! Hearts to Heaven, 190
Ask Ye What Great Thing I Know? 521
At the Lamb's High Feast We Sing, 326
At the Name of Jesus (Belle Rive), 208
At the Name of Jesus (Wye Valley), 207
Because He Lives, 192
Christ Arose! 182
"Christ the Lord Is Risen Today", 184
Christ, Whose Glory Fills the Skies, 573
Come, Ye Faithful, Raise the Strain! 181
Crown Him with Many Crowns, 46
Go to Dark Gethsemane, 158
Hail Thee, Festival Day!187
He Is Lord, 196
He Lives 526
Hosanna to the Living Lord, 48
I Know Not How That Bethlehem's Babe, 527
I Will Sing of My Redeemer, 262
In Christ Alone, 390
Jesus Christ Is Risen Today, 183
Lift High the Cross, 203
O Sing a Song of Bethlehem, 146
One Day, 150
The Day of Resurrection! (Ellacombe), 186
The Day of Resurrection! (Lancashire), 185
The Power of the Cross, 166
The Risen Christ, 189
The Strife Is O'er, 191
Thine Be the Glory, 188
To God Be the Glory, 31

JESUS, HIS RETURN
Are You Washed in the Blood? 256
At the Name of Jesus (Belle Rive), 208
At the Name of Jesus (Wye Valley), 207
Christ Returneth! 215
He Is Lord, 196
How Great Thou Art! 27
Is It the Crowing Day? 214
Lo! He Comes with Clouds Descending
    (Helmsley), 211
Lo! He Comes with Clouds Descending
    (Regent Square), 210
One Day, 150

What If It Were Today? 213
When He Cometh, 212
While We Are Waiting, Come, 73

JESUS, SAVIOR
A Great and Mighty Wonder, 85
All for Jesus! All for Jesus! 480
All the Way My Savior Leads Me, 421
Baruch Hashem Adonai, 252
Blessed Assurance, 362
Come, Ye Sinners, Poor and Needy, 291
For God So Loved Us, 253
Glorious Is Thy Name, 38
Jesus, Savior, Pilot Me, 391
May the Mind of Christ, My Savior, 497
Our Great Savior, 248
Pass Me Not, O Gentle Savior, 311
Savior, Like a Shepherd Lead Us, 373
Savior, More Than Life to Me, 419
Shout to the Lord, 71
What a Wonderful Savior, 257
Wonderful, Merciful Savior, 7

JESUS, SHEPHERD
Ah, Holy Jesus, 176
Bring Them In, 361
Lamb of God, 175
My Shepherd Will Supply My Need, 372
Only Believe, 432
Praise Him! Praise Him! 64
Savior, Like a Shepherd Lead Us, 373
Shepherd of Souls, Refresh and Bless, 331
The King of Love My Shepherd Is
  (Dominus Regit Me), 371
The King of Love My Shepherd Is
  (St. Columba), 370
The Lord's My Shepherd, I'll Not Want, 369

JOY
All the Way My Savior Leads Me, 421
Alleluia, Alleluia! Hearts to Heaven, 190
Blessed Assurance! 362
For the Beauty of the Earth, 239
How Great Our Joy! 117
In the Garden, 456
Jesus Is All the World to Me, 534
Jesus, Our Lord and King, 325
Jesus, the Very Thought of Thee, 55
Joy Has Dawned, 101
Joy to the World! The Lord Is Come, 92
Joyful, Joyful, We Adore Thee, 235
Leaning on the Everlasting Arms, 397
Like a River Glorious, 412
O Love That Will Not Let Me Go, 389
O Perfect Love, 546
O Thou Joyful, O Thou Wonderful, 113
O What the Joy and the Glory Must Be, 548
Since Jesus Came into My Heart, 514
Sunlight, 537
There Is Sunshine in My Soul, 536
We're Marching to Zion, 584

JUDGEMENT (See Warning & Judgement)

JUSTICE & SOCIAL CONCERN
I Would Be True, 500
Jesus, Thou Divine Companion, 148
Once to Every Man and Nation, 598
Where Cross the Crowded Ways of Life, 149

KINGDOM OF GOD (See God, Kingdom of)

KYRIE ELEISON
God, Be Merciful to Me (Stanza 1), 290
Kyrie Eleison (Lord, Have Mercy), 611

LENT
Ah, Holy Jesus, 176
Alas! And Did My Savior Bleed? 177
Amazing Grace! *(New Britain)*, 280
Amazing Grace! *(Land of Rest)*, 281
As Longs the Deer for Cooling Streams, 368
At the Cross, 525
Be Still and Know, 365
Breathe on Me, Breath of God, 225
Come, Ye Sinners, Poor and Needy, 291
Dear Lord and Father of Mankind
  (Repton), 475
Dear Lord and Father of Mankind *(Rest)*, 474
From Every Stormy Wind That Blows, 468
God, Be Merciful to Me, 290
Have Thine Own Way, Lord! 298
Holy God - Trisagion, 612
I Know a Fount, 267
I Lay My Sins on Jesus, 294
I Surrender All, 305
Just As I Am, 293
Kyrie Eleison (Lord, Have Mercy), 611
Lord Jesus, Think on Me, 467
Lord, Who Throughout These Forty Days,
  151
Not I, but Christ, 312
O for a Closer Walk with God, 471
Search Me, O God *(Maori)*, 295
Search Me, O God *(Ellers)*, 296
Take My Life, and Let It Be *(Hendon)*, 302
Take My Life, and Let It Be *(Yarbrough)*, 301
Take Time to Be Holy, 472
There's a Wideness in God's Mercy, 273
Where Cross the Crowded Ways of Life, 149
Wonderful, Merciful Savior, 7

LIBERTY (See Freedom & Liberty)

LIFE & MINISTRY
(See Jesus, His Life and Ministry)

LORD'S SUPPER
According to Thy Gracious Word, 332
Alas! And Did My Savior Bleed? 177
All for Jesus! All for Jesus! 480
Alleluia! Sing to Jesus, 195
At the Lamb's High Feast We Sing, 326
Beneath the Cross of Jesus, 170
Break Thou the Bread of Life 231
Christ, We Do All Adore Thee, 180
Cross of Jesus, 168
Glory Be to Jesus, 173
God, Be Merciful to Me, 290
Hail, Thou Once-Despised Jesus, 201
Here at Thy Table, Lord, 327
How Deep the Father's Love for Us, 157
I Know a Fount, 267
It Is Finished, 629
Lamb of God - Agnus Dei *(Nancarrow)*, 634
Lamb of God *(Lamb of God)*, 175
Lead Me to Calvary, 165
Let All Mortal Flesh Keep Silence, 82
Let Thy Blood in Mercy Poured, 329
Let Us Break Bread Together, 330
Lift Up Your Hearts! 333
My God, Thy Table Now Is Spread, 328
My Song Is Love Unknown, 164

O Sacred Head Now Wounded, 169
Shepherd of Souls, Refresh and Bless, 331
The Risen Christ, 189
The Power of the Cross, 166
We Remember His Death, 630
Wonderful, Merciful Savior, 7

LOVE, GRACE AND MERCY
A Child of the King, 403
Abide with Me, 575
Alas! And Did My Savior Bleed? 177
All the Way My Savior Leads Me, 421
Amazing Grace *(New Britain)*, 280
Amazing Grace! *(Land of Rest)*, 281
And Can It Be? 247
As Longs the Deer for Cooling Streams, 368
As the Deer, 52
At the Cross, 525
Baruch Hashem Adonai, 252
Begin, My Tongue, Some Heavenly Theme, 30
Blessed Assurance! 362
Cast Thy Burden upon the Lord, 617
Come, Thou Fount of Every Blessing
  (Nettleton), 13
Come, Thou Fount of Every Blessing
  (Warrenton), 14
Day by Day, 416
Depth of Mercy! Can There Be? 292
For God So Loved Us, 253
For the Beauty of the Earth, 239
Glorious Things of Thee Are Spoken, 319
God of Grace and God of Glory, 337
God, Be Merciful to Me, 290
God the Omnipotent! 17
Grace Greater than Our Sin, 279
Great God of Wonders! 283
Great Is Thy Faithfulness, 33
How Deep the Father's Love For Us, 157
Here Is Love, Vast as the Ocean, 254
I Love Thee, 60
Jesus Loves Even Me! 275
Jesus Loves Me! 274
Jesus Paid It All, 265
Jesus, Our Lord and King, 325
Joyful, Joyful, We Adore Thee, 235
Love Divine, All Loves Excelling *(Beecher)*, 40
Love Divine, All Loves Excelling
  (Blaenwern), 41
Love Divine, All Loves Excelling
  (Hyfrydol), 42
Love Is the Theme, 278
My Jesus, I Love Thee, 61
My Song Is Love Unknown, 164
Near the Cross, 288
O How He Loves You and Me, 277
O Love That Will Not Let Me Go, 389
O Master, Let Me Walk with Thee, 485
O the Deep, Deep Love of Jesus, 272
Oh, How I Love Jesus, 62
Once for All, 285
Rock of Ages, 284
Saved by Grace, 556
Savior, Like a Shepherd Lead Us, 373
Sweeter as the Years Go By, 289
The Great Physician, 286
The Lord's My Shepherd, I'll Not Want, 369
The Love of God, 276
There's a Wideness in God's Mercy, 273
Wonderful Grace of Jesus, 282
Wonderful, Merciful Savior, 7

LOYALTY AND COURAGE

A Charge to Keep I Have, 495
All for Jesus, 481
Am I a Soldier of the Cross? 439
"Are Ye Able?" Said the Master, 473
Come, Labor On, 354
Faith Is the Victory, 434
Follow On, 452
Footsteps of Jesus, 445
For All the Saints, 547
Give of Your Best to the Master, 450
Go Forward, Christian Soldier, 437
God of Grace and God of Glory, 337
He Who Would Valiant Be, 453
Higher Ground, 447
Lead On, O King Eternal, 451
O Jesus, I Have Promised, 446
Once to Every Man and Nation, 598
Onward, Christian Soldiers, 438
Rise Up, O Men of God! (Festal Song), 340
Rise Up, O Men of God! (St. Thomas), 341
Soldiers of Christ, Arise, 449
Stand Up, Stand Up for Jesus (Geibel), 440
Stand Up, Stand Up for Jesus (Webb), 441
"Take Up Thy Cross", the Savior Said, 484
The Banner of the Cross, 443
True-Hearted, Whole-Hearted, 448
We Rest on Thee, 444
Who Is on the Lord's Side? 436

MAJESTY & POWER

A Mighty Fortress Is Our God (Isometric), 22
A Mighty Fortress Is Our God (Rhythmic), 23
Come, Thou Almighty King, 4
Come, Ye Faithful, Raise the Strain! 181
God of Grace and God of Glory, 337
God the Omnipotent! 17
Great God of Wonders! 283
He Is Exalted, 63
He's Got the Whole World in His Hands, 409
Holy God, We Praise Thy Name, 3
Holy, Holy, Holy! (Nicaea), 1
Holy, Holy, Holy - Sanctus (Darnell), 627
Holy, Holy, Holy - Sanctus
  (Heilig Ist Der Herr), 628
How Great Thou Art! 27
I Sing the Mighty Power of God
  (Ellacombe), 241
I Sing the Mighty Power of God (Forest
  Green), 242
Immortal, Invisible, God Only Wise, 18
Lead On, O King Eternal, 451
Lo! He Comes with Clouds Descending
  (Helmsley), 211
Lo! He Comes with Clouds Descending
  (Regent Square), 210
Look, Ye Saints! The Sound Is Glorious
  (Bryn Calfaria), 205
Look, Ye Saints! The Sound Is Glorious
  (Regent Square), 240
Majesty, 197
O Worship the King, 10
Praise the Lord, Ye Heavens, Adore Him, 238
Ride On! Ride On in Majesty! 156
Shout to the Lord, 71
The God of Abraham Praise, 16
The Spacious Firmament, 240
We Will Glorify, 66

MARRIAGE & FAMILY

Be Present at Our Table, Lord, 544
Father, We Thank Thee, 545

For the Beauty of the Earth, 239
He's Got the Whole World in His Hands, 409
O Perfect Love, 546
Precious Memories, 539

MAUNDY THURSDAY/TENNEBRAE

According to Thy Gracious Word, 332
At the Lamb's High Feast We Sing, 326
Go to Dark Gethsemane, 158
In the Garden, 456
Lead Me to Calvary, 165
Let Thy Blood in Mercy Poured, 329
Let Us Break Bread Together, 330
My God, Thy Table Now Is Spread, 328
There Is a Fountain, 259
Tis Midnight, and on Olive's Brow, 159
Where He Leads Me, 477

MEMORIAL ACCLAMATIONS

It Is Finished -
  Memorial Acclamation Prayer A, 629
We Remember His Death -
  Memorial Acclamation Prayer B, 630

MERCY (See Love, Grace & Mercy)

MIRACLES
(See Jesus, His Miracles and Wonders)

MISSIONS (See Evangelism & Missions)

MORNING

All Creatures of Our God and King, 236
All Things Bright and Beautiful
  (All Things Bright and Beautiful), 244
All Things Bright and Beautiful
  (Royal Oak), 243
Be Thou My Vision, 386
Christ, Whose Glory Fills the Skies, 573
Come, Christians, Join to Sing! 45
Great Is Thy Faithfulness, 33
Holy, Holy, Holy! (Nicaea), 1
Sing Praise to God Who Reigns Above, 29
Still, Still with Thee, 574
The Church in the Wildwood, 582
May Jesus Christ Be Praised! 51

MUSIC & SINGING

All Creatures of Our God and King, 236
Alleluia, Alleluia! Hearts to Heaven, 190
Alleluia! Sing to Jesus, 195
Begin, My Tongue, Some Heavenly Theme, 30
Blessing and Honor and Glory and Power, 194
"Christ for the World!" We Sing, 344
Come, Christians, Join to Sing, 45
Come, Thou Fount of Every Blessing
  (Nettleton), 13
Come, Thou Fount of Every Blessing
  (Warrenton), 14
Guide Me, o Thou Great Jehovah, 413
He Keeps Me Singing, 508
His Eye Is on the Sparrow, 378
Holy, Holy, Holy! (Nicaea), 1
Holy Ground (Beatty), 67
How Can I Keep from Singing? 509
How Great Thou Art! 27
I Sing the Mighty Power of God
  (Ellacombe), 241
I Sing the Mighty Power of God
  (Forest Green), 242
I Will Sing of My Redeemer, 262
I Will Sing the Wondrous Story, 507
Joyful, Joyful, We Adore Thee, 235

Let the Whole Creation Cry, 245
Lift Every Voice and Sing, 602
May Jesus Christ Be Praised! 51
O Could I Speak the Matchless Worth, 44
O for a Thousand Tongues to Sing
  (Azmon), 49
O for a Thousand Tongues to Sing
  (Lyngham), 50
O Praise Ye the Lord! 26
O Sing a Song of Bethlehem, 146
On Christmas Night All Christians Sing, 128
Praise the Lord, His Glories Show, 25
Rejoice, Ye Pure in Heart, 24
Since I Have Been Redeemed, 511
Sing Praise to God Who Reigns Above, 29
Sing to the Lord of Harvest, 593
Sing We Now of Christmas, 127
Singing Songs of Expectation, 321
The Great Physician, 286
There's a Song in the Air! 135
What Wondrous Love Is This, 174
When in Our Music God Is Glorified, 56
Wonderful Words of Life, 234
Wonderful, Wonderful Jesus, 420

NATIONAL HYMNS

America the Beautiful, 601
Battle Hymn of the Republic, 603
Eternal Father, Strong to Save, 600
God of Our Fathers, 597
Lift Every Voice and Sing, 602
My Country, 'Tis of Thee, 599
O Canada, 606
Once to Every Man and Nation, 598
The Star-Spangled Banner, 605

NATURE (See Creation)

NEW YEAR

All the Way My Savior Leads Me, 421
Another Year Is Dawning, 596
Day by Day, 416
Guide Me, O Thou Great Jehovah, 413
If Thou but Trust in God to Guide Thee, 387
Lead On, O King Eternal, 451
Now Thank We All Our God, 589
O God, Our Help in Ages Past, 28
Savior, Like a Shepherd Lead Us, 373
Yesterday, Today, Forever, 427

OBEDIENCE

A Charge to Keep I Have, 495
All for Jesus, 481
Am I a Soldier of the Cross? 439
Draw Me Nearer, 309
I Have Decided to Follow Jesus, 300
I Surrender All, 305
I Would Be True, 500
If Thou But Trust in God to Guide Thee, 387
Jesus Calls Us (Restoration), 479
Jesus Calls Us (Galilee), 478
Jesus, I My Cross Have Taken, 483
Kneel at the Cross, 310
Lead Me to Calvary, 165
Lord, Dismiss Us with Thy Blessing, 585
May the Mind of Christ, My Savior, 497
My Jesus, I Love Thee, 61
Spirit of the Living God, 221
Take My Life and Let It Be (Hendon), 302
Take My Life and Let It Be (Yarbrough), 301
Take Time to Be Holy, 472
Trust and Obey, 504

OFFERING (See Service & Stewardship)

OPENING HYMNS
Brethren, We Have Met to Worship, 581
Christ Is Made the Sure Foundation
   (Regent Square), 317
Christ Is Made the Sure Foundation
   (Westminster Abbey), 318
Hosanna to the Living Lord! 48
Hosanna, Loud Hosanna, 153
The Church in the Wildwood, 582
We're Marching to Zion, 584

ORDINATION
A Charge to Keep I Have, 495
Be Thou My Vision, 386
Come, Holy Ghost, Our Souls Inspire, 218
How Firm a Foundation, 392
Lift High the Cross, 203
O Jesus, I Have Promised, 446
The Church's One Foundation, 316

PALM SUNDAY/PASSION SUNDAY
All Glory, Laud, and Honor
   (St. Theoldulph), 154
All Glory, Laud, and Honor
   (St. Theodulph - with Refrain), 155
All Hail the Power of Jesus' Name!
   (Coronation), 57
All Hail the Power of Jesus' Name!
   (Diadem), 58
All Hail the Power of Jesus' Name!
   (Miles Lane), 59
Glorious Is Thy Name, 38
Glory Be to Jesus, 173
Hallelujah! What a Savior! 178
Hark the Glad Sound! The Savior Comes, 78
He Is Exalted, 63
Hosanna to the Living Lord, 48
Hosanna, Loud Hosanna , 153
Majesty, 197
My Savior's Love, 518
My Song Is Love Unknown, 164
Ride On! Ride On in Majesty! 156
Tell Me the Stories of Jesus, 152
The Old Rugged Cross, 167
Were You There? 161
What Wondrous Love Is This, 174
When I Survey the Wondrous Cross
   (Hamburg), 171
When I Survey the Wondrous Cross
   (Rockingham), 172
When Jesus Left His Father's Throne, 147

PASSION & DEATH
(See Jesus, His Passion & Death)

PASSION SUNDAY
(See Palm Sunday/Passion Sunday)

PEACE
All the Way My Savior Leads Me, 421
All Your Anxiety, 469
A Peaceful Night, 580
Blessed Quietness, 228
"Christ for the World!" We Sing, 344
Dear Lord and Father of Mankind
   (Repton), 475
Dear Lord and Father of Mankind *(Rest)*, 474
God the Omnipotent! 17
He Keeps Me Singing, 508

How Can I Keep from Singing? 509
I Am His and He Is Mine, 398
I Need Thee Every Hour, 459
It Is Well with My Soul, 363
Leaning on the Everlasting Arms, 397
Like a River Glorious, 412
Near to the Heart of God, 457
O Love That Will Not Let Me Go, 389
O Master, Let Me Walk with Thee, 485
Peace Like a River, 408
Peace, Perfect Peace, 405
Savior, Again to Thy Dear Name We Raise,
   588
There's a Wideness in God's Mercy, 273
Thou Wilt Keep Him in Perfect Peace, 407
Wonderful Peace, 404

PENITENCE
Ah, Holy Jesus, 176
Comfort, Comfort Ye My People, 81
God, Be Merciful to Me, 290
I Surrender All, 305
Kyrie Eleison (Lord, Have Mercy), 611
Let Thy Blood in Mercy Poured, 329
Lord Jesus, Think on Me, 467
Lord, Who Throughout These Forty Days,
   151
My Jesus, I Love Thee, 61
Rock of Ages, 284
Search Me, O God *(Ellers)*, 296
Search Me, O God *(Maori)*, 295

PENTECOST
Breathe on Me, Breath of God, 225
Bring Your Vessels, Not a Few, 224
Channels Only, 498
Come Down, O Love Divine, 216
Come, Every One That Is Thirsty, 226
Come, Holy Ghost, Our Souls Inspire, 218
Fill Me Now, 219
God of Grace and God of Glory, 337
Hail Thee, Festival Day! 187
His Way with Thee, 313
Holy Ghost, with Light Divine, 223
O Breath of Life, 339
O to Be Like Thee! 470
Open My Eyes, That I May See, 229
Open the Wells of Salvation, 494
Pentecostal Power, 222
Revive Us Again, 338
Shine, Jesus, Shine, 348
There Shall Be Showers of Blessing, 342
Spirit of God, Descend upon My Heart, 217
Spirit of the Living God, 221
The Comforter Has Come! 220

PILGRIMAGE
All the Way My Savior Leads Me, 421
Amazing Grace! *(New Britain)*, 280
Amazing Grace! *(Land of Rest)*, 281
Be Thou My Vision, 386
Day by Day, 416
Deep River, 555
Follow On, 452
Footsteps of Jesus, 445
For All the Saints, 547
God Leads Us Along, 422
Guide Me, O Thou Great Jehovah, 413
He Leadeth Me, 374
He Who Would Valiant Be, 453
Higher Ground, 447
Jerusalem, My Happy Home, 549

Just a Closer Walk with Thee, 461
Lead, Kindly Light, 433
Lead On, O King Eternal, 451
Lift Every Voice and Sing, 602
Lord, Dismiss Us with Thy Blessing, 585
Now Thank We All Our God, 589
O God, Our Help in Ages Past, 28
O Master, Let Me Walk with Thee, 485
On Jordan's Stormy Banks
   (Evergreen Shore), 564
On Jordan's Stormy Banks
   (Promised Land), 565
Rejoice, Ye Pure in Heart, 24
Shall We Gather at the River? 559
Savior, Like a Shepherd Lead Us, 373
Shepherd of Souls, Refresh and Bless, 331
Singing Songs of Expectation, 321
The Sands of Time Are Sinking, 550
Trust and Obey, 504
We're Marching to Zion, 584
When I Can Read My Title Clear, 551
When We All Get to Heaven, 557
Where He Leads Me, 477

POWER (See Majesty & Power)

PRAISE & ADORATION
A Mighty Fortress Is Our God (Isometric), 22
A Mighty Fortress Is Our God (Rhythmic), 23
Ah, Holy Jesus, 176
All Creatures of Our God and King, 236
All Glory, Laud, and Honor
   (St. Theoldulph), 154
All Glory, Laud, and Honor
   (St. Theodulph - with Refrain), 155
All Hail the Power of Jesus' Name!
   (Coronation), 57
All Hail the Power of Jesus' Name!
   (Diadem), 58
All Hail the Power of Jesus' Name!
   (Miles Lane), 59
All People That on Earth Do Dwell, 21
All Things Bright and Beautiful
   (All Things Bright and Beautiful), 244
All Things Bright and Beautiful
   (Royal Oak), 243
Alleluia, Alleluia! Hearts to Heaven, 190
As the Deer, 52
At the Name of Jesus *(Belle Rive)*, 208
At the Name of Jesus *(Wye Valley)*, 207
Beautiful Savior, 54
Begin, My Tongue, Some Heavenly Theme, 30
Bless the Lord, O My Soul, 36
Blessed Assurance! 362
Blessed Be the Name, 37
Brightest and Best of the Stars, 142
Christ Is Made the Sure Foundation
   (Regent Square), 317
Christ Is Made the Sure Foundation!
   (Westminster Abbey), 318
"Christ the Lord Is Risen Today", 184
Come as a Child, 106
Come, Christians, Join to Sing! 45
Come, Thou Almighty King, 4
Creator of the Stars of Night, 76
Crown Him with Many Crowns, 46
Fairest Lord Jesus, 53
For the Beauty of the Earth, 239
Glorious Is Thy Name, 38
Glory Be to Jesus, 173
Glory Be to the Father - Gloria Patri
   (Greatorex), 614

Glory Be to the Father - Gloria Patri
(Gloria Patri), 615
Glory to the Father - Gloria Patri, 616
Down at the Cross, 524
God Is So Good, 517
God, Our Father, We Adore Thee! 2
Great God of Wonders! 283
Hallelujah! What a Savior! 278
He Is Exalted, 63
His Name Is Wonderful, 69
Holy God, We Praise Thy Name, 3
Holy Ground (Beatty), 67
Holy Ground (Holy Ground), 68
Holy, Holy, Holy! (Nicaea), 1
Holy, Holy, Holy - Sanctus (Darnell), 627
Holy, Holy, Holy - Sanctus
(Heilig Ist Der Herr), 628
Hosanna to the Living Lord! 48
Hosanna, Loud Hosanna, 153
How Great Thou Art! 27
How Sweet the Name of Jesus Sounds! 399
I Will Praise Him! 510
I Will Sing of My Redeemer, 262
Jesus Shall Reign, 39
Jesus, Our Lord and King, 325
Jesus, the Very Thought of Thee, 55
Join All the Glorious Names, 43
Joyful, Joyful, We Adore Thee, 235
Let the Whole Creation Cry, 245
Lift Up Your Heads, Ye Mighty Gates! 77
Love Divine, All Loves Excelling (Beecher), 40
Love Divine, All Loves Excelling
(Blaenwern), 41
Love Divine, All Loves Excelling
(Hyfrydol), 42
Majesty, 197
May Jesus Christ Be Praised! 51
My Jesus, I Love Thee, 61
Now Thank We All Our God, 589
O Come, All Ye Faithful, 90
O Come, Let Us Adore Him, 47
O Could I Speak the Matchless Worth, 44
O for a Thousand Tongues to Sing
(Azmon), 49
O for a Thousand Tongues to Sing
(Lyngham), 50
O God, Our Help in Ages Past, 28
O Praise Ye the Lord! 26
O Worship the King, 10
Of the Father's Love Begotten, 86
Oh, How I Love Jesus, 62
Praise God, from Whom All Blessings Flow
(Dedication Anthem), 623
Praise God, from Whom All Blessings Flow
(Lasst Uns Erfreuen), 624
Praise God, from Whom All Blessings Flow
(Old 100th, original), 622
Praise God, from Whom All Blessings Flow
(Old 100th, altered), 621
Praise Him! Praise Him! 64
Praise the Lord! Ye Heavens, Adore Him, 238
Praise the Savior, 65
Praise to the Lord, the Almighty, 11
Praise Ye the Triune God! 8
Rejoice, the Lord Is King! 206
Shout to the Lord, 71
Sing Praise to God Who Reigns Above, 29
The Church's One Foundation, 316
The God of Abraham Praise, 16
To God Be the Glory, 31
We Praise Thee, O God, Our Redeemer, 32
We Praise Thee, O God, (Revive Us Again), 338

We Will Glorify, 66
We Worship and Adore You, 70
When in Our Music God Is Glorified, 56
Wonderful, Merciful Savior, 7
Worship the Lord in the Beauty of Holiness,
143
Worthy of Worship, 9
Ye Servants of God, 209
Yesterday, Today, Forever, 427

PRAYER & GUIDANCE
Abide with Me, 575
All Your Anxiety, 469
Be Still and Know, 365
Be Thou My Vision, 386
Cast Thy Burden upon the Lord, 617
Dear Lord and Father of Mankind
(Repton), 475
Dear Lord and Father of Mankind (Rest), 474
Draw Me Nearer, 309
Eternal Father, Strong to Save, 600
From Every Stormy Wind That Blows, 468
God Is So Good, 517
Hear Our Prayer, O Lord, 618
I Am Praying for You, 464
I Must Tell Jesus! 462
I Need Thee Every Hour, 459
I Would Be True, 500
If Thou But Trust in God to Guide Thee, 387
In the Garden, 456
Just a Closer Walk with Thee, 461
Leave It There, 466
More Love to Thee, O Christ, 463
My Faith Looks Up to Thee, 417
Near to the Heart of God, 457
O for a Closer Walk with God, 471
O to Be Like Thee! 470
Open My Eyes, That I May See, 229
Savior, Like a Shepherd Lead Us, 373
Spirit of God, Descend upon My Heart, 217
Sunlight, 537
Sweet Hour of Prayer, 458
Take Time to Be Holy, 472
The Beautiful Garden of Prayer, 455
Turn Your Eyes upon Jesus, 297
What a Friend We Have in Jesus, 460

PRAYER RESPONSES
Be Still and Know, 365
Cast Thy Burden upon the Lord, 617
God Is So Good, 517
Hear Our Prayer, O Lord, 618
I Know a Fount, 267
Lead Me, Lord, 620
Let the Words of My Mouth, 619
O Come, Let Us Adore Him, 47
O How He Loves You and Me, 277
Thou Wilt Keep Him in Perfect Peace, 407
Turn Your Eyes upon Jesus - Refrain, 297

PRAYERS
A Peaceful Night, 580
Come Down, O Love Divine, 216
Come, Holy Ghost, Our Souls Inspire, 218
Christ Be with Me, 6 (second part)
Christ, We Do All Adore Thee, 180
Dear Lord and Father of Mankind
(Repton), 475
Dear Lord and Father of Mankind (Rest), 474
Eternal Father, Strong to Save, 600
Kyrie Eleison (Lord, Have Mercy), 611
Lord, Jesus, Think on Me, 467

Lord, Speak to Me, that I May Speak, 465
O Breath of Life, 339
O for a Closer Walk with God, 471
Our Father in Heaven - The Lord's Prayer, 632
Search Me, O God (Ellers), 296
Search Me, O God (Maori), 295
Spirit of the Living God, 221
Teach Me Your Way, O Lord, 476
The Lord Bless You and Keep You, 636
The Lord's Prayer
(Conditor Alme Siderum), 631
The Lord's Prayer (Malotte), 632
The Risen Christ, 189

PROCESSIONALS
A Mighty Fortress Is Our God (Isometric), 22
A Mighty Fortress Is Our God (Rhythmic), 23
All Creatures of Our God and King, 236
All Glory, Laud, and Honor, 154
All Glory, Laud, and Honor (with Refrain),
155
All Hail the Power of Jesus' Name!
(Coronation), 57
All Hail the Power of Jesus' Name!
(Diadem), 58
All Hail the Power of Jesus' Name!
(Miles Lane), 59
All People That on Earth Do Dwell, 21
Alleluia! Alleluia! Hearts to Heaven, 190
Christ Is Made the Sure Foundation
(Regent Square), 317
Christ Is Made the Sure Foundation
(Westminster Abbey), 318
Christ, Whose Glory Fills the Skies, 573
Come, Christians, Join to Sing! 45
Come, Thou Almighty King, 4
For All the Saints, 547
For the Beauty of the Earth, 239
From All that Dwells Below the Skies
(Duke Street), 20
From All that Dwells Below the Skies
(Lasst Uns Erfreuen), 19
Glorious Things of Thee Are Spoken, 319
God, Our Father, We Adore Thee! 2
God the Omnipotent! 17
Hail to the Lord's Anointed, 79
Holy, Holy, Holy! (Nicaea), 1
I Sing the Mighty Power of God
(Ellacombe) 241
I Sing the Mighty Power of God
(Forest Green), 242
Immortal, Invisible, God Only Wise, 18
Jesus Shall Reign, 39
Join All the Glorious Names, 43
Joyful, Joyful, We Adore Thee, 235
Let the Whole Creation Cry, 245
Lift Up Your Heads, Ye Mighty Gates! 77
Majesty, 197
May Jesus Christ Be Praised! 51
Now Thank We All Our God, 589
O Bless the Lord, My Soul! 35
O For a Thousand Tongues to Sing
(Azmon), 49
O God, Our Help in Ages Past, 28
O Praise Ye the Lord! 26
O Worship the King, 10
Praise, My Soul, the King of Heaven, 12
Praise the Lord, His Glories Show, 25
Praise the Lord! Ye Heavens, Adore Him, 238
Praise to God, Immortal Praise, 595
Praise to the Lord! the Almighty, 11
Praise Ye the Triune God! 8

Rejoice, Ye Pure in Heart, 24
Rejoice, the Lord Is King! 206
Sing Praise to God Who Reigns Above, 29
The Church's One Foundation, 316
The Day of Resurrection! *(Ellacombe)*, 186
The Day of Resurrection! *(Lancashire)*, 185
The God of Abraham Praise, 16
The Spacious Firmament, 240
Thine Be the Glory, 188
Thou, Whose Almighty Word, 5
To God Be the Glory, 31
We Praise Thee, O God *(Kremser)*, 32
Ye Servants of God, 209

PSALM SETTINGS - Alpha

A Mighty Fortress Is Our God (Isometric) (Psalm 46), 22
A Mighty Fortress Is Our God (Rhythmic) (Psalm 46), 23
All People That on Earth Do Dwell (Psalm 100), 21
As Longs the Deer for Cooling Streams (Psalm 42), 368
From All That Dwell Below the Skies *(Duke Street)* (Psalm 117), 20
From All That Dwell Below the Skies *(Lasst Uns Erfreuen)* (Psalm 117), 19
Hail to the Lord's Anointed (Psalm 72), 79
Jesus Shall Reign (Psalm 72), 39
Joy to the World! The Lord Is Come (Psalm 98), 92
Lift Up Your Heads, Ye Mighty Gates! (Psalm 24), 77
My Shepherd Will Supply My Need (Psalm 23), 372
Praise, My Soul, the King of Heaven (Psalm 103), 11
O Bless the Lord, My Soul (Psalm 103:1-5), 35
O God, Our Help in Ages Past (Psalm 90:1-5), 28
O Praise Ye the Lord! (Psalm 148 & 150). 26
On Eagle's Wings (Psalm 92), 366
The King of Love My Shepherd Is *(Dominus Regit Me)* (Psalm 23), 371
The King of Love My Shepherd Is *(St. Columba)* (Psalm 23), 370
The Lord's My Shepherd, I'll Not Want (Psalm 23), 369
Unto the Hills (Psalm 121), 15

PSALM SETTINGS - Numerical

Psalm 23 - My Shepherd Will Supply My Need, 372
Psalm 23 - The King of Love My Shepherd Is *(Dominus Regit Me)*, 371
Psalm 23 - The King of Love My Shepherd Is *(St. Columba)*, 370
Psalm 23 - The Lord's My Shepherd, I'll Not Want, 369
Psalm 24 - Lift Up Your Heads, Ye Mighty Gates! 77
Psalm 42- As Longs the Deer for Cooling Streams, 368
Psalm 46 - A Mighty Fortress Is Our God (Isometric), 22
Psalm 46 - A Mighty Fortress Is Our God (Rhythmic), 23
Psalm 72 - Hail to the Lord's Anointed, 79
Psalm 72 - Jesus Shall Reign, 39
Psalm 90:1-5 - O God, Our Help in Ages Past, 28
Psalm 92 - On Eagle's Wings, 366

Psalm 98 - Joy to the World! The Lord Is Come, 92
Psalm 100 - All People That on Earth Do Dwell, 21
Psalm 103 - Praise, My Soul, the King of Heaven, 11
Psalm 103:1-5 - O Bless the Lord, My Soul, 35
Psalm 117 - From All That Dwell Below the Skies *(Duke Street)*, 20
Psalm 117 - From All That Dwell Below the Skies *(Lasst Uns Erfreuen)*, 19
Psalm 121 - Unto the Hills, 15
Psalm 148 & 150 - O Praise Ye the Lord! 26

RECESSIONALS

All for Jesus! All for Jesus! 480
At the Name of Jesus *(Belle Rive)*, 208
At the Name of Jesus *(Wye Valley)*, 207
Battle Hymn of the Republic, 603
Come, Labor On, 354
Crown Him with Many Crowns, 46
Eternal Father, Strong to Save, 600
Glorious Things of Thee Are Spoken, 319
God of Grace and God of Glory, 337
God the Omnipotent! 17
Guide Me, O Thou Great Jehovah, 413
How Firm a Foundation, 392
In Christ Alone, 390
In Christ There Is No East or West *(McKee)*, 336
In Christ There Is No East or West *(St. Peter)*, 335
Jesus Shall Reign, 39
Lead On, O King Eternal, 451
Lift Every Voice and Sing, 602
Lift High the Cross, 203
Like a River Glorious, 412
Love Divine, All Loves Excelling *(Beecher)*, 40
Love Divine, All Loves Excelling *(Blaenwern)*, 41
Love Divine, All Loves Excelling *(Hyfrydol)*, 42
O God, Our Help in Ages Past, 28
O, Zion Haste, 343
Onward, Christian Soldiers, 438
Rise Up, O Men of God! *(Festal Song)*, 340
Rise Up, O Men of God! *(St. Thomas)*, 341
Singing Songs of Expectation, 321
The Church's One Foundation, 316
The Sands of Time Are Sinking, 550
There Is a Redeemer, 249
We've a Story to Tell, 353

RECONCILIATION

Blest Be the Tie, 334
From Every Stormy Wind That Blows, 468
In Christ There Is No East or West *(McKee)*, 336
In Christ There Is No East or West *(St. Peter)*, 335
Lord, Speak to Me That I May Speak, 465
O Master, Let Me Walk with Thee, 485
Once to Every Man and Nation, 598

REDEMPTION

A New Name in Glory, 266
And Can It Be? 247
Arise, My Soul, Arise, 246
Christ, We Do All Adore Thee, 180
Crown Him with Many Crowns, 46
Glory Be to Jesus, 173
Hallelujah, What a Savior! 178

He the Pearly Gates Will Open, 568
Here Is Love, Vast as the Ocean, 254
I Will Sing of My Redeemer, 262
Jesus Paid It All, 265
Jesus, Thy Blood and Righteousness, 251
Lamb of God *(Lamb of God)*, 175
Let Thy Blood in Mercy Poured, 329
Lift Up Your Heads, Ye Mighty Gates! 77
Love Found a Way, 520
My Jesus, I Love Thee, 61
My Savior's Love, 518
O Boundless Salvation, 250
Once for All, 285
Redeemed, How I Love to Proclaim It! 268
Since I Have Been Redeemed, 511
The Love of God, 276
The Power of the Cross, 166
There Is a Fountain, 259
There's a Wideness in God's Mercy, 273
There Is a Redeemer, 249
To God Be the Glory, 31
What a Wonderful Savior, 257
When I See the Blood, 260
Wonderful, Merciful Savior, 7

REFORMATION SUNDAY & CHURCH HISTORY

A Mighty Fortress Is Our God (Isometric), 22
A Mighty Fortress Is Our God (Rhythmic), 23
For All the Saints, 547
Faith of Our Fathers, 322
God of Our Fathers, 597
Holy God, We Praise Thy Name, 3
How Firm a Foundation, 392
I Love Thy Kingdom, Lord, 320
Onward, Christian Soldiers, 438
O God, Our Help in Ages Past, 28
Singing Songs of Expectation, 321
The Church's One Foundation, 316

RENEWAL & REVIVAL

Bring Your Vessels, Not a Few, 224
God of Grace and God of Glory, 337
O Breath of Life, 339
Revive Us Again, 338
Rise Up, O Men of God! *(Festal Song)*, 340
Rise Up, O Men of God! *(St. Thomas)*, 341
Search Me, O God *(Ellers)*, 296
Search Me, O God *(Maori)*, 295
Spirit of the Living God, 221
The Risen Christ, 189
There Shall Be Showers of Blessing, 342

REPENTANCE & COMMITMENT

All Your Anxiety, 469
Breathe On Me, Breath of God, 225
Bring Your Vessels, Not a Few, 224
Come Down, O Love Divine, 216
Come, Ye Sinners, Poor and Needy, 291
Comfort, Comfort Ye My People, 81
Dear Lord and Father of Mankind *(Repton)*, 475
Dear Lord and Father of Mankind *(Rest)*, 474
Depth of Mercy! Can There Be? 292
Draw Me Nearer, 309
God, Be Merciful to Me, 290
Grace Greater than Our Sin, 279
Have Thine Own Way, Lord! 298
Have You Any Room for Jesus? 308
His Way with Thee, 313
I Am Resolved, 315
I Have Decided to Follow Jesus, 300

I Lay My Sins on Jesus, 294
I Need Thee Every Hour, 459
I Surrender All, 305
I Would Be Like Jesus, 314
Jesus Is Calling, 304
Jesus, I Come, 299
Just As I Am, 293
Kneel at the Cross, 310
Lord Jesus, Think on Me, 467
Lord, I'm Coming Home, 307
Make Me a Captive, Lord, 488
My Faith Looks Up to Thee, 417
Not I, But Christ, 312
Only Trust Him, 306
Pass Me Not, O Gentle Savior, 311
Search Me, O God *(Ellers)*, 296
Search Me, O God *(Maori)*, 295
Softly and Tenderly, 303
Take My Life and Let It Be *(Hendon)*, 302
Take My Life and Let It Be *(Yarbrough)*, 301
Turn Your Eyes upon Jesus, 297
Yield Not to Temptation, 454

REST
A Shelter in the Time of Storm, 396
Dear Lord and Father of Mankind
   (Repton), 475
Dear Lord and Father of Mankind *(Rest)*, 474
I Heard the Voice of Jesus Say
   (Kingsfold), 530
I Heard the Voice of Jesus Say
   (Vox Dilecti), 531
Jesus, I Am Resting, Resting, 367
Jesus, Priceless Treasure, 388
Jesus, the Very Thought of Thee, 55
Near to the Heart of God, 457
Now the Day Is Over, 576
O Love That Wilt Not Let Me Go, 389
O the Deep, Deep Love of Jesus, 272
On Eagle's Wings, 366
The Day Thou Gavest, Lord, Is Ended, 578
The King of Love My Shepherd Is
   (Dominus Regit Me), 371
The King of Love My Shepherd Is
   (St. Columba), 370
We Rest on Thee, 444
We'll Work Till Jesus Comes, 505

RESURRECTION (See Jesus, Resurrection of)

RETURN (See Jesus, Return of)

SANCTUS
Day Is Dying in the West (Refrain), 579
Holy, Holy, Holy! *(Darnell)*, 627
Holy, Holy, Holy *(Heilig Ist Der Herr)*, 628
Holy, Holy, Holy *(Nicaea)* (Stanza 4), 1

SALVATION
A Great and Mighty Wonder, 85
A New Name in Glory, 266
Ah, Holy Jesus, 176
All for Jesus, 481
All for Jesus! All for Jesus! 480
All My Heart This Night Rejoices, 111
Alleluia! Sing to Jesus, 195
Amazing Grace *(New Britain)*, 280
Amazing Grace! *(Land of Rest)*, 281
And Can It Be? 247
Are You Washed in the Blood? 257
Arise, My Soul, Arise, 246
Ask Ye What Great Thing I Know? 521

At Calvary, 523
Baruch Hashem Adonai, 252
Blessed Assurance, 362
Break Forth, O Beauteous Heavenly Light, 88
Brightest and Best of the Stars, 142
"Christ for the World!" We Sing, 344
Christ, We Do All Adore Thee, 180
Christians, Awake! 112
Comfort, Comfort Ye My People, 81
Creator of the Stars of Night, 76
For God So Loved Us, 253
Glorious Things of Thee Are Spoken, 319
Glory Be to God on High, 613
God Is My Strong Salvation, 431
Great God of Wonders! 283
Here Is Love, Vast as the Ocean, 254
I Am Not Skilled to Understand, 263
I Am Trusting Thee, Lord Jesus, 429
I Know a Fount, 267
I Know Not How That Bethlehem's Babe, 527
I Will Praise Him! 510
I Will Sing of My Redeemer, 262
I Will Sing the Wondrous Story, 507
In Christ Alone, 390
Jesus Paid It All, 265
Jesus, Thy Blood and Righteousness, 251
Join All the Glorious Names, 43
Joy Has Dawned, 101
Lift High the Cross, 203
Lo! He Comes with Clouds Descending
   (Helmsley), 211
Lo! He Comes with Clouds Descending
   (Regent Square), 210
Love Lifted Me! 516
My Faith Has Found a Resting Place, 418
Nothing but the Blood, 255
O Boundless Salvation, 250
O Happy Day, 323
O How He Loves You and Me, 277
Of the Father's Heart Begotten, 80
One Day, 150
Open the Wells of Salvation, 494
Our Great Savior, 248
Redeemed, How I Love to Proclaim It! 268
Saved, Saved! 512
The Cleansing Wave, 261
The Way of the Cross Leads Home, 270
There Is a Fountain, 259
There Is a Redeemer, 249
There Is Power in the Blood, 258
What a Wonderful Savior, 257
When I See the Blood, 260
Whiter Than Snow, 264
Ye Must Be Born Again, 276
Ye Servants of God, 209

SECOND COMING (See Return)

SERVICE AND STEWARDSHIP
A Charge to Keep I Have, 495
All for Jesus, 481
All for Jesus! All for Jesus! 480
All Things Come of Thee, O Lord, 626
"Are Ye Able," Said the Master, 473
Close to Thee, 493
Dear Lord and Father of Mankind
   (Repton), 475
Dear Lord and Father of Mankind *(Rest)*, 474
Deeper and Deeper, 502
Deeper, Deeper, 503
Give Me Thy Heart, 489
Give of Your Best to the Master, 450

I Gave My Life for Thee, 482
I Have Decided to Follow Jesus, 300
I Would Be True, 500
I'll Go Where You Want Me to Go, 352
I'll Live for Him, 491
In the Bleak Midwinter, 122
Jesus Calls Us *(Restoration)*, 479
Jesus Calls Us *(Galilee)*, 478
Jesus, I My Cross Have Taken, 483
Jesus, Thou Divine Companion, 148
Lead Me to Calvary, 165
Little Is Much When God Is in It, 490
Living for Jesus, 492
Make Me a Captive, Lord, 488
May the Mind of Christ, My Savior, 497
More About Jesus, 499
Must Jesus Bear the Cross Alone? 486
O Jesus, I Have Promised, 446
O Master, Let Me Walk with Thee, 485
Our Best, 496
Savior, Like a Shepherd Lead Us, 373
Something for Thee, 487
Take My Life and Let It Be *(Hendon)*, 302
Take My Life and Let It Be *(Yarbrough)*, 301
Take Up Thy Cross, 474
Teach Me Your Way, O Lord, 476
Trust and Obey, 504
Turn Your Eyes upon Jesus, 297
We'll Work Till Jesus Comes, 505
When I Survey the Wondrous Cross
   (Hamburg), 171
When I Survey the Wondrous Cross
   (Rockingham), 172
Where He Leads Me, 477
Work, for the Night Is Coming, 506

SERVICE MUSIC
Amens
   Amen - Twofold (Dresden), 637
   Amen - Twofold (Greek), 638
   Amen - Threefold (Danish), 639
   Amen - Fourfold, 640
   Amen - Sevenfold, 641
   also:
   Amen - Onefold - final 2 measures, 635
   Amen - Sevenfold - final 10 measures, 636
Agnus Dei
   Lamb of God *(Nancarrow)*, 634
   also:
   Lamb of God (Lamb of God), 175
Benediction
   God Be in My Head, 635
   The Lord Bless You and Keep You, 636
   also:
   A Peaceful Night, 580
   Christ Be with Me, 6 - second part
   God Be with You Till We Meet Again
      (Endeavor), 586
   God Be with You Till We Meet Again
      (Randolph), 587
   O for a Closer Walk with God, 471
   Thou Wilt Keep Him in Perfect Peace,
      407
   Will the Circle Be Unbroken? 572
Gloria In Excelsis
   Glory Be to God on High, 613
   also:
   Angels We Have Heard on High (Refrain),
      99
   Ding Dong! Merrily on High (Refrain), 120
   Glorious Is Thy Name (Refrain), 38

Gloria Patri - Traditional Language
Glory Be to the Father *(Greatorex)*, 614
Glory Be to the Father *(Meineke)*, 615
Gloria Patri - Contemporary Language
Glory to the Father, 616
Introit
Be Still, 609
Bless the Lord, 610
The Lord Is in His Holy Temple, 609
also:
All Glory, Laud, and Honor (Refrain), 155
Bless the Lord, O My Soul, 36
The Strife Is O'er (Refrain), 191
Kyrie
Kyrie Eleison (Lord, Have Mercy), 611
also:
God, Be Merciful to Me (Stanza 1), 290
Lord's Prayer - Traditional Language
The Lord's Prayer *(Malotte)*, 632
The Lord's Prayer
(Conditor Alme Siderum), 631
Lord's Prayer - Contemporary Language
Our Father in Heaven, 633
Memorial Acclamation Prayer A
It Is Finished, 629
Memorial Acclamation Prayer B
We Remember His Death, 630
Prayer Response
Cast Thy Burden upon the Lord, 617
Hear Our Prayer, O Lord, 618
Lead Me, Lord, 620
Let the Words of My Mouth, 619
also:
Be Still and Know, 365
God Is So Good, 517
I Know a Fount, 267
O Come, Let Us Adore Him, 47
O How He Loves You and Me, 277
Thou Wilt Keep Him in Perfect Peace, 407
Turn Your Eyes upon Jesus - Refrain, 297
Presentation of Offering
All Things Come of Thee, O Lord, 626
Bless Thou the Gifts, 625
Praise God, from Whom All Blessings Flow *(Dedication Anthem)*, 623
Praise God, from Whom All Blessings Flow *(Lasst Uns Erfreuen)*, 624
Praise God, from Whom All Blessings Flow *(Old 100th, original)* , 622
Praise God, from Whom All blessing Flow *(Old 100th, altered)* , 621
also, Doxology from last stanza:
All Creatures of Our God and King, 236
All People That on Earth Do Dwell, 21
Alleluia, Alleluia! Hearts to Heaven, 190
As Longs the Deer for Cooling Streams, 368
Christ Is Made the Sure Foundation *(Regent Square)*, 317
Christ Is Made the Sure Foundation *(Westminster Abbey)*, 318
Come, Ye Faithful, Raise the Strain, 181
Creator of the Stars of Night, 76
God, Our Father, We Adore Thee! 2
Holy God, We Praise Thy Name, 3
I Will Praise Him, 510
Now Thank We All Our God, 598
O Christ, Our Hope, 198
O What the Joy and the Glory Must Be, 548
Of the Father's Love Begotten, 86

See the Conqueror Mounts in Triumph, 199
The Risen Christ, 189
Sanctus
Holy, Holy, Holy *(Darnell)*, 627
Holy, Holy, Holy *(Heilig Ist Der Herr)*, 628
also:
Day Is Dying in the West (Refrain), 579
Holy, Holy, Holy! *(Nicaea)* (Stanza 4), 1
Trisagion
Holy God, 612

SIN
Agnus Dei - Lamb of God, 634
Ah, Holy Jesus, 176
Amazing Grace! *(New Britain)*, 280
Amazing Grace! *(Land of Rest)*, 281
Alas! And Did My Savior Bleed? 177
At the Cross, 525
Christ Receiveth Sinful Men, 345
Depth of Mercy! Can There Be, 292
God, Be Merciful to Me, 290
Grace Greater than Our Sin, 279
How Deep the Father's Love For Us, 157
I Lay My Sins on Jesus, 294
It Is Well with My Soul, 363
Jesus, I Come, 299
Jesus Paid It All, 265
Lamb of God *(Lamb of God)*, 175
Nothing but the Blood, 255
O Boundless Salvation, 250
Rock of Ages, 284
Search Me, O God *(Ellers)*, 296
Search Me, O God *(Maori)*, 295
There Is a Fountain, 259
What a Wonderful Savior, 257
Wonderful Grace of Jesus, 282

SORROW (See Suffering & Sorrow)

SPIRITUALS
Deep River, 555
Give Me Jesus *(Spiritual)*, 435
Go, Tell It on the Mountain, 132
He's Got the Whole World in His Hands, 409
I'm So Glad Jesus Lifted Me, 543
Let Us Break Bread Together, 330
Peace Like a River, 408
Rise Up, Shepherds, and Follow, 133
The Old Time Religion, 533
There Is a Balm in Gilead, 383
Were You There? 161

STEWARDSHIP (See Service & Stewardship)

SUFFERING & SORROW
Be Still, My Soul! 364
Comfort, Comfort Ye My People, 81
Cross of Jesus, 168
Day by Day, 150
Does Jesus Care? 400
How Firm a Foundation, 392
I Must Tell Jesus! 462
I Need Thee Every Hour, 459
It Is Well with My Soul, 363
Like a River Glorious, 412
Moment by Moment, 376
My Faith Looks Up to Thee, 417
Oh, How I Love Jesus, 62
Trust and Obey, 504
What a Friend We Have in Jesus, 460
Whispering Hope, 406

SOCIAL CONCERN (See Justice & Social Concern)

SURRENDER
All for Jesus! All for Jesus! 480
At the Name of Jesus *(Belle Rive)*, 208
At the Name of Jesus *(Wye Valley)*, 207
Breathe On Me, Breath of God, 225
Bring Your Vessels, Not a Few, 224
Come Down, O Love Divine, 216
Deeper and Deeper, 502
Give Me Thy Heart, 489
Give of Your Best to the Master, 450
Have Thine Own Way, Lord! 298
Himself, 528
His Way with Thee, 313
I Am Resolved, 315
I Surrender All, 305
I'll Go Where You Want Me to Go, 352
Jesus, I My Cross Have Taken, 483
Jesus Calls Us *(Restoration)*, 479
Jesus Calls Us *(Galilee)*, 478
Jesus, Our Lord and King, 325
Kneel at the Cross, 310
Living for Jesus, 492
Make Me a Captive, Lord, 488
Moment by Moment, 376
Not I, But Christ, 312
O for a Closer Walk with God, 471
O Happy Day, 323
O to Be Like Thee! 471
Open the Wells of Salvation, 494
"Take Up Your Cross", the Savior Said, 484
Trust and Obey, 504
Yield Not to Temptation, 454

TEMPTATION
A Charge to Keep I Have, 495
Abide with Me, 575
All the Way My Savior Leads Me, 421
Come, Thou Fount of Every Blessing *(Nettleton)*, 13
Come, Thou Fount of Every Blessing *(Warrenton)*, 14
Day by Day, 416
Hiding in Thee, 381
I Must Tell Jesus! 462
I Need Thee Every Hour, 459
Just a Closer Walk with Thee, 461
Lord Jesus, Think on Me, 467
Lord, Who Throughout These Forty Days, 151
No, Not One! 401
Savior, Again to Thy Dear Name We Raise, 588
Spirit of God, Descend upon My Heart, 217
Sweet Hour of Prayer, 458
We'll Understand It Better By and By, 569
What a Friend We Have in Jesus, 460
Yield Not to Temptation, 454

TENNEBRAE
(See Maundy Thursday/Tennebrae)

TESTIMONY
A Child of the King, 403
A New Name in Glory, 266
All Things Bright and Beautiful *(All Things Bright and Beautiful)*, 244
All Things Bright and Beautiful *(Royal Oak)*, 243
As Ye What Great Thing I Know? 521

At Calvary, 523
At the Cross, 525
Baruch Hashem Adonai, 252
Count Your Blessings, 594
Down at the Cross, 524
God Is So Good, 517
He Is So Precious to Me, 540
He Keeps Me Singing, 508
He Lifted Me! 519
He Lives 526
Himself, 528
His Eye Is on the Sparrow, 378
His Name Is Wonderful, 69
How Can I Keep from Singing? 509
I Am Not Skilled to Understand, 263
I Heard the Voice of Jesus Say
  (Kingsfold), 530
I Heard the Voice of Jesus Say
  (Vox Dilecti), 531
I Know Whom I Have Believed, 535
I Love to Tell the Story, 522
I Will Praise Him! 510
I Will Sing of My Redeemer, 262
I Will Sing the Wondrous Story, 507
I Would Be Like Jesus, 314
I've Found a Friend, 515
Jesus Is All the World to Me, 534
Jesus Is the Sweetest Name I Know, 529
Love Found a Way, 520
Love Lifted Me! 516
Majestic Sweetness Sits Enthroned, 200
My Savior's Love, 518
O Boundless Salvation, 250
Precious Memories, 529
Satisfied, 541
Saved, Saved, 512
Since I Have Been Redeemed, 511
Since Jesus Came into My Heart, 514
Stand Up and Bless the Lord, 34
Tell Me the Old, Old Story, 532
The Light of the World Is Jesus, 542
The Lily of the Valley, 538
The Old-Time Religion, 533
The Power of the Cross, 166
There Is Sunshine in My Soul, 536
When the Roll Is Called Up Yonder, 552

THANKSGIVING
(See Harvest & Thanksgiving)

TRANSFIGURATION
Beautiful Savior, 54
Fairest Lord Jesus, 53
Holy Ground *(Beatty)*, 67
Holy Ground *(Holy Ground)*, 68
Immortal, Invisible, God Only Wise, 18
O Worship the King, 10
Open My Eyes, That I May See, 229
Shine, Jesus, Shine, 348
Songs of Thankfulness and Praise, 144
Sun of My Soul, 577
The God of Abraham Praise, 16
Turn Your Eyes upon Jesus, 297
We Worship and Adore You, 70
Worthy of Worship, 9

TRINITY
All Creatures of Our God and King, 236
All People That on Earth Do Dwell, 21
Alleluia, Alleluia! Hearts to Heaven, 190
Arise, My Soul, Arise! 246
At the Lamb's High Feast We Sing, 326

Christ Is Made the Sure Foundation
  (Regent Square), 317
Christ Is Made the Sure Foundation
  (Westminster Abbey), 318
Come, Holy Ghost, Our Souls Inspire, 218
Come, Thou Almighty King, 4
Eternal Father, Strong to Save, 600
For All the Saints, 547
Glory Be to the Father - Gloria Patri
  (Greatorex), 614
Glory Be to the Father - Gloria Patri
  (Meineke), 615
Glory to the Father - Gloria Patri, 616
God, Our Father, We Adore Thee! 2
Holy God, We Praise Thy Name, 3
Holy, Holy, Holy! *(Nicaea)*, 1
I Bind Unto Myself Today, 6
I Will Praise Him! 510
Join All the Glorious Names, 43
Lord Jesus, Think on Me, 467
Now Thank We All Our God, 589
Of the Father's Love Begotten, 86
Praise God, from Whom All Blessings Flow
  (Dedication Anthem), 623
Praise God, from Whom All Blessings Flow
  (Lasst Uns Erfreuen), 624
Praise God, from Whom All Blessings Flow
  (Old 100th, original), 622
Praise God, from Whom All Blessings Flow
  (Old 100th, altered), 621
Praise Ye the Triune God! 8
See the Conqueror Mounts in Triumph, 199
The God of Abraham Praise, 16
The Risen Christ, 189
There Is a Redeemer, 249
Thou, Whose Almighty Word, 5
Wonderful, Merciful Savior, 7
Worthy of Worship, 9

TRISAGION
Holy God, 612

TRUST (See Faith & Trust)

UNITY
Blest Be the Tie, 334
"Christ for the World!" We Sing, 344
Christ Is Made the Sure Foundation
  (Regent Square), 317
Christ Is Made the Sure Foundation
  (Westminster Abbey), 318
God of Grace and God of Glory, 337
In Christ There Is No East or West
  (McKee), 336
In Christ There Is No East or West
  (St. Peter), 335
Joyful, Joyful, We Adore Thee, 235
Lift Up Your Hearts! 333
O Perfect Love, 546
Onward, Christian Soldiers, 438
The Church's One Foundation, 316

VICTORY
A Mighty Fortress Is Our God *(Isometric)*, 22
A Mighty Fortress Is Our God *(Rhythmic)*, 23
At the Lamb's High Feast We Sing, 326
Be Thou My Vision, 386
Because He Lives, 192
Faith Is the Victory, 434
For All the Saints, 547
Go Forward, Christian Soldier, 437
God of Grace and God of Glory, 337

He Who Would Valiant Be, 453
Hail to the Lord's Anointed, 79
Lead On, O King Eternal, 451
Look, Ye Saints! The Sight Is Glorious
  (Bryn Calfaria), 205
Look, Ye Saints! The Sight Is Glorious
  (Regent Square), 204
Make Me a Captive, Lord, 488
Onward, Christian Soldiers, 438
Soldiers of Christ, Arise, 449
Stand Up, Stand Up for Jesus *(Geibel)*, 440
Stand Up, Stand Up for Jesus *(Webb)*, 441
The Banner of the Cross, 443
The Church's One Foundation, 316
The Strife Is O'er, 191
We Gather Together, 590
We Praise Thee, O God, 32
We Rest on Thee, 444
When I Can Read My Title Clear, 551
Who Is on the Lord's Side, 436
Yield Not to Temptation, 454

WARNING & JUDGEMENT
A Charge to Keep I Have, 495
Battle Hymn of the Republic, 603
Hail to the Lord's Anointed, 79
Is It the Crowning Day? 214
Lo! He Comes with Clouds Descending
  (Helmsley), 211
Lo! He Comes with Clouds Descending
  (Regent Square), 210
When I See the Blood, 260

WEDDING HYMNS
Be Thou My Vision, 386
Day by Day, 416
Great Is Thy Faithfulness, 33
Joyful, Joyful, We Adore Thee, 235
In Christ Alone, 390
Love Divine, All Loves Excelling *(Beecher)*, 40
Love Divine, All Loves Excelling
  (Blaenwern), 41
Love Divine, All Loves Excelling
  (Hyfrydol), 42
O God, Our Help in Ages Past, 28
O Perfect Love, 546
Praise, My Soul, the King of Heaven, 12
Praise to the Lord, the Almighty, 11
Savior, Like a Shepherd Lead Us, 373
The King of Love My Shepherd Is
  (Dominus Regit Me), 371
The King of Love My Shepherd Is
  (St. Columba), 370
The Lord's Prayer *(Malotte)*, 632

WITNESS (See Evangelism & Missions)

WONDERS (See Jesus, Miracles of)

WORD OF GOD
Break Thou the Bread of Life, 231
Holy Bible, Book Divine, 233
How Firm a Foundation, 392
Jesus Loves Even Me! 275
My Faith Has Found a Resting Place, 418
O Word of God Incarnate, 230
The Risen Christ, 189
Thou, Whose Almighty Word, 4
Thy Word Have I Hid in My Heart, 232
Wonderful Words of Life, 234

WORSHIP (See Praise & Adoration)

A Charge to Keep I Have, 495 (Bb)
A Child of the King, 403 (C)
A Great and Mighty Wonder, 85 (D)
A Mighty Fortress Is Our God (Isometric), 22 (C)
A Mighty Fortress Is Our God (Rhythmic), 23 (C)
A New Name in Glory, 266 (G)
A Peaceful Night, 580 (D minor)
A ruler once came to Jesus by night, 271 (C)
A Shelter in the Time of Storm, 396 (Eb)
A wonderful Savior is Jesus my Lord, 382 (C)
Abide with Me, 575 (D)
According to Thy Gracious Word, 332 (Eb)
Ah, Holy Jesus, 176 (E minor)
Alas! And did my Savior bleed (Hudson), 525 (Eb)
Alas! And Did My Savior Bleed? *(Martyrdom)*, 177 (F)
All Creatures of Our God and King, 236 (C)
All for Jesus, 481 (Eb)
All for Jesus! All for Jesus! 480 (C)
All Glory, Laud, and Honor, 154 (Bb)
All Glory, Laud, and Honor (with Refrain), 155 (Bb)
All Hail the Power of Jesus' Name! *(Coronation)*, 57 (F)
All Hail the Power of Jesus' Name! *(Diadem)*, 58 (F)
All Hail the Power of Jesus' Name! *(Miles Lane)*, 59 (G)
All My Heart This Night Rejoices, 111 (F)
All my life-long I had panted, 541 (C)
All People That on Earth Do Dwell, 21 (F)
All the Way My Savior Leads Me, 421 (F)
All Things Bright and Beautiful
   (All Things Bright and Beautiful), 244 (C/G)
All Things Bright and Beautiful *(Royal Oak)*, 243 (F)
All Things Come of Thee, O Lord, 626 (G)
All to Jesus I surrender, 305 (C)
All Your Anxiety, 469 (C)
Alleluia, Alleluia! Hearts to Heaven, 190 (F)
Alleluia! Sing to Jesus, 195 (Eb)
Almighty Lord, grant unto us, 580 (D minor)
Am I a Soldier of the Cross? 439 (F)
Amazing Grace! *(Land of Rest)*, 281 (F)
Amazing Grace! *(New Britain)*, 280 (F)
Amen — Fourfold, 640 (G)
Amen — Sevenfold, 641 (F)
Amen — Threefold *(Danish)*, 639 (G)
Amen — Twofold *(Dresden)*, 637 (C)
Amen — Twofold *(Greek)*, 638 (G)
America the Beautiful, 601 (Ab)
And Can It Be? 247 (F)
Angels, from the Realms of Glory, 98 (Ab)
Angels We Have Heard on High, 99 (F)
Another Year Is Dawning, 596 (D)
Anywhere with Jesus I Can Safely Go, 375 (C)
"Are Ye Able," Said the Master, 473 (G)
Are you longing for the fullness, 224 (C)
Are You Washed in the Blood? 257 (G)
Arise, My Soul, Arise! 246 (F)
As Longs the Deer for Cooling Streams, 368 (F)
As the Deer, 52 (C)
As with Gladness Men of Old, 141 (F)
Ask Ye What Great Thing I Know? 521 (Eb)
At Calvary, 523 (Bb)
At the Cross, 525 (Eb)
At the Lamb's High Feast We Sing, 326 (C)

At the Name of Jesus *(Belle Rive)*, 208 (D minor)
At the Name of Jesus *(Wye Valley)*, 207 (F)
Away in a Manger *(Away in a Manger)*, 105 (F)
Away in a Manger *(Cradle Song)*, 104 (Eb)

Baruch Hashem Adonai, 252 (E minor)
Battle Hymn of the Republic, 603 (Ab)
Be not dismayed, whate're betide 393 (Ab)
Be Present at Our Table, Lord. 544 (F)
Be Still, 609 (F)
Be Still and Know, 365 (Bb)
Be Still, My Soul! 364 (Eb)
Be Thou My Vision, 386 (D)
Beautiful Savior, 54 (E minor)
Because He Lives, 192 (G)
Begin, My Tongue, Some Heavenly Theme, 30 (F)
Beneath the Cross of Jesus, 170 (C)
Beulah Land, 567 (Eb)
Bless the Lord, 610 (Eb)
Bless the Lord, O My Soul, 36 (G)
Bless Thou the Gifts, 625 (F)
Blessed Assurance, 362 (C)
Blessed Be the Name, 37 (G)
Blessed Quietness, 228 (Bb)
Blessed Redeemer! 179 (C)
Blessed Savior, we adore Thee, 38 (F)
Blessing and Honor and Glory and Power, 194 (F)
Blest Be the Tie, 334 (Eb)
Break Forth, O Beauteous Heavenly Light, 88 (D)
Break Thou the Bread of Life, 231 (C)
Breathe on Me, Breath of God, 225 (Eb)
Brethren, We Have Met to Worship, 581 (F)
Brightest and Best of the Stars, 142 (F)
Brightly beams our Father's mercy, 357 (F)
Bring a Torch, Jeannette, Isabella! 134 (F)
Bring Them In, 361 (F)
Bring Your Vessels, Not a Few, 224 (C)
Bringing in the Sheaves, 360 (Bb)

Cast Thy Burden upon the Lord, 617 (D)
Channels Only, 498 (F)
Child in the Manger, 115 (Bb)
Children of the Heavenly Father, 379 (C)
Christ Arose! 182 (Bb)
"Christ for the World!" We Sing, 344 (F)
Christ has for sin atonement made, 257 (G)
Christ Is Made the Sure Foundation *(Regent Square)*, 317 (G)
Christ Is Made the Sure Foundation
   (Westminster Abbey), 318 (F)
Christ our Redeemer died on the cross, 260 (Bb)
Christ Receiveth Sinful Men, 345 (Bb)
Christ Returneth! 215 (Bb)
"Christ the Lord Is Risen Today", 184 (Bb)
Christ, We Do All Adore Thee, 180 (Bb)
Christ, Whose Glory Fills the Skies, 573 (C)
Christians, Awake! 112 (Bb)
Close to Thee, 493 (F)
Come As a Child, 106 (F)
Come, Christians, Join to Sing 45 (G)
Come Down, O Love Divine, 216 (C)
Come! Everyone Who Is Thirsty, 226 (F)

Come, every soul by sin oppressed, 306 (F)
Come, Holy Ghost, Our Souls Inspire, 218 (C)
Come, Holy Spirit, Dove Divine, 324 (D♭)
Come, Labor On, 354 (G)
Come, Thou Almighty King, 4 (F)
Come, Thou Fount of Every Blessing *(Nettleton)*, 13 (C)
Come, Thou Fount of Every Blessing *(Warrenton)*, 14 (C)
Come, Thou Long-Expected Jesus *(Hyfrydol)*, 74 (E♭)
Come, Thou Long-Expected Jesus *(Stuttgart)*, 75 (E♭)
Come, We That Love the Lord *(Festal Song)*, 583 (A b)
Come, we that love the Lord (Marching to Zion), 584 (E♭)
Come, Ye Disconsolate, 402 (B♭)
Come, Ye Faithful, Raise the Strain, 181 (E♭)
Come, Ye Sinners, Poor and Needy, 291 (E minor)
Come, Ye Thankful People, Come, 591 (E♭)
"Comfort, Comfort Ye My People", 81 (F)
Count Your Blessings, 594 (C)
Creator of the Stars of Night, 76 (D)
Cross of Jesus, 168 (E♭)
Crown Him with Many Crowns, 46 (D)

Day by Day, 416 (C)
Day Is Dying in the West, 579 (F)
Dear Lord and Father of Mankind *(Repton)*, 475 (E♭)
Dear Lord and Father of Mankind *(Rest)*, 474 (C)
Deep River, 555 (D)
Deeper and Deeper, 502 (C)
Deeper, Deeper, 503 (G)
Depth of Mercy! Can There Be, 292 (D)
Ding! Dong! Merrily on High, 120 (G)
Does Jesus Care? 400 (B♭)
Down at the Cross, 524 (F)
Down in the valley, 452 (F)
Doxology — Praise God, from Whom All Blessings Flow
　(Dedication Anthem), 623 (G)
Doxology — Praise God, from Whom All Blessings Flow
　(Lasst Uns Erfreuen), 624 (D)
Doxology — Praise God, from Whom All Blessings Flow
　(Old 100th, altered) , 621 (G)
Doxology — Praise God, from Whom All Blessings Flow
　(Old 100th, original), 622 (G)
Draw Me Nearer, 309 (F)
Dwelling in Beulah Land, 428 (Ab)
Dying with Jesus, by death reckoned mine, 376 (E♭)

Earthly pleasures vainly call me, 314 (F)
Encamped along the hills of light, 434 (C)
Eternal Father, Strong to Save, 600 (C)

Face to Face, 553 (G)
Fairest Lord Jesus, 53 (D)
Faith Is the Victory, 434 (C)
Faith of Our Fathers, 322 (G)
Far and near the fields are teeming, 358 (F)
Far away in the depths of my spirit tonight, 404 (F)
Far away the noise of strife, 428 (A♭)
Father, We Thank Thee, 545 (G)
Fear not, little flock, 432 (C)
Fill Me Now, 219 (F)
Follow On, 452 (F)
Footsteps of Jesus, 445 (D)
For All the Saints, 547 (F)
For God So Loved Us, 253 (C)
For the Beauty of the Earth, 239 (F)

Fourfold Amen, 640 (G)
Free from the law, O happy condition, 285 (C)
From All That Dwell Below the Skies *(Duke Street)*, 20 (C)
From All That Dwell Below the Skies *(Lasst Uns Erfreuen)*, 19 (D)
From Every Stormy Wind That Blows, 468 (A♭)

Gentle Mary Laid Her Child, 109 (F)
Give Me Jesus *(Give Me Jesus/Spiritual)*, 435 (B♭)
Give Me Jesus *(Give Me Jesus/Sweney)*, 385 (E♭)
Give me that old-time religion, 533 (G)
Give Me Thy Heart, 489 (E♭)
Give of Your Best to the Master, 450 (D)
Glorious Is Thy Name, 38 (E♭)
Glorious Things of Thee Are Spoken, 319 (D)
Glory Be to God on High, 613 (F)
Glory Be to Jesus, 173 (F)
Glory Be to the Father — Gloria Patri *(Greatorex)*, 614 (C)
Glory Be to the Father — Gloria Patri *(Meineke)*, 615 (F)
Glory to the Father — Gloria Patri, 616 (B♭/C/B♭)
Go Forward, Christian Soldier, 437 (C)
Go, Tell It on the Mountain, 132 (E♭)
Go to Dark Gethsemane, 158 (C)
God Be in My Head, 635 (G)
God, Be Merciful to Me, 290 (D)
God Be with You Till We Meet Again *(Endeavor)*, 586 (B♭)
God Be with You Till We Meet Again *(Randolph)*, 587 (C)
God Bless Our Native Land, 604 (F)
God Is My Strong Salvation, 431 (C)
God Is So Good, 517 (D)
God Leads Us Along, 422 (C)
God of Grace and God of Glory, 337 (F)
God of Our Fathers, 597 (D)
God, Our Father, We Adore Thee! 2 (A♭)
God Rest Ye Merry, Gentlemen, 116 (D minor)
God save our gracious Queen, 607 (G)
God Save the Queen, 607 (G)
God sent His Son, they called Him Jesus, 192 (G)
God the Omnipotent! 17 (C)
God Will Take Care of You, 393 (A♭)
Good Christian Friends, Rejoice, 94 (E♭)
Good King Wenceslas, 139 (F)
Grace Greater than Our Sin, 279 (F)
Gracious Spirit, Dwell with Me, 227 (E♭)
Great God of Wonders! 283 (C)
Great Is Thy Faithfulness, 33 (C)
Guide Me, O Thou Great Jehovah, 413 (F)

Hail the Day That Sees Him Rise, 193 (F)
Hail Thee, Festival Day! 187 (F)
Hail, Thou Once-Despised Jesus! 201 (F)
Hail to the Lord's Anointed, 79 (F)
Hallelujah, What a Savior! 178 (A♭)
Hark the Glad Sound! The Savior Comes, 78 (E♭)
Hark! The Herald Angels Sing, 93 (F)
Hark, the Voice of Jesus Calling, 350 (G)
Hark! 'Tis the Shepherd's voice I hear, 361 (F)
Have Thine Own Way, Lord! 298 (D♭)
Have You Any Room for Jesus? 308 (A♭)
Have you been to Jesus, 256 (G)
He Hideth My Soul, 382 (C)
He Is Able to Deliver Thee, 287 (F)
He Is Born, 102 (F)
He Is Exalted, 63 (F)
He Is Lord, 196 (F)

He Is So Precious to Me, 540 (F)
He Keeps Me Singing, 508 (F)
He Leadeth Me! O Blessed Thought, 374 (B♭)
He Lifted Me! 519 (F)
He Lives, 526 (G)
He the Pearly Gates Will Open, 568 (F)
He Who Would Valiant Be, 453 (E♭)
Hear Our Prayer, O Lord, 618 (D)
Hear ye the Master's call, 496 (A♭)
Here at Thy Table, Lord, 327 (D)
Here Is Love, Vast As the Ocean, 254 (F)
He's Got the Whole World in His Hands, 409 (D)
Hiding in Thee, 381 (D)
Higher Ground, 447 (F)
Himself, 528 (E♭)
His Eye Is on the Sparrow, 378 (B♭)
His Name Is Wonderful, 69 (F)
His Way with Thee, 313 (F)
Ho, Everyone That Is Thirsty; *see*
   Come! Everyone Who Is Thirsty, 226 (F)
Holy Bible, Book Divine, 233 (E♭)
Holy Ghost, with Light Divine, 223 (G)
Holy God — Trisagion, 612 (D/F)
Holy God, We Praise Thy Name, 3 (F)
Holy Ground *(Beatty)*, 67 (D)
Holy Ground *(Holy Ground)*, 68 (D)
Holy, Holy, Holy! *(Nicaea)*, 1 (C)
Holy, Holy, Holy — Sanctus *(Heilig Ist Der Herr)*, 628 (D)
Holy, Holy, Holy — Sanctus *(Darnell)*, 627 (D)
Hosanna, Loud Hosanna, 153 (G)
Hosanna to the Living Lord! 48 (F)
Hover o'er me, Holy Spirit, 219 (F)
How Can I Keep from Singing? 509 (F)
How Deep the Father's Love for Us, 157 (E♭)
How Firm a Foundation, 392 (F)
How Great Our Joy! 117 (A♭)
How Great Thou Art! 27 (A♭)
How I praise Thee, precious Savior, 498 (F)
How Sweet the Name of Jesus Sounds! 399 (C)

I Am His, and He Is Mine, 398 (C)
I Am Not Skilled to Understand, 263 (C)
I Am Praying for You, 464 (F)
I Am Resolved, 315 (A♭)
I am so glad that our Father in heaven, 275 (F)
I am Thine, O Lord, 309 (F)
I Am Trusting Thee, Lord Jesus, 429 (G)
I am weak but Thou art strong, 461 (G)
I Belong to the King, 561 (F)
I Bind Unto Myself Today, 6 (G minor/G)
I can hear my Savior calling, 477 (E♭)
I come to the garden alone, 456 (G)
I Gave My Life for Thee, 482 (B♭)
I have a Savior, He's pleading in glory, 464 (F)
I have a song I love to sing, 511 (E♭)
I Have Decided to Follow Jesus, 300 (B♭)
I have found a friend in Jesus, 538 (E♭)
I hear the Savior say, 265 (C)
I Heard the Bells on Christmas Day, 126 (C)
I Heard the Voice of Jesus Say *(Kingsfold)*, 530 (D minor)
I Heard the Voice of Jesus Say *(Vox Dilecti)*, 531 (F minor/F)
I Know a Fount, 267 (C)
I Know Not How That Bethlehem's Babe, 527 (F)
I know not why God's wondrous grace, 535 (C)

I know of a name, a beautiful name, 130 (F)
I Know Whom I Have Believed, 535 (C)
I Lay My Sins on Jesus, 294 (C)
I Love Thee, 60 (D)
I Love Thy Kingdom, Lord, 320 (E♭)
I Love to Tell the Story, 522 (F)
I must needs go home, 270 (F)
I Must Tell Jesus! 462 (C)
I Need Thee Every Hour, 459 (F)
I serve a risen Savior, 526 (G)
I Sing the Mighty Power of God *(Ellacombe)*, 241 (G)
I Sing the Mighty Power of God *(Forest Green)*, 242 (E♭)
I stand amazed in the presence, 518 (G)
I Surrender All, 305 (C)
I wandered in the shades of night, 537 (D)
I was once a sinner, but I came, 266 (G)
I was sinking deep in sin, 516 (A♭)
I Will Praise Him! 510 (C)
I Will Sing of My Redeemer, 262 (F)
I Will Sing the Wondrous Story, 507 (C)
I Would Be Like Jesus, 314 (F)
I Would Be True, 500 (E♭)
If Jesus Goes with Me, I'll Go, 355 (B♭)
If the world from you withhold, 466 (F)
If Thou but Trust in God to Guide Thee, 387 (F minor)
If We Never Meet Again, 562 (E♭)
I'll Go Where You Want Me to Go, 352 (E♭)
I'll Live for Him, 491 (F)
I'm pressing on the upward way, 447 (F)
I'm So Glad Jesus Lifted Me, 543 (G)
Immortal, Invisible, God Only Wise, 18 (F)
Immortal Love, Forever Full, 513 (C)
In Christ Alone, 390 (D)
In Christ There Is No East or West *(McKee)*, 336 (B♭)
In Christ There Is No East or West *(St. Peter)*, 335 (C)
In loving-kindness Jesus came, 519 (F)
In shady, green pastures, 422 (C)
In the bleak midwinter *(Castle)*, 123 (B♭)
In the Bleak Midwinter *(Cranham)*, 122 (F)
In the Cross of Christ I Glory *(Crucifixion)*, 162 (C)
In the Cross of Christ I Glory *(Rathbun)*, 163 (B♭)
In the Garden, 456 (G)
In the harvest field now ripened, 490 (C)
In the little village of Bethlehem, 136 (F)
In the morning when I rise, 435 (B♭)
In the Sweet By and By, 560 (F)
Infant Holy, Infant Lowly, 119 (G)
Into the heart of Jesus, 502 (C)
Is It the Crowning Day? 214 (B♭)
Is there a heart o'er-come by sorrow? 469 (C)
It Came upon the Midnight Clear, 100 (G)
It Is Finished — Memorial Acclamation Prayer A, 629 (C)
It Is Well with My Soul, 363 (B♭)
It may be at morn, 215 (B♭)
It may be in the valley, 355 (B♭)
It may not be on the mountain's height, 352 (E♭)
I've a home prepared, 558 (G)
I've found a Friend who is all to me, 512 (F)
I've Found a Friend, 515 (F)
I've got peace like a river, 408 (G)
I've reached the land of joy divine, 567 (E♭)
I've wandered far away from God, 307 (F)

Jerusalem, My Happy Home, 549 (F)

Jesus Calls Us *(Galilee)*, 478 (F)
Jesus Calls Us *(Restoration)*, 479 (E minor)
Jesus Christ Is Risen Today, 183 (C)
Jesus, I Am Resting, Resting, 367 (F)
Jesus, I Come, 299 (F)
Jesus, I My Cross Have Taken, 483 (F)
Jesus Is All the World to Me, 534 (F)
Jesus Is Calling, 304 (A♭)
Jesus is coming to earth again, 213 (B♭)
Jesus Is the Sweetest Name I Know, 529 (C)
Jesus, keep me near the cross, 288 (E♭)
Jesus, Lover of My Soul *(Aberystwyth)*, 395 (D minor)
Jesus, Lover of My Soul *(Martyn)*, 394 (E♭)
Jesus Loves Even Me! 275 (F)
Jesus Loves Me! 274 (C)
Jesus may come today, glad day, 214 (B♭)
Jesus, Our Lord and King, 325 (E♭)
Jesus Paid It All, 265 (C)
Jesus, Priceless Treasure, 388 (B minor)
Jesus Saves! *(Jesus Saves)*, 346 (F)
Jesus Saves! *(Limpsfield)*, 347 (B♭)
Jesus, Savior, Pilot Me, 391 (G)
Jesus Shall Reign, 39 (C)
Jesus, the Very Thought of Thee, 55 (G)
Jesus, Thou Divine Companion, 148 (E♭)
Jesus, Thy Blood and Righteousness, 251 (G)
Jesus, what a Friend for sinners! 248 (D)
Join All the Glorious Names, 43 (B♭)
Joy Has Dawned, 101 (E♭)
Joy to the World! The Lord Is Come, 92 (C)
Joyful, Joyful, We Adore Thee, 235 (G)
Joys are flowing like a river, 228 (B♭)
Just a Closer Walk with Thee, 461 (G)
Just As I Am, 293 (C)
Just Over in the Glory-Land, 558 (G)

King of my life, I crown Thee now, 165 (C)
Kneel at the Cross, 310 (G)
Kyrie Eleison, (Lord, Have Mercy), 611 (D minor)

Lamb of God *(Lamb of God)*, 175 (C)
Lamb of God — Agnus Dei *(Nancarrow)*, 634 (E♭)
Lead, Kindly Light, 433 (G)
Lead Me, Lord, 620 (D)
Lead Me to Calvary, 165 (C)
Lead On, O King Eternal, 451 (B♭)
Leaning on the Everlasting Arms, 397 (G)
Leave It There, 466 (F)
Let All Mortal Flesh Keep Silence, 82 (D minor)
Let the Lower Lights Be Burning, 357 (F)
Let the Whole Creation Cry, 245 (E♭)
Let the Words of My Mouth, 619 (F)
Let Thy Blood in Mercy Poured, 329 (B♭)
Let Us Break Bread Together, 330 (D)
Lift Every Voice and Sing, 602 (F)
Lift High the Cross, 203 (C)
Lift Up Your Heads, Ye Mighty Gates! 77 (C)
Lift Up Your Hearts! 333 (C)
Like a River Glorious, 412 (E♭)
Little Is Much When God Is in It, 490 (C)
Living for Jesus, 492 (Eb)
Lo! He Comes with Clouds Descending *(Helmsley)*, 211 (G)
Lo! He Comes with Clouds Descending
    (Regent Square), 210 (B♭)

Lo, How a Rose E'er Blooming, 84 (E♭)
Look, Ye Saints! The Sight Is Glorious
    (Bryn Calfaria), 205 (F minor)
Look, Ye Saints! The Sight Is Glorious
    (Regent Square), 204 (A♭)
Lord, as of old at Pentecost, 222 (F)
Lord, Dismiss Us with Thy Blessing, 585 (C)
Lord, I am fondly, earnestly longing, 494 (F)
Lord, I'm Coming Home, 307 (F)
Lord Jesus, I long to be perfectly whole, 264 (F)
Lord Jesus, Think on Me, 467 (D minor)
Lord, Lay Some Soul upon My Heart, 349 (C)
Lord, Speak to Me, that I May Speak, 465 (F)
Lord, the light of Your love is shining, 348 (A♭)
Lord, Who Throughout These Forty Days, 151 (F)
Love Came Down at Christmas, 91 (Eb)
Love Divine, All Loves Excelling *(Beecher)*, 40 (A♭)
Love Divine, All Loves Excelling *(Blaenwern)*, 41 (F)
Love Divine, All Loves Excelling *(Hyfrydol)*, 42 (F)
Love divine, so great and wondrous, 568 (F)
Love Found a Way, 520 (G)
Love Is the Theme, 278 (G)
Love Lifted Me! 516 (A♭)
Loved with everlasting love, 398 (C)
Low in the grave He lay, 182 (B♭)

Majestic Sweetness Sits Enthroned, 200 (D)
Majesty, 197 (G)
Make Me a Captive, Lord, 488 (C)
"Man of Sorrows!" what a name, 178 (A♭)
Marvelous grace of our loving Lord, 279 (F)
Master, the Tempest Is Raging! 424 (B♭)
May Jesus Christ Be Praised! 51 (B♭)
May the Mind of Christ, My Savior, 497 (D♭)
Mine eyes have seen the glory, 603 (A♭)
Moment by Moment, 376 (E♭)
More About Jesus, 499 (F)
More Love to Thee, O Christ, 463 (F)
Morning Star, O Cheering Sight, 118 (F)
Must Jesus Bear the Cross Alone? 486 (G)
My Country, 'Tis of Thee, 599 (F)
My Faith Has Found a Resting Place, 418 (F)
My Faith Looks Up to Thee, 417 (C)
My Father is rich in houses and lands, 403 (C)
My God, Thy Table Now Is Spread, 328 (C)
My hope is built on nothing less (Melita), 411 (B♭)
My hope is built on nothing less (Solid Rock), 410 (E♭)
My Jesus, I Love Thee, 61 (E♭)
My Jesus, my Savior, 71 (B♭)
My life flows on in endless song, 509 (F)
My life, my love I give to Thee, 491 (F)
My Savior First of All, 554 (F)
My Savior's Love, 518 (G)
My Shepherd Will Supply My Need, 372 (B♭)
My Song Is Love Unknown, 164 (F)

Near the Cross, 288 (E♭)
Near to the Heart of God, 457 (C)
Nearer, My God, to Thee, 426 (E♭)
Nearer, Still Nearer, 380 (C)
No, Not One! 401 (E♭)
Not I, But Christ, 312 (C)
Nothing Between, 501 (F)
Nothing but the Blood, 255 (F)

Now Thank We All Our God, 589 (D)
Now the Day Is Over, 576 (A♭)

O beautiful for spacious skies, 601 (A♭)
O Bless the Lord, My Soul! 35 (F)
O Boundless Salvation, 250 (G)
O Breath of Life, 339 (C)
O Canada! 606 (D)
O Christ, Our Hope, 198 (C)
O Come, All Ye Faithful, 90 (F)
O Come, Let Us Adore Him, 47 (G)
O Come, Little Children, 103 (C)
O Come, O Come, Emmanuel, 72 (D minor)
O Could I Speak the Matchless Worth, 44 (C)
O for a Closer Walk with God, 471 (E♭)
O for a Thousand Tongues to Sing *(Azmon)*, 49 (F)
O for a thousand tongues to sing *(Blessed Name)*, 37 (G)
O for a Thousand Tongues to Sing *(Lyngham)*, 50 (F)
O God, Our Help in Ages Past, 28 (B♭)
O Happy Day, 323 (E♭)
O Holy Night! 129 (B♭)
O How He Loves You and Me, 277 (G)
O Jesus, I Have Promised, 446 (E♭)
O land of rest for thee I sigh! 505 (E♭)
O Little Town of Bethlehem *(Forest Green)* 96 (F)
O Little Town of Bethlehem *(St. Louis)*, 95 (F)
O Lord my God, 27 (A♭)
O Love That Will Not Let Me Go, 389 (F)
O Master, Let Me Walk with Thee, 485 (C)
O Perfect Love, 546 (D)
O Praise Ye the Lord! 26 (A♭)
O Sacred Head Now Wounded, 169 (C)
O safe to the Rock that is higher than I, 381 (D)
O say, can you see, 605 (G)
O Sing a Song of Bethlehem, 146 (E minor)
O soul, are you weary and troubled? 297 (E♭)
O spread the tidings 'round, 220 (B♭)
O That Will Be Glory for Me, 566 (G)
O the Deep, Deep Love of Jesus, 272 (D minor)
O they tell me of a home, 563 (F)
O Thou Joyful, O Thou Wonderful, 113 (C)
O to Be Like Thee! 470 (C)
O What Their Joy and Their Glory Must Be, 548 (E♭)
O Word of God Incarnate, 230 (C)
O Worship the Lord in the Beauty of Holiness; *see*
    Worship the Lord in the Beauty of Holiness, 143 (C)
O Worship the King, 10 (F)
O Zion, Haste, 343 (A♭)
O, Breath of God, come fill this place, 189 (D)
Of Jesus' love that sought me, 289 (G)
Of the Father's Heart Begotten, 80 (E♭)
Of the Father's Love Begotten, 86 (D)
Of the themes that men have known, 278 (G)
Oh, How I Love Jesus, 62 (F)
Oh! Now I see the crimson wave, 261 (D♭)
Oh, to see the dawn of the darkest day, 166 (C)
On a hill far away, 167 (A♭)
On Christmas Night All Christians Sing, 128 (F)
On Eagle's Wings, 366 (D)
On Jordan's Stormy Banks *(Evergreen Shore)*, 564 (E♭)
On Jordan's Stormy Banks *(Promised Land)*, 565 (C)
On This Day Earth Shall Ring, 114 (D Dorian)
Once for All, 285 (C)
Once in Royal David's City, 83 (F)

Once it was the blessing, 528 (E♭)
Once to Every Man and Nation, 598 (E minor)
One Day, 150 (B♭)
Only Believe, 432 (C)
Only Trust Him, 306 (F)
Onward, Christian Soldiers, 438 (D)
Open My Eyes, That I May See, 229 (G)
Open the Wells of Salvation, 494 (F)
Our Best, 496 (A♭)
Our Father in Heaven — The Lord's Prayer, 633 (G/A♭/D♭)
Our Father, Who art in heaven
    (Conditor Alme Siderum), 631 (D)
Our Father, Who art in heaven (Malotte), 632 (A♭)
Our Great Savior, 248 (D)
Out of my bondage, sorrow and night, 299 (F)

Pass Me Not, O Gentle Savior, 311 (F)
Peace Like a River, 408 (G)
Peace, Perfect Peace, 405 (A♭)
Pentecostal Power, 222 (F)
Praise God, from Whom All Blessings Flow — Doxology
    (Dedication Anthem), 623 (G)
Praise God, from Whom All Blessings Flow — Doxology
    (Lasst Uns Erfreuen), 624 (D)
Praise God, from Whom All Blessings Flow — Doxology
    (Old 100th, altered) , 621 (G)
Praise God, from Whom All Blessings Flow — Doxology
    (Old 100th, original), 622 (G)
Praise Him! Praise Him! 64 (F)
Praise, My Soul, the King of Heaven, 12 (C)
Praise the Lord! His Glories Show, 25 (E♭)
Praise the Lord! Ye Heavens, Adore Him, 238 (F)
Praise the Savior, 65 (F)
Praise to God, Immortal Praise, 595 (G)
Praise to the Lord, the Almighty, 11 (F)
Praise ye the Father! 8 (F)
Praise Ye the Triune God! 8 (F)
Precious Memories, 539 (F)

Redeemed, How I Love to Proclaim It! 268 (G)
Rejoice, the Lord Is King! 206 (B♭)
Rejoice, Ye Pure in Heart, 24 (E♭)
Rescue the Perishing, 359 (A♭)
Revive Us Again, 338 (E♭)
Ride On! Ride On in Majesty! 156 (A♭)
Ring the Bells of Heaven! 269 (G)
Rise Up, O Men of God! *(Festal Song)*, 340 (G)
Rise Up, O Men of God! *(St. Thomas)*, 341 (F)
Rise Up, Shepherd, and Follow, 133 (C)
Rock of Ages, 284 (G)

Satisfied, 541 (C)
Saved by Grace, 556 (E♭)
Saved, Saved! 512 (F)
Savior, Again to Thy Dear Name We Raise, 588 (F)
Savior, Like a Shepherd Lead Us, 373 (C)
Savior, More Than Life to Me, 419 (F)
Savior, Thy dying love Thou gavest me, 487 (F)
Savior's Lullaby, 108 (F)
Search Me, O God *(Ellers)*, 296 (F)
Search Me, O God *(Maori)*, 295 (F)
See, Amid the Winter's Snow, 121 (F)
See the Conqueror Mounts in Triumph, 199 (F)
Send the Light! 356 (F)

Sevenfold Amen, 641 (F)
Shall We Gather at the River? 559 (C)
Shepherd of Souls, Refresh and Bless, 331 (F)
Shine, Jesus, Shine, 348 (A♭)
Shout to the Lord, 71 (B♭)
Silent Night! 89 (A♭)
Simply trusting every day, 415 (E♭)
Since I Have Been Redeemed, 511 (E♭)
Since Jesus Came into My Heart, 514 (G)
Sing Praise to God Who Reigns Above, 29 (C)
Sing the wondrous love of Jesus, 557 (A♭)
Sing them over again to me, 234 (F)
Sing to the Lord of Harvest, 593 (G)
Sing We Now of Christmas, 127 (D Dorian)
Singing Songs of Expectation, 321 (E minor)
Sinners Jesus will receive, 345 (B♭)
So precious is Jesus, my Savior, my King, 540 (F)
Soft as the voice of an angel, 406 (B♭)
Softly and Tenderly, 303 (F)
Soldiers of Christ, Arise, 449 (C)
Some day the silver cord will break, 556 (E♭)
Something for Thee, 487 (F)
Songs of Thankfulness and Praise, 144 (C)
Soon we'll come to the end of life's journey, 562 (E♭)
Sowing in the morning, 360 (B♭)
Spirit of God, Descend upon My Heart, 217 (B♭)
Spirit of the Living God, 221 (D)
Stand Up and Bless the Lord, 34 (F)
Stand Up, Stand Up for Jesus *(Geibel)*, 440 (F)
Stand Up, Stand Up for Jesus *(Webb)*, 441 (G)
Standing on the Promises, 430 (G)
Stepping in the Light, 425 (B♭)
Still, Still, Still, 107 (C)
Still, Still with Thee, 574 (D)
Sun of My Soul, 577 (E♭)
Sunlight, 537 (D)
Sweet Hour of Prayer, 458 (C)
Sweeter as the Years Go By, 289 (G)
Sweetly, Lord, have we heard Thee calling, 445 (D)

Take My Life, and Let It Be *(Hendon)*, 302 (E♭)
Take My Life, and Let It Be *(Yarbrough)*, 301 (E♭)
Take the Name of Jesus with You, 377 (G)
Take the world, but give me Jesus, 385 (E♭)
Take Time to Be Holy, 472 (E♭)
"Take Up Thy Cross," the Savior Said, 484 (E♭)
Teach Me Your Way, O Lord, 476 (D)
Tell Me the Old, Old Story, 532 (B♭)
Tell Me the Stories of Jesus. 152 (A♭)
That Beautiful Name, 130 (F)
The Banner of the Cross, 443 (G)
The Beautiful Garden of Prayer, 455 (C)
The Birthday of a King, 136 (G)
The Call for Reapers, 358 (F)
The Church in the Wildwood, 582 (A♭)
The Church's One Foundation, 316 (C)
The Cleansing Wave, 261 (D♭)
The Comforter Has Come! 220 (B♭)
The Day of Resurrection! *(Ellacombe)*, 186 (A♭)
The Day of Resurrection! *(Lancashire)*, 185 (B♭)
The Day Thou Gavest, Lord, Is Ended, 578 (F)
The First Noel, 97 (C)
The God of Abraham Praise, 16 (E minor)
The Great Physician, 286 (C)

The Head That Once Was Crowned, 202 (F)
The King of Love My Shepherd Is *(Dominus Regit Me)*, 371 (F)
The King of Love My Shepherd Is *(St. Columba)*, 370 (C)
The Light of the World Is Jesus, 542 (E♭)
The Lily of the Valley, 538 (E♭)
The Lord Bless You and Keep You, 636 (C)
The Lord Is in His Holy Temple, 608 (D)
The Lord's My Shepherd, I'll Not Want, 369 (E♭)
The Lord's our rock; in Him we hide, 396 (E♭)
The Lord's Prayer *(Conditor Alme Siderum)*, 631 (D)
The Lord's Prayer *(Malotte)*, 632 (A♭)
The Love of God, 276 (C)
The Old Rugged Cross, 167 (A♭)
The Old-Time Religion, 533 (G)
The Power of the Cross, 166 (C)
The Risen Christ, 189 (D)
The Sands of Time Are Sinking, 550 (D)
The Solid Rock *(Melita)*, 411 (B♭)
The Solid Rock *(Solid Rock)*, 410 (E♭)
The Son of God Goes Forth to War, 442 (G)
The Spacious Firmament, 240 (F)
The Star-Spangled Banner, 605 (G)
The Strife Is O'er, 191 (C)
The Unclouded Day, 563 (F)
The Way of the Cross Leads Home, 270 (F)
The whole world was lost, 542 (E♭)
There have been names, 529 (C)
There Is a Balm in Gilead, 383 (F)
There Is a Fountain, 259 (B♭)
There Is a Green Hill Far Away, 160 (C)
There Is a Land of Pure Delight, 570 (E♭)
There is a name I love to hear, 62 (F)
There is a place of quiet rest, 457 (C)
There Is a Redeemer, 249 (C)
There is never a day so dreary, 420 (F)
There Is Power in the Blood, 258 (G)
There Is Sunshine in My Soul, 536 (D)
There Shall Be Showers of Blessing, 342 (A♭)
There's a call comes ringing, 356 (F)
There's a church in the valley, 582 (G)
There's a garden where Jesus is waiting, 455 (C)
There's a land beyond the river, 571 (D)
There's a land that is fairer than day, 560 (F)
There's a royal banner given for display, 443 (G)
There's a Song in the Air! 135 (C)
There's a star in the East on Christmas morn, 133 (C)
There's a Wideness in God's Mercy, 273 (A♭)
There's not a friend like the lowly Jesus, 401 (E♭)
There's within my heart a melody, 508 (F)
Thine Be the Glory, 188 (C)
This is holy ground, 67 (D)
This Is My Father's World, 237 (D)
Thou Didst Leave Thy Throne, 137 (C)
Thou, my everlasting portion, 493 (F)
Thou, Whose Almighty Word, 5 (E♭)
Thou Wilt Keep Him in Perfect Peace, 407 (B♭)
Throw Out the Life-Line! 351 (E♭)
Thy Word Have I Hid in My Heart, 232 (D)
Thy word is a lamp to my feet, 232 (D)
'Tis Midnight, and on Olive's Brow, 159 (G)
'Tis So Sweet to Trust in Jesus, 414 (F)
'Tis the grandest theme through the ages rung, 287 (F)
To God Be the Glory, 31 (F)
True-hearted, Whole-hearted, 448 (D)

Trust and Obey, 504 (E♭)
Trusting Jesus, 415 (E♭)
Trying to walk in the steps of the Savior, 425 (B♭)
Turn Your Eyes upon Jesus, 297 (E♭)
Twofold Amen, 637 (C)
Twofold Amen, 638 (G)
Threefold Amen, 639 (G)

Under a velvet blanket of starlight, 108 (F)
Under His Wings, 385 (B♭)
Unto the Hills, 15 (E♭)
Unto Us Is Born a Son, 87 (C)
Up Calvary's mountain one dreadful morn, 179 (C)

We are often tossed and driven, 569 (E♭)
We are standing on holy ground, 68 (D)
We Gather Together, 590 (C)
We Have an Anchor, 423 (E♭)
We have heard the joyful sound (Jesus Saves), 346 (F)
We have heard the joyful sound (Limpsfield), 347 (B♭)
We Plow the Fields and Scatter, 592 (F)
We Praise Thee, O God *(Kremser)*, 32 (C)
We praise Thee, O God (Revive Us Again), 338 (E♭)
We Remember His Death — Memorial Acclamation
    Prayer B, 630 (A minor)
We Rest on Thee, 444 (D)
We Three Kings of Orient Are, 140 (D minor)
We Will Glorify, 66 (D)
We Wish You a Merry Christmas, 138 (F)
We Worship and Adore You, 70 (G)
We'll Understand It Better By and By, 569 (E♭)
We'll Work Till Jesus Comes, 505 (E♭)
We're Marching to Zion, 584 (E♭)
Were You There? 161 (D)
We've a Story to Tell, 353 (D)
What a fellowship, what a joy divine, 397 (G)
What a Friend We Have in Jesus, 460 (E♭)
What a wonderful change, 514 (G)
What a Wonderful Savior! 257 (C)
What Can I Give Him? 123 (B♭)
What can wash away my sin? 255 (F)
What Child Is This? 110 (E minor)
What If It Were Today? 213 (B♭)
What Wondrous Love Is This, 174 (D Dorian)
When all my labors and trials are o'er, 566 (G)
When He Cometh, 212 (C)
When I Can Read My Title Clear, 551 (F)
When I saw the cleansing fountain, 510 (C)
When I See the Blood, 260 (B♭)
When I Survey the Wondrous Cross *(Hamburg)*, 171 (F)
When I Survey the Wondrous Cross *(Rockingham)*, 172 (C)
When in Our Music God Is Glorified, 56 (F)
When Jesus Left His Father's Throne, 147 (D minor)
When morning gilds the skies, 51 (B♭)
When my lifework is ended, 554 (F)
When peace like a river, 363 (B♭)
When the Roll Is Called Up Yonder, 552 (F)
When the trumpet of the Lord shall sound, 552 (F)
When They Ring the Golden Bells, 571 (D)
When upon life's billows, 594 (C)
When We All Get to Heaven, 557 (A♭)
When we walk with the Lord, 504 (E♭)
Where Cross the Crowded Ways of Life, 149 (G)

Where He Leads Me, 477 (E♭)
While by the sheep we watched at night, 117 (Ab)
While Shepherds Watched Their Flocks *(Christmas)*, 125 (B♭)
While Shepherds Watched Their Flocks
    (Winchester Old), 124 (E♭)
While We Are Waiting, Come, 73 (F)
Whispering Hope 406 (B♭)
Whiter Than Snow, 264 (F)
Who am I to be part of your people, 252 (E minor)
Who Is He in Yonder Stall? 145 (G)
Who Is on the Lord's Side? 436 (B♭)
Why should I feel discouraged? 378 (B♭)
Will the Circle Be Unbroken? 572 (F)
Will your anchor hold in the storms of life, 423 (E♭)
Wonderful Grace of Jesus, 282 (B♭)
Wonderful love that rescued me, 520 (G)
Wonderful, Merciful Savior, 7 (C)
Wonderful Peace, 404 (F)
Wonderful, Wonderful Jesus, 420 (F)
Wonderful Words of Life, 234 (F)
Work, for the Night Is Coming, 506 (D)
Worship the Lord in the Beauty of Holiness, 143 (C)
Worship the Newborn King. 131 (F)
Worthy of Worship, 9 (F)
Would you be free from your burden of sin? 258 (G)
Would you live for Jesus, 313 (F)

Ye Must Be Born Again, 271 (C)
Ye Servants of God, 209 (F)
Years I spent in vanity and pride, 523 (B♭)
Yesterday, Today, Forever, 427 (G)
Yield Not to Temptation, 454 (F)
You who dwell in the shelter of the Lord, 366 (D)
Your only Son no sin to hide, 175 (C)